MW01284383

Colonial Institutions and Civil War

What explains the peculiar spatial variation of Maoist insurgency in India? Mukherjee develops a novel typology of colonial indirect rule and land tenure in India, showing how they can lead to land inequality, weak state, and Maoist insurgency. Using a multi-method research design that combines qualitative analysis of archival data on Chhattisgarh and Andhra Pradesh states with sub-district datasets, Mukherjee demonstrates path dependence of land/ethnic inequality leading to Maoist insurgency. This is nested within a quantitative analysis of a district-level dataset of India which uses an instrumental variable analysis to address potential selection bias in colonial choice of princely states. The author also analyzes various Maoist documents, and interviews with key human rights activists, police officers, and bureaucrats, providing rich contextual understanding of the motivations of agents. Furthermore, he demonstrates the generalizability of his theory to cases of colonial frontier indirect rule causing ethnic secessionist insurgency in Burma, and the Taliban insurgency in Pakistan.

SHIVAJI MUKHERJEE is Assistant Professor in Political Science at the University of Toronto, Mississauga. He has published articles in journals including *Civil Wars, Journal of Conflict Resolution, World Development*, and *Asian Security*.

Cambridge Studies in Contentious Politics

General Editor

Doug McAdam   *Stanford University and Center for Advanced Study in the Behavioral Sciences*

Editors

Mark Beissinger, *Princeton University*
Donatella della, *Porta Scuola Normale Superiore*
Jack A. Goldstone, *George Mason University*
Michael Hanagan, *Vassar College*
Holly J. McCammon, *Vanderbilt University*
David S. Meyer, *University of California, Irvine*
Sarah Soule, *Stanford University*
Suzanne Staggenborg, *University of Pittsburgh*
Sidney Tarrow, *Cornell University*
Charles Tilly (d. 2008), *Columbia University*
Elisabeth J. Wood, *Yale University*
Deborah Yashar, *Princeton University*

Colonial Institutions and Civil War

Indirect Rule and Maoist Insurgency in India

SHIVAJI MUKHERJEE

University of Toronto

CAMBRIDGE
UNIVERSITY PRESS

CAMBRIDGE
UNIVERSITY PRESS

University Printing House, Cambridge CB2 8BS, United Kingdom

One Liberty Plaza, 20th Floor, New York, NY 10006, USA

477 Williamstown Road, Port Melbourne, VIC 3207, Australia

314–321, 3rd Floor, Plot 3, Splendor Forum, Jasola District Centre, New Delhi – 110025, India

79 Anson Road, #06–04/06, Singapore 079906

Cambridge University Press is part of the University of Cambridge.

It furthers the University's mission by disseminating knowledge in the pursuit of education, learning, and research at the highest international levels of excellence.

www.cambridge.org
Information on this title: www.cambridge.org/9781108844994
DOI: 10.1017/9781108954266

First published 2021

A catalogue record for this publication is available from the British Library.

ISBN 978-1-108-84499-4 Hardback

Contents

Figures

Tables

Acknowledgments

I started this project during my PhD dissertation at Yale, but my intellectual debts go far back in time. It was during my years as an MA student in the School of International Studies at Jawaharlal Nehru University (JNU) that I met Kanti Bajpai, who was a great teacher and exhorted me to become an academician. I would like to thank him and other scholars at JNU, including Anuradha Chenoy, Kamal Chenoy, Om Bakshi, Amitabh Mattoo, and Rajesh Rajagopalan for guiding my initial steps into the world of international relations and comparative politics. JNU's progressive environment stimulated my interest in radical politics and conflict, which was fermented further at the Institute for Conflict Management in New Delhi under its director Ajai Sahni, where I was a research associate working on insurgency. My journey continued at the University of Michigan, Ann Arbor, where I learned a great deal from Allen Hicken, Arthur Lupia, James Morrow, Ashu Varshney, and in particular Jennifer Widner, whose advice that it is good to have more than one research question in your head during dissertation fieldwork, in case one does not work out, was indeed useful!

The idea behind the book was born when I was a grad student at Yale: looking at some Election Commission maps of Maoist insurgency in Chhattisgarh I had gathered during fieldwork, I realized they shared a very high correlation with maps of British direct/indirect rule in the Central Provinces. I could not have brought these nascent ideas to fruition without the help and guidance of my dissertation committee. I would like to thank Steven Wilkinson for his patience in listening to my half-baked ideas and pushing me to improve them and for sharing his comprehensive knowledge on archival data, maps, and Indian history and politics. Libby Wood has always been an inspiration on how to do fieldwork, and her suggestion to think of how historical legacies created *political opportunities* was key in creating the theoretical framework. Ken Scheve's encouragement and guidance with the project was crucial, especially his help in developing the instrument to address selection bias with indirect rule. I would like to thank Tariq Thachil for discussions on Indian politics, for suggestions on how to simplify the theory, and for motivating me to go and collect more data and tweak the research question when needed.

Nicholas Sambanis and Jason Lyall provided many helpful suggestions and ideas on civil war and conflict. James Scott was a role model to follow on how to study rebellion; several early conversations with him were helpful in conceptualizing the project. I also had the opportunity to learn from many other scholars at Yale, including Thad Dunning, Matthew Kocher, Adria Lawrence, Karuna Mantena, John Roemer, and Susan Stokes. K. Sivaramakrishnan as chair of the Center for South Asian Studies was always generous with his time and advice and created a stimulating environment for South Asian studies scholars.

I would like to sincerely thank Onur Bakiner, Eddie Camp, Nathaniel Cogley, Valerie Frey, Radhika Govindrajan, Theo Grigoriadis, Alex Kirschner, Dominika Koter, Xiaobo Lu, Joel Middleton, Shambaditya Saha, and Kang Yi for their friendship and company as fellow PhD students at Yale. The number of PhD students who provided comments are too many to list but include Ana Arjona, Laia Balcells, Gina Bateson, Mario Chacon, Karisa Cloward, Madhavi Devasher, Nandini Deo, Nikhar Gaikwad, Nancy Hite, Gareth Nellis, Leonid Peisakhin, Jonah Schulhofer-Wohl, Ryan Sheely, Paolo Spada, and Rory Truex.

I am indebted to numerous individuals and institutions that helped make my fieldwork and data collection on the Maoist insurgency possible in India. It is challenging and sometimes risky to do fieldwork on a politically sensitive topic like the Maoist conflict, especially meeting people on different sides of the conflict and gaining their trust. This book would not have been possible without all the people I met in West Bengal, Chhattisgarh, Andhra Pradesh, and New Delhi, who were willing to take time to talk to me, share their ideas, and give me access to data, without my being able to give much back in return except a remote promise of telling their story at some point in the future!

In Chhattisgarh, I first met Binayak Sen and Ilina Sen during pre-dissertation fieldwork; they graciously invited me to their home and talked to me on development issues affecting tribals and the Maoist conflict in Chhattisgarh. When I arrived later for dissertation fieldwork, Binayak was in Raipur jail in connection with the case of the Maoist leader Narayan Sanyal, where I saw him briefly. I still remember my trip with my wife to Raipur Central Jail to meet the arrested Maoist leader Narayan Sanyal, who asked the jailor to offer us a cup of tea and chatted about Maoist ideology. Several human rights activists like Rajendra Sail and Sudha Bhardwaj took time from their schedules to meet for interviews. Lalit Surjan allowed access to the archives of the *Deshbandhu* newspaper, which had old articles on Maoist activity and some letters to the editor from Maoists. Many thanks are due to the staff of the Vidhan Sabha library in Raipur for their assistance in researching official discussions on the Maoist issue. Comrade C. P. Bakshi of the Communist Party of India spoke to us and gave useful political data and connected us to cadres and activists of Communist Party of India (CPI) in Jagdalpur and Dantewada. I would also like to thank the many bureaucrats and police officers who granted interviews and helped me understand the state side of the story, in particular the Director General of Police Vishwa Ranjan, who gave his insights into rebellion and politics and was very helpful with logistics and data collection. IGP (Naxal) Giridhari Naik shared his experiences in tackling the Maoist insurgency and provided police data. Rahul Sharma, who was then superintendent of police Dantewada, met me on one of my last days in Dantewada and gave his candid thoughts about the Maoist conflict and why it persists. Bithihotra Sahu became a good friend who helped us in so many ways to settle into Raipur and introduced us to his friends in the law school, as well as good restaurants. A big thank you is due to Brigadier Basant K. Ponwar at the Counter Terrorism and Jungle Warfare School in Kanker district for interviews and data on counterinsurgency. I would also like to thank journalists Krishna Das, Raja Das, and especially Ruchir Garg who have covered the Maoist conflict for valuable discussions. Swami Satyarupananda and Swami Nikhilatmananda shared the experiences of the R. K. Mission Ashram in Narayanpur deep within Maoist territory where they create fair price shops and teach farming to Gond tribals.

In Andhra Pradesh, I am deeply indebted to Professor G. Haragopal at the University of Hyderabad for talking to us about the history of the Maoist movement in Telangana and introducing me to other professors in Hyderabad and Kakatiya University in Warangal. I met K. Balagopal several times for interviews and benefited greatly from his encyclopedic knowledge of the political economy and history of Andhra Pradesh and Maoist violence (his death is a sad loss). Kodandaram Reddy at Osmania University drew maps to explain to me the historical land tenures in Hyderabad state and discussed the recent politics surrounding the Maoist conflict. My most treasured memory is meeting the revolutionary poet Gaddar, who burst into song several times and related poignant accounts of his experiences as an underground activist in the past and explained the various factors behind the rise of Naxalism in Telangana. In Kakatiya University in Warangal, I would like to thank Professor Balaramulu for hosting us and literally saving my life after a snake bit me by pressing the venom out and taking me quickly to a local nursing home. Human rights organizations like Andhra Pradesh Civil Liberties Committee (APCLC) and Human Rights Forum (HRF) provided me with documents and data. I am thankful to the State Election Commission office in Hyderabad for providing data on elections and the chief election commissioner for sharing photos of Maoist posters he had picked up from election booths. On the police side, I would like to thank Swaranjit Sen for sharing his experiences as chief of police fighting the Maoist movement in Andhra Pradesh, and the National Police Academy for allowing me to use its library. It was great to meet Bela Bhatia in Hyderabad, whose ethnographic work on the Maoists in Bihar has been an inspiration, and she exhorted me to go and meet people during fieldwork and not just read books and stay in Hyderabad.

In New Delhi, I would like to thank Pralay Kanungo and Siddartha Malavarappu for helping me with access to the library and guest house at JNU. The Contemporary History Archives in the JNU library was useful to locate old Maoist and human rights documents and the staff was very helpful, as was the staff at the National Archives of India in accessing historical documents on Bastar and Hyderabad states. Rohini Somanathan provided an affiliation with the Delhi School of Economics in the initial phase of research and helped conceptualize the dataset and shared census data. I am grateful to Rajat Kujur and Saroj Giri for chatting about Maoist conflict, and especially Nandini Sundar whose work on Bastar has been an inspiration and for all her advice on the project. G. N. Saibaba of the Revolutionary Democratic Front gave a valuable interview from an activist's perspective, and I am thankful to Tapas and Kaustav Banerjee in JNU for talking from the Communist Party of India-Marxist Leninist perspective. Ajai Sahni was willing as ever to discuss insurgency and suggested several data sources on www.satp.org that were helpful.

In West Bengal, I would like to thank Ajay Nand, SP West Midnapore for interviews, and Shyam Singh, DSP Midnapore district for sharing Maoist documents and taking me to police outposts in Maoist-affected areas. Jayanta Choudhury, director of state IB, West Bengal, shared from his knowledge of the subject. B. D. Sharma, IG (Prisons) made possible a trip to Midnapore Jail. I would like to thank Suniti for taking us to his village in Salboni in West Midnapore where the Maoists had carried out a landmine blast on Chief Minister Buddhadeb Bhattacharya's convoy. Choton Das of the Bandi Mukti Samiti gave interviews on the topic and was helpful in developing more contacts with human rights groups.

The book was largely written at the University of Toronto, where the Political Science Department and Center for South Asian Studies provided funding for a book manuscript workshop. I am indebted to Melani Cammett, Aditya Dasgupta, and Anirudh Krishna for reading the book chapters and providing extensive comments at the workshop, which played a major role in improving the quality of the manuscript. I would also like to thank Joseph Wong for chairing the workshop and for being a great mentor who is always supportive, Dickson Eyoh for critical comments and practical advice, and Noel Anderson for suggestions on generalizability of my theory. Several PhD students attended the workshop and provided feedback on the manuscript – Adam Casey, Karol Czuba, Anika Ganness, Kevin Luo, and Yao Wen. I could not have done without the excellent research assistance from the following students: Sanjida Amin, Faisal Kamal, Nidhi Panwar, Alex Paquin-Pelletier, and Siddhartha Sengupta. Asya Bidordinova provided valuable assistance with creating maps.

Several people at the University of Toronto deserve a special mention – Lee Ann Fujii for all her mentorship and encouragement (she is missed); Aisha Ahmad, Jacques Bertrand, Diana Fu, Seva Gunitsky, and Lynette Ong for discussions about research and being great colleagues; and Ronnie Beiner, Aurel Braun, Antoinette Handley, Andrea Olive, Ed Schatz, and Erin Tolley for their advice. Ritu Birla pushed me to think more deeply about different forms of colonial rule in India. A big thanks to Christoph Emmrich, the director of the Center for South Asian Studies for his warmth and support for my book workshop. Zaheer Babbar, Kanishka Goonewardena, Kristin Plys, and Ajay Rao of the Center for South Asian Civilizations (CSAC) at University of Toronto, Mississauga, organized several workshops on radical politics in South Asia and created a vibrant intellectual culture; Dean Amrita Daniere deserves thanks for supporting these initiatives.

I will always be grateful to the Kroc Institute of Peace Studies, University of Notre Dame, for giving me the opportunity to be a visiting fellow in 2018–19, where I revised and polished the manuscript. I would like to thank Asher Kaufman, the director of the Kroc Institute, and Michel Hockx, the director of the Liu Institute of Asian Studies, for their support. Gary Goertz gave extensive comments at the Kroc-Kellogg workshop and valuable advice on research methods, and he kept the conversation going at the group dinners in different restaurants in South Bend. Occasional meetings with Guillermo Trejo in the Hesburgh Library would turn into impromptu chats on political violence and interesting new research questions. Michael Desch helped organize a panel on the Kashmir crisis and had good advice on scholarship in general. I also had opportunities to chat about my research with Jaimie Bleck, David Campbell, Eugene Gholz, Karrie Koesel, Jason Klocek, James McAdams, Mahan Mirza, Ibrahim Moosa, Anibal Perez-Linen, and Victoria Tin-bor Hui. The South Asia group at Notre Dame, composed of Amitava Datta, Madhav Joshi, Nikhil Menon, and Susan Ostermann, provided a sense of intellectual community. Several discussions with Lakshmi Iyer helped sharpen the theory and empirics of the manuscript further. Leonard Wantchekon was a visiting fellow at Kellogg, and I had stimulating conversations about rebel movements and social networks with him over lunch.

I benefited from presenting earlier versions of the research project at various conferences and workshops and would like to thank everyone who provided comments along the way. At the Harvard/Brown/MIT South Asia series, I received valuable early feedback on the manuscript from Gina Bateson, Chappell Lawson, Akshay Mangla, and Vipin Narang. Ashutosh Varshney's questioning the ability of my theory to explain Kerala and Karnataka led me to develop a more fine-grained typology of princely states to explain these exceptional cases. I had the opportunity to present at the Institute for the Study of International Development Speaker Series, McGill University, where I got useful feedback from Erik Kuhonta, Narendra Subramanian, and Juan Wang. I would especially like to thank Matthew Lange not only for his comments at this workshop but also for helping me think about different forms of indirect rule in India when I emailed him as a PhD student. I would like to thank Jan Pierskalla for inviting me to a workshop on comparative colonialism at Ohio State University. For comments at the workshop, I would like to thank Roberto Foa, Jenny Guardado, Anne Meng, Tom Pepinsky, Philip Roessler, Nic Van deWalle, and in particular Alex Lee, whose insights on colonial legacies in India continue to be helpful. I would like to thank Jake Shapiro and Oliver Vanden Eynde for inviting me to a workshop on Maoist insurgency at Princeton University where I received useful feedback on my project from Kanchan Chandra, Kishore Gawande, Devesh Kapur, Shankar Satyanath, and Rumela Sen. This group has produced some of the best articles on Maoist insurgency, and I am thankful to them for helping improve the quality of my arguments. I would like to thank Devesh Kapur for inviting me to present my work at the CASI Security Studies workshop at the University of Pennsylvania, where I received great comments from my discussants Paul Staniland and Sameer Lalwani and several participants including Manjari Chatterjee-Miller, Chris Clary, Devin Finn, Yogesh Joshi, Anit Mukherjee, Rohan Mukherjee, Srinath Raghavan, and Ashley Tellis. For a chance to present at the APSA 2019 preconference on South Asia at the World Bank, I would like to thank the co-hosts Jennifer Bussell, Saad Gulzar, Irfan Nooruddin, and Biju Rao, and Naveen Bharathi, Dipin Kaur, and Gautam Nair for comments.

Many scholars of comparative politics have provided comments and advice on different aspects my project at various conferences over the years. I am thankful for these conversations to Leonardo Arriola, Michael Albertus, Kristin Bakke, Volha Charnysh, Mark Dincecco, Kristine Eck, James Fearon, Scott Gates, John Gerring, Alisson Hartnett, Ron Hassner, Paul Huth, Saumitra Jha, Kathleen Klaus, Jeffrey Kopstein, Peter Krause, David Laitin, Janet Lewis, Evan Lieberman, Zach Mampilly, Dan Mattingly, Didac Queralt, Cyrus Samii, Rudra Sil, Kathleen Thelen, Andreas Wimmer, Robert Woodberry, Daniel Ziblatt, and Sarah Zukerman-Daly. I would particularly like to thank James Robinson for his insights into colonial legacies and conflict, James Mahoney for giving useful advice on framing the India puzzle within the broader literature, and Catherine Boone and Lars Erik Cederman for their critical inputs on the theoretical framework of the project. Erik Wibbels and Adria Lawrence gave comments on the book proposal.

Several senior scholars of South Asian politics like Arun Agrawal, Abhijit Banerjee, Sanjib Baruah, Thomas Blom-Hansen, Christine Fair, John Harriss, Ron Herring, Christophe Jaffrelot, Atul Kohli, Rahul Mukherji, Sanjay Ruparelia, Kunal Sen, and Aseema Sinha continue to be an inspiration. Conversations with Ram Guha and Jairam Ramesh proved helpful in deciding which cases in India to study. I am particularly indebted to Devesh Kapur from whom I have learned a lot about Indian politics and for all his advice and guidance over the years. Sumit Ganguly always provided encouragement to study political violence in South Asia. For discussions and camaraderie, I thank the group of junior scholars working on South Asian politics who have produced interesting new scholarship, including Amit Ahuja, Adam Auerbach, Yelena Biberman, Nicolas Blarel, Rachel Brule, Ahsan Butt, Poulomi Chakrabarti, Phil Hultquist, Gabrielle Kruks-Wisner, Bethany Lacina, Sameer Lalwani, Alex Lee, Aditi Malik, Irfan Nooruddin, Manjeet Pardesi, Anoop Sarbahi, Mark Schneider, Prerna Singh, Pavithra Suryanarayan, Manny Teitelbaum, and Maya Tudor. Rikhil Bhavnani has always been willing to read and give comments on different aspects of my research. Discussions with Adnan Naseemullah about different forms of colonial indirect rule have been helpful. Paul Staniland has been a commentator on different versions of this project at countless workshops and conferences, and the book is better because of that.

I would like to thank the Mary Parker Follett Prize Committee of the Politics & History Section of APSA composed of Jennifer Dixon, Nicole Mellow, and Jason Wittenberg for awarding an Honorable Mention to my article on this topic in the *Journal of Conflict Resolution* and to Nancy Bermeo and Rob Mickey for organizing a dinner for the award winners.

I would like to thank my editor at Cambridge University Press, John Haslam, for his faith in the project and his advice and encouragement throughout the process of manuscript submission and publication, and David Meyer and Mark Beissinger for agreeing to include the book in the Contentious Politics Series. I would also like to thank Tobias Ginsburg, senior editorial assistant, for his help with the production of the book, and Qudsia Ahmad for support with the South Asia edition. I am indebted to the two anonymous reviewers for their comments that greatly improved the manuscript.

I received financial support for fieldwork and data collection from the United States Institute of Peace (USIP) Dissertation fellowship, the McMillan Center dissertation fellowship from Yale University, and an NSF Dissertation Improvement Grant. For pre-dissertation research, I received funding through the George W. Leitner pre-dissertation grant and the Agrarian Studies Summer Grant at Yale. At the University of Toronto, I have received funding from the Connaught New Scholars Grant and the UTM Research Scholars Activity Fund (RSAF) fellowship. The Shastri-Indo Canada Institute (SICI) awarded me a book publication grant for which I am grateful.

Some of the quantitative analysis in Chapter 6 was published in "Colonial Origins of Maoist Insurgency in India," *Journal of Conflict Resolution,* Volume 62, Issue 10, October 2018, https://doi.org/10.1177/0022002717727818; an expanded version of the quantitative analysis of Maoist insurgency in Chhattisgarh in Chapter 7 was published in "Historical Legacies of Colonial Indirect Rule: Princely States and Maoist insurgency in Central India," *World Development,* 2018, 111 (113–29), https://doi.org/10.1016/j.worlddev.2018.06.013. I would like to thank the publishers of these journals for their permission to use some of these materials.

I would like to end by thanking my family for their immense support over the years. My mother Sutapa Mukherjee instilled in me a work ethic and made many sacrifices, and my father Prasun Mukherjee inculcated in me a love for books and ideas and an awareness of larger social and political issues that influenced me indirectly into becoming a political scientist. My brother Ranajit Mukherjee helped me with logistics and meeting people, and we shared many conversations on politics in India. Various other family members helped by providing much needed help with housing and food, in particular Joy and Manjari Chakrabarty in Hyderabad and Soma and Pranab Chakrabarty in New Delhi. Hironmoy Mukherjee and Saibal Mukherjee helped with contacts in Raipur. Last, I would like to thank my wife Nandini, who traveled with me to Maoist zones in Andhra Pradesh, Chhattisgarh, and West Bengal; endured the ups and downs of fieldwork and the many adventures and struggles of a dissertation; and read parts of the manuscript and kept encouraging me. She has patiently persevered while I was busy writing the dissertation and book and taken care of us as a family and given advice on a wide range of issues that often stopped me from making mistakes! To her and our son Shrihan, I give all my gratitude for making this project possible.

PART I

THEORY

Colonial Institutions and Civil War

> As the British imperialists had kept intact hundreds of feudal ties in order to ensure
> their own survival and decided the model of production in India to serve their own
> country's industrial needs, some regions were developed while some other regions
> remained backwards. ... As Andhra, Telangana regions were living as separate
> units for centuries, there is a vast difference in development in the economic,
> political and social spheres of these two regions. Andhra region is more advanced
> in these spheres. ... The important factors which had facilitated the development
> are: the people's struggles against the Zamindari system in Madras Presidency and
> Andhra regions, the Ryotwari system introduced by the British, irrigation
> facilities.
>
> – Central Committee, CPI-ML People's War, pp. 1–2

I   INTRODUCTION

1.1   Do Current Insurgencies Have Deep Roots in History?

With the end of World War II and decolonization since the 1950s, civil
war and insurgencies have replaced interstate wars as the main form of
conflict. However, a fundamental question remains unanswered by
theorists of civil war – do historical institutions play a role in creating
conditions for civil wars and insurgencies? Are there deeper processes of
state formation, so far ignored by scholars of civil war, that have created
structural and ethnic fault lines within states that have erupted into ethnic
conflict and rebellion in recent years? In contrast to the scholarship on civil
wars that tends to focus on proximate causes of insurgency and rebellion,
this book proposes that many insurgencies around the world have origins
in deep historical institutions and processes.

For example, once the NATO/US forces started defeating the Taliban in
Afghanistan in 2001, the Taliban migrated to bordering areas in Pakistan.
They emerged as different groups as part of the umbrella Tehrik-e-Taliban in
Pakistan in the Federally Administered Tribal Areas (FATA) in the North
Western Frontier Province (NWFP), which were previously under an indirect
form of governance by the British, and where a relatively weaker state with

a different set of laws had persisted. They were not as successful in neighboring districts in the NWFP that was formerly part of British direct rule. This suggests that while the timing of the onset of this insurgency in Pakistan was in response to international intervention and conflict across the border, once the Taliban insurgency emerged in Pakistan, it found more fertile ground in areas formerly under British indirect rule.

One of the longest insurgencies that recently negotiated a peace agreement is the leftist Revolutionary Armed Forces of Colombia (Fuerzas Armadas Revolucionarias de Colombia; FARC) insurgency in Colombia, which started in the 1960s. This insurgency was initially located in areas of historically low state penetration (Robinson 2013). Zukerman-Daly (2012) shows how the La Violencia conflict from the past left organizational legacies that led to the FARC insurgency. This leads one to suspect that while proximate geographic factors, ethnic grievances, and natural resources like cocaine have spurred recent conflict, institutional and organizational legacies from the past may have played some role in the emergence and persistence of the FARC insurgency in the areas where it succeeded.

Some African countries like Sierra Leone did not abolish colonial indirect rule systems, and this created grievances that led to ethnic insurgencies. Others like Uganda were able to reduce the powers of pre-colonial–era chiefs and avoid such problems (Acemoglu et al. 2013). Studies have noted the role of British indirect rule in allowing the Islamic caliphate and sharia law to continue in the north of Nigeria, and more direct rule creating a Western secular Christian/animist culture in the south, thus creating conditions for Islamic movements since 1980s and more recently the emergence of the Boko Haram insurgency in Nigeria's north (Babalola, 2013: 13–16; Sampson 2014: 312–15).

Many of the ethnic secessionist insurgencies in India's northeastern states including Mizoram, Nagaland, Tripura, and Manipur can be traced back to discontent and identity formation emerging from policies of indirect rule and the chieftaincy system set up by the British (Baruah 2005), and such long-term effects need to be investigated further. While studies focus on the role of ethnic grievances and endemic rebellion in Burma's peripheral regions, what has been less analyzed is that the multiple ethnic secessionist insurgencies in Kachin, Shan, Karen, and other provinces occur in what were formerly "frontier areas" under British indirect rule (Smith 1999). The Chittagong Hill Tracts (CHT) "sons of the soil" insurgency in Bangladesh beginning in the 1970s saw indigenous tribal people who considered themselves original inhabitants of the Hill Tracts region oppose immigration by Bengali settlers into their homeland. Colonial indirect rule policies under the British that declared the CHT to be an Excluded Area with autonomy for the Hill tribes helped create a distinct tribal ethnic identity, which persisted and was later mobilized against the majority Bengali ethnic group (Mohsin 2003; Qanungo 1998).

Most studies of the Maoist insurgency in Nepal find that factors like poverty (Do & Iyer 2010) or ethnic inequality explain why the insurgency occurred. While the timing of onset of the Maoist insurgency in 1996 may have been due to election results in 1995, longer-term effects may have been due to historical legacies of indirect land tenure through *zamindars* or landlords that created land inequalities that persisted and created conditions that were later exploited by the Maoist leaders in Nepal (Joshi & Mason 2010; Regmi 1976). Similarly, in a recent study, Boone (2017) analyzes how land tenure systems in Africa may have created conditions for land-related conflict, but there could be long-term effects of colonial-era land tenure on the possibility of sons of the soil conflicts in Africa that need to be investigated.

The Liberation Tigers of Tamil Eelam (LTTE) insurgency in Sri Lanka occurred because of Tamil grievances against Sinhalese dominance and ethnic exclusion (Fearon & Laitin 2011). However, this conflict may have had deeper historical roots that scholars of insurgency ignore. Schools set up by American missionaries in northeastern Sri Lanka during British colonialism made the Tamils more educated than the Sinhalese and set the conditions for future ethnic riots and insurgency (Horowitz 1985: 156). Similarly, while most studies point to the role of exploitation of natural resources by the Indian state and the emergence of Assamese nationalism as the cause for the emergence of the United Liberation Front of Asom–led insurgency in Assam in India, colonial era migration into the tea estates in the state of Assam also set up ethnic competition and created conditions for sons of the soil-type insurgency (Weiner 1978).

Even though the effects of past institutions influenced many of these insurgencies, scholars have not adequately explored the long-term legacies of historical institutions on postcolonial insurgency. In this book, I show that both opportunity to rebel and ethnic grievances are endogenous to colonial patterns of state building. Bringing history back into the study of civil wars can provide a deeper understanding of the roots of some insurgencies. It can also explain the persistence and recurrence of civil conflict (Besley & Reynal Querol 2014; Jha & Wilkinson 2012), which existing theories of civil war that focus on more proximate determinants cannot explain. I do this by analyzing the important case of the Maoist insurgency in India, the world's largest democracy, which reveals that different forms of colonial indirect rule created structural conditions for insurgency. Following this, I outline how colonial institutions can create conditions for insurgency in other cases beyond India, which need to be explored in future research.

1.2 Analyzing Subnational Variation within the Case of the Maoist Insurgency in India

I analyze the case of the Maoist insurgency in India, which exemplifies how different forms of colonial indirect rule and indirect revenue collection created land and ethnic inequalities that persisted and created the conditions for rebellion. Thinking more broadly beyond the Maoist conflict, India has experienced several ethnic secessionist insurgencies, whether in Kashmir, the various northeastern states like Nagaland, Manipur, and Tripura, and in Punjab. Except for Punjab, which was annexed into direct rule around 1848 soon after the death of Maharaja Ranjit Singh, all these states with ethnic insurgency also historically experienced some form of British indirect rule. The northeastern states like Manipur and Tripura were small frontier-type states, while Kashmir was a large princely state with a ruler from a different ethnic-religious group than majority of subjects.

Why focus on the Maoist insurgency, which is an ideological, center-seeking insurgency that wants to overthrow the Indian state, and not on the other secessionist insurgencies?[1] One reason is methodological. Unlike the secessionist insurgencies that are concentrated in one province, the Maoist conflict during its expansionist phase from 2005 to 2012 spread to almost ten provinces and developed some level of influence in almost 25 percent to 30 percent of districts in India. This allows us to exploit subnational variation across different provinces and districts within India, which studying the secessionist insurgencies located in one province would not.

Another reason for studying the Maoist insurgency is that it has high policy importance and was considered to be the most important internal security threat by the former Indian Prime Minister Manmohan Singh, as the conflict started escalating beginning in 2005.[2] The Maoist conflict represents an attempt by armed violent groups to fight for the rights of lower castes, tribes, and other subaltern groups that were historically neglected by the state and points to a schism in the rural political economy of the world's largest democracy. Unlike ethnic secessionist insurgencies like those in Kashmir and Punjab that are localized in their province and do not pose a threat to the very fabric of Indian democracy (Varshney 1998), the Maoist insurgency mobilizes lower castes and tribes that are spread across different states of India and thus becomes an important internal threat to the very idea of a stable and "substantive" democracy (Kohli 2001).

With the leftist FARC insurgency in Colombia negotiating a peace agreement in 2016, and the Maoist insurgency in Nepal having ended in 2006, the Maoist conflict in India remains one of the longest-running leftist insurgencies today and needs to be better analyzed and understood. Also, the long-term effects of colonial indirect rule are very visible in the Maoist insurgency case, since the descendants of *zamindars* (landlords) from colonial times in Bihar and Chhattisgarh started various vigilante groups like the Ranvir Sena and Salwa

---

[1] Sambanis, "Do Ethnic and Non-Ethnic Civil Wars Have the Same Causes?" differentiates between secessionist insurgencies that want to separate or secede from the state and center-seeking insurgencies that want to overthrow the central state. He suggests that they may have different types of causes for onset.

[2] *The Economist*, "Ending the Red Terror."

Judum, which led to human rights violations against underprivileged ethnic groups like *Dalits* and *Adivasis*. The land inequality created through the *deshmukhs* who collected land revenue under the Nizam of Hyderabad was difficult for the postcolonial Indian government to reverse through land reforms and created ideal structural conditions for Maoist rebels. The direct policy significance of colonial indirect rule for the current Indian state is clear, both for counterinsurgency and land reform policies.

1.3 Brief History of the Maoist Conflict in India

While details of the political history and patterns of violence of the Maoist movement are discussed in Chapter 4, a brief outline follows.[3] The Maoist insurgency in India initially started in 1967 in a village called Naxalbari in the state of West Bengal, and the Marxist-Leninist ideology rapidly spread to various parts of India. The Indian government crushed this initial phase by 1973. Following this, the movement fractured, and it was in the late 1970s that different factions regrouped to reemerge in different parts of India, particularly in the states of Bihar and Andhra Pradesh.

Three main Maoist groups used violence and consolidated their control – the Maoist Communist Center (MCC) in Bihar, the People's War Group (PWG) in Andhra Pradesh and Chhattisgarh, and the People's Unity (PU) operating mostly in Bihar/Jharkhand. In 2004, the PWG and MCC factions unified to form the Communist Party of India–Maoist (CPI-Maoist); since then, the level of guerrilla activities as well as the geographic zone of influence expanded rapidly, which prompted the Indian Prime Minister Manmohan Singh to repeatedly call it "India's number one security threat." By 2008–9, the insurgency had expanded to almost 150 or more of India's 600-odd districts, and it represents both a serious security threat and a developmental challenge to India's politicians. While the level of violence has declined since 2012, a cyclical pattern of violence has occurred every twenty years, and it is not clear if the insurgency is coming to an end or simply entering a dormant phase.[4] In fact, attacks in 2016 and early 2017 on Central Reserve Police Force (CRPF) soldiers lend credence to the idea that the Maoists are only in a phase of "tactical retreat."

1.4 A Puzzling Spatial Variation within India

As shown in the map in Figure 1.1, at its peak period in 2005–12, the long-lasting Maoist insurgency in India (1967–72 and 1980–ongoing) generates

---

[3] For an overview of the Maoist insurgency in India, see Singh, *The Naxalite Movement in India*, and various articles in the *Economic and Political Weekly* especially by scholars such as Bela Bhatia, "The Naxalite Movement in Central Bihar"; K. Balagopal, "Maoist Movement in Andhra Pradesh"; Nandini Sundar, "Bastar, Maoism and Salwa Judum."

[4] See Mukherjee, "Insurgencies in India – Origins and Causes."

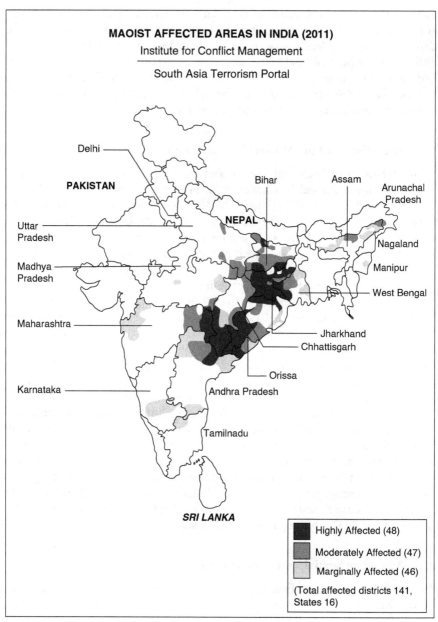

FIGURE 1.1 Map of Maoist insurgency in India, 2011–2012
Source: www.satp.org/satporgtp/sair/images/10_35/Maoist_2012map.html

a puzzle not easily solved by conventional theories of civil war – why did the insurgency emerge and consolidate along certain territories in the central-eastern part of India and not in other parts? Why are certain provinces and districts affected by the insurgency and not others? Is it, as Fearon and Laitin (2003) would argue, purely because opportunities for rebellion are present in some areas of India in the form of forest cover or hilly terrain or weak state presence? Is it because rebellious tribes or oppressed lower castes facing horizontal inequalities live there, as theorized by Murshed and Gates (2005), or because these tribes or lower castes have been excluded from political power (Cederman, Wimmer, & Min 2010)?

Yet, other areas of the country have similarly high forest cover, hilly terrains, poverty, and socioeconomically deprived ethnic groups like *Dalits* (lower castes) and *Adivasis* (tribal people), and yet no Maoist insurgency. For example, the Western Ghats areas in the state of Karnataka are ridged and hilly; Maoist documents show that they targeted these areas in 2005, but failed.[5] While it is true that in Chhattisgarh, the areas of highest Maoist control occur in the deeply forested Dandakaranya areas, there is dense forest cover in the neighboring state of Madhya Pradesh and famous tiger reserves, but no Maoist insurgency. While lower castes live in Maharashtra and Uttar Pradesh (UP), these areas have not seen Maoist mobilization, except for a few districts like Gadchiroli in Maharashtra bordering neighboring Chhattisgarh and districts like Chandauli in UP bordering Bihar, which are highly affected, probably due to spillover effects.

While these proximate measures of *rebel opportunity* and *grievances* are important parts of the causal chain, they are *neither necessary nor sufficient conditions* to explain Maoist insurgency. These existing theories of civil war and rebellion are part of the causal framework, but they cannot fully explain the entire spatial variation in Maoist insurgency in India. There must be some other omitted variable that is key to explaining this unusual spatial variation. Looking into the past, these same areas that have the Maoist insurgency today tended to have various kinds of agrarian and peasant rebellions and unrest during British colonial rule, and sometimes even during pre-colonial times (Gough 1974). Could it be some long-term lingering effect of past institutions, which makes these areas intrinsically more prone to peasant rebellion?

1.5   Answer to the Puzzle – Two Types of Colonial Indirect Rule Created Structural Conditions for Maoist Insurgency in India

To fully explain this puzzling spatial variation of initial areas of Maoist control in India, it is necessary to include a crucial omitted variable – colonial indirect rule. Using subnational qualitative and quantitative data from the Maoist insurgency in India, I demonstrate that different forms of colonial indirect

---

[5] CPI-ML (PW), *"Karnataka: Social Conditions."*

rule, whether *informal indirect rule* through landlord-based *zamindari* land revenue system (see Dirks 2001; Kohli 2004: 225–26; Lange 2009) or more *formal indirect rule* through certain types of native princely states (Fisher 1991; Iyer 2010; Lee-Warner 1910), created long-term persistent and path-dependent effects conducive to leftist ideological insurgency in India.

These two forms of indirect British colonial rule coincided with two epicenters of Maoist insurgency, one in northeastern and another in south-central India. The northern epicenter of the insurgency was near the conjunction of the states of Bihar/Jharkhand/Bengal, where the MCC was the dominant rebel faction. In these areas, which were formerly part of the Bengal presidency during British rule, informal indirect rule through the *zamindari* land tenure system chosen by the colonizers created the mechanism of land and caste inequality, which became a structural cause for radical leftist mobilization. As Kohli (2004) points out in his analysis of effects of colonial institutions on development, the *zamindari* land revenue system based on local political elite like landlords (*zamindars*) required less expansion of the colonial bureaucracy than the *ryotwari* land revenue system in Bombay and Madras Presidencies in which the colonial state directly collected tax and revenue from the villagers or *ryots*.[6] Thus, using *zamindars* as local intermediaries to collect taxes and revenue led to the creation of both grievance and state weakness mechanisms that persisted over time.

The southern epicenter of the insurgency occurred near the borders of the states of Andhra Pradesh/Chhattisgarh/Maharashtra/Madhya Pradesh/southern Orissa, where the PWG was the dominant rebel faction. In this area, the more formal type of indirect rule was established through princes/native rulers in the form of the large princely state of Hyderabad and the smaller feudatory states of Chhattisgarh and Orissa and Eastern State Agencies. The areas in Chhattisgarh that were part of the former princely states of Bastar and Surguja had *Adivasi* or tribes staying there, which from pre-colonial times had not been part of the state formation process (Scott 2009). These areas saw the colonial state not providing sufficient levels of development, and only exploiting the region for land and natural resources, which continued into the postcolonial period. Also in the princely state of Hyderabad, which was one of the largest princely states in India besides Kashmir, the Nizam of Hyderabad depended on *deshmukhs* to collect land revenue on his behalf. This led to their behaving in a despotic manner like the *zamindars* in Bihar/Bengal areas and resulted in high levels of land/caste inequalities and created horizontal intergroup inequalities (Cederman, Gleditsch, & Buhang 2013). Maoist guerrillas later used these land/ethnic inequalities, ethnic grievances due to natural resource exploitation, and

---

[6] Lee, "Land, State Capacity, and Colonialism," provides empirical support that the *zamindari/*landlord areas had lower tax and bureaucratic capacity than the *ryotwari/*non-landlord tenure areas.

state weakness to mobilize these lower castes and tribes successfully and establish zones of rebel control.

In contrast, states in the southern and western regions of India, like Maharashtra and Tamil Nadu, had not only been annexed into direct British rule but also had the more direct *ryotwari* land tenure system, in which land revenue was collected directly through colonial administrators from the *ryots* or *peasants*. These areas were both de facto and de jure direct rule, and had higher levels of development and lower levels of land inequality, and no Maoist insurgency. Though these areas also had opportunity for rebellion through forest cover, and presence of ethnic groups like *Adivasis* and *Dalits*, they did not have high levels of land inequality and state weakness created by British indirect rule in the form of princely states or *zamindari* land tenure. These other proximate factors are part of a longer causal chain that leads to insurgency and are neither necessary nor sufficient conditions. However, almost all areas that experienced Maoist insurgency had been previously exposed to some form of indirect rule, which makes it a *necessary condition* for Maoist insurgency.[7]

The analysis of the Maoist insurgency in India provides evidence that colonial institutions of indirect rule through princely states and *zamindari* land tenure institutions created the structural conditions that favor insurgency. Not including colonial institutions creates a potential omitted variable bias in the econometric analysis of Maoist insurgency onset in India, as well as in the study of civil war onset/spatial variation. It also prevents us from understanding why there is persistent conflict in some areas of a country. By analyzing the spatial variation of insurgency in the Maoist case in India, I demonstrate that the literature on civil war does not give enough attention to historical factors and colonial institutions, even though many of the conditions that give rise to insurgency have historical origins.

2 WHY HISTORICAL INSTITUTIONS MATTER TO EXPLAIN CIVIL WARS

What kind of lessons can we draw from the analysis of the Maoist conflict in India to understand why it is important to analyze the long-term legacies of historical institutions for insurgency? While insurgencies often seem to be triggered by proximate events, resource shocks, and ethnic grievances, several deficiencies in the literature on civil wars are addressed by analyzing the long-term legacies of historical institutions on insurgency.

---

[7] Colonial indirect rule is not a sufficient condition since there are some cases with formal indirect rule through princely states but no insurgency, like Kerala and Karnataka. However, deeper analysis in Chapter 9 reveals that these are not really exceptions, but what Gerring, *Case Study Research* calls *influential cases* and had a different type of princely state than that found in Hyderabad or Bastar.

2.1 Proximate Triggers of Insurgency Endogenous to Historical Institutions

In an influential analysis of civil war onset, Fearon and Laitin (2003) focus on the role of *rebel opportunity* and argue that the effects of *ethnic grievances* as suggested by previous literature on rebellions were overemphasized. Following from earlier theories of social movements that had focused on "opportunity structures" (Tarrow 1998; Tilly 1978) and "resource mobilization" (McCarthy & Zald 1977), Fearon and Laitin (2003) proposed that it was more important to focus on opportunities for rebellion than on grievances. They proceed to interpret opportunity structure in terms of proximate measures of weak state capacity measured by per capita income, as good predictors of onset of insurgency.[8] However, they do not ask whether proximate levels of state capacity could have been influenced by past colonial institutions of governance.

Recent studies have argued against this perspective of *rebel opportunity*, and suggest that it is *ethnic exclusion* of certain groups from political power which creates grievances and the structural conditions for insurgency (Cederman et al. 2010; Cederman et al. 2013). However, it is possible that past colonial policies of divide and rule had created institutions of ethnic exclusion that were causally prior to current levels of ethnic exclusion and ethnic inequality and grievances that led to insurgency in the postcolonial period. Both *rebel opportunity* as well as *ethnic grievances* are possibly endogenous to the long-term process of state formation triggered by colonial choices and institutions.

Even the growing literature on civil war using sub-national designs, which tries to overcome some of the weaknesses of the cross-national literature like over-aggregation and measurement error, mostly neglects the effect of historical institutions.[9] In a prominent study, Kalyvas (2006) focuses on the importance of current levels of rebel versus government control as explaining patterns of selective and indiscriminate violence. However, this still begs the question – what explains variation in rebel control in the first place? Historical institutions like colonial land tenure, indirect rule, forest policy, and inclusiveness of ethnic groups in colonial armies or bureaucracies could have long-term effects on patterns of rebel control, which then could influence patterns of insurgency-related violence.

Whether the colonial institution chosen was more or less extractive (Acemoglu et al. 2001), created more or less inclusive ethnic identities (Mamdani 2001; Chandra & Wilkinson 2008), was more or less direct in

---

[8] In an older 2001 APSA version of their paper, Fearon and Laitin, "Ethnicity, Insurgency and Civil War," cite the resource mobilization literature, but their 2003 APSR paper does not refer to the social movements and revolutions literature, though they still use the framework of political opportunity structures.

[9] See Blattman and Miguel, "Civil War," for a critical appraisal of this stream of research.

setting up bureaucracy and police capacity (Lange 2009), or facilitated more or less development (Kohli 2004; Mahoney 2010) is a determinant of current subnational variation of these factors that then become proximate causes of current insurgency. By ignoring these deep-rooted determinants of conflict, the civil war literature fails to explain the underlying long-term causal processes that generate postcolonial insurgencies.

2.2 Historical Institutions as Omitted Variables for Analysis of Civil War Onset

Many of the dominant theories on civil war onset/incidence, like Fearon and Laitin (2003), Collier and Hoeffler (2004), Sambanis (2001, 2004), Hegre et al. (2001), and Cederman, Wimmer and Min (2010), use cross-national data and focus on the importance of state capacity, rebel opportunity, democracy, or ethnic exclusion to explain civil war. This literature does not refer to historical institutions, though anti-colonial conflicts are sometimes part of the model specifications.[10] Overlooking the role of historical institutions creates potential omitted variable bias in the civil wars literature, because these colonial institutions affect subnational variation in levels of postcolonial state capacity, economic development, and ethnic inequalities, which then become proximate factors that affect the ability of rebel leaders to start and sustain insurgency. This could create the problem of omitted variable bias because past historical institutions could jointly determine state capacity/income/male literacy/ethnic exclusion and inequalities on the one hand, as well as the chance of insurgency on the other.

Miguel, Satyanath and Sergenti (2004) recognize that in addition to the problem of endogeneity of socioeconomic factors to the process of conflict that is not adequately addressed by the cross-national literature on civil wars, "omitted variables – for example, governmental institutional quality – may drive both economic outcomes and conflict, producing misleading cross-country estimates" (Miguel et al. 2004: 726). Extending this analysis to the potential role of historical institutions, it is possible that colonial institutions of different types are one such omitted variable (Z) that is driving postcolonial state capacity, ethnic inequalities, and natural resource extraction (X), as well as conflict occurrence (Y).

Colonial institutions can influence civil war onset through these intermediating mechanisms of current state capacity/ethnic grievances, which are the usual mechanisms theorized by civil war scholars and also have a separate effect through other unobserved mechanisms. By including such omitted variables that are causally prior to the more proximate processes of weak state capacity, or exploitation of natural resources, or creation of ethnic

---

[10] The dataset in Fearon and Laitin, "Ethnicity, Insurgency, and Civil War," has anti-colonial wars that they include in their analysis.

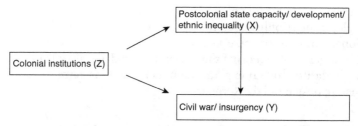

FIGURE 1.2 Colonial institutions as omitted variables to explain civil war

grievances into explanations of civil war, it may be possible to reduce some of the endogeneity issues and have a more holistic explanation for conflict. This is described graphically in Figure 1.2.

As Djankov and Reynal-Querol (2010: 1039) note, "some historical factors could jointly determine the development path and the political stability path of countries and could explain the positive correlation we observe between poverty and civil wars." To control for such possible omitted variables, and building on Acemoglu et al. (2001), they include different proxies of colonizer strategy in the model, like log of European settler mortality rates, population density in 1500, and European settlement in 1900, in cross-national models of civil war onset. They find that the effect of state capacity as measured by per capita income on civil war disappears. This hints at the possibility of omitted variable bias. However, they do not outline a theory or the possible causal mechanisms linking these colonial institutions with postcolonial civil war.

Unlike Djankov and Reynal-Querol (2010) who use cross-national data and analyze the general effects of colonial institutions, I focus specifically on one significant type of colonial institution, namely colonial indirect rule, and use fine-grained subnational data for the important case of Maoist insurgency in India. I find that colonial indirect rule has effects mostly through the channels of *ethnic inequalities* and *weak state capacity*, but there could be a direct effect on insurgency through other unobserved channels. This could be causing omitted variable bias in studies of Maoist insurgency that do not include such historical institutions in their models.

2.3 Civil War Literature Cannot Explain Long-Term Persistence and Conflict Recurrence

Another advantage of analyzing the effects of past institutions on conflict today is that these insurgencies are sometimes symptomatic of persistent conflict from colonial and pre-colonial times in these regions. For example the FARC insurgency in Colombia recurred in areas that had La Violencia in the 1940s (Zukerman-Daly 2012) and happened in areas that were historically of weak state capacity (Robinson 2013). The Sendero Luminoso insurgency in Peru occurred in areas where the Spanish colonizers used the *mita* system of forced exploitation of indigenous labor for mining that created unequal land tenure structures, lower public good distribution, and anti-colonial rebellions in the past (Dell 2010; Guardado 2016). Similarly, Besley and Reynal-Querol (2014) find that areas in Africa that had pre-colonial conflict also tend to have insurgencies and conflict in the postcolonial era. Areas within India that had colonial-era tribal rebellion led by the messianic tribal leaders Birsa Munda in Jharkhand and Gunda Dhar in Chhattisgarh later saw recurrence of tribal rebellion beginning in the 1980s but this time led by Maoist intellectuals (Sundar 2007). Analyzing the role of historical institutions and previous legacies of conflict allows us to explain the persistence and recurrence of certain conflicts today, which the civil war literature cannot do because of its focus on proximate causes.

3 CONTRIBUTION TO LITERATURE ON COLONIAL LEGACIES

Besides filling important gaps in the literature on civil wars, this project contributes to the literature on colonial legacies in South Asia and beyond. A large body of research has focused on how different historical institutions explain postcolonial development and democracy (Acemoglu et al. 2001; Jha & Wilkinson 2012; Lange 2009; Mahoney 2010), but this literature does not focus on insurgency. There is also literature that studies the effect of colonial institutions on ethnic identity formation (Dirks 2001; Laitin 1986), but it does not analyze if such ethnic identities or ethnic exclusion can potentially create conditions that enable insurgency.

A few studies have used cross-national datasets to test for the effects of colonial institutions on rebellion and insurgency (Djankov & Reynal Querol 2010; Lange & Dawson 2009). However, these studies have very broad measures of colonial institutions and are too aggregate in measurement to produce fine-grained theory sensitive to regional complexities. Given the nascent stages of the literature analyzing effects of colonial legacies on insurgency, focusing on an important colonial institution and using fine-grained subnational data to study its long-term effect on conflict in one or more countries or regions would be fruitful. As Mahoney and Goertz (2006) have suggested, there may be a lot of unit heterogeneity in cross-national data, and so countries in different regions experiencing different types of colonial legacies may have very different sets of mechanisms. It is better to focus on particular regions to understand how specific colonial institutions have effects in certain regions of the world, before generalizing to other regions.

My study tries to do this by analyzing subnational variation in colonial institutions of indirect rule and land tenure and Maoist insurgency in India. Future research can try to use the theoretical insights that emerge from my study to analyze colonial indirect rule in other regions.[11] In his study of the effects of degree of Spanish colonialism in Latin America, Mahoney (2010) has suggested that one productive direction of research would be to focus on colonial institutions that produce hierarchical forms of domination and recommends that scholarly attention must turn to "colonial rules for securing indigenous labor, for assigning land rights, and for designating local political power holders. These institutions ... can make ethnic identities into highly enduring axes of contention for the people designated by the identities" (Mahoney 2010: 19). Colonial indirect rule is one such institution, and I focus on how it created multiple causal pathways that led to revolutionary insurgency in the world's largest democracy.

Traditionally, scholars have analyzed the long-term effects of colonial indirect rule on development (Kohli 2004; Mahoney 2010), state capacity (Lange 2009), nationalism (Hechter 2000), and genocide (Mamdani 1996). Only a few studies have explored the effects of colonial indirect rule on insurgency, but they have contradictory results relying on cross-national datasets and focus on Africa. A paper by Wucherpfennig et al. 2016) uses country-level statistical analysis to show that British indirect rule over peripheral interior areas gave local power to pre-colonial–era chiefs in Africa, which resulted in higher ethnic inclusion of these peripheral ethnic groups into political power in postcolonial electoral politics, and lower chances of insurgency. In contrast, French direct rule in Africa caused higher levels of cultural and institutional assimilation of ethnic groups that prevented much autonomy and power for the chiefs of ethnic groups in interior areas. So post-independence, these peripheral ethnic groups were excluded from power, which created grievances and higher chances of insurgency.[12]

In contrast, Blanton, Mason, and Athow (2001) find that British indirect rule in Africa led to more ethnic conflict and civil war than French direct rule: British indirect rule led to a decentralized power structure that did not interfere as much with the indigenous institutions; it was easier for rebels to overcome collective action problems and mobilize because the indigenous social structures and institutions were left relatively unchanged. The French on the other hand used a more centralized form of direct rule and bureaucratic structures that interfered with the indigenous social and political institutions that were replaced with the modern nation-state; as a result, future rebels found it more difficult to mobilize and overcome collective action problems because direct rule had destroyed indigenous social institutions. This prevented ethnic minorities from having the "mobilizing structures necessary to mount an

---

[11] Chapter 10 starts the process of generalization by analyzing how British colonial indirect rule created conditions for the Taliban insurgency in Pakistan, and ethnic secessionist insurgency in Burma, and how Spanish colonialism created conditions for the NPA insurgency in the Philippines and Zapatistas in Mexico.

[12] Wucherpfennig et al., "Who Inherits the State? Colonial Rule and Post-colonial Conflict."

organized challenge to the post-colonial state, regardless of the extent of their grievances against the state" (Blanton et al. 2001: 475).[13]

These studies have opposite predictions because they emphasize different mechanisms being generated by the same institutions of British indirect versus French direct rule. While the Blanton et al. (2001) paper focuses on how French direct rule destroyed the *opportunities for rebel mobilization* in peripheral ethnic groups while British indirect rule left indigenous institutions and mobilization structures intact, Wucherpfennig et al. (2016) focus on how French direct rule created *ethnic exclusion* and grievances in these peripheral ethnic groups, while British indirect rule allowed their political inclusion. This suggests that the literature on effects of colonial indirect rule on insurgency is still in its early stages, and further theoretical and empirical analysis needs to be done before we can reach a scholarly consensus. Also, these studies focus on indirect rule and insurgency in Africa, which was colonized much later by the British, besides having much lower population density than South Asia.

Of more direct relevance would be a study that analyzes the legacies of colonial indirect rule on insurgency in Pakistan by Naseemullah (2014), which shows that British colonial indirect rule in the frontier regions of Pakistan led to different structures of administration and law, and lower levels of state control over the Federally Administered Tribal Areas (FATA) in North West Frontier Province (NWFP) of Pakistan. These different institutions in these peripheral areas of Pakistan persisted into the postcolonial period, since the Pakistani state found it convenient to continue such indirect or *hybrid* forms of governance in these frontier areas. In 2001, following the war against the Taliban in Afghanistan by NATO/US troops, the Tehrik-e-Taliban emerged and was able to consolidate in those districts of the FATA in NWFP, which had historically been under colonial indirect rule with lower levels of state capacity. This paper is a step in the right direction, since it uses micro-level qualitative and quantitative analysis to show the effects of indirect rule on insurgency. However, it does not address the issue of selection bias created by British colonizers intentionally choosing poor tribal regions that were difficult to administer for indirect rule.

My project advances this emerging literature on the historical legacy of colonial indirect rule on insurgency by focusing on the case of the Maoist insurgency and exploits fine-grained quantitative and qualitative subnational data within India. This allows my study to address issues of selection bias unlike Naseemullah (2014) and conceptualize different types of indirect rule and princely states, which other studies do not analyze.

Another major contribution of my book is to engage in a debate among scholars on the effects of direct versus indirect rule on state capacity, development, and insurgency in South Asia. Scholars like Kohli (2004), Lange (2009), and Mahoney (2010) suggest that British indirect rule *on average* produces worse development outcomes and weaker state capacity than areas

---

[13] Blanton et al., "Colonial Style and Post-Colonial Ethnic Conflict in Africa", p. 475

under British direct rule. Similarly, Naseemullah (2014) finds that hybrid colonial indirect rule in the frontier provinces of Pakistan set up conditions for Taliban insurgency in the future. In contrast, a quantitative analysis by Iyer (2010) uses an instrumental variable strategy and finds that districts within India that were indirectly ruled as princely states have better development outcomes. Similarly, a recent article by Verghese (2016a) interprets Bastar princely state to have been directly ruled and suggests therefore it had Maoist conflict. Verghese (2016b) analyzes the effects of colonial indirect versus direct rule on both Hindu-Muslim riots and caste/tribe-based conflict and also proposes that Bastar princely state was directly ruled at certain points by the British and had Maoist insurgency. Teitelbaum and Verghese (2019) also provide quantitative evidence that it was districts under former colonial direct rule that had better outcomes and lower Maoist insurgency.

My book joins this debate by noting several empirical and conceptual flaws in Verghese's (2016a, 2016b) and Teitelbaum and Verghese's (2019) studies and providing evidence in favor of Mahoney (2010), Kohli (2004), and Lange's (2009) theoretical position.[14] First, these studies fail to explain why there was no Maoist insurgency in Maharashtra and Tamil Nadu states, which were ruled directly by the British as Bombay and Madras Presidency. These areas also saw the more direct *ryotwari* land tenure system that was more egalitarian than the indirect *zamindari* land tenure system in the east in Bengal province, and so logically they should have had high Maoist insurgency according to these studies.

Second, they also cannot explain why the strongest areas of Maoist rebel control occurred in the southern epicenter composed of the indirectly ruled Bastar princely state area in current Chhattisgarh state, and also in the Telangana region of the indirectly ruled large princely state of Hyderabad, which saw a despotic land tenure system under the Nizam and his *deshmukhs*.

Third, studies like Verghese (2016a, 2016b) and Teitelbaum and Verghese (2019) conceptualize the eastern districts in Bengal and Bihar state as direct rule and having Maoist insurgency. However, they mischaracterize the *zamindari* tenure system prevalent in these areas as direct rule, when in reality this was a more indirect revenue collection system in which the British colonizers depended on intermediaries like landlords to collect land revenue on their behalf. Studies of the effect of colonial indirect rule on India's economy (Kohli 2004: 225–26) and British colonial indirect rule on state capacity (Lange 2009) characterize the *zamindari* tenure system as a different shade of indirect rule in which rulers depend on intermediaries to collect land revenue, rather that collect it directly as in the *ryotwari* system in Madras and Bombay.

The main problem in these studies is that they conceptualize direct-indirect rule as a binary concept, when in reality there is a lot of variation within the

---

[14] For more detailed criticisms of these studies, see Chapter 2 and Mukherjee, "Historical Legacies of Colonial Indirect Rule."

category of indirect rule in India. Wilkinson (2017) has criticized studies of indirect revenue collection and indirect rule in India, for example, Iyer (2010) and Verghese (2016a, 2016b), for not sufficiently disaggregating the different types of indirect rule, and questioned whether "we can squeeze the fluidity and complexity of history into the hard categories of social science and especially statistical analysis" (Wilkinson 2017).

One of the major conceptual contributions of my project is that I disaggregate the concept of colonial indirect rule compared with these theories of indirect rule and development/insurgency in South Asia and develop a more fine-grained typology of different types of indirect rule. First, I introduce a conceptual innovation by proposing that two broad types of indirect rule exist within India – the more formal type of indirect rule through princely or native states and also the informal type of indirect rule through *zamindars* in Bengal-Bihar province in the east, which could be compared with the direct revenue collection through the *ryotwari* non-landlord tenure system in Bombay-Madras in the southwest.

A second major conceptual contribution of this book is that I delineate variation between types of princely states within India, by showing how *feudatory/tributary* princely states in Bastar and Orissa had ethnic outsiders as rulers who were protected by the British, which resulted in despotic extraction and Maoist insurgency, while *warrior/conquest* princely states in Travancore and Mysore that challenged the British had lower levels of land exploitation and more state capacity and less successful Maoist insurgency (Ramusack 2004).[15] This is the first study to analyze such internal variation within the category of formal indirect rule within princely states in South Asia, which helps explain some of the fallacies in the existing studies of indirect rule and insurgency in South Asia.

This book also makes a major empirical contribution. The literature on the effect of colonial land tenure systems on development outcomes in India only measures land tenure for British direct rule areas from official sources and does not have measures of land tenure for those districts in India that were under formal indirect rule (Banerjee & Iyer (2005).[16] Here, I measure and describe land tenure institutions within the indirectly ruled princely states of Bastar and Hyderabad and show how such land tenure institutions created land revenue exploitation. Future studies could similarly measure land tenure in other princely states like Kashmir or Mysore to fill this gap in measurement of land tenure in princely India.

---

[15] Chapter 6 does quantitative testing of the effects of these different types of princely states. Then Chapters 7 to 9 qualitatively analyze these different types of princely states in Bastar, Hyderabad, and Travancore/Mysore and how that created different trajectories leading to Maoist insurgency.

[16] Banerjee and Iyer, "History, Institutions and Economic Performance," measure land tenure from Baden-Powell's *Land Tenure Systems in British India,* volumes 1 to 3, which are the official colonial measures of land tenure in British direct ruled India.

4 CONTRIBUTION TO LITERATURE ON POLITICAL VIOLENCE AND MAOIST INSURGENCY IN INDIA

The third and final contribution of my book is to the literature on political violence in the world's largest democracy, which has debated the causes behind Hindu and Muslim ethnic riots (Brass 1997; Varshney 2002; Wilkinson 2004) and explored the dynamics and patterns of ethnic insurgencies in Kashmir, North East, and Punjab (Baruah 2005; Ganguly 1996; Staniland 2014) but lacks comprehensive analysis of leftist insurgency. This is the first comparative politics study of such leftist insurgency and is an important contribution to understanding political violence in South Asia.

Several excellent recent articles on India's Maoist insurgency use district-level econometric analyses. Gawande, Kapur, and Satyanath (2017) and Vanden Eynde (2018) explain variation in patterns of Maoist and state violence by focusing on how rainfall shocks change forest cover and have an adverse effect on opportunity costs to rebel recruitment. Dasgupta, Gawande, and Kapur (2017) find that implementing the National Rural Employment Guarantee Scheme (NREGS) program increases rural employment and thus reduces Maoist recruitment in states like Andhra Pradesh and Chhattisgarh, which is supported by my quantitative analysis in later chapters, which find that male unemployment is positively correlated with Maoist control. Gomes (2015) analyzes the role of the *zamindari* land tenure system in creating land inequality but also forest cover and scheduled castes and tribes in allowing conditions for Maoist insurgency. Hoelscher, Miklian, and Vadlamannati (2012) find that mining, scheduled castes/tribes, and NREGS all have an effect on Maoist violence. Chandra and Garcia-Ponce (2019) find that areas in India that had subaltern ethnic parties of lower castes and tribes saw Maoists being prevented from successfully recruiting from these lower castes and tribes, a finding reflected in my analysis of Chhattisgarh, where there were no local tribal parties that emerged to represent indigenous tribes.[17]

My analysis is complementary to these studies by focusing on historical determinants of these more proximate causal factors for Maoist insurgency that these studies analyze. However, my study is also distinct from this emerging quantitative literature in several ways. First, while these studies focus on proximate factors like political parties, ethnic grievances, state weakness, forest resources, and recent government welfare policies to explain current patterns of violence, my study analyzes the omitted variable of colonial indirect rule that is the underlying deeper cause of some of these proximate factors that determine Maoist conflict. Second, while these studies use *Maoist violence* as their dependent variable, I use a different dependent variable of *Maoist control,* which tries to measure actual rebel control of a district. As

---

[17] A more detailed engagement with this literature on the Maoist insurgency can be found in Chapter 2.

Kalyvas (2006) notes, areas with the highest rebel control may have low violence, so not using measures of violence can avoid potential measurement errors for rebel control. Third, these articles use quantitative analysis based on district-level datasets, while my book leverages qualitative and quantitative analysis and novel sub-district datasets for the states of Andhra Pradesh and Chhattisgarh.

5 TESTING THE COLONIAL LEGACIES EXPLANATION: RESEARCH DESIGN, DATA COLLECTION, AND ENDOGENEITY CONCERNS

5.1 Why India and Why the Maoist Insurgency Case?

Why study the case of India? It is the world's most populous democracy where democracy coexists with persistent insurgency in some parts of the country (Ganguly 1996; Mukherjee 2018), and it has significant subnational variation in state capacity, with highly developed urban areas coexisting with poor rural areas (Kohli 2012; Krishna 2017). It was in India, known as the jewel in the crown of the British Empire, that the British colonizers first developed the institution of colonial indirect rule between 1757 and the late 1800s, before implementing indirect rule in Nigeria and Africa in late nineteenth century (Lee-Warner 1910).

India has subnational variation in types of colonial direct and indirect rule, and also variation in the types of insurgency. It thus allows us the opportunity to develop nuanced theories of types of indirect rule and also test its correlation with subnational variation in patterns of rebel control. It allows us to understand how the British developed patterns of direct and indirect rule, before they applied them in practice to other contexts like Africa, the Middle East, and South East Asia.

Also, uncovering the underlying causal mechanisms linking colonial indirect rule to insurgency requires a careful qualitative case study approach that allows process tracing and demonstrating that path dependence sets in at a certain point of time. Given the nascent stage of research on colonial institutions and their impact on civil wars, it is necessary to develop fine-grained measures of different types of colonial institutions at the subnational level to analyze various mechanisms through which they could affect insurgency, before studying the effects of colonial institutions using cross-national datasets.

My study takes a step in these directions by analyzing the puzzle of the peculiar spatial variation in the Maoist insurgency in India to develop more disaggregated measures of colonial indirect rule and conflict. Making use of subnational data on one of the most important ideological insurgencies in the world's largest democracy also allows me to conceptualize a theory of different types of colonial indirect rule and revenue collection, thus heeding the plea by Wilkinson (2017) and Gerring et al. (2011) to think of colonial indirect rule as a non-dichotomous category.

5.2   Subnational Comparative Analysis – Nested Research Design and Case Selection

To test my theory, I exploit subnational spatial variation in Maoist insurgency and colonial indirect rule in India, a method that has been used successfully in the study of insurgencies (Staniland 2014; Weinstein 2007; Wood 2003), and ethnic riots in India (Varshney 2002; Wilkinson 2004). This method allows a controlled environment to develop and test theory and yields more accurate and micro-level measurements of different variables.

I test my theory by nesting qualitative analysis of Maoist insurgency in two Indian provinces – Andhra Pradesh and Chhattisgarh – within a larger all-India district-level econometric analysis of Maoist insurgency. This is similar to the "nested analysis" strategy of Lieberman (2005, 2015). It follows in the tradition of recent books on Indian politics like Thachil (2014) and Singh (2016), which also use mixed methods designs.

Level 1: Large N Quantitative Analysis Using District-Level Dataset Complemented by Qualitative Analysis

According to nested analysis design, we first need to attempt a preliminary large N analysis to "explore as many appropriate, testable hypotheses as is possible with available theory and data" (Lieberman 2005: 438). I test my theory of different types of colonial indirect rule and revenue collection on an all-India district-level dataset, which is the large N analysis (LNA) part of the research design. The dependent variable of *rebel control* is measured based on the Indian Ministry of Home Affairs (MHA) estimate of Maoist control in each district, coded from government documents collected during fieldwork. The independent variables of *princely state* and *land tenure* are collected from the Iyer (2010) dataset, and the coding is further improved by consulting other historical sources. Control variables like forest cover, elevation, land inequality, and population density are measured from the Census of India 1991 and other data sources. I also develop a new instrument for the choice of colonial indirect rule in India based on European wars creating exogenous constraints on the ability to fight wars and sign treaties in India. The IV-2SLS analysis allows me to address the issue of selection bias and is a significant empirical contribution.

Level 2: Small N Two-State Micro-Level Quantitative and Qualitative Analysis

Nested within this all-India analysis, I focus on the small N analysis (SNA) and use rich qualitative archival and fieldwork data to process trace the underlying causal mechanisms linking colonial indirect rule to insurgency in two states in India where the causal pathway of formal indirect rule through princely states leading to insurgency is prominent, namely Andhra Pradesh (A.P.) and Chhattisgarh. The cases of Chhattisgarh and A.P. represent crucial pathway cases (Gerring 2007) for my theory of colonial indirect rule creating weak state capacity and exploitation of land and natural resources, which are then exploited by rebel leaders to create and sustain rebellion. I also test the theory using novel sub-district assembly constituency-level datasets for these two states. This lower level quantitative analysis allows more fine-grained measurement of variables and removes the problem of over-aggregation.

Fieldwork in Maoist Zones: My project makes significant contributions in terms of data to the subnational analysis of insurgency. During fifteen months of fieldwork, I interviewed 120 police officers, bureaucrats, army officers, politicians, journalists, human rights activists, and Maoist sympathizers in Andhra Pradesh and Chhattisgarh. I interviewed villagers near Kirandul deep inside Dantewada district in the heart of Maoist country in Chhattisgarh, where the Bailadilla iron ore mines are located: the Maoists claim that there has been significant iron ore extraction and exploitation by the state from these tribal areas. I also interviewed at the Counter Terrorism and Jungle Warfare (CTJW) School in the Kanker district in Chhattisgarh, where the army trains police to fight the Maoists. Besides interviews, I collected a significant amount of data of different types that are not available through secondary sources or media, including police data on arrests and violence, State Assembly (Vidhan Sabha) discussions on the Maoist issue, old Naxal letters to the editor, and old news articles from archives of *Deshbandhu*, the oldest regional newspapers from Raipur, capital of Chhattisgarh. I have collected Maoist documents and posters and a large amount of Maoist literature from the police that they obtained from Maoists they arrested, and copies of the official mouthpiece of the CPI-Maoist called *People's March*. This data allows me to analyze the strategy and ideology of the Maoist movement in Chapter 4. I have also been collecting archival data to measure land tenure patterns within princely states, as well as types of indirect rule.

6 PLAN OF THE BOOK

This chapter asks a fundamental question that remains unanswered by theorists of civil war – do colonial institutions matter in explaining civil wars? It proposes that the puzzle of spatial variation of Maoist insurgency in India can be explained by legacies of British colonial indirect rule of different types. The case of the Maoist insurgency in India provides novel theoretical insights that can be extended to analyze other similar cases of how colonial indirect rule creates structural conditions for insurgency.

The rest of the book is divided into two parts. The first part uses qualitative and quantitative analysis with an all-India scope to demonstrate how different forms of colonial indirect rule created structural conditions for leftist insurgency. In Chapter 2, I engage with alternate explanations to show that they cannot explain the entire spatial variation of Maoist insurgency in India. I then outline the broad theoretical framework of how colonial indirect rule creates opportunity structures and ethnic mobilization networks for insurgency, and how these structural conditions in conjunction with rebel agency in the form of previous rebel networks and ideological frames of rebellion could create successful insurgency.

Then in Chapter 3, I trace the history of British colonial expansion in India and develop the theoretical framework specific to India by proposing that there are two types of colonial indirect rule, namely – (1) informal indirect rule or revenue collection through *zamindars* in the landlord revenue system, and (2) formal indirect rule through various princely states. In Chapter 4, I present qualitative evidence drawn from interviews with police, Maoist sympathizers, and other key actors, as well as textual analysis of Maoist documents to analyze the role of rebel agency and demonstrate that the Maoists failed to consolidate rebel control in areas considered strategically viable by them but which were under former direct rule. Instead, they were able to establish successful rebel control in the Bihar/Jharkhand epicenter where the *zamindari* land tenure system existed or in the Andhra/Chhattisgarh epicenter that had been part of princely states.

I test the theory on an all-India district-level dataset, which I present in two parts. In Chapter 5, I present the OLS analysis showing that princely state and *zamindari* land tenure are positively correlated with Maoist control. Then in Chapter 6, I address potential selection bias due to the possibility that the British selected for indirect rule those areas that were worse off in terms of governance, rebellion, and revenue potential by presenting a comparative case study of two similar princely states of Hyderabad and Awadh to demonstrate that historical contingency prevented selection in certain cases, and also using a novel instrument based on European wars to do an IV-2SLS analysis. I also develop a typology of different types of princely states and test it quantitatively to show that there is internal variation among princely states in their effects on state capacity, land tenure, and Maoist insurgency.

Following this all-India-level analysis, I move to the second part of the nested analysis research design. Chapter 7 describes how feudatory princely states like Bastar created structural conditions of land revenue extraction and low state capacity in Chhattisgarh, causing tribal grievances. The chapter then uses process tracing to show path dependent persistence of power of landlords and princely elites (Mahoney 2000) and continued exploitation of natural resources of these areas by the Indian state, which was exploited by the PWG Maoists to mobilize in south Chhattisgarh in 1990–2000s. The qualitative analysis is complemented by a quantitative analysis of a novel assembly constituency–level dataset.

Chapter 8 focuses on the neighboring state of Andhra Pradesh, where colonial indirect rule through the successor princely state of Hyderabad created extractive institutions and land inequalities, compared with areas that were part of British direct rule. Politics in the postcolonial period created path dependent mechanisms that prevented the government from doing land reforms and removing the unequal effects of these colonial institutions, and the PWG

Maoists were successful in the Telangana districts of the former princely state of Hyderabad.

Chhattisgarh and Andhra Pradesh are crucial pathway cases (Gerring 2007), which are well predicted by my theory. However, the path dependent process through which areas previously exposed to colonial indirect rule end up having structural conditions necessary for Maoist insurgency is not deterministic (Lange 2009). In certain states within India, princely states and *zamindari* tenure do not lead to Maoist insurgency, like Kerala and Karnataka. Closer qualitative analysis of these cases in Chapter 9 shows that these are not really exceptions but rather influential cases (Gerring 2007: 108) where "apparent deviations from the norm are not *really* deviant, or do not challenge the core of the theory, once the circumstances of the special case or cases are fully understood."

Chapter 10 tests the portability of my theory to other insurgencies in South Asia, and beyond. Within Pakistan, both the Tehrik-e-Taliban insurgency since mid-2000s in the FATA region, and the Baluchi secessionist insurgency movements since the 1960s have occurred in areas of erstwhile indirect rule under the British (Ali 2005; Naseemullah 2014). Another case I analyze is secessionist insurgency by the Kachin, Karen, Shan, and other ethnic groups in former British indirect rule areas in Myanmar (Callahan 2003). I also briefly analyze the effects of Spanish colonialism for the Zapatista insurgency in Mexico and the New People's Army (NPA) insurgency in the Philippines to look beyond British colonialism. Future studies should analyze in more detail these and other such cases of how colonial indirect rule created structural conditions of inequality and insurgency like the Nepal Maoist insurgency where there were unequal land tenure institutions, as well as the Boko Haram insurgency in northern Nigeria, which the British ruled indirectly through the Sokoto Caliphate. Chapter 11 concludes by discussing policy implications of my theory and explaining why the Maoist insurgency has declined in its level of violence in recent times.

2

Legacies of Colonial Indirect Rule: Weak State, Ethnic Inequality, and Insurgency

> *Much of the developing world was dragged into the modern era by colonialism. However one judges it, this is a historical legacy with which all scholars interested in the political economy of development, especially political economy over the long duration, must come to terms.*
>
> – Atul Kohli, *State Directed Development*

I   INTRODUCTION

What explains the peculiar spatial variation of Maoist insurgency in India? In this chapter, I outline this puzzle and show that existing theories of Maoist insurgency and colonial legacies in South Asia cannot explain the full spatial variation of Maoist control in India. It is necessary to develop a more nuanced theory of different forms of colonial indirect rule that created the ethnic inequalities and weak state capacity that the Maoist rebels exploited to foment insurgency. While ethnic inequalities were present in the western and southern parts of India, they were not as acute because of colonial direct rule in these areas, and so there was no Maoist insurgency there. It is the eastern region of Bihar/Bengal and the south-central regions of Orissa/Chhattisgarh/Andhra Pradesh where different forms of colonial indirect rule and revenue collection were used by the British that severe land inequalities, ethnic exclusion of Dalits and tribes from development, and weak state capacity created conditions favorable for insurgency in the future.

Colonial legacies are an ignored variable in most theories of civil war and insurgency and including it in a model of civil war increases the explanatory power. Chapter 1 outlined the various ways in which taking history seriously would contribute to the study of civil wars – for example it would allow us to explain the persistence and recurrence of rebellion, besides helping explain the sub-national variation in ethnic inequality and weak state capacity which are precursors for rebellion. In this chapter, I outline the theoretical mechanisms of despotic extraction, weak state capacity, and ethnic exclusion created by colonial indirect rule in South Asia and beyond, which could create conditions of insurgency. I engage with the literature on social movements/ rebellion to develop a general theoretical framework of how colonial indirect rule can create opportunity structures in the form of weak states and ethnic mobilization networks in the form of excluded ethnic groups with grievances, and how these structural conditions are then exploited by rebel leaders who provide ideological frames to start and sustain rebellion.

While none of these conditions is individually sufficient to produce rebellion, rebel agency in the form of ideological frames in conjunction with such opportunity structures and ethnic networks is a jointly sufficient condition to explain insurgency. The theory in this generalizable form could be used to explain how colonial indirect rule and land tenure can create causal pathways that potentially can lead to insurgency in various regions, whether in Pakistan, Burma, Nigeria, or the Philippines. In the next chapter, I use this theoretical lens to develop a schematic outline specific to the Maoists in India.

Unlike the cross-national dataset-based literature on civil wars that describes rebel opportunity in terms of more proximate determinants such as weak state capacity (Fearon & Laitin 2003), natural resource availability (Ross 2004), and ethnic exclusion (Cederman et al. 2010), my theoretical framework borrows from the earlier literature on rebellion and conceptualizes rebel opportunity as well as ethnic grievances as more long term, persistent, and sticky. This opens conceptual space to think of rebellion and insurgency as part of a long-term process of state formation and moves beyond the current myopic frameworks of civil war theory.

2 THE RED CORRIDOR ALONG INDIA'S EAST – EXPLAINING THE PUZZLE OF SPATIAL VARIATION

2.1 India's Red Corridor or Compact Revolutionary Zone

A glance at spatial variation of the Maoist insurgency on the map of India in Figure 2.1 reveals that during the peak period of insurgency in 2005–10, a long zone of Maoist influence ran from Andhra Pradesh in the south all the way up through Chhattisgarh and Jharkhand and Bihar to almost the border of Nepal in the north. The Maoists call this a Compact Revolutionary Zone (CRZ), sensationalized by the media as a "red corridor."

Figure 2.1 reveals two epicenters of Maoist mobilization along the CRZ. There is a northern epicenter around the Jharkhand and southern Bihar area and extending into some districts of northern Orissa and western West Bengal. This area is forested and hilly; while the parts in Jharkhand and West Bengal are scheduled tribe (ST) dominated, the districts in Bihar are scheduled caste (SC) dominated. There is also a southern epicenter near the Andhra Pradesh and

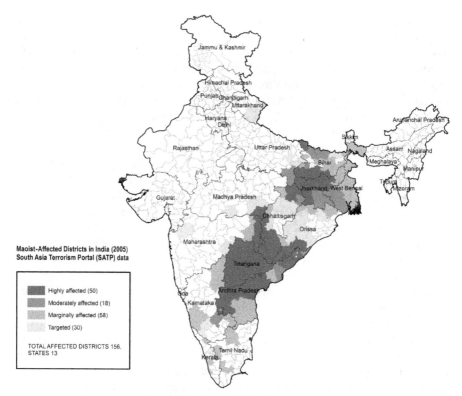

Maoist-Affected Districts in India (2005)
South Asia Terrorism Portal (SATP) data

Highly affected (50)
Moderately affected (18)
Marginally affected (58)
Targeted (30)

TOTAL AFFECTED DISTRICTS 156,
STATES 13

FIGURE 2.1 Spatial variation of Maoist mobilization, 2005
Source: www.satp.org/satporgtp/countries/india/images/naxalitemap.htm

Chhattisgarh borders, with diffusion of the movement into the surrounding districts of Maharashtra, Madhya Pradesh, Orissa, and Karnataka. This is a heavily forested region centered on the Dandakaranya forests, populated by Gond tribals or *Adivasis* who have been exploited by the state and ethnic outsiders. Within this lies the deeply forested Abujhmarh area in Bastar district south of Chhattisgarh, considered by the Maoists to be the center of their alternate people's government (*janathana sarkar*) and one of the few base areas they have been able to create.

It seems that the epicenters are close to state and district borders and populated by poor scheduled castes or tribes, with low public goods and infrastructure and hilly or forested terrain. Before the unification of the two main Maoist groups, the People's War Group (PWG) and the Maoist Communist Center (MCC) in 2004 to form the Communist Party of India-Maoist (CPI-Maoist), the People's Unity (PU) and the MCC dominated the northern epicenter, and the PWG dominated the southern one.[1]

---

[1] See Chapter 4 for detailed organizational history of the Maoist insurgency since the 1960s.

The Puzzle of Spatial Variation: This particular spatial variation in the map raises the following questions: Why have the different factions of Maoists been successful in creating this CRZ along this southeastern corridor but not in the west or south of India? Within this larger CRZ, why has Maoist control consolidated around these two epicenters of insurgency, namely along the Chhattisgarh-Orissa-Andhra Pradesh epicenter in the southeast and the Bihar-Jharkhand-Bengal epicenter in the northeast? What factors are common between these two geographic epicenters, which are not present in any of the other areas of India, which also have poor tribes and Dalits, forest cover, and inequalities?

What factors are different between this central-eastern red corridor and other parts of India where the Maoists did not succeed? Why is it that there has been a high level of Maoist mobilization in Bihar but less in neighboring Uttar Pradesh, which also has lower castes with grievances, and none in Rajasthan? Why is there high support for the Maoists in the Bastar region of Chhattisgarh, which has Gond tribes with grievances but not much in neighboring Madhya Pradesh and Maharashtra, which also have similar tribes and forests? Why did the Maoists succeed in the Telangana region of Andhra Pradesh but not so much in the Rayalseema and Coastal Andhra districts of the same state? Finally, why has there been no Maoist influence in the western state of Maharashtra, which was the Bombay Presidency under the British or in Tamil Nadu, which was earlier part of Madras Presidency under the British?

2.2   Engaging with Alternate Explanations

As briefly explained in Chapter 1, the peculiar spatial variation in Maoist insurgency in India is best explained by historical legacies of colonial British indirect rule. This makes the Maoist case an important one that highlights the role colonial legacies play in explaining insurgency.

I now engage with several alternate explanations for this peculiar spatial variation in Maoist control in India. Most of these explanations are not rival but complementary to my theory, even though they focus on more proximate factors of ethnic inequality and state weakness and not colonial indirect rule. However, they cannot explain the entire spatial variation, which is why it becomes important to conceptualize the role of colonial legacies.

2.2.1   *Complementary Explanations Based on Quantitative Analyses of Maoist Insurgency Are Neither Necessary nor Sufficient to Explain Spatial Variation*

Several recent studies of the Maoist insurgency in India use quantitative analysis based on district-level datasets, and find that both rebel opportunity (Collier & Hoeffler 2004; Fearon & Laitin 2003) and ethnic and political grievances (Gurr 1970; Sambanis 2001; Cederman et al. 2010) matter to explain Maoist violence. These studies use measures of violence and killings as their dependent variable drawn from the latter phases (2000–10) of the insurgency from media sources and analyze the effect of socioeconomic and geographic factors, natural resources, poverty, land inequality, and government policy on Maoist violence.

Gawande, Kapur, and Satyanath (2017) develop a new dataset on the Maoist insurgency for the 2000–10 period, which incorporates events from regional and vernacular newspapers, besides English-language newspapers, and thus is more comprehensive than other datasets like the SATP data that is based on urban media sources. Gawande et al. (2017) use rainfall as an instrument for forest cover and find that sudden reduction in forest cover or vegetation leads to more conflict deaths, which implies that it is lack of access to forest products and livelihood that decreases opportunity costs for tribals and *Adivasis* staying in these areas and increases their chances of joining the Maoists.

Using the same dataset, Dasgupta et al. (2017) analyze the effects of the National Rural Employment Guarantee Scheme (NREGS) program on Maoist recruitment and find that those districts where the NREGS were rolled out tended to see a reduction in the level of Maoist violence. They suggest that the reason providing employment opportunities to poor people reduces Maoist recruitment could be working through both the opportunity cost mechanism (Collier & Hoeffler 2004; Fearon & Laitin 2003) and the political/economic grievance mechanism (Cederman et al. 2013; Gurr 1970), and that both "originate in poverty and underdevelopment as a root cause" and yield the same observable implications (Dasgupta et al. 2017: 608).

In another district-level analysis using conflict data from 1980 to 2009, Gomes (2015) finds that districts with scheduled castes and tribes have higher levels of Maoist violence, which is support for the ethnic grievances hypothesis (Cederman et al. 2010; Gurr 1970). Gomes (2015) however also finds that forest cover percentage as well as barren and rocky terrain tends to have a positive correlation with Maoist conflict and suggests that this could be because forests allow rebels a place to hide and fight, which would be support for the rebel opportunity hypothesis. Hoelscher et al. (2012) find that mining, scheduled castes/tribes, and NREGS all have an effect on Maoist violence, similar to the Dasgupta et al. (2017) study.

Unlike these studies, which focus on socioeconomic, demographic, and natural resource factors, Chandra and Garcia-Ponce (2019) argue that where ethnic political parties reach subaltern groups like the scheduled castes and tribes first and recruit young men from these subaltern group into the party system, Maoists are preempted from recruiting, since these ethnic groups from which they recruit are already incorporated into the political mainstream.

In Chapter 5, I do a similar district-level quantitative analysis, though my dependent variable is *rebel control* in the initial period of insurgency before the unification of the MCC and PWG in 2004, which is conceptually different from insurgency-related violence, which is the dependent variable used by these studies. In this regression analysis, I control for many of these proximate factors like forest cover, hilly terrain, male unemployment, literacy, scheduled caste, and tribe percentage that are analyzed as proximate causes of Maoist insurgency in these studies and find that *colonial indirect rule* is still a statistically significant predictor of *Maoist rebel control*. While these more proximate factors matter a great deal in explaining current patterns of violence and recruitment in Maoist insurgency, colonial indirect rule institutions are a long-term underlying cause of these proximate factors, which are intermediate mechanisms that can explain Maoist rebellion. Once the British chose indirect rule for particular areas, these institutions had an independent effect on the probability of insurgency beyond that created by proximate opportunity structures like forest cover and hilly terrain.

There is a second reason why analyzing effects of proximate socioeconomic, ethnic, and state capacity factors is not enough, and it is important to include the omitted variable of colonial institutions. While the Maoist insurgency occurs in areas that have rough terrain or forest cover, mineral resources, weak state capacity, socioeconomically exploited lower castes and tribes, and fewer subaltern ethnic political parties, other areas also have these same characteristics but no Maoist insurgency. This makes these factors not sufficient and sometimes not even necessary conditions, to explain the full breadth of Maoist mobilization in India. For example, while in Chhattisgarh the Bastar region controlled by the Maoists is in the dense Dandakaranya forested zone, the central plains of Bihar do not have forests, but do have a long history of Maoist conflict. In the large forested and hilly tracts in the Western Ghats along India's western coast in Karnataka state, Maoists have tried in the past but not succeeded in establishing rebel control, as they have in the Chhattisgarh-Andhra-Orissa border area.[2] This shows that forested or hilly terrain is neither a necessary nor sufficient condition.

Similarly, while the Maoists are known to recruit tribal *Adivasis* with grievances in states like Chhattisgarh and Jharkhand, poor tribes live in other neighboring states like Maharashtra and Madhya Pradesh where the Maoists have not succeeded, except for a few districts like Gadchiroli, and Balaghat near their borders with Chhattisgarh state. In fact, the tribal belt of India stretches from east to west across central India, and the western states of Madhya Pradesh, Maharashtra, and Gujarat have tribes but no Maoist conflict. Also, Maoist mobilization has been successful in Bihar and in parts of Andhra Pradesh, where the Maoists have recruited lower castes or *Dalits* and not *Adivasi* tribals. This demonstrates that tribes/*Adivasis* are neither necessary nor sufficient to explain Maoist mobilization.

There are lower castes/*Dalits* with grievances in Bihar and Andhra Pradesh, and different Maoist groups have mobilized them and to address their needs. However, there are lower castes/*Dalits* in Maharashtra, Madhya Pradesh, Punjab, and Tamil Nadu; while they have been involved with other kinds of

[2] See CPI-ML (People's War), "Karnataka: Social Conditions and Tactics."

social and political movements, the Maoists have not succeeded in mobilizing them, which implies that lower caste is not a sufficient condition either.

So, the usual explanations for civil war based on state weakness, rough terrain, and rebel opportunity (Collier & Hoeffler 2004; Fearon & Laitin 2003) and ethnic exclusion of tribes/lower castes (Cederman et al. 2010) cannot fully explain this peculiar spatial variation of the Maoist insurgency. In contrast, almost all the districts that had Maoist control until the unification of the PWG and MCC in 2004 previously experienced colonial indirect rule of some type, thus making this a necessary condition for successful mobilization.[3] This is demonstrated in the qualitative analysis of Maoist documents in Chapter 4, which shows that while strategic factors like access to forests and presence of tribals and *Dalits* were important to the Maoists, a close look at the core areas of Maoist control in Bihar/Jharkhand/Bengal and Chhattisgarh/Andhra/Orissa until 2004 reveals that their movement succeeded *only* if historical institutions of indirect rule through *zamindars* or princely states were also present. So colonial indirect rule in conjunction with more proximate factors explains spatial variation of Maoist control until the unification of MCC and PWG and rapid expansion since 2004. My theory is not rival to but is complementary to these other explanations that focus on more proximate ethnic, geographic, political, and socioeconomic factors to explain Maoist violence.

How My Study Is Complementary to These Studies but Also Distinct from Them While complementary, my study is also distinct from this quantitative literature on India's Maoist insurgency. First, while these studies focus on proximate factors that explain current patterns of violence, my study analyzes the omitted variable of colonial indirect rule. Second, I use rebel control of the initial core areas, before the insurgency expands with the unification of the MCC and PWG groups in 2004, as my dependent variable. This makes my study distinct from these studies on the Maoist insurgency that use insurgency violence from 2005 to 2010 as their dependent variable. As Kalyvas (2006) notes, areas with the highest rebel control may have low violence, so not using measures of violence can avoid potential measurement errors for rebel control. Third, my theory focuses on how colonial indirect rule creates structural constraints for rebel leaders before the insurgency suddenly expands following unification of the PWG and MCC factions in 2004 and is distinct from these other studies that explain levels and patterns of violence in the latter phase of insurgency (2005–12). Finally, my study has a mixed-method design that combines archival data and field interviews based on extensive fieldwork in Maoist-affected areas in India to demonstrate path dependence, with IV-2SLS

---

[3] Indirect rule may not be a sufficient condition by itself because there are exceptional cases like Kerala and Karnataka that had princely states or *zamindars* but not very successful Maoist movement, but this is explained as "influential cases" (Gerring 2007a) in Chapter 9.

regression analysis to address selection bias (Lieberman 2015). In contrast, these other studies use mainly quantitative analysis.

2.2.2 Addressing Competing Explanations Based on Colonial Legacies

Some studies analyze the effects of colonial legacies in South Asia on development, or more directly on Maoist conflict in India. I engage with these studies and show that they either cannot explain the Maoist insurgency or can only partly explain it.

Theories Showing Effect of Colonial Land Tenure and Indirect Rule on Development in India In a well-known paper, Banerjee and Iyer (2005) find that districts in India that had the *zamindari* system of land revenue where the British colonizers used landlords as intermediaries to collect land revenue on their behalf have lower rates of economic performance and public goods, than districts that had *ryotwari* and *mahalwari* types of non-landlord systems of land revenue in which the British colonizers collected land revenue directly from the *ryots* or peasants and villages. The more unequal *zamindari* land tenure system created not only land inequality but also political inequality between landed and landless groups. While these authors do not analyze effects of colonial land tenure on insurgency, they do mention in passing that "the areas most associated with Maoist peasant uprisings (known as 'Naxalite' movements) ... are West Bengal, Bihar, and the Srikakulum district of Andhra Pradesh, all landlord areas" (Banerjee & Iyer 2005: 1198).

My project draws inspiration from this study to understand how colonial legacies matter for explaining the second phase of the Maoist insurgency since the 1980s, by conceptualizing the *zamindari* landlord tenure system as indirect revenue collection systems. However, this study of colonial land tenure has two shortcomings when applying it to explain the spatial variation of Maoist insurgency in the 1980s–90s. First, it can explain the northern epicenter of the Maoist insurgency in Bihar/Bengal/Jharkhand, where land inequalities intensified caste conflicts and allowed the Maoists to mobilize lower castes. However, it cannot explain why there was Maoist conflict in the southern epicenter of Andhra Pradesh/Chhattisgarh/Orissa where it is not *zamindari* tenure but rather colonial indirect rule through princely states that sets up structural conditions that were exploited by PWG Maoists to create zones of rebel control (Sundar 2007). In fact, the areas with Maoist rebellion in Telangana in Andhra Pradesh that were part of the former Hyderabad princely state were officially *ryotwari* type of tenure and not *zamindari*.[4] Another problem with this study is that it only measures colonial land tenure for British direct rule areas and does not have measures of colonial land tenure for princely states. I describe land tenure in the princely states of Bastar and Hyderabad in Chapters 7 and 8, thus making an important empirical contribution.

---

[4] Interview with K. Balagopal, 2008, noted human rights activist and former Maoist sympathizer.

A second paper that makes a significant contribution to understanding the political economy of colonial legacies in South Asia is Iyer's (2010) IV-2SLS analysis using an all-India dataset, which shows that indirect ruled areas under former princely states had better development and agricultural outcomes than districts under former British direct rule. While this paper is valuable for the colonial legacies literature on South Asia, it fails to explain why the PWG Maoists operated successfully in the princely state (indirect rule) areas of Hyderabad in Andhra Pradesh, and Bastar/Kanker in Chhattisgarh, which saw some of the strongest core areas of guerrilla zones and base areas. The issue with this study is that it assumes all princely states are the benevolent type like Baroda and Travancore and uses a 0–1 measure for indirect rule, while in reality there is a lot of variation between different types of princely states, as Wilkinson (2017) has suggested, and some princely states like Bastar and Hyderabad are more despotic, as I demonstrate in Chapters 7 and 8.[5]

Theories Showing Effect of Colonial Indirect Rule on Maoist Insurgency in India A more recent explanation based on colonial institutions that fails to explain the spatial variation of the Maoist insurgency is a paper by Teitelbaum and Verghese (2019), which is similar to Iyer's (2010) conclusion and hypothesizes that the districts that had direct British rule tend to have more Maoist insurgency and tests this empirically on a district-level dataset. In a different paper, Verghese (2016a: 1621) notes that these tribal conflicts continued to happen in former areas of direct British rule and suggests that the princely state of Bastar experienced tribal Maoist insurgency because it was not really indirect rule since the British intervened often. In a separate book, Verghese (2016b: 149) has a broader theory that claims that in the directly ruled provinces, the British protected religious minorities through a policy of neutrality and discriminated against low castes and *Adivasis*, while in the princely states, native kings protected the low castes and tribals and discriminated against non-coreligionists. Thus former British provinces like Ajmer and Malabar experienced caste and tribal violence while the former princely states like Jaipur and Travancore experienced considerable Hindu-Muslim religious violence. He also spends a chapter on the outlier case of Bastar princely state that contradicted his theory and had tribal rebellions led by the Maoists.

These studies suffer from several conceptual and empirical weaknesses. First, an empirical problem with Teitelbaum and Verghese's (2019) theory is that it cannot explain why the PWG Maoists operated in the southern epicenter of the

---

[5] There is also a potential problem with the IV2SLS analysis in Iyer, "Direct versus Indirect Colonial Rule in India," since the instrument is based on random deaths of rulers during Lord Dalhousie's Doctrine of Lapse period (1847–56), but this strategy leaves out the northern epicenter of Maoist insurgency in Bihar-Bengal annexed between 1757 and 1846 from the IV-2SLS analysis. See the quantitative analysis in Chapter 6 for details.

insurgency in indirect rule areas of Bastar/Surguja in Chhattisgarh state and in the Telangana region of the former indirect ruled princely state of Hyderabad in Andhra Pradesh state, and the feudatory princely states in Orissa/Chota Nagpur/Jharkhand areas, which were core areas of insurgency and make up a significant chunk of the Maoist red corridor. These were areas of high inequality, and exploitation of tribal *Adivasis*, due to the despotic rule of the Nizam of Hyderabad and the princes of Bastar and other eastern feudatory states in Orissa. Inability to explain the entire southern epicenter of insurgency leads to a major weakness in their theory since subnational variation within India clearly shows that it was areas with certain types of British indirect rule, and not direct rule, that create conditions for the PWG to mobilize successfully in Telangana and Bastar/Kanker and some Orissa princely states.

In fact, in his article, Verghese (2016a) recognizes this in a footnote, "Bastar is not the only former princely state that experiences tribal conflict – the Naxalites are also active in Orissa and Telangana."[6] However, he does not have a convincing explanation for why these areas of former indirect rule through princely states had and continue to have tribal rebellion. In both his book and article, Verghese (2016a, 2016b) suggests that Bastar princely state was direct rule because the British often intervened and controlled the administration through their officers. But this is not persuasive, since this happened in many princely states where the British used the Residency system to control and intervene in case of maladministration or for other strategic reasons (Fisher 1991). This does not mean that these princely states were direct rule as in Madras and Bombay Presidencies where the British used their own bureaucracy and police and allowed provincial elections since the 1920s, though it hints at variation between types of princely states.

The second empirical problem with these studies' claim that colonial direct rule causes Maoist insurgency is that it cannot explain why there is no Maoist insurgency and relatively higher development in the western and southern states of Maharashtra, Tamil Nadu, and so on, which were formerly British direct rule with *ryotwari* (peasant based) land revenue systems in Bombay and Madras Presidency, respectively. So the theory fails to explain large chunks of territory that were directly ruled by the British and yet had relatively higher levels of development and no Maoist insurgency. In fact, these were the areas that were not only directly ruled but also had direct land tenure systems like the *ryotwari* system and so based on their theory should have had maximum Maoist and tribal conflict. Yet it has the least Maoist conflict, which shows a serious weakness in the predictive power of these studies.

Third, Teitelbaum and Verghese (2019) make the conceptual error of interpreting the *zamindari* landlord tenure in the northern epicenter of the Maoist insurgency in Bihar/Jharkhand as British direct rule. In his article, Verghese (2016a: 1621; emphasis mine) similarly notes that these "tribal

---

[6] Verghese, "British Rule and Tribal Revolts in India," p. 1623.

conflicts continued to occur ... especially in former areas of *direct British rule* like Bengal, Bihar, and Jharkhand." This is in contrast to scholars like Kohli (2004: 225–26), Lange (2009), and Dirks (2001), who conceptualize the *zamindari* tenure system as a type of indirect revenue collection or rule, under which the overburdened colonial state depended on native intermediaries to collect land taxes on their behalf, instead of collecting land taxes directly as in the *ryotwari* tenure system in Bombay and Madras provinces.

As explained in greater detail in the next chapter, the *zamindari* land tenure system in Bengal/Bihar provinces in the east is a type of informal indirect rule, since the British depended on intermediaries to collect land revenue and carry out administration on their behalf, as compared with the *ryotwari* type of land tenure system in Madras or Bombay province in the west/south where the British collected land revenue directly from the *ryots* or peasants in the villages and thus required a more penetrative bureaucratic setup (Kohli 2004; Lange 2009). Verghese (2016a, 2016b) and Teitelbaum and Verghese (2019) are wrong to characterize the *zamindari* system as direct rule, just because it is part of formal British direct rule in Bengal and Bihar provinces. It was the *indirect revenue collection* systems through *zamindars* used in Bengal/Bihar by the British that created land and caste inequalities; areas in Bombay or Madras provinces in the southwest of India, where the British used more direct and equitable *ryotwari* land tenure system that was truly direct rule and direct revenue collection did not see tribal/peasant rebellions in colonial or postcolonial times.

The main problem in these studies is that they conceptualize direct-indirect rule as a binary concept, when in reality there is a lot of variation within the category of indirect rule in India. In his review of Verghese's (2016b) book, Wilkinson (2017) builds on Verghese's suggestion that Bastar princely state was often directly controlled by the British for periods of time and agrees that there is a lot of variation between different types of princely states. Wilkinson (2017) states, "as Verghese's qualitative analysis makes clear, some states such as Hyderabad had enormous autonomy, others much less so, while in other states rulers were autonomous for some periods but were under heavy British supervision or even direct rule for others." From this, Wilkinson draws the conclusion that the binary distinction between direct versus indirect rule by Verghese (2016b) is inaccurate, and we need to think of indirect rule as a continuous concept and disaggregate between the different types of indirect rule. Wilkinson questions whether the complexity of history can be quantified easily into binary measures of direct versus indirect rule in statistical analysis.[7]

Unlike previous studies like Verghese (2016b) and Iyer (2010) that measure indirect rule as a 0–1 variable in their quantitative analysis, I address this issue

---

[7] See Steven Wilkinson, "Looking Back at the Colonial Origins of Communal and Caste Conflict in India."

by disaggregating the concept of colonial indirect rule and developing a more nuanced typology of different types of indirect rule. In the next chapter I develop a theory of different types of indirect rule in India – formal indirect rule through princely states and informal indirect rule through *zamindars*. In later Chapters 6–8, I further differentiate between different types of princely states in India, some having more land and natural resource exploitation than others.

Theories of Colonial Indirect Rule and Conflict in South Asia In a recent paper that takes a step in the direction of disaggregating types of indirect rule, Naseemullah and Staniland (2016: 15–16) criticize the literature on colonial legacies by Banerjee and Iyer (2005) and Lange (2009) for conceptualizing indirect rule as a dichotomous or binary 0–1 concept. To make better sense of the "bewildering diversity" of indirect rule in South Asia, the paper proposes a typology of three types of indirect rule governance arrangements – suzerain rule, hybrid, and de jure rule.[8] The *suzerain* type of indirect rule "represents a relationship in which princely or tribal states are nominally independent and constitutionally free to order their internal affairs, yet maintain allegiance to an overarching imperial power" (Naseemullah and Staniland 2016: 17). It seems that various small and large princely states that had signed formal treaties or *sanads* with the British, like Hyderabad, Bastar, Baroda, Mysore, and Kashmir, would fit in here. In the second type of indirect rule, *hybrid governance*, "the state explicitly shares authority with social actors" so as to maintain control over a strategically important territory, without having to deploy a monopoly of force and often relies on militias and constabularies for maintaining order, for example, in the frontier territories in northwest Pakistan bordering Afghanistan (Naseemullah and Staniland 2016: 17). The third category of indirect rule is *de jure governance*, under which the state maintains de jure direct rule over a territory, but "in reality coercion is enforced locally by intermediate political elites" (Naseemullah and Staniland 2016: 17).

The authors, however, recognize one of the limitations of their typology, since there is "significant variation *within* the subcategories presented here, such as between suzerain territories of radically different sizes" (Naseemullah and Staniland 2016: 18, emphasis in original). Applying this framework to the case of the Maoist insurgency in India would be useful since their category of de jure governance is similar to the *zamindari* land tenure system in Bengal province, which was officially directly ruled, but in reality the colonial officers depended on the *zamindars* to collect taxes and rule on their behalf, thus creating land inequality and Maoist insurgency. However, this typology does not differentiate between types of princely states in the suzerain governance category and so cannot explain why there was successful Maoist insurgency in former princely states like Hyderabad and Bastar, but not in princely states like Travancore and Mysore. To explain the complete spatial variation in levels of

---

[8] Naseemullah and Staniland, "Indirect Rule and Varieties of Governance."

Maoist rebel control in India would require even more fine-grained differentiation between types of princely states, which I present in later chapters.

3   EXPLAINING THE ENTIRE SPATIAL VARIATION: COLONIAL INDIRECT RULE AND INSURGENCY

These existing theories cannot fully explain the entire spatial variation of Maoist insurgency across all the districts of India. To explain both epicenters of Maoist insurgency in India, I develop a theory that conceptualizes two types of British indirect rule – both formal (princely states) and informal (*zamindari* land tenure) – and show how they create mechanisms that help set up long-term opportunity structures for leftist mobilization in the future.

Many of the dominant theories on civil war onset, like Fearon and Laitin (2003), Collier and Hoeffler (2004), Sambanis (2001, 2004), and Hegre et al. (2001), use cross-national data and focus on the importance of state capacity, rebel opportunity, and ethnic heterogeneity to explain civil war, without referring to historical institutions. What is missing from these theories of civil war onset is a broader interpretation of state capacity/rebel opportunity/ethnic identity in terms of historical institutions and their long-term effect on postcolonial institutions, ethnic structures, and rebel networks.

To explain this peculiar spatial variation of Maoist insurgency in India, I conceptualize colonial indirect rule institutions as an omitted variable from models of civil war, since it affects subnational variation in levels of postcolonial state capacity, economic development, and ethnic inequalities, which then become proximate factors that influence the ability of rebel leaders to start and sustain insurgency. This implies one of the weaknesses of studies on civil war onset – that various predictors of conflict onset – whether weak state capacity measured by per capita income (Fearon & Laitin 2003), or rebel opportunity measured by primary commodity exports or male school enrollment (Collier & Hoeffler 2004), or ethnic polarization (Reynal-Querol 2002a), or ethnic exclusion (Cederman et al. 2010) – are potentially endogenous to historical processes of state formation.

Miguel, Satyanath, and Sergenti (2004: 726) recognize that the cross-national literature on civil wars fails to incorporate "omitted variables – for example, governmental institutional quality" that "may drive both economic outcomes and conflict, producing misleading cross-country estimates." Extending this analysis to historical institutions, we can visualize colonial indirect rule as one such omitted variable (Z) that is driving both postcolonial state capacity/ethnic inequalities/natural resource extraction (X) on the one hand, and insurgency occurrence (Y) on the other (see Figure 1.2 in Chapter 1). By including such an omitted variable that is causally prior to the more proximate processes of weak state capacity, or exploitation of natural resources, or creation of ethnic grievances into explanations of civil war, it may be possible to reduce some of the endogeneity issues and have a more holistic explanation for conflict.

In the rest of this chapter, I define the concept of colonial indirect rule and then begin to sketch out the mechanisms created by indirect rule that can possibly create conditions for insurgency in South Asia and beyond.

3.1 Defining Indirect Rule

In his comprehensive study of the British Residency System in India, Fisher (1991: 2) defined indirect rule broadly as "indirect control over other peoples through indigenous political structures" and mentions that it has been used by the Roman, Chinese, and Egyptian empires to try and govern far-flung parts of the empire with different ethnic groups. Not only emperors from Alexander to Caesar to Napoleon but also corporate merchants like the French and Dutch East India Companies in the 1600s experimented with different forms of indirect rule that used "indigenous political institutions" to some degree.

In this book, I am specifically interested in British colonial indirect rule that was developed in India and then applied in Western Africa and the Middle East by British administrators in their efforts to conquer and control an expanding empire, and how this particular type of colonial rule created conditions for postcolonial insurgency. The British started developing control over African countries with the "scramble for Africa" toward the end of the nineteenth century. Most of these British colonies including Nigeria, Sierra Leone, Uganda, Tanzania, Ghana, Kenya, Botswana, and Malawi used different types of indirect rule (Lange 2009: 25).

The well-known architect of British indirect rule in West Africa was Lord Lugard, who was suspicious of the introduction of representative government in India and preferred for Western Africa the system of "rule by native chiefs, unfettered in their control of their people" but "subordinate to the control of the protecting power in certain well-defined directions" (Lugard 1926: 197). The epitome of this system of indirect rule through native chiefs was northern Nigeria, which Lugard describes as follows: "The object in view is to make each 'Emir' or paramount chief, assisted by his judicial council, and effective ruler over his own people. He presides over a 'Native Administration.' ... The area over which he exercises jurisdiction is divided into districts under the control of 'Headmen,' who collect the taxes in the name of the ruler, and pay them into the 'Native Treasury'" (pp. 200–201).

This ideal form of indirect rule in Nigeria was a unified system in which there is one government in which the native chiefs have well-defined duties within an overall structure of rule and were considered of equal status with the colonial officers (Lugard 1926: 203). What emerged in reality in most African countries was what Mamdani (1996: 16) called a "bifurcated state" in which two separate and incompatible forms of rule existed: an urban directly ruled core dominated by colonial officials in which natives were excluded from civil freedoms and the more rural periphery controlled through different indigenous authorities that tried to incorporate natives into a state-enforced customary order.

This was a little different from the type of indirect rule that had evolved in India, where the British East India Company arrived much earlier and started conquering territories beginning in 1757 and faced the unique situation of a country of much higher population density than in Africa, with diverse ethnicity and complex pre-colonial institutions of little and big kingdoms. To control this large and diverse population, the British developed a hybrid mix of territories of high colonial state penetration mixed with areas of relative sovereignty (Mahoney 2010: 240). The former type of rule was the directly ruled areas of Madras in the south, Bombay in the west and the Bengal Presidency in the east where the British tried to implant institutions of rule like police, bureaucracy, and tax collection as in Britain, and later even introduced provincial elections beginning in the 1920s. The latter type of rule included the various types of native states and other native elites on whom the colonial administrators depended to control the diverse political and ethnic landscape that was India and can be broadly grouped under the rubric of *indirect rule*. Even in some of the officially directly ruled areas like Bengal Presidency in the east, the British depended on *zamindars* to collect land revenue on their behalf, and depending on such intermediaries was also a form of indirect rule.

In his study of the British Residency System in the princely states in India, Fisher (1991: 6–7) defined indirect rule in India as "the exercise of determinative and exclusive political control by one corporate body over a nominally sovereign state, a control recognized by both sides," and the imposing power must recognize to some degree the sovereignty of the local state. Lange (2009: 4) builds on this definition by Fisher (1991) and proposes that indirect rule is

a form of colonial domination via collaboration with indigenous intermediaries who controlled regional political institutions. It created bifurcated colonial states based on two radically different organizational principles. Like direct rule, the central legal-administrative institutions in indirectly ruled colonies were relatively bureaucratic, yet these institutions were usually miniscule and isolated in the colonial capital and areas of European settlement. In peripheral regions, chiefs, princes, sultans, and other indigenous leaders controlled "customary" legal-administrative institutions that were organized along patrimonial lines.

In his classic work on colonial legacies in Latin America, Mahoney (2010) briefly discusses British colonialism in India. According to Mahoney (2010: 239–40), although the British may have wanted to use a single bureaucratic system for the whole of India, the existence of pre-colonial kingdoms and the Great Indian Mutiny of 1857 made them realize they could not ignore local institutions; thus, they decided to strengthen "alliances with traditional elites" and deploy those elites "for collecting taxes and maintaining political order." This resulted in "a hybrid colony that combined indirect and direct forms of colonialism. Some six hundred princely states, comprising approximately two-fifths of colonial India, were ruled indirectly. The remainder of the colony continued to be dominated by a direct form of administration that did not incorporate indigenous institutions into the overall system of governance." One difference between the indirectly ruled areas in India and those in Africa was that the central administration in colonial India was more bureaucratically organized than in the African colonies, which had more comprehensive indirect rule. So, state capacity varied within India, but the state had higher capacity for policy implementation and reforms, a point also raised by Kohli (2004), who compares the patrimonial state of Nigeria with the mixed colonial legacy in India.

3.2 Mechanisms Created by Colonial Indirect Rule That Are Relevant to Explain Insurgency

There is a literature that debates the effects of colonial indirect rule on development, state capacity, and ethnic identity/exclusion in South Asia and Africa. Different types of colonial indirect rule and indirect revenue collection were created by the British, and these resulted in lower levels of state capacity and development and more land inequality *on average*, which then persisted into the postcolonial period through path dependent mechanisms (Kohli 2004; Lange 2009; Mahoney 2010). While these studies do not analyze the effects of indirect rule on insurgency, the effects on state capacity, level of development, ethnic exclusion, and land inequality could be considered intermediate mechanisms leading to insurgency in some countries.

Weak state capacity or ethnic/land inequalities created historically by colonial indirect rule of different types persist into the postcolonial period and then are exploited by rebel leaders to create and sustain insurgency, whether the leftist ideological insurgency of the Maoists in India or Nepal, Islamic ideological insurgencies like those of the Taliban in Pakistan, or ethnic secessionist insurgency that is seen in cases like Kashmir in India, or the Baluchis in Pakistan, or the Kachin and Shan insurgents in Burma. These mechanisms created by colonial indirect rule can also be used to explain insurgency in regions beyond South Asia like the Boko Haram insurgency in Nigeria, the leftist NPA insurgency in Philippines, and the leftist Zapatista rebellion in Mexico.

This section outlines the three main types of mechanisms suggested by this literature that could be intermediate mechanisms that create the structural conditions for insurgency. In the next section, I propose a general theory linking colonial indirect/ direct rule with insurgency in South Asia and beyond.

*Mechanism 1: Colonial Indirect Rule Creates Low State Capacity and Low
Development That Facilitates Insurgency*

Some canonical studies analyze how the choice of indirect versus direct rule has
long-term ramifications in terms of variation in levels of state capacity and
development, thus setting up the structural conditions for low state
penetration and low development, which are some of the main mechanisms
explaining civil war onset (Collier & Hoeffler 2004; Fearon & Laitin 2003).

Various scholars like Kohli (2004), Lange (2009), and Mahoney (2010)
suggest that *on average* British direct rule areas had more development and
infrastructure, while indirect rule areas had lower state penetration and lower
levels of development. Kohli (2004) uses comparative historical analysis to
demonstrate that the type of colonizer and variation in colonizer ideology are
important factors to explain why developing countries varied in their types of
state structures. According to Kohli (2004: 18), the Japanese colonizers used
direct state intervention for agricultural development and industrial growth in
Korea and had a colonial impact that was "intense, brutal and deeply
architectonic" and resulted in high levels of bureaucratic capacity and police
capacity. . . . This was even more developed and penetrative than the British civil
service in India, often called the "steel frame of the British empire." They also
developed a penetrative police force that was used to incorporate the village
elders and local elites into the ruling coalition, instead of relying on such local
elites through indirect rule. Such direct forms of colonialism in South Korea left
administrative and state capacity legacies that persisted and shaped the
institutional foundations for what Kohli calls a "cohesive-capitalist" state in
South Korea, thus leading to subsequent high levels of state-driven
development.

In contrast, British colonialism in Nigeria was quite minimalist and used
indirect rule, relying on traditional chiefs to control the country, since the
British wanted to rule Nigeria on the cheap. There was some variation in
colonial rule, with the northern part of Nigeria that was previously part of the
Islamic Sokoto Caliphate being ruled indirectly through the existing emirs. The
level of colonial police forces was low in the north, and the traditional chiefs
were given the responsibility of maintaining a native police force, with only
a "handful of British civil servants" used to "supervise the emirs, primarily in . . .
tax collection and expenditure" (Kohli, 2004: 306). Colonial rule in the
Yorubaland regions in southern Nigeria was a little more direct, with the
police force recruited based on the "martial races" theory, with some 3,000
policemen and about 80 British officers (Kohli 2004: 305).

This indirect type of colonialism "reinforced a pattern of patrimonial and
personalistic rule that failed to centralize authority, to develop an effective civil
service, and relatedly, to develop even such minimal political capacities as the
ability to collect direct taxes" (Kohli 2004: 18). This produced a weak state that
readily evolved into a *neo-patrimonial* state after Nigeria gained independence,
with "weakly centralized and barely legitimate authority structures,

personalistic leaders unconstrained by norms or institutions, and bureaucracies of poor quality" (p. 9). While Kohli (2004) focuses on the effects of colonial indirect versus direct rule on state formation and development, it is possible that the use of indirect rule through the Sokoto Caliphate in the north of Nigeria also made northern Nigeria more open to an Islamic ideology that persisted and led to various Islamic movements and finally the Boko Haram insurgency in northern Nigeria in more recent times. Weaker state capacity in northern Nigeria allowed the Boko Haram to establish rebel control (Babalola, 2013: 13–16; Sampson 2014: 312–15).

Similarly, Lange (2009: 6) analyzes British colonialism across different countries and suggests that direct rule created more bureaucratic and state capacity and had a more positive effect on social and economic development than indirect rule.[9] Lange (2009) tests his theory on a dataset of former British colonies and finds that those colonies that were more indirectly ruled have lower levels of postcolonial development and governance, as measured by per capita GDP, school attendance, and infant mortality. He also does case studies and finds that British indirect rule in Sierra Leone "impaired the state's legal-administrative capacities" and prevented the state from providing developmental goods to its citizens and also caused state officials to be despotic and predatory (Lange 2009: 7). Lange (2009: 103) describes anti-chief revolts that broke out in 1955–56 in response to "chiefly misrule." Acemoglu et al. (2013: 6) describe how the traditional chiefs were allowed to persist in local politics and not abolished by the postcolonial politicians, and the RUF insurgency in Sierra Leone was "in many ways a reaction by alienated youth against the institutions of indirect rule."[10] The weak state presence in rural areas, a result of indirect rule, also facilitated the success of the rebellion (Lange 2009: 111). In contrast, British direct rule in Mauritius led to high levels of bureaucratic organization and infrastructural power, as well as dense associational ties among the natives because the colonial state supported the working classes and allowed them to free themselves from the hierarchical relationship of dependency on plantation elite (Lange, 2009: 68–75).

Mechanism 2: Colonial Indirect Rule Creates Despotic Extraction and Grievances That Can Be Exploited by Rebels

A second type of mechanism relevant for civil war onset has been discussed by scholars like Boone (1994, 2014), Mamdani (1996), Migdal (1988), Banerjee and Iyer (2005), and Acemoglu et al. (2001), who focus on the despotic rule and predatory extraction of revenue surplus from peasants by the native chiefs or other political intermediaries appointed by the colonizers. This creates

[9] Lange, *Lineages of Despotism and Development*, p. 6.
[10] Acemoglu et al., "Indirect Rule and State Weakness in Africa."

grievances due to land inequality and other kinds of ethnic and class-based grievances (Horowitz 1985; Wood 2003) to explain revolution and rebellion.

Mamdani (1996) in *Citizen and Subject* discusses how the British depended on preexisting chiefs to collect taxes, govern, and provide labor on behalf of the colonizers in sub-Saharan Africa. The colonial state undermined traditional and popular checks on the chiefs' power and thus liberated the chiefs from all institutional constraints, which resulted in institutionalizing "decentralized despotism," in which the chiefs were able to extract and exploit the tribes under their control. Mamdani (1996: 53) cites Padmore about the chiefs in Nigeria, that "No oriental despot ever had greater power than these black tyrants, thanks to the support which they receive from the white officials who quietly keep in the background." The result was several anti-colonial peasant rebellions that were often struggles against the native authorities created by the colonial state (Mamdani 1996: 24) For example, the insurgency by the Rogo peasantry in Hausaland in Nigeria saw themselves as *talakawa* or the oppressed commoners and in opposition to the *masu sarauta*, who were the aristocratic class who allied themselves with the colonial power during indirect rule (Mamdani 1996: 202).

Other scholars of African state formation like Boone (1994) suggest that the "colonial state's dependence on local intermediaries and allies created new privileged groups within African societies or allowed established powerholders to sustain their status and wealth."[11] In a more recent study, Boone (2014) mentions two types of land tenure systems in Africa: the more direct form of *statist land tenure regime* and the *neo-customary land tenure* system that was a type of indirect rule in which the colonial state builders used "trusted local intermediaries ... through whom they could govern the rural masses" (Boone, 2014: 26–27). Through such neo-customary land tenure institutions, the colonizers "taxed, conscripted, imposed *corvee,* and used coercion to prop up the colonial chiefs" (Boone 2014: 44). As a consequence, there were a number of anti-tax revolts, anti-chief revolts, and other forms of "rural resistance against colonial impositions and extractions." Boone (2014: 44) also mentions the occurrence of peasant uprisings against local chiefs, for example, in western Nigeria in 1968–69 and in parts of the Niger Delta region today, in western Cote d'Ivoire in 1970, and in Burundi in 1972 and 1988. The Casamance secessionist movement in Senegal starting in 1982 and the rural insurgency that brought Museveni to power in Uganda in 1986 are also cases of rebellion against postcolonial landed elites.

Similar to Boone's (2014) analysis of land tenure systems in Africa, in a study using a district-level dataset, Banerjee and Iyer (2005) suggest that districts in India that were exposed to the more unequal *zamindari*-type land tenure system had less economic development and more class conflict after independence because of exploitation of the lower-caste peasants and laborers by the upper-

[11] Boone, 'States and Ruling Classes in Postcolonial Africa," pp. 117–18.

caste landlords. They suggest in passing that this could also explain why the areas of initial Naxalite rebellion in the 1960s had occurred in these areas of extortion of taxes from peasants by landlords.[12] As discussed in more detail in the next chapter, many scholars conceptualize this *zamindari* land tenure system as a form of indirect rule (Dirks 2001; Kohli 2004; Lange 2009).

Mahoney (2010: 240) proposes that in the indirectly ruled princely states in India,

the British actively protected oppressive local elites, who otherwise likely would have faced major rebellion from the rural producers they exploited. ... In turn, the concentration of these duties and powers in elite hands made possible the hyper-exploitation of the peasantry, something that appears to have retarded agricultural production and stultified investment in public goods, even after the end of colonialism.

In particular, the feudatory princely states in Orissa, Chhattisgarh area as well as the successor princely states like Hyderabad resulted in despotic extraction from peasants and various rebellions in the colonial period, and the Maoist insurgency since 1980s.

Mechanism 3: Colonial Indirect Rule Creates Ethnic Identities and Ethnic Minority Exclusion That Facilitates Insurgency

A third group of studies, including those by Laitin (1985, 1986), Mamdani (2001), and Lange (2009), focuses on the effect of indirect/direct rule on ethnic grievances, nationalism, and ethnic conflict. These studies demonstrate how indirect rule led to the creation of ethnic identities as politically salient, and even ethnic exclusion of certain groups at the cost of others, thus causing ethnic conflict. While these studies do not theorize how this could lead to insurgency, it is possible that such historically created ethnic identity and ethnic exclusion could lead to ethnic grievances that persist and are mobilized by rebel leaders to start insurgency (Cederman et al. 2010; Wucherpfenning et al. 2016).

Lange (2009: 39) mentions that "although all British colonial states had relatively low levels of inclusiveness throughout the majority of the colonial period, indirect rule obstructed inclusiveness to a greater extent than direct rule, and direct rule created the institutional foundations for the subsequent expansion of inclusiveness." Inclusive political structures keep the state accountable and responsive to broad segments of the population and prevent one societal group from using the state for its own purposes and excluding other groups. Studies of civil war onset like Cederman et al. (2010) have emphasized the importance of ethnic inclusion in political power of peripheral ethnic groups to prevent grievances and insurgency; Lange's theory suggests that this could be one mechanism leading from colonial indirect rule to insurgency.

An example of colonial indirect rule leading to ethnic exclusion of minority groups and hence ethnic insurgency is Burma, discussed in detail in Chapter 10.

---

[12] Banerjee and Iyer, "History, Institutions and Economic Performance."

The British used direct rule in "Ministerial Burma" and indirect rule in the peripheral frontier regions. Colonial indirect rule facilitated insurgency through the crystallization of ethnic identities and divisions between the majority Bamars, who started a nationalistic movement and Burmanization of schools, and the ethnic minorities like Shans/Karens/Kachins, who felt threatened by this (Silverstein 1959: 98). Following independence in 1949, attempts by the majority Burman-dominated government in the plains to extend control into these peripheral areas have met with armed resistance and ethnic insurgencies by the ethnic minority Karen, Kachin, and Shan, who had been historically part of frontier rule (Smith 1999: 27).

In Nigeria, Laitin (1985) theorized that the colonial strategy of indirect rule set up by Lord Lugard in western Nigeria led the British to find the ancestral city kings to have become devoid of actual political power though having social legitimacy, and they decided to infuse these ancient tribal kings with political and economic power to assist them in their colonial rule. In contrast, religion was found to be too "noisy" for the British and was deemphasized. This colonial policy led to "reification of the tribe and the depoliticization of religion" (Laitin 1985: 306). This pattern persisted into the postcolonial period, thus ensuring that religion was not used for intra-Yoruba competition and conflict in western Nigeria.[13] However, the indirect rule emphasis on tribe could have led to policies of ethnic exclusion of certain tribes and inclusion of others into political power, and this may have led to the Biafran secessionist insurgency by the Igbo tribe in eastern Nigeria in 1967–70.

Mamdani (2001) theorizes that the Rwandan genocide was the result of oppositional political identities of settler versus native forged during Belgian colonialism. In Rwanda, Belgian rule was more of a halfway house between indirect and direct rule (Mamdani 2001: 99). Colonial law in Rwanda recognized only race (indigenous Hutus versus alien Tutsis), and not ethnicity as a political identity; the priming of race over ethnicity by Hutu nationalists after independence meant that Hutus could be made to think of Tutsis as outsider settlers who needed to be driven out of the country or killed, and not as neighbors belonging to another ethnic group. This shows that the type of identities created by Belgian colonial indirect rule created the structural conditions for one of the most horrific genocides in recent history in Africa, which was followed by civil war.

4 THE ARGUMENT: COLONIAL INDIRECT RULE AND ITS LONG-TERM EFFECTS ON INSURGENCY

I now propose a general theoretical framework linking colonial indirect rule with insurgency. The theory is developed by building on the literatures on social

---

[13] Laitin, "Hegemony and Religious Conflict."

movements and revolutions and linking them to existing theories of colonial indirect rule discussed earlier.

4.1 Colonial Indirect Rule and Rebellion

The effects of direct/indirect rule can vary greatly depending on the context and the colonizer type. Colonial institutions, through a variety of mechanisms, can possibly create conditions for conflict and insurgency. It is more useful to develop a theory that is specific to a particular type of colonizer in a particular region and operates within certain scope conditions (Mahoney & Goertz 2006). Overgeneralization of theory at this nascent stage of theory building can lead to conceptual stretching (Sartori 1970). The Maoist conflict in India, which is the analytical focus of this study, represents one set of mechanisms that leads to insurgency in a specific context of British colonial indirect rule in India.

Based on the theories outlined earlier, I argue that within South Asia, the different types of institutions of British colonial indirect rule often lead to the creation of territories within a country that have low bureaucratic penetration (Lange 2009) and lower levels of development (Kohli 2004) and have socially and politically excluded indigenous groups residing in them (Cederman et al. 2010). Compared with this, areas that have colonial direct rule have higher levels of state capacity, development, and governance on average. Colonial indirect rule also led to dependence on local preexisting indigenous elites, which can lead to despotic behavior by these elites, who often create extractive institutions to fleece land revenue and taxes from the rural peasants (Boone 1994; Mahoney 2010; Mamdani 1996). This results in land inequality, thus impoverishing the weaker classes or ethnic groups in society. These lower levels of development, less-integrated ethnic groups, and higher levels of land inequality then tend to persist into the postcolonial period through path dependent mechanisms (Mahoney 2000; Pierson 2000), because very often the political elites of the postcolonial state lack the political will or ability to overcome the lower-quality institutions and land and ethnic inequalities prevailing in these regions of colonial indirect rule.

To summarize, colonial indirect rule creates both opportunity (Collier & Hoeffler 2004; Fearon & Laitin 2003) and grievance (Cederman et al. 2010, 2013; Gurr 1970) based mechanisms leading to postcolonial insurgency. The opportunity is structural in nature and comes from existing lower levels of bureaucratic and police capacity and development created during the colonial period. The grievance mechanism is also structural in nature and comes from the higher levels of land and interethnic inequalities and ethnic exclusion (Cederman et al. 2010, 2013). The native elites like princes and landlords who ruled and collected revenue on behalf of the colonizer often used their autonomy with local society to exploit the poorer and politically less powerful groups in society, thus creating a relatively unequal society.

4.2   A Theory of Colonial Indirect Rule Creating Political Opportunity Structures, Ethnic Mobilization Networks, and the Role of Rebel Agency to Create Rebellion

I make use of a theoretical framework drawn from the literature on social movements and revolutions to develop a general model for how rebels make use of these mechanisms of weak state capacity and ethnic grievances created by historical institutions to start and sustain rebellion. According to McAdam, McCarthy, and Zald (1996), three factors that matter are the *political opportunity structures* confronting the movement, the *mobilizing structures*, and the *framing processes* of social movements. Adapting this framework, I propose that colonial indirect rule creates *opportunities structures* in the forms of low levels of bureaucratic and police institutions, which make effective counterinsurgency difficult and provide rebels with better opportunities to succeed. Colonial institutions also create grievances by excluding ethnic groups from economic and political power or creating land inequality and exploitation of resources, which provide the rebels with *ethnic mobilization structures* from which to create rebel organizations. The rebels have their own ideological frames of rebellion, repertoires of struggle or *framing processes* that they use to mobilize the ethnic groups to create insurgency.

Figure 2.2 synthesizes the various elements of my theory, and how their conjunction creates a sufficient condition for insurgency. While the exact nuances and details will vary from case to case, this represents the overall framework that can be used to understand how colonial indirect rule creates conditions conducive for insurgency. Future studies should analyze how colonial indirect rule creates conditions for insurgency in other contexts, where the exact mechanisms could vary, but the broad theoretical framework can be applicable.

Opportunity Structures

Scholars of social movements, like Tilly (1978) and Tarrow (1998), had emphasized "political opportunity structures," a concept that focused on institutional structures, elite alliances, and weaknesses that made states more or less vulnerable to protest movements and rebellion. Most early work by scholars tried to explain the emergence of a social movement on the basis of *"changes in the institutional structure or informal power relations of a given national political system"* (McAdam, McCarthy, & Zald, 1996: 3).

In an earlier version of their well-known paper on insurgency onset, Fearon and Laitin (2001: 2) write that they want to develop "an explanation for civil war in this period that like the earlier social movements perspective stresses opportunities over specific motivations affecting groups of people. However, we attempt to specify the 'opportunity structure' more precisely, as it exists for the particular problem of civil war in the period since 1945."[14] While the final

---

[14] Fearon and Laitin, "Ethnicity, Insurgency and Civil War," APSA 2001 conference paper.

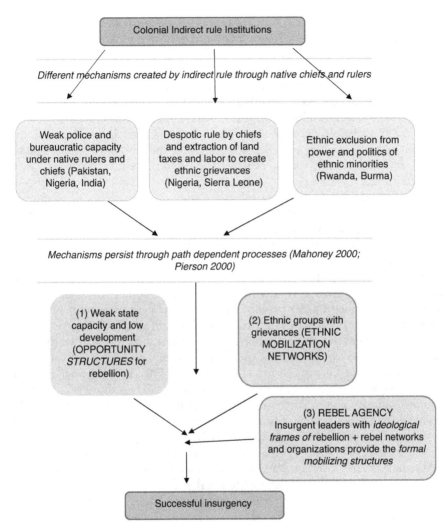

FIGURE 2.2 Mechanisms from colonial indirect rule to postcolonial ideological insurgency

version of the Fearon and Laitin (2003) paper does not cite these earlier theorists of rebellion and social movements, they take the idea of opportunity structures from earlier social movements theorists like Tarrow (1998) and Tilly (1978). However, they did not think of historical institutions having path dependent effects to create current opportunity structures for insurgency. Instead, Fearon and Laitin (2003) interpreted opportunity structures for insurgency onset in terms of more proximate state capacity for counterinsurgency, defined in terms of policing and information-gathering capacity or opportunity for rebels to hide in forests or hilly terrain. What is missing from these theories of civil war onset, by Fearon and Laitin (2003) or Collier and Hoeffler (2004), is a broader interpretation of rebel opportunity in terms of long-term institutions and their effects.

My theory proposes that different forms of colonial indirect rule set up the opportunity structures for postcolonial ideological insurgency, through path dependent causal processes, which create low levels of police and bureaucratic capacity, and lower development (Kohli 2004; Lange 2009; Mahoney 2010). If there are historically determined low levels of state penetration and weak police and bureaucracy in a region, it becomes easier for the rebels to hide and sustain their activities because, as Fearon and Laitin (2003) theorize, state counterinsurgency capacity is closely related to the ability of the state to gather information about where rebels are hiding. Areas that due to indirect rule historically developed low police and bureaucratic capacity, whether in the northwestern frontiers of Pakistan, or the eastern frontiers of Burma, or the interior but neglected regions like Chhattisgarh in India, or northern Nigeria, prevent security forces from controlling and collecting information and thus become safe havens for rebels to develop their capacity and organizational networks. As long as this low state penetration is not changed through a reversal of policy by the postcolonial state, these areas remain politically created opportunity structures for rebels to start and sustain insurgency.

This argument interprets opportunity structures more broadly than the original theorists of revolution and social movements (McCarthy & Zald 1973, 1977; Skocpol 1979, 1982; Tarrow 1998; Tilly 1978). The theories of social movements conceptualize opportunity structures as more proximate to conflict and also assume that sudden changes in political factors open up the opportunity for political mobilization. In contrast, my theory lends stickiness to certain institutions and processes, and it is the persistence and path dependence of these institutions rather than their change that sets up the structural opportunities for conflict. While earlier social movement theories were analyzing proximate changes in institutional and political capacity, my theory focuses on how opportunity structures for rebellion like weak states were created due to choices by colonial bureaucrats in the past. My theory is thus able to explain the institutional origins of variation in state capacity and development within a country, which are the intermediary mechanisms that are used by scholars of civil war to explain civil war onset.

Ethnic Mobilization Networks

While the opportunity structures in the form of weak state capacity are necessary for successful rebellion, it is also important that the rebels can create the *mobilizing structures* in the form of overground and underground insurgent organizations. Skocpol (1982) suggests that insurgent organizations play a crucial role in creating rebellion, and the nature or class structure of peasants does not matter as much. While colonial institutions may set up the structural conditions necessary for rebel recruitment, rebellion will not happen without the ability of rebel leaders to set up organizational networks.

Social movement scholars have called these mobilizing structures necessary for the successful emergence of an insurgency movement as the actual "forms of organization (informal as well as formal), available to insurgents" (McAdam, McCarthy, & Zald (1996: 2). These are both formal organizations and informal networks that are necessary for social movements and revolutions to succeed (McAdam et al. 1996: 3). While the resource mobilization theories propounded by McCarthy and Zald (1973, 1977) focused on the mobilization processes, the formal social movement organizations (SMOs) theorists like Tilly (1978) developed the *political process theory* that focused on informal and grassroots institutions and local networks like churches and social networks. The role of organizational and informal networks in social movements has also been discussed by scholars like Snow, Zurcher, and Eklkand-Olson (1980), McAdam (1986), and Gould (1991).

To overcome collective action problems and recruit people from the deprived ethnic groups or oppressed classes to join their rebel groups, whether by providing *selective incentives* (Lichbach 1994) or public goods (Arjona 2017), insurgent leaders need such formal and informal networks and mobilizing structures. Colonial indirect rule and indirect land tenure institutions often lead to land and ethnic inequality and grievances among the underprivileged ethnic groups, which are exploited through the predatory rule of the native elites whom the colonizers depend on to rule. These exploited ethnic groups provide the informal ethnic mobilization networks/structures that rebel leaders can then mobilize to create insurgent groups. Such high levels of land and economic inequalities due to extractive institutions set up by native chiefs and landlords as part of indirect rule thus form the ideal conditions to mobilize grievances of deprived ethnic groups, as Gurr (1970) and Cederman et al. (2010, 2013) suggest.

As long as the postcolonial government does not introduce any radical policy changes to try and incorporate these tribal groups or lower-caste landless or other historically exploited or neglected ethnic groups into mainstream modern society and politics, they remain available as the mobilizing networks/structures that rebel leaders can easily motivate and mobilize from to create and then sustain their insurgent movement. Blanton et al. (2001) similarly suggest that British indirect rule in Africa left the indigenous ethnic structures intact that could then be mobilized by insurgent leaders to create rebel groups. This provides the ideal structural conditions for rebel leaders to recruit from the socially excluded and deprived ethnic groups with grievances who provide the ethnic mobilization networks for rebellion.

Other than such informal ethnic mobilization networks, rebel organizational capacity is also influenced by whether or not there are preexisting social or political networks in that area or neighboring areas on which the rebel leaders can draw to quickly build a nascent organization with a sufficient number of leaders and cadres who can carry out the initial tasks of organizing the peasants and indigenous groups, and indoctrinating them into the ideology of the rebel group. Such preexisting networks are usually formed by radical/religious political parties in the postcolonial period and often become the ideological and organizational base for later more extremist insurgency movements. For example, Zukerman-Daly (2012) demonstrates that regions in Colombia that have previous exposure to rebel groups during the earlier La Violencia period were more prone to successful FARC-led insurgent mobilization beginning in the 1980s. Staniland (2012a) shows that in Kashmir in India in the 1990s, the Hizbul Mujahideen (HuM) insurgent group was built on preexisting quasi-religious organizations that were tightly knit together in strong horizontal and vertical linkages and thus remained cohesive and well organized in the face of Indian counterinsurgency. In contrast, the Jammu Kashmir Liberation Front (JKLF) had more popular support in Kashmir; however, because its urban student leadership lacked preexisting organizations with tight horizontal and vertical linkages, it soon became factionalized and non-cohesive.

Earlier rebellions in colonial periods can sometimes leave organizational residues. For example, certain areas within India have a "strong tradition of rebellion" in Bengal, Bihar, and Andhra Pradesh where there were various colonial-era peasant and tribal rebellions (Gough 1974: 1406), and these possibly left organizational legacies of rebellion that persisted and provided informal grassroots networks that were available to Maoist rebels to mobilize. Similarly, Johnson and Mason (2008: 53–54) describe a long history of rebellion by the various frontier Pashtun tribes against the British colonizers in the North Western Frontier Province (NWFP), for example, the long rebellion by the legendary Fakir of Ipi, who was remarkably similar to the Taliban leader Mullah Mohammed Omar. Naseemullah (2014: 518) notes that militant Islamic religious figures and later the Taliban were able to exploit these "traditions of resistance to the state and tribal authority."

In case there are no preexisting political/social networks to help create successful insurgent organization, then the chances of successful rebel mobilization are lower, even if the area is an enclave of low stateness and ethnic grievances created through colonial indirect rule.

Ideological Frames of Rebellion and Rebel Agency

So far, my theoretical framework has only focused on the opportunity structures created by colonial indirect rule and the *mobilization structures/ networks* based on informal ethnic tribal/ caste networks as well as rebel formal organizations. However, McAdam et al. (1996: 2–3) note the importance of framing processes to explain social movement, and define them as "the collective processes of interpretation, attribution and social construction that mediate between opportunity and action." It is the ideological beliefs of the rebel leaders and their techniques of rebellion, alongside their organizational networks, that form what scholars of social movements call the *framing processes* for successful insurgency. It is not just structural conditions but also *rebel agency* that matters in explaining how insurgency succeeds in mobilizing the socially excluded ethnic groups.

Rebel leaders need to convince the ethnic groups with the grievances that they have been exploited in some ways and that if they act collectively they can redress the situation. According to McAdam et al. (1996: 5), this requires a "collective attribution" and "social construction" by the rebel leaders, which is referred to as framing processes by Snow et al. (1980). This refers to the role of ideology and indoctrination and how that is used to mobilize individuals with grievances and convince them to join and participate in the insurgency in different ways. However, McAdam et al. (1996: 6) summarize the social movements literature's efforts to analyze the role of ideas and culture in overcoming collective action by returning to Snow et al.'s (1980) original concept and define "framing rather narrowly as referring to the *conscious strategic efforts by groups of people to fashion shared understandings of the world and of themselves that legitimate and motivate collective action.*"

The more recent literature on rebellion and insurgency has debated the role of *selective incentives* in the form of private benefits (Lichbach 1994) versus the role of public goods (Arjona 2017; Mampilly 2011) in mobilizing people to join the rebellion. Other scholars have analyzed the role of emotions (Peterson 2002), symbolic values like religious and sacred spaces (Hassner 2003), and the role of non-instrumental motivations like pleasure of participation (Wood 2003) in overcoming collective action problems. The importance of ideology as part of the framing processes of rebellion has not been well analyzed.

Gutiérrez, Sanin, and Wood (2014) propose that *ideology* should be seriously considered by civil war scholarship and not ignored, since it can explain variation in type of violence and recruitment and is often used by rebel groups for socialization of cadres to make them more disciplined and efficient, as well as for instrumental reasons to develop support among recruits and civilians. Oppenheim and Weintraub (2017) analyze variation in ideological commitment across subunits of the FARC insurgency and find that those FARC units that received ideological training that emphasized the strategic and tactical importance of restraint toward civilian population did not use indiscriminate violence toward civilians. Kalyvas and Balcells (2010) show that rebellions in the Cold War era driven by Marxist ideology were longer and more lethal, compared to non-Marxist rebellions, because of the long time horizons of their leaders and their ideological commitment to protracted war.

In my theoretical framework in the next section, I incorporate both the importance of rebel organizational networks and ideology as *rebel agency* that mobilizes the ethnic mobilization networks among tribes and lower castes. Chapters 7 and 8 on the PWG Maoists in Chhattisgarh and Andhra Pradesh use rich qualitative data to analyze the role of rebel ideology and strategy, as does Chapter 4, which focuses on how Maoist strategy/tactics are constrained by structural conditions created by indirect rule in India.

4.3   Building a General Model of Colonial Indirect Rule and Insurgency – Necessity and Sufficiency of These Conditions for Successful Rebellion

How do these political opportunity structures, ethnic mobilization networks, and rebel agency in the form of mobilizing structures and framing processes combine to allow conditions that are favorable for the emergence of successful rebellion? When the rebel leaders start recruiting, their success in mobilization is influenced partly by whether or not they faced weak state capacity and ethnic inequalities created by colonial indirect rule institutions, and also partly by whether the rebel agents have the ability to create organizational capacity through social networks and convince the ethnic group with grievances of their ideological goals. It is easier to overcome collective action problems and sustain insurgency in areas that were inherently exploitative due to unequal colonial land tenure system, or inherently low state penetration due to colonial indirect rule, or with indigenous populations that are alienated and prone to rebellion because of extractive colonial forest policy combined with indirect rule.

However, while these various opportunity structures in the form of weak police and bureaucratic capacity created by historical institutions, and the ethnic mobilization structures in the form of aggrieved ethnic groups that feel excluded from the political and economic process due to these inequitable effects of colonial institutions may be necessary conditions for successful rebellion, they are not sufficient conditions. It is possible that a place that had colonial indirect rule has both these conditions but no rebel agents or leaders to mobilize the ethnic groups, and so there may be a few protests and ethnic violence but no sustained insurgency. The third and final necessary condition is autonomous and well-organized rebel organizations with clear ideologies and repertoires of violence in these areas that are able to exploit these structural opportunities and create enough recruitment and mobilization among the exploited ethnic groups.

While colonial institutions create political opportunity structures in the form of weak state capacity and also ethnic mobilization networks in the form of tribes and ethnic groups with grievances, and rebels develop their organizational capacity, none of these are sufficient conditions for insurgency, though each of them is individually necessary. However, in combination they create conditions for successful rebellion. It is thus the conjunction of political opportunity structures and ethnic mobilization networks/structures shaped by colonial legacies, and rebel organizations as framing processes, that are sufficient for successful ideological rebellion. This is similar to causation conceptualized as INUS conditions, where none of these causes is individually necessary or individually sufficient but are jointly sufficient for the outcome of Maoist insurgency (Mahoney & Goertz 2006).[15]

This broad theoretical framework is applied to the specific case of the Maoist insurgency in India in the next few chapters, but the exact mechanisms could vary to explain other cases of how colonial indirect rule could create conditions of insurgency, for example, in Burma, Pakistan, Nigeria, or Mexico, as discussed in Chapter 10 on generalizability.

5 CONCLUSION

This chapter reviews various studies that have suggested that colonial indirect rule has long-term effects on development, state capacity, ethnic exclusion, and land and resource inequality. While the exact effect varies by country and colonizer, scholars outline three main mechanisms. One is the mechanism of weak state capacity, another is despotic extraction by native chiefs, and the third is ethnic exclusion of minority ethnic groups. While most of these previous studies of colonial direct/ indirect rule do not analyze possible effects on insurgency, I develop a theoretical framework in which these effects of colonial indirect rule become intermediate mechanisms that are then exploited by rebel leaders.

I engage with the literature on social movements and rebellions and use that theoretical framework to conceptualize these mechanisms of state weakness as opportunity structures, and the ethnic groups with grievances as providing the ethnic mobilizing networks/structures that are then mobilized by the rebel leaders with their ideological frames to indoctrinate and mobilize these ethnic groups. Unlike the more recent cross-national dataset-based literature on civil wars that portrays rebel opportunity in terms of more proximate determinants as weak state capacity (Fearon & Laitin 2003) and natural resource availability (Ross 2004), my theoretical framework borrows from the earlier literature on rebellion and conceptualizes rebel opportunity as more long term, persistent, and sticky. This opens up conceptual space to think of rebellion and insurgency as part of a long-term process of state formation and moves beyond the current theories of civil war that only analyze more proximate causes of rebellion.

Chapter 1 motivated the reasons why it was important to bring colonial institutions back into the study of civil war. In this chapter, I focused on colonial indirect rule as an important type of historical institution and presented a plausible general model of how causal pathways starting from these colonial institutions lead to insurgency and conflict. In the next chapter, I turn to the case of the Maoist insurgency in India and outline how the general theoretical framework developed in this chapter plays out in this important case.

---

[15] According to Mahoney and Goertz, "A Tale of Two Cultures," p. 232, fn. 4: An INUS condition is "an *insufficient* but *nonredundant* part of an *unnecessary* but *sufficient* [combination of conditions]."

3

Varieties of Indirect Rule and Causal Pathways to Maoist Insurgency in India

I INTRODUCTION

What explains the peculiar spatial variation of Maoist insurgency in India? In Chapter 2 I raised the puzzle of why the Maoist insurgency occurs along the central-eastern "red corridor" belt of India. Why not in the western and southern parts of the country, which also have forest cover, hilly terrain, and exploited lower castes and tribes in some regions? I theorized that colonial indirect rule institutions created the structural conditions of weak state capacity, land inequality, and ethnic grievances, which could be deep-rooted causes for insurgency. In this chapter, I outline two types of indirect rule in India and show how they created distinct causal pathways that led to Maoist mobilization.

In Section 2, I describe the colonial history of direct and indirect rule, and how the British slowly extended their rule by annexing certain Indian states into direct rule and signing treaties of indirect rule with other Indian princes. Following this, Section 3 develops the theory of different types of indirect rule and revenue collection within India – a formal type of indirect rule through princely states and an informal type of indirect rule through *zamindars*/landlords. In Section 4, I then outline the theoretical framework of how these types of colonial indirect rule set up the *opportunity structures* and *ethnic mobilization networks* that persisted into the postcolonial period through path dependent causal pathways and led to Maoist insurgency since the 1980s. While the *zamindari* landlord tenure system created conditions of land and caste inequality and also lower bureaucratic penetration, the *princely states* in central-eastern India tended to have lower state capacity and the exploitation of land and natural resources in tribal areas.

While the type of colonial institution varied in different regions, it produced similar mechanisms of *despotic extraction* and a *weak state* and led to the same outcome of Maoist insurgency. This demonstrates the *equifinality* of outcomes (Mahoney & Goertz 2006), outlined in the schematic diagram in Figure 3.3, which describes how colonial indirect rule created different causal pathways of structural inequalities and low state capacity, which then persisted through path dependent mechanisms into the postcolonial period to result in Maoist insurgency.

While the theory outlined so far is based on structural constraints created by historical institutions, I address the importance of rebel agency in Section 5. Rebel agency and the emergence of Maoist leaders and organizations are still dependent on structural conditions created by colonial indirect rule even in the first phase of Maoist rebellion. So, rebel agency cannot be considered independent of *structural factors* created by historical institutions, and it is the potential interaction of rebel agency with the structural conditions created by indirect rule that creates *conjunctural causation* for Maoist insurgency (Mahoney & Goertz 2006). The interaction of rebel agency with structural conditions is further analyzed in Chapters 7 and 8 using qualitative data on Maoist rebellion for the states of Chhattisgarh and Andhra Pradesh.

2 TIMELINE OF ANNEXATION INTO COLONIAL DIRECT RULE AND SIGNING OF TREATIES OF INDIRECT RULE

Before laying out the theoretical framework of how indirect rule through princely states and *zamindari* land tenure within India created the structural conditions for Maoist insurgency, it is important to sketch the evolution of these types of indirect rule and indirect revenue collection within India. This section outlines the sequence of British conquest and timeline of the emergence of different forms of direct and indirect rule.

2.1 Timeline of British Conquest and Choice of de Jure Indirect Rule through Princely States

British conquest of India initially was oriented around the commercial interests of the East India Company. The Mughal emperor Jahangir granted a *firman* or imperial edict to the English East India Company in 1613 that gave it permission to trade in Surat. Following from this humble beginning, the East India Company started to expand commercially; by 1647, it had twenty-three trading posts, or factories, on the Indian coast and by 1665 had acquired sovereignty over small areas around Madras and Bombay.[1] Political domination started with the Battle of Plassey in 1757, in which the British forces under the Company were able to defeat the Nawab of Bengal Shiraj Ud Daula and gain an initial political toehold in the Indian subcontinent. In 1764, the East India Company defeated the combined forces of the Mughal emperor, the Nawab of Awadh Shuja Ud Daula, and the deposed Nawab of Bengal Mir Kasim in the Battle of Buxar. Following this victory, in 1765 the British received

---

[1] Jeffrey, *People, Princes and Paramount Power*, p. 4

the *diwani* or revenue-collecting rights in Bengal and captured the first of many territories. This allowed the East India Company to establish itself as a major regional player among other Indian states.[2] By 1797, Bengal, Bihar, and the Benaras region had been integrated into the direct rule administration with its capital at Calcutta, although the Nawab of Bengal remained nominally as the ruler, under the supervision of a British Resident appointed to the Court of the Nawab.[3]

According to Lee-Warner (1910), there were three distinct periods of British political expansion in India. Each period saw both annexations of certain princely states into direct rule and the creation of indirect rule through signing treaties of collaboration with various Indian princes, to assist them in controlling this vast territory. This finally led to a patchwork of areas of indirect rule next to direct rule areas by the time the British stopped conquering following the Indian Mutiny in 1857 and the Crown took over from the East India Company.

First Phase: The first phase was characterized by the *ring fence* policy of nonintervention by the British in the internal affairs of Indian states. During this phase, the British entered into treaties of "mutual alliance" with rulers who were on the borders/frontiers of the areas already under British control, to act as a ring or buffer against more aggressive Indian rulers who might take away the initial territories the British had conquered. This phase started with the initial period of conquest under Robert Clive from 1757 to 1767 and was continued by Warren Hastings (1772–85) during his time as first governor-general. Having first defeated the Nawab of Awadh, Shuja ud Daula, in the Battle of Buxar in 1764, Robert Clive then allied with the Nawab and signed a treaty in 1765 to maintain a buffer state between the Company's new base in Bengal and the Marathas. Hastings further developed this policy of ring fence in 1773 when he rented a subsidiary force to Shuja Ud Daula, which the Awadh ruler used to attack the Afghan Rohillas who had not paid their tribute (Ramusack 2004: 65).

This was followed by the governor-generalships of Lord Cornwallis (1786–93) and Sir John Shore (1793–98), which were periods of nonintervention and consolidation rather than annexation. Expansionism returned with Lord Wellesley (1798–1805), who started the policy of "subsidiary alliance," during which treaties were signed with princes like the Nizam of Hyderabad, the Nawab of Awadh, and several Maratha chiefs in which the native ruler was forced to maintain subsidiary forces on behalf of the British; in return, the British promised to provide protection from external enemies (Ramusack

---

[2] Ramusack, *The Indian Princes and Their States*, p. 25
[3] Fisher, *Indirect Rule in India: Residents and the Residency System*, p. 125

2004, pp. 68–71).[4] Lord Minto (1807–13), who followed Wellesley, did not pursue the treaties of subsidiary alliance as ruthlessly. The treaty of offensive and defensive alliance with Ranjit Singh, the ruler of Punjab, was signed in 1809, as was a treaty with the small cis-Sutlej princely states, which would provide a buffer against the powerful Punjab state. See Figures 3.1a and 3.1b for the different phases of British conquest into direct rule and treaties of indirect rule with different Indian princely states.

Second Phase: The second phase started with Lord Hastings returning as the governor general (1813–23) and was called *subordinate alliance*. In this phase, the East India Company signed treaties of subsidiary alliance or protection with several Indian rulers, which provided British protection of these states and nonintervention in the internal affairs of their Indian allies, while these native states recognized the "paramountcy" of British power in India. The Indian rulers who entered treaties of subsidiary alliance could not declare war or employ Europeans without British permission.

While in the first phase of ring fence, the treaties were between equals, now the treaties were between unequal powers, and the Indian states entered dependent status. The most important one under Hastings was with the Maratha rulers, who were defeated in battle and signed various treaties of subsidiary alliance, starting with Scindia in 1817, who was allowed to retain the tribute of his tributary states but had to fight on behalf of the British. Another treaty with the Bhonsle ruler of Nagpur soon followed in 1818, which was more humiliating, and finally with the Peshwa Baji Rao, thus ending Maratha power and the threat to the British in India.

By the end of Hastings's rule, the broad outline of princely India had been formed with three large blocks of native state territories. The first was the "massive conglomeration of Rajput and Maratha ruled states, which spread from Gujarat in the west through Rajasthan to Malwa and Rewa in central India" (Ramusack 2004: 79). This included several small states with aboriginal tribal groups. The second group of states were in the East, comprising Maratha-ruled Nagpur and the Orissa states, constituting the Tributary Mahals of Chota Nagpur, and had significant tribal populations. The third was a group of states in the south, with Hyderabad and Mysore being the largest, and Travancore and Cochin on the southwest coast.

After Hastings, there was a string of governors general, under whom a number of annexations into direct rule were carried out, though some followed more noninterventionist policies. For example, the province of lower Burma were annexed in 1826 and Sind in 1843, and the British defeated the rulers of Punjab and annexed parts of it in 1846. This phase of *subordinate alliance* finally ended with the more aggressive annexation policies of Lord

---

[4] Wellesley was an annexationist by temperament and often went against the official policy of caution and ring fence of the East India Company.

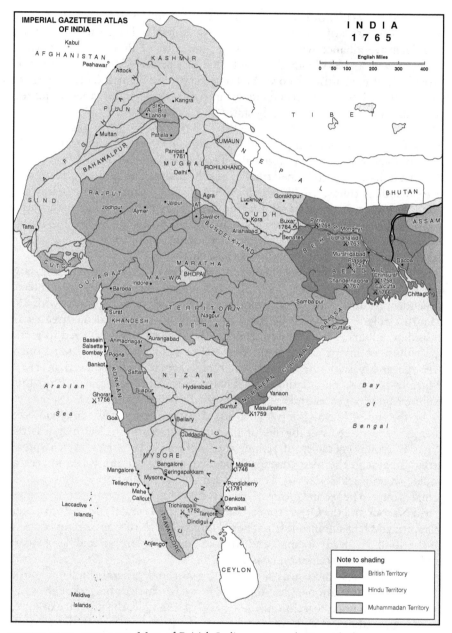

FIGURE 3.1A AND 3.1B Map of British India, 1765 and 1837 (dark gray areas were
direct British rule, lighter gray areas were Indian princely states)
Source: Imperial Gazetteer of India (1909), Volume 26 – Atlas. Oxford University Press.
http://dsal.uchicago.edu/reference/gaz_atlas_1909/fullscreen.html?object=33)

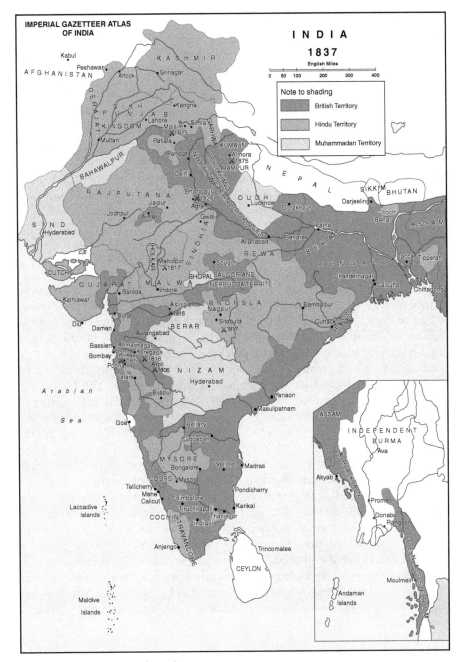

FIGURE 3.1A AND 3.1B (cont.)

Dalhousie (1848–56), which brought several states under direct rule. Dalhousie fought a second war against Punjab and annexed the rest of this province in 1849, and Pegu province of Burma in 1852. More controversially, he initiated the "Doctrine of Lapse," under which any Indian ruler who died without a male heir would have to forfeit his kingdom to the British. Using this doctrine, under which adopted sons were no longer recognized as legitimate heirs, Dalhousie was able to annex the princely states of Satara, Nagpur, Jhansi, and Sambalpur by 1856. However, this policy proved to be unpopular to some Indian princes and was part of the reason for a major mutiny by Indian soldiers and princes against British forces in 1857.

See Figures 3.2a and 3.2b for the different princely states and British direct rule areas at the time of the Indian Mutiny in 1857 and the final consolidated map of 1909 which persisted till Indian independence in 1947.

Third Phase: This munity of 1857–59 was a major shock to the British. Post 1858, annexation as a policy was abolished, and this started the third phase of British rule in India. The administration of British India so far had been under the East India Company, and it was transferred to the British government headed by Queen Victoria in 1858. In appreciation of the fact that many Indian princes had actually assisted the British forces during the mutiny, as well as recognizing that excessively aggressive policies of annexation were unpopular, the British Parliament passed the Government of India Act, 1858, which declared that areas that had not yet been annexed into direct rule by 1858, would remain under indirect rule as princely states. The British did intervene in the internal affairs of princely states by appointing Residents or sometimes replacing an inefficient or inconvenient ruler with a relative but did not officially annex territories into direct rule after 1858.[5] Thus, the Indian Sepoy Mutiny of 1857 froze the political map of British India and resulted in a hybrid patchwork of indirect- and direct-ruled territories across the Indian subcontinent, which remained as such until Indian independence in 1947.

The British formally categorized as indirect rule these existing princely states. While initially there were around 40–50 such ruling princes in 1858, by the end of the nineteenth century, almost 600 such princely states made up two-fifths of the area of colonial India, since several smaller native rulers were provided *sanads* and recognized as princes by governors general like Lord Canning in the 1860s. Some of these were large like Hyderabad and Kashmir, but many small states were concentrated in western or central India, where the British policy converted many petty chieftains and *zamindars* to small feudatory princely states.

---

[5] See Fisher, *Indirect Rule in India,* for details of the Residency System in which the British had Residents in the courts of different native states to supervise and monitor administrative affairs of state.

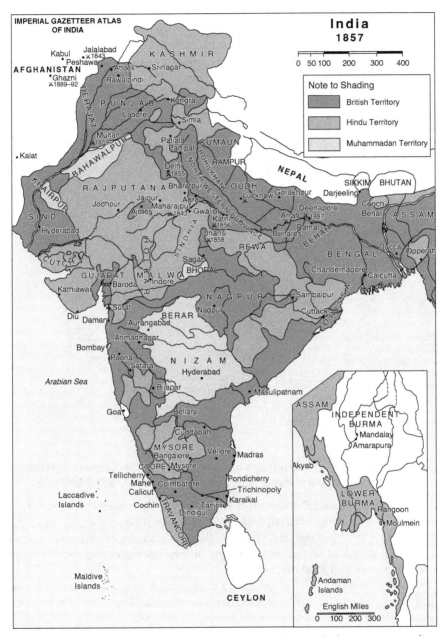

FIGURE 3.2A AND 3.2B Map of British India, 1857 and 1909 (dark gray areas are direct British rule, lighter gray are Indian princely states)
Source: Imperial Gazetteer of India (1909), Volume 26 – Atlas. http://dsal.uchicago.edu/reference/gaz_atlas_1909/fullscreen.html?object=34 and http://dsal.uchicago.edu/reference/gaz_atlas_1909/pager.html?object=26)

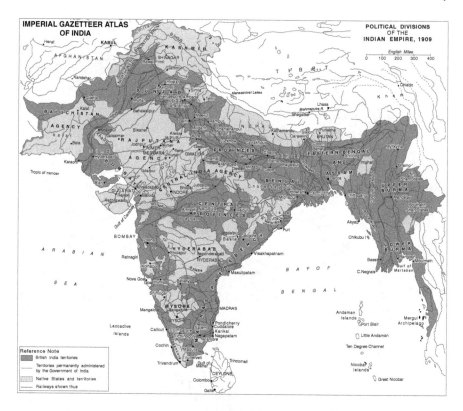

FIGURE 3.2A AND 3.2B (cont.)

2.2 Timeline of British Implementation of Types of Land Tenure Systems, Including de Facto Indirect Rule through *Zamindars* and *Malguzars*

In the areas of official British direct rule, the British colonial officers set up several administrative, judicial, legal, and police institutions, which created a higher degree of state capacity. Once the British decided to annex an area into direct rule, they had to decide what type of land tenure collection system to implement to collect land revenue taxes.

In this subsection I briefly summarize the historical origins of these different forms of land tenure systems used by the British. The British developed three main types of land tenure systems in all lands in India under their official direct rule.[6]

---

[6] Description of the land tenure systems is available in Baden-Powell, *The Land-Systems of British India*, Vols. 1–3. Banerjee and Iyer, "History, Institutions and Economic Performance," summarize these different land revenue systems and their dates of establishment in their appendix table 2.

Zamindari *and* Malguzari *Land Tenure:* In the initial phase of British rule from 1757 to the 1790s, in the eastern areas of Bengal and Bihar that the British annexed, even within these so-called officially direct ruled territories, the British were forced to depend on political intermediaries like landlords, locally called *zamindars* (owners of land or *zamin*) to collect land revenue and carry out other administrative tasks on their behalf. The colonial administration did not have sufficient personnel and capacity initially, and it decided to depend on preexisting landlords to collect the land taxes on their behalf. Thus was born the famous *zamindari* or landlord-based system, which in reality was a type of indirect rule or revenue collection system.

In a landlord-based system, the right and responsibility to collect land revenue from a group of villages in a given area was given to a single landlord. The landlord was allowed to set the revenue rates for the villages under his control, collect the land revenue, pay the British their revenue rent, and kept the rest for himself. This gave local *zamindars* power over the peasants in their villages and often exposed them to manipulation .

The landlord tenure system was implemented in British provinces like Bengal, Bihar, Orissa, Central Provinces, and some parts of Madras Presidency (which later became Tamil Nadu and Andhra Pradesh states). In some areas like Bengal, the Permanent Settlement of 1793 under Lord Cornwallis as governor-general meant the revenue rate the landlords had to pay to the British was fixed permanently; in other areas, there was a temporary settlement whereby the revenue rate was fixed only for short periods of time, after which it was revised by the British administrators.

Another type of landlord system was the *malguzari* system, which was created in the Central Provinces. After the initial attempt to set up the *mahalwari* or village-based tenure system in the Central Provinces in the 1860s failed, the British adapted and created an entirely new system based on the old Maratha system of using intermediaries called *malguzars* or *patels* to collect the land revenue. These *malguzars* developed enough proprietary rights to become similar to the *zamindari* system in Bengal and often exploited excess land revenue from the peasants, which led to discontent and sometimes rebellion.[7] This is discussed in greater detail in Chapter 7.

Ryotwari *Land Tenure:* Later on, in the 1810–20s, as the British annexed more territories and the colonial infrastructure expanded, the British developed the *ryotwari* land tenure system that did not depend on landlords and tried to develop its own revenue collection infrastructure to collect land taxes directly from the peasants. The *ryotwari* system was the second major type of land tenure system and was a more direct form of land tenure collection and rule by the British. It was so called because the revenue settlement was made directly with the *ryots* or individual cultivators, with each *ryot* directly holding his

---

[7] Baden-Powell, *Land Tenure Systems*, Vol. 2, p. 456–58.

own land. The revenue commitment was not fixed and was changed periodically depending on circumstances and changing productivity of land and varied from place to place depending on soil type and productivity. Overall, it was more flexible than the *zamindari* system, and more sensitive to the productivity of the individual peasant (Banerjee and Iyer 2005: 1193).

Different parts of Madras Presidency were changed to *ryotwari* tenure from *zamindari* tenure under the influence of Thomas Munro from 1815 to the 1820s. The influence of the *ryotwari* administration in Madras was felt in Bombay, where Lord Elphinstone, though not initially in favor of a direct settlement with the *ryots*, because of his sympathy for Munro's system and also because of geographical contiguity, pushed for the introduction of a similar system (Mukherjee 1962: 372). Another reason for the introduction of the *ryotwari* system into Bombay was pragmatic concerns like removing the undue influence of the local Indian intermediaries (*desais*) at the district and village levels by having a more direct assessment of land revenue, which would make revenue collection more efficient (Rabitoy 1975: 532). So both ideological imperatives and more pragmatic concerns of increased efficiency in revenue collection led the British to choose this more direct form of land revenue collection.

Mahalwari *Land tenure:* The third type of tenure system was a village- or *mahal*-based system called *mahalwari*. Under this system, village bodies collectively owned the revenue for the entire village and were responsible for collecting the land revenue. Stokes (1978) notes that often a flexible and pragmatic approach to measuring the rent due from *mahals* or villages was used, ranging from reviewing the tract's revenue history over the previous twenty years to developing an overall rent for the entire district and then distributing the sum over individual villages based on soil quality.[8] The *mahalwari* system of tenure was more flexible and sensitive than the *zamindari* system and can be considered a non-landlord type of tenure system (Banerjee & Iyer 2005).

The *mahalwari* system was initially set up in North West Provinces (currently Uttar Pradesh) in the 1820s and later Punjab after its conquest in the 1840s. Its initial selection in the North West Provinces was the result of vigorous debate among British administrators in 1802–19. Initially, temporary *zamindari* tenures were implemented in the North West Provinces. While the Court of Directors of the East India Company were more cautious about using the permanent settlement of the *zamindari* tenure system as in Bengal, the Board of Commissioners setup to evaluate the ideal land tenure system was in favor of *zamindari* tenure.

The decision was clinched by a brilliant minute written in 1819 by Holt Mackenzie, the secretary of the Board of Revenue, which suggested, "no

---

[8] Stokes, *The Peasant and the Raj*, pp. 98–99.

Settlement should be declared in perpetuity which did not give proper recognition to the customary sub-proprietary rights of the cultivating classes" (Misra 1942: 25–26).[9] The result was Regulation VII of 1822, which created the *mahalwari* settlement in the United Provinces and recognized the old customary rights of village communities. This demonstrates that the East India Company was becoming concerned about the original *zamindari* landlord-based tenures and wanted to move toward more direct land tenure like *ryotwari* and *mahalwari* that required direct interaction with and collection from the peasants.

3 DIFFERENT TYPES OF COLONIAL INDIRECT RULE AND REVENUE COLLECTION IN INDIA

As discussed in earlier chapters, I propose that indirect rule can set up *opportunity structures* and *ethnic mobilization networks* for insurgencies. The existing literature, which analyzes the effects of indirect/direct rule on development outcomes (Iyer 2010) and Maoist insurgency (Teitelbaum & Verghese 2019; Verghese 2016b), measures indirect rule as a dichotomous or binary (0–1) concept. The problem with these studies is that they treat all princely states as uniformly having benevolent rulers, but in reality there is variation among the types of princely states. Wilkinson (2017) has criticized these and other studies of colonial legacies in South Asia for ignoring the more fine-grained variations in types of indirect rule within India and has questioned whether it is possible to classify the huge variation in types of colonial indirect rule and land revenue systems in India into a few categories that make it amenable to statistical analysis.

Mahoney (2010) discusses different levels of colonial rule, which could be centralized territories versus peripheral territories in the Spanish Empire, or the direct versus indirect rule regions in the British Empire. While it is possible to think of level or degree of colonial penetration in dichotomous terms, Mahoney (2010) admits that it is more of a continuous gradation of colonial penetration. Gerring et al. (2011: 378) analyze the reasons for choice of direct versus indirect rule and propose a "key conceptual move ... to understand systems of rule along a continuum that reflects the degree of central control." Lange (2009: 176) notes that there were several variations of both direct and indirect rule within "the administrative hodgepodge of colonial India," which supports the suggestion that there was a lot of variation within the categories of direct and indirect rule and it should not be conceptualized as a binary measure.

---

[9] Misra, *Land Revenue Policy in the United Provinces under British Rule*, pp. 20–6. For Holt Mackenzie's minute, which argued in favor of Indian village communities, see Holt Mackenzie, Memorandum, 1 July 1819, para. 550, *Selections from the Revenue Records of the N.W. Provinces 1818–1820*, p. 117.

The reason the British administrators had to depend on indirect forms of rule was the large size of the country. While the central state was relatively large in absolute terms when compared with other British colonies, it was quite small relative to the huge population of India, and this "prevented it from reaching down to the local level and often required additional tiers of colonial control that depended on local intermediaries" (Lange 2009: 176). However, the type of local intermediary they depended on varied by the particular type of administrative function they needed to fulfill and also by the type of native elites available in that context. Synthesizing concepts from Kohli (2004) and Lange (2009) with the existing historiographical understanding of indirect rule in South Asia (Fisher 1991; Ramusack 2004), I posit that there were two main types of indirect rule in India, depending on the type of native intermediary being used by the British in a particular context to assist them in ruling or collecting revenue. One type was formal indirect rule through princely states and the other was informal indirect rule through *zamindari* and *malguzari* land tenure system. These could be compared with areas in Bombay and Madras Presidency, where the British colonizers not only ruled directly but also used the more direct form of land revenue collection through the *ryotwari* tenure system.

3.1   Different Types of Colonial Indirect Rule Create Different Mechanisms and Opportunity Structures for Insurgency

Type 1: Formal/Official (de Jure) Indirect Rule through Princely States Causing Low State Capacity, Low Development, and Despotic/Extractive Rule

The most commonly understood form of dependence on preexisting native rulers is that of formal (de jure) indirect rule in which the British signed different treaties with various small and large Indian rulers or native princes, to rule or administer on behalf of the colonizers. This was the official/formal/de jure type of indirect rule in which the colonizers ruled through preexisting native rulers called princes, *nizams*, *nawabs*, or *rajahs*. This form of rule allowed substantial autonomy in the sphere of administration, taxation, land revenue, and law, while keeping foreign policy under the direct control of the colonial administration (Copland 1982; Fisher 1991; Lee-Warner 1910). The formal/legal relations are usually defined through treaties or *sanads*, which summarized the duties and responsibilities of the native ruler to the colonial power. Usually, the colonizer would keep some level of control over the internal affairs of the native state administration through British political appointees called Residents in the court of the native chief, and interference by the colonial state would reduce the actual internal autonomy and reduce the de facto nature of indirect rule.[10] But in majority of cases, this was genuine indirect rule, and the

---

[10]   As Fisher, *Indirect Rule in India*, describes in detail, British officials were appointed as Residents in the courts of the Indian princes. In a few cases, like Mysore, the British Resident would

prince had autonomy over land tenure, the judiciary, the administration, and the police.

Given the large population and miniscule colonial army and bureaucracy, the colonizers found it difficult to administer and tax certain areas within their colonies and preferred to use formal de jure indirect rule to get whatever revenue they could without spending much money on creating large administrative structures (Lange 2009). Sundar (2007: 91) in her study of the princely state of Bastar notes that indirect rule allowed the political consolidation of vast areas "without the attendant difficulties and costs of administration." Another function of using indirect rule was to "deflect rebellion," which could be blamed on the local king's lack of concern for his subjects (Sundar 2007: 103).

These princely states, especially the feudatory/tributary states in central/ eastern India, developed weaker state capacity and saw exploitation of land and natural resources, which I discuss in more detail in Section 4.

Type 2: Informal/ Unofficial but de Facto Indirect Rule through Zamindars, Leading to Despotic Extraction of Taxes and Land/Income Inequality

Another type of indirect rule occurs in areas that the colonizer has officially annexed into direct rule. However, because of the difficulty of governing or collecting taxes/revenue, the colonial administrators depend on local pre-colonial elites to carry out land revenue collection and other functions of government on their behalf, thus leading to de facto indirect rule or indirect revenue collection, under the official rubric of de jure direct rule.

One of the most important aspects of rule for which the British depended on Indian elites was land revenue or land tax collection, which formed the economic bedrock of their sustainability in India. Within British India, this informal type of indirect rule often resulted when the British conquered an area and annexed it into direct rule but then found it convenient to rely on preexisting native political intermediaries called *zamindars* or *taluqdars* or *malguzars* to collect land revenue/taxes on its behalf. As discussed in more detail in Section 2.2 on the history of evolution of land tenure systems under the British, this first happened in Bengal Presidency in the east, in the initial period of British annexation in India from 1765 onward, when the British did not have sufficient power to penetrate into rural society, and was formalized under Lord Cornwallis's permanent settlement policy in Bengal in 1793.

As Levi (1988) notes, revenue collection is an important form of rule, and it is conceptually fruitful to think of any kind of pre-colonial elite in India who assisted the colonizers in ruling or revenue collection as a form of colonial indirect rule (Sartori 1970). While in an official or de jure sense, it was only

informally take over administration of the princely state, due to alleged misgovernance, minority status of the ruler, or other political reasons.

the native or princely states that were thought of as experiencing indirect rule, in reality on the ground, *zamindari* and other such landlord- or intermediary-based land revenue systems were different shades of de facto indirect rule or indirect revenue collection by the colonizer.

Lange (2009: 176–77) hints at this variation of de facto indirect rule within de jure direct rule areas when he mentions that the British in India tried to officially characterize the different forms of administration that emerged and

some of these collaborative forms of rule were formally recognized as indirect rule, while others were categorized as direct despite some telltale signs of indirect rule (e.g. administrative dependence on patrimonial collaborators). Whether classified by colonial officials as direct or indirect, all forms of collaboration severely limited the state's infrastructural power and level of bureaucratization and empowered local intermediaries.

Lange (2009: 177) thus suggests that the British were forced to depend on pre-colonial Indian elites like *zamindars,* taluqdars, and other tax-collecting landlords to help them rule and collect land revenue in much of the directly ruled territories like Bihar and Bengal, and such forms of collaboration was also a type of indirect rule.

Besides Lange (2009), other scholars also interpret the landlord type of tenure system as a manifestation of indirect rule and control by the British administrators. Mahoney (2010: 240), when discussing British colonization in India, also proposes the following:

Even in the directly ruled areas, officials relied on indigenous elites for a number of functions because of the general absence of the colonial administration, especially in the countryside. In many instances, local elites were also given rights to large tracts of land and were thereby able to control villages technically under British administration. ... In turn, the concentration of these duties and powers in elite hands made possible the hyper-exploitation of the peasantry, something that appears to have retarded agricultural production and stultified investment in public goods, even after the end of colonialism.

Kohli (2004) too describes these arrangements of indirect rule between the British colonizers and indigenous elites and categorizes the choice of *zamindars* and other intermediaries to collect land revenue as a type of indirect revenue collection and hence rule. According to Kohli (2004: 225–26),

After subduing one area and then another, the British entered into a variety of arrangements with influential "natives" – generally members of traditional ruling classes – to facilitate the essential tasks of collecting taxes and securing order. In some parts of India (e.g., in the Bengal presidency) this arrangement involved British rulers in alliance with Indian zamindars (landlords). ... This ingenious arrangement of indirect rule served the British purpose very well in securing predictable revenues and long-term ruling allies. ... At the same time, however, the arrangement also limited the downward reach of state power, leaving much influence in the hands of traditional elites, and it was also detrimental to the development of the agrarian economy. In other parts of India, especially in Western India, for example, British rule was more direct and reached deeper into Indian society, with British civil servants being directly responsible for collecting taxes from peasant proprietors.

Anthropologists like Dirks (2001: 15) also suggest that these land revenue systems were in reality different forms of indirect rule and writes, "By indirect rule in this context I mean the mechanisms that were used both to buttress and to displace colonial authority. In the early years of colonial rule, these mechanisms were organized principally through 'land systems' that were linked to models of property, agrarian relations, and revenue collection."[11] A historian of South Asia, Ramusack (2004: 56) suggests that even in Saran district of Bihar, which was part of the directly ruled province of Bengal since 1765, the British rule was limited and required collaboration with the maharaja of Hathwa, a local *zamindar*. This *zamindar* maintained local control over the peasantry and produced the revenue for both himself and the British.

These *zamindari* land tenure systems created high levels of land/caste inequality and also lower levels of state capacity and prevented "the ability of the peasants to pursue their well-being" (Lange 2009: 177), which is discussed later in Section 4.

Type 3: Both Direct Rule and Direct Land Revenue Systems

These two types of indirect rule are in contrast to the rule in other areas in the south and west of India that the British annexed areas into direct rule and then used a more progressive and interventionist land revenue collection system called the *ryotwari* (peasant-based) tenure, in which land revenue was collected directly from the *ryots* or peasants, thereby cutting out native elites who could establish exploitative land relations. This was carried out in the later phases of British rule in Bombay Presidency in the west and Madras Presidency in the south, from 1820 to 1850.[12] Another form of land tenure system used in these areas was the *mahalwari* system, also discussed in Section 2, which was more village based but also did not have landlords as intermediary land revenue collectors. These areas represent both de jure and de facto direct rule, where both administration and land revenue collection were executed through institutions created by the British.

It resulted in lower levels of land and agrarian inequality, since there were no native elites who had an incentive to exploit the peasants and keep the extra revenue for themselves. Eliminating such native intermediaries, who would do revenue collection and rule on behalf of the colonizers, reduced the characteristic despotism of indirect rule (Mamdani 1996) to some extent in these *ryotwari* and *mahalwari* land tenure areas.

Another positive effect of directly collecting land revenue was that the colonial administration was forced to increase levels of administrative and institutional penetration into the rural areas: the British colonial administrators had to create

---

[11] Dirks, *Castes of the Mind*, p. 15   [12] Rabitoy, "System v. Expediency," p. 532.

their own bureaucratic networks and institutions to reach out to the village level so that they could accurately estimate the changing value of land and agricultural production, and also so that they could collect land revenue directly from the peasants or *ryots* or from the villages (*mahals*). This required a far greater degree of state penetration and creation of institutions up to the village level, which the indirect revenue tenure system in Bengal and Bihar did not, since it depended on the existing landlords or *zamindars* or *malguzars* to do the tax/revenue collection for the colonizers.

Also, since these areas were formally de jure direct rule, there was a much higher level of bureaucratic capacity and governance. These areas of direct British rule in the west and south were divided into different subregions called Madras and Bombay Presidencies. The office of secretary of state was created in London to assist the British Crown in the administration of her colonial direct ruled territories in India, and a governor-general or viceroy was appointed and put in charge of daily administrative functions in directly ruled provinces. A large and complex system of administration was set up in these directly ruled British provinces, which included the bureaucratic administration called the Indian Civil Service (ICS), which was in charge of running the actual administration on a daily basis and was made up mainly of British-origin civil servants, though Indians did begin to qualify for the ICS exam and join the bureaucracy in later stages. Other institutions implanted by the British in these direct ruled territories were the judiciary and the Imperial Police.

4   THEORY AND MECHANISMS LINKING DIFFERENT TYPES OF INDIRECT RULE AND REVENUE COLLECTION TO SPATIAL VARIATION IN MAOIST MOBILIZATION

4.1   Theory Linking These Types of Indirect Rule to Maoist Insurgency

These forms of colonial indirect rule and revenue collection set up the long-term structural conditions conducive to Maoist insurgency. Areas of initial Maoist control in the 1990s–2000s were correlated with districts that had colonial indirect rule through princely states in Chhattisgarh, Andhra Pradesh, and southern Orissa, and with districts that had colonial indirect revenue collection through *zamindars* in Bihar, Jharkhand, and West Bengal. While the princely state areas in Chhattisgarh and Andhra Pradesh were formal or de jure manifestations of indirect rule, the *zamindari* land tenure systems in Bihar, Jharkhand, and West Bengal were informal but de facto indirect forms of economic and political control, in which land revenue was collected and local governance was conducted by the British colonizers through intermediary landlords and local political elites. Both areas had some form of Maoist insurgency in the 1980s and 1990s.

The British colonial history of administration using indirect rule and indirect revenue systems released certain mechanisms that had an impact on postcolonial institutions, state capacity, and development trajectories in different areas of India, thus indirectly affecting spatial variation in Maoist mobilization today. In many of these former *zamindari* or princely state areas in the eastern and central-southern parts of India, the effects of weak state penetration, low bureaucratization, inter-caste inequality, or socioeconomic alienation of the tribals persisted and became path dependent even after India became independent in 1947. With the exception of certain princely states that had benevolent despots, or in which there were progressive postcolonial governments that tried to reverse the effects of indirect colonial rule, these negative effects of bad governance and state weakness in the more extractive princely states like Chhattisgarh and Hyderabad in south-eastern India could not be reversed.[13]

A deeper analysis would reveal that such historically rooted structural variables to a large extent influenced the possibility of successful Maoist mobilization in the 1980s. The British colonial institutions of indirect rule and indirect revenue collection set into motion causal pathways that persisted after independence and set up the *political opportunity structures* that were needed for the successful Maoist rebellion in the 1980s, after the initial failure of Naxalism in the late 1960s. Other opportunity variables like access to forest cover and mining resources played a crucial role, as did various grievance-related factors like levels of underdevelopment and literacy, the presence of socioeconomically exploited scheduled castes and neglected scheduled tribes, and the level of natural forest produce in assisting the Maoist leaders to recruit. The effects of government development programs like NREGS and also counterinsurgency programs like the Salwa Judum campaign also mattered.[14] But these opportunity and grievance variables are not sufficient to explain the full breadth of Maoist mobilization in India. They were only parts of a long causal chain tracing back to these colonial institutions of different types of indirect rule.

This argument interprets political opportunity structures more broadly than the original theorists of revolution, social movements, and civil wars. While theories of civil war like that of Fearon and Laitin (2003) try to apply the idea of opportunity structure to the outcome of civil wars, what is missing from most theories of civil war onset/incidence (e.g., Collier & Hoeffler 2004; Fearon & Laitin 2003; Hegre et al. 2001; Sambanis 2001) is a broader and deeper

---

[13] There are exceptional cases like the princely states of Mysore and Travancore that had enlightened despots/rulers who created higher-quality administrative and bureaucratic institutions and produced more public goods than the average Indian princely state ruler. These are influential cases that are discussed in Chapter 9 and can be explained as part of the theoretical framework outlined in Figure 3.3.

[14] See Chapter 2 for an analysis of studies of Maoist insurgency highlighting these factors.

interpretation of *rebel opportunity* in terms of long-term institutions and their effects. In contrast, my theory conceptualizes opportunity for rebellion more broadly and shows how such opportunities are sometimes the outcomes of persistence and path dependence of the effects of colonial institutions.

4.2   Schematic Diagram of Two Causal Pathways Leading from Indirect Rule to Insurgency

Figure 3.3 presents a schematic diagram that outlines the causal links between different forms of indirect rule by the British colonizers and the dependent variable of postcolonial Maoist control. The two geographic epicenters of Maoist mobilization represent two causal pathways that led to successful Maoist mobilization in India.

The first epicenter of insurgency occurred in areas of erstwhile informal de facto British indirect rule through *zamindari*-type tenure, which also had a

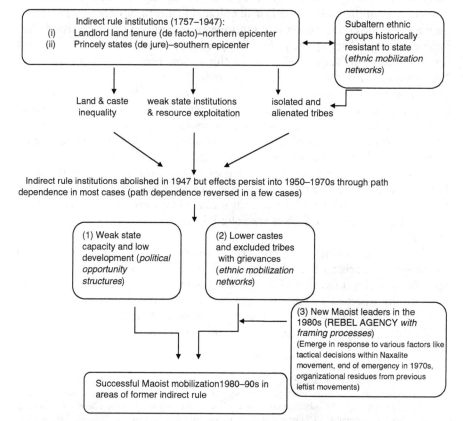

FIGURE 3.3 **Different causal pathways from colonial indirect rule to Maoist insurgency in India**

social structure consisting of a ranked caste system with oppressed *Dalits*, and these led to the Maoist mobilization in the plains of central Bihar, eastern Uttar Pradesh, and western Bengal. The southern Bihar area, which later on became Jharkhand had this same combination of colonial institutions, except that the ethnic structure was dominated by tribes, not lower castes, and there was more natural resource exploitation. Both these areas had successful Maoist mobilization post 1980s, mainly by the Maoist Communist Center (MCC) but also by the People's War Group (PWG) and many other smaller Communist Party of India-Marxist Leninist (CPI-ML) factions. This was the northern epicenter of the movement and is explained in detail in the discussion of the organizational history of the Naxal or Maoist movement in Chapter 4.

The second geographic epicenter of the insurgency representing the second causal pathway occurred in areas of formal de jure British indirect rule through princely states, and these were mostly areas with different *Adivasi* (tribal) populations, as well as some *Dalit* populations in central-southern India. These areas coincide geographically with the indirect ruled princely state areas of Bastar and Surguja in the current state of Chhattisgarh, the Telangana region of former Hyderabad princely state in the former state of Andhra Pradesh, and some princely state areas in Orissa. In this southern epicenter of the insurgency, in the deeply forested area popularly called the Dandakaranya zone by the Maoists, near the borders of the states of Chhattisgarh, Andhra Pradesh, Maharashtra, and Orissa, the PWG emerged as the main Maoist rebel group beginning in the 1980s, though other Maoist factions like Party Unity (PU) also operated here, until it united with the PWG. (See Figure 1.1 for a recent map of Maoist insurgency.)

4.3 Mechanisms Created by Formal Indirect Rule in the Southern Epicenter

In the southern zone, the PWG Maoists succeeded in those areas that were under indirect rule by the British, in the form of princely states, and were not as successful in the areas the British ruled directly. In these central-south Indian areas of Andhra Pradesh, Chhattisgarh, and Orissa, the British chose indirect rule with the help of the native rulers in the *successor* princely state of Hyderabad, part of which remained in the state of Andhra Pradesh, and the *feudatory* princely states of Bastar, which was in the southern part of the current state of Chhattisgarh.[15] These types of princely states in this region created several mechanisms of low state capacity and despotic extraction of land and natural resources, which created the structural conditions for leftist ideological insurgency.

---

[15] The British also had the princely states of Surguja, Koriya, Changbhakar, and Udaipur in the northern tip of Chhattisgarh, but these were effectively part of the northern epicenter of insurgency.

Mechanism 1: Weak State/Bureaucratic Capacity

The first mechanism is that colonial indirect rule through native rulers tended to produce lower levels of development, weaker bureaucratic and police capacity (Hurd 1975; Kohli 2004; Lange 2009; Mahoney 2010).[16] This laid the ground for low state penetration and weak bureaucratic/police capacity. Most of the princely states in central-southern India in the Chhattisgarh and Andhra Pradesh area were not as efficient in creating structures of bureaucracy, roads, revenue and tax collection, and other institutions of modern state, as the British administration did in areas of British direct rule.

These areas of formal indirect rule through princely states had different systems of administration and institutions than those in British direct rule areas. The British created the Indian Political Service through which political officers and Residents were appointed to the court of native princely states to advise and influence the princes and gather information about the political and other affairs in these states (Fisher 1991). This political service often attracted British Indian Civil Service (ICS) and military officers who did not like the increasing democratization in Britain and directly ruled India and were often attracted to the Indian Political Service in the princely states, as an escape (Ramusack 2004: 101–2). These political officers were less sensitive to the needs of the peoples of these states and made them more dependent on the nature of the prince/ruler for the quality of rule (Ramusack 2004: 103).

As a consequence, the bureaucratic, judiciary, legal, tax collection, and public works institutions in these central-southern princely states were not as efficient and intrusive as the ICS in the British provinces. None of the administrative, police, judicial, or tax collection institutions that prevailed in British India was present in the princely states, with the exception of certain progressive states like Travancore, Mysore, and Baroda. Hurd (1975) matches princely states with neighboring British districts that are similar in ecological factors like soil, topography, water supply, and cultural patterns and finds that the majority of princely states fell below their matching British districts for four indices of development: (1) percentage of male workers employed in nonagricultural jobs, (2) percentage of males born outside the political unit, (3) percentage of males literate, and (4) percentage of population living in urban areas.[17]

This created enclaves of state weakness in these areas, and the postcolonial governments often lacked the political incentives or ability to overcome this deficit of state capacity in these areas and build complex bureaucracies, police, roads, and tax institutions into these historically underdeveloped and remote

---

[16] In contrast, Iyer, "Direct versus Indirect Rule in India," suggests indirect rule produces better outcomes in India, but there are potential problems with her IV-2SLS analysis since it covers only the 1847–56 period for a truncated sample and cannot address selection for the 1757–1846 period of annexation. See Chapter 5 for more detailed analysis.

[17] Hurd, "The Economic Consequences of Indirect Rule in India."

areas. This created path dependent development of areas of endemic state weakness, which provided ideal opportunity structures for the PWG Maoists to mobilize and set up their guerrilla zones by motivating and recruiting the different tribal groups living in these areas.

Mechanism 2: Despotic Exploitation of Land/Natural Resources of Tribes

The second mechanism in these formal indirect rule areas was *despotic and extractive rule* by the native prince or chief, leading to exploitation of land, labor, and natural resources of subaltern ethnic groups (Boone 1994; Mamdani 1996). In most princely states, the *diwan* or chief minister oversaw collection of taxes and land revenues (Ramusack 2004: 171). The land revenue systems in princely states was divided into *khalsa/diwani* or crown lands that paid land revenue directly to the ruler to support the state administration, and *non-khalsa* lands that were beyond the control of the prince or state where *jagirdars* (feudal military allies of the prince/ruler), state officials, relatives of the ruler, and other appointed officials collected revenues. The administrators in these *khalsa/ diwani* areas often extracted high levels of revenue and exploited the peasants. The *jagirdars* and other feudal lords in the *non-khalsa* lands were also exploitative of labor and other land-related resources (Ramusack 2004: 171).

While the institutions of indirect rule and land revenue were abolished following Indian independence in these areas, their effects became path dependent and persisted, since the local elites continued to have power in agrarian societies and prevented land reforms. As demonstrated in the cases of Chhattisgarh and Andhra Pradesh in later chapters, the landed elites had a vested interest in preventing land reforms, and so this land inequality persisted and was not changed through a reversal of policy by the postcolonial state. This provided the ideal opportunity structures and ethnic mobilization networks for ideologically driven Maoist rebel leaders to mobilize and recruit from these exploited ethnic groups by providing them with public goods, protection from the oppressive state and landed elites, as well as selective incentives (Lichbach 1994).

4.4   Mechanisms Created by Indirect Revenue Collection in the Northern Epicenter

In the northern epicenter of the insurgency, in the hilly and forested plains of central and southern Bihar and northern Orissa and western Bengal, the Maoist Communist Center (MCC) emerged as the strongest Maoist faction in the 1980s and 1990s. These were areas where the British had informally depended on the *zamindars* to carry out revenue collection, and local administration on their behalf. There are two mechanisms through which this type of de facto indirect rule through the *zamindari* system of land tenure shaped the historical legacies for successful Maoist mobilization in this region.

Mechanism 1: Land/Caste Inequality

First, there was *despotic extraction* by the *zamindari* elites, which caused rural inequalities and class polarization in agrarian society between these landowning native elites and the landless agrarian poor. This kind of colonial land tenure system introduced intermediaries between the colonizer and the lower-caste landless peasants. This created increasing land inequality and exploitation of these lower-caste peasants by these landlords/*zamindars* because the landlords were protected by the colonizer and could carry out extractive and predatory land revenue taxation and create oppressive institutions of labor extraction (Boone 1994; Mamdani 1996). Such a system increased land inequality as well as political inequality between ethnic groups along caste lines, as the landlords were often upper caste and the peasants and landless laborers were lower caste, and it was a ranked ethnic system (Horowitz 1985). This led to ethnic exclusion from power of lower castes, which persisted into the 1970s (Cederman et al. 2010).

Previous scholarship has theorized land inequality and landlessness to be important preconditions for leftist insurgency and revolution (Mitchell 1967, 1968; Paige 1975; Wood 2003), and the colonial landlord tenure system may be a structural determinant of such conflict. In the Indian context, Banerjee and Iyer (2005: 1198) show that Indian districts that had colonial landlord tenure systems (*zamindari* or *malguzari*) tended to have lower levels of public goods, because the landlord tenure systems increased class-based political antagonisms, which created collective action problems and led to lower public good provision in these districts. Banerjee and Iyer (2005: 1198) mention in passing that such class and political inequality may also have led to peasant support for land redistribution and that "the areas most associated with Maoist peasant uprisings ... are West Bengal, Bihar, and the Srikakulam district of Andhra Pradesh, all landlord areas." While some of the land inequality was removed by postcolonial provincial governments, class-based antagonism between peasants and landlords from the colonial era persisted into the 1980s and allowed for the grievances of the landless class to be mobilized for effective violent collective action by the Maoists.

Mechanism 2: Weaker Bureaucratic and State Capacity

Another mechanism was that the *zamindari* land revenue system required less expansion of the colonial bureaucracy than the *ryotwari* land revenue system in which the colonial state directly collected tax and revenue from the villages. The *ryotwari* system required more British and Indian personnel on the ground to evaluate land values and a larger rural infrastructure to support this, while in *zamindari* areas the local *zamindars* did the land tax collection and evaluations on behalf of the British. According to Lange (2009: 177), the landlords who were chosen as revenue collectors carried out their own form of patrimonial administrations, and "this personal system of administration severely limited state bureaucratization, infrastructural power, and inclusiveness."

According to Mukherjee (1962), "The ryotwari system naturally resulted in an intimate contact between the people and the Government. The ryots had to come in daily touch with the revenue officials, small and big. ... Under a permanent Zemindary settlement or a village rent system, the people had few occasions to come in direct contact with the Government." So compared with the *ryotwari* system in Madras and Bombay in the west and south, the *zamindari* system in the east in Bengal and Bihar had lower levels of state penetration and bureaucratic networks. Mukherjee (1962: 363–64) mentions that the initial introduction of the *ryotwari* settlement in the ceded districts in Madras in the early 1800s under Read and Munroe resulted in better law and order outcomes, besides more revenue.

Using historical data from the 1930s and 1960s, Lee (2019) demonstrates that *zamindari* land tenure districts had lower levels of bureaucratic and tax capacity than *ryotwari* districts. Lee (2019: 425) finds that directly ruled areas with *ryotwari* land tenure were forced to develop a professional uniformed police service, known as the police *patil* in Bombay, the village *headman* in Madras, and the *lambradar* in Punjab province, all of whom were "responsible for ensuring that taxes were collected, and crimes reported." In contrast, in *zamindari* areas like Bengal, the *zamindars* retained police authority as they had under the Mughals, and they appointed and paid the village watchmen or *chaukidars*, and the British found it very difficult to replace this decentralized law enforcement force with an official police force in Bengal. Lee's (2019) study thus shows that colonial land tenure affects not just development and land inequality as earlier studies like Banerjee and Iyer (2005) claim but also subnational variation in state capacity in India, which influences insurgency onset (Fearon & Laitin 2003).

4.5 Mechanisms Became Path Dependent and Persisted into the 1980s

Once India became independent in 1947, these princely states and *zamindaris* were formally abolished, and so the effects of these institutions should have withered away and there should have been convergence between districts under indirect and direct rule by 1980s. Yet, in many of these former *zamindari* districts in Bihar/Jharkhand/Bengal in eastern India or princely state areas in Hyderabad, Bastar, and Orissa in central-southern India, the causal mechanisms of weak state penetration, intercaste inequality, or tribal alienation combined with exploitation of natural resources, became path dependent and persisted even after 1947.

The various reasons for path dependent persistence of these institutional legacies are demonstrated in more detail in Chapters 7 and 8 where the cases of Chhattisgarh and Andhra Pradesh are analyzed. The first is similar to Mahoney's (2000: 521) "power-based" explanation for path dependent institutional persistence, in which an institution can persist when an elite benefiting from it has sufficient strength to promote its reproduction.

Postcolonial governments in areas previously ruled by landlords in Bihar and Andhra Pradesh found it difficult to do serious land reforms, as land reforms are proposed by the ruling elites who are largely composed of, or structurally dependent upon, agrarian elites (Besley & Burgess 2000). The tenancy reforms introduced by the Congress party government in Andhra Pradesh in the 1950s lacked political will because the rich peasant landlord castes, like the Kammas and Reddys, wielded a lot of influence on the politicians from their own castes.[18] The reemergence of the Maoist movement in the 1970s and 1980s in Andhra Pradesh was partly to "complete the unfinished agenda of the Telangana armed struggle in the 1940s."[19] In other places, tribal leaders like Mahendra Karma in Chhattisgarh and Shibu Soren in Jharkhand "promoted policies that not only increase their personal wealth, but also intensified the very exploitative processes that form the core of *Adivasi* grievances" (Kennedy & Purushottam 2012: 853).

A second means for persistence of these mechanisms is that areas of formal indirect rule through princely states in central India were often treated as administrative backwaters by the colonial administrators, and postcolonial provincial governments in Madhya Pradesh continued to treat these as areas of "punishment postings" for police officers and bureaucrats, thus leading to persistence of lower levels of police and bureaucratic capacity in these former princely state areas.[20] According to a police officer who served in these Maoist-affected areas in the south of Chhattisgarh: "in a batch of Assistant Sub Inspectors (ASI)s, those who are the toppers in the batch or best officers, they are not sent to the Naxal areas, the others who are not the best officers are sent."[21]

A third mechanism of persistence was that the colonial state had only been interested in the revenue and natural resources it could exploit from these areas (Kennedy & Purushotham 2012: 840). The Bastar princely state area in south Chhattisgarh "contains one of the most deciduous forests of the country, consisting of sal, teak and mixed forests" and by 1909 the first commercial exploitation of these forests began with a lease given to Becket and Co. for extraction of 25,000 railway sleepers from sal trees, and operations increased during World War II.[22] The Indian state has similarly been interested in exploiting the rich deposits of bauxite and iron ore in southern Chhattisgarh through the National Mineral Development Corporation since the 1960s, and more recently allowing Multi national Corporations (MNCs) like Essar into the Kirandul/Bacheli area in Dantewada district, without building adequate roads and providing sufficient development, thus showing another continuity in state

---

[18] *Economic and Policy Weekly*, "Andhra Pradesh: Peasants Struggle for Land," p. 1693.
[19] Haragopal, "The Telangana People's Movement," p. 54.
[20] Interview with superintendent of police (district not revealed), Chhattisgarh, 2009.
[21] Interview with deputy superintendent of police, Kanker district, Chhattisgarh, 2009.
[22] People's Union of Civil Liberties (PUCL), *Bastar: Development and Democracy*, p. 5

policy.[23] According to human rights activists, village clearing during the Salwa Judum vigilante movement (2005–2009) also served the purpose of making land easily available for mining projects by private companies that were interested in the rich iron ore resources in the Dantewada area.[24]

5 TIMING OF ONSET OF INSURGENCY AND REBEL AGENCY

What explains the timing of insurgency onset in 1980s? Since there is no temporal variation in the explanatory variable of indirect rule since the Indian Mutiny of 1857 stopped the policy of annexation, this question of onset of insurgency cannot be answered by focusing only on colonial indirect rule. The final part of the theoretical framework in Figure 3.3 is the reemergence of *rebel agency* in the form of Maoist groups in the 1980s in Andhra Pradesh and Bihar. These initial rebel leaders and their cadres provided the *ideological frames of rebellion*. The timing of the Maoist reemergence is linked to factors like the release of Maoist leaders from jail with the end of Indira Gandhi's Emergency period in 1977 and ideological and strategic rethinking within the radical leftist movement in India in the 1970s leading to the emergence of four main factions – MCC, PWG, PU, and CPI-ML (Liberation) (Bhatia 2005; Kujur 2008). The initial onset of the Maoists in the 1980s occurred before economic liberalization was launched in India in the 1990s; so this can be ruled out as a potential explanation, though it could possibly explain the later expansion of the movement from 2000 to 2010.

The emergence of the Maoists is not explained by historical institutions but by other political, economic, and organizational factors that are complementary to my theory. However, once the new rebel organizations emerged in 1980–90s, their ability to succeed in an area was largely constrained by the opportunity structures in the form of low state capacity and development, and the ethnic mobilization networks in the form of tribes and lower castes with grievances created by colonial indirect rule institutions (McAdam et al. 1996). Colonial institutions thus provide the structural constraints that influence the initial spatial variation in rebel control and not the timing of emergence or onset of rebellion.

5.1 Scope Conditions

Some scope conditions for my theory make it analytically distinct from the other recent studies of Maoist insurgency (Chandra & Garcia-Ponce 2019; Dasgupta et al. 2017; Gawande et al. 2017; Vanden Eynde 2018) and not rival to them in

---

[23] Interview with human rights activist Dr. Binayak Sen, Raipur, Chhattisgarh, 2008. Also, focus group discussion with villagers, Village X (pseudonym), near Kirandul town, Dantewada district, 2009.

[24] Interview with PUCL activist Sudha Bhardwaj, Bhilai, Chhattisgarh, 2009. Also see PUCL, *Where the State Makes War on its Own people*, pp. 7–8.

explanation. My theory of colonial indirect rule and revenue institutions only explains variation in rebel control until 2004, before the rapid spatial expansion and increase in violence beginning with the unification of the MCC and PWG to form the CPI-Maoist. Once an insurgency consolidates itself, it develops sufficient organizational and military capacity so that it may no longer be constrained by historically created inequalities and low state capacity and can possibly expand even into areas with fewer inequalities and higher state capacity. The unification of the main Maoist groups to form CPI-Maoist in 2004 represents a sudden increase in the organization's ability and capacity, which allowed it to expand geographically beyond the initial areas of historic indirect rule and use higher levels of violence than was possible when the movement was still fragmented. However, in Chapter 6, the theory is also tested using measures of Maoist control for 2005, 2011, and 2016, and *princely state* variable is still a robust predictor of Maoist control for these later periods of expansion of insurgency.

The other studies on Maoist insurgency (Dasgupta et al. 2017; Gawande et al. 2017; Gomes 2015; Vanden Eynde 2018) explain levels and patterns of violence (2005 to 2010) in this later phase of the insurgency, when the CPI-Maoist became a unified and organizationally much stronger group. In later phases of the insurgency, various environmental factors explain violence patterns and diffusion in rebel control, like failure of peace negotiations and intensification in counterinsurgency in Andhra Pradesh in 2003–4, use of vigilante groups like Salwa Judum in Chhattisgarh in 2006–10 and discovery of mineral resources (Gomes 2015; Vanden Eynde 2018), covert deals between the Trinamul Congress party and the Maoists in West Bengal in 2009–10, strategic decisions within the CPI-Maoist to expand operations after unification in 2004, implementation of NREGS developmental programs (Dasgupta et al. 2017), or the presence of subaltern ethnic parties (Chandra & Garcia-Ponce 2019). Such proximate factors can explain the escalation in levels of violence as the insurgency expanded geographically since 2005, but the initial core areas of rebel control are better explained by persistent structural conditions created by colonial indirect rule interacting with initial rebel agency.

6 CONCLUSION – REBEL AGENCY AND IDEOLOGICAL FRAMES OF REBELLION

In this chapter, I outlined a theory of how different colonial institutions of indirect rule trigger different mechanisms that persist into the postcolonial period and create structural conditions for Maoist insurgency in India. These mechanisms persisted because many postcolonial governments of states within India that had districts previously under either form of colonial indirect rule did not or could not reverse the effects of these institutions. The result was areas with opportunity structures in the form of low state capacity and underdevelopment and the presence of tribes or lower castes with grievances in these districts that provided ethnic mobilization networks for leftist rebels to exploit.

I conclude this chapter by focusing on rebel agency in the form of previous organizational legacies and leftist networks from past rebellions, and how that interacts with the structural conditions created by indirect rule, as shown in the schematic diagram in Figure 3.3. This sets the agenda for the analytical discussion in the next chapter on Maoist rebel strategy and tactics and their interaction with structurally created ethnic and land inequalities.

Previous leftist networks of the 1940s–60s may have created some of the organizational legacies that the more radical Maoist rebel leaders built upon in the 1980–90s to start rebellion in places like Bihar and Andhra Pradesh. According to noted human rights activist K. Balagopal, the areas in Andhra Pradesh where there had been previous leftist mobilization during the Telangana peasant revolts in the 1940s–50s provided the organizational nucleus to restart the Maoist movement under the aegis of the PWG in the 1980s. According to Balagopal, in Telangana,

in 1946 there was a major Communist uprising here. That in turn was because the Nizam's administration had created these Deshmukhs who were very powerful land-lords. ... And that in turn has left a remnant of a Communist way of looking at things, which therefore was a politically a convenient ambience for the Naxalites to take over in the 1970s.[25]

Zukerman-Daly (2012: 474) similarly finds that regions in Colombia that were "plagued by the organizational legacies of past violence prove six times more likely to experience rebellion than areas without co-optable receptacles of prior collection action." This implies that not only opportunity structures created by institutions of colonial indirect rule but also rebel agency in the form of preexisting leftist/tribal networks also matters in explaining the successful mobilization of the Maoists. Those districts in India with past leftist/agrarian mobilization had a higher chance of successful Maoist mobilization in the 1980s–90s. This rebel agency in the form of ideological or organizational legacies could be considered part of the framing processes in the theoretical framework presented in Figure 3.3.

However, the emergence of agrarian rebellions in the past was itself in response to the structural conditions set up by different forms of indirect rule. For example, as shown in Chapter 8, the Telangana rebellion in Andhra Pradesh in 1940s occurred in response to the land and labor exploitation by the *deshmukhs* and *jagirdars* under the Nizam of Hyderabad. The Tebhaga rebellion in West Bengal in the 1940s was in response to the land inequality due to the *zamindari* tenure system. Thus, these preexisting organizational networks were themselves a result of the prevailing structural conditions created by different types of indirect rule,

---

[25] Interview with K. Balagopal, Hyderabad, February 12, 2008.

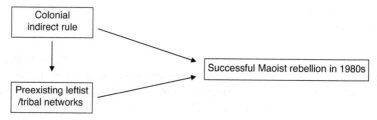

FIGURE 3.4 Indirect rule and previous leftist organizational mobilization

and not entirely exogenous to the causal pathways leading from indirect rule to insurgency. This is shown in Figure 3.4.

It is possible to conceptualize both the structural condition of indirect rule and the agency condition of whether there were preexisting leftist mobilization as INUS conditions, that is, neither cause is either individually necessary or sufficient, but they are jointly unnecessary but sufficient conditions for the outcome of Maoist insurgency.[26] Areas that had indirect rule through *zamindari* land tenure or through princely states but had no previous history of communist or agrarian rebellion, like Rajasthan or Gujarat, did not have Maoist insurgency in the 1980s. Areas that had some form of indirect rule and also a past history of extreme communist/peasant mobilization, like Andhra Pradesh, Bengal, and Bihar, ended up having successful Maoist mobilization beginning in the 1980s.

In the next chapter, using qualitative analysis based on field-based interviews and textual analysis of Maoist documents, I demonstrate that the Maoist leaders are very strategic about their choice of area, based on local politics, terrain, ethnic composition, and economic development. However, even within those areas they considered favorable based on terrain, level of inequality, and politics, they were successful only where the British colonial institutions of *zamindari* land tenure or certain type of princely states were present. This demonstrates that rebel agency is an important part of the story but is finally constrained by whether or not inequalities created by historical institutions/structures were or were not present in an area.

---

[26] See Mahoney and Goertz, "A Tale of Two Cultures," p. 232, fn. 4 for definition of an INUS condition.

PART II

QUALITATIVE AND QUANTITATIVE TESTING

4

Qualitative Analysis of Maoist Strategy and Rebel Agency

I INTRODUCTION

Chapters 1–3 (the theory section) showed that scholars have not explored the links between colonial institutions and postcolonial insurgency. To explain the deeper roots of insurgencies in historical processes of state formation and persistence of conflict in some regions, it is crucial to take the role of colonial and other historical legacies on conflict seriously. In the previous chapter, I addressed the puzzle of the peculiar spatial variation in Maoist insurgency in India and theorized that this is best explained by historical legacies of colonial British indirect rule. This makes the Maoist case an important one that highlights the role colonial legacies play in explaining insurgency.

The schematic diagram in Figure 3.3 outlined the two causal pathways to Maoist insurgency, and the importance of structural conditions created by colonial indirect rule. It also emphasized that rebel agency plays an equally important role in mobilizing the ethnic networks of lower castes and tribes that had developed grievances. However, rebel agency in the form of ideological frames and organizational legacies are ultimately constrained by whether or not weak state or land/ethnic inequalities created by historical institutions are present. It is the combination of rebel agency and historical legacies that creates the ideal conditions for Maoist insurgency to succeed.

In this chapter, I provide qualitative evidence to demonstrate this interaction between rebel agency and structural conditions created by colonial institutions. I use fieldwork interviews and textual analysis of Maoist documents to demonstrate that the Maoists are strategic about their choice of area, based on local politics, terrain, ethnic composition, and level of economic development. However, even within those areas they considered favorable based on terrain, level of inequality, and politics, they were successful only where the British colonial institutions of *zamindari* or *malguzari* (landlord-based) land tenure or certain type of princely states were present. This demonstrates that rebel agency and ideological frames are useful to mobilize subaltern groups like *Dalits* and *Adivasis*, who are the ethnic mobilization networks for rebellion. However, rebel agency is constrained by the opportunity structures of land/ethnic inequality available in areas of former indirect rule and revenue collection. (See Figures 3.3 and 3.4)

The rest of this chapter is as follows: in Section 2, I outline the organizational evolution of the low-scale but persistent Maoist insurgency in different parts of India. Then in Section 3, I draw on qualitative evidence drawn from interviews with key actors, as well as discursive analysis of Maoist documents gathered during fieldwork, to demonstrate that the Maoist groups have been successful along a belt of India that contained erstwhile British indirect rule institutions and were less successful in areas they have strategically targeted but were colonial direct rule. In Section 4, I show that the Maoist ideology-driven language demonstrates their understanding that the "semi-feudal" structure of indirect rule used by the British in the form of *zamindari* systems and princely states resulted in inequalities and that these inequalities were not removed and have persisted with new dimensions into the postcolonial period. Section 5 concludes by engaging with the next chapter, in which I use a district-level dataset to test for the effects of colonial indirect rule on Maoist control.

2   HISTORY OF THE MAOIST INSURGENCY: IDEOLOGICAL FRAMING PROCESSES AND ORGANIZATIONAL RESIDUES FROM PAST REBELLION

As shown in the theoretical framework in Figure 3.3, rebel agency in the form of ideological framing processes and organizational networks in conjunction with political opportunity structures in the form of weak state and land inequality create conditions for successful Maoist mobilization. In this section, I present a brief history of the organizational and ideological evolution of the Maoist insurgency in India, which will be an account of how this rebel agency developed and interacted with the structural conditions of land and ethnic inequality. Given that the Maoist insurgency in India is one of the longest leftist conflicts, along with the FARC insurgency in Colombia and the New People's Army (NPA) rebellion in Philippines, it is not possible to provide all the nuances of its trajectory of development. The goal of the section is to provide only the broad contours of the evolution of the various strands of Maoist ideology and groups that are most crucial to understand why they were successful in some areas of India and not others. The later chapters on Chhattisgarh and Andhra Pradesh include more detailed political histories of the People's War Group (PWG) Maoists in those two states.

While different scholars have focused on different time periods of the Maoist/Naxalite insurgency (Kennedy & Purushottam 2012), I divide it into four phases.

First Phase: The original Naxal movement started in 1969 and in some ways provided the ideologies and organizational networks that future Maoist movements built upon.[1] It emerged out of ideological differences within the broader Communist movement. Following India's independence in 1947, the Communist Party of India (CPI) was initially banned, but it later joined the mainstream and participated in elections. In 1957, the CPI was able to win elections in the state of Kerala, under the leadership of E. M. S. Namboodiripad, who became the first democratically elected Communist chief minister in the world, but this government was soon overthrown by the Congress Party in power at the national level. In 1962, India fought and lost a war with China over a border dispute. This led to an ideological split in the CPI, resulting in the formation of the CPI-Marxist in 1964. After winning provincial elections in the state of West Bengal in 1967, the CPI and CPI-Marxist formed a coalition United Front government. While the CPI-Marxist started a process of land tenure reforms in West Bengal, extremist elements within the CPI-Marxist remained dissatisfied with the "reformist" and "parliamentary" trends within the Communist movement and wanted more radical changes and armed revolution.[2]

In this scenario, an incident in Naxalbari in the Darjeeling district of West Bengal allowed this nascent radical left to organize effectively. The local landlords and police assaulted a tribal youth over his right to plough his land, and this led to a spontaneous local tribal backlash against the police, with one policeman being killed. This soon triggered a chain of events that led to the formation of the All India Coordination Committee of Communist Revolutionaries (AICCCR) in May 1968, and later the Communist Party of India (Marxist-Leninist) (CPI-ML) under the ideological leadership of Charu Mazumdar in 1969. With the help of able organizers like Kanu Sanyal and Jangal Santhal, the so-called Naxal movement rapidly spread to rural parts of West Bengal and Andhra Pradesh; there was also an intense urban guerrilla struggle in the city of Kolkata. The initial focus was on individual "annihilation of class enemies" like policemen and landlords. However, the United Front government in West Bengal, with the help of the Congress government at the center in New Delhi, was able to crush the movement. After the capture and killing of Charu Mazumdar in 1972, the movement collapsed, and many of the surviving leaders were jailed (Banerjee 1980; Mishra 2007).

Besides Naxalbari in Bengal, another region where there was Maoist insurgency in this phase was the Srikakulum district in Andhra Pradesh,

---

[1] The Maoist insurgency is also called the Naxal movement because the initial Marxist-Leninist version of this movement emerged in a small village called Naxalbari in the state of West Bengal in 1969.

[2] This section developed from the following studies: Kujur, *Naxal Movement in India: A Profile*; Bhatia, "The Naxalite Movement in Central Bihar"; Singh, *The Naxalite Movement in India*; and profiles of the Naxal groups at www.satp.org and www.massline.info/India/Indian_Groups.htm

where a different group of activists mobilized the Girijan tribals against exploitation by landlords and moneylenders, and they linked up with Charu Mazumdar. In 1967–74, the Andhra Pradesh Revolutionary Communist Committee (APRCC) movement led by Chandra Pulla Reddy and T. Nagi Reddy in Andhra Pradesh also occurred in the Telangana region of former Hyderabad princely state.[3] The interesting thing about the geographical location of the Naxalite movement in this first phase is that it started in Bengal, where the effects of land inequalities due to the *zamindari* land tenure system was evident, and in Andhra it occurred in princely state areas of Telangana and *zamindari* areas of Srikakulam. So, the different Marxist-Leninist groups that emerged succeeded in either the informal type of indirect revenue collection through *zamindari* land tenure or in formal indirect rule areas of former princely states, as my theoretical framework proposes.

Second Phase: Following the death of Charu Mazumdar, the movement factionalized into several splinter groups and many of the leaders were jailed. In 1977, after the lifting of the Emergency in India, many of these leaders were released from jail, followed by a lot of ideological and strategic rethinking and self-criticism. While the movement remained factionalized based on individual personalities and ideological differences, four main groups emerged, which can be used to understand the main ideological and strategic trends that have dominated the extreme radical leftist movement in India since that point. These were the Dakshin Desh, which soon became the Maoist Communist Center (MCC); the People's War Group (PWG); the Party Unity (PU); and the CPI-Marxist Leninist (Liberation). These groups were able to develop rebel control in different rural areas of India beginning in the 1980s, leading to the current situation where the PU, PWG, and MCC have united to form the CPI-Maoist, which completely rejects parliamentary democracy and has become the biggest armed threat to the Indian government, and the CPI-ML (Liberation), which has become less dominant, takes part in elections, and focuses more on mass movements.

Certain leaders like Kanhai Chatterjee from West Bengal differed with the Naxal guru Charu Mazumdar over the question of annihilation of class enemies and urban warfare and believed such individual targeting should only be undertaken after building up a mass base among peasants, workers, and tribals. Separating from the CPI-ML, Kanhai Chatterjee and Amulya Sen formed the Dakshin Desh group on October 20, 1969, which in 1975 became the Maoist Communist Center (MCC). The MCC believed in the development of mass movements, alongside armed struggle. The guiding philosophy of the MCC was Mao's revolutionary strategy of creating rural guerrilla base areas, and then slowly encircling the urban areas.

---

[3] For details of the Telangana movement, see Chapter 8 on Andhra Pradesh.

While in its initial period in the 1970s, Dakshin Desh had been active mainly in the Jangal Mahal area of Burdwan district, Midnapore, and Twenty-four Pargana districts of West Bengal, in the 1980s, the MCC spread its activities to Bihar. It began to develop its guerrilla zones in Bihar and Jharkhand, creating several front organizations, such as the Krantikari Chhatra League (Revolutionary Student's League), Naari Mukti Sangh (Women's Liberation Committee), and Mazdoor Mukti Sangh (Worker's Liberation Committee). It also had a military wing called Lal Raksha Dal, which had armed squads called *dastas*, drawing its recruits from the landless and poor peasants who belonged to the backward and scheduled castes.[4] The movement expanded; between 1987 and 1990, more than 7,000 acres of land in Chhotanagpur were confiscated and distributed among the villagers. In 1991, the landlords formed the *Sunlight Sena* – a private army – to combat the MCC. Within a year, Maoist armed squads liquidated the *Sena*.[5] By 2002, the MCC was active in six Naxalism-hit districts of Bihar and fourteen districts in Jharkhand.[6]

Besides the MCC, other groups emerged out of the old CPI-ML. In 1974, a group of erstwhile leaders of the CPI-ML started ideological "course correction" and renamed themselves as CPI-ML (Liberation). They critiqued Charu Mazumdar's line of annihilation of class enemies and decided that more important than armed struggle was the development of mass movements. The CPI-ML (Liberation) followed Lenin's theory that it may be necessary to take part in political elections to further the revolution in the future and started participating in democratic elections. It won its first seat in the Lok Sabha elections from Ara district in the state of Bihar in 1989 through its front organization, the Indian People's Front (IPF). The CPI-ML was initially strong in the central districts of Bihar. However, it later lost ground to the MCC and the PWG, as the latter groups were able to use their armed cadres to gain support of the poor lower castes and tribals, which the CPI-ML was unable to do.

Some Naxal leaders like Kondapalli Sitaramaiah (Andhra Pradesh) and Navin Prasad (Bihar) broke away to form their own parties. While Prasad, alias Narayan Sanyal, formed the CPI-ML (Unity Organization), Sitaramaiah started the People's War Group (PWG) on April 22, 1980, Lenin's birthday. The PWG criticized the CPI-ML (Liberation) as "revisionist" and opposed all forms of democratic participation. The PWG developed its strongholds in the northern Telangana districts of Andhra Pradesh, where the *Rayatu Coolie Sangham* (Agricultural Laborers Association) and the *Singareni Karmika Samakhya* (Singareni Collieries Workers Federation) emerged as front organizations with mass followings in the 1980s. In the 1990s, in response to increased state counterinsurgency, the PWG started developing the People's

---

4 "*Echoes of Spring Thunder,*" Report by Left Wing Extremism Cell, West Bengal Police, p. 30.

5 Banerjee, *Inside MCC Country,* June 2003, p. 11

6 See www.massline.info/India/Indian_Groups.htm#MCCI.

Guerrilla Army, which was composed of armed squads called *dalams* and developed a dual focus on both mass organizations and guerrilla-armed action.[7]

The Central Organizing Committee (COC) CPI-ML led by M. Appalasuri of Andhra Pradesh and the Unity Organization of CPI-ML led by Navin Prasad alias Narayan Sanyal of Bihar and Bhavani Roy Chowdhury of Bengal united in 1983 to form the CPI-ML (Party Unity). This group was opposed to any electoral participation and believed in combining overground and underground functioning, like the MCC and the PWG. It carried out armed struggle, advocating attacks on upper castes as a means of mobilizing *Dalits* for agrarian reform. In Gaya-Aurangabad, a call was issued for all landlords to deposit their weapons with the Kisan Samitis. Those who refused found their houses attacked and their weapons seized.[8] Simultaneously, CPI-ML (Party Unity) launched the Mazdoor Kisan Sangram Samiti (MKSS) or Worker-Peasant Struggle Association, which was successful among the peasants and active in the seven central districts of Bihar.[9] Party Unity (PU) was strongest in the district of Jehanabad as well as Gaya and Patna districts in Bihar.[10]

In 1998, PU merged with PWG, to form the CPI-ML (People's War). After this merger, PWG was able to expand its areas of influence to Bihar, Jharkhand, and other areas where the PU had influence. Gradually, CPI-ML (Liberation) began to lose its control over the districts in Bihar, and CPI-ML (People's War) gained ascendancy, as People's War attacked and killed Liberation cadres.[11] The other outcome of the unification of the PWG with Party Unity was that it led to clashes between PWG and the MCC in their common areas of operation in Bihar, and this period is referred to as the "black chapter" by these two largest Maoist groups.

Since 2001, peace attempts between the MCC and PWG culminated in their unification in 2004. At the time of unification, the two parties released their joint self-criticism to signal their mutual acceptance of their mistakes leading to these internecine killings (See Figure 4.6). The PWG Central Committee wrote, "This wrong approach of ours … was avoidable had we adopted the proper Leninist style of work and Maoist guidelines to rectify our own mistakes. … For nearly half a decade (1996–2001) in the B-J, the class struggle against the class enemy was badly affected."[12]

---

[7] Chapter 8 on Andhra Pradesh develops the history of the PWG movement in great detail.

[8] *30 years of Naxalbari – An Epic of Heroic Struggle and Sacrifice*, Revolutionary Publications, Kolkata

[9] http://en.wikipedia.org/wiki/Central_Organising_Committee,_Communist_Party_of_India_%28Marxist%E2%80%93Leninist%29_Party_Unity and Singh, *The Naxalite Movement in India*, p. 159.

[10] Bhatia, "The Naxalite Movement in Central Bihar," pp. 1536–37.

[11] Singh, *The Naxalite Movement in India*, p. 155.

[12] Central Committee (P) CPI-Maoist, *We Humbly Bow Our Heads – Self-Criticism of the MCCI and the CPI-(ML) [PW] on Strained Relations*, pp. 6–7

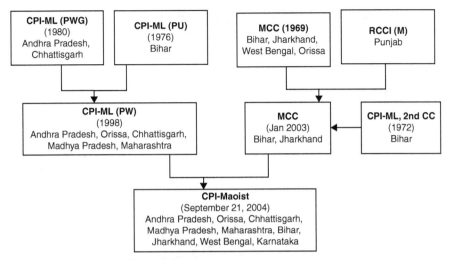

FIGURE 4.1 Evolution chart of the CPI-Maoist
Source: Adapted from D. M. Mitra, *Genesis and Spread of Maoist Violence and Appropriate State Strategy to Handle It,* Bureau of Police Research and Development, Ministry of Home Affairs, Government of India, p. 59.

Figure 4.1 summarizes some of the main unifications between various radical leftist groups within India and how that led to the evolution of the CPI-Maoist in 2004.

Third Phase: The new phase of the movement started with the merger of the MCC and the PWG on October 14, 2004, to form the Communist Party of India-Maoist (CPI-Maoist). The MCC and PWG, in spite of factional conflict, were quite similar in their ideologies, and this possibly helped them unite. The goal of the MCC is to "establish a 'people's government' through 'people's war.' It traces its ideology to the Chinese Communist leader Mao Tse Tung's dictum of organized peasant insurrection."[13] The PWG also traces its ideology to Mao's theory of organized peasant insurrection and believes in "capturing political power through protracted armed struggle based on guerrilla warfare."[14] The PWG adhered to "a Marxist-Leninist line," while the MCC embraced Maoism. These differences were ironed over, with Maoism prevailing, in the words of PWG Andhra Pradesh state "secretary" as "the higher stage of the M-L (Marxist-Leninist) philosophy."[15]

Figures 4.2 and 4.3 provide aggregate-level figures of Maoist violence, based on Ministry of Home Affairs data, which is the official government data, though

---

[13] www.satp.org/satporgtp/countries/india/terroristoutfits/MCC.htm
[14] www.satp.org/satporgtp/countries/india/terroristoutfits/PWG.htm
[15] www.satp.org/satporgtp/countries/india/terroristoutfits/CPI_M.htm

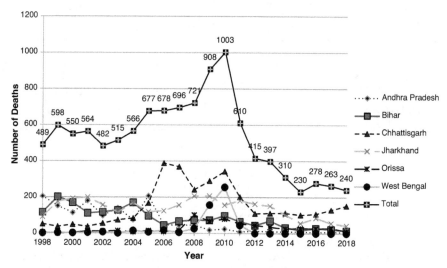

FIGURE 4.2 All-India and state-level patterns of Maoist violence (deaths)
Source: Data for 1998 and 1999 from "*Echoes of Spring Thunder*," Report prepared and compiled by Left Wing Extremist Cell, Special Branch, Kolkata, p. 41. Data for 2000 to 2010 from various Annual Reports, Ministry of Home Affairs, Government of India. Data for 2011 to 2015 from *Annual Report, MHA, 2016*, and also available from the MHA website currently http://mha.nic.in/sites/upload_files/mha/files/LWEViolanceStatistic2016. PDF. Data for 2016 to 2018 from *Annual Report, MHA, 2018–19*, at https://mha.gov.in/documents/annual-reports.

not the most comprehensive.[16] During the 1998–2003 period, around fifty-five districts were affected by one or more Naxal groups. As evident from Figure 4.2, violence remained at around 500 deaths per year in the late 1990s to early 2000s. The MCC and the PWG accounted for most of the violence; the PWG accounted for 59 percent of countrywide violence in 2001, 64 percent in 2002, and 65 percent in 2003. The MCC accounted for 23 percent of violence in 2003.[17]

After 2004, there seems to have been an upward trend in patterns of deaths/incidents: following the unification of the main Maoist factions to form the CPI-Maoist, the Maoist leadership changed its tactics and started intensifying violence.

---

[16] The Indian Ministry of Home Affairs (MHA) provides one source of Maoist violence data. A problem with this data is that it only adds security forces and civilians killed in Maoist-related incidents, and not the number of Maoists killed. The most comprehensive events data source on the Maoist conflict is the one collected by the CASI team under Devesh Kapur and published in Gawande et al. (2017) in their *JCR* article on the effects of rainfall shocks on Maoist conflict. This dataset not only uses English national newspapers but also vernacular newspapers like *Prabhat Khabar* and *Deshbandhu* from states affected by Maoist insurgency.

[17] "*Echoes of Spring Thunder*," p. 43.

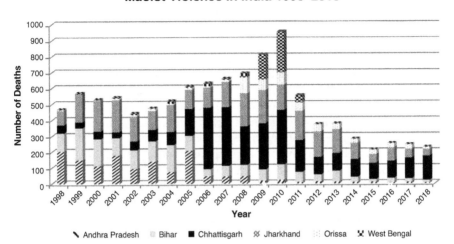

FIGURE 4.3 Level of Maoist violence (deaths) in the main states affected by Maoist insurgency relative to total violence in India

Source: Data for 1998 and 1999 from "*Echoes of Spring Thunder*," Report prepared and compiled by Left Wing Extremist Cell, Special Branch, Kolkata, p. 41. Data for 2000 to 2010 from various Annual Reports, Ministry of Home Affairs, Government of India. Data for 2011 to 2015 from *Annual Report, MHA, 2016*, and also available from the MHA website http://mha.nic.in/sites/upload_files/mha/files/LWEViolanceStatistic2016 .PDF. Data for 2016 to 2018 from *Annual Report, MHA, 2018–19*, at https://mha .gov.in/documents/annual-reports.

In 2007, the new CPI-Maoist stated, "In the past two years our unified Party ... tried to intensify the ongoing people's war with a firm determination to transform the guerrilla war into a mobile war, PLGA into PLA, and guerrilla zones into base areas."[18] Since 2004, the number of districts affected by the combined CPI-Maoist increased rapidly, and a phase of rapid diffusion and expansion of the movement into different parts of India started. An estimate based on the number of districts to be included in the Security Related Expenditures (SRE) scheme of the Indian Ministry of Home Affairs, shows 55 districts around 2003, 77 districts in 2005, and 83 districts in 2012.[19] According to former home minister P. Chidambaram,

---

[18] *Political Organization Review of CPI (Maoist) (Passed in the Unity Congress-9th Congress in January 2007)*, p. 30.

[19] The Security Related Expenditures (SRE) scheme is a funding scheme used by the central government to fund state government expenses regarding anti Naxal counterinsurgency. The 2003 and 2005 data are from the following report obtained from police during fieldwork: "Revision of Guidelines for Re-Imbursement of Security Related Expenditure (S.R.E) to Naxal Affected States under S.R.E. Scheme," MHA Memo Number 11–18015/4/03-IS.III, February 11, 2005. The 2012 data are from "Revised Guidelines for Re-Imbursement of Security Related Expenditure (S.R.E) to Naxal Affected States under S.R.E. Scheme," available

more than 2,000 police station areas in 223 districts were "partially or substantively affected by the menace" by 2009, while violence, "the most visible aspect of Naxal menace," had been consistently witnessed in about 400 police station areas of around 90 districts in 13 of these states.[20]

Another possible reason for this sudden increase in violence levels in the 2004–12 period was the state's response to expanding Maoist control by escalating counterinsurgency. As is clear from Figure 4.2 and 4.3, part of the overall increase in levels of violence was due to escalation in violence in the states of Chhattisgarh and West Bengal, even as violence in Andhra Pradesh fell, following the failure of the peace negotiations between the Andhra Pradesh government and the PWG in 2004 and the subsequent police crackdown on the PWG in that state. CPI-Maoist General Secretary Ganapathy explained the collapse of the movement in North Telangana region of Andhra Pradesh in 2005–6, and its expansion into other parts as follows: "In any protracted peoples war, there will be advances and retreats. ... Confronted with a superior force, we chose to temporarily retreat our forces from some regions of Andhra Pradesh, extend and develop our bases in the surrounding regions and then hit back at the enemy. ... Our war in is the stage of strategic defence."[21]

As the Maoist leadership shifted its focus to the jungles of Chhattisgarh, the Bharatiya Janata Party (BJP) government in Chhattisgarh in cooperation with a tribal landlord in the Congress Party, Mahendra Karma, launched the vigilante *Salwa Judum* movement from 2005 to 2009, which tried to use tribal civilians to target the Maoists. This resulted in large-scale displacement and deaths in villages that were accused of being supporters of the Maoists. The Maoists admitted that the *Salwa Judum* was the single biggest threat to their movement in base areas since the 1970s. To survive, the Maoists retaliated with a series of equally brutal attacks on some of the *Salwa Judum* camps in 2006–7 killing many policemen and Special Police Officers (SPOs) as well as some civilians, which slowed down the *Salwa Judum* campaign.[22]

In another major offensive, from 2009 to 2012, former Central Government home minister P. Chidambaram launched Operation *Green Hunt*, which targeted the Maoists in their core areas in Jharkhand and Chhattisgarh by coordinating police forces across all states with the central paramilitary forces. The Maoists responded with several high-profile attacks, including a major one on April 6, 2010, at Chintalner in Dantewada district, where the Maoists ambushed and killed seventy-five Central Reserve Police Force (CRPF)

at http://mha.nic.in/pdfs/nm_pdf1.pdf, from the Naxal Management Division site at http://mha.nic.in/uniquepage.asp?Id_Pk=540.

[20] Speech of Home Minister P. Chidambaram on September 14, 2009, on the Occasion of the DGPs/IGPs Conference, 2009.

[21] Interview with Ganapathy, general secretary, CPI-Maoist, by Rahul Pandita, October 17, 2009, pp. 5, 9–10.

[22] Human Rights Watch, *Being Neutral Is Our Biggest Crime*, pp. 109–10.

soldiers, which was one of the largest attacks and signaled intelligence failure by the security forces.[23] This led to public uproar and destroyed political consensus within the government, leading to the stalling of Operation *Green Hunt* and a stalemate with lower levels of violence.

Fourth Phase: Endgame or Temporary Rollback?

As Figures 4.2 and 4.3 indicate, the level of violence and overall incidents related to the Maoist insurgency declined with the end of Operation *Green Hunt*; in 2013–15, the levels of violence dipped below the usual average of around 400 deaths in the 1990s. Since the new BJP government formed the national government under Narendra Modi as prime minister in 2014, the levels of violence have declined and the insurgency has entered a more dormant phase, with total violence plateauing at around 250 deaths on average per year.

There are two possible reasons for this recent decline in Maoist violence that can be tentatively proposed, though further research is needed. One reason could be that the counterinsurgency efforts by the central and state governments have finally succeeded. The previous Congress-led governments (2005–9 and 2009–14) had developed a strategy of using both counterinsurgency funded by Security Related Expenditure (SRE) projects and several development programs like the Integrated Action Plan (IAP), road building projects, and National Rural Employment Guarantee Scheme (NREGS) projects to increase rural employment. The current BJP government, in power since 2014, has been continuing these policies and adding some new ones. All these could have created more state capacity and development in these historically neglected areas, thus reducing Maoist support.

The counterinsurgency strategy also has possibly been a success, with arrests of several top-level Maoist leaders since 2010. However, looking at the SATP database, of the 708 Maoist leaders killed, arrested, and surrendered between 2010 and June 2016, only 4 are from the Politburo and 6 are from the Central Committee, and the large majority are zonal commanders, sub-zonal commanders, and area commanders, who are in the lower to middle ranks of the organization.[24] Another source shows that between 2007 and June 2016, only fifteen members of the Politburo and Central Committee were arrested or killed.[25] There are still large numbers of top Maoist leaders who have not yet been arrested or killed, and this puts some doubt to theories of *leadership decapitation* being the cause of the sudden decrease in levels of Maoist violence.

---

[23] Biswas, "Scores of Indian soldiers killed in Maoist ambushes," *BBC World News*, April 6, 2010.

[24] See www.satp.org/satporgtp/countries/india/maoist/data_sheets/LWE_2016.htm for compilation of numbers of deaths, arrests, and surrenders of different levels of Maoists.

[25] See www.satp.org/satporgtp/countries/india/maoist/data_sheets/Central_level_leaders_CPI-Maoist .htm

The second possible reason could be that the Maoist central leadership realized that the expansionist strategy it adopted following the creation of CPI-Maoist in 2004 was too adventurous and they did not have the capacity to sustain the movement. Some top leaders and cadres were being arrested or eliminated, and the organization was getting infiltrated, one of the most significant being the killing of politburo member Kishenji in 2011, who was covertly allying with the Trinamul Congress (TMC) to rebuild Maoist strength in Bengal. Kishenji's death was probably the result of his adopting a high-profile strategy and engaging openly with the media, making it easy to track him; this led to collapse of the resurgence of the Maoists in the western districts of Bengal from 2009 to 2011, which the Maoists had painstakingly built up. Faced with this problem, the Maoist leadership possibly decided to change to a strategy of "tactical retreat," focusing on a reconsolidation of strengths and the "construction of alternative communication channels to prevent leakage of information."[26] Increasing surrenders since 2016 and government counterinsurgency pressures reducing recruitment of cadres led to the CPI-Maoist Central Committee leadership in a meeting in February 2017 to acknowledge that the movement was undergoing a "difficult phase" in different regions of India.[27]

A close observer of the movement suggests that there was a cyclical pattern of violence, with peaks of violence in 1971, 1991, and 2001, with the exception of 1981 when there were only 325 incidents causing 92 deaths and the second phase was starting with the PWG and MCC just emerging.[28] Given that violence peaked again in 2010–11, it does seem that there is a pattern of recurrence of escalation over time, and the insurgency may escalate again in the future. For more detailed analysis of the current phase of low intensity violence, see Chapter 11.

3   WHY HAS THE SUCCESS OF THE MAOIST INSURGENCY IN INDIA BEEN RESTRICTED TO THE AREAS THAT WERE COLONIAL INDIRECT RULE?

While the onset of the insurgency and patterns of violence in different phases were dependent on counterinsurgency tactics and strategic decisions by the Maoist leadership, the spatial variation of emergence of guerrilla zones in the initial 1980s–90s period was constrained to areas that were former indirect rule. In this section, I use fieldwork interviews and textual analysis of Maoist documents to show that while the Maoists were very strategic in their choice

---

[26] Pradhan, "Maoists: Tactical Retreat."

[27] Reddy, "CPI-Maoist admits to tough phase for revolutionary movement," *Telangana Today*, September 27, 2017.

[28] Singh, *The Naxalite Movement in India*, pp. 164–65.

of areas of operation, they were finally constrained by deep-rooted structural factors created by different forms of indirect rule.

3.1 Maoists Are Strategic Actors, but Feudal Exploitation and History of Rebellion Matter More than Poverty

Why have the different factions of Maoists been successful along the so-called red corridor, known as the Compact Revolutionary Zone (CRZ) by the Maoists? Within this larger CRZ, why has Maoist power consolidated around these two epicenters of insurgency? A member of the *Bandi Mukti Samiti* (Free Prisoner's Movement) in Kolkata suggested that the Maoists are quite strategic in choosing their areas of operation. According to him, the Maoists in Bengal had tried to recruit people and consolidate their influence in Arambagh subdivision in Hooghly district of West Bengal, but they were forced to withdraw because the CPI-Marxist party cadres were already too strong there, even though Arambagh was as poor as some of the areas in West Midnapore district where the Maoists had been quite successful.[29] In another interview with him, he said:

ROBI: Suppose I had ten cadres. I have myself been in CPI-Marxist earlier, so I know some of their strategies, the Maoists would use similar strategy. So if someone had ten cadres, it would be better to focus all ten cadres on one issue, rather than spread the resources. Focus on those issues which are *shombhabona purno* [those issues that have greater chance of being useful to mobilize people successfully].

AUTHOR: What do you mean by *shombhabona purno*?

ROBI: You see, backwardness only is not enough; there also needs to be some history of movement in the past. In Bihar, there have been a lot of peasant movements in the past and so those areas which have had such a history of rebellion are more prone to getting mobilized again. Areas where the people had been suffering from *oshomman* and *bonchona* [disrespect and deprivation]. *Oshomman* [disrespect] is even more important than *bonchona* [deprivation].[30]

This basic intuition that the Maoists were strategic was reiterated by the deputy superintendent of police (DSP), West Midnapore district, West Bengal, who noted that the Maoists carefully choose villages according to whether they (1) are underdeveloped, (2) have tribal populations that do not consider themselves to be part of mainstream India, (3) have inaccessible terrain (mountain, forest, or river), and (4) are near district or state borders. He emphasized that the Maoists in Bengal had initially tried to enter the forested

---

[29] Interview with Robi (pseudonym), member Bandi Mukti Samiti, Kolkata, West Bengal, June 27, 2006. The police in West Bengal consider the Bandi Mukti Samiti to be a Maoist front organization, though this is denied by its members, who claim it fights for the release of political prisoners and prisoners undergoing trial of all types.

[30] Interview with Robi (pseudonym), member of Bandi Mukti Samiti, Kolkata, West Bengal, January 11, 2008.

areas of Sundarban in southern Bengal, which has high levels of poverty, but found that the terrain was not conducive due to the mangrove forests and they withdrew.[31] In a later visit to West Midnapore district, the then superintendent of police (SP) suggested the role of forests and tribal populations but also mentioned the importance of jurisdictional boundaries, like district and state boundaries that were exploited by the Maoists:

AUTHOR: I had come last time, and the DSP had given me an area map. So one of the things I am trying to understand is the spatial variation, that is, why the movement is strong in some districts and not in others, and within each district why it is happening in some police station areas and not in others? Is it poverty which causes it, or the Maoists have other factors in mind when they choose the areas of operation.

R: Actually they choose the areas of operations, based on various factors. For a revolutionary to function, he needs to exploit the administrative set up which we have in this country. We have interstate boundaries, we have inter district boundaries; we have inter block boundaries. Block means . . . police station boundaries. Because . . . the in-charge of two police stations, they don't work together. They have their own . . . er . . . differences. Differences of opinion. If something happens in a neighboring police station, the OC [officer in charge], although he is legally bound to help him, unless the OC . . . the other OC of the other police station, asks for any help, this fellow will not *suo moto* go for any help. Because as he will say, that is not my jurisdiction. We as civil servants are bound by jurisdictional responsibilities. Naxalites . . . these Maoists, they have no jurisdiction. So they can . . . they exploit this kind of mind-set, which we bureaucrats or the government servants have.[32]

Interviews with both the police and Maoist supporters in Andhra Pradesh confirmed that the Maoists were quite strategic in choosing their areas of operation, and there was no strong correlation between the poverty level of an area and whether that would become a Maoist stronghold. According to K. Balagopal, noted human rights activist and lawyer in Andhra Pradesh (he had been shot twice by the AP police in his early days advocating the cause of the tribals and doing human rights investigations against the police), there is no direct link between level of development and Naxalism. Lack of development was not a necessary condition; rather, it was the presence of the Communist Party of India-Marxist cadres who converted to the Naxal ideology in the 1970s that mattered in explaining the success of Naxalism in a region. As Balagopal mentioned,

The geographic variation will not have any one to one relation with backwardness. . . . [E]ven in Telangana the most backward district is Mahbubnagar. Mahbubnagar yes, it has a Naxalite presence, but it came much later. See if you are going to look at Naxalism as a straightforward response to backwardness, Mahbubnagar would have been the first

---

[31] Interview with Shyam Singh, deputy superintendent of police, June 7, 2006, at police headquarters, Midnapore district. Midnapore, Bankura, and Purulia are the three districts in West Bengal that are Maoist affected and are on the western side of Bengal near the Jharkhand and Bihar border.

[32] Interview with superintendent of police, West Midnapore district headquarters, West Bengal, January 29, 2008.

district. Anantpur and Rayalseema would have been the first districts. It did not happen that way because [inaudible] ... it was a political decision, which then went looking for areas where the idea could be implemented.[33]

When I further pursued this question of a link between poverty and Naxalism, Balagopal said, "If you have any amount of backwardness in Gujarat, it may not give rise to Naxalite movement, because the political ambience is quite different there."[34]

As the following excerpts from an interview with the famous Maoist sympathizer and balladeer Gaddar indicate, one reason the PWG was successful in the eastern districts of Telangana in Andhra Pradesh and not as successful in the western districts could be because the eastern districts are closer to the Dandakaranya forests that border Chhattisgarh; this made it easier for the cadres to escape. Also the eastern districts had a previous history of revolt, and there was a higher revolutionary consciousness among the people. Finally, the eastern districts of Telangana also had higher levels of feudal exploitation than the western districts because of the Nizam of Hyderabad allowing *zamindar*-type political intermediaries called *deshmukhs* in the eastern districts of Telangana.

AUTHOR: Within the Telangana region, we see that the Northern and Eastern districts ... Adilabad, Karimnagar, Warangal these were affected, while Mahbubnagar, Medak (in the west) were less affected. And I was talking with an intellectual and he said ... he is from Mahbubnagar, he said Mahbubnagar is actually poorer than Warangal, and it continues to remain so. And yet the movement started more in Warangal and Karimnagar. So what are the factors based on which the cadres and the comrades decide which areas to start the movement and not others?

GADDAR: Only poverty, or only the backwardness ... it is not the criteria of the movement. ... Actually when they started in Karimnagar, Warangal, they must have a retreating place. *Woh pichhe bahar nikalne ka terrain bhi dekhna hain*. Why not in Calcutta, why only in Naxalbari? The tribal Santhals, they had land issues, and the movement started in the backward areas of the country.... Mahbubnagar is very backward, the poorest of the poor, but as terrain, to start a movement, *usko bachane ke liye dekhna hain*. ... So they have taken the more politically enlightened people. Warangal, Karimnagar, the more enlightened, they will face anything. They started there, they made the movement, they made the leadership. Those people who are leading the movement, they are from there, from Karimnagar, Warangal only. All politburo members.

AUTHOR: But why is it that ...

GADDAR: So in Telangana, ... where the more feudal exploitation is there, at the same time where more revolutionary enlightenment is also there, there you have to start. .... They must be not only the poor, simple poor, every poor fellow will not revolt, they must be enlightened mentally. Revolutionary feeling is also necessary. So Warangal, Karimnagar, and the other parts, which have a history of revolt, yes Adilabad, history

---

[33] Interview with K. Balagopal, Hyderabad, February 8, 2008.
[34] Interview with K. Balagopal, Hyderabad, February 12, 2008.

of revolt. . . .So in Telangana, the terrain, as well as the history, as well as the feudal exploitation. Feudal exploitation *harek jagah hain, lekin feudal se larne ki himmat bhi hona na organize karne ke liye. Aur usko terrain bhi hona chahiye, bhag jana hain* [feudal exploitation is in every place, but to fight against the feudals you need courage to organize. And you also need the right terrain to be able to escape]. Because this is a guerrilla war, otherwise they would not have retreated into the forest.[35]

   The ex-director general of police (DGP) of Andhra Pradesh, Swaranjit Sen, who was chiefly responsible for crushing the PWG in Andhra Pradesh in 2005–6, when asked about why there is more poverty in Mahbubnagar and yet less Naxal influence than in other districts of Telangana suggested that if a district is too poor, then it is not possible to sustain a Naxal movement in that area, which also needs resources to recruit people:

ME: But within Telangana we see there is some geographical variation. We see the movement has been more in Warangal, Nizamabad, Adilabad, but not in Mahbubnagar which is poor, and not in Medak . . .
SEN: Mahbubnagar is closer to Hyderabad; it also falls on the line to Rayalseema; it's also not such a rich district, as other districts.
AUTHOR: So if it is poorer logically there should be a link between poverty and the movement . . .
SEN: Yes there is a link, but you know you also need to have the resources also, to feed the Naxals. That I don't think Mahbubnagar offers that much, but these other places do. And there are more tribals in these other areas of Telangana than in Mahbubnagar, so there are certain demographic reasons.[36]

In another interview with a member of the Revolutionary Democratic Front, it was similarly pointed out to me that Maoists have their roots in areas where there were *Adivasis*, because they were never part of the British system and could never understand becoming part of the modern state system, and the state is historically weak there. According to this person, other than tribal areas, wherever the movement grew is where the feudal system is very strong, for example, Telangana and Bihar. The history of peasant rebellions against the British also mattered. In western Uttar Pradesh, Haryana, and Rajasthan, there were no such earlier movements, and lack of such previous movements historically meant lack of previous networks to build on. In Uttar Pradesh, since there was no Communist movement, the Bahujan Samaj Party (BSP), a lower-caste party, grew and in these areas no previous social movements

---

[35] Interview with Gaddar, Hyderabad, February 18, 2008. Parts of the interview in Hindi are left in that language and italicized. Gaddar is the famous poet and balladeer who left the underground Maoist movement and came overground and formed his own cultural troupe, the *Jana Natya Mandali*, which used to go around singing revolutionary songs and acting out dance dramas that appealed directly to the coal miners and rural people of Andhra Pradesh.

[36] Interview with Swaranjit Sen, ex-DGP of Andhra Pradesh, Hyderabad, February 26, 2008. Sen was the police chief of Andhra Pradesh in the 2005–7 period, when the CPI-Maoist was ruthlessly crushed in Andhra Pradesh, and he is credited with playing a crucial role in this counterinsurgency operation.

arose. Once the BSP emerged, the Maoists never tried.[37] This suggests that there could be deeper roots to this insurgency than can be perceived by the usual theories of rebellion and insurgency that focus on only proximate factors (Cederman et al. 2010; Collier & Hoeffler 2004; Fearon & Laitin 2003).

Most of these interviews suggest that the Maoists are strategic in choosing the areas in which to rebel, and they think not only of poverty but also of favorable terrain like forest cover and presence of *Adivasis* or tribal people with grievances. Several of these Maoist sympathizers and human rights activists also suggested that a history of revolutionary consciousness as well as colonial feudal oppression through *zamindars* also matters.

3.2 Maoist Strategy Constrained by Deep Structural Institutions

This section analyzes Maoist documents gathered from the police during fieldwork to try and understand whether Maoist intellectuals were aware of the deeper structural effects of these colonial institutions on their tactical choices at the ground level.

When analyzing the Maoist documents, it becomes clear that they have long-term plans to select certain areas as their base areas and guerrilla zones, based on careful surveys of the main socioeconomic grievances and opportunity structures. This supports the views expressed in the interviews with key police and human rights activists that I presented earlier.

Maoists' strategic documents indicate that they carry out extensive socioeconomic analyses of the areas into which they are planning to expand. One example is a socioeconomic survey of Karnataka in 2001 made once they decided to try to expand into this new area.[38] The PWG Maoists did a similar social investigation of the South Bastar area of Chhattisgarh in 2004, where they tried to reevaluate their level of control since the 1990s before deciding to escalate their level of activity further.[39] Similarly, in an evaluation of the North Telangana region of Andhra Pradesh in the year 2000, the PWG did a social investigation and analyzed Warangal district; the report states the following:

Twenty years back there was one SI with one old cycle motor, ten constables and a dilapidated building. Now there are 60 to 80 CRPF or APSP police in one station. . . . MRPS and Ambedkar organizations are seen in the developed villages. But the dalits are voting to the bourgeois political parties during elections and not to the petty bourgeois parties. . . . So according to the above changes we have to bring changes in the struggle and organizational forms.[40]

---

[37] Interview with Lenin (pseudonym), member of the Revolutionary Democratic Front (RDF), New Delhi, January 17, 2008.

[38] CPI-ML (People's War), "Karnataka: Social Conditions and Tactics."

[39] CPI-ML (People's War), "Social Investigation – South Bastar," March 2004.

[40] CPI-ML (People's War), "Social Investigation of North Telangana," p. 9.

The Maoists clearly differentiate between guerrilla zones, base areas, and liberated zones. The guerrilla zones are areas where they have initially started operations and security forces have high level of control.[41] Once the Maoists have been able to establish control over a guerrilla zone for a sufficient period of time and security forces have reduced ability to enter into this area, it is considered a base area, and the final goal is to convert these base areas into liberated areas, where the Maoists have complete political and military control, with minimal state penetration and presence.[42]

In their main document *Strategy and Tactics*, adopted after the unification of the PWG, MCC, and PU in 2004 to form the CPI-Maoist, the Maoists write,

Basing on the laws of protracted people's war in India, in order to confront an enemy who is far superior in strength, the revolutionary forces will have to select areas, in which the enemy is relatively weaker and which are favorable to the revolutionary forces. . . . Our country has many such areas that are strategically important for the people's war where the Liberated Areas can be established. . . . These strategic areas are hilly regions with dense forest cover, have sufficient economic resources, a vast population, and a vast forest area spreading over thousands of square kilometers. In such areas the enemy is weak, and these areas are very favorable for the maneuvers of the people's army.[43]

Figure 4.4 shows the first page of this Maoist document.

The names of these strategic areas are listed as "The Dandakaranya; the Eastern Ghats, ranging from the river Godavari in Andhra to Koraput district in Orissa; Jharkhand – which is the converging point of the Bihar, Bengal, MP, Orissa states; the Western Ghats, ranging from Tamil Nadu – Kerala – Karnataka-Maharashtra; the Himalayan borders; the Vindhya-Satpura ranges; the Chambal valley; etc."[44] In an earlier document called *Guerilla Zones – Our Perspective*, the PWG Maoists list a second type of terrain as candidates for strategic base areas:

Backward rural plain areas, with a semi-forest cover and with hills and hillocks come under the second category – areas like North Telangana, South Telangana, Rayalaseema, Nallamala (in AP), Marathwada (MR), Maharashtra-Gujarat border region, Hyderabad-Karnataka, Dharmapuri-North Arcot-Salem (TN), Magadh, North Bengal etc. . . . These are also areas with relatively higher population, strong feudal base and acute class contradictions. . . . By utilizing the first category areas as rears, these areas will be able to withstand enemy onslaught. . . . Extensive mass movements should be built in these regions which have vast population and acute class contradictions. The military recruits and leadership generated by these movements should be sent to strategic areas.[45]

[41] CPI-ML (People's War), *Strategy and Tactics*, March 2001 (preliminary draft), p. 45
[42] CPI-ML (People's War), *Strategy and Tactics*, pp. 55–56.
[43] CPI-Maoist Central Committee, *Strategy and Tactics of the Indian Revolution*, 2004 (final version), pp. 50–51.
[44] CPI-ML (People's War), *Strategy and Tactics*, March 2001 (preliminary draft), p. 59.
[45] CPI-ML (People's War) Central Committee, *Guerilla Zones – Our Perspective*, draft, May 1999, pp. 7–8.

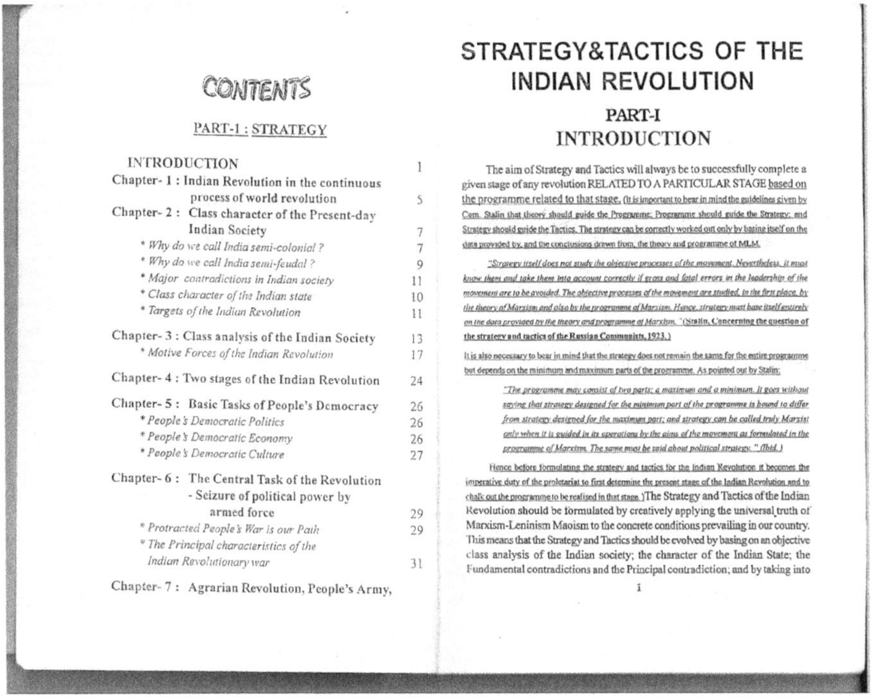

STRATEGY&TACTICS OF THE INDIAN REVOLUTION

PART-I

INTRODUCTION

The aim of Strategy and Tactics will always be to successfully complete a given stage of any revolution RELATED TO A PARTICULAR STAGE based on the programme related to that stage. (It is important to bear in mind the guidelines given by Com. Stalin that theory should guide the Programme; Programme should guide the Strategy; and Strategy should guide the Tactics. The strategy can be correctly worked out only by basing itself on the data provided by, and the conclusions drawn from, the theory and programme of MLM.

"*Strategy itself does not study the objective processes of the movement. Nevertheless, it must know them and take them into account correctly if gross and fatal errors in the leadership of the movement are to be avoided. The objective processes of the movement are studied, in the first place, by the theory of Marxism and also by the programme of Marxism. Hence, strategy must base itself entirely on the data provided by the theory and programme of Marxism.* "(Stalin, Concerning the question of the strategy and tactics of the Russian Communists, 1923.)

It is also necessary to bear in mind that the strategy does not remain the same for the entire programme but depends on the minimum and maximum parts of the programme. As pointed out by Stalin:

"*The programme may consist of two parts: a maximum and a minimum. It goes without saying that strategy designed for the minimum part of the programme is bound to differ from strategy designed for the maximum part; and strategy can be called truly Marxist only when it is guided in its operations by the aims of the movement as formulated in the programme of Marxism. The same must be said about political strategy.* " (Ibid.)

Hence before formulating the strategy and tactics for the Indian Revolution it becomes the imperative duty of the proletariat to first determine the present stage of the Indian Revolution and to chalk out the programme to be realised in that stage.)The Strategy and Tactics of the Indian Revolution should be formulated by creatively applying the universal truth of Marxism-Leninism Maoism to the concrete conditions prevailing in our country. This means that the Strategy and Tactics should be evolved by basing on an objective class analysis of the Indian society; the character of the Indian State; the Fundamental contradictions and the Principal contradiction; and by taking into

1

FIGURE 4.4 First page of *Strategy and Tactics,* the main tactical document of the CPI-Maoist
Source: Obtained from West Midnapore district police, West Bengal.

However, of all these places identified by the Maoists, the ones where they have been able to establish successful base areas or even guerrilla zones, were either in the Bihar/Jharkhand/Bengal area where informal colonial indirect rule in the form of the *zamindari* land tenure system dominated or in the North Telangana part of Andhra Pradesh and the southern Chhattisgarh and Orissa areas which were under formal indirect colonial rule of princely states. The other areas mentioned in their documents and targeted for their strategic value – like Rayalseema in Andhra Pradesh, Marathwada in Maharashtra, the Chambal Valley in Madhya Pradesh, and the Western Ghats crossing several states – may have possessed many of the other characteristics deemed desirable by the Maoists to set up strategic areas like hilly terrain and forest cover or lower castes and tribes, but they were not formerly part of colonial indirect rule, and the Maoists were not successful there. See the map of spatial variation in Maoist movement in Figure 2.1 to see these two epicenters of the insurgency in the year 2005, just after the formation of the CPI-Maoist.

It is only in the areas that had colonial indirect rule institutions present and had created inequitable land ownership patterns or low levels of development that the Maoists were actually successful in consolidating base areas in the initial phase. This shows that the role of rebel agency and ideological frames of rebellion, outlined in the theoretical framework in Chapter 3, did play a significant role in mobilization but were successful only when the structural conditions of inequality (political opportunity structures) created by indirect rule institutions were *also* present.

While the CPI-ML (People's War) had established strongholds in the 1990s in the North Telangana region of the erstwhile Hyderabad princely state area in Andhra Pradesh, which was their second type of strategic base area, the AP government crushed the insurgency by the mid-2000s. After the severe police repression carried out in Andhra Pradesh, the Maoist Central Committee took a decision to focus its efforts in developing a base area in the Bastar region, which was even more deeply forested than the Telangana regions, and consisted of princely states that were smaller than Hyderabad princely state and had even lower state penetration.

Ganapathy, general secretary of CPI-Maoist, admitted as much when he said,

AP, particularly the region of North Telangana, has been an important center of revolutionary movement for a long period. ... But we have to keep in mind that so far as the question of establishing base areas goes, it has been the more backward areas falling in central and eastern India that were selected by the Party with the immediate task of liberating these vast areas. Hence the focus of our movement had gradually shifted to Dandakaranya and Bihar-Jharkhand.[46]

The Dandakaranya forested zone was part of the princely states of Hyderabad and Bastar, and the Bihar-Jharkhand area was part of the *zamindari* land tenure regime in colonial times. These two regions best represent the colonial influence of indirect rule through princely states and indirect revenue collection through *zamindari* land tenure, respectively. While Ganapathy, the leader of CPI-Maoist, may or may not have been theoretically aware of this, his own statement shows that the Maoists strategically relocated and converged to areas that had experienced colonial indirect rule.

See Figures 4.5 and 4.6 for examples of Maoist letters and documents collected during fieldwork.

3.3 Maoist Strategy Constrained by Whether or Not Structural Inequalities Created by Colonial Indirect Rule Were Present

These interviews and documents suggest that the Maoists are strategic in choosing their areas of operation. While poverty and forest cover matter, so do other factors. The Maoists try to choose those villages where the state and other political actors have minimal reach and those that have a high level of

---

[46] Interview with Ganapathy, general secretary, CPI-Maoist. Text of the interview was released by Azad, Spokesperson, CPI-Maoist in April 2007.

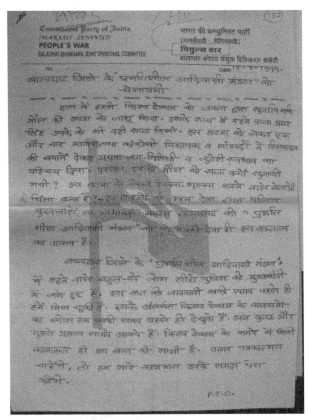

FIGURE 4.5 Letter written by CPI-ML (People's War)
Source: *Deshbandhu* newspaper archives, Raipur, Chhattisgarh. Photo taken by author.

easily mobilizable grievances among *Adivasis* (tribals) who believe they are not part of mainstream Indian culture, or among *Dalits* (scheduled castes) who feel socially and politically discriminated against by the hierarchical caste-based society. They also try to situate their areas of operation close to adequate forest cover, and close to district and state borders so as to exploit borders as opportunities for escape since bureaucratic red-tapism between state governments and sometimes even different district administrations of the same state prevent coordinated counterinsurgency responses across administrative borders. Rebels can cross over from Jharkhand, do their operations on the West Bengal side, and escape back to the forests in Jharkhand.

However, these demographic, geographic, administrative, and socioeconomic characteristics do not fully explain variation in successful Maoist mobilization. A forested and tribal belt in the western states of Rajasthan and Gujarat is quite underdeveloped but does not have Maoist mobilization. As the Maoist

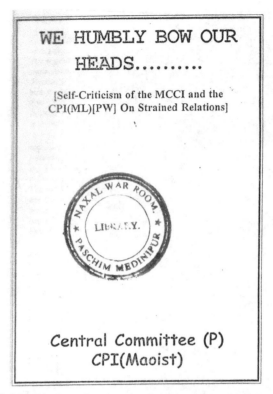

FIGURE 4.6 "We Humbly Bow Our Heads": Document in which the MCC and PWG do self-criticism for fighting each other before their unification in 2004
Source: Scan of first page of document. Obtained from West Midnapore police, West Bengal.

documents indicate, there is a forested belt in Karnataka and Kerala where the Maoists have tried but not succeeded as much as they have in the Chhattisgarh-Andhra-Orissa border area.[47] Scheduled castes in western parts of Uttar Pradesh suffer from poverty and inequality and yet there is no Maoist mobilization there, though there is relatively successful mobilization in some of the eastern districts of Uttar Pradesh bordering Bihar, like Balia, Gorakhpur, and Mirzapur due to spillover effects.

So the usual opportunity factors considered important in the civil war literature, like forest cover, hilly terrain, tribal or scheduled caste concentration, and underdevelopment, may be necessary but not sufficient conditions for successful Maoist mobilization. The additional factor that differentiates those forested, tribal-dominated areas where the Maoists have been successful in

---

[47] Maoist failure in Karnataka and Kerala is analyzed in Chapter 9.

establishing base areas from those forested, tribal-dominated areas where they have not succeeded is the colonial institution of indirect rule, either the formal type of indirect rule through princely states or the less formal type through *zamindari* estates. It is only when colonial indirect rule institutions have *also* been present in an area along with various other proximate factors like forest cover, natural resources, tribes, and castes, that there has been successful Maoist control of the area.

This is the *omitted variable* that is necessary to fully explain the peculiar geographic variation in Maoist influence in India. Though neglected by the literature on Maoist rebellion as well as by the civil war onset literature, colonial indirect rule could explain a high proportion of the variation in Maoist control.

4 ARE MAOIST INTELLECTUALS CONSCIOUS OF THE ROLE OF HISTORICAL INSTITUTIONS AFFECTING THEIR ABILITY TO MOBILIZE THE ETHNIC NETWORKS OF SUBALTERN GROUPS?

The Maoist leaders were agents who were making decisions according to their Marxist-Leninist ideology and strategy, adapted to the unique ethnic and developmental circumstances of India. These ideologies and strategies are part of the *ideological frames of rebellion* outlined in Chapter 3, and they interact with the structural legacies of indirect rule to create successful rebellion. It is important to ask whether the agents were aware of the larger structural constraints imposed on them by the historical legacies of colonial institutions.

As shown in greater detail in Chapter 8, the Maoist movements under the APRCC failed to succeed in the coastal Andhra region of former British direct rule, and only succeeded in the Telangana region of the former Hyderabad princely state. The PWG, which emerged as the most powerful group after 1980 in Andhra Pradesh, has also acknowledged the impact of colonial indirect rule (Telangana) vs. direct rule (Coastal Andhra) on differences in future economic and political inequalities between these regions. According to the PWG:

As the British imperialists had kept intact hundreds of feudal ties in order to ensure their own survival and decided the model of production in India to serve their own country's industrial needs, some regions were developed while some other regions remained backwards. ... As Andhra, Telangana regions were living as separate units for centuries, there is a vast difference in development in the economic, political and social spheres of these two regions. Andhra region is more advanced in these spheres. ... The important factors which had facilitated the development are: the people's struggles against the Zamindari system in Madras Presidency and Andhra regions, the Ryotwari system introduced by the British, irrigation facilities.[48]

---

[48] "Separate Telangana Movement," *Central Committee, CPI (ML) People's War*, pp. 1–2.

The PWG notes:

When compared with the growth of the coastal Andhra regions, Telangana is relatively backward. ... Because of Nizam's rule, Telangana region did not undergo much development. ... As the land was concentrated in the hands of the Nizam feudal class, economic development did not take place, and most of the land is less fertile, the soil rocky and also due to lack of irrigation facilities the agricultural development in Telangana was also very less.[49]

The Maoists have suggested in their writings that forms of indirect rule have been continued by the rulers of independent India, thus hinting at the continuation of some of these mechanisms of exploitation started by the British. Shah (2013: 426) writes:

The CPI (Maoist) formed in 2004, ... reaffirmed their analysis that contemporary Indian society is semi-colonial and semi-feudal, under neo-colonial forms of indirect rule, exploitation and control. British colonialism, according to the Maoists, arrested the independent development of capitalism in Indian society, transforming it from feudal to colonial and semi-feudal. They argue that separation from Britain in 1947 turned India from colonial and semi-feudal into a semi-colonial and semi-feudal society, in which several imperialist powers took the place of British imperialism. ... These powers, according to the Maoists, operate through indirect rule ... dependent on Indian "compradors" who were nurtured by them in the colonial period.

Writing in the banned Maoist journal *People's March*, Bhaskar mentions the following:

[A]fter the Indian exploitative classes became heir to the political power of the outgoing colonial rulers in 1947, they and the imperialists have concentrated more and more land in their hands by using state power. In the wake of the growing democratic consciousness of the people of India, acquired in the course of anti-colonial struggle, it was no longer possible to rule the old way. The old form of direct colonial rule, control and exploitation gave way to a neo-colonial form of indirect rule, control and exploitation. ... Princely states, kings, zamindars, landlords of the old type, all of them were becoming obsolete and therefore had to give way. Abolition of Zamindari Act, Land Ceiling Act, etc. were promulgated. More than six hundred states and all zamindari estates, the colonial legacy of the hated Permanent Settlement, were formally abolished. ... Even some land reform programmes were initiated by various ruling class governments in the next decades, most notably in Kashmir, Keralam, Karnataka and, to a lesser degree, in Paschim Banga. ...

These measures were more to hoodwink the people; they have not fundamentally changed the prevailing land relations in the last 67 years of so-called independence. Over these decades, the peasant's land has been grabbed by the ruling classes, using the state directly, under the guise of "public" purposes as defined by draconian laws like the colonial Land Acquisition Act of 1894. Land has been acquired in the name of the nation, the country and progress.[50]

---

[49] "Separate Telangana Movement," *Central Committee, CPI (ML) People's War*, pp. 2–3.

[50] Bhaskar, "A Decade of 'Developing' Displacement," in *People's March Supplement*, September 2014.

It is clear that even Maoist ideologues are aware of the role of princely states and *zamindari* systems and how they created land inequality. Bhaskar suggests that though land reforms were carried out in several states like Kashmir, Kerala, Karnataka, and West Bengal, it did not fundamentally alter the land relations in postcolonial independent India. This implies a certain path dependency and old forms of what he called direct rule but are basically different forms of indirect rule within a feudal set up which Shah (2013) mentions have been replaced by indirect rule of colonizers through "comprador" classes or capitalists within India.

As Chapter 8 on Andhra Pradesh and Chapter 7 on Chhattisgarh demonstrate, there is some variation in the level of state penetration in the princely state areas of these two provinces, with Hyderabad being a larger state and historically having slightly higher levels of state penetration than Bastar, which was a smaller and more remote princely state. However, the underlying similarity is that the historical effect of political decisions to not penetrate into the politics and society of tribals in these erstwhile princely states, the exploitation of natural and land resources under these Indian princes, and the continued decision by postcolonial governments of India to persist with such policies into the 1960s and 1970s set up the political opportunity structures and ethnic mobilization networks for successful Maoist mobilization beginning in the 1980s.

The excerpts from Maoist documents suggest that while local Maoist cadres may not have been aware of the role of historical structures, Maoist intellectuals were well aware of the role historical institutions played in setting up structural conditions of inequality and low state penetration in these areas. The Maoists tend to emphasize the language of "semi-feudal and semi-colonial" India, which is the typical Marxist-Leninist terminology used by leftist rebels. However, the semi-feudal structures they are referring to are the various types of indirect rule through native princes that Fisher (1991) and Ramusack (2004) discuss, and the different types of indirect revenue collection through *zamindaris* analyzed by Kohli (2004) and Lange (2009).

5   CONCLUSION: REBEL AGENCY VS. HISTORICAL STRUCTURAL CONSTRAINTS

Historical institutions chosen during colonial times have long-term path dependent effects, which persist and create some of the proximate levels of state weakness and ethnic inequalities in these parts of India, which were then exploited by the Maoists. However, the role of Maoist leaders as strategic actors who make use of their ideological doctrines to convince and recruit *Adivasis* and *Dalits* to join their movement is equally important to understand.

In this chapter, I first outlined a history of the ideological and organizational evolution of the various Maoist groups in the two epicenters in India. Then using interviews with key human rights activists, former Maoists, and police and also analyzing documents of the Maoists in India collected during fieldwork, I showed that the Maoists are strategic in choosing their areas of operation and do careful surveys before moving into an area over a period of time. However, their documents reveal that of the various areas targeted by them, they have only succeeded in consolidating rebel control, where there were erstwhile colonial institutions of indirect rule like princely states or landlord/ *zamindari* systems. In the other areas, though many of the other criteria like favorable terrain, subaltern ethnic groups like *Dalits* and *Adivasis* were present, the Maoists failed. This indicates that deep-rooted political opportunity structures in the form of weak states, exploitation of land and natural resources created by colonial indirect rule, and their persistence through path dependence constrained the ability of Maoist rebel agency to succeed.

This chapter demonstrated the role of rebel agency and the inability of Maoist entrepreneurs to use their ideological frames of rebellion successfully in areas where such historically created inequalities were absent, but success in those areas where such historically created structural conditions were present. Previous experience with rebellion seems to have also left revolutionary consciousness in the tribals in these areas, and possibly organizational remnants and memories that also made it easier to start rebellion there later.

In Chapter 5, I will test the theory of different types of colonial indirect rule creating structural conditions for Maoist insurgency on a district-level dataset of India, to check for the overall generalizability of my theory within India. This will be the large N analysis (LNA) part of the research design, outlined in Chapter 1. To address the possibility of selection bias in this all-India district-level econometric analysis, I use a new instrument in an IV-2SLS regression analysis in Chapter 6. The IV-2SLS regression analysis shows that both *zamindari* land tenure and *princely states* are statistically significant predictors of Maoist insurgency in India.

The rigorous quantitative testing of my theory in Chapters 5 and 6 combined with the qualitative analysis of Maoist documents and interviews in this chapter shows that the Maoists have been successful in establishing base areas and guerrilla zones only in those areas of India that were previously exposed to some form of indirect rule. In contrast, they have been less successful in regions which had not been exposed to any form of colonial indirect rule or indirect land tenure institutions.

5

Quantitative Testing of Effects of British Indirect Rule on Maoist Insurgency

I INTRODUCTION

This book engages with the broader question of how colonial indirect rule has long-term causal effects on insurgency by trying to answer the puzzle of why the Maoist insurgency in India occurs in certain districts in India and not others. To restate the puzzle, why did the Maoist insurgency emerge and consolidate along certain districts in the central-eastern part of India and not in other areas? I propose that different forms of colonial indirect rule and indirect revenue collection created the long-term structural conditions for Maoist insurgency in India.

As I described earlier in more detail, there were two main types of British indirect rule. The more formal (de jure) one was indirect rule through princely states, which involved the British allowing an Indian prince, or rajah, or Nawab to continue to rule in the area where his ancestors had ruled, while the British had control over foreign and financial policy of the state. The less formal (de facto) one was indirect rule through *zamindari* landlord tenure in which the British officially ruled directly by setting up their own governance, but even then they depended on local political intermediaries or landlords to collect land revenue and do some basic administration on their behalf. I argued that these two forms of British colonial indirect rule – (1) *zamindari* (*zamindar* or landlord intermediary based) land tenure and (2) princely states (states ruled by Indian princes under British paramountcy) – created the opportunity structures of weak state capacity and ethnic mobilization networks of tribal and *Dalit* groups with grievances that persist into the postcolonial period though path dependent causal pathways and lead to Maoist insurgency in the postcolonial period.

While Chapter 4 provides qualitative evidence drawn from Maoist documents and interviews to show how Maoist rebel agency is constrained by these structurally created inequalities, in this chapter, I test the theory on a district-level dataset of India. I use Ministry of Home Affairs (MHA) data as a measure of the dependent variable of *Maoist control*. Unlike other quantitative studies of Maoist insurgency like Dasgupta et al. (2017), Gawande et al. (2017), Gomes (2015), Chandra and Garcia-Ponce (2019), Vanden Eynde (2018), and Teitelbaum and Verghese (2019), which use measures of violence from 2005 to 2010 as their dependent variable, I do not use such violence data as my dependent variable for two reasons.[1] First, violence is only the most visible aspect of insurgency and does not measure actual Maoist rebel control, which is a more multidimensional concept. Second, violence data used by these studies does not measure the initial core areas of insurgency before its sudden expansion following unification of the People's War Group (PWG) and Maoist Communist Center (MCC) in 2004, which my dependent variable tries to measure.

When testing for the effect of colonial indirect rule institutions on postcolonial insurgency, it is important to think of possible causes for the British choice of some regions or districts for indirect rule, and how this could bias our ability to estimate the causal effects of indirect rule. There could be a variety of reasons why the British chose indirect rule and not direct rule in a region of India. The paper by Gerring et al. (2011) suggests that previous levels of state institutional capacity determined colonial choice of rule, but this does not really apply to the case of India, where other factors played a more prominent role in determining selection of indirect vs. direct rule.[2]

The most commonly known reasons for the British administrators intentionally selecting certain kingdoms or districts for indirect rule included whether the princely state was considered governable or known to be more prone to rebellion. Another primary criterion used by the British to decide whether to annex into direct rule or sign a treaty with a native ruler to govern on their behalf was the economic value and agricultural productivity of the kingdom or region, and how much revenue it would generate. Access to ports and coasts to allow trade was another consideration, and the British tried to annex into direct rule most of coastal India.

To get at the correct causal effect of colonial indirect rule, in Section 3.2 in this chapter, I control for some well-known and observable pre-colonial determinants of indirect rule choice, like forest cover, terrain, soil quality, and pre-colonial agrarian rebellion and find that the explanatory variable *princely state* is still a statistically significant predictor of *Maoist control*. This means that while these pre-colonial qualities may have played a role in the choice of institutions, once in place such colonial indirect rule had an independent causal effect on postcolonial insurgency beyond that caused by terrain, revenue potential, and conflict proneness.

---

[1] This literature using quantitative analysis of the Maoist insurgency in India is discussed in detail in Chapter 2.

[2] Gerring et al., "An Institutional Theory of Direct and Indirect Rule," p. 492, note that India is dropped from their analysis because of coding issues, so their theory does not apply there. See discussion that follows in Section 3 of this chapter.

However, it is not possible to observe, measure, and control for all pre-colonial factors that could affect why the British selected some areas and not others for indirect rule. To fully address the issue of selection bias, in Chapter 6 I first present qualitative case studies that demonstrate historical contingencies that prevent such selection by the British. I also create a new instrument for the British choice of indirect rule through princely states and present IV-2SLS analysis to address the issue of selection bias. The instrument relies on the fact that when the British government had to fight wars against other European powers, it created financial constraints that affected its ability to wage costly wars of annexation into direct rule in India and increased the probability that it would rather sign treaties of indirect rule with rulers of Indian states on the frontiers of territories already under British direct rule. Based on this intuition, I use the frontier districts in India at the time of major wars against the great powers in Europe as an instrument for the choice of indirect rule in India.

2 QUANTITATIVE ANALYSIS – ALL-INDIA DISTRICT-LEVEL TESTING OF THEORY

2.1 Hypotheses

The following hypotheses are proposed based on the theory outlined in previous chapters and explained briefly in the introduction to this chapter. They are tested on district-level data on the Maoist insurgency in India.

Hypotheses

Colonial institutions theories

Hypothesis 1.a: Areas that had indirect rule through princely states tend to have higher probability of Maoist insurgency in the future.
Hypothesis 1.b: Areas that had indirect revenue collection through zamindari *(landlord) type land tenure systems tend to have higher probability of Maoist insurgency in the future.*

2.2 Data and Variables

Unit of Analysis: The unit of analysis is the district, which is the basic unit of administration and distribution of government funds within each state/province in India. I develop a district-level dataset for measures of Maoist control and various socioeconomic, political, and state capacity factors. There are some disadvantages to using the district as the unit of analysis. First, it hides sub-district spatial variation in Maoist insurgency, since there are intra-district variations in rebel control. For example, it is the western part of Kanker district that is Maoist affected, not the eastern parts, but a district-level dataset measures the whole of Kanker district as under high rebel control and is unable to measure this fine-grained sub-district variation. Second, the district is at a high level of aggregation and prone to the problem of imputing individual preferences from aggregate data. While ethnographic studies of the Maoist movement like Bhatia's (2005) study of the MCC in Bihar or Shah's (2010) study of the Maoists in Jharkhand are better able to understand individual motivations for joining, imputing such individual preferences from district-level qualities may lead to incorrect ecological inference problems (Chandra 2004). Third, there are regional variations in the dynamics of the Maoist insurgency in India and using the district for an all-India analysis could lead to over-generalization and glossing over such regional variations.

To overcome these problems, I use sub-district datasets (assembly constituency level) for the two states of Chhattisgarh and Andhra Pradesh in later chapters.[3] However, in this chapter, the district is used as a unit of analysis for two reasons. First, district-level socioeconomic data is easily available for the whole of India, and by using an all-India district-level dataset, it is possible to test the extent to which my theory explains geographic variation in the insurgency across all states, thus broadening the geographic scope of the theory. Second, the recent econometric analyses of the Maoist insurgency in India – Chandra and Garcia-Ponce (2019), Teitelbaum and Verghese (2019), Vanden Eynde (2018), Gawande et al. (2017), Dasgupta et al. (2017), Gomes (2015) – all use the district as the unit of analysis. There are similar district-level dataset-based studies for the Maoist insurgency in Nepal (Do & Iyer 2010; Murshed & Gates 2005). I use a district-level analysis in this chapter to engage with these recent studies on the Maoists in South Asia.

Dependent Variable – Rebel Control: Unlike most of these district-level analyses of Maoist insurgency that use *violence* as the dependent variable, I prefer to use a measure of *Maoist rebel control* for two reasons. First, as Kalyvas (2006) and other scholars have noted, areas with high rebel control could sometimes have low total violence and are distinct concepts, and violence should not be used as a measure of rebel control. In fact, in areas under very high rebel control, the insurgents may need to use little violence. In addition, media-based events data may not record violent events deep inside rebel territories due to information not filtering out from such zones of high rebel control (Zukerman-Daly 2012). So, using *total violence* could mis-measure rebel control, and it is important to try and measure Maoist control using other kinds of indicators of rebel organizational capacity.

Second, as discussed in the scope conditions of the theory in Chapter 3, historical institutions like indirect rule could be used to predict the initial phase of rebellion and the core areas in which the rebels were successful in

---

[3] These chapters test my theory in the two Maoist-affected states of Chhattisgarh and Andhra Pradesh, using more fine-grained data and local histories of the Maoist movement and are sensitive to such sub-district variations in Maoist insurgency.

consolidation of their movement. However, such long-term institutions may not predict the spatial expansion of an insurgency in its latter phases: once the movement has consolidated, other dynamics within the movement and its environment influence the expansion of the insurgency. Most of the measures of insurgency violence used by these studies to do econometric analysis of the Maoist insurgency are for the period of 2005–10. But the Maoist movement starts rapidly expanding geographically after 2004–5 with the unification of the MCC and PWG, and so it is not correct to use such late measures of violence as a proxy for initial core areas of rebel control. It may still be acceptable to use measures of violence between say 1995 and 2003, when the movement had not expanded much beyond its original bases.

Measuring Rebel Control Based on Government Perception: I follow the precedence of Mitchell (1968) and Kalyvas and Kocher (2009) and measure *Maoist control* based on government perception. The dependent variable is a binary 0–1 measure of Maoist control by the Ministry of Home Affairs (MHA), Government of India. This particular measure was published in 2005 and was available in a circular from the MHA to all district administrations in India on the issue of Security Related Expenditures (SRE) for tackling the Maoist problem.[4] It codes fifty-five districts for the 2000–2003 period as under Maoist control and notes that the number of districts would be increased to seventy-seven beginning in 2005 to reflect the expanding Maoist influence in this period following the merger of the People's War Group (PWG) and the Maoist Communist Center (MCC) to form the CPI-Maoist. These fifty-five districts can be used as a measure of initial Maoist control before the sudden geographic expansion and diffusion of the movement since 2005.[5] See Figure 5.1 for a scan of the relevant page from the SRE document with this list of districts.

The specific measure of Maoist rebel control that I use is based on the MHA's threat perception. It mentions five criteria for inclusion of districts under the SRE scheme. These criteria consider several other aspects of rebel organizational capacity and influence besides level of violence and are a multi-faceted measure of the concept of *rebel control*:

---

[4] "*Revision of guidelines for Re-Imbursement of Security Related Expenditure (S.R.E) to Naxal affected states under S.R.E. Scheme,*" MHA Memo Number 11–18015/4/03-IS.III, February 11, 2005. The Security Related Expenditures scheme is a funding scheme used by the central government to fund state government expenses regarding counterinsurgency, like purchase of vehicles or development programs in Maoist-affected areas, and even providing money to ex-Maoists who surrendered to the police through a special surrender scheme.

[5] In 2005, the insurgency was crushed in Andhra Pradesh and started expanding to other parts of Andhra Pradesh, as well as into other neighboring states like Orissa, West Bengal, Jharkhand, and Karnataka. However, this measure from 2005 is still limited to fifty-five core districts, so it is not capturing this surge of expansion, and it can be used as a reasonably good measure of initial core areas of Maoist control and consolidation.

(3) States and Districts covered under the SRE Scheme:

The names of the States and the Districts to which the revised scheme
would be applicable are given in the following table:

S. No.	State	Districts
1.	Andhra Pradesh	Warangal, Karimnagar, Adilabad, Khammam, Medak, Nalgonda, Nizamabad, Mehboobnagar, **Guntur, Prakasam, Anantapur, Kurnool, Vizianagaram, Visakhapatnam, East Godavari** and **Srikakulam.**
2.	Bihar	Aurangabad, Gaya, Jehanabad, Rohtas, Nalanda, Patna, Bhojpur, Kaimur, **East Champaran, West Champaran, Sitamarhi, Arwal, Nawada** and **Jamui.**
3.	Jharkhand	Hazaribagh, Lohardagga, Palamu, Chatra, Garhwa, Ranchi, Gumla, Simdega, Latehar, Giridih, Koderma,Bokaro, Dhanbad, **East Singhbhum, West Singhbhum** and **Saraikela–Kharaswan.**
4.	Madhya Pradesh	Balaghat, Dindori and **Mandla.**
5.	Chhattisgarh	Bastar, Dantewada, Kanker, Kawardha, Rajnandgaon, Sarguja, Jashpur and **Korea (Baikunthpur).**
6.	Maharashtra	Gadchiroli, Chandrapur, Bhandara and Godia.
7.	Orissa	Malkangiri, Ganjam, Koraput, Gajapati, Rayagada, Navrangpur, Mayurbhanj, **Sundargarh** and **Keonjhar.**
8.	Uttar Pradesh	Sonebhadra, Mirzapur and Chandauli.
9.	West Bengal	Bankura, Midnapore and Purulia.

The districts shown in the bold have been approved for inclusion w.e.f. Financial
Year 2004–05.

FIGURE 5.1 Dependent variable: Scan of list of districts from SRE document under
Maoist control
Source: "Revision of guidelines for Re-Imbursement of Security Related Expenditure (S.
R.E) to Naxal affected states under S.R.E. Scheme," MHA Memo Number 11–18015/4/
03-IS.III, 11 February 2005. (Obtained from Midnapore district headquarters, West
Bengal police during fieldwork.)

(1) Intensity of naxal violence over a period of say, five years. . . . (2) The organizational
consolidation attained by the various naxal outfits in the affected district. Whether the
districts are having "liberated areas" or "guerilla zones" where the extremist outfit(s)
virtually run a parallel administration even though the overall violence profile may not be
very high. (3) The presence of armed dalams, their free movement and their fire power which
would determine the potentiality of an extremist outfit to commit violent acts and be
a serious threat. . . . (4) The spread of active mass front organizations of the naxal groups
that lend . . . effective support in terms of logistics and safe refugee to the armed cadres. . . .
(5) Extent of pro-active measure initiated by the police/ administration to counter the naxal
extremist.[6]

It is important to note that the MHA is conscious that in areas where rebel
control was high and considered Maoist liberated areas or guerrilla zones, the
level of violence could actually be low. This is similar to Kalyvas's (2006)

---

[6] See http://mha.nic.in/sites/upload_files/mha/files/NM-SRE-Scheme_160614.pdf for the latest
MHA SRE scheme, which uses the same criteria to include districts as Maoist controlled as earlier
years.

suggestion and implies total violence may not be linearly related to actual rebel control. By focusing on guerrilla zones, armed *dalams*, which represent rebel organizational capacity, as well as overground mass organizations of Maoists, the MHA has a multi-faceted measure of rebel control that better captures this abstract concept than just relying on violence.

Possible Bias in Dependent Variable Maoist Control: This data is similar to the Kalyvas and Kocher (2009) data on rebel control in the Vietnam insurgency, which is also based on government perception. Like other measures of rebel control based on government perception (Kalyvas and Kocher 2009; Kocher, Pepinsky, & Kalyvas 2011; Mitchell 1968), there may be a certain amount of bias due to overestimation or underestimation of rebel control by the states reporting to the MHA. For example, Kalyvas and Kocher (2009) use the Hamlet Evaluation System (HES) data created by the US military during the Vietnam war to measure rebel control, but note that "Bole & Kobata (1975) find evidence that the HES was biased in the direction of government control (the so-called 'optimistic bias'), perhaps in response to bureaucratic incentives to show 'progress' in the pacification effort" (Kalyvas & Kocher 2009, p. 342). In the Indian case, the list of fifty-five districts for the 2000–2003 period seems like the expected districts under Maoist control and there does not seem to be much bias.

There is of course a chance that state governments intentionally overestimate the number of districts under Maoist control in their state to ensure that the MHA provides more counterinsurgency funds to their state, to make it easier for them to fight the Maoists, or sometimes to extract resources for rent.[7] It could go the other direction too, where states underestimate the districts under Maoist control to generate the "optimistic bias" that Kalyvas and Kocher (2009) mention. However, the error in the measure of political sensitivity would not be correlated with the independent variables of historical indirect rule, since the MHA and Intelligence Bureau officers do not have colonial indirect rule in mind when perceiving the level of Maoist control. So, the OLS estimators are unbiased and consistent, though there will be larger variance in the error terms.[8]

Timing of Measure of Rebel Control: The measure of the fifty-five districts that I use as my primary measure of Maoist control from 2000 to 2003 accurately indicates the core areas of Maoist control before the sudden geographic expansion since 2004 with the unification of the PWG and MCC, and the increase in its organizational capacity. This reflects the scope conditions of my theoretical framework, that colonial institutions could be used to predict initial areas of rebel control but not sudden spatial diffusion of an insurgency once it consolidated. In general, historical institutions are more useful to predict the initial areas of rebel control but not the timing of onset of insurgency, which is

---

[7] Interview with Alok Shukla, chief election commissioner of Chhattisgarh, Raipur, November 2008.
[8] See Woolridge, *Introductory Econometrics*, pp. 302–3.

influenced by several factors like state counterinsurgency, government policy changes that suddenly increase grievances, and international factors like insurgency in neighboring regions or countries.

In the next chapter, I present IV-2SLS results using similar models as the OLS results in this chapter. Robustness tests using the IV-2SLS analysis show that the results are robust to using later measures of Maoist control based on SRE documents from 2005, 2011, and 2016, which show an expansion of the insurgency to 76, 83, and 106 districts respectively. Figure 5.2 shows the expansion of Maoist control for these different years as measured by the MHA data.

Key Independent Variables: The two independent variables are *princely state*, which is a variable measuring formal indirect rule, and *landlord tenure*, which is a measure of indirect revenue collection.

(1) Princely State: This is a 0–1 measure of whether a district was under formal indirect rule as a princely state or under direct British rule. It is based on the measure of *princely state* in Iyer (2010), which is coded from several volumes and maps in *The Imperial Gazetteers of India*, Volumes 1–26. The data is cross checked by comparing 1991 Indian districts map to the map of direct/indirect rule from Volume 26.[9] Some corrections of errors in coding are made for the *princely state* variable in the Iyer (2010) dataset.[10] This dichotomous measure of princely state is sufficient for an initial test of the theory, but in the next chapter I discuss a more fine-grained typology of different types of princely states and show that only certain types of princely states lead to Maoist conflict, which answers the call by Wilkinson (2017) to develop more fine-grained measures of colonial direct/indirect rule.

(2) Landlord Tenure: This is the informal type of indirect rule, or rather indirect revenue collection system using landlords or intermediaries to collect land revenue. It is measured as a proportion of area in each district under the *zamindari* and *malguzari* land tenure systems, which are considered the two main types of landlord type tenure systems. The data is from Iyer (2010) and for the areas under direct British rule is coded from Baden-Powell (1892), *Land Tenure Systems of British India*, Volumes 1–3. However, Baden Powell (1892)

---

[9] The 1991 district map of India is from the *Census of India 2011 Administrative Atlas*, p. 117, Map 51. The map for British direct vs. indirect rule is from *Imperial Gazetteer of India*, vol. 26, Atlas 1909 edition, Political Divisions, p. 20, http://dsal.uchicago.edu/reference/gaz_atlas_1909/pager.html?object=26

[10] In the Iyer, "Direct versus Indirect Colonial Rule in India" dataset, Bastar and Rajnandgaon districts of 1991 census are coded as *britdum* = 1, which is incorrect because they are princely states and so *britdum* should be coded as 0, according to the map of British direct/indirect rule in *Imperial Gazetteer of India*, vol. 26, Political Divisions, p. 20. Other errors I have noticed for this variable are some districts in the state of Orissa, which I have changed.

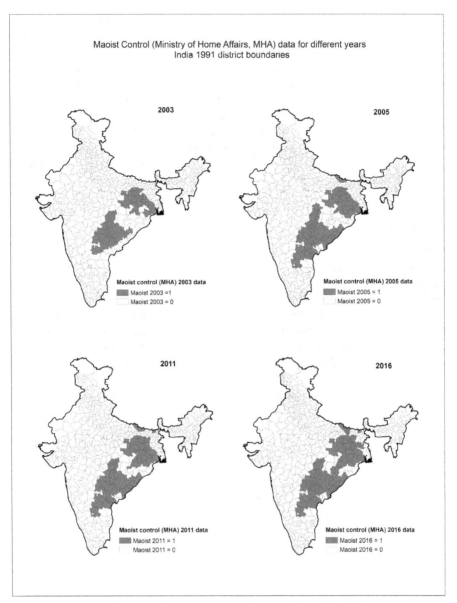

FIGURE 5.2 Dependent variable: Maoist control (MHA data) for different years
Source: Security Related Expenditure (S.R.E) Scheme, Ministry of Home Affairs (MHA)
data. (Obtained from MHA Annual Reports and from police during fieldwork.)

only provides us with descriptions and maps of land tenure within directly ruled British India and not for indirect rule areas, and Iyer (2010) measures land tenure type in princely states using *Imperial Gazetteer* volumes (1909).[11]

Scholars like Wilkinson (2017) have noted that the measures of land tenure coded in Banerjee and Iyer (2005) from official British gazetteers and maps are not accurate measures of how land tenure actually operated de facto on the ground.[12] A much more detailed and accurate measure of *zamindari, ryotwari,* and other types of land tenure is required, but it is not feasible to accurately measure land tenure for all districts in India using other archival sources, as that would be a huge data collection effort beyond the scope of this project. Instead, in the following chapters on Chhattisgarh and Andhra Pradesh, more fine-grained measures of land tenure are developed at the sub-district level from archival sources for these two states, which is the first such accurate measure of land tenure variable at the sub-district level.

Control Variables. I use various district-level measures like altitude; male literacy; percentage of scheduled caste and scheduled tribe; caste fractionalization; and public goods like access to electricity, schools, tanks, land Gini, and so on that are available in the Iyer (2010) dataset for each district of India. These are measures from various sources like the Census of India 1991, Topalova (2005), and Indian Database Project by Vanneman and Barnes (2000). See Online Appendix A of this chapter for a listing of data sources. These are measures of ethnicity, inequality, and terrain that are the usual explanations for civil war onset.

All variables are measured by 1991 census districts, and there are a total of 415 districts in 17 major states of India.[13] It is better to use 1991 and not 2001 census measures of socioeconomic and political variables as controls, since the dependent variable of *Maoist control* is measured around 2003, and so measuring the socioeconomic and political control variables temporally prior to the dependent variable will reduce concerns about reverse causality (Hegre & Sambanis 2006).

2.3   OLS/Logit Model Specification:

I present results for both OLS and logistic regressions for comparison, and the results are similar. Also, it is not possible to do instrumental variable regressions

[11] In email correspondence (dated March 2, 2011), Iyer mentioned that the data for land tenure for native/princely state areas were derived from the *Imperial Gazetteers of India.*

[12] Wilkinson, "Looking Back at the Colonial Origins," notes that the method of clubbing *mahal-wari* and *ryotwari* land tenure systems as being both non-landlord type of tenure is not accurate, since these are different types of non-landlord tenure and can have different effects.

[13] The states in the Iyer, "Direct versus Indirect Colonial Rule in India," dataset are Andhra Pradesh, Assam, Bihar, Gujarat, Haryana, Himachal Pradesh, Jammu and Kashmir, Karnataka, Kerala, Madhya Pradesh, Maharashtra, Orissa, Punjab, Rajasthan, Tamil Nadu, Uttar Pradesh, and West Bengal. These states accounted for 96 percent of India's population in 2001.

using logistic regression models, so it is necessary to present OLS results that can be compared with the IV-2SLS regressions in the next chapter.

The OLS regressions are of the form:

$$Y_i = \alpha + \beta \text{ princely state}_{i} + \gamma \text{ landlord tenure}_i + \delta X_i + \varepsilon_i,$$

where Y_i is the dependent variable of *Maoist control* for district *i*; *princely state$_i$* is the dummy for whether the *i* th district was earlier part of a princely state (indirect rule) or British India (direct rule); *landlord tenure$_i$* is the continuous measure of what fraction of the district was under landlord type of land tenure (*zamindari/ malguzari* or *ryotwari/mahalwari*); and X_i stands for other district characteristics controlled for, including altitude, forest cover, population density, land inequality (*gini*), access to public goods like primary schools and water tanks and public health centers, and variables measuring ethnicity like percentage of scheduled castes and tribes, caste fractionalization in each district in India. These are measures of opportunity for rebellion, as well as possible grievance factors that could lead to Maoist rebellion in India; ε_i represents the error term.

Similarly, the logistic regressions are of the form:

$$\text{logit } (\pi) = \alpha + \beta \text{ princely state}_{i} + \gamma \text{ landlord tenure}_i + \delta X_i + \varepsilon_i,$$

where *logit* (π) is the logistic function of probability that a district *i* is under *Maoist control*, and *princely state$_i$* and *landlord tenure$_i$* are respective measures of the two forms of indirect rule (as explained earlier), and X_i stands for other district characteristics previously described.

Table 5.1 shows the summary statistics including average values of all variables included in the analysis. Table 5.2 presents both OLS/Linear Probability Model (Models 1–2) and logistic regression (Models 3–4) models. Different states in India have different political cultures, political parties, and ethnic groups, and their own separate histories of colonial and even pre-colonial rule. To control for such unobservable qualities of individual states in India, I include state fixed effects in Model 1 (OLS/LPM) and Model 3 (Logit).[14] I also present results of random effects in Model 2 (OLS/LPM) and Model 4 (Logit) in Table 5.2.

2.4 Discussion of Results

In Table 5.2, the baseline models that include only *princely state* (formal indirect rule) and *landlord tenure* (informal indirect rule) with state fixed effects (Models 1

---

[14] I do not cluster by state, but for the IV-2SLS regressions in the next chapter, I also use robust cluster by state. In Table 5.2, the state fixed effects with logit (Model 3) drop some of the states from the analysis, probably because of lack of variation of the *landtenure* variable within these states. The fixed effects analysis with logit drops the following states: Gujarat, Haryana, Himachal Pradesh, Karnataka, Kerala, Punjab, Rajasthan, Tamil Nadu. However, the random effects model with logit (Model 4) does not drop these states, and also the OLS/Linear Probability Model with fixed effects (Model 1) and random effects (Model 2) does not drop these states, and the results hold for these other models, thus providing robustness to these empirical results.

TABLE 5.1 *Summary statistics*

Variables	Obs.	Mean	Std. Dev.	Min	Max
Dependent Variable					
Maoist control	395	0.093671	0.29174	0	1
Independent Variables					
Princely State	395	0.336709	0.473184	0	1
Landlord Tenure	355	0.457245	0.433363	0	1
Control Variables					
Altitude	354	396.9075	379.9965	0	5480
Population Density	391	297.6832	238.9936	2.261944	1929.291
Scheduled Caste Percentage	391	0.176692	0.084373	0.001755	0.545097
Scheduled Tribe Percentage	391	0.110891	0.18086	0	0.982891
Caste Fragmentation	391	0.926741	0.069278	0.595493	0.999737
Land Gini Coefficient	391	0.465091	0.092177	0.065742	0.604849
Primary School	391	1050.736	650.0054	42	6008
Riots	391	243.7033	252.4767	0	2303
Access to Water Tanks	391	207.5381	398.9598	0	3187
Primary Health Center	391	43.46061	32.20434	2	392
Electricity	391	366.8386	383.6679	0	2865
Scheduled Tribe Percentage * Electricity	391	31.66806	71.85854	0	612.6927
Alluvial Soil	357	0.507003	0.500653	0	1
Black Soil	357	0.207283	0.405929	0	1
Red Soil	357	0.179272	0.384118	0	1
Barren Rocky Soil	378	0.007434	0.019487	0	0.265584
Forest Cover 1991	301	16.54485	17.39211	0	85.83
Pre-Colonial Agrarian Rebellion	395	0.159494	0.3666	0	1

and 3) show that both measures of colonial indirect rule are significant and positively correlated with Maoist insurgency. This result shows that once I control for unobserved heterogeneity of different Indian states, both indirect rule and indirect revenue collection have significant and positive correlations with Maoist control. The results hold for both OLS in Model 1 and logistic regression in Model 3. The results are similar for the random effects models for both OLS (Model 2) and logistic regression (Model 4), and indirect rule through *princely state* is statistically significant at the 95 percent confidence level and have a positive regression coefficient, and indirect revenue collection through *zamindari landlord tenure* has a positive coefficient at the 99 percent confidence level.

TABLE 5.2 *All-India district-level estimates of impact of colonial institutions on Maoist rebellion*

Dependent variable: Maoist control (Ministry of Home Affairs 2000–2003 measure of Maoist control in each district)

	Models			
	(1) OLS State FE	(2) OLS State RE	(3) LOGIT State FE	(4) LOGIT State RE
Princely State	0.1046	0.0756	2.0128	1.60487
	(0.008)***	(0.031)**	(0.005)***	(0.017)**
Landlord Tenure	0.1115	0.1204	3.0426	3.0391
	(0.015)**	(0.002)***	(0.011)**	(0.002)***
Constant	−0.0073	−0.0005		−5.6884
	(0.797)	(0.987)		(0.000)
N	355	355	207	355
R^2	0.0336	0.0320		
Log Likelihood			−54.767	−79.185

*** $p < 0.01$, ** $p < 0.05$, * $p < 0.10$. P-values in parentheses.

Note: For the logistic regression with state level fixed effects in Model 3, nine groups were dropped because of all positive or all negative outcomes. This is discussed in footnote 15.

I conduct a Hausman test to check whether the random effects model is significantly different from a fixed effects model. Comparing OLS with fixed effects (Model 1) and OLS with random effects (Model 2), the Hausman test provides a p value of 0.2253, which means that it is not possible to reject the null hypothesis that the difference in coefficients between fixed effects and random effects models is not systematic. However, in Table 5.4, which includes more control variables, the Hausman test comparing OLS with fixed effects (Model 1) and OLS with random effects (Model 2) provides a p value of 0.0000 and rejects the null hypothesis that the difference in coefficients between fixed and random effects is not systematic. Including control variables thus indicates that the coefficients of the fixed effects model is different, and it is probably more realistic to assume that there is some unobservable quality about each state that could possibly influence propensity for Maoist rebellion. I use the fixed effect models to interpret results and to control for possible unobserved heterogeneity between Indian states.

A certain amount of unobserved heterogeneity is controlled for by using state fixed effects (FEs). However, there may be other unobserved qualities of these districts that may have prompted the British to select them for indirect rule that are not controlled for, so the regression coefficients in Table 5.2 cannot be interpreted as measures of causal effect of indirect rule on postcolonial Maoist insurgency.

3 SELECTION BIAS IN CHOICE OF COLONIAL INDIRECT RULE

3.1 Controlling for Causes of Choice of Indirect Rule by British

What are the causes for the British choosing certain areas for direct rule and other areas for indirect rule within India? In a well-known study, Gerring et al. (2011) try to explain why British colonizers chose indirect rule vs. direct rule. They propose that the British would choose indirect rule where the pre-colonial state had higher levels of political development and state institutional capacity. They would choose direct rule where the pre-colonial polity had lower levels of political and institutional complexity, and it was easier to replace these institutions with their own. The reason for colonizers choosing indirect rule for colonies with preexisting complex political organization is that this allowed for a clear political leader with legitimacy, who can be held accountable, so enforcement is easier. Also, a well-developed political organization can help the colonizer by providing public goods like maintaining order, collecting revenue, preventing disease and provide population control like prevent emigration.

However, this theory of colonial choice of indirect rule does not explain colonial choices in India for two reasons. First, Gerring et al. (2011) test their theory using Lange's (2009) country-level dataset on indirect rule in former British colonies, but they mention that they leave out India from their analysis because of "coding difficulties it poses" for both the type of colonial rule chosen and their independent variable of "degree of pre-colonial institutional complexity" (Gerring et al. 2011: 392, footnote 49). This is because the Lange (2009) dataset has country-level data, while for India we need subnational variation in direct/indirect rule.

Second, Gerring et al.'s (2011) prediction does not explain this subnational variation in British choices within India, since the British chose indirect rule in the large state of Hyderabad in the south that was a *successor state* of the Mughals but chose to annex the other successor states of Awadh in the north and Bengal in the east into direct rule (Ramusack 2004). These were large states with complex bureaucracies and tax collection systems inherited from the Mughal Empire; according to Gerring et al.'s (2011) theory, the British should have applied indirect rule in all these cases. The fact that they did not do so implies the colonial officers had other calculations in mind when making decisions about whether or not to sign a treaty of indirect rule. Similarly, the British chose to sign treaties of indirect rule with a large variety of Indian princes – some were small interior *feudatory states* in Central India and Chhattisgarh, and others were frontier states in the northeast like Tripura and Manipur and in the northwest frontier like Kalat and tribal maliks of North West Frontier Province (NWFP). These states had much lower levels of pre-colonial institutional capacity than the large Mughal successor states of Awadh and Hyderabad, or warrior states like Marathas and Mysore. Gerring et al.'s (2011) theory would incorrectly predict that the British chose direct rule in these frontier states. This shows that the colonial officers based their decisions on geostrategic calculations and not pre-colonial institutional complexity.

A similar study by Lange, Mahoney, and Vom Hau (2006) compares the choices of Spanish and British colonizers regarding whether to rule more or less directly. The Lange et al. (2006) study suggests that the Spanish were mercantilist and tended to choose more direct rule where pre-colonial political and economic institutions were more complex, which is the opposite of the British who believed in liberal free market ideology and preferred to choose indirect rule where pre-colonial institutional complexity was high. Their theory is more nuanced than the Gerring et al. (2011) study and has a more accurate prediction for British choices in Asia. Unlike Gerring et al. (2011) who leave out settler colonies like the United States, Australia, Canada, and New Zealand from their analysis, Lange et al. (2006) proposed that the British chose settler colonialism in those countries with low population density and pre-colonial institutions that were not complex. In African countries with more complex pre-colonial institutions as in Botswana, Ghana, Nigeria, Kenya, Sierra Leone, and Uganda, the British chose mostly indirect rule, which also confirms their theoretical prediction.

However, Lange et al. (2006: 1429) admit that many of Britain's Asian colonies did not "conform to the predicted inverse relationship between precolonial development and level of British colonialism." These Asian colonies generally showed intermediate and high levels of pre-colonial institutions but resulted in "intermediate to high levels of colonial influence because of the presence of exploitable resources and markets." One example would be Hong Kong, where the British used direct rule even though the levels of pre-colonial institutions and population density were quite high, but the pre-colonial institutions were trade oriented and capitalist. Also, within the largest colony of India, the British used *hybrid colonialism* that combined a patchwork of territories of direct rule and indirect rule (Lange 2009; Mahoney 2010), even though the theory would predict that because of the complex bureaucracy and institutions left behind by the Mughal Empire, the colonizers should have chosen only indirect rule.

What explains this subnational variation in choice of British indirect vs. direct rule within India? Lange et al. (2006: 1433) suggest that this is probably because the Asian colonies offered the chance of "capitalist accumulation" and resources, so the British were willing to try and establish more direct forms of rule and institutions, despite the challenges of doing so. This colonial calculus can be further explained by referring to the large historiography of colonial indirect rule in India.

Historians like Ramusack (2004: 79–80) suggest, "The British were … anxious to control most coastal tracts, the hinterland of their major entrepots, and economically productive areas such as the Gangetic Plain." Other historians like Robin Jeffrey (1978) note that the Zamorin of Calicut, whose dynasty had been ruling for hundreds of years, was turned into a landlord and the British took over more of a direct rule. In contrast, once Tipu Sultan of Mysore was defeated, his territory was given to the Hindu family of the Wodeyars, who had once ruled only a small portion of the state, and the British remained satisfied with indirect rule. According to Jeffrey (1978: 7), "much depended on the value of the country" and the Zamorin's Malabar was rich pepper country, while much of Mysore was dry and unprosperous. Clearly, in a lot of cases, the British were driven by motivations of profit and acquiring productive and governable lands when they chose to annex a state or district and introduce direct rule. Ramusack (2004: 87) mentions that the British directly ruled a combination of "those parts of India held by any major aspirant to a centralized imperial status, from the Mauryan Empire to the Congress Party, with those parts of India prized by seaborne traders, whether foreigners such as Arabs or indigenous south Indian kings."

However, neither the British nor any other central claimant to authority on the Indian subcontinent

ever sought to govern directly the Thar desert of Rajasthan, the remote salt flats of Cutch, or the jungly tracts of central India and Orissa. The British system of indirect rule over Indian states and a limited raj even in directly ruled areas such as Bihar and the United provinces provided a model for the efficient use of scarce monetary and personnel resources that could be adopted to imperial acquisitions in Malaya and Africa. (Ramusack 2004: 87)

For those regions that were not coastal and had difficult terrain or potentially rebellious tribes in Rajasthan, Gujarat and central India, and Orissa, the British preferred to use different treaties of indirect rule with various princes. In these places, the British colonial motivation was driven by ruling on the cheap through collaboration with princes whose lands were not as easily governable or were not deemed as profitable or strategically important to control. Nandini Sundar (2006: 203) in her anthropological work on the feudatory state of Bastar in Chhattisgarh state writes, "Indirect rule had several advantages for the British." First, it was useful for areas that are "too poor to justify direct management" by the colonial state. Second, it is less expensive than direct rule that entails setting up colonial administration and officials. Third, it helps deflect the blame of any rebellions that occur to the prince's unpopular policies, rather than a response to British rule.

Based on this historiography, it seems that the British administrators in India intentionally selected those areas for direct rule that were more economically and agriculturally productive and had fewer rebellious tribes and terrain more suited to governance. In contrast, they chose for indirect rule those areas that were more difficult to govern or not very resource rich and productive, and hence more prone to rebellion. This raises a concern of *selection bias* while trying to estimate long-term causal effects of colonial indirect rule on insurgency.

It may be that the pre-colonial attributes of the district increase its chances of postcolonial rebellion, and not the institution of indirect rule. This would cause the regression estimates to be biased and the OLS coefficients to overestimate the causal effect of indirect rule. In contrast, it is also possible that the British were sometimes forced by geostrategic or other contingencies to select stronger states or ones that had more revenue potential for indirect rule, for example, the state of Hyderabad, in which case the OLS coefficients would underestimate the effect of indirect rule.

This concern has some validity because the western region of Cutch in Gujarat and the small princely states of the Rajput kings that form Rajasthan do not have Maoist rebellion today because contingent historical circumstances did not ever allow the Communist movement to be strong in those parts. However, the "jungly tracts" of central India and Orissa that Ramusack mentions did have a Communist influence beginning in the 1960s and developed successful Maoist insurgency later in the 1980s. Even the parts that were officially under direct rule but had a "limited raj" through the help of *zamindars* in Bihar/Bengal had some form of Communist mobilization in the past and successful Maoist consolidation since the 1980s.

3.2 Controlling for Pre-Colonial Factors to Address Selection Effect

In this section, I control for some observable and expected determinants of the choice of indirect rule by the British to try and demonstrate that while these pre-colonial qualities of districts may have influenced the British decision about whether to annex it into direct rule or to sign a treaty of indirect rule, once the choice was made the type of colonial rule chosen also had its own separate long-term effect on the chances of conflict by creating different levels of state capacity and ethnic inequalities.

I measure and include controls for some of these pre-colonial factors in Table 5.3, and both these pre-colonial and some postcolonial factors in Table 5.4. I use a measure of *barren rocky* nature of soil and *soil type (red, alluvial, or black soil)*, which is available in the Iyer (2010) dataset. I also developed a measure of *forest cover* as the percentage of each district that is covered by forest from the *Forest Survey of India Report, 1991* as another measure of rough terrain (Fearon & Laitin 2003).[15] Finally, following from the study by Besley and Reynal-Querol (2014), which suggests that pre-colonial conflicts in Africa have long-term effects on postcolonial conflicts, I control for pre-colonial conflict. However, most of the pre-colonial conflicts for India in the Brecke (1999) dataset used by Besley and Reynal-Querol (2014) are big and small wars between princes and kings, and not

[15] Forest Survey of India's *State of Forest Report 1991 report*, Table 2.3, pp. 51–63. See www .fsi.nic.in/

TABLE 5.3 *All-India district-level estimates of impact of colonial institutions on Maoist rebellion*
Dependent variable: *Maoist control* (Ministry of Home Affairs 2000–3 measure of Maoist control)
Including only pre-colonial factors as controls

	Model 1 – OLS with state FE	Model 2 – including forest cover	Model 3 – including types of soil	Model 4 – including forest cover and types of soil	Model 5 – including pre-colonial conflict
Princely State	0.105***	0.150***	0.115***	0.148***	0.154***
	(0.008)	(0.001)	(0.007)	(0.001)	(0.001)
Landlord Tenure	0.112**	0.136***	0.115**	0.123**	0.123**
	(0.015)	(0.009)	(0.030)	(0.019)	(0.019)
Altitude		-0.0000405		-0.0000373	-0.0000111
		(0.687)		(0.768)	(0.931)
Forest Cover		0.00530***		0.00446***	0.00454***
		(0.000)		(0.000)	(0.000)
Alluvial Soil			0.0193	-0.0612	-0.0678*
			(0.607)	(0.134)	(0.098)
Black Soil			0.0669	0.0410	0.0366
			(0.173)	(0.395)	(0.447)
Red Soil			0.193***	0.187***	0.169**
			(0.001)	(0.006)	(0.014)
Barren & Rocky			-0.631	-0.0447	-0.105
			(0.567)	(0.968)	(0.925)
Pre-Colonial (Mughal) Agrarian Rebellion					0.0665
					(0.134)
Constant	-0.00736	-0.0902	-0.0592	-0.0766	-0.0965
	(0.797)	(0.126)	(0.197)	(0.297)	(0.196)
Observations	355	240	305	232	232
R^2	0.034	0.134	0.082	0.183	0.192

P-values in parentheses
All models include state fixed effects.
* $p < 0.10$, ** $p < 0.05$, *** $p < 0.01$

TABLE 5.4 *All-India district-level estimates of impact of colonial institutions on Maoist rebellion*
Dependent variable: *Maoist control* (Ministry of Home Affairs 2000–3 measure of Maoist control)
Including both pre-colonial and postcolonial measures as controls

	Model 1 – OLS with state FE	Model 2 – including forest cover	Model 3 – including types of soil	Model 4 – including forest cover and types of soil	Model 5 – including pre-colonial conflict
Princely State	0.160***	0.172***	0.160***	0.170***	0.172***
	(0.000)	(0.000)	(0.000)	(0.000)	(0.000)
Landlord Tenure	0.119*	0.129**	0.104*	0.111**	0.110**
	(0.016)	(0.013)	(0.041)	(0.034)	(0.036)
Altitude	-0.0000554	-0.0000344	0.0000529	0.0000411	0.0000629
	(0.560)	(0.745)	(0.671)	(0.754)	(0.633)
Popln Density	-0.000205**	-0.000133	-0.000147	-0.0000195	-0.0000211
	(0.049)	(0.393)	(0.187)	(0.909)	(0.901)
Scheduled Caste Percentage	0.832***	0.640*	0.641**	0.702**	0.703**
	(0.004)	(0.066)	(0.033)	(0.046)	(0.045)
Scheduled Tribe Percentage	0.526***	0.371**	0.383**	0.310*	0.299*
	(0.001)	(0.033)	(0.021)	(0.078)	(0.089)
Caste Fragmentation	-0.144	-0.0499	-0.201	0.0178	-0.0389
	(0.672)	(0.883)	(0.576)	(0.960)	(0.913)
Land Gini	0.374	0.355	0.282	0.405	0.394
	(0.136)	(0.250)	(0.301)	(0.219)	(0.230)
Primary School	0.000163***	0.000143***	0.000186***	0.000165***	0.000168***
	(0.000)	(0.005)	(0.000)	(0.002)	(0.001)
Ethnic Riots	-0.0000996	-0.0000983	-0.0000739	-0.0000997	-0.000114
	(0.187)	(0.226)	(0.346)	(0.229)	(0.173)
Access to Water Tanks	-0.000312***	-0.000207**	-0.000326***	-0.000186**	-0.000190**
	(0.000)	(0.020)	(0.000)	(0.041)	(0.037)

(*continued*)

TABLE 5.4 (continued)

	Model 1 – OLS with state FE	Model 2 – including forest cover	Model 3 – including types of soil	Model 4 – including forest cover and types of soil	Model 5 – including pre-colonial conflict
Public Health Center	0.000996 (0.135)	0.000818 (0.364)	0.000886 (0.193)	0.000430 (0.642)	0.000262 (0.778)
Electricity	-0.0000914 (0.155)	-0.0000665 (0.355)	-0.0000985 (0.137)	-0.0000723 (0.325)	-0.0000712 (0.331)
ST% * Electricity	-0.000586* (0.058)	-0.000505 (0.107)	-0.000624* (0.051)	-0.000604* (0.061)	-0.000613* (0.057)
Forest Cover		0.00412*** (0.001)		0.00397*** (0.002)	0.00404*** (0.002)
Alluvial Soil			0.00104 (0.978)	-0.0631 (0.134)	-0.0662 (0.115)
Black Soil			0.0422 (0.393)	0.0379 (0.447)	0.0382 (0.443)
Red Soil			0.162*** (0.007)	0.150** (0.031)	0.135* (0.053)
Barren & Rocky			-1.188 (0.276)	-0.524 (0.632)	-0.570 (0.601)
Pre-Colonial (Mughal) Agrarian Rebellion					0.0606 (0.171)
Constant	-0.275 (0.439)	-0.421 (0.253)	-0.231 (0.543)	-0.556 (0.153)	-0.506 (0.194)
Observations	309	234	294	230	230
R^2	0.263	0.263	0.283	0.299	0.305

P-values in parentheses
All models include State Fixed Effects.
* $p < 0.10$, ** $p < 0.05$, *** $p < 0.01$

pre-colonial agrarian rebellions, and do not seem very relevant to predict future leftist rebellions.[16] I developed a new measure of agrarian/peasant rebellion in India during the pre-colonial Mughal period (1556–1707), which logically should be the most politically relevant type of pre-colonial conflict that should matter for postcolonial Maoist insurgency.[17] See Online Appendix B for list of sources used for coding *precolonial agrarian conflict*.

It would be useful to control for pre-colonial population density as in Besley and Reynal-Querol (2014: 327), and pre-colonial political centralization as in Michalopoulos and Papaioannou (2013) and Gennaioli and Rainer (2007), but it is not possible because of the absence of district-level data on population density and political centralization in pre-colonial India.[18]

While Table 5.3 only includes the pre-colonial factors that may have influenced choice of indirect rule, Table 5.4 includes both these pre-colonial as well as postcolonial controls like literacy, percentage of scheduled castes and tribes, access to various public goods, and land inequality that are considered to be proximate determinants of Maoist insurgency onset. Controlling for these observable factors that might have influenced the British administrators to be selective in their choice of direct/indirect rule, Tables 5.3 and 5.4 show that both princely state and landlord tenure are statistically significant predictors of Maoist control. These results are similar to the baseline models in Table 5.2. *Forest cover* has a statistically significant and positive regression coefficient, but the size of the coefficient is much smaller than that of *colonial institutions*. Of the different types of soil, *red soil* has a positive and statistically significant correlation with Maoist insurgency, while *alluvial soil* and *black soil* are not statistically significant. It is possibly because *red soil* is bad for crops and tends to create lower agricultural productivity and hence increases the chances of leftist agrarian unrest, which provides support for grievance-based theories. *Barren & rocky terrain* has no statistically significant correlation with Maoist control and is a measure of revenue potential of the region as well as terrain.

Precolonial agrarian rebellion (Mughal period) does not have a significant correlation with the areas of Maoist insurgency: the areas where there were peasant and other types of agrarian rebellions during Mughal times, like the

---

[16] The Brecke (1999) dataset is available at www.cgeh.nl/data#conflict.

[17] This measure is developed from various sources like Habib, *The Agrarian System of Mughal India* and *Peasant and Artisan Resistance in Mughal India;* Rana, "Agrarian Revolts in Northern India during the Late 17th and Early 18th Century"; Alam and Subrahmanyam, *The Mughal State, 1526–1750;* Mayaram, *Against History, Against State.*

[18] Various papers like Besley and Reynal Querol, "The Legacy of Historical Conflict"; and Nunn and Puga, "Ruggedness: The Blessing of Bad Geography in Africa" use pre-colonial population density measures from McEvedy and Jones, *Atlas of World Population History* and Maddison, *The World Economy: Historical Statistics,* but these are available only at the country level. Similarly, there are no sources for district-level measures of pre-colonial centralization, or pre-colonial institutional complexity in India, though Jha, "Trade, Institutions, and Ethnic Tolerance: Evidence from South Asia" has data on trade routes and mints in the Mughal period, which could be used as proxies for pre-colonial political centralization.

Satnami rebellion or the Sikh rebellions in North India, or the many agrarian rebellions that occurred in the regions of Rajasthan and Mewat and Agra *suba*, do not coincide with the areas in Bihar/Jharkhand or Chhattisgarh/Andhra Pradesh where the Maoist rebellion flourished beginning in the 1980s (Habib 1984; Rana 1981).[19] Unlike Africa, where the colonizers relied on previous chiefs to control areas (Besley and Reynal Querol 2014), in India the British used higher levels of direct rule and relied less on preexisting rulers for indirect rule (Lange 2009), and so possibly colonial choices and institutions override pre-colonial institutions and state capacity.

The results imply that while these observable pre-colonial qualities of districts may have played a role in the choice of the institutions, once in place the institutions of colonial indirect rule and indirect revenue collection had an additional effect on creating low governance, weak state, and ethnic inequalities, which persisted into postcolonial times, creating the opportunity structures for Maoist insurgency. Geography, forest cover, revenue, and other qualities are important determinants of inequality and rebellion, but colonial institutions once put into place also create a further set of conditions that can be useful for fomenting rebellion (Acemoglu et al. 2001).

4   CONCLUSION

In this chapter, I described the data sources for my dependent variable of *Maoist control* and my two independent variables of *princely states* and *land tenure institutions* in India. I then presented OLS and logistic regression analysis to show that both these measures of indirect rule are positively correlated with Maoist control. I also discussed the various factors that could have been potential causes for the British choosing indirect rule in some areas and direct rule in other areas. It is possible that the British intentionally selected those areas that were not agriculturally productive, had difficult terrain, and rebellious tribes difficult to govern for indirect rule. This creates potential *selection bias* which I try to address by controlling for some of these pre-colonial determinants of indirect rule.

However, this still may not be enough to address selection bias as there could be other unobservable determinants of choice of indirect rule, and we cannot control for all these factors. To address the issue of selection bias, I adopt a multi-method approach in the next chapter. First, I do a comparative case study of two princely states – Awadh and Hyderabad – using a Most Similar Systems research design (Ragin 1987; Slater & Ziblatt 2013). Comparing these two princely states which were very similar on many characteristics yet diverged in their outcomes of whether they remained under indirect rule or were annexed

---

[19] See map in Habib, *Peasant and Artisan Resistance*, p. 15. Many of the agrarian rebellions at this time are mixed and often see local *zamindars* or chiefs rebelling against the Mughal Empire, but these also involve local tribes, or peasants, or lower castes joining them. Some of these rebellions are purely peasant based.

into direct rule demonstrates that historical contingencies and geostrategic considerations sometimes played a crucial role in the choice of indirect rule and prevented the British officers from carefully selecting areas according to their calculus. So, selection was not as universal and there was a certain randomness and contingency that forced the hand of colonial administrators.

Following this, the next chapter also presents an instrumental variable analysis to deal with the issue of selection bias in choice of indirect rule and presents a new instrument for the British choice of indirect rule through princely state.[20] The instrument is based on the idea that during the period of the great power wars in Europe, the British in India were both financially constrained and felt threatened by France or Russia through Central Asia. This led them to fight fewer wars of annexation to create direct ruled provinces and increased their propensity to sign treaties of indirect rule with the Indian states bordering their areas of control. That these states were contiguous to areas of British direct rule during times of the great power wars is used as an instrument for the choice of colonial indirect rule in India. This shows that external geostrategic considerations in Europe that were totally unrelated to qualities of regions or districts in India were exogenous determinants of choice of indirect rule and helps address the issue of selection bias.

Finally, the next chapter also deals with another thorny empirical issue that needs to be addressed. Scholars like Wilkinson (2017) have suggested that there is much more fine-grained variation within the category of land tenure and princely states than previous scholars like Iyer (2010) and Banerjee and Iyer (2005) have measured. My empirical measure of princely state and landlord tenure relies on these well-known studies and datasets, and I use a 0–1 measure of princely state. This may not adequately measure the heterogeneity among the different types of formal colonial indirect rule through princely states within the Indian subcontinent. To squarely address this issue, I develop a more fine-grained typology of *princely states* in the next chapter by looking at different types of princely states and how they vary in their effect on state capacity and land revenue exploitation and Maoist insurgency.

---

[20] This is similar to previous studies like Banerjee and Iyer, "History, Institutions and Economic Performance" and Acemoglu et al., "The Colonial Origins of Comparative Development" and various others that develop innovative instruments to address selection problems related to choice of colonial institutions.

6

Colonial Choice or Random Contingency? Addressing Selection Bias in British Indirect Rule

I   INTRODUCTION

In the previous chapter, I presented a quantitative analysis of how *zamindari* land tenure and *princely state* had significant effects on *Maoist control* in late 1990–early 2000s before the rapid expansion of the insurgency following the formation of CPI-Maoist in 2004. I used Ministry of Home Affairs (MHA) data to measure Maoist control, and OLS regression results showed that my measures of indirect rule were strongly and positively correlated with Maoist control even after including various factors that are commonly associated with civil war onset.

I also considered the possibility that the British intentionally selected those areas for indirect rule that were difficult to govern due to rebellious ethnic groups, or had bad soil quality and low agricultural productivity, or had difficult terrain that made it unattractive for direct rule. I controlled for some of these pre-colonial qualities of districts in the OLS analysis. However, it is not possible to observe, measure, and control for all possible pre-colonial factors that could have affected the decisions of colonial administrators on which areas to leave for indirect rule through native princes and which areas to annex and rule directly and set up colonial governance infrastructure. This means the OLS regression coefficients could still be biased. In this chapter, I address the issue of *selection bias* more directly in several ways.

First, I present a comparative case study using a Most Similar Systems research design (Ragin 1987; Slater & Ziblatt 2013) between the two similar princely states of Awadh and Hyderabad, which shows that it was historical contingency determined by external geopolitical circumstances that influenced British choice of direct vs. indirect rule and prevented Governor General Lord Dalhousie from being selective in 1856.

Second, I develop a new instrument for the British choice of indirect rule through princely states. The instrument relies on the fact that when the British government had to fight major European wars, it faced budget constraints and perceived security threats to India from France and Russia. This increased the tendency of British administrators to sign treaties of indirect rule with rulers of Indian states on the frontiers of British direct rule and reduced their willingness to fight wars of annexation into direct rule. Since European wars and their causes were exogenous to local politics in India, the interaction of timing of major European wars and frontier districts bordering British territory in India is a plausible instrument for the British choice of indirect rule in India.

The British often could not be selective, and choices were forced on the colonial officials because of external geostrategic constraints or even financial constraints that forced a treaty with an Indian ruler instead of annexing into direct rule. The IV-2SLS analysis shows that those districts that had *zamindari* land tenure or princely state rule had higher probability of Maoist control in the postcolonial period. This provides greater confidence that the effects of these two types of indirect rule on Maoist control are causal in nature and not merely correlations. The IV-2SLS analysis in this chapter is a major empirical contribution and allows an estimate of the causal effects of colonial indirect rule on Maoist insurgency.

There is another possible weakness in the quantitative OLS analysis in the previous chapter. Scholars like Wilkinson (2017) have proposed that the measures of indirect rule and land tenure system that have been used by previous scholarship like that of Banerjee and Iyer (2005), Iyer (2010), and Verghese (2016a) do not reflect the nuanced variation in types of land tenure systems and indirect rule in India. There is a lot of heterogeneity between different types of princely states than that captured in the measures in the Iyer (2010) or Verghese (2016a) papers. Yet, my analysis in the previous chapter used the 0–1 binary measure of princely states from Iyer (2010). This is to allow comparison with previous studies, and for analytical simplicity.

In this chapter, I try to address this by developing a novel typology of different types of princely states in India, partly based on the historiography of Ramusack (2004). This typology looks at the pre-colonial qualities of Indian kingdoms and differentiates between *successor states* like Hyderabad and Bengal that were less efficient and despotic; *warrior states* like Mysore, Marathas, and Travancore that tried to fight the colonizers and developed centralized and more efficient states and bureaucracies; and *feudatory / tributary states* in the Chhattisgarh and Orissa region that were not annexed by the British and saw inefficient and despotic rule by princes and *diwans* who were ethnic outsiders.

I test for the effects of these types of princely states, and results show that the effect on Maoist control varies depending on the type of princely state. This is a major empirical contribution to the literature on colonial legacies in South Asia, which answers the call by Wilkinson (2017) to further disaggregate the category of indirect rule. Future research can build on this and analyze fine-grained variation in types of land tenure systems that the current categories of *zamindari, mahalwari* and *ryotwari* do not measure.

2   ADDRESSING SELECTION BIAS USING CASE STUDIES AND IV-2SLS ANALYSIS

2.1   Case Study Comparison to Show Historical Contingency in Selection into Indirect Rule

Most historians of South Asia agree that the British wanted to control economically productive areas such as the Gangetic Plain and coastal regions under direct rule and use indirect rule through native rulers to control those areas that were less productive and difficult to govern. However, as the historian Ramusack (2004: 79–80) admits, "Historical contingencies were partly responsible for which areas were annexed and which remained under princes." Robin Jeffrey suggests that there was "an awesome arbitrariness about who got a treaty and who did not" (Jeffrey 1978: 6). In certain cases, the choice of indirect rule was influenced by arbitrary factors, or contingencies, that had nothing to do with the intrinsic quality of the district or province. By locating such cases and the causes of such contingent events, it is possible to take the first step in addressing the issue of selection bias.

Case Study Comparison of Hyderabad and Awadh Provinces, circa 1798–1856

I present a case comparison of how historical contingencies and external geostrategic factors influenced the variation in British choice regarding annexation between Hyderabad and Awadh provinces. This is a Most Similar Systems research design (Ragin 1987; Slater & Ziblatt 2013), which is used to compare two princely states that were similar on a lot of characteristics yet diverged in the outcome of whether they remained under indirect rule or were annexed into direct rule.[1] This paired comparison of similar cases shows that historical contingencies rather than internal qualities of districts or states played an important role in the choice of indirect rule. This prevented colonial administrators from selecting areas for indirect rule based on a strict cost-benefit calculus and shows that contingency often dictated the choices of colonial administrators.

While Governor General Lord Dalhousie wanted to annex both princely states into direct rule, contingent circumstances allowed Awadh to be annexed into direct rule but prevented doing so for Hyderabad, which remained under indirect rule. Later the Telangana region of Hyderabad state

---

[1] While this is not a perfect method approximating experimental conditions, it continues to be a popular method in use in comparative politics (see Slater & Ziblatt, "The Enduring Indispensability of the Controlled Comparison").

saw People's War Group (PWG) led Maoist insurgency in the 1980s. If Dalhousie had been able to annex Hyderabad into direct rule as he had wanted to, then the counterfactual outcome would have probably been no Maoist insurgency in the future in the Telangana region.[2]

The reason the British allowed the state of Hyderabad to continue under indirect rule and did not annex it in 1856 had to do with external geopolitical factors that influenced the financial relations between the Nizam of Hyderabad and the British officials, and not to do with the intrinsic qualities of Hyderabad state. Enough evidence exists that the British very much wanted to annex Hyderabad because it had high agricultural productivity and was rich in revenue. Fisher (1991: 400–401) notes that in 1848, Dalhousie threatened the Nizam of Hyderabad that unless he reformed his administration, "the Company would displace him from control over it." Yet for reasons related to financial obligations of the Nizam and British connections with the ruler, the Company did not. It remained under indirect rule, not because the area was unproductive or had bad soil or high tribal rebellion, but because external circumstances prevented the British administrators from annexing it and setting up institutions of direct rule.

This becomes clearer when the fate of Hyderabad is compared with that of Awadh, which was another large state ruled by a Muslim prince that was annexed into direct rule by the British in 1856. The extremely similar qualities of Awadh and Hyderabad in the eyes of the British governor general, and their divergent outcomes in terms of indirect and direct rule, make this a compelling comparative analysis using the Most Similar Systems research design. First, according to Ramusack's (2004) typology of princely states, both Awadh and Hyderabad were successor states to the Mughal Empire, which means their rulers were initially appointed as governors by the empire but later became independent kingdoms by declaring sovereignty from the Mughals. Second, both were Muslim rulers who ruled over Hindu subjects, though Awadh was Shia and Hyderabad was Sunni. Third, both were landlocked and close enough to British centers of political and military power–while Awadh was close to Calcutta, the capital and center of the Bengal Presidency in the east, Hyderabad was close to Madras, the capital of Madras Presidency in the south. Fourth, both had relatively high tax capacities and were rich in terms of crops and other natural resources and similar in size and wealth. Fifth, the East India Company regarded both Awadh and Hyderabad as sources of financial gain and extracted as much revenue in as many different forms as possible from both states.[3] The

---

[2] In Chapter 8, I analyze the spatial variation in the Maoist insurgency in the Telangana region of the erstwhile princely state of Hyderabad.

[3] Both states had to give up their own armies and pay for the maintenance of subsidiary troops for the British on their territories. Awadh had to cede half its territory in 1801 to satisfy these subsidiary payments. Hyderabad had to cede the Northern Circars in 1766, and the cotton-rich area of Berar in 1853 to the British to pay for these subsidiary forces.

Company threatened to annex Hyderabad, as it did Awadh several times. Yet Hyderabad remained under the rule of the Nizam, while the British annexed Awadh in 1856.

Fisher (1991: 389) notes that while for Awadh, the East India Company contracted for massive loans from the ruler at very low interest rates, in contrast, in Hyderabad, the Nizam "borrowed vast sums for his state from private British firms and individuals." The Nizam of Hyderabad developed debts and arrears of payment for the Hyderabad Contingent, which was an armed force the British were to maintain for Hyderabad according to the Subsidiary Alliance Treaty of 1798 (Ramusack 2004: 27). These financial obligations and debts were particularly to a joint stock company called William Palmer and Company, which had some 5,000 stockholders, mostly Europeans in the Company's or British government's service. Also various British officials had provided loans in a personal capacity to the Nizam. Fisher suggests that "Hyderabad's substantial debt to these individuals in their private capacity undoubtedly gave the Ruler influence over them as Company officials" (Fisher 1991: 389). These personal connections and debts reduced the possibility of annexation of Hyderabad by the British, since such action "would kill a goose that laid golden eggs" (Ramusack 2004: 68).

In contrast, the Company owed money to the Nawab of Awadh for the loans taken from him, and annexing Awadh would reduce the financial debt owed to that state. As a result of this "contrasting financial relationships which developed between the Company and each state" (Fisher 1991: 388), Awadh was annexed in 1856 under the reason of 'mis-governance' by Lord Dalhousie, but in spite of "Dalhousie's expressed wish, the Company did not annex Hyderabad" (Fisher 1991: 399). The Nawab of Awadh, "by loaning money to the Company, and placing prominent members of his family, court, and administration under the Resident's protection, compromised their loyalty to his dynasty. The Nizam, by allowing his state to owe money to the Resident and prominent officials of the Company personally, compromised them" (Fisher 1991: 400).

The real reason for the difference in British choice of rule between Hyderabad and Awadh is to be found in the difference in geo-political constraints facing these two otherwise similar states, which in turn influenced the different financial relations between the British and these two states. Awadh was located in North India and did not have many external threats from other Indian rulers. The British in north India already had defeated Bengal and Awadh in the Battle of Buxar in 1764. After the defeat of Awadh in 1764, the British chose to sign a treaty with the Nawab of Awadh rather than annex it into direct rule, because they felt the need for a buffer state against the Marathas and Afghans from the south and west respectively. So from a relatively early period of British expansion in India, Awadh entered a relationship of military and political dependence on the British, and the Nawabs of Awadh were more pliable to British demands for finances, and tolerant of British interference in internal politics of the state.

In contrast, Hyderabad was in South India and faced other strong Indian rival states like the Marathas and Mysore. The task for the British in south India was more difficult when faced with competition from the French till the 1770s and from the Marathas and Tipu Sultan of Mysore, who were powerful threats to the ambition of British expansion. This complicated geopolitical situation meant that the British needed to ally with the Nizam of Hyderabad at different times to counter the French influence or the even stronger threat from Tipu Sultan. It was only when Tipu Sultan was defeated in 1799 and the Marathas were finally defeated in 1819 that the British were strong enough in South India to adopt a more aggressive approach toward Hyderabad. Because of these geopolitical differences between the situations of Awadh and Hyderabad, the Nizam of Hyderabad was able to maintain a more independent political and military trajectory than the Nawab of Awadh for a longer period. The Nizam was more resistant to British interference in internal politics of the state and less willing to provide loans and finances to the British administration (Fisher 1991: 399–400).

Based on this different external geopolitical circumstance, the Nizams of Hyderabad always tried to maintain more autonomy from British influence and prohibited their court officials from having much contact with the British Resident. Fisher (1991: 393) states:

In Awadh, the Ruler provided loans to the Company – albeit reluctantly – and nominated courtiers to receive the interest and protection of the Company. In Hyderabad, the Ruler consistently evidenced hostility towards any links between the Resident and his officials. In light of the Ruler's objections, the Governor-General forbade the issuance of any secret guarantees, although he added that the minister was free to purchase Company bonds and other commercial paper openly, should he choose. Therefore, while the Awadh Resident disbursed some Rs 5,000,000 annually in pensions and remittances to local inhabitants in 1821, the Hyderabad Resident paid out only Rs 4,500.

It was this same overall policy of independence pursued by the Nizam of Hyderabad that led to the Nizam borrowing money and compromising the British, thus preventing the East India Company from allowing Lord Dalhousie to annex Hyderabad into direct rule. In contrast, political dependence led to the Nawabs of Awadh to loan money to the British, which only increased the incentive of the Company to annex Awadh into direct rule. The overall reason for this difference had to do with the very different external geopolitical and geostrategic circumstances of threats and alliances facing these two large Indian states. It is possible to conclude that this particular geopolitical situation, which was external to the princely state of Hyderabad and not based on its internal qualities like chance of tribal rebellion or difficult terrain or poor soil quality, was the determinant of the status of Hyderabad's indirect rule.

2.2   IV-2SLS Analysis to Address Selection Effect

Another way to address the problem of selection of areas by the colonial administrators is an instrument that is correlated with the choice of direct vs. indirect rule but has no direct effect on postcolonial outcomes of insurgency, except its effect through direct/indirect rule institutions. As discussed in Chapter 1, the studies of civil war onset using cross-national datasets tend to suffer from possible endogeneity issues and omitted variable bias (Sambanis & Hegre 2006). Analyzing the long-term causal effects of historical institutions and using an instrument for the choice of such historical institutions can address this problem. Within the econometrics-based literature on civil wars, only a few studies like that of Miguel et al. (2004) deal with the issue of endogeneity of economic variables to the process of civil wars by using an instrumental variable strategy that relies on the effects of weather-induced shocks like the effect of rainfall on income in rural areas and its effects on insurgency. The only econometric analysis of Maoist insurgency in India that uses instrumental variables to deal with the endogeneity of economic variables to civil war process is Gawande et al. (2017), which uses change in rainfall to instrument for changes in natural forest resources, that in turn is supposed to affect livelihood and employment opportunities of tribals and thus patterns of Maoist recruitment in India.

For the purpose of the all-India econometric analysis presented in this chapter, I need instruments for the two main possibly endogenous measures of indirect rule – *princely state* and *zamindari* land tenure. Studies like Miguel et al. (2004) in the context of Africa and Gawande et al. (2017) as well as Bhavnani and Lacina (2015) in the Indian context have exploited rainfall variation as an instrument for factors which lead to conflict. However, Dunning (2008) and other studies have criticized the use of rainfall as an instrument since this would apply only to countries where income is heavily dependent on agriculture and crops; the Indian Maoist-affected states have other channels of rural income for poor tribals and *Dalits*.[4] Another possible issue is that rainfall variation could directly affect counterinsurgency as well as Maoist strategy in some states in India like Chhattisgarh, and so the instrument is directly related to the dependent variable of conflict, and the exclusion restriction is possibly violated.

Instead of using weather-induced shocks as an instrument for institutions that finally lead to conflict, I delve deeper into history to develop an instrument for the choice of indirect rule based on historical contingencies that throw up natural experiment-like situations and randomly prevent the British from being selective in their choice of indirect rule. The comparative case study analysis of Hyderabad and Awadh princely states revealed that external geostrategic factors often played a big role in the strategic choices by the British of

---

[4] Dunning, "Model Specification in Instrumental-Variables Regression."

whether or not they could annex into direct rule. Following up on this logic, I try to look for factors exogenous to the qualities of districts that forced the British to choose the type of rule, without in any way being related to pre-colonial qualities of districts.

Instrument for Zamindari *Landlord Tenure (Indirect Revenue Collection)*

I use the instrument for *zamindari* land tenure developed in the paper by Banerjee and Iyer (2005), where they estimate the effects of colonial land tenure systems on postcolonial agricultural productivity and development outcomes in India. They use the fact that between 1820 and 1856, certain British policy makers and intellectuals like Munro and Elphinstone were influenced by ideological trends in Europe and in their turn influenced the choice of land tenure systems in India based on their personal ideological convictions. According to Banerjee and Iyer (2005), these British policy makers were convinced that the village-based *ryotwari* land tenure system, which tried to collect land revenue directly from the *ryots* or peasants, was superior and more equitable than the existing *zamindari* or landlord-based tenure system. Under their influence, this new individual cultivator-based *ryotwari* tenure system was initially applied to Madras Presidency in 1819. Following this, between 1820 and 1856, the older *zamindari* land tenure was no longer imposed; instead, almost all provinces annexed in this period and brought under direct rule had the individual cultivator-based *ryotwari* or the village-based *mahalwari* tenure system implemented. Since the choice of land tenure in this period was influenced by European intellectual sway on British policy makers, and exogenous to the local characteristics of the Indian provinces/districts, a time period dummy for 1820–56 is used as an instrument for the choice of land tenure systems by the British in India by Banerjee and Iyer (2005). I use this instrument for the *zamindari* land tenure measure of indirect rule/revenue collection from this widely cited paper. For more details see Banerjee and Iyer (2005: 1204–6), and Online Appendix A for this chapter.

Problem with Existing Instrument for Indirect Rule through Princely States

In a study of the impact of indirect rule through princely states on economic development at the all-India district level, Iyer (2010: 693) suggests a high level of selection by the British. To deal with the issue of selection, Iyer (2010) develops an instrument that exploits the fact that random deaths of certain Indian rulers led their princely states to be annexed by Lord Dalhousie (1848–56) using the policy of Doctrine of Lapse. Under this controversial policy, the kingdom of any Indian ruler who died without a male heir would lapse into British direct rule.

However, closer analysis reveals potential problems with this instrument, as it does not cover the entire time period of British annexation from 1757 to 1856 but only for the 1847 to 1856 period for a truncated sample, which casts some doubt on the validity of the IV-2SLS results in Iyer (2010). The Doctrine of Lapse policy of Lord Dalhousie occurred only in the 1847 to 1856 period, and so Iyer (2010) leaves all districts annexed between 1757 and 1846 out of the IV-2SLS analysis, thus reducing the sample size as compared with her OLS analysis. While this is not necessarily a problem when using princely states to explain developmental outcomes, which is the focus of the Iyer (2010) paper, it is a more serious problem when explaining *Maoist control* as the dependent variable: the entire northern epicenter of the insurgency in Bihar/Bengal/Jharkhand was annexed into direct rule after the Battle of Buxar in 1764 and is left out of the IV-2SLS sample, so the IV-2SLS sample in Iyer (2010) does not address selection issues for large chunks of territories in India that were later affected by Maoist insurgency.

To overcome the problem with the instrument in Iyer (2010), I develop a new instrument for the choice of direct or indirect rule by the British, which makes use of the idea that during onset of major European wars, budget constraints and also increasing threat perceptions from Russia and France were exogenous factors influencing British decisions to sign treaties of indirect rule within India. This instrument is for the much longer time period from 1764 to 1857 and thus covers the timing of selection into direct or indirect rule of most districts that are today part of the Maoist insurgency zone.

New Instrument for Indirect Rule through Princely States

For princely state, I develop a new instrument, based on external geostrategic imperatives like wars in Europe that prevent the British from being selective in their choice of type of rule to use in India at certain points of time. Historical contingencies and geostrategic necessities and financial constraints often influenced the decisions of British officers to either fight a war and annex the area into direct rule or sign a treaty of indirect rule, rather than the revenue potential or governability of a territory. An example of this is the policy of *ring fence* from 1765 to 1813 (Lee-Warner 1910), during which the British East India Company preferred signing treaties with Indian rulers to create a buffer ring around the territories it already controlled.[5] While such internal geostrategic factors could still be considered endogenous to competition within India, external factors like warfare between Britain and other Great Powers like France and Russia in the eighteenth and nineteenth centuries can be treated as exogenous determinants of signing treaties with and annexations of Indian states, and hence an instrument for the *princely state* variable.

There is a twofold logic behind the instrument. First, during the time periods of major wars in Europe that involved Britain like the Napoleonic

---

[5] Ramusack, *The Indian Princes and Their States,* p. 65, notes that this policy started when Robert Clive, after defeating Awadh in 1765 did not annex it, in spite of its high agricultural potential, because he wanted it as a buffer territory between the British province of Bengal and the Maratha threat from the west.

Wars (1792–1815), the resources available to the British Empire were constrained, and this influenced British ability to fight wars of annexation in India. Second, during these European wars, the British also perceived threats from France and Russia to frontier regions in India. Such resource constraints and perceived threats led the British administrators to sign treaties of indirect rule with Indian rulers in frontier areas contiguous to British territories, at the onset of major European Great Power wars. Since the location of the Indian states near the frontiers of British rule at the start of a major European war was random and not related to the possibility of leftist rebellion in the future, it can be used as an instrument. There is some precedence for the use of warfare as an instrument; for example, Dincecco and Prado (2012) look at the effects of war casualties as an instrument for fiscal capacity and its effects on economic growth.

Budget Constraints: Various historical documents show evidence that during these periods of war in Europe, there was pressure on military and economic resources available for use in the colonies including India, and so the British would prefer to sign treaties and bring geostrategically important states on the frontiers of British direct rule areas into indirect rule as buffer states in India, rather than fight wars of annexation.

For example, Lyall (1910: 200–202) recounts the financial constraints during the American revolutionary war period (1775–83), when Britain found it difficult to annex new territories in India:

> In 1781 England, without an ally, and with great odds against her, was confronted by all the great naval powers of Europe, France, Spain and Holland, and by the North American colonies. ... It is no wonder that during such a struggle, and for some time afterwards, our territorial landmarks in India were stationary; since our resources in men and money barely sufficed to preserve Madras and Bombay from destruction.[6]

This period of the American Revolution coincided with the *ring fence* policy of the East India company (Lee-Warner 1910) in India during which the East India Company signed treaties of indirect rule with Indian states to create buffer zones around areas it controlled in Bengal. Looking at data on annexations and treaties signed in this time period of 1772–85, which was under the governor generalship of Lord Hastings/Moira, there was only one state that entered direct rule through ceding (not by annexation): in 1775, Nawab of Awadh ceded seven districts. The core region of Awadh had been handed back to the Nawab by treaty following his defeat in the Battle of Buxar in 1764. Another six states that signed treaties of indirect rule were Kuch Behar (1773), Bhutan (1774), Dholpur (1779), Gwalior (1781), Nagpore and Berar (1781).[7]

---

[6] Lyall, *The Rise and Expansion of the British Dominion in India*, pp. 200–202.
[7] Data on treaties signed taken from Lee-Warner, *The Native States of India*, pp. 53–57, and data on states that entered direct rule through annexation, ceding, lapse, and so on are taken from Iyer, "Direct versus Indirect Colonial Rule in India," and Banerjee and Iyer, "History, Institutions and

Similarly, during the French Revolution and Napoleonic Wars (1793–1815), the British had to devote considerable materials and finances to their naval campaigns to contain Napoleon's territorial ambitions, which could have affected their financial ability to annex territories in India. For the later period of the French Revolution from 1797 to 1800 when Tipu Sultan of Mysore was finally defeated in the third battle of Seringapatnam, Kohli mentions, "The Company's and King's forces in India depended for supplies of arms and other military stores almost entirely on imports from England. During the time of war, however, this mode of supply did not always prove to be adequate or satisfactory."[8] This indicates continuing constraints of military and financial supplies during this period of French revolutionary wars before and under Napoleon. For a list of Great Power wars involving Britain during the period of 1765–1858, see Online Appendix B for this chapter, where I also provide more qualitative evidence of financial constraints during the Napoleonic wars.

Perceived External Threats: There is a second reason why the British would try to sign treaties of indirect rule with Indian states at the frontiers of British direct rule. During these time periods of external wars in Europe, the British occasionally perceived external security threats from their European rivals to territories within India that were contiguous to provinces under direct British rule. Examples of this include the British fear in the 1790s of an alliance between Tipu Sultan, the ruler of Mysore, and Napoleon, during the initial years of the Napoleonic Wars. This fear became most acute during Napoleon's campaign in Egypt in 1798, at the same time as the War of the Second Coalition (1798–1801) between France and other European powers, following which Napoleon planned to invade India (Lyall 1910: 236). Tipu Sultan was hoping that Napoleon would win in Egypt and then come toward India. But Napoleon's navy was defeated in the Battle of the Nile by Admiral Nelson on August 1, 1798, and so Napoleon could not invade India to assist Tipu Sultan. Soon after, the British in alliance with Hyderabad and the Marathas in the Fourth War against Mysore (1798–99) defeated Tipu Sultan in 1799; the British then signed a treaty with Mysore bringing it under British indirect rule.[9] The decision to defeat Mysore and then keep it as indirect rule in 1799 was prompted by British fears of French interference in India. The fact that Mysore was an independent princely state when India became independent in 1947 was for reasons exogenous to the quality of the districts within it.

Another example would be perceived threats from Russia during the War of the Fourth Coalition (1806–7), especially after Napoleon defeated Russia and

Economic Performance," who extracted this data from Baden-Powell, *The Land-Systems of British India.*
[8] Kohli, *Fort William-India House Correspondence (Military Series), Vol. XXI: 1797–1800*, p. xxi.
[9] See Lee-Warner, *Native States of India*, pp. 78–80.

Prussia and signed the Treaty of Tilsit in 1807, which allied France with Russia against Britain and Sweden. This alliance between Russia and France became a source of concern for the British policy makers in India, since it allowed a land route through central Asia to directly threaten Britain's colonies in India, especially through the northwestern border states of Punjab, Sind, and Afghanistan.[10] Since the British had annexed large parts of Awadh by this time, the natural frontier of British territories in India was now Punjab and Lahore. This caused the British to make a Treaty of Alliance with Ranjit Singh, the ruler of Punjab, in 1809, to create a buffer zone, for which purpose the governor general Lord Minto had sent Charles Metcalfe to negotiate.[11] Thus, external wars in Europe and the imperialist ambitions of Napoleon and Russia influenced the patterns of treaty making with Indian states contiguous to British direct rule.

Online Appendix C provides more detailed qualitative evidence of the effect of Britain's wars against European Great Powers on British administrators' decision making regarding annexing or signing treaties with princely states in India due to perceived security threats from these foreign European powers. For a detailed table with a list of different governors general and different time periods of European war, a list of states annexed into direct rule, and states with which treaties of indirect rule were signed in each time period, see Online Appendix D. This table shows how conquest varied by whether the governor general was annexationist or pacifist, but also whether there was major European war in this period.

To summarize, during these periods of European wars, those Indian native states that were contiguous to British direct rule territories had higher chances of getting treaties of indirect rule. The timing of war in Europe was exogenous to politics in India, and the location of these particular Indian states near the frontiers of British rule was random and not related to the possibility of leftist rebellion in the future. Thus, the geostrategic location of Indian states on frontiers of British direct rule, at the onset of major wars between Britain and other European Great Powers in the eighteenth to nineteenth centuries, can be used as an instrument for choice of indirect rule.

Exclusion Restriction: Wars between European great powers were driven by balance of power politics and the need for resources and prestige. They were orthogonal or exogenous to the qualities of territories in India, in terms of their governability and revenue potential. The only possible effect such European wars have on the potential of future leftist rebellion in India is through the choice of colonial direct or indirect rule of territories in India. However, a counterargument could be that the need to fight wars and control territory in

---

[10] See Lyall, *The Rise and Expansion of the British Dominion in India*, pp. 273–79, and Lee-Warner, *Native States of India*, p. 88.

[11] Lepel Griffin, *Ranjit Singh and the Sikh Barrier between Our Growing Empire and Central Asia*, pp. 175–81, for description of the negotiations between Ranjit Singh and Metcalfe.

India, the "jewel in the crown of the British Empire," affected the decisions and resources available to the British to fight against their European rivals. But European competition was a greater threat to the national sovereignty of England, especially during the time period of the Napoleonic Wars, and it was only British naval supremacy that prevented Napoleon from invading Egypt and even Britain.[12] So the first consideration when deciding how many military resources to devote to India and other colonial areas was the defense and security of the home country. The imperative to conquer territories within India came second and did not really affect Britain's decisions in Europe.

Coding Procedure and Data Sources: The instrument is coded as a dummy variable that is given a value of 1 for those districts in the all-India dataset that were in the frontier region and contiguous to the outer bounds of British direct ruled areas at the onset of a major European war involving Britain and other Great Powers, between 1765 and 1858. This is coded at three slices of time at the onset of the three major periods of war – American Revolution (1775–83), Napoleonic Wars (1804–15), First Anglo Afghan War (1837–42) – and also combined to form the main instrument, called *Instru Euro_War Frontiers (1765–1858)*. For detailed coding procedure and data sources, see Online Appendix E, and for a list of Great Power wars involving Britain during the period of 1765–1858, see Appendix B.

Relevant Time Period for Coding Instrument: The British won the Battle of Plassey in 1757, which led to British control over a large amount of territory within India for the first time. This started a period of British annexation of other Indian states into direct rule. The British continued annexing territories in different ways till 1857, when the Indian Mutiny occurred, following which the British territories in India were taken over from the East India Company by the British Crown, and the policy of annexation was abandoned in 1858. So, 1757 to 1858 is the period of time when the British annexed territories in India, and this is the relevant time frame for analyzing the effect of European Great Power wars on British choice of direct vs. indirect rule in India.

Even though the British annexed their first large territory in India in 1757, the period more relevant for the coding of this instrument is 1765 to 1858. The reason for this coding decision is that the logic of the instrument is not valid for the Seven Years' War in Europe (1756–63), which coincided with the Third Carnatic War in India (1757–63), leading to annexations of Bengal and Northern Circars and signing of a treaty of indirect rule with Awadh in 1765.[13] There was an element of British-French competition within India in the Third Carnatic War for good territories since the French were still strong

---

[12] See Knight, *Britain against Napoleon: The Organization of Victory, 1793–1815*, and Hall, *British Strategy in the Napoleonic War, 1803–15*.

[13] The Seven Years' War was the first "world war" involving competition between Britain and France and was fought in different parts of the world, as well as in India where the British and French fought the Third Carnatic War.

and not yet defeated by the British in India. It was during the Third Carnatic War that the British were able to eliminate the French as serious contenders for power in India.

While there was a major European power still competing with the British for territories within India, the effect of European Great Power wars cannot be considered fully exogenous to the British choice of direct vs. indirect rule inside India. Hence it is best to analyze the effect of European Great Power wars on British decision making in the post-1765 period when the British became the sole European colonial power in India. The ending date of 1858 following the Indian Mutiny in 1857 is relevant, since the British Crown stopped annexation from 1858.

IV-2SLS Regression Results and Discussion
In Tables 6.2 and 6.3, I replicate the OLS models in Table 5.3 that use pre-colonial controls, but this time using IV-2SLS strategy. I use the Banerjee and Iyer (2005) instrument for the *zamindari* land tenure (*Instru LandTenure 1820–1850*) in all models. I instrument for *princely state* using *Instru Euro_War Frontiers (1765–1858)* in Table 6.3, which combines the three periods. I use the individual periods of 1765–1802, 1804–15, and 1837–58 for the version of the instrument that captures these smaller slices of time called *Instru Euro Wars (Three Periods)* in Table 6.2.[14]

Before doing the second stage of the IV2SLS, I present the first stage of the IV-2SLS.

First stage results: The results of the first stage are presented in Table 6.1. The first stage regression for the IV strategy is:

$$princely\ state_i = \alpha + \beta\ instru\_EuropeanWar\_frontiers\ (1765\text{--}1858\ or\ 3\ periods)_{i} + \gamma\ instru\_landtenure1820\text{-}1850_i + \theta\ X_i + \varepsilon_i$$

$$landlord\ tenure_i = \alpha + \beta\ instru\_EuropeanWar\_frontiers\ (1765\text{--}1858\ or\ 3\ periods)_{i} + \gamma\ instru\_landtenure1820\text{-}1850_i + \theta\ X_i + \varepsilon_i,$$

where *princely state$_i$*, *landlord tenure$_i$*, and X_i stand for the same variables as in the OLS models in Table 5.3.

In Table 6.1, I present the first stage results of Model 5 from both the *Instru Euro Wars (Three Periods)* from Table 6.2 and the combined *instru_EuropeanWar_frontiers1765–1858* from Table 6.3. For Model 5 from Table 6.3, the first stage relationship between the *instru_EuropeanWar_frontiers1765–1858* and *princely state* is strongly positive and statistically significant at the 99 percent confidence interval level. This implies that districts in India that were ever frontiers of British rule at the onset of a major European Great Power war between 1765 and 1858 tended to have been signed into indirect rule by the British. Also, the first stage

---

[14] The three measures of frontiers individually are called *Instru Euro_War Frontiers (1765–1802)*, *Instru Euro_War Frontiers (1804–1815)*, and *Instru Euro_War Frontiers (1837–58)*.

TABLE 6.1 *First stage of IV-2SLS estimates of impact of colonial institutions on Maoist rebellion*
Dependent variable: Indirect colonial British rule (princely state or landlord tenure)
First Stage of Model 5 from Tables 6.2 and 6.3

	Model 5 (Instru Euro Wars 1765–1858) – DV Princely State	Model 5 (Instru Euro Wars 1765–1858) – DV Landlord Tenure	Model 5 (Instru 3 time periods) – DV Princely State	Model 5 (Instru 3 time periods) – DV Landlord Tenure
Forest Cover	−0.00234 (0.167)	−0.000964 (0.580)	−0.00486*** (0.002)	−0.000595 (0.669)
Altitude	−0.000119 (0.371)	−0.000102* (0.080)	−0.000538*** (0.000)	0.000127 (0.364)
Alluvial Soil	−0.0769 (0.238)	−0.172*** (0.002)	0.0232 (0.635)	−0.00737 (0.893)
Black Soil	0.0397 (0.570)	−0.283*** (0.000)	0.0508 (0.427)	−0.0521 (0.402)
Red Soil	−0.0575 (0.506)	0.0342 (0.645)	0.0701 (0.274)	0.0790 (0.251)
Barren & Rocky	3.542 (0.100)	−0.272 (0.882)	−0.0606 (0.961)	−1.656 (0.239)
Pre-Colonial (Mughal) Agrarian Rebellion	−0.0743 (0.291)	0.0161 (0.809)	−0.129** (0.024)	−0.000277 (0.996)
Instru Euro_War Frontiers (1765–1858)	0.480*** (0.000)	0.0645 (0.224)		
Instru LandTenure (1820–50)	−0.140 (0.107)	−0.385*** (0.000)	−0.175** (0.033)	−0.142* (0.085)
Instru Euro War Frontier (1765–1802)			−0.136* (0.054)	0.214*** (0.004)
Instru Euro War Frontier (1804–1815)			0.172** (0.029)	0.00575 (0.951)
Instru Euro War Frontier (1837–58)			0.416*** (0.000)	−0.0504 (0.604)
Constant	0.300*** (0.000)	0.678*** (0.000)		
Observations	232	232	232	232
Adjusted R^2	0.246	0.163	0.283	−0.022

TABLE 6.1 (*continued*)

	Model 5 (Instru Euro Wars 1765–1858) – DV Princely State	Model 5 (Instru Euro Wars 1765–1858) – DV Landlord Tenure	Model 5 (Instru 3 time periods) – DV Princely State	Model 5 (Instru 3 time periods) – DV Landlord Tenure
Weak Instrument Diagnosis:				
Angrist Pischke F statistic	58.58	46.51	29.63	7.43
Angrist Pischke p value	(0.0000)	(0.0000)	(0.0000)	(0.0001)
Kleibergen-Paap Wald statistic	5.00		5.413	

P-values in parentheses. * p < 0.10, ** p < 0.05, *** p < 0.01
All models include Robust Standard Errors.

relationship between *instru_landtenure1820–1850* and *landlord tenure* is negative and statistically significant at the 99 percent confidence level, which implies that most of the districts were assigned non-landlord type (either *ryotwari* or *mahalwari*) land tenure by the British during the period of 1820–50, because of ideological convictions of British policy makers in India, as expected by Banerjee and Iyer (2005).

For Model 5 from Table 6.2, the first stage relationship between *instru_landtenure1820–1850* and *landlord tenure* is also negative and statistically significant at the 90 percent confidence level. However, the first stage relationship between the *Instru Euro Wars (Three Periods)* and *princely state* is more nuanced. While *Instru Euro War Frontier (1765–1802)* has a negative correlation with *princely state*, *Instru Euro War Frontier (1804–1815)* and *Instru Euro War Frontier (1837–1858)* have the expected positive and significant correlation with *princely state*. This may imply that my assumption that the British colonizers tend to sign treaties of indirect rule on bordering districts/states is more valid for the later periods of Napoleonic Wars and the competition with Russia in central Asia than the early period.

Bound, Jaeger, and Baker (1995) show how IV-2SLS estimates may be somewhat biased in the same direction as OLS estimates in finite samples if there is weak correlation in the first stage between the instrument and the endogenous independent variables. In Table 6.1, the Angrist-Pischke multivariate F test of excluded instruments for first stage regressions for Table 6.2, model 5 is 58.58 (p-value of 0.000) for *princely state*, and 46.51 (p-value of

0.000) for *landlord tenure (p_landlord)*, which is larger than 10, the usual F statistic value required to suggest that instruments are sufficiently strong. The Angrist-Pischke F test values are similarly 29.63 for *princely state* and 7.43 for *landlord tenure* for Table 6.3, model 5.[15] So, it is possible to reject the null hypothesis of no correlation between instrument and endogenous regressors at the 95 percent confidence level, and it implies the instruments are not weak.[16]

Second Stage: The second stage regression for the IV strategy estimates the impact of the two measures of indirect rule – *princely state* and *landlord tenure* – on *Maoist control*:

$$Y_i = a + b \text{ } princely \text{ } state_i + c \text{ } landlord \text{ } tenure_i + d \text{ } X_i + u_i,$$

where Y_i is the dependent variable of *Maoist control* for district *i*. The two endogenous independent variables are *princely state$_i$* and *landlord tenure$_i$*, measured for district *i*, and X_i stands for the same set of district characteristics controlled for as in OLS, and u_i represents the error term.

The second stage IV-2SLS regression results are presented in Tables 6.2 and 6.3, which show the IV-2SLS effects of colonial institutions with only pre-colonial controls and do not include postcolonial controls. They are similar to the model specification in Table 5.3 using OLS. This makes it possible to interpret the effect of *princely* and *p_landlord* even after controlling for pre-colonial terrain, soil quality and conflict-proneness. Models 1 to 5 in Table 6.2 include *instru_landtenure1820–1850* as an instrument for *p_landlord* and include three separate time periods of *instru_EuropeanWar_ frontiers* as instrument for *princely state* to allow over-identification tests. Table 6.3 has the same model specifications as Table 6.2, except that I use *instru_EuropeanWar_ frontiers (1765–1858)* as the instrument for *princely state*.

State fixed effects are included, and standard errors are robust to heteroskedasticity, though the results do not include standard errors robust to clustering by state.[17]

---

[15] According to Angrist and Pischke, *Mostly Harmless Econometrics*, in a model with multiple endogenous regressors and multiple instruments, the overall equation F test statistic is not as useful. Since my models include more than one instrument, the Angrist Pischke F test is better. I report the Angrist-Pischke multivariate F-test as described in Angrist and Pischke and as reported by the user-written *xtivreg2* command in Baum, Schaffer, and Stillman, "*ivreg2*: Stata Module for Extended Instrumental Variables."

[16] See Stock, Wright, and Yogo, "A Survey of Weak Instruments," and Baum et al., "*ivreg2*: Stata Module for Extended Instrumental Variables" for detailed discussion about weak instruments. The results are generated using the *ivreg2* command developed by Baum et al.

[17] Since there are only fifteen states, the baseline specifications in Tables 6.2 and 6.3 do not report standard errors clustered by state, since there may not be enough clusters to produce accurate standard errors. Estimating identical specifications with clustered standard errors by state generates qualitatively similar results with the *princely state* coefficient significant at the 0.10 error level.

TABLE 6.2 *IV-2SLS estimates of impact of colonial institutions on Maoist rebellion: Including only pre-colonial factors as controls*
Dependent variable: *Maoist control* (MHA measure – SRE scheme 2000–3)

	Model 1 – IV-2SLS Instru Euro Wars (Three Periods)	Model 2 – IV-2SLS Instru Euro Wars (Three Periods)	Model 3 – IV-2SLS Instru Euro Wars (Three Periods)	Model 4 – IV-2SLS Instru Euro Wars (Three Periods)	Model 5 – IV-2SLS Instru Euro Wars (Three Periods)
Princely State	0.286***	0.260***	0.298***	0.271***	0.264***
	(0.001)	(0.008)	(0.004)	(0.004)	(0.004)
Landlord Tenure	0.493***	0.792***	0.839***	0.722***	0.701***
	(0.002)	(0.002)	(0.001)	(0.002)	(0.002)
Forest Cover		0.00569***		0.00533***	0.00532***
		(0.000)		(0.001)	(0.001)
Altitude		0.0000689		-0.0000215	0.00000571
		(0.530)		(0.872)	(0.997)
Alluvial Soil			0.0495	-0.0378	-0.0455
			(0.385)	(0.480)	(0.388)
Black Soil			0.102	0.0615	0.0566
			(0.102)	(0.265)	(0.305)
Red Soil			0.118	0.115	0.0998
			(0.180)	(0.277)	(0.353)
Barren & Rocky			1.229	1.258	1.141
			(0.279)	(0.280)	(0.316)
Pre-Colonial (Mughal) Agrarian Rebellion					0.0678
					(0.179)
Observations	355	240	305	232	232

(continued)

TABLE 6.2 (*continued*)

	Model 1 – IV-2SLS Instru Euro Wars (Three Periods)	Model 2 – IV-2SLS Instru Euro Wars (Three Periods)	Model 3 – IV-2SLS Instru Euro Wars (Three Periods)	Model 4 – IV-2SLS Instru Euro Wars (Three Periods)	Model 5 – IV-2SLS Instru Euro Wars (Three Periods)
R^2	-0.205	-0.495	-0.546	-0.339	-0.292
Adjusted R^2	-0.269	-0.624	-0.660	-0.486	-0.441
Endogeneity & Overidentification Test Diagnosis:					
No. of Instruments	4	4	4	4	4
Kleibergen-Paap Wald	3.916	6.17	5.039	5.465	5.413
Hansen's J statistic	11.230	3.237	5.512	3.162	3.596
Hansen's J (p-value)	(0.0036)	(0.1982)	(0.0636)	(0.2058)	(0.1657)
Anderson-Rubin	6.76	5.90	7.67	5.57	5.49
Anderson-Rubin (p-value)	(0.000)	(0.0002)	(0.0000)	(0.0003)	(0.0003)

Note: P-values in parentheses.
* p < 0.10, ** p < 0.05, *** p < 0.01
All models include State Fixed Effects and Robust Standard Errors.

TABLE 6.3 *IV-2SLS estimates of impact of colonial institutions on Maoist rebellion: Including only pre-colonial factors as controls*
Dependent variable: Maoist control (MHA measure – SRE scheme 2000–3)

	Model 1 – IV-2SLS Instru Euro Wars (1765–1858)	Model 2 – IV-2SLS Instru Euro Wars (1765–1858)	Model 3 – IV-2SLS Instru Euro Wars (1765–1858)	Model 4 – IV-2SLS Instru Euro Wars (1765–1858)	Model 5 – IV-2SLS Instru Euro Wars (1765–1858)
Princely State	0.196*** (0.008)	0.168** (0.026)	0.223*** (0.008)	0.210*** (0.008)	0.209*** (0.008)
Landlord Tenure	0.133*** (0.001)	0.187*** (0.005)	0.161** (0.013)	0.159* (0.056)	0.151* (0.076)
Forest Cover		0.00430*** (0.001)		0.00392*** (0.004)	0.00403*** (0.004)
Altitude		-0.0000181 (0.566)		-0.0000184 (0.675)	-0.0000182 (0.681)
Alluvial Soil			-0.00518 (0.896)	-0.0244 (0.564)	-0.0273 (0.528)
Black Soil			0.0481 (0.370)	0.0453 (0.430)	0.0426 (0.463)
Red Soil			0.136** (0.037)	0.118 (0.115)	0.117 (0.118)
Barren & Rocky			-1.115 (0.204)	-0.798 (0.399)	-0.809 (0.399)
Pre-Colonial (Mughal) Agrarian Rebellion					0.0270 (0.586)
Constant	-0.0454** (0.013)	-0.116** (0.016)	-0.0914* (0.067)	-0.122* (0.094)	-0.122* (0.091)

(continued)

TABLE 6.3 (continued)

	Model 1 – IV-2SLS Instru Euro Wars (1765–1858)	Model 2 – IV-2SLS Instru Euro Wars (1765–1858)	Model 3 – IV-2SLS Instru Euro Wars (1765–1858)	Model 4 – IV-2SLS Instru Euro Wars (1765–1858)	Model 5 – IV-2SLS Instru Euro Wars (1765–1858)
Observations	355	240	305	232	232
R^2	-0.031	0.043	-0.022	0.048	0.052
Adjusted R^2	-0.037	0.027	-0.042	0.014	0.013
Endogeneity & *Overidentification Test* *Diagnosis:*					
No. of Instruments	2	2	2	2	2
Kleibergen-Paap Wald	43.784	25.112	27.850	17.523	17.298
Hansen's J statistic	†	†	†	†	†
Hansen's J (p-value)	†	†	†	†	†
Anderson-Rubin	13.54	7.40	9.86	6.81	6.91
Anderson-Rubin (p-value)	(0.0000)	(0.0008)	(0.0001)	(0.0013)	(0.0012)

Note: P-values in parentheses. * p < 0.10, ** p < 0.05, *** p < 0.01

All models include Robust Standard Errors, but no state fixed effects, since state fixed effects prevent us from estimating the effects of landlord tenure when used with combined instrument for this specification. This is because landlord tenure has an effect on development and rebellion due to inter state differences and so state FE prevents us from estimating that.

† Hansen J Statistic (over-identification test of all instruments) is 0.000, since the equation is exactly identified because the number of endogenous regressors equals the number of instruments.

In Table 6.2, Model 1, which has only the two measures of *indirect rule,* the instrumental variable estimate yields a point estimate of 0.286 on *princely state* that is significant at the 99 percent confidence level, and 0.493 on *landlord tenure* that is significant at the 99 percent confidence level. These coefficients are larger than the OLS estimates in Model 1 of Table 5.3. This is common in many studies using IV-2SLS and could imply that *negative attenuation bias* is more relevant than positive bias due to omitted variable.[18] The results in Table 6.2, Model 1, show the causal effect of colonial indirect rule without any controls and suggest that a district that was previously exposed to indirect rule as *princely state* increases the probability of Maoist insurgency by 28.6 percentage points, and a district formerly exposed to some form of indirect revenue collection has 49.3 percentage points higher chance of insurgency. The results are similar in Models 2 to 5, in which I control for various pre-colonial measures of geography, opportunity, soil quality, and finally pre-colonial agrarian rebellions.

Table 6.3 has the same models except it uses *instru_EuropeanWar_frontiers (1765–1858),* and the results are quite similar. By using an instrument for the historical institutions of indirect rule, addressing selection issues, and controlling for pre-colonial factors, I am able to address the concerns of omitted variable bias and endogeneity that affect the cross-national literature on civil wars.

Diagnostics of the IV-2SLS regressions indicate that the instruments are valid. In case there are more instruments than endogenous regressors, it is possible to perform a Hansen's *J* Test for over-identifying restrictions. This tests whether all instruments are exogenous and satisfy the exclusion restriction, assuming that at least one of the instruments is exogenous, which is a reasonable assumption in this case since Banerjee and Iyer's (2005) instrument for *landlord tenure* is valid.[19] It is possible to report this test statistic for the Models in Table 6.2, since they have more instruments than endogenous regressors. The Hansen J-statistic (Sargan test) for Table 6.2, Model 5, cannot reject the joint null hypothesis that the instruments are valid instruments, that is, uncorrelated with the error term, and that the excluded instruments are correctly excluded from the estimated equation. This provides support for my argument that the instrument for *princely state* is exogenous to my dependent variable.

The Anderson-Rubin (A-R) statistic tests the significance of the endogenous regressors in the structural equation being estimated. The statistic rejects the joint null hypothesis that the coefficients of the endogenous regressors (the two measures of colonial indirect rule) in the structural equation are jointly equal to zero. The tests are equivalent to estimating the reduced form of the equation

[18] Dinecco and Prado, "Warfare, Fiscal Capacity, and Performance," similarly find that the IV-2SLS estimates are larger than the OLS estimates and reach a similar conclusion.

[19] Kurt Schmidheiny, "Short Guides to Microeconometrics: Instrumental Variables," at www .schmidheiny.name/teaching/iv.pdf

(with the full set of instruments as regressors) and testing that the coefficients of the excluded instruments are jointly equal to zero.[20] This statistic is important in assessing the results when instruments are weak. The rejection of the null is perhaps not surprising in this case since frontiers in India at the time of European wars have strong correlations with indirect rule through princely states, and the instruments are not weak.

I also include postcolonial measures of state capacity and inequalities as controls in Table 6.3B in Online Appendix F, and colonial *indirect rule* is still statistically significant. I also analyze the effects of colonial indirect rule on the intermediary mechanisms of state capacity and land inequality, and find that *princely state* and *landlord tenure* have a negative effect on *paved road* (measure of state capacity for counterinsurgency), on *land inequality* (measure of landlord-based extraction), and also on *female literacy*, which are in Table 6.3C in Online Appendix G.

3   ROBUSTNESS TESTS FOR IV-2SLS ANALYSIS

3.1   Alternate Measures of Dependent Variable *Maoist Control*

A possible concern is that I use only one measure of *Maoist control* for 2000–2003 from the Ministry of Home Affairs (MHA) Security Related Expenditures (SRE) scheme. I test for the robustness of these findings by using (1) a continuous measure of SRE (2000–3) using Integrated Action Plan (IAP) measures of most-affected districts; (2) other time periods for the same SRE-based measure for 2005, 2011, and 2016; and (3) alternate measures of *Maoist control* and *Maoist violence* from SATP database. The model specification is the same as in Tables 6.2 and 6.3, Model 3 (IV-2SLS European Wars), which allows Hansen's *J* Test for over-identifying restrictions. The results are presented in Tables 6.4 and 6.5 and show colonial indirect rule measures to be significant for these alternate measures and time periods.[21]

Continuous Measure of the Dependent Variable

While the MHA SRE scheme uses a list of five criteria to measure *Maoist control*, it unfortunately only provides a binary 0–1 measure. The IAP introduced by the Congress government in 2010 to provide development funds to underdeveloped areas was initially started for a smaller number of around thirty-three to thirty-five districts that were supposed to be more severely

---

[20]   See Baum et al., "*ivreg2*: Stata Module for Extended Instrumental Variables" p. 491. The *ivreg2* helpfile in STATA mentions that the null hypothesis tested by the Anderson-Rubin (1949) test is that "the coefficients of the endogenous regressors in the structural equation are jointly equal to zero, and, in addition, that the overidentifying restrictions are valid."

[21]   More detailed discussions of these robustness tests are in Online Appendix H.

TABLE 6.4 IV-2SLS estimates of impact of colonial institutions on Maoist rebellion – using a continuous measure of the MHA (SRE) 2000–2003 measure and different time periods of the MHA (SRE) measure of Maoist control as DV

	Model 1 – IV2SLS Instru Euro Wars (Three Periods) – DV: Maoist control MHA (SRE) 2003 continuous	Model 2 – IV2SLS Instru Euro Wars (Three Periods) – DV: Maoist control MHA (SRE) 2005	Model 3 – IV2SLS Instru Euro Wars (Three Periods) – DV: Maoist control MHA (SRE) 2011	Model 4 – IV2SLS Instru Euro Wars (Three Periods) – DV: Maoist control MHA (SRE) 2016
Princely State	0.423***	0.164*	0.216**	0.238***
	(0.001)	(0.063)	(0.019)	(0.009)
Landlord Tenure	0.983***	0.504**	0.538**	0.503**
	(0.004)	(0.035)	(0.033)	(0.047)
Altitude	−0.00000644	−0.0000370	−0.00000810	0.0000185
	(0.961)	(0.641)	(0.921)	(0.825)
Population Density	−0.000257*	−0.000265***	−0.000356***	−0.000435***
	(0.083)	(0.007)	(0.001)	(0.000)
Scheduled Caste Percentage	0.616	0.338	0.198	0.249
	(0.269)	(0.373)	(0.618)	(0.538)
Scheduled Tribe Percentage	0.656**	0.429**	0.187	0.318*
	(0.040)	(0.026)	(0.290)	(0.092)
Caste Fragmentation	−0.772	−0.169	−0.0545	0.134
	(0.265)	(0.661)	(0.886)	(0.727)
Land Gini	1.212***	0.313	0.380	0.246
	(0.007)	(0.332)	(0.249)	(0.494)
Primary School	0.000220**	0.000138**	0.000115*	0.0000595
	(0.021)	(0.019)	(0.077)	(0.363)

(continued)

TABLE 6.4 (*continued*)

	Model 1 – IV2SLS Instru Euro Wars (Three Periods) – DV: Maoist control MHA (SRE) 2003 continuous	Model 2 – IV2SLS Instru Euro Wars (Three Periods) – DV: Maoist control MHA (SRE) 2005	Model 3 – IV2SLS Instru Euro Wars (Three Periods) – DV: Maoist control MHA (SRE) 2011	Model 4 – IV2SLS Instru Euro Wars (Three Periods) – DV: Maoist control MHA (SRE) 2016
Ethnic Riots	-0.0000946	-0.0000763	-0.0000524	-0.0000616
	(0.401)	(0.344)	(0.521)	(0.465)
Access to Water Tanks	-0.000572***	-0.000371***	-0.000381***	-0.000254**
	(0.000)	(0.000)	(0.000)	(0.015)
Public Health Center	0.00297***	0.00147**	0.00176**	0.00199***
	(0.010)	(0.036)	(0.024)	(0.008)
Electricity	-0.000201**	-0.000106*	-0.0000996*	-0.0000563
	(0.032)	(0.064)	(0.097)	(0.368)
ST% * Electricity	-0.000709	-0.000542**	-0.0000573	-0.000192
	(0.115)	(0.050)	(0.875)	(0.576)
Observations	309	309	309	309
R^2	-0.025	0.093	0.019	-0.003
Adjusted R^2	-0.131	-0.001	-0.083	-0.106

P-values in parentheses
All models include state fixed effects and robust standard errors.
* $p < 0.10$, ** $p < 0.05$, *** $p < 0.01$

TABLE 6.5 *IV-2SLS estimates of impact of colonial institutions on Maoist rebellion – using alternate measures of Maoist control and Maoist violence (SATP data) as dependent variable*

	Model 1 – IV2SLS Instru Euro Wars (Three Periods) – DV: Maoist control SATP 2003	Model 2 – IV2SLS Instru Euro Wars (Three Periods) – DV: Maoist control SATP 2000	Model 3 – IV2SLS Instru Euro Wars (Three Periods) – DV: Maoist violence SATP 2000
Princely State	0.298***	0.256***	1.628**
	(0.004)	(0.002)	(0.012)
Landlord Tenure	0.760***	0.523**	2.668**
	(0.004)	(0.012)	(0.038)
Altitude	0.0000792	0.0000230	0.000693
	(0.429)	(0.766)	(0.146)
Population Density	−0.000112	−0.0000470	−0.0000219
	(0.343)	(0.616)	(0.957)
Scheduled Caste Percentage	0.369	0.356	1.532
	(0.372)	(0.296)	(0.389)
Scheduled Tribe Percentage	0.459**	0.402**	1.319
	(0.039)	(0.047)	(0.117)
Caste Fragmentation	−0.440	−0.709	−3.129
	(0.378)	(0.105)	(0.158)
Land Gini	0.711*	0.616**	2.819**
	(0.054)	(0.027)	(0.043)
Primary School	0.0000576	0.00000354	−0.0000198
	(0.401)	(0.945)	(0.947)
Ethnic Riots	0.0000134	0.0000251	0.000277
	(0.879)	(0.708)	(0.430)

(continued)

TABLE 6.5 (*continued*)

	Model 1 – IV2SLS Instru Euro Wars (Three Periods) – DV: Maoist control SATP 2003	Model 2 – IV2SLS Instru Euro Wars (Three Periods) – DV: Maoist control SATP 2000	Model 3 – IV2SLS Instru Euro Wars (Three Periods) – DV: Maoist violence SATP 2000
Access to Water Tanks	-0.000297***	-0.000254***	-0.000749***
	(0.000)	(0.000)	(0.005)
Public Health Center	0.00216**	0.000979	0.00379
	(0.014)	(0.169)	(0.335)
Electricity	-0.000127*	-0.0000150	-0.000159
	(0.083)	(0.795)	(0.602)
ST% * Electricity	-0.000381	-0.000369	-0.000475
	(0.234)	(0.168)	(0.735)
Observations	309	309	309
R^2	-0.232	-0.231	-0.150
Adjusted R^2	-0.360	-0.358	-0.269

P-values in parentheses
All models include state fixed effects and robust standard errors.
* $p < 0.10$, ** $p < 0.05$, *** $p < 0.01$

affected by Maoist insurgency among the districts then under the SRE scheme.[22] I code these thirty-five focused districts as higher Maoist control or a 2 as compared to the rest of the districts that are coded as 1, and non-affected districts coded as 0, to create a more continuous 0–1–2 measure of Maoist control.[23] The result is presented in Table 6.4, Model 1, and shows that *princely state* and *landlord tenure* are statistically significant predictors of this more continuous measure of Maoist control.

Other Years of Maoist Control Based on MHA Security Related Expenditures Data (2005, 2011, 2016)

The measure of *Maoist control* from SRE counterinsurgency document is for the 2000–2003 period, which satisfies the scope conditions of my theory that colonial institutions can be thought of as constraints on rebel mobilization before they develop organizational capacity to expand. To recount the scope conditions outlined earlier in Chapter 3, my theory based on colonial institutions only explains the initial core areas of the Maoist insurgency and does not claim to explain changing patterns of spatial variation or patterns of violence, since once an insurgency persists, various other factors related to counterinsurgency and rebel strategy start playing a more important role.

However, it is important to check if the results are robust to measures of *Maoist control* once the insurgency expanded after the creation of CPI-Maoist in 2004. I measure *Maoist control* from same SRE scheme documents for 2005, 2011, and 2016 that were downloaded from the MHA website. For the 2016 MHA data on the SRE scheme, see http://mha.nic.in/sites/upload_files/mha/files/NM-SRE-Scheme_160614.pdf. The 2011 data were downloaded earlier in 2012 from http://mha.nic.in/pdfs/nm_pdf1.pdf and are no longer on the MHA website but are presented in Online Appendix I. The 2005 data are available from the SRE documents gathered during fieldwork to measure my dependent variable and are cited earlier in Chapter 5.

The results are presented in Table 6.4, Models 2, 3, and 4. An interesting finding is that the level of statistical significance is reduced for *princely state* in 2005, following the initial expansion of the insurgency, but it is again strongly significant by 2016 when the insurgency contracts to some of its previous core areas in Andhra Pradesh and also expands into princely state areas in Orissa. *Zamindari land tenure* is less statistically significant for 2011 and 2016, which could be because the Maoists concentrate more on tribal areas under former princely states in later periods than in the original landlord areas in Bihar and

---

[22] See Medha Chaturvedi, "Integrated Action Plan in Naxal-Affected Districts: A Critique," IPCS, Article No. 3743, October 31, 2012. www.ipcs.org/article/india/integrated-action-plan-in-naxal -affected-districts-a-critique-3743.html

[23] The 33/35 districts are available in letter no. J-12012/1/2007-RH, Ministry of Rural Development, October 7, 2010. http://iapmis.planningcommission.nic.in/writereaddata/Reports/GuideLines/G_guidelines_flagship.pdf

Andhra Pradesh. The results reflect the fact that the Maoists initially expanded following the 2004 merger of the PWG and MCC to form CPI-Maoist; later following decline in violence and weakening of insurgency, the levels of Maoist control contracted to the initial core areas of indirect rule.

Alternate Measures of the Dependent Variable: Maoist Rebel Control and Maoist Violence

I also develop an alternate measure of *Maoist control* based on events data from the South Asia Terrorism Portal (www.satp.org) for the years 2003 and 2000, to get a media-based measure of which districts had Maoist activity. While Gawande et al. (2017) and Chandra and Garcia-Ponce (2019) have rightly critiqued the SATP dataset for missing data from vernacular newspapers, many studies of the Maoist conflict like Gomes (2015) and Vanden Eynde (2018) use the SATP data, and it is sufficient for the purpose of developing an overall measure of which districts were Maoist affected. The results in Table 6.5, Models 1 and 2, show both *princely state* and *landlord tenure* to be statistically significant.

I use a measure of *Maoist violence* for the year 2000 before the unification of the MCC and the PWG from the www.satp.org dataset. The results in Table 6.5, Model 3, show both measures of indirect rule – *princely state* and *p_landlord* – to have a statistically significant and positive effect on this measure of Maoist violence.[24] This measure of the number of *violent incidents* in a district from the SATP events data from the year 2000 allows comparability of my analysis to most of these other analyses of Maoist insurgency like Gawande et al. (2017), Dasgupta et al. (2017), Chandra and Garcia-Ponce (2019), Vanden Eynde (2018), and Gomes (2015), which use violence as the dependent variable.

4   VARIATION IN TYPES OF PRINCELY STATES

4.1   A Typology of Different Types of Princely States That Explains Subnational Variation in Maoist Insurgency

The IV-2SLS analysis just described addresses the issue of selection bias, and the robustness tests show that the analysis applies even to other measures of Maoist control and other time periods of Maoist insurgency. However, an important issue of measurement of indirect rule remains unresolved.

---

[24] Gawande et al., "Renewable Natural Resource Shocks and Conflict Intensity," use the most comprehensive dataset on Maoist insurgency violence for 2001–2010, since they include vernacular newspaper sources like *Prabhat Khabar*, thus capturing more local newspaper-based incidents than in the www.satp.org data, which uses English newspaper sources. Using the Gawande et al. data for the 2001–2003 period gives similar results.

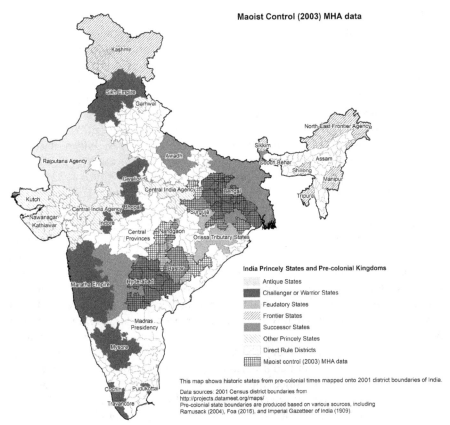

FIGURE 6.1 Types of princely states and pre-colonial kingdoms in India
Source: Boundaries of princely states and pre-colonial empires based on maps from
Ramusack (2004), Foa (2016), *Imperial Gazetteers of India* (1909), and other
historical sources.

In this book, I have so far theorized that there are different types of indirect
rule within India – the more formal type through the various princely states and
the less formal one through *zamindari* land tenure in Bengal, Bihar, in the east.
This takes seriously the suggestion by scholars like Gerring et al. (2011) and
Wilkinson (2017) that the concept of indirect vs. direct rule is not a binary (0–1)
one. Yet, there is further variation between different types of princely states
within India, which is not captured by the 0–1 binary measure used in the
quantitative analysis so far. It is important to take seriously the cautionary
note by Wilkinson (2017) that the existing studies fail to account for the
heterogeneity of indirect rule in India, and to go beyond the binary 0–1
coding of princely states in previous studies like Iyer (2010) and use a more
continuous or categorical measure.

In this section, I present a typology that further differentiates between different types of princely states within the Indian subcontinent, which varied in their level of state capacity and development and land tenure systems. I then use quantitative analysis to show that those types of princely states that had higher state capacity and more equal land tenure systems had lower chance of Maoist insurgency, while other types that had lower levels of state capacity and more land inequality had higher chances of Maoist insurgency.

This typology of princely states builds on the historiography of Barbara Ramusack's (2004) *The Indian Princes and Their States*, which describes different types of princely states at the time of collapse of the Mughal Empire following Emperor Aurangzeb's death in 1707.[25] In this typology, Ramusack (2004) focuses on the pre-colonial qualities of the kingdoms that later became different princely states, especially their relationship with the collapsing Mughal Empire and the increasingly powerful British East India Company.

These different categories according to Ramusack (2004, pp. 13–38) were as follows: (1) *successor states* such as Bengal, Awadh, and Hyderabad, which were originally ruled by governors of the Mughal Empire, who then started their own local kingdoms as the Mughal Empire declined but were unable to resist the emerging British colonial power, thus becoming militarily weak and developing despotic land tenure systems that created conditions for peasant and Maoist rebellions; (2) *antique states* such as the Rajput kingdoms in the west and the Tamil poligars (military chiefs) in the south that were local kingdoms from old times that had limited fiscal and regulatory authority – these states did not see much rebellion since the tribes and castes from these states had a tradition of being part of the central state and bureaucracy; and (3) *warrior* or *conquest states* like Mysore, the Marathas, Travancore, and Bhopal, which challenged the Mughals as well as Europeans by creating centralized bureaucratic regimes, efficient tax collection systems, and armies that could fight and defeat even the European powers like the British and Dutch. These states later had higher state capacity and development that made it difficult for Maoist rebels to succeed.

A fourth category of princely states not discussed in Ramusack (2004) but relevant to explaining low state capacity and exploitation of land revenues leading to tribal and Maoist rebellion included the *tributary* or *feudatory* states in Orissa tributary and Chhattisgarh feudatory state areas in central-eastern India, where there were often Rajput or Maratha princes ruling over indigenous tribal populations. These rulers were relatively weak and protected by the British colonial authorities and caused underdevelopment and land revenue exploitation from their tribal subjects. This later led to the PWG Maoist–led insurgency mobilizing indigenous tribals in these areas.

---

[25] Ramusack, *The Indian Princes and Their States*, The New Cambridge History of India, Volume III.6.

A fifth category of princely states also not discussed in Ramusack (2004) involved the *frontier states* in the northwest and northeast, which are used as buffer states for strategic purposes by the British. Examples would be the Federally Administered Tribal Areas (FATA) in the North West Frontier Province (NWFP) of Pakistan, which experienced the subsequent Taliban insurgency in 2001–2008 (Naseemullah (2014), or the small princely states in India's northeast like Manipur and Tripura or the North East Frontier Agency (NEFA), which experienced different types of secessionist insurgencies post-independence. While not relevant to explain Maoist insurgency, these states did have other types of insurgency in the postcolonial period.

The criterion used to develop the typology is based on (1) the relationship between the princely state and the British colonial masters – in some cases like successor states, princes were subservient to the colonizer and protected by the colonial power thus allowing them to be despotic and use feudalistic and inequitable land revenue systems, while in others like warrior states the princes fought the colonial powers and had to build up military and state capacity and were not inefficient rulers and tended to use more direct land revenue systems; and (2) the co-ethnicity between the rulers of the princely state and their subjects, that is, whether the rulers were of same religion or ethnicity as the subjects as in warrior states like the Marathas and Travancore and thus chances were higher that they would not be despotic, or of different ethnicity as in the feudatory states in Chhattisgarh that had Rajput or Maratha rulers over tribal subjects or successor states like Bengal, Hyderabad, and Awadh that had Muslim rulers over Hindu subjects (Lee 2017).

These differences explain why these warrior or conquest princely states of Travancore and Cochin that later were part of the post-independence state of Kerala and Mysore state that was later part of the post-independence state of Karnataka were different and more developed and progressive than the interior protected tributary/feudatory princely states of Bastar, Kanker, and Surguja that were part of the state of Chhattisgarh, or the successor states of Hyderabad and Bengal that were part of the states of Andhra Pradesh and West Bengal, respectively. This variation in type of princely state explains why there was more development and a more centralized state historically in Travancore and Mysore states that translated into higher levels into the postcolonial period in Kerala and Karnataka. This led to very different patterns of state formation and land inequality in these states, which decreased the chances of success of radical Maoist insurgency later. In contrast, the feudatory states of Bastar/Kanker/Surguja in the Chhattisgarh and Jharkhand areas continued to have weak state capacity and exploitation of land and natural resources by the state that created ideal conditions for successful radical Maoist insurgency since the 1980s. The successor state of Bengal was annexed by the British and became directly ruled but had feudal land tenure systems from the time of its Mughal governors that persisted under the British as *zamindari* land tenure and led to conditions of weaker state capacity and more land inequality that made it ripe for leftist insurgency. Similarly, the successor state of Hyderabad remained indirectly ruled till 1947, but it became militarily weak and subservient to the colonial power and also developed a feudal land tenure system dependent on *jagirdars* and *deshmukhs* from its Mughal era roots that created land inequality and therefore subsequent peasant rebellion. See Figure 6.1 for map of different types of princely states.

4.2   Description of These Types of Princely States

I now describe in more detail these types of princely states and their effects on state capacity and land resource exploitation, and how this either facilitated or prevented future Maoist rebels in their mobilization of lower castes and indigenous tribes.

(1) *Successor States:* According to Ramusack (2004: 24–26), Awadh, Bengal, and Hyderabad were all former Mughal provinces that became successor states of the declining Mughal Empire. These were all initially administered by governors or *subedars* of the Mughal emperor; gradually with the decline of Mughal power following the death of Emperor Aurangzeb in 1707, these former governors established their independence by appointing their own revenue officers, nominating their own successors, and reducing the amount of tribute being sent to the Mughal court in Delhi. Fisher (1991: 377) also mentions that as the Mughal Empire fragmented over the eighteenth century, "imperial governors and hereditary regional powers established *de facto* states out of its constituent parts."

Hyderabad: The princely state of Hyderabad was the most long-lived of the successor states of the Mughal Empire. Asaf Jah I was appointed *subedar* of the Deccan Plateau province in 1713. Having been *wazir* of the empire for some time, he became disgusted with the political infighting in Delhi and returned to the Deccan capital in Aurangabad and appointed his own revenue officers (Ramusack 2004: 25). Following his death in 1748, his son Salabat Jang became the Nizam with the support of the French in 1751. However, his younger brother Nizam Ali Khan replaced him in 1761 with the help of the British, who ruled from 1762 to 1803 and established his capital at Hyderabad city.[26] He signed treaties of *subsidiary alliance* in 1798 with Governor-General Lord Wellesley requiring that Hyderabad disband its foreign troops and maintain a subsidiary force for the British, thus starting the process of subservience to the British (Ramusack 2004: 60–62). His heirs continued the Asaf Jah dynasty but lost the capacity to fight the British and never developed a highly centralized state bureaucracy and tax capacity like Mysore did under Tipu Sultan or the Marathas did under Shivaji's heirs and the Peshwas.

Also, the Nizam of Hyderabad was Muslim while the majority of his subjects were Telugu-speaking Hindus. When Nizam-ul-Mulk formed the Asaf Jahi

---

[26] *Imperial Gazetteer of India*, Hyderabad State, 1909, pp. 15–17.

dynasty in Hyderabad, the land revenue collectors called *deshmukhs* were already powerful from pre-colonial times, and he continued to use them as land revenue collectors and contractors. The *deshmukhs* became exploitative of the peasants and this culminated in an agrarian crisis in Telangana in the mid-nineteenth century and forced the British Resident at Hyderabad to appoint Salar Jung I as the new prime minister to carry out land reforms in 1853.[27] However, the *deshmukhs* continued their exploitative practices that finally led to the Telangana rebellion of 1946, which was a precursor to the Maoist-led rebellion in the same region beginning in 1980.[28] Thus, the pattern of land revenue administration developed under the Nizam's administration was like the feudal landlord-based tenure system that developed under the British in Bengal. It led to despotic extraction and land inequality and grievances among *Dalits* and *Adivasis* that the Maoists were able to mobilize successfully much later.

Awadh: After Hyderabad disengaged from the politics in North India in 1713, Awadh remained the most important and valuable province engaged in the political conflict surrounding the declining Mughal Emperor (Fisher 1991: 377). Sadat Khan was the governor of Awadh in the 1720s, and he appointed his own revenue officers and nominated his son-in-law Safdar Jang as his successor, who later appointed his son Shuja-ud-Daula as heir. In the Battle of Buxar that was fought in 1764, the English East India Company led by Robert Clive defeated the combined forces of Awadh, the Mughal Emperor, and Mir Kasim the deposed Nawab of Bengal (Ramusack 2004: 24). The Nawab of Awadh, Shuja-ud-Daula, was forced to yield territories, but due to the policy of ring fence used by the British in this period, Clive allowed him to continue ruling a smaller kingdom, as a buffer state to protect the British direct ruled areas of Bengal province from the hostile forces of the Marathas and invading Afghans (Fisher 1991: 377–78).

After defeat in the Battle of Buxar in 1764, the Nawab of Awadh recognized the superiority of European military arms and strategy and started recruiting European military advisers. In response, the British forced the Nawab to sign a treaty in 1768 to restrict the size of his army and accept that less than a third could be modernized on a "European model." Another treaty in 1801 further limited the size of the Awadh army and forced the Nawab to cede more territories. The British replaced the Awadh army with its own troops, which would guarantee protection of Awadh from external enemies, and this made the Nawab of Awadh militarily dependent, and no longer a threat (Fisher 1991: 380–81). Unlike the warrior states like Mysore and the Marathas that were able to fight the British for some time, the successor state of Awadh became a militarily weak state that survived by not fighting the British and being

[27] Thirumali, *Against Dora and Nizam*, pp. 22–25.
[28] Reddy, *Economic History of Hyderabad State*, p. 104.

subservient to the colonial power. In 1856, Awadh was finally annexed into direct rule on charges of misadministration by Governor General Lord Dalhousie, and so it no longer remained a princely state, but the effects of the pre-colonial period persisted.

Also, like Hyderabad, Awadh was a "classic Mughal successor state" where a "small elite of Mughal warriors, literati and gentry stood poised over a vast Hindu countryside ruled by petty chieftains of Rajput origin" (Bayly 1988: 90–91). These petty chieftains or landlords were called *taluqdars* and were mostly Rajputs who had migrated there earlier, and they had strong local roots in the villages under their control. Some of these *taluqdars* survived the annexation of Awadh by the British East India Company in 1857 and "became members of a hereditary, privileged and protected landlords class under the British" (Fisher 1987: 4) and formed a landlord-type land tenure system. The taluqdars often abused their power over the peasants by levying excessive taxes called *nazarana* and exploiting them for *begar* or forced labor. All this led to peasant movements in 1917–21 mobilized by the Kisan Sabhas, which opposed the exploitation of the *taluqdars*.[29]

Following independence in 1947, the current state of Uttar Pradesh, which contains the region that used to be Awadh, did not have much Maoist insurgency, except in the eastern districts of Chandauli, Mirzapur, and Sonbhadra, which bordered Bihar. This was because lower-caste parties like the Bahujan Samaj Party (BSP) came to power in the state (Chandra 2004) and prevented Maoists from attracting *Dalits* to their cause. However, this region did have historically created conditions of weak state and land revenue exploitation.

Bengal: The province of Bengal in the east was the bridgehead of the British Empire and the first large territory annexed by the East India Company into direct rule when Robert Clive defeated the Nawab of Bengal, Siraj-ud-Daulah, in the Battle of Plassey in 1757. The defeat of the Nawab of Awadh in the Battle of Buxar in 1764 led to the Company getting the *diwani* rights in Bengal and further strengthened the control of the Company in this rich province.

While Banerjee and Iyer (2005) attribute the *zamindari* land tenure system to the British, these landlords were elites from the pre-colonial Mughal era who were co-opted later by the colonial administrators. In 1704, the Mughal emperor sent Murshid Kuli Khan as governor to Bengal to manage the finances of this rich province. He "consolidated and brought to obedience the great Hindu and Muslim zamindars of Bengal." One of his successors, Nawab Alivardi Khan (1740–56), started conferring revenue grants to dependents and stopped sending revenue to Delhi after Nadir Shah's invasion of Delhi in 1739 and converted Bengal into a successor state (Bayly 1988: 19). To control the

---

[29] Leanne Bennett, "The Origins of the Peasant Agitation in Oudh," MA Thesis, Concordia University, August 1997.

revenue administration, these Mughal governors encouraged the consolidation of about thirty great *zamindaris*, some of whom were long-established Hindu chiefs and others were servants of the court like in Burdwan and Rajshahi (Bayly 1988: 49).

Later when Lord Cornwallis was sent to Bengal in 1786 to reform Bengal's administration and land revenue system, he decided to create a stable "hereditary landed aristocracy" that would allow increased agrarian productivity. He introduced the Permanent Settlement in 1791, whereby *zamindars* or landlords would have to pay a fixed amount of land revenue. This resulted in the demise of many of the older feudal landlords from Mughal times who could not pay these very high revenue rates, and a major redistribution of control of land and emergence of new landlords followed. About thirty new families rose to prominence through purchases of land rights post-1793 (Marshall 1987: 146–47).

This created a system of indirect rule in which the British depended on these *zamindars* to help them with administration as well as land revenue collection (Kohli 2004). The *zamindari* land tenure system resulted in exploitation of peasants and created the conditions for peasant rebellions like the Tebhaga rebellion in the 1940s and the initial Naxalite movement in Naxalbari in West Bengal in 1967–73.

(2) *Warrior or Conquest States:* A second category of princely states described by Ramusack (2004) were the warrior or conquest states like the princely state of Mysore under Tipu Sultan which formed the rump of the current states of Karnataka, Travancore under Martanda Varma which later became part of Kerala, and the core Maratha state ruled by the Peshwa around Poona and Satara on the west coast and also various other Maratha confederacies like the Scindias at Gwalior, the Holkar at Indore, the Gaikwad and Baroda, and the Bhonsle at Nagpur ruling over Gonds of Central India. Other Indian kingdoms that Ramusack (2004) includes in this category of warrior states are the Sikh kingdom that Ranjit Singh built in northwest India that was able to resist British annexation till 1848, and the kingdom of Bhopal that was founded by the Afghan warrior Dost Mohammad Khan (1703–28) and continued by a series of successors including Mamola Begum (1763–80). Bayly (1988: 21–22) also refers to these "great non-Muslim warrior states," especially the Marathas, Sikhs, and Jats, as reflecting popular peasant insurgency against the Indo-Muslim aristocracy of the Mughals.

According to Ramusack (2004: 27), these were states that were "established by warrior groups who contested with an overarching authority to establish new political entities by offering military protection to local populations." Foa (2016: 20–21) mentions that what distinguished these various types of warrior states from the successor states of the Mughal Empire was that they

adopted European military tactics, developed salaried bureaucracies, and engaged in territorial expansion. While former Mughal provinces such as Awadh and Bengal were quick to cede to European suzerainty, challenger regimes did not. The Mysore Empire for example fought four wars against the East India Company between 1767 and 1799, the Marathas fought three wars from 1775 to 1818, and Travancore fought, and defeated, the Dutch East India Company in 1741.

This resulted in the expansion of bureaucratic and tax capacity and resulted in "military fiscalism" and a more direct land tenure system.

These states like Travancore, Mysore, and the Marathas did not ally with European powers and did not get protection from them. This forced them to be responsive to their own populations and prevented them from developing the pattern of despotic extraction (Mamdani 1996), as happened in successor states like Hyderabad and Bengal. The rulers of Travancore, Cochin, and Maratha core region ruled by the Peshwa provided more development to the people who were from their own ethnic group (Lee 2017), as compared with the rulers of Hyderabad, Awadh, and Bengal who were Muslim rulers over Hindu subjects. Even in Mysore, while Haider Ali and Tipu Sultan were Muslim rulers of Hindu subjects, they engaged many Hindu Brahmin officials and ministers. On Tipu's defeat in Seringapatnam in 1799, Mysore was returned to the Hindu Wadiyar dynasty by the British, who ruled Mysore directly for a certain period when the Wadiyar prince was a minor in the 1800s.

A final effect of these warrior states was that they tended to use more direct and intrusive land revenue systems, which resulted in expansion of bureaucratic and tax capacity and were later adopted by the British to form the direct *ryotwari* land tenure system in South India (Baden-Powell 1892). According to Kulke and Rothermand (2004: 254): "In the South, Tipu Sultan and the Marathas had established a rather rigorous direct assessment of the peasants ... The British continued, nearly everywhere, the type of assessment set up by their immediate predecessors." In contrast, the Mughal successor states like Bengal and Hyderabad had developed a more indirect intermediarybased land tenure system that led to more exploitation.

I briefly sketch some of the major warrior states.

Mysore: The kingdom of Mysore was originally ruled by the Hindu Wadiyar dynasty whose leaders were petty chieftains of the ancient Vijayanagara Empire (Ramusack 2004: 29–30). The state saw an increase in military capacity and revenue collection under Chikkadevaraja Wadiyar who ruled from 1672 to 1704 (Stein 1985: 400–401). During an internal war of succession, Krishnaraja Wadiyar II (1734–65) sought help of the Muslim general Haidar Ali (1722–82), who then took control of Mysore in 1761 and became the de facto ruler (Ramusack 2004: 30). It was under Haidar Ali that the military modernization of Mysore intensified, and he modernized his army by using European tactics and armed his infantry with muskets and hired mercenary Eurasian officers (Roy 2005: 668).

Lee-Warner (1910: 69) notes that Haidar Ali's "military genius" was inherited by his son Tipu Sultan, who ruled from 1782 to 1799 following his father's death, which allowed Mysore to create a formidable army that was able to defeat the British several times. He contrasts "the rabble army defeated at Plassey and the Mysore cavalry that overran Madras within sight of the British factory, " which shows the difference in military capacity of Mysore's warrior state and the much weaker successor states of Bengal and Awadh. To fund his various wars against the Marathas, the Nizam of Hyderabad, and the British East India Company, Tipu Sultan tried to create a centralized state that extracted land revenue directly from rural areas by appointing central officers to collect land revenue in place of petty chiefs who earlier used to siphon off much of the land revenue (Ramusack, 2004: 31). This created a more direct land revenue system that British officials like Alexander Reade and Thomas Munro later adapted to create the *ryotwari* land tenure system in South India districts that the British annexed from Tipu Sultan in 1791 (Bayly 1988: 64). The *ryotwari* tenure system was more egalitarian than the *zamindari* and *taluqdari* systems that emerged in the successor state regions of Awadh, Hyderabad, and Bengal, and so the Maoists failed in the future in Karnataka state where Mysore used to be located.[30]

Travancore: Another warrior state in South India was Travancore, which was ruled by Martanda Varma between 1729 and 1758. Varma converted the ancient kingdom of Venad into a "new type of centralized state" by conquering the territories of neighboring chiefs and bringing in Tamil and Maratha brahmins from outside to create a new bureaucracy to replace the local chiefs (Ramusack 2004: 33–34). He invited the main Nayar chiefs to his palace and executed them, sold their families into slavery, and then used the Brahmins to create an efficient bureaucracy (Foa 2016: 93).

To fund his increasing military expenditures, Martanda Varma introduced a low land tax in 1739, but the majority of revenues was generated from an "elaborate system of personal taxes and fines, covering not only life rituals such as marriages, childbirth and death, but also the consumption and export of commodities (salt and pepper), personal and capital goods such as country boats, ploughs" (Foa 2016: 93–94). The net effect was that in 1853 per capita taxation in Travancore was among the highest in India, even though land revenue was low. This high level of revenues allowed Travancore state to build a "highly centralized military force" and invest large amounts for construction of fortification and temples. Varma defeated the Dutch East India Company in 1741 and modernized the army along European lines by employing the defeated captain of the Dutch army, Eustace de Lannoy (Foa 2016: 94; Ramusack 2004: 33).

Since Travancore later became part of the princely state of Kerala, this historically created higher state capacity, along with land reforms carried out by the CPI-Marxist party in Kerala starting in the 1960s, partly explains why Maoists have not succeeded as much in Kerala.[31]

---

[30] See Chapter 9 for detailed analysis of Mysore state and Maoist failure in Karnataka.

[31] See Chapter 9 for more detailed analysis of Travancore and Cochin princely states and lack of Maoist success in Kerala.

Maratha Empire: The other Indian kingdom that fought several wars and built up a strong administration and tax capacity was the Maratha Empire started by Chhatrapati Shivaji and continued under his descendants and the Peshwas. Shivaji (1630–80) came from a *deshmukh* family and by the time of his death had built up a powerful base through "adroit military campaigning, administrative reforms and ritual innovation" (Ramusack 2004: 35). The Marathas under him used two main sources of revenue – the *chauth*, which was one-fourth of land revenue, and the *sardeshmukh*, which was one-tenth of the produce and implied accepting Shivaji as head of the *deshmukhs* (Ramusack 2004: 35). Following Shivaji's death, the Maratha Empire started expanding, especially under Peshwa Baji Rao I (1720–40) who was an efficient administrator and general and annexed various territories and challenged the Nizam of Hyderabad. His son Peshwa Balaji Baji Rao continued the expansion of the Maratha Empire till its defeat to the Afghans in the Battle of Panipat in 1761 (Gordon 1993).

While the core of the Maratha Empire was the Peshwa-ruled regions of Poona and Satara in the west, other Maratha chiefs who accepted the suzerainty of the Peshwa kept expanding control of other territories. This created the "Maratha confederacy" and led to two levels of state formation – within the core or heartland region where the Peshwa claimed authority and outside this core region where various other Maratha chiefs had acquired or delegated authority (Seshan, 2014: 39).

Foa (2016: 100–101) notes that to achieve fiscal centralization, the land revenue collection system in the core Maratha region in the west became quite intrusive and direct and tried to remove the influence of intermediaries. He cites the *Satara District Gazetteer* (p. 242) that "Shivaji never permitted the deshmukhs (village headmen) and deshpandes to interfere in the management of the country; nor did he allow them to collect their dues until the amount had been ascertained, when as order was annually given for the amount. The patils, khots and kulkarnis were strictly superintended."

Gordon (1993: 140) notes that as the Maratha confederacy expanded, it started removing local *zamindars* and replacing them with a more direct land administration system, in which the Peshwa appointed a *kamavisdar* who had broad powers to collect taxes and adjudicate disputes, assisted by a staff of clerks and messengers, and troops.

All this required the expansion of the bureaucratic capacity to keep track of land surveys. Gordon (1993: 141) notes the following about this pre-colonial Maratha state: "Based on the kamavisdar's on-the-ground surveys, the body of information flowing from the district to the Peshwa's clerks at Pune dramatically increased in volume and specialization. … Six-months accounts were replaced by one-month accounts for the larger and more stable places (like Sironj and Bhilsa)." The pre-colonial Maratha core state thus developed an expansive bureaucratic infrastructure to fund their constant warfare, and this left pre-colonial legacies of higher state capacity and intrusive land tenure systems, which the British colonizers built upon once they annexed this region to direct rule in 1820s. It prevented the chance of many peasant rebellions or Maoist rebellion in the future.

(3) *Tributary* or *Feudatory States:* Another category of princely states is not described in Ramusack (2004) but also tended to have weak state capacity and despotic rule by Indian rulers. These were the smaller princely states in the central-eastern regions of Orissa, Chhattisgarh, and Chhota Nagpur (Jharkhand) that could be categorized as *tributary* or *feudatory states* and were often ruled by Rajput and Maratha princes from outside the region, whose ancestors defeated the Gond and Bhil tribes in central-eastern India and were thus ethnically quite different from the native tribal populations of these regions. Unlike the warrior states, they were subservient to the colonial power. Hence, they were given protection by the British, which allowed them to be despotic and extractive of land and natural resources from their subjects.

Several of these feudatory or tributary states were created in the region of the Central Provinces, near the borders of current Chhattisgarh, Maharashtra, Orissa, and Madhya Pradesh states, following the Indian Mutiny in 1857–59. To pacify the Indian princes, the controversial Doctrine of Lapse policy of the previous governor general Lord Dalhousie (1848–56) was reversed. In 1862, the new Governor General Lord Canning (1856–62) gave adoption *sanads* (treaties) to many Indian princes to assure them of their right to adopt male heirs.[32] In a report in 1863, the chief secretary of the Central Provinces, Richard Temple, suggested that many of these *zamindars* of the Central Provinces qualified to be given adoption *sanads* and converted into princely states.[33] So this policy was applied by the Governor General Sir John Lawrence (1864–69) to around fifteen *zamindaris* in the Central Provinces, which were elevated to the status of princely states, given these adoption *sanads*, and became feudatory states with direct tributary relations with the British Crown. The largest *zamindari* was the Raja of Bastar, who was granted the adoption *sanad* in 1862. In 1865, the adoption *sanads* were given to eleven *zamindaris* inside Sambalpur state, which is in Orissa, and Kalahandi (Karond), Kanker, Kawardha, Khairagarh, Nandgaon, and Chhuikhadan (Kondka) *zamindaris*, which belonged to the group called Nagpur State Zamindars. Finally, Raigarh and Sarangarh Garhjat *zamindaris* belonging to Sambalpur State were given *sanads* and made princely states in 1867.[34]

---

[32] For overview of Lord Canning's policies, see Cunningham, *Earl Canning*, and Maclagan, 'Clemency' Canning.

[33] Temple, *Report on the Zamindaris and Other Petty Chieftaincies in the Central Provinces in 1863*, pp. 19–20.

[34] See C. U. Aitchison, *A Collection of Treaties, Engagements, and Sanads relating to Indian and Neighbouring Countries*, Vol. VIII, pp. 500–514. Also see De Brett, *Chhattisgarh Feudatory States*, p. 8.

These feudatory states were dependent on the British and developed lower state capacity and development (Kohli 2004; Lange 2009) and despotic extraction through *zamindars* or *malguzars* who collected land taxes from indigenous tribes living in these areas (Boone 1994; Mamdani 1996). Bastar was the largest of the feudatory/tributary states in the Chhattisgarh area and best represents the dynamics of despotic extraction in these types of princely states; since the 1980s, it has become a stronghold of the PWG Maoists.[35] The Rajas of Bastar were Rajputs from outside the region. The scourge of Bastar state was that the rajas depended on *diwans* appointed by the British who often were despotic and inefficient and this led to tribal rebellions (Joshi 1990: 28–31). For example, during the reign of *Diwan* Gopinath Kapurdar who took over in 1867, the administration became more corrupt and despotic. He introduced exploitative land taxes that led to a tribal rebellion in 1876, and the British authorities had to intervene and remove him from office. The Additional Commissioner, Chhattisgarh, Colonel Ward, went to investigate and wrote a report in 1883 that criticized Raja Bhairam Deo as "a man who … takes no sort of interest in any branch of administration."[36] Ward suggested dismissing the raja and introducing British direct management of Bastar state.

However, the chief commissioner of the Central Provinces, W. B. Jones, did not agree with Colonel Ward's suggestions because he believed that maladministration was ubiquitous in the feudatory states of Chhattisgarh, and using that as a cause for deposing the Bastar raja would mean none of the feudatory chiefs of the region could be allowed to rule.[37] This shows that the British were aware of the weak administrative capacity and despotic nature of the princes and *diwans* of these feudatory states but still decided to continue indirect rule, thus allowing oppression of the indigenous Gond tribals, because they did not consider it worth the cost of directly administering these areas (Sundar 2007). This finally led to the famous *Bhumkal* tribal rebellion of 1910 in Bastar and recurrence of rebellion in the 1980s, but this time led by Maoist rebels exploiting historically created tribal grievances.

4.3   Coding Different Types of Princely States:

The measure of *princely state* that I used for the OLS analysis in the last chapter and IV-2SLS analysis in previous sections in this chapter was coded based on whether a district was under formal indirect rule as a princely state (coded 1) or

---

[35] For detailed analysis of Bastar princely state in Chhattisgarh and how it later became the epicenter of the Maoist insurgency, see the next chapter.

[36] "Report on the Administration of Bastar State," Prog. No 122, Paragraphs 90–96, by H. C. E Ward, Addl. Commissioner, Chhattisgarh Division, in *Foreign A-Political-I, January 1884, Prog. Nos. 117–125, NAI.*

[37] "Memo by Chief Commissioner, Central Provinces," Prog. 118, para 40, in *Foreign A-Political-I, January 1884, Prog. Nos. 117–125, NAI.*

under direct British rule (coded 0). It is taken from the measure of *princely state* in the Iyer (2010) dataset, which was coded from several volumes and maps in *The Imperial Gazetteers of India*, Volumes 1–26. I cross-checked the data by comparing a 1991 India districts map with the map of direct/indirect rule from Volume 26 of the *Imperial Gazetteers* and corrected a few errors.[38]

To go beyond this 0–1 binary measure of *princely states* and code the different types of princely states, I consulted the following sources to calculate the boundaries of pre-colonial kingdoms in India:

1. William Lee-Warner, *The Native States of India,* Treaty Map of India, p. 53. This shows the princely state boundaries as different treaties are being formed but is not as useful for this purpose since these are not the final boundaries of states formed after 1857.
2. A map of princely states in Ramusack (2004: xiv), which provides the boundaries of British and princely districts in 1912, by which time the boundaries had become the post-1857 final boundaries.
3. *Imperial Gazetteers of India* (1909 edition), Volume 26, Political Divisions Map, p. 20, http://dsal.uchicago.edu/reference/gaz_atlas_1909/pager.html?object=26 which has the post-1857 final boundaries.

For the 1991 district boundaries of India, I use the following atlas:

1. Census of India, *India Administrative Atlas, 1872–2001: A Historical Perspective of Evolution of Districts and States in India,* Technical direction, R. P. Singh; general direction, Jayant Kumar Banthia. New Delhi: Controller of Publications, 2004.

This Census of India publication, *India Administrative Atlas, 1872–2001* is very useful to compare district boundaries over time, as it has all the state and district boundaries of India for all censuses from 1872 to 2001. The maps show that the state and district boundaries of British provinces and princely states remained the same in 1891, 1911, 1921, 1931, and 1941 and are similar to the *Imperial Gazetteers of India,* Volume 26, *Political Divisions Map,* p. 20. In the 1951 census following independence, state and districts were renamed but have almost the same boundaries as they had during the colonial periods. From 1961 census, we find that following the linguistic reorganization of Indian states, new states were formed as they still exist today and state boundaries changed, though district boundaries remained similar as they were during the colonial period.

To code the 1991 districts as different types of princely states, I compared the district boundaries of British provinces and princely states

---

[38] The 1991 district map of India is from the *Census of India 2011 Administrative Atlas,* p. 117, Map 51. The map for British direct vs. indirect rule is from *Imperial Gazetteer of India,* v. 26, Atlas 1909 edition, Political Divisions, p. 20, http://dsal.uchicago.edu/reference/gaz_atlas_1909/pager.html?object=26

from the 1941 Administrative Divisions map in this *India Administrative Atlas, 1872–2001* (which is the same as the map of direct and indirect rule in the *Imperial Gazetteers of India*, 1909, Volume 26) with the district boundaries of modern Indian states and districts in the Administrative Map of 1991 districts. The list of districts in India that fit within Ramusack's (2004) classification of different types of princely states, and the coding using STATA are listed in Online Appendix J.

4.4   Discussion of Quantitative Results

Based on this coding of different types of princely states, I do OLS regression analysis to test my theory of variation in how the different types of princely states affect the probability of Maoist insurgency. For my dependent variable, I continue to use the measure of *Maoist control* as in my earlier quantitative analysis. I present my analysis in the tables that follow.

Testing within the Category of Princely States and Excluding British Direct Rule Districts

In Table 6.6, I analyze the effects of these different types of princely states on Maoist insurgency while constraining the sample to princely states and excluding districts that were under British direct rule. This allows us to focus the analysis within the broader category of formal indirect rule through princely states and then see the relative effect of one type of princely state vs. the other types. The *ancient states* category is made up of the Rajputana princely states like Mewar, Jaisalmer, and Jodhpur that were all part of the Indian state of Rajasthan and is dropped from the analysis that used state fixed effects. The reason is that all these princely states became part of the same state of Rajasthan, and so there is no internal variation in them within the state of Rajasthan. However, the other types of princely states, like the *warrior states* of Hyderabad or Mysore or the *feudatory states* of Bastar or Mayurbhanj, were divided across boundaries of different states in independent India or were part of a larger state that also had other direct rule territories in them and so it is possible to use state fixed effects for them.

In Table 6.6, Model 1A tests for the effects of *successor states* against other types of princely states while controlling for forest cover, while Model 1B includes a few more pre-colonial factors in the model, like pre-colonial agrarian rebellion and red soil, which are often positively correlated with Maoist insurgency. Similarly, Models 2A and 2B test for the effects of *feudatory princely states* in Chhattisgarh and the Orissa area, controlling for some pre-colonial factors. Models 3A and 3B test for the effects of *warrior states* on Maoist insurgency, controlling for the same pre-colonial factors.

The results in Table 6.6 show that within the category of princely states, both *feudatory princely states* and *successor princely states* tend to have positive correlation with *Maoist control*, with *feudatory state* being statistically significant at the 99 percent error level. In contrast, *warrior states* have

TABLE 6.6 *Effects of types of princely states on Maoist rebellion – within the category of princely states (excluding British direct rule districts)*
Dependent variable: *Maoist control* (MHA measure – SRE scheme 2000–3)

	Model 1a – Successor States	Model 1b – Successor States	Model 2a – Feudatory States	Model 2b – Feudatory States	Model 3a – Warrior States	Model 3b – Warrior States
Successor States	0.125 (0.311)	0.145 (0.252)				
Feudatory States			0.607*** (0.000)	0.595*** (0.000)		
Warrior States					−0.147** (0.027)	−0.143** (0.035)
Forest Cover	0.00663*** (0.000)	0.00767*** (0.000)	0.00349*** (0.009)	0.00406*** (0.007)	0.00592*** (0.000)	0.00680*** (0.000)
Pre-Colonial (Mughal) Agrarian Rebellion		0.0380 (0.601)		0.0416 (0.501)		0.0388 (0.587)
Red Soil		−0.0462 (0.661)		−0.0273 (0.761)		−0.0417 (0.688)
Constant	−0.0120 (0.744)	−0.0187 (0.643)	0.00818 (0.742)	0.00447 (0.873)	0.0654* (0.086)	0.0626 (0.130)
Observations	124	119	124	119	124	119
R^2	0.148	0.174	0.393	0.403	0.178	0.199
Adjusted R^2	0.029	0.035	0.309	0.302	0.064	0.064

P-values in parentheses
* $p < 0.10$, ** $p < 0.05$, *** $p < 0.01$
All models include state fixed effects.
Antique states are all part of the state of Rajasthan and so dropped from analysis when using state fixed effects.
The analysis is constrained to only princely states and excludes all British direct rule districts

a negative correlation with *Maoist control* statistically significant at the 95 percent error level. This provides support for my hypotheses that the warrior states like Travancore, Mysore, Marathas, and Sikhs develop higher state capacity and provide more public goods, while the feudatory states in Orissa and the Chhattisgarh area like Bastar and Mayurbhanj have weaker state capacity and are more despotic, thus being more prone to tribal and Maoist rebellions. The result for successor states like Bengal, Awadh, and Hyderabad may not be statistically significant but is positively correlated with *Maoist control*, and we know from qualitative evidence that the Maoist Communist Center (MCC) succeeded in states like Bihar and Jharkhand that were part of the former *successor state* of Bengal, and the PWG-Maoists succeeded in the Telangana districts of the former *successor state* of Hyderabad. As we see in Table 6.7, successor states are statistically significant and positively correlated with Maoist control as expected based on my typology.

Testing Effects of Different Types of Princely States for the Entire Dataset of Indian Districts

Unlike Table 6.6, which looks for the effects of princely states only within the population of princely states, Table 6.7 includes the entire dataset of both direct and indirect ruled areas in the analysis. I also include all the different types of princely states in the model. To test if the effects of the pre-colonial qualities of these different types of princely states survive even after including colonial institutions, I control for colonial direct vs. indirect rule.

Both *successor states* and *feudatory states* are statistically significant and positively correlated with *Maoist control* even after controlling for colonial indirect rule through *princely state* (1–0). This means that the pre-colonial qualities of different types of princely states have an effect on the chances of Maoist insurgency, even after controlling for whether they were under British direct rule or indirect rule in colonial times. *Warrior states* has a negative coefficient as expected, but it is not statistically significant, and *antique states* also have a negative correlation that has a very low level of significance, probably because we are using state fixed effect. Even when controlling for several pre-colonial controls in Models 2A and 2B, these results persist.

Looking at the results in Tables 6.6 and 6.7, there seems to be support for the typology of princely states that I developed based on Ramusack's (2004) historical analysis. *Feudatory states* seem to have a very strong positive correlation with Maoist insurgency and so does *successor states*. The effect of *Warrior states* is less strong in Table 6.7 but is statistically significant in Table 6.6 where it is included individually in the model specification and with fewer pre-colonial controls. It is not possible to estimate the effects of *antique states* but the native states in Jaisalmer, Jodhpur, Ajmer, and so on that became part of Rajasthan and survived colonial rule are in India's northwest and far from the theater of Maoist insurgency.

TABLE 6.7 *Effects of types of princely states on Maoist rebellion – all types of princely states (including both direct rule and indirect rule districts)*
Dependent variable: *Maoist control* (MHA measure – SRE scheme 2000–3)

	Model 1A	Model 1B	Model 2A	Model 2B
Princely State vs. Direct Rule (1–0)		0.0451 (0.319)		0.0394 (0.397)
Successor States	0.182*** (0.001)	0.164*** (0.005)	0.186*** (0.001)	0.172*** (0.004)
Feudatory States	0.491*** (0.000)	0.454*** (0.000)	0.474*** (0.000)	0.442*** (0.000)
Warrior States	−0.0131 (0.798)	−0.0365 (0.517)	0.0159 (0.775)	−0.00311 (0.959)
Antique States	−0.00591 (0.981)	−0.0506 (0.840)	0.0190 (0.939)	−0.0208 (0.934)
Forest Cover	0.00254** (0.014)	0.00267** (0.011)	0.00269** (0.012)	0.00281*** (0.009)
Pre-Colonial (Mughal) Agrarian Rebellion	0.0525 (0.225)	0.0534 (0.216)	0.0554 (0.205)	0.0569 (0.194)
Red Soil	0.198*** (0.001)	0.195*** (0.001)	0.233*** (0.000)	0.229*** (0.000)
Altitude			−0.000086 (0.204)	−0.000077 (0.262)
Alluvial Soil			−0.0642 (0.119)	−0.0639 (0.121)
Black Soil			0.0235 (0.624)	0.0213 (0.658)
Barren and Rocky			−0.0805 (0.920)	−0.0905 (0.910)
Constant	−0.0231 (0.549)	−0.0307 (0.436)	0.0243 (0.664)	0.0142 (0.804)
Observations	278	278	263	263
R^2	0.195	0.198	0.236	0.238
Adjusted R^2	0.129	0.129	0.155	0.154

P-values in parentheses * $p < 0.10$, ** $p < 0.05$, *** $p < 0.01$
All models include state fixed.
The analysis used the entire sample of all districts in India, both direct and indirect rule. Antique states are also included in the analysis.

This answers the call by scholars like Wilkinson (2017), and Gerring et al. (2011) to conceptualize the direct-indirect rule dichotomy as a nonbinary concept. I develop the first typology of different types of indirect rule within the Indian subcontinent, based on the pre-colonial qualities of these kingdoms and whether they had rulers who tried to fight the British or were weak and subservient to them. This typology is able to differentiate between different types of princely states that the typology suggested by Naseemullah and Staniland (2016) does not. Future research should try to test this typology on its effects on other factors like state capacity and levels of development.

5   CONCLUSION

This chapter started by presenting a comparative case study analysis of the two states of Awadh and Hyderabad, which were similar in many aspects, except that Awadh was annexed into direct rule and Hyderabad was not. This structured comparison shows that it was external geostrategic considerations and not internal qualities of districts that determined the choice of indirect vs. direct rule. I then presented a new instrument based on the exogenous effects of Great Wars in Europe on patterns of choosing indirect rule vs. attempts to annex states into direct rule in India. The IV-2SLS analysis shows that the two measures of indirect rule – through *zamindari* landlords and through princely states – are both statistically significant predictors of Maoist insurgency. This allays concerns of selection bias in the OLS quantitative analysis in the previous chapter on the effects of colonial indirect rule on Maoist insurgency.

I also developed a novel typology of different types of historical princely states in India. This is a major empirical contribution to the study of colonial indirect rule in India and goes beyond what previous studies by Iyer (2010), Banerjee and Iyer (2010), Verghese (2016), and even Lange (2009) have proposed. Most of these studies think of formal indirect rule through princely states as homogenous and do not account for heterogeneity within the category of formal indirect rule through princely states.

I demonstrated that the conquest/warrior states like Mysore, Marathas, the Sikh Empire, and Travancore, which tended to challenge the authority of the Mughals and then the British colonial power, had higher levels of state centralization and tax capacity and more direct land revenue collection systems. This prevented the Maoist rebellion from being as successful in states like Karnataka, which had the Mysore kingdom, and Kerala, which had Travancore as part of their territory. In contrast, the feudatory and smaller princely states in the Chhattisgarh and Chota Nagpur areas had lower levels of state centralization and more despotic rule through *diwans* who were ethnic outsiders. This created the structural conditions for tribals with grievances that the Maoist rebels were able to exploit more easily. Also, the larger successor princely states of Hyderabad, Bengal, and Awadh were forced to sign treaties of subsidiary alliance. This prevented their military and tax capacity from growing; at the same time, their rulers were protected by the British and they allowed *zamindars* and *deshmukhs* to become despotic in their collection of land revenue, thus creating structural conditions of inequality, which were later conducive for Maoist rebellion. The ancient states of Rajasthan were too far away from the epicenter of the Maoist insurgency for rebellion to diffuse there. Also, these were small states where many of the Rajput elites had collaborated with the Mughals and then the colonial state, and even the tribals and lower castes like Meenas were incorporated as part of the administrative services, and not prone to rebellion.

Following the broad analysis of the typology of princely states in this chapter, the next chapters on the states of Chhattisgarh, Andhra Pradesh, and Karnataka/ Kerala follow as examples of these different types of princely states that led to Maoist insurgency. Chapter 7 analyzes the feudatory princely states in Chhattisgarh, Chapter 8 analyzes the successor state of Hyderabad in Andhra Pradesh, while Chapter 9 analyzes the warrior or conquest princely states of Mysore and Travancore that later were part of the states of Karnataka and Kerala. Chapter 10 discusses the frontier states like the Federally Administered Tribal areas (FATA) in North West Frontier Province (NWFP) in Pakistan which had Taliban insurgency, and the eastern frontier of Shan, Karen, and Kachin states in Burma, which had ethnic insurgencies. The following chapters serve two purposes – first to use rich qualitative data to outline how conditions created by historical institutions became path dependent and how rebel agency mobilized it and, second, to demonstrate that there was internal variation within princely states that created heterogeneous effects on chances of insurgency.

7

Maoist Insurgency in Chhattisgarh: The Raja of Bastar and Tribal Rebellion

I INTRODUCTION

In the past few chapters, I outlined a theory of how different types of indirect rule within India created different causal pathways to Maoist insurgency in India and tested the theory using a district dataset of India. Nested within this large N analysis (LNA), I now focus on different types of princely states in India and do process tracing of how the structural conditions of inequality and weak state created by colonial indirect rule persisted and caused Maoist insurgency (Lieberman 2005, 2015). In this chapter, I analyze the case of the Maoists in the tribal state of Chhattisgarh in central India, and in the next chapter on Andhra Pradesh.

In Chhattisgarh, the northern and southern parts of the state had colonial indirect rule through feudatory princely states, which created weak state capacity (Lange 2009; Lee 2019) and despotic extraction of land revenue and natural resources through landlords and feudatory chiefs (Boone 1994; Mahoney 2010; Mamdani 1996). This created tribal grievances that persisted in the postcolonial period in the 1950s to 1980s through path dependence of these mechanisms in the northern and southern parts of the state. These were mobilized by the People's War Group (PWG) Maoists, leading to high levels of Maoist rebel control by 1990s. In contrast, the central districts of Raipur and Bilaspur in Chhattisgarh had been under British direct rule as part of the Central Provinces and had relatively higher levels of development and less exploitation of forest and natural resources of tribals, and so the Maoists did not succeed there.

I use archival and fieldwork-based qualitative data to do process tracing of the causal mechanisms of this process tracing case (Goertz 2017). While indirect rule through princely states and *zamindars*/landlords was abolished following Indian independence in 1947, the effects of these institutions persisted into the 1980s in these areas in central India through different mechanisms. First, the political and economic power of tribal and non-tribal landed elite persisted through path dependent mechanisms of *elite persistence* (Mahoney 2000) and resulted in *ethnic exclusion* of poor tribals from power (Cederman et al. 2010, 2013). This combined with policies of natural resource extraction through landlords and outsiders continued even under the postcolonial Indian state, which used policies similar to *internal colonialism* (Baruah 1999) that echoed the indirect rule used by colonizers in the past. This resulted in indigenous tribals with grievances, who thus formed the ethnic mobilization networks that Maoist rebels could successfully recruit.

Second, indirect rule created weak state capacity that persisted through path dependence, and these areas of former indirect rule continued to have weak state capacity (Lange 2009), thus creating *political opportunity structures* that allowed space for successful rebel organization. These mechanisms leading from colonial institutions to insurgency are outlined more generally in Figure 3.3, and this chapter outlines the mechanisms of persistence specific to the case of Chhattisgarh.

In this chapter, I also present a history of the PWG Maoists in Chhattisgarh, and how the rebels contributed to the welfare of the tribals and opposed natural/forest resource exploitation by the state and outside companies. This allows us to understand the importance of rebel agency and ideological frames of rebellion, and how PWG rebels exploited these historically created structural inequalities to develop high rebel control since 1980s. The same rebels were constrained and not successful in fomenting rebellion due to the lack of such high levels of inequalities in central districts of Bilaspur and Raipur in Chhattisgarh, which were colonial direct rule and relatively more developed. This complements the analysis in Chapter 4, where I analyzed Maoist documents and rebel strategy, and how rebel agency was ultimately constrained by whether or not structural conditions created by colonial indirect rule/revenue collection were present or absent.

A final contribution of this chapter is that it complements this process tracing with a quantitative analysis of a novel sub-district level dataset for Chhattisgarh, which shows that those assembly constituencies that were part of indirect rule through princely states tend to have a strong positive correlation with Maoist control. There is potential selection bias, since it is possible that the British administrators selected those areas in Chhattisgarh that were forested and prone to tribal rebellion for indirect rule. I address this by using an instrument for the British choice of indirect rule based on random deaths of rulers in the princely state of Nagpur, which led to the switch of central districts in Chhattisgarh to direct rule. The IV-2SLS analysis shows that *princely state* has a significant and positive correlation with *Maoist control*, which suggests that historical institutions have a causal effect on postcolonial inequalities and insurgency.

The chapter outline is as follows. In Section 2, I explain case selection of Chhattisgarh and describe the history of Bastar state. In Section 3, I describe the mechanisms released by the historical institution of indirect rule in Chhattisgarh. In Section 4, I show how they persisted into the postcolonial period through path dependence and created the political opportunity structures and ethnic grievances and mobilization networks for insurgency. Section 5 outlines a history of the PWG Maoists in Chhattisgarh, and how rebel agency tries to make use of the structural conditions of *opportunity* and *inequality*. In Section 6, I briefly describe the Assembly Constituency dataset and IV-2SLS econometric analysis. Section 7 suggests policy implications, and Section 8 concludes.

2   THE CASE OF CHHATTISGARH

2.1   Why Choose Chhattisgarh?

The quantitative large N analysis (LNA) in the previous chapter provides broad statistical evidence that districts that were formerly princely states and landlord tenure had high levels of Maoist control. In this chapter, nested within this broader quantitative analysis (Lieberman 2005, 2015), I focus on the Maoist insurgency in Chhattisgarh. This is a crucial pathway case (Gerring 2007) that allows us to trace the causal pathway of how *formal* colonial indirect rule through princely states can create grievances among indigenous tribals due to land and natural resource exploitation (Boone 1994; Mamdani 1996) as well as ethnic exclusion from power (Cederman et al. 2010), facilitated by weak state capacity (Fearon & Laitin 2011). The crucial pathway case is best used according to Gerring (2007b: 238–39) when a causal hypothesis is already established prior to case study investigation, but the causal mechanisms are not yet clear, and so the case serves to "elucidate causal mechanisms." Focusing on the case of Chhattisgarh, which is well predicted by the broader quantitative analysis in Chapters 5 and 6, allows us to understand better the underlying path dependent mechanisms created by formal colonial indirect rule that persist into the postcolonial period (Mahoney 2000).[1]

Another reason for studying Chhattisgarh is that it represents the feudatory/tributary type of princely states, which is prone to despotic rule. I take seriously the suggestion of Wilkinson (2017) and Gerring et al. (2011) that direct-indirect rule is not a dichotomy and should be conceptualized as a continuum.[2] In Chapter 6, I distinguished between different subtypes of princely states based on Ramusack's (2004) historical analysis of indirect rule in India and

---

[1] Thachil, "Embedded Mobilization," similarly uses Chhattisgarh as a case to elucidate mechanisms for his broader theory of why the Bharatiya Janata Party (BJP) wins votes among poor tribals in India.

[2] Wilkinson, "Looking Back at the Colonial Origins of Communal and Caste Conflict in India," criticizes Iyer, "Direct versus Indirect Colonial Rule in India," and Verghese (2016b) for failing to differentiate between different types of indirect rule.

developed a typology of indirect rule and pre-colonial states in South Asia. In this typology, warrior or conquest states like Travancore and Mysore that were ruled by kings who challenged the British and Dutch and built armies and bureaucracies resulted in more state capacity and less land inequality and had less Maoist insurgency in the future. Also, there were the successor states of Hyderabad and Bengal that had Muslim rulers who were formerly vassals of the Mughal emperor, but later became autonomous suzerain rulers. These Muslims kings ruled over Hindu subjects and developed despotic regimes and exploitative land tenure systems that caused Maoist rebellions. Finally, the tributary or feudatory states in Orissa and Chhattisgarh areas often had outsider Rajput princes who were protected by the British and also tended to be despotic, resulting in exploitation and future Maoist conflict.

If we apply this typology to Maoist insurgency, it seems that the Maoists succeeded in the tributary or feudatory princely states in Orissa/Chhattisgarh area, and also in the Bengal and Hyderabad areas of former successor states to the Mughal Empire, because there were different forms of despotic rule in these areas. They did not succeed as much in the state of Karnataka that had Mysore princely state, which was stronger in capacity because Tipu Sultan had made it a warrior state. Neither did the Maoists succeed as much in Kerala in the second part of the 1980s onward, because of various reasons, one of them being that Martanda Varma of Travancore was efficient and had fought wars and made his state more centralized.[3]

In this chapter, I use historical analysis to focus on the Chhattisgarh *feudatory* princely state of Bastar in central India, which exemplifies the mechanisms of lower state capacity and development (Kohli 2004; Mahoney 2010) and despotic extraction through *zamindars/malguzars* who extracted land taxes, as well as natural resources from *Adivasis* (Banerjee & Iyer 2005; Boone 1994). The next chapter will analyze another type of princely state, namely the successor state of Hyderabad and how that also leads to exploitation of land revenue. These two chapters study two types of princely states in India that result in despotism and lower development, which allows us a glimpse into the diversity of princely state types, which still led to the same outcome of Maoist insurgency, thus suggesting *equifinality* (Mahoney & Goertz 2006).

2.2 History of the Feudatory State of Bastar in South Chhattisgarh

As discussed in Chapter 3 above, several studies suggest that *on average* princely states often had despotic rulers who produced weaker state capacity (Lange

---

[3] Other reasons, discussed in Chapter 9, for why the Maoists did not succeed in Kerala were that the mechanisms of inequality created by the *zamindari* land tenure system were reversed because the Communist Party of India did land reforms in the state.

2009) and concomitantly lower development (Kohli 2004; Mahoney 2010).[4] The feudatory states in Chhattisgarh, particularly Bastar and Kanker in the south, clearly fit into this pattern.

Bastar was the largest of the feudatory/tributary states in the Chhattisgarh area and best represents the dynamics of despotic extraction in these type of princely states. When Bhopal Deo was the Raja of Bastar in the 1840s, the British resident of Nagpur state, T. Wilkinson, appointed Dalganjan Singh as the *Diwan* of Bastar in 1846. Dalganjan Singh turned out to be overbearing and despotic and acquired extensive *jagir* lands for himself and earned the ire of the raja. With the death of Raja Bhopal Deo in 1853, his minor son Bhairam Deo became the raja but was under the control of Dalganjan Singh who continued to control the raja while the quality of administration declined (Joshi 1990: 28–31).

With the death of *Diwan* Dalganjan Singh in 1863, *Diwan* Motisingh was appointed and was able to stop the abuse of power and introduced several reforms in judiciary and land tenure laws. However, he was soon replaced by *Diwan* Gopinath Kapurdar in 1867 due to court intrigue, and Gopinath along with other officials took complete control over the administration and became corrupt and despotic and introduced land taxes that were exploitative. All this resulted in a tribal rebellion in Bastar in 1876 (described later), and the British authorities had to intervene and remove *Diwan* Gopinath from office. The deputy commissioner of Sironcha District, H. MacGeorge, when investigating the tribal rebellion found Gopinath to be in complete control of the Raja and while he "did very well at first, but latterly … he has managed to raise the feelings of the whole peasantry against himself."[5] The chief commissioner of Central Provinces warned the Raja of Bastar that if he "neglects the business of administration, denies access to his subjects … and leaves the conduct of affairs in the hands of unscrupulous subordinates," then the British government would be forced to intervene.[6]

MacGeorge found in his next visit in 1877 that the raja had engaged in a new land revenue settlement in 1877–78 and had also promised to give a number of villages to the Muria tribals and take away villages from some Kayasth outsiders, who had been taking land from the raja.[7] However, these improvements were short lived due to the *diwans* continuing to abuse their powers. The new *diwan* in 1879 was Durjan Singh, who was an illegitimate brother of the raja, and he

---

[4] Iyer, "Direct versus Indirect Colonial Rule in India" suggests that princely states did better in terms of development and agricultural outcomes, but there is a lot more variation between types of princely states than her analysis captures.

[5] Letter from MacGeorge to Chief Commissioner, Central Provinces, "Disturbances at Bastar," Program No. 165, *Foreign Political-A, August 1876*. Prog. No. 170, Para. 16, *NAI*.

[6] T. Thornton, Secretary to Govt. of India, Foreign Dept., in "Disturbances at Bastar," Program No. 163–172, *Foreign Political-A, August 1876, NAI*.

[7] "Memo by Chief Commissioner, Central Provinces," Prog. 118, para 6, in *Foreign A-Political-I, January 1884, Prog. Nos. 117–125, NAI*.

continued to be in the same mold as the previous *diwan,* and the Chief Commissioner Jones referred to him as "dissolute and extravagant" who emptied the treasury and oppressed and looted people in Jagdalpur.[8]

Durjan Singh died in 1881 of his excesses, and the next *diwan* appointed was Lall Kalendra Singh, who was a cousin of the raja and son of the late Dalganjan Singh. A 1882 report on Bastar by a British official found that Kalendra Singh was misusing "his power to oppress the people and to extort as much money . . . for his own gratification."[9] In 1883, the British decided to intervene to prevent another rebellion. The Additional Commissioner, Chhattisgarh, Colonel Ward went to investigate and wrote a report in 1883 that noted that the treasury was empty, and he criticized Raja Bhairam Deo as "a man who . . . takes no sort of interest in any branch of administration."[10] Ward suggested dismissing the raja and introducing British direct management of Bastar state.

However, Chief Commissioner of the Central Provinces W. B. Jones did not agree with Ward's proposal; he decided to give Raja Bhairam Deo another chance to reform his administration and agreed to the raja's request to reinstate *Diwan* Kalendra Singh and to allow appointment of Tehsildar Sher Mohammad to help him gain experience with administration.[11] This was based on the chief commissioner's belief that maladministration was ubiquitous in the feudatory states of Chhattisgarh, and using that as a cause for deposing the Bastar raja would mean "no one of the Feudatory Chiefs would be left on the *gadi*" or throne.[12] The chief commissioner warned the raja if he did not reform his administration, there would be "no alternative but to assume . . . the direct management of Bastar."[13]

In the immediate aftermath, we find the Commissioner of Chhattisgarh Division J. W. Chisholm visiting Bastar and reporting in February 1884 that in spite of the best efforts of *Diwan* Kalendra Singh, the state "was bankrupt, its treasury empty, its servants unpaid," with huge debts.[14] The Gond tribals think of the harmless raja as a "Deo" or deity, and it would be difficult to depose him, so he suggested the solution was to give a loan to Bastar to help reform the

---

[8] "Memo by Chief Commissioner, Central Provinces," Prog. 118, para 19, in *Foreign A-Political-I,* January 1884, Prog. Nos. 117–125, *NAI.*

[9] "Memo by Chief Commissioner, Central Provinces," Prog. 118, para 29, in *Foreign A-Political-I,* January 1884, Prog. Nos. 117–125, *NAI.*

[10] "Report on the Administration of Bastar State," Prog. No 122, Paragraphs 90–96, by H. C. E Ward, Addl. Commissioner, Chhattisgarh Division, in *Foreign A-Political-I, January 1884, Prog. Nos. 117–125, NAI.*

[11] Letter from W. B. Jones, Chief Commissioner, Central Provinces to Raja Bhyro Deo, Bastar, Prog. No. 120, in *Foreign A-Political-I, January 1884, Prog. Nos. 117–125, NAI.*

[12] "Memo by Chief Commissioner, Central Provinces," Prog. 118, para 40, in *Foreign A-Political-I,* January 1884, *NAI.*

[13] "Memo by Chief Commissioner, Central Provinces," Prog. 118, para 43, in *Foreign A-Political-I,* January 1884, *NAI.*

[14] Chisholm to Chief Commissioner, Central Provinces, Prog. No. 101, in *Foreign A-Political-I,* April 1884, Nos 99–103, *NAI.*

financial system. Chief Secretary Jones agreed and a loan of Rs. 70,000 without interest was commissioned to Bastar, with which some salaries and debts were paid off.[15] However, *Diwan* Kalendra Singh continued to be inefficient, pleasure seeking, and addicted to opium and could not reform the administration.[16] The British replaced Kalendra Singh and tried to carry out several reforms between 1886 and 1891 and sent four *diwans* to Bastar – namely, Krishna Rao, Ganpat Rao Gokle, Gopinath Guru, and Pandit Alamchand – but none of them proved effective.[17]

On July 28, 1891, Raja Bhairam Deo died, leaving minor prince Rudra Pratap Deo to succeed. During this minority period, from November 1, 1891, to 1908, Bastar state was under direct British management.[18] Various English and Indian officers served as superintendents and administrators to carry out indirect rule under direct British management from 1891 to 1903. From 1903 to 1908, Panda Bajinath was made superintendent of Bastar and served efficiently. When the minor prince Rudra Pratap Deo was installed as raja in 1908, Panda Bajinath was made the *diwan*. The former *diwan* Kalendra Singh was left out of the Bastar administration.[19] During this period, many innovations were introduced and administrative reforms were made, but at the local level exploitation of tribals by officials and traders continued (Joshi 1990: 76).

Soon thereafter, the outbreak of the *Bhumkal* tribal rebellion of 1910 occurred, which saw "looting of foreigners and burning of their houses and of State buildings," as well as murder of policemen and forest officials.[20] The local Gond tribals had been "subjected to many petty acts of oppression and tyranny by the subordinates of the forest, police, educational and revenue departments in the State, and by lessees of villages and petty traders from up country" and reservation of their forests.[21] The tribal leaders visited Kalendra Singh to ask for help, but he was nursing his own grievances against the raja and *Diwan* Bajinath for not being allowed back into a position of power, and he took this opportunity to motivate them into rebelling. It was clear that the Gond tribals had "grievances which have aroused in them a strong feeling of resentment against the foreign employees of the State" and in the Kuakonda pargana (district) where the "riotous crowds were most bloodthirsty," they were led by their indigenous leader Gunda Dhurwa.[22]

[15] Chisholm to Chief Commissioner, Central Provinces, Prog. No. 101, in *Foreign A-Political-I*, April 1884, Nos 99–103, *NAI*.

[16] *Foreign Political-I*, September 1884, Prog. No. 32, paras 9, 18 (memo), *NAI*.

[17] *Foreign Political-I*, September 1884, Prog. No. 34, paras 9, 18 (memo), *NAI*.

[18] *Foreign Political-I*, November 1891, Pros. Nos. 103–106, *NAI*.

[19] *Foreign Secret-I*, September 1910, *Progs. No. 16, Enclosure 1, paras. 3–4*.

[20] Report by E. A. DeBrett, in *Foreign Secret-I, August 1911, Prog. No 37. Enclosure no. 1, para 7*.

[21] "Report on connection … " in *Foreign Secret-I, September 1910*, Prog. No 16 Enclosure 1, Para 16, *NAI*.

[22] R. H. Craddock, Chief Commissioner, Central Provinces, "Note on connection of Lal Kalendra Singh with the rebellion in Bastar State … " in Prog. No 16, Enclosure 3, Para 5 in *Foreign Secret-I, September 1910, NAI*.

This history of administration in Bastar feudatory state shows that despotic and inefficient *diwans* and a raja who was not interested in administration led to exploitation of tribals, and poor administration. This view was expressed by the Secretary, Government of India: "Bad Diwans have been the curse of Bastar" and he states that it "would not be reasonable to expect from Bastar the same standard of administration which may be looked for and insisted on in other more favored States."

This shows that the British government was aware of the different types of princely states, with the feudatory states in Central India being more despotic and providing poor governance. Part of the reason for despotic rule in feudatory princely states was that the British would allow such inefficient rulers/*diwans* to continue, since they thought that it would not be profitable enough for the British to install direct rule. This comes up clearly in Commissioner of Chhattisgarh Chisholm's comment about Bastar that "we could not directly manage the State without a heavy expenditure ... the best plan is ... of managing through a Diwan with an official adviser."[23] It reflects Mahoney's (2010: 240) suggestion that "In the indirectly ruled areas, the British actively protected oppressive local elites, who otherwise likely would have faced major rebellion from the rural producers they exploited."

3 BRITISH INDIRECT RULE: SETTING UP CAUSAL PATHWAYS TO MAOIST INSURGENCY

3.1 Mechanisms Created by Colonial Indirect Rule in Chhattisgarh That Facilitated Maoist Insurgency

The type of rule in these feudatory princely states since the late 1800s contributed to making the princely states of Surguja, Koriya, Udaipur, and Jashpur in the north and Kanker and Bastar in the south of Chhattisgarh low state capacity areas with little public good provision and exploitation of land and natural resources of the indigenous tribes by landlords. These conditions persisted over time due to path dependence and created ideal structural conditions that Maoist rebel agents were able to use to foment leftist rebellion in the north and south of Chhattisgarh. The largest feudatory state in the Central Provinces area in the south of Chhattisgarh was Bastar, and Sundar (2007: 4) states, "In Bastar, as in other cases, the roots of this conflict can be traced to the colonial period" when structures of indirect rule created conditions for conflict.

In contrast, the central districts of Raipur, Bilaspur, and Durg were annexed in 1854 into British direct ruled Central Provinces due to death of the Raja of Nagpur without male heirs during the Doctrine of Lapse policy of Lord

---

[23] Chisholm to Chief Commissioner, Central Provinces, Prog. No. 101, para. 10, in *Foreign A-Political-I*, April 1884, *NAI*.

Dalhousie (1848–57). They had much higher levels of state capacity and less exploitation of land/natural resources and did not have insurgency later.

3.1.1   *MECHANISM 1: Colonial Indirect Rule and Despotic Extraction through* Zamindari *and* Malguzari *Land Tenure System*

Land Revenue Exploitation in the Khalsa *and* Zamindari *Lands in Bastar Princely State:* Indirect rule through the princely state of Bastar created unequal land tenure systems that increased power of landlords/*zamindars* and *diwans* who exploited land revenue and labor from the indigenous tribals. This is similar to despotic extraction in Africa, where Boone (1994: 117–18) suggests that the "colonial state's dependence on local intermediaries and allies created new privileged groups" who "were able to use their positions in the colonial system to their own advantage, often in ways that were not fully consistent with colonial ambitions."

The land tenure system under the princely states was made of up two types of land revenue systems – (1) *khalsa* lands that were under direct control of the prince, where the prince collected land revenue directly through the *diwan* and his bureaucracy, and (2) *zamindari* lands under landlords who paid fixed tributes to the prince (Joshi 1990:18).[24] See Figure 7.1 for *zamindari* estates in Bastar state.

(1) Khalsa Lands: The *khalsa* lands are officially supposed to be *ryotwari* land tenure, and initially they had village headmen collect land revenue and pass it on to *pargana majhis* who then passed it on to the king's officials. However, when Gopinath Kapurdar became the *diwan* of Bastar in 1867, he introduced the *malguzari* or *thekedari* land tenure system. This system was similar to the exploitative landlord type tenure systems in which the *malguzar* or *thekedar* collected the land revenue from the peasants and passed on a fixed rate, instead of a proportion of revenue collected (Sundar 2007: 94–96).

Diwan Gopinath Kapurdar, along with his close friend Adit Prasad, who was chief of the criminal court, oppressed the tribal *ryots* in the area and allowed excessive extraction of land taxes and labor. This resulted in a tribal uprising when the raja was traveling out of the state to attend a ceremonial meeting with the Prince of Wales in March 1876, and he refused to listen to his peasants' requests to not leave them at the mercy of the *diwan*. The raja telegrammed for help and when the British arrived with troops and enquired, the tribal leaders peacefully explained to Captain Eastall that they had "no ill-feeling against the Raja, but spoke very bitterly against the Diwan and Moonshee" and believed the *diwan* had a bad influence on the raja.[25] Further investigations by Deputy Commissioner of

---

[24] For details of land tenure systems in Chhattisgarh feudatory states, see E. A. de Brett, *Central Provinces Gazetteers: Chhattisgarh Feudatory States.*

[25] Letter from Captain Eastall, Acting Special Assistant Agent, Vizagapatnam, March 25, 1876, in Program No. 165, *Foreign Political-A, August 1876, NAI.*

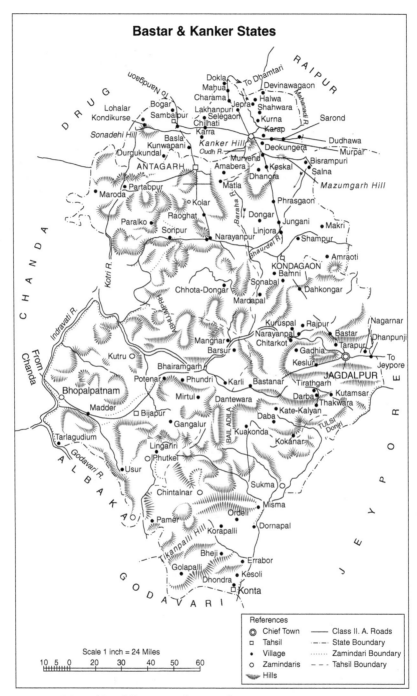

FIGURE 7.1 Map of Land Tenure and *Zamindaris* in Bastar
Source: E. A. DeBrett. 1909. *Central Provinces Gazetteers: Chhattisgarh Feudatory States*. Bombay: *The Times Press*. pp. 24–25.

Sironcha District H. MacGeorge, who traveled to Bastar and spoke with the tribals, revealed that Gopinath Kapurdar, along with Adit Prasad, had been "guilty of general oppression, indolence and injustice," and he found that "every Mooria I met and questioned, complained of their oppression." So the deputy commissioner proceeded to dismiss and remove them from Bastar, which satisfied the tribal peasants and ended the rebellion.[26]

The main reason for this tribal rebellion in 1876 was the sudden increase in land revenue rates under the *malguzari* system. Since the introduction of *malguzari* land tenure, the land settlements in Bastar "have been exceptionally favourable to malguzars" so that in many villages the malguzars "subsisted on the rents of ploughs in excess of the state demand" and did not do farming any more.[27] Additional Commissioner of Chhattisgarh H. C. E. Ward, after touring Bastar in 1883 wrote in his report that the revenue system in Bastar had been settled since 1877–78, and leases were fixed at Rs. 3 plus 5 annas per rupee per plough. In 1882, there were complaints from the peasants about *begar* or forced labor as well as taxes on "Thora Banat" and the *Diwan* Lal Kalandar Singh had to reduce "the State demand by Rs. 1 per plough."[28]

An element of exploitation of resources and land by ethnic outsiders was also a cause of grievance for the tribals. Sundar (2007: 97) mentions that many of the *thekedars* and *malguzars* were Oriya brahmins, and many of the clerks and accountants were Marathi brahmins. Many of the *tehsildars* (revenue colletors) of the various *tehsils* (sub-districts) had names such as Sheo Mangal Singh of Dongar tehsil, Jaikishen of Narayanpur tehsil, Mahadeo of Pertabpur tehsil, who were all upper-caste non-tribal immigrants.[29] These immigrant *thekedars/ malguzars/traders* and government officials exploited the tribals, and these groups were the target of attacks during rebellions. The "seven parganas that were closest to Jagdalpur had many of their villages given to foreigners, and it was here that the oppression complained of was mostly exercised," and the tribal rebellion of 1876 occurred in these areas.[30] The tribal *ryots* also complained that there were "foreigners in this part of the country" to whom the raja had given "grants of villages to the exclusion of the natives" and this had caused grievances among the tribals.[31]

---

[26] Report from H. MacGeorge, Deputy Commissioner to Secretary to the Chief Commissioner, Central Provinces, 22 April 1876, in Program No. 170, *Foreign Political-A, August 1876, paras 12–16, NAI.*

[27] de Brett, *Chhattisgarh Feudatory States*, p. 62.

[28] "Report on the Administration of Bastar State," Paragraph 33, by H. C. E Ward, Addl. Commissioner, Chhattisgarh Division, in *Foreign A-Political-I, January 1884, Prog. Nos. 117–125, NAI.*

[29] "Report on the Administration of Bastar State," Paragraph 34–36, by H. C. E Ward, Addl. Commissioner, Chhattisgarh Division, in *Foreign A-Political-I, January 1884.*

[30] Report from H. MacGeorge, in "Disturbances at Bastar," Program No. 170, *Foreign Political-A, August 1876, para 40, NAI.*

[31] Report from H. MacGeorge, in "Disturbances at Bastar," *para 21.*

The *ryots* in the *khalsa* tracts held by the state had to pay several direct and indirect taxes imposed by the greedy officers at lower levels of government, which resulted in their exploitation.[32] The state also allowed additional taxes on the *ryots,* and the contractors collected far more taxes than they deposited to the state treasury, pocketing the extra amount, thus fleecing and rack-renting the *ryots* (Joshi 1990: 47).

Commissioner of Raipur A. H. L. Fraser, in his tour report in 1892, states, "the system of leasing a whole tract of even hundreds of villages to one man to realize the revenue must be abandoned. It is utterly unsound and mischievous." He also suggests that the *muafi* tenures, which were revenue-free land grants for religious purposes, given to various feudal lords that did not require them to pay land revenue must be assessed and reduced.[33] This shows that the *malguzari/thekedari* land tenure system continued to be exploitative. One of the causes of tribal grievances that led to the 1910 *Bhumkal* rebellion was "exaction of excessive *begar* by malguzars." De Brett in his report on the 1910 rebellion agreed that while the *malguzar's* or *lessee's* right was restricted to three days of *begar* labor from his ryots, they were forcing the tribal *Adivasis* to work for more than a month of *begar.*[34]

(2) Zamindari Estates: Besides *khalsa lands,* there were ten *zamindari* estates in the Bastar/Kanker princely state areas south of the Indrawati River (see Table 7.1), and they paid tribute known as *takoli* to the raja. They had internal autonomy in terms of police, judicial, and revenue administration in their area, and usually the raja or prince did not interfere in the administration of these *zamindari* estates as long as they paid their tribute and there was no breakdown of law and order.[35]

In the *zamindari estates* within Bastar princely state, there was some level of oppression, similar to that in the *zamindari* areas in Bihar and Bengal. The PUCL 1989 report states, "during the colonial period, people in Kutru and Bhopalpatnam zamindaris had to abandon their fields due to Zamindari oppression. They fled to neighboring areas. After independence and zamindari abolition, they returned to find that their fields were now notified as forests, under the newly introduced Forest Act."[36] B. D. Sharma, scheduled castes and scheduled tribes commissioner in late 1980s and former collector of Bastar, wrote in his 1986–87 annual report: "In the pre-independence period, a number of villages were deserted by the people because of the depredations of the local zamindars who were taking advantage of the inaccessibility and remoteness.

---

[32] *Foreign Political-I, September 1886, Progs. Nos. 32 (memo), paras 6–8, NAI.*

[33] A. H. L. Fraser, "Tour Notes on the Bastar State," 1892, Paragraphs 21–22.

[34] Report no. 4417 by E. A. De Brett, in *Foreign, Secret-I, August 1911, Prog. No 37. Enclosure no. 1, para 36.*

[35] "Report on the Administration of Bastar State," by H. C. E Ward, Addl. Commissioner, Chhattisgarh Division, Paragraphs 5–6, in *Foreign A-Political-I, January 1884, Prog. Nos. 117–125.*

[36] PUCL, *Bastar: Development and Democracy,* 1989, p. 3

TABLE 7.1 *Zamindari estates in Bastar princely state*

Zamindari name	Area (square miles)	*Takoli* (Rs.)
Bhopalpatnam	1170	1400
Kutru	1072	1135
Beji (khalsa)	855	1900
Bijapur (khalsa)	705	3050
Kotapalli	408	300
Sukma	408	1255
Chintalnur	486	500
Patibul or Phhotkal	375	300
Pinlakot	Not known	450
Kokawarra	50	200

Source: "Report on the Administration of Bastar State," by H. C. E Ward, Addl. Commissioner, Chhattisgarh Division, Paragraph 6, in *Foreign A-Political-I, January 1884*, Prog. Nos. 117–125.

The agricultural lands in these areas were reclaimed by the forests which in due course came to be classified as protected and even reserved forests."[37] In the 1980s, increasing Maoist activity in these former *zamindari* areas of Kutru and Bhopalpatnam in Bijapur tehsil shows the persistence of the effects of such historic inequalities (PUCL, 1989: 9).

NATURAL AND FOREST RESOURCE EXTRACTION Extraction from tribal areas in Bastar did not happen only through land taxes. Another source of extraction was through natural resources like timber, minor forest products, and minerals. The Forest Act of 1878 gave the colonial state the right to reserved forests in colonial India and to keep original forest dwellers out; it also created three classes of forests – reserved forests, protected forests, and village or *nistari* forests.[38] There has been no consistent system of forest management in Bastar prior to its coming under British indirect rule, and the Forest Act of 1878 was applied to Bastar in the 1890s, when the British coerced the raja and *diwan* of Bastar state to introduce the new forest laws.

According to the People's Union of Civil Liberties (PUCL) report, the Bastar princely state area south of Chhattisgarh "contains one of the most deciduous forests of the country, consisting of sal, teak and mixed forests."[39] In 1908, the Bastar Forest Manual came into effect; by 1909, the first commercial exploitation of these forests began with a lease given to Beckett and Co. for extraction of 25,000 railway sleepers from sal trees, and operations increased during World

[37] Cited in Amit Baruah, "Bastar of the Tribals," *Frontline*, May 12–25, 1990, p. 5.
[38] Guha, "Forestry in British and Post-British India"; Sivaramakrishnan, *Modern Forests*.
[39] PUCL, *Bastar: Development and Democracy*, p. 5.

War II with increases in demand.[40] According to Sundar (2007: 107), felling of sal trees and their use in railway sleepers began in "1897 in the Kokawada range of Jagdalpur tehsil, 65,000 sleepers being supplied to the Southern Maratha railways from there alone. ... In 1906 the state was able to contract a lease for 100,000 sleepers to the Madras Timber Co, ... and 12,500 sleepers to another company." This showed extraction of timber for colonial projects like railways and exploitation using indirect forms of rule.

One of the reasons for the various tribal rebellions was that the British declared large areas as reserved forests under the new Forest Act, thus denying the *Adivasis* access to their forest resources and land, and supported the influx of outsiders into the area. Following the tribal rebellion of 1876, when Berry, the political agent, was in Bastar making enquiries, he found that there had been a reckless system of contracts for cutting the teak in Bhejji that had been "ruinous to the forests and bad for the revenue."[41] In the *Bhumkal rebellion* of 1910, tribals rebelled "led by their 'majhis' and village headmen. Bazaars were looted, the houses of officials, traders, and police stations – all those associated with the state – were burnt and robbed and grain redistributed."[42] While investigating the 1910 rebellion, Chief Commissioner Craddock stated, "reservation of certain forest areas – an innovation ... undoubtedly very distasteful to the aborigines – was the prime cause of the rising."[43] According to a British officer stationed in Bastar, L. W. Reynolds, "In his telegram of the 17th March 1910 the Chief Commissioner stated that one of the objects of the rising was the eviction of foreigners. I believe it to be the case that in connection with the exploitation of the forests Messrs. Gillanders, Arbuthnot and Company, who have a contract in the State, have introduced a large number of workmen from Bengal ... the (tribes) resent the introduction of these foreigners."[44]

LESS LAND REVENUE EXPLOITATION IN NEIGHBORING DIRECT BRITISH RULE DISTRICTS OF BILASPUR/RAIPUR IN CENTRAL CHHATTISGARH The central districts of current Chhattisgarh state – Raipur, Bilaspur, Durg – were part of Maratha-ruled Nagpur state. They lapsed to British direct rule and became part of the Central Provinces, due to the death of the Maratha king Raghuji III in 1854 without a male heir, under Lord Dalhousie's (1848–56) Doctrine of Lapse policy in which any Indian ruler who died without a male heir

---

[40] PUCL, *Bastar: Development and Democracy*, p. 5.

[41] Chisholm to Chief Commissioner, Central Provinces, Prog. No. 101, para. 12, in *Foreign A–Political–I*, April 1884, Nos 99–103, *NAI*.

[42] Nandini Sundar, "Bastar, Maoism and Salwa Judum," *Economic and Political Weekly* July 22, 2006.

[43] R. H. Craddock, Chief Commissioner, Central Provinces, "Note on connection of Lal Kalendra Singh with the rebellion in Bastar State," in *Foreign Secret–I, September 1910*, Prog. No 16, Enclosure 3, Para 7, *NAI*.

[44] Cited in Verghese (2016a: p. 1633), Report by Chief Commissioner L. W. Reynolds. April 19, 1910, British Library, IOR/R/1/1/415, 1910, p. 15.

would forfeit his kingdom to British rule (Iyer 2010).[45] When the choice of type of land tenure system for the Central Provinces was made in 1860s, the British erred and imposed the *mahalwari* tenure, because of the influence of Holt Mackenzie, secretary of the Board of Revenue, who had written a brilliant minute in 1819 in strong support of village-based/*mahalwari* settlements in India.[46]

Unfortunately, the villages in the central provinces "were not of the landlord or joint type, but represented aggregates of cultivators, each claiming his own holding and nothing more, like the villages of Bombay and Madras ... and so a *raiyatwari* Settlement like in Madras or Bombay, would not only have been possible but also highly advantageous."[47] So the *mahalwari* system failed and the British administrators adapted by falling back on the old Maratha system of using *malguzars* or *patels* to collect the land revenue on behalf of the village. This became known as the *malguzari* tenure and was a hybrid between the *zamindari* system of Bengal and the *ryotwari* (non-landlord) system of Bombay and Madras.

However, certain British administrators considered the *malguzari* tenure system a mistake, and the British government tried to limit the proprietary right of the *malguzar* and protected the rights of individual cultivators by making them plot-proprietors (*Malik-makbuza*) (Baden-Powell, Vol.1, p. 388). The tenants were also protected because in these malguzari villages, the landlords were not given power of eviction over a large number of original tenants (Baden-Powell 1892, Vol. 1, p. 313). Portions of the province were "left purely raiyatwari" (Baden-Powell 1892, Vol. 2, pp. 456, 476) – Berar, Nimar, and Chhindwara districts were mostly *ryotwari*, while Bilaspur and Raipur districts in central Chhattisgarh had a mix of *zamindari* and *khalsa/ryotwari* lands.[48] According to the 1909 *Gazetteer*, within Raipur district, Raipur and Dhamtari *tahsils* had no *zamindaris* and only *khalsa* areas, while Mahasamund and BalodaBazar *tehsils* had some *zamindaris* mixed with *khalsa* areas.[49] However, the majority of the *zamindars* were Raj-Gonds and so ethnically similar to the indigenous tribes of this region, in contrast to the *zamindars* in Bastar princely state.[50] Compared with the dominant *zamindari/malguzari* land tenure system in the Bastar princely state region, the mix of modified *malguzari* and *ryotwari* land tenure systems in neighboring direct rule districts of Bilaspur and Raipur thus allowed more equality of land holdings and was less extractive,

---

[45] Baden-Powell, *Land Tenure Systems of British India, Volume 1*, p. 47.
[46] Holt Mackenzie, Memorandum, July 1, 1819, para. 550, *Selections from the Revenue Records of the N.W. Provinces 1818–1820* (Calcutta, 1866), p. 117.
[47] Baden-Powell, *Land Tenure Systems of British India, Volume 1*, pp. 311–13.
[48] *Report on Administration of Central Provinces & Berar*, 1904–1905, pp. 6–9.
[49] *Central Provinces District Gazetteer: Raipur District*, 1909, pp. 70–72.
[50] *Central Provinces District Gazetteer: Raipur District*, 1909, p. 123.

and the tenants were relatively well off.[51] As a result of lower levels of exploitation, and more equitable land tenure, these directly ruled areas in central Chhattisgarh did not see tribal and peasant rebellions.

3.1.2   MECHANISM 2: Colonial Indirect Rule Created Weak State Capacity

Besides leading to exploitation of land and forest/mineral resources that created tribal grievances, indirect rule in these feudatory princely states resulted in low levels of road network and police capacity, and low public goods distribution, as compared with neighboring areas that were under direct British rule as part of the Central Provinces. Roads and police are useful for counterinsurgency in rural areas and are a proxy for local state capacity and rebel opportunity (Fearon & Laitin 2003). This historically created weak state capacity allowed political opportunity structures that facilitated Maoist rebels in sustaining insurgency later. According to renowned human rights activist K. Balagopal: "Abujhmarh in Chhattisgarh area was allowed to remain un-administered as a decision ... and unsurveyed also ... And the ... areas of today's Kanker, Bastar and Dantewada are so backward that administering was possible by the Maoists."[52]

Fewer Roads/Railways in Bastar Princely State: In the 1880s, Bastar was underdeveloped because of the lack of good communication links with the outside world and the inaccessibility of the state, which made it difficult to conduct trade and develop markets linking it to other regions (Joshi 1990: 17). This was probably because of the forests and difficult terrain, though Ward in his 1883 report on Bastar mentioned that "there is no reason, except the backward state and ignorance of its rulers, why Bastar should not have been made ... accessible for traffic, for much of the country is peculiarly favorable for road construction."[53] Commissioner of Raipur Fraser toured the various parts of Bastar state in 1892 and wrote a scathing report in which he suggested that the complaint that the terrain was rough and the interiors were difficult to reach was a myth, created by the officers themselves.[54]

Not only roads but also railway networks connecting Bastar princely state to the outside world were less developed. In response to a request by Tata Steel to renew its iron ore prospecting license in 1926 for a further three years, the British officials had requested the Bengal National (B. N.) Railways to see if it was possible to construct a line from Durg district (direct rule) to Kanker district (indirect rule). In response the B. N. Railways had "stated that the construction

---

[51] *Central Provinces District Gazetteer: Raipur District*, 1909, p. 166.

[52] Interview with K. Balagopal, Hyderabad, February 8, 2008.

[53] "Report on the Administration of Bastar State," Prog. No 122, Paragraphs 90–96, by H. C. E Ward, Addl. Commissioner, Chhattisgarh Division, in *Foreign A–Political–I*, January 1884, Prog. Nos. 117–125, *NAI*.

[54] A. H. L. Fraser, "Tour Notes on the Bastar State," 1892, Compilation No. XXXVIII, Jagdalpur Collectorate Records Room. Paragraph 6.

of the Raipur-Vizianagram line has removed entirely the necessity for the Durg-Bastar-Jeypur-Kotavalasa line as a connection link between the Central Provinces and the east coast."[55] This suggests greater priority given to connecting direct rule areas like Raipur to the coastal city of Vizianagram in directly ruled Madras Presidency, and lower priority to indirectly ruled Bastar/Kanker.

More Roads/Railways in British Direct Rule Areas: In contrast, Bilaspur, Raipur, and Durg districts in the center of Chhattisgarh that were under British direct rule as part of the Central Provinces had relatively higher levels of road networks, which made it difficult for Maoists to succeed there in the future. Administrative reports of the Central Provinces mention high expenditures on roads, post offices, and railways. For example, the Annual Report of 1909–10 mentions the "widening of the remaining 47 miles of the ... principal roads in the Nagpur district, which was left unfinished during 1908–09. ... Several roads in Berar were stone-metalled at the cost of Rs. 28,437."[56] A few years later, the Annual Report of 1915–16 mentions that "the Nagpur section of the Nagpur-Amraoti road and the Anji-Wardha road were practically completed. ... A submerged bridge of the Raipur-Bilaspur road over the Sheonath river was completed at a cost of over Rs. 84,000."[57]

Comparing Maps of Roads/Railways of Princely States and Direct Rule: This variation in road/railway networks between direct ruled areas in Central Provinces and the indirect rule areas of Bastar in the south, and other feudatory princely states like Surguja in the north of Chhattisgarh, becomes clear when comparing historical maps of this region. First, Figure 7.2 shows a historical map of colonial direct rule in the Central Provinces and various feudatory princely states. Then Figure 7.3 shows a map of the Central Provinces' roads and railway lines for 1920–21, and Figure 7.4 shows the spread of railway lines and electricity stations soon after India's independence in 1947. Comparing Figure 7.2 with Figures 7.3 and 7.4, it is evident that such state penetration and public goods were lowest in the Bastar and Surguja districts in the south and north, respectively, of the eastern part of the Central Provinces that later became Madhya Pradesh following independence in 1947. Relative to these regions, the direct rule districts in the west like Nagpur, Balaghat, Chhindwara, Mandla, and even the Bilaspur and Raipur districts have a denser network of roads and railway lines.

[55] "Renewal of the prospecting license for iron ore in the Bastar State in favour of the Tata Iron and Steel Company, Ltd., for one year at a time, for a further period of three years." *Foreign and Political Department, Internal Branch, File No. 328-I, 1926, NAI.*

[56] *Report on the Administration of the Central Provinces and Berar, for the year 1909–10.* Nagpur: Printed at the Secretariat Press, 1911. pp. 33–34.

[57] *Report on the Administration of the Central Provinces and Berar, for the year 1915–16.* Nagpur: Printed at the Secretariat Press, 1917, p. 36, para 121.

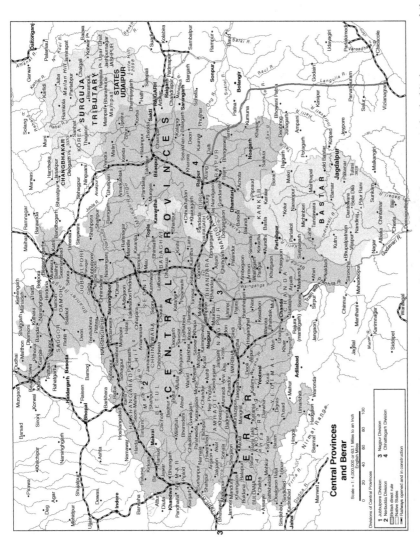

FIGURE 7.2 Map of princely states and British direct rule in Central Provinces: Princely states are shaded lighter grey, while British direct rule districts are shaded darker grey

Source: *The Imperial Gazetteer of India: Volume 26 – Atlas*, Plate 39. 1909. Available at Digital South Asia Library, University of Chicago at https://dsal.uchicago.edu/maps/gazetteer/images/gazetteer_V10_pg112.jpg

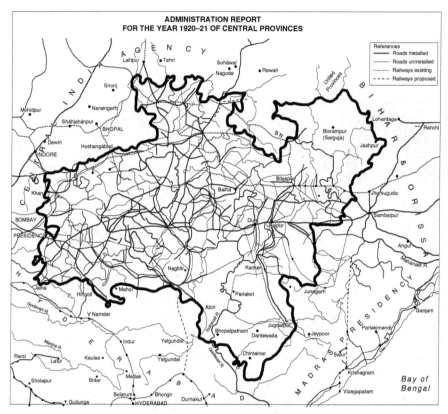

FIGURE 7.3 Map of roads and railway in Central Provinces, 1920–21
Source: *Report on the Administration of the Central Provinces and Berar, for the year 1920–21.* Printed at Government Press, Nagpur, 1922, page ii (before the Contents page) Available through CRL at https://dds.crl.edu/crldelivery/18265

LOWER POLICE CAPACITY IN PRINCELY STATE AREAS AS COMPARED TO DIRECT RULE AREAS: Another important measure of local counterinsurgency capacity is police capacity that allows the state to collect local information about insurgents. Similar to variation in road networks, the Central Provinces directly ruled districts had higher quality police forces than the princely state areas of Bastar and Surguja. I briefly provide data on this variation here (more details on police capacity variation are in Online Appendix A for this chapter).

Low Police Capacity in Bastar: Bastar in the 1880s had a corrupt police force, which was "the bane of the local administration, the men being poorly paid and badly supervised; they preyed on the local people, particularly the tribals. Many

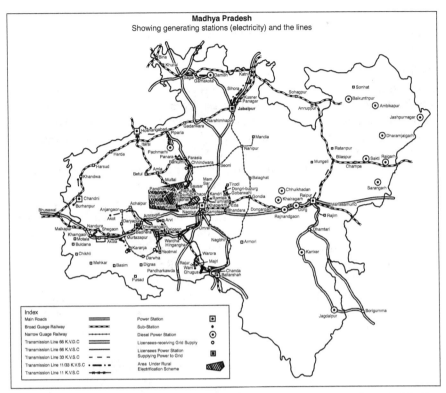

FIGURE 7.4 Map of roads, railways, and electricity-generating stations in Madhya Pradesh (erstwhile Central Provinces), 1951
Source: Census of India, 1951, *Volume VII, Madhya Pradesh, Part 1-A Report.* Nagpur, Government Printing, 1953.

interior areas had no police posts at all."[58] Raja Bhairam Deo had written to the commissioner of the Chhattisgarh Division in 1884 mentioning that "I do not require any Police force to preserve peace within my State, because there is tranquility in other parts of the state" except the highway between Jagdalpur and Sihawa, which was troubled by those opposed to him politically, for which he requested the help of the British.[59] This shows low interest by the raja in creating police capacity. According to de Brett (1909), in Bastar in 1908, the police force "strength is one man to 948 of the population and 40 square miles of country," which was not adequate for a large state like Bastar.[60] In 1944, it

[58] Joshi, *Tribal Bastar and British Administration*, p. 49, cites Bastar Annual Report 1886–87, para 46. Also Annual Report 1887–88, para 47.

[59] Letter from Raja Bhairo Deo to Chief Commissioner Bastar, No. 100, in *Foreign A-Political-I, April 1884*, NAI.

[60] E. A. de Brett, *Central Provinces Gazetteers: Chhattisgarh Feudatory States*, Bombay: Time Press, 1909, p. 67, paragraph 62.

"amounts to *one Police Officer to every 47 square miles and every 2,149 persons.*"[61] This shows that the *police:area ratio* became worse in 1944 as compared to 1909.

Higher Police Capacity in Neighboring British Direct Rule Districts: Comparing police force strength using the various *Annual Reports on the Police Administration of the Central Provinces,* from 1907 to 1912 and 1920 to 1921, shows that British direct ruled districts of the Central Provinces like Raipur, Durg, Bilaspur, Balaghat, Mandla, Nagpur, and Chhindwara had higher *police to area ratio* as compared with Bastar and Surguja princely states. Table 7.2 presents comparative data for Bastar state and British direct rule districts of Chhattisgarh division and shows that for 1909, just before the tribal rebellion in Bastar in 1910, the police to area ratio for Bastar was around 1:40 square miles, but for Raipur, Bilaspur, and Durg districts it was around 1:13, 1:15, and 1:8, respectively.[62] In 1909–10, "construction of offices for the District Superintendents of Police at Nagpur and Balaghat was taken in hand . . . a station house and quarters at Bhatapara in the Raipur district were begun."[63] In the *Annual Reports* of 1920, Inspector General of Police K. W. Deighton mentions that the total strength of the force was increased by 258, including an increase to the Special Armed Force of 8 head and 106 constables for Nagpur and Jubbulpore.[64]

4   PERSISTENCE OF THE EFFECTS OF THESE INSTITUTIONS INTO POSTCOLONIAL TIMES

Following India's independence in 1947, the princely states and *zamindars* were officially abolished by the 1950s. However, due to path dependence of the effects of these institutions, low state penetration combined with extraction of land revenue and natural resources from tribal lands continued. Consequently, the northern and southern parts of Chhattisgarh, which were former princely states of Surguja and Bastar, respectively, remained areas of low stateness, with low provision of public goods, and continued exploitation of land/natural resources, and experienced successful Maoist movement since 1980s. Districts in central Chhattisgarh like Bilaspur and Raipur, which had been formerly part of British direct rule, had higher state capacity and lower levels of land resource exploitation and did not see Maoist insurgency.

The Chhattisgarh region was in the eastern part of the larger Central Provinces during colonial rule. In the first census of independent India in 1951, the Central Provinces was renamed Madhya Pradesh, with the state and

---

[61] *Report on the Administration of Bastar state, for the year 1944*, pp. 8–10.

[62] Table 7.2B in Online Appendix A has data on police strength in the 1920s.

[63] *Report on the Administration of the Central Provinces and Berar, for the year 1909–10*. Nagpur: Secretariat Press, 1911, pp. 32–33, paragraph 122.

[64] *Annual Report on the Police Administration of the Central Provinces*, 1920, pp. 33–34.

TABLE 7.2 *Police strength (proportion of police to area) in different districts of Central Provinces and Berar, compared with princely states of Bastar and Surguja in 1910s*

Name of district/princely state and year	Number of senior officers (SPs, ASPs, DSPs, DIGs)	Number of Inspectors and sub-inspectors	Number of head/chief constables	Number of constables	Total police	Area (in square miles)	Population	Proportion of police to area	No. of police stations and outposts
Chhattisgarh division (1909)									
Raipur	4	45	109	566	724	9,831	11,96,858	13	29
Bilaspur	2	23	76	412	513	7,605	833,308	15	38
Durg	2	29	58	293	382	3,137	676,313	8	19
Nagpur division (1909)									
Nagpur	4	34	128	704	870	3,840	751,844	4	42
Bhandara	1	14	52	280	347	3,965	663,062	10	25
Balaghat	1	10	39	213	263	3,139	326,521	11	15
Chanda	3	24	92	523	642	9,911	554,105	15	43
Wardha	1	17	52	283	353	2,428	385,103	7	24
Berar Division (1909)									
Amraoti	3	45	114	612	774	4,754	809,499	6	27
Akola	3	41	104	540	688	4,109	754,804	5	24

TABLE 7.2 (*continued*)

Name of district/ princely state and year	Number of senior officers (SPs, ASPs, DSPs, DIGs)	Number of Inspectors and sub-inspectors	Number of head/chief constables	Number of constables	Total police	Area (in square miles)	Population	Proportion of police to area	No. of police stations and outposts
Buldana	3	36	86	468	592	3,663	613,756	6	22
Yeotmal	2	38	85	463	588	5,183	575,957	8	23
Chhattisgarh feudatory princely states (indirect rule)									
Bastar (1889)	0	1	36	184	221	13,062	N.A.	59	7
Bastar (1909)	0	4	57	274	335	13,062	3,06,501	40	10
Surguja (1909)	0	16	44	153	213	6,089	3,51,011	29	9
Kanker (1909)	0	4	13	58	75	1,429	103,536	19	2
Raigarh (1909)	0	1	3	107	111	1486	174,929	13	3
Nandgaon (1909)	0	5	17	94	116	906	19,548	7.81	

Sources: Data on Central Province districts from "Statement D: Showing sanctioned strength and cost of police of the Central Provinces for the year 1909" in Appendices of *Report on the Police Administration of the Central Provinces and Berar for the Year 1910.* Nagpur: Government Press. 1911. Data on Bastar and other princely states like Surguja, Kanker, Raigarh, Udaipur, etc. for the year 1909, from de Brett (1909). Data on Bastar for 1889 from Joshi (1990).

district boundaries remaining almost the same, as is clear from the maps in Figure 7.2. The new name Madhya Pradesh was a literal translation, since Madhya means "central" and Pradesh means "provinces" in Hindi, the official language of India, and shows another continuity from colonial times. Discussing the Madhya Pradesh area in 1951, a census officer remarked that the

railway line passes through all the districts of the State except Bastar ... a proposal to connect it with a railway line either from Dhamtari in the Raipur district or Rajnandgaon in the Durg district was examined during the decade but for financial reasons the matter could not be pursued further. ... These backward districts as we have seen are full of practically untapped natural resources and as soon as the Railway projects materialize they will develop fast.[65]

This implies that the bureaucrats of the new postcolonial Indian government soon after independence in the 1950s recognized that the areas in the north and south of the Chhattisgarh region in eastern Madhya Pradesh that were former princely states had lower state penetration/capacity and also had huge amounts of natural resources that could be exploited but had not been explored yet. This reveals continuities in the administrative mind-set of the postcolonial bureaucrats with that of colonial bureaucrats. In the same way as colonial officers thought of these areas in Bastar and Surguja as valuable in terms of land and natural resources but best ruled indirectly through their preexisting native rulers because it was not worth the cost to administer them directly, postcolonial bureaucrats and politicians believed that these far-flung areas of Madhya Pradesh with *indigenous Adivasis* were valuable in terms of their resources, but not important enough to provide public goods.

Path Dependence Mechanism 1: Continuation of Power of *Zamindars* and Tribal Elites and Path Dependence through Elite Vested Interests

During colonial times, the British relied on native princes from Rajput dynasties and various *zamindars* and *malguzars*, often from ethnic groups outside the region, to collect land revenue and extract forest and mineral resources from the Bastar region. Following Indian independence in 1947, electoral democratic institutions were introduced in Bastar as in the rest of India, and the Raja of Bastar and the various *zamindaris* were abolished. However, from the 1950 to 1970s, these former landlords, chiefs, and tribal elites continued to remain powerful in Chhattisgarh. They joined the mainstream political parties like the Congress and Bharatiya Janata Party (BJP) and allowed the central government to control votes and resources in this area through them. This persistence of power of landed elites that allowed continuation of exploitation of land and natural resources resulted in what Mahoney (2000: 521) calls "power-based" path dependent institutional persistence, in which the effects of a former institution can persist when an elite benefiting from it has sufficient strength to promote its reproduction.

---

[65] Census of India, 1951, *Volume VII, Madhya Pradesh*, Part 1-A Report, p. 211.

The persisting power of former landed elites from colonial times manifested in Chhattisgarh in two ways. First, these former elites continued to have political power and this resulted in ethnic exclusion of the poor indigenous *Adivasis* from genuine political representation in democratic politics and power (Cederman et al. 2010). This led to grievances and created ethnic mobilization networks for Maoist rebels. Kennedy and Purushottam (2012) mention that unlike the scheduled castes that were relatively larger in population and more concentrated in certain areas, the scheduled tribes in India were fewer in population and probably too dispersed, and thus they have not been as successful in furthering their cause through electoral politics. Most of these former landlords and tribal elites were co-opted and joined either the Congress or the BJP, thus preventing any indigenous political party representing the poorer "sons of the soil" from emerging in Chhattisgarh, even after the formation of the state in the year 2000 out of the larger state of Madhya Pradesh on the basis of tribal demands.

A key example would be Mahendra Karma, a well-known tribal landlord who initially started his political career with the leftist Communist Party of India (CPI) in 1978, but later switched to the mainstream Congress Party and was the mastermind behind the *Salwa Judum* movement, which started in 2005 to fight the Maoists.[66] The right-wing Bharatiya Janata Party was elected in the state in the 2003, 2008, and 2013 elections, before being defeated by the Congress in the 2019 Assembly elections; the BJP always had non-tribal Raman Singh as the chief minister and many of the ministers like Brijmohan Agarwal and Prem Prakash Pandey were non-tribals too.[67] This has not been perceived as beneficial to tribal welfare by tribal leaders of the BJP like Nandkumar Sai.[68]

While there is a sons of the soil party named the Prithak Bastar Rajya Party in Chhattisgarh, which claims to represent the needs of poor tribals in Bastar, it has never succeeded electorally in Chhattisgarh, thus denying the Gond tribes of political representation.[69] The Gondwana Ganatantra Party (GGP) represents Gond tribes in central India. Although it has had some electoral success in the neighboring state of Madhya Pradesh, it has not had much success electorally in south Chhattisgarh districts. Chandra and Garcia-Ponce (2019) show that prior inclusion of subaltern ethnic groups through ethnic parties prevents the Maoists from being successful; in Chhattisgarh the inability of political parties to provide proper representation to demands of poor tribals meant their ethnic exclusion from power, which created grievances mobilized by the Maoists.

The second way in which continuing power of non-tribal and tribal landed elites manifested was through continuing land inequality and former landlords

---

[66] PUDR et al., *When the State Makes War on Its Own People*, p. 12.
[67] www.newincept.com/chhattisgarh/council-of-ministers-of-chhattisgarh.html
[68] Suvojit Bagchi, "Chhattisgarh needs a tribal Chief Minister," *The Hindu*, September 26, 2013.
[69] Interview with Prabhat Pattawi, Prithak Bastar Rajya Party leader, Raipur, Chhattisgarh, 2009.

controlling land. Even elites from within tribal society, for example, tribal landlords like Mahendra Karma, "have promoted policies that not only increase their personal wealth, but also intensified the very exploitative processes that form the core of *Adivasi* grievances" (Kennedy & Purushottam 2012: 853). The long-term legacy of colonialism becomes clear from the fact that Mahendra Karma's father Bodda Majhi and grandfather Mashal were village headmen (*jalil mukhiya*) and landlords who used to work for the British during colonial times.[70]

By the late 1980s, the Maoist-led mass organizations like the *Dandakaranya Adivasi Kisan Majdoor Sangh* (Tribal Peasant and Workers Association, DAKMS) started addressing inequality in land ownership. This inequality was highest in parts of Konta tehsil (which had formerly been part of the Sukma/Konta *zamindari*). The DAKMS carried out distribution of part of larger land holdings controlled by a "few families in the village … to those without land, and redistribution of the most fertile lands was carried out in some areas."[71] In 1989–90, the Maoist-backed DAKMS started attacking landlords and taking away their landholdings, and the Maoists started removing the traditional village headmen or *mukhiyas* from power. In response, the Bastar region saw two *Jan Jagran Abhiyans* (public awareness campaigns) by landed elites against the Maoists' attempts to take away their land and redistribute it to the poorer tribals.[72]

The first *Jan Jagran Abhiyan* started in July-August 1990, in response to the killing of a village headman in Kutru. Several local leaders including Mahendra Karma led this movement that attacked villages and threatened villagers to hand over members of the Maoist *sanghams* (organizations), looted villages, and beat and raped women. The PWG Maoists retaliated and within some months the *Abhiyan* ended and Maoist control over villages in Kutru was reestablished.[73] A second such *Jan Jagran Abhiyan* started in 1998, in villages around Pharsapal, Mahendra Karma's native village, where there was substantial inequality in land ownership. Karma again led the movement against the Maoists and the pattern of mobilization was similar to that in 1991. But this second *Abhiyan* was localized and did not last long.[74]

These movements were examples of political opposition to the Maoist attempts to redistribute land to peasants from the dominant and landed groups in society, both tribal and non-tribal. The removal from positions of power of the village headman and the priest due to the creation of *sanghams* by the Maoists led to grievances of the former traditional elite, which led to support for these *Jan Jagran Abhiyans*. Also, traders and contractors in

---

[70] CPI-Maoist, *Jan Jagran Nahi, Jan Daman Abhiyan*, p. 12.
[71] PUDR et al., *When the State Makes War on Its Own People*, p. 11.
[72] CPI-Maoist, *Jan Jagran Nahi, Jan Daman Abhiyan*, p. 5.
[73] PUDR et al., *When the State Makes War on Its Own People*, pp. 12–13.
[74] PUDR et al., *When the State Makes War on Its Own People*, p. 13.

"trading towns and tehsil headquarters such as Bijapur and Bhairamgarh – who were mostly non-tribals – added to this constituency against the Maoists."[75]

The most recent such anti-Maoist vigilante movement has been the *Salwa Judum* or "purification hunt" movement that started in June 2005 in Kutru and mobilized tribals against the Maoists. Mahendra Karma along with Rajendra Pambhoi and Kedar Kashyap started the *Salwa Judum*, but unlike previous movements this time there was stronger support from the ruling BJP government, which used the police and paramilitary and underage tribals called Special Police Officers (SPOs) for logistical support of the *Salwa Judum*.[76] It resulted in a lot of violence against civilians who were forced to leave their villages and settle in camps, and increasing killings between the Maoists and the *Salwa Judum*.[77]

Besides Mahendra Karma, the top-level leadership of the *Salwa Judum* was composed of "those in traditional positions of authority within the village, those whose lands have been redistributed" and non-tribal immigrant traders whose profits have been hit by the struggles over tendu patta and forest produce by Maoists.[78] According to Lakshman Kashyap, a local *Salwa Judum* leader, the *Salwa Judum* leadership primarily consisted of (a) some village headmen, and *sarpanches*, along with their clans, and (b) non-tribal immigrants who stood to lose the most from the Maoist insurgency.[79] Some of the *Salwa Judum* leaders like Ram Bhuvan Kushawa in Dornapal and Ajay Singh in Bhairamgarh were non-tribal immigrants from Uttar Pradesh, who worked as contractors and traders and had been targeted by Maoists.[80]

The persistence of political influence of landlords is also evident in states like Bihar and Andhra Pradesh where upper-caste landed elites continued to have a vested interest and prevented politicians of their castes from carrying out serious land reforms, causing continuing land inequality (Herring 1983). In central Bihar in the 1980s, upper-caste landlords started anti-Maoist vigilante groups like *Ranvir Sena* to stop land redistribution to *Dalit* peasants (Bhatia 2005; Louis 2002), similar to the *Salwa Judum* in Chhattisgarh.

Continuing Exploitation of Natural Resources in Bastar

Besides exploitation of land revenue by the landlord class, there was also continuity in exploitation of natural resources from this region. Exhibiting similar policies as the colonial state, the postcolonial Indian government decided to start extracting these rich natural resource deposits through the

---

[75] PUDR et al., *When the State Makes War on Its Own People*, pp. 11–12.
[76] CPI-Maoist, *Jan Jagran Nahi*, pp. 5–7.
[77] Human Rights Forum, *Death, Displacement and Deprivation: The War in Dantewada*.
[78] PUDR et al., *When the State Makes War on Its Own people*, pp. 15–17.
[79] PUDR et al., *When the State Makes War on Its Own People*, p. 15.
[80] Independent Citizen's Initiative, *War in the Heart of India*, pp. 15–16.

FIGURE 7.5 Single-bore railway line near Kirandul town in Dantewada district where iron ore was extracted. It was used to take the iron ore all the way to Vishakhapatnam, and then to Japan, and is symbolic of exploitation of natural resources of this tribal area by the Indian state
Source: Photograph by author during fieldwork.

National Mineral Development Corporation's (NMDC) iron ore mining project, which was started in 1968 in Kirandul and Bacheli towns in the Bailadilla Hills in the Dantewada district of Bastar.[81] The government of India had entered into an agreement to export 40 million tons of iron ore from Bailadilla mines, starting in 1966, to Japan Steel Mills Association, with the target of 4 million tons annually to be exported.[82] To overcome the poor communication links between Bastar and surrounding regions, the Indian government decided to build the Kottavalasa-Bailadilla broad gauge railway line to link the iron ore areas of Bailadilla with Visakhapatnam port in the Andhra Pradesh state coast by 1966.[83] See Figure 7.5 for a picture of this railway line.

There has been a lot of criticism of the NMDC and other mines in the region for being exploitative of the natural resources of Bastar. By the 1990s, the tribal

[81] "Dinesh Singh inaugurates Bailadilla Mines," October 13, 1968, *Dandakaranya Samachar*.
[82] "Railways to start Construction." November 27, 1960, *Dandakaranya Samachar*.
[83] *"Hindustan Steel Limited,"* January 1963, in *"Proposal for the setting up of a steel plant in Bailadilla,"* Dept: Railways, Branch: Planning, Year: 1963. File No: 63/PL/4/4 (5)/ 1–22, NAI.

population of Kirandul was just about 2 percent, showing significant displacement of indigenous tribals by the NMDC government project, which became one of India's largest foreign exchange earning units.[84] The PUCL report (1989) mentions that the iron ore slurry from the iron ore plants in Bailadilla was dumped into the Sankhini River, and this "mass of red slime is spreading through the southern river system. Some 40,000 people living in about 51 villages are its immediate victims, deprived of even drinking water."[85]

More recently agreements were reached in 2005 between the BJP in Chhattisgarh and the Essar group that were supposed to set up a pipe line to transport 8 million tons of iron ore slurry per annum to the Vishakhapatnam port; also steel plants were to be set up in Bhansi and Dhurli. There were also plans for a new NMDC steel plant to be set up at Nagarnar village in Bastar, which faced local protests.[86] A memorandum of understanding (MoU) was similarly signed with Tata Steel to set up a steel plant in Lohandiguda in Dantewada district; it included a confidentiality clause that prevented the terms of the agreement from being made public, and even the MP from Lohandiguda was not aware of the terms.[87] The state made use of the Land Acquisitions Act of 1894 and contacts with politicians to acquire tribal land to set up the development projects and factories of Tata Steel and other MNCs (Kennedy & Purushottam 2012: 853).

According to human rights activist Sudha Bharadwaj, the ulterior motive behind the controversial *Salwa Judum* vigilante movement was to drive out *Adivasi* supporters of Maoists from their villages and make land easily available for mining projects by private companies like Tata and Essar in the Dantewada area.[88] According to journalist Aman Sethi, "In an instance of truly Orwellian coincidence, the Memorandum of Understanding (MoU) for the Tata steel plant was signed on June 4, 2005, two days after the formal launch of the controversial *Salwa Judum* programme in the Bastar and Dantewada districts. . . . The State government also signed an MoU with the Essar group the same day."[89] Maoist writers like Nitin (pseudonym) suggest that the *Salwa Judum* campaign was used by the state to create schisms within and weaken the support of the Adivasis for the Maoist rebellion which was targeting the companies trying to extract iron ore and various other minerals in Dantewada region.[90] Even the police chief of Chhattisgarh agreed that the reason the BJP government of Raman Singh had supported the *Salwa Judum* movement against the Maoists was that

---

[84] PUCL, *Bastar: Development and Democracy*, p. 5.
[85] PUCL, *Bastar: Development and Democracy*, p. 9.
[86] PUDR et al., *When the State Makes War on Its Own people*, p. 8.
[87] Ilina Sen, "Ground-clearing with the Salwa Judum," *Himal South Asian*, November 2006: 42–44.
[88] Interview with PUCL activist Sudha Bhardwaj, Bhilai, Chhattisgarh, 2009.
[89] Aman Sethi, "New battle zones," *Frontline*, Vol. 24, Issue 18.
[90] Nitin, "The Forest Is Ours," p. 8.

the Bastar region was rich in minerals, and the BJP government could not develop and use the natural resources without insurgency being controlled.[91]

The well-known social activist Dr. Binayak Sen points out that these multinational corporations (MNCs) like Tata and Essar in the Kirandul/Bacheli area in Dantewada district have been setting up plants to extract iron ore without building adequate roads and providing sufficient development.[92] In a focus group discussion in a village near Kirandul town, several villagers reported that health facilities were insufficient and proper roads were lacking; in addition, the pollution coming from the neighboring Essar plant was making it risky for them to take baths.[93]

There has been local opposition to these proposed steel plants under the aegis of the *Adivasi Mahasabha*, a mass-based indigenous rights organization. There were several *gram sabhas* (village electorate meetings) in Dhurli opposing the land acquisition by the Essar Plant in 2006, and several people were taken into police custody and pressured to not oppose the plant in the next *gram sabha* meeting. Similarly, villagers in Nagarnar opposed the proposed NMDC steel plant, and were lathi charged (baton charged) by the police, and some were arrested and released only on the condition that they would accept the compensation package offered for giving up their lands. The Maoists attacked the NMDC complex in Dantewada in June 2017 several times and carried out a successful economic blockade late June in Chhattisgarh and Jharkhand to protest the economic policies of creating special economic zones (SEZs) on tribal lands.[94]

Path Dependent Mechanism 2: Persistence of Poor Road Network and Weak Police Capacity

Much like the colonial bureaucrats, the new Indian state officials were not interested in developing the infrastructure, roads, or railway networks of this area. This resulted in the continuing weak state capacity in the form of lower levels of road/railway networks and lower police/bureaucratic capacity in these areas in Madhya Pradesh state that were previously part of the princely states of Bastar/Kanker in the south and Surguja/Koriya/Jashpur in the north. This allowed opportunity structures for Maoist rebels to create successful rebellion. Compared with this, the areas in the central parts of Chhattisgarh, which were formerly part of British direct rule Central Provinces, continued to further develop their levels of road and infrastructure, and the state was able to increase the provision of public goods in these areas.

[91] Interview with Vishwaranjan, director general of police, Raipur, Chhattisgarh, 2008.
[92] Interview with human rights activist Dr. Binayak Sen, Raipur, Chhattisgarh, 2008.
[93] Focus group discussion with villagers, Village X (pseudonym), near Kirandul town, Dantewada district, 2009.
[94] Aman Sethi, "New battle zones," *Frontline*, Vol. 24, Issue 18, 21 September 2017.

What explains the reproduction of these mechanisms of low state capacity and development in the areas that were former princely states? One reason is that there is a certain path dependence of these mechanisms, and it was easier for the postcolonial state to build on and expand the already existing higher levels of roads, railways, and other physical infrastructure in the former British direct rule districts. But it was more difficult for the postcolonial state to expand on the preexisting low levels of roads and infrastructure in the former princely state areas. Herbst (2000), in his analysis of road networks in Africa, finds that those African countries that had a high level of colonial-era road density continued to expand, while those countries with low levels of road networks were really not able to expand very much.

Continuing Weak Police Capacity: Another reason for persistence of low state capacity in the former princely state areas was that the postcolonial Indian state and bureaucracy continued to perceive these areas as administrative backwaters, which were not easy to control and not as important in terms of their projects of state formation. The low levels of colonial bureaucratic and police capacity continued into postcolonial times, because these areas continued to be considered "punishment postings" to which poor-quality officers or those being punished for their recalcitrant political positions were sent by politicians.[95] According to a police officer who works in Maoist affected south Chhattisgarh: "in a batch of Assistant Sub-inspectors of Police (ASI)s, those who are the toppers in the batch or best officers . . . are not sent to the Naxal areas, the others who are not the best officers are sent."[96] According to another senior police officer, when the new state of Chhattisgarh was created, the best-quality officers stayed in Madhya Pradesh, and most did not want to go to the new state of Chhattisgarh.[97]

Baruah (1990: 4) cites a joke often used in official circles:

[A]ppointment in Bastar is governed by three Ps: probation, promotion or punishment. As soon as the order is received, invariably officers go on leave and make frantic efforts to get the posting cancelled before the expiry of leave. They will join duty only if they are unsuccessful in their attempts and somehow carry on their work anxiously awaiting the transfer. Generally, the officers . . . invariably take a posture of martyrs, who are carrying a burden of improving the life of the people and in the process suffering hard life.

Miklian (2009: 443–44) mentions that Chhattisgarh police lag "far behind other Indian states in both quantitative and qualitative terms," and most policemen view Chhattisgarh positions as bad for their career.

Continuing Lack of Road Network in Bastar: A study by the Census Department of Madhya Pradesh in the 1980s mentions that while roads and

---

[95] Interview with superintendent of police (district not revealed), Chhattisgarh, 2009.
[96] Interview with Balaji Rao, additional superintendent of police (Kanker district), Chhattisgarh, 2009.
[97] Interview with A. N. Upadhyaya, inspector general of police, Jagdalpur, Chhattisgarh, 2009.

railway have been developed in the Bastar region to exploit the iron ore resources in the south Bastar region of Bailadilla Hills, there are still large parts that remain isolated, in particular the Abujhmarh Hills area in southern Bastar where there are few roads because of the physiographic conditions.[98]

Journalist, D. N. Tiwari wrote in 1973 that the only railway line linking Bastar to the outside world was the one constructed in late 1960s connecting the Bailadilla Hills (Kirandul) with the port city of Vishakhapatnam in Andhra Pradesh for the export of iron ore to Japan, but this railway line "has not allowed other activities to profit from it." According to Tiwari, on March 1973, "Bastar had a P.W.D. road length of 4.5 kilometers per hundred sqr. Km, as against more than 16 km. for Madhya Pradesh and 27 km. for the country as a whole."[99] Amit Baruah writes in 1990, "What strikes any visitor to Bastar is the lack of a road network. Forest roads hardly exist. And with the forest guards being the only form of Government known to the people ... the Adivasis were subjected to their whimsical depredations."[100] This impression of a journalist in the 1990s seems almost the same as that expressed by A. H. L. Fraser, the chief commissioner of Central Provinces in 1892.[101]

The Preface to the *Chhattisgarh State Assembly Election 2003 Report* by the Chief Election Commission of Chhattisgarh mentioned that "Out of the 1838 polling stations in the entire Bastar area, 684 were hyper sensitive (under high Maoist threat). ... About 367 polling stations had to be approached on foot because of the difficult geographical terrain."[102] The Maoists set many of the roads up with mines, and road-clearing operations had to be carried out by security forces before the Election Commission teams could arrive in these areas. This suggests that even in 2003, there were not sufficient metaled roads in these interior areas in Bastar, which made it difficult to conduct elections safely in these Maoist-controlled areas.

5 POSTCOLONIAL MAOIST INSURGENCY IN CHHATTISGARH

5.1 Maoist Rebel Agents Exploit These Historically Created Political Opportunity Structures and Ethnic Mobilization Networks

Due to persistence of these colonial-era policies under the postcolonial Indian government, these former princely state areas remained low in bureaucratic/ police capacity into the 1970s. This provided ideal political opportunity

---

[98] B. K. Roy and Vijay Verma, IAS, "Regional Divisions of India – A Cartographic Analysis: Occasional Papers," Series 1, Volume XI, Madhya Pradesh, p. 514.

[99] D. N. Tiwari, "Bastar needs a railway line connecting North," *Dandakaranya Samachar*, March 31, 1974.

[100] Amit Baruah, "Bastar of the tribals," *Frontline*, May 12–25, 1990, p. 3.

[101] A. H. L. Fraser, "Tour Notes on the Bastar State," 1892, Paragraph 6.

[102] Chief Electoral Officer, Chhattisgarh, in the Preface to *State Assembly Election, 2003, Chhattisgarh*. State Election Commission, Raipur during fieldwork.

structures for the PWG Maoists to exploit in the 1980s. Also the continuing policy of extraction of forest and natural resources created tribal grievances, and the Maoists used these tribal networks as ethnic mobilization structures. When the PWG Maoists emerged in the Telangana region of the neighboring state of Andhra Pradesh and moved into the southern Chhattisgarh region of Bastar in the early 1980s, they brought with them the ideological frames and repertoires of revolution (McAdam et al. 1996). These initial rebel agents could successfully exploit these historically created structures of ethnic inequalities/ exclusion (Cederman et al. 2010; Gurr 1970) and state weakness (Fearon & Laitin 2003) and create successful core areas of Maoist control.

In contrast, the PWG did not try to build up Maoist control in the central districts of Raipur and Bilaspur in Chhattisgarh, since these areas were more developed, had higher state capacity, and were flat plains and not hilly or forested terrain, which made it difficult to sustain rebellion. The central districts of Bilaspur and Raipur also had lower levels of land inequality due to more egalitarian *ryotwari* type land tenure systems historically. The Maoists also operated in some districts in neighboring states like Balaghat district in Madhya Pradesh, and Gadchiroli and Bhandara districts in Maharashtra state, since these were geographically contiguous to the Bastar district of the state of Chhattisgarh. However, this occurred because of spatial diffusion of the insurgency into neighboring districts, which were not really areas of high control. I address this in the quantitative analysis in Section 6 by using spatial regression techniques.

Maoist intellectual Nitin (pseudonym), writing in the Maoist journal *People's March*, said that *Adivasi* support of the PWG since the 1980s opposing government policies that deprive them of their rights over forests and land was a "continuation of their 150 year long tradition of militant protests and armed rebellions."[103] According to Sundar (2006), the Maoists are the true heirs to the Bhumkal rebellion by Gond tribals in 1910 against land and forest resource exploitation. They have tried to mobilize the tribals by providing them protection from the outsider *thekedars* and forest guards and a state that exploits their resources.[104] They have provided leadership and organizational structure to the resistance of the *Adivasis* against non-tribal migrants and police forces. Ilina Sen pointed out that although the Maoists in Bastar are critiqued by some as "outsiders" from Andhra Pradesh, it would be wrong to speak of them as "external agents" since they had tried to integrate into tribal society, and to fight against the exploitation of these tribals of their natural and land resources by steel plants like Tata and Essar, and by the police and forest officials historically who were also non-tribals and outsiders.[105]

---

[103] Nitin, "The Forest Is Ours," *People's March*, Vol. 7, No. 1, 2006, p. 8.
[104] Nandini Sundar, "Bastar, Maoism and Salwa Judum," *Economic and Political Weekly*, July 22, 2006.
[105] Interview with Ilina Sen, Raipur, 2007.

5.2 Emergence of PWG Maoist Organizational Networks and Levels/Patterns of Violence

In this section, I sketch a history of the Maoist insurgency as it developed in the Abujhmarh forested areas of the former princely state of Bastar/Kanker in the south of Chhattisgarh. While there were a few sporadic incidents of Maoist activity in the 1960s to 1970s in the Bastar region, the armed struggle in Bastar region really started in 1980. The People's War Group (PWG) Maoists had started operating in the Telangana region of the former princely state of Hyderabad, just south of the border of Bastar in 1980, under the leadership of K. Sitaramaiah.[106] In 1979, a PWG squad was sent to Dandakaranya to conduct a reconnaissance mission, and another five squads were sent in the subsequent year. These initial Maoists, from Andhra Pradesh, numbered twenty-five, and none of them knew the *Adivasi* Koya language. They found this region to be heavily forested, with very low state or police presence, and various Gond tribes staying there, with grievances related to exploitation of their land and forest resources, and exploitation of their livelihood resources by forest guards.[107]

The PWG Maoists started developing their base areas deep inside the Abujhmarh forest areas of Bastar in the south of the state of Chhattisgarh; by the 1990s, they had developed strong zones of rebel control. Except for a few short escalations in the 1990s, violence had remained low in this area, which became a Maoist stronghold. Drawing on data from a newspaper interview with former Bastar Superintendent of Police Paswan, Table 7.3 shows low levels of violence for this initial period of Maoist activity. The slow buildup of Maoist capacity and alternate governance had gone virtually unnoticed till the sudden escalation of violence in 2005 due to the *Salwa Judum* movement that caused the national media to focus on the region, as shown in Figure 7.6.

Between 1985 and June 1989, the encounters between the police and Maoists slowly started increasing; thirteen Maoists were killed; ten were arrested; and the Maoists killed six civilians, two police personnel, and one *sarpanch* (village head).[108] In 1989–90, the insurgency intensified, and in the south and west Bastar areas anti-landowner movements were launched; a lot of land was confiscated by the Maoists with the help of the tribals, and Maoist governance in the villages started replacing the control of the village *mukhiyas*. The landed elite also responded and there were two *Jan Jagran Abhiyans* against the Naxals in 1990–91 and 1997–98, but neither succeeded and Maoists crushed both.[109]

---

[106] CPI-Maoist, *Jan Jagran Nahi, Jan Daman Abhiyan*, August 12, 2005, p. 6.
[107] C. Vanaja, "Janatana Sarkar: A Parallel Government in the Dandakaranya," *Andhra Jyothi*, April 10, 2005.
[108] "Bastar mein Naxal gatividhiyan," *Deshbandhu*, July 31, 1989.
[109] CPI-Maoist, *Jan Jagran Nahi, Jan Daman Abhiyan*, August 12, 2005, pp. 1–7. See also PUDR et al., *When the State Makes War on Its Own People*, pp. 11–12.

TABLE 7.3 *Naxal-related events in South Chhattisgarh from 1974 to 2001*

	Total	Bastar district	Dantewada district (includes Bijapur)	Kanker district
1. Landmine Explosions	26	5	18	3
2. Encounter	116	30	67	19
3. Arrested Naxals	126	21	90	15
4. Killed Naxals	29	14	10	5
5. Surrendered Naxals	115	7	102	6
6. Killed Villagers	165	43	66	26
7. Killed Police (in landmine blast)	85	38	43	4
8. Killed Police (in encounter)	12	1	11	N.A.

Source: "Police dwara Naxalio ko Muhtor jawab dene se vardato mein kami ain–Paswan," *Deshbandhu*, December 20, 2001.

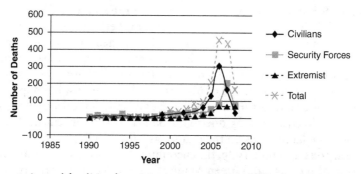

FIGURE 7.6 Annual fatalities from Maoist insurgency in Chhattisgarh: 1990–2008
Source: Data from 1990 to 1999 is from Madhya Pradesh police records and from 2000 to 2008 is from Chhattisgarh police records.

In the 9th Congress of the CPI-ML (People's War) held in 2001, a decision was taken to convert the Dandakaranya region into a base area and intensify the "people's struggle."[110] In June 2005, the anti-Maoist vigilante movement *Salwa Judum* emerged, led by the Congress leader Mahendra Karma and indirectly supported by the BJP government in Chhattisgarh. This was on a much larger scale than the *Jan Jagran Abhiyans* of the 1990s, and led to escalation of violence. The *Salwa Judum* movement recruited underage tribals called Special Police Officers (SPOs) to fight against other tribals who were with the Maoists. This led

[110] CPI-Maoist, *Jan Jagran Nahi* . . ., p. 2.

to displacement of tribals into camps, massive dislocation of tribals who escaped to Andhra Pradesh, and brutal attacks by *Salwa Judum* on villages known to be Maoist bases causing human rights violations, rapes, and other atrocities.[111]

One possible reason for the state using a vigilante movement like the Salwa Judum rather than the army is because the army is politically costly to use in interior tribal areas in a democracy like India. According to Giridhari Naik, a senior police officer with lot of expertise in counter insurgency operations against the Maoists in Chhattisgarh, the army is a "very expensive commodity" and it is better to use the police adapted to counter insurgency purposes. [112] Brigadier Ponwar echoed this sentiment and mentioned that the army was to fight external enemies and it was best to leave internal threats like the Maoists to the police, who need to be better trained to "fight the guerrilla like a guerrilla."[113] However, other reasons the BJP government allowed the emergence of the vigilante *Salwa Judum* movement helped by Mahendra Karma was that it was lower cost and also allowed the state plausible deniability from any direct involvement in using civilians to fight the Maoist rebels. The SPOs were also valuable to provide local information.

Threatened in their core base area, the Maoists retaliated with equally brutal attacks on some of the *Salwa Judum* camps, including the attacks on Errabore camp on July 17, 2006, in which at least twenty-five people including civilians were killed, and an even bigger attack on the Ranibodli camp on March 16, 2007, where at least fifty-five policemen and SPOs were burnt to death.[114] This broke the momentum of the *Salwa Judum* campaign. According to Rahul Sharma, who was superintendent of police in Dantewada district, for the CPI-Maoist, "Rani Bodli was basically a message to the SPOs, and to the people who had joined Salwa Judum ... that we are still a potent force and we can hit with vengeance" and such large-scale attacks were desperate attempts by the Maoists to stop the *Salwa Judum*, which was one of the biggest security threats to their movement.[115] Justifying the brutal counterattack by the Maoists at Rani Bodli, CPI-Maoist General Secretary Ganapathy said it was "an inevitable consequence of the brutal reign of terror unleashed by the state ... in the name of Salwa Judum."[116]

[111] See Committee Against Violence on Women (CAVOW), *Salwa Judum and Violence on Women in Dantewara, Chhattisgarh*, December 2006; Human Rights Forum, *Death, Displacement and Deprivation*, December 2006.

[112] Interview with Giridhari Naik, inspector general of police (Naxal operations), Raipur, 2008.

[113] Interview with Brigadier Basant Ponwar, director, Counter Terrorism and Jungle Warfare College, Kanker district, Chhattisgarh, 2009.

[114] Human Rights Watch, *Being Neutral Is Our Biggest Crime*, July 2008, pp. 109–10.

[115] Interview with Rahul Sharma, superintendent of police, Dantewada district, Dantewada Police Headquarters, 2009.

[116] Interview with Ganapathy, general secretary, CPI-Maoist. Text of the interview was released by Azad, Spokesperson, CPI-Maoist in April 2007.

With the failure of the vigilante *Salwa Judum* movement, the central Congress government Home Minister Chidambaram mobilized paramilitary forces and launched a massive counterinsurgency operation called *Green Hunt* in 2009–10 in different Maoist-affected parts of India, with the goal of destroying Maoist power in their core areas of Abujhmarh in Chhattisgarh. On February 1, 2010, at Silda in Midnapore district of West Bengal, the Maoists attacked an Eastern Frontier Rifles camp and killed twenty-four policemen, which the Maoist leader Kishenji called a response to Operation *Green Hunt.*[117] Then on April 6, 2010, at Chintalner, Dantewada district, the Maoists ambushed and killed seventy-five Central Reserve Police Force (CRPF) personnel of Alpha Company, 62nd Battalion, which was the largest single attack in the history of the insurgency.[118] This led to public uproar and destroyed political consensus in the government, leading to stalling of Operation *Green Hunt.*

Since 2014, with the BJP under Narendra Modi coming to power in the federal government, the Maoist insurgency in Chhattisgarh is in a stalemate with lower levels of violence. Successful counterinsurgency efforts by the state as well as large-scale surrenders by Maoist cadres and leaders seem to have reduced the Maoist threat. While the ability of the Maoists to recruit seems to have decreased in recent years, they still have the capacity to carry out the occasional large-scale attacks. On April 24, 2017, the Maoists attacked a CRPF convoy and killed twenty-five *jawans* and injured six in an ambush in Sukma in Chhattisgarh. This incident happened more than a month after thirteen CRPF *jawans* were killed in a similar ambush on the Injeram-Bhejji stretch, around 60 km from this ambush spot.[119] The CPI-Maoist has recently replaced its aging General Secretary Ganapathy, and this shows attempts to revive the organizational capacity, while acknowledging recent reverses.

5.3   Rebel Agency Mobilizing the Ethnic Grievances of the *Adivasi* Tribals

While the Gond tribes with their ethnic grievances formed the ethnic mobilization networks, the PWG Maoists brought their ideological frames of rebellion to mobilize the indigenous tribes. In the initial period of low violence from 1980 to 2005, the PWG Maoists worked hard to build organizational networks, and recruit from the tribals by trying to address the grievances of the Gond *Adivasi* tribes staying in this area of Bastar, which they framed in terms of their radical Maoist ideology of trying to help the poor tribals from being exploited by the forest guards, landlords, and the Indian state. Three main

---

[117] Raktima Bose, "Maoists kill 20 jawans in West Bengal," *The Hindu*, February 16, 2010.
[118] Soutik Biswas, "Scores of Indian soldiers killed in Maoist ambushes," BBC World News, April 6, 2010.
[119] Deeptiman Tiwary, Dipankar Ghose, and Rahul Tripathi, "Worst in Chhattisgarh in seven years: 25 CRPF men killed by Maoists in Sukma," *Indian Express*, April 25, 2017.

areas in which Maoist rebel agency addressed ethnic grievances of the Gond tribes are outlined below.

Providing Protection from Exploitative Landlords and Forest Guards and Other Public Goods: The PWG started the *Dandakaranya Adivasi Kisan Majdoor Sangh* (Tribal Peasant and Workers Association, DAKMS) and the *Krantikari Adivasi Mahila Sangh* (Revolutionary Tribal Women's Association, KAMS) in the 1980s. Tribals in villages joined these overground organizations and were called *sangham* members. In this initial period, the Maoists focused on issues of justice for the tribals and tried to integrate themselves into tribal culture and society though intermarriage and developmental work.[120]

The Gond *Adivasis* used to collect firewood and various other minor forest products; the changed Forest Laws introduced by the British and continued by the postcolonial Indian government in the form of the Forest Act (1980) made it a crime to collect forest products. This allowed police to extort the tribals for money and poultry for such crimes and to take away one of their natural sources of livelihood. The Maoists beat up, and even killed, some of the forest guards and local police, thus spreading fear among state officials and reducing the exploitation of tribals.[121] According to human rights activist Balagopal (2006), one of the reasons for the Gond *Adivasis* joining the Maoist movement in the Dandakaranya forested regions of Chhattisgarh was that the Maoists used violence against the state to stop the "harassment the adivasis suffered at the hands of forest and police officials for cultivating land in the reserve forests."[122]

The Maoists also initiated armed action against the *zamindari*/landlord class, which had emerged as actors during the colonial period of indirect rule and whose political and economic power had persisted in this former princely state area. In 1986, the DAKMS had forced the landowners of Chintalnar village in Konta tehsil to reduce the price of the goods they were selling in the weekly markets they controlled. On July 18, 1988, three hundred villagers participated in a mass *dacoity* (robbery) led by a Naxalite *dalam* on the houses of these landowners, and while the *dalam* snatched six guns from the *thakurs*, the *Adivasis* stole a lot of salt. Salt is a most precious commodity in the *Adivasi* areas of Bastar, since it is not easily available, and the traders usually cheated the *Adivasis* and charged them large amounts for a small quantity of salt.[123] The official interpretation of this incident was that the Maoists had lured the *Adivasis* to join them with the promise of providing them with rice due to shortage of food.[124]

---

[120] P. Shankar, *Yeh Jangal Hamara Hain*, New Vitas Publications, 2006, pp. 222–26; PUCL, *Bastar: Development and Democracy*, July 1989, p. 13.

[121] PUDR et al., *When the State Makes War on Its Own People*, pp. 10–11.

[122] K. Balagopal, "Chhattisgarh: Physiognomy of Violence," *Economic and Political Weekly*, June 3, 2006, pp. 2183–86.

[123] PUCL, *Bastar: Development and Democracy*, 1989, p. 16.

[124] "Chintalnar dacoity kand," *Deshbandhu*, August 8, 1988.

By the late 1980s, Maoist-led mass organizations like the DAKMS started addressing inequality in land ownership, which was a legacy from colonial times, and tried to redistribute land to the landless.[125] In Antagarh in Bastar district, in November 1995, if a farmer had a very large harvest of crops, then the Naxals redistributed the excess amount to poorer farmers; if they refuse to give the excess amount, then the Naxals threatened them.[126]

To regulate social and political life, the Maoists created *sanghams* in villages, which were overground organizations that villagers could join. The purpose of these *sanghams* was to replace the traditional structures of feudal authority at the village level and also to settle disputes in a more democratic way. The Salwa Judum targeted these sanghams in the 2005–9 period, because they challenged the traditional structures of authority of landlords and the rich elites.[127]

The Maoists have been criticized for sometimes opposing development projects and road building by the government. According to Swami Nikhilatmananda of the Ram Krishna Mission Ashram in Narayanpur district in the south Chhattisgarh region, where the monks of this Hindu missionary order provide schools and fair price shops and teach the tribals farming, the Maoists initially opposed the provision of such social goods to the tribals, and did not provide such goods like education themselves.[128] While it was difficult for the PWG Maoists to provide public goods since they lacked resources available to the state, they did try to provide various types of services to the tribals like medicines, basic education, though they opposed construction of roads since that would facilitate incursion of security forces into these areas under their control.[129] Also, the protection from exploitation by the police and forest officers could be considered another type of public good provided by Maoists.[130] Figure 7.7 shows a Maoist cadre giving an injection to a sick tribal villager, which is an example of small-scale public goods provided by the Maoist groups to tribal people living in these areas, which helped them get civilian support for their rebel activities. Figure 7.8 shows girls who joined the Maoist movement in the Bastar/Gadchiroli region, which shows that Maoists recruit many women into their organization and allow them some form of relief from a patriarchal society.

Increasing Price of Tendu Leaves and Other Natural Forest Products: An area in which the Maoists made a significant contribution was in the organized trade in minor forest produce like *tendu* leaves, which are used to make local cigarettes called *bidis*. *Tendu* leaves are collected by the local *Adivasis* and then sold at really low prices to non-tribal contractors, who then sell them at much higher

---

[125] PUDR, *When the State Makes War on Its Own People*, p 11.

[126] "Zameen ka batwara ab Naxalion ke aadesh se," *Deshbandu*, November 28, 1995.

[127] PUDR, *When the State Makes War on Its Own People*, p. 11.

[128] Interview with Swami Nikhilatmananda, Ram Krishna Mission Ashram, Narayanpur, 2007.

[129] Interview with Ilina Sen, human rights activist and scholar, Raipur, 2007.

[130] For recent literature on how rebel groups provide governance and public goods in areas they control, see Ana Arjona, *Rebelocracy*, and Zachariah Mampilly, *Rebel Rulers*.

FIGURE 7.7 A Maoist fighter gives an injection to a sick villager he met while on patrol
Source: Photo taken by Ishan Tankha in Bastar/Gadchiroli region (Copyright Ishan Tankha)

FIGURE 7.8 "Comrades" – Women cadres make up a large part of the Maoist force
Source: Photo taken by Ishan Tankha in Bastar/Gadchiroli region (Copyright Ishan Tankha)

rates to companies to make a huge profit. According to Garg (2008: 36–37), the *tendu* collectors' agitation for better wages and against exploitation in the Dandakaranya forests began in 1982 and was instrumental in generating support for the Maoists among the Gond tribals.[131] In one of the first such efforts, a CPI-ML leader named Ganapati with his companions toured the villages in Bastar and organized meetings to raise the demand for increasing the wage rate. In response, the contractors in the Bandhe-Tarveli area increased the wage rate to Rs. 11 per 100 bundles in the 1984 season. However, in the next season wage rates fell again, and paramilitary forces were brought into the area to provide protection to the contractors; on March 5, 1985, Ganapati was killed in an encounter with security forces in Tarveli village in Narayanpur district.[132]

However, the PWG put pressure on the *tendu*-leaf contractors and forest officials and threatened violence or labor strikes. Succumbing to the pressure of the Maoists, the contractors were forced to provide higher wages to the *Adivasi* laborers. While for two decades, "the wages remained at 3 paise to 8 paise per *gaddi* (bundle of 50 leaves)," from "about 1982 it has risen dramatically to 30 paise in 1988, while . . . in rest of the state remained at 8 paise."[133] See Table 7.4 for increasing wages for collecting *tendu* leaves.

TABLE 7.4 *Rate for 100 bundles of* Tendu *leaves (in rupees; translated from Hindi)*

Year	Rate declared by government	Rate decided by tribals after struggle with contractors
1990	25	55
1991	28	65
1992	33	75
1993	35	90
1994	41	105
1995	46	110
1996	46	120
1997	50	130
1998	53	133
1999	58	136

Source: P. Shankar, *Yeh Jangal Hamara Hain,* New Vistas Publications, 2006, p. 39.

[131] Ruchir Garg, "Roots and Causes: The Case of Dandakaranya," in P. V. Ramana (ed.), *The Naxal Challenge.*
[132] PUCL et al., *Bastar: Ek Muthbher ki Jaanch (Investigation into an Encounter),* pp. 10–12.
[133] PUCL, *Bastar: Development and Democracy,* p. 13.

On the night of December 10, 1991, in Barsur in Jagdalpur district in Bastar, Naxalites attacked a *tendu* leaf deposit of the Forest Department but failed to set it on fire and the police forced them to retreat.[134] In 1996, the local *Adivasis* set fire to the *tendu* godown (store) of contractors in places like Kodispalli, Narekal, and Pottegaon. They also beat up those workers of these *tendu patta* companies who were sexually abusing and harassing the female *tendu* leaf pickers, and this spread fear and stopped such activities.[135]

Besides *tendu* leaves, the Maoists opposed exploitation of other kinds of forest resources. On April 7, 1992, in Narayanpur district, Naxalites set fire to a Forest Department storage of timber and wood that caused a loss of Rs. 2 lakhs worth of timber.[136] On April 5, 1994, in Narayanpur district, Naxalites again set fire to a Forest Department timber depot that resulted in loss of Rs. 8 lakhs worth of timber. They also left some pamphlets and notes, signed in the name of the DAKMS, saying they opposed the newly launched police program *Sadbhavna Yatra*, which was supposed to be a public welfare march.[137]

Trying to Stop Exploitation of Natural Resources Like Iron Ore and Bauxite: The Maoists have often opposed extractive mining and attacked companies that extract such natural resources from Bastar. In the 1990s, there was a lot of opposition to the mining of bauxite in Keshkal. On March 9, 1994, Naxalites burnt a truck belonging to the Koya Mines Company and threatened three workers by rubbing their nose six feet on the ground as a form of punishment. The Naxalites also warned the contractors and the laborers to leave and work the mines because the bauxite belonged to the *Adivasi* tribals.[138] In two separate incidents on March 10, 1994, Naxalites set fire to a truck belonging to Govindpur Bauxite Company carrying bauxite from the mines in Keshkal, and thirty-five Naxalites attacked this bauxite mine and set fire to the camp.[139]

Opposing the Tata and Essar Steel plants, top Maoist leader Kosa released a press statement in 2006: "The indigenous people of Bastar hold ownership rights over the natural resources of Bastar . . . we demand the scrapping of the Salwa Judum."[140] In June 2009, Vimal Meshram, a tribal supporter of the Tata Steel project, was shot dead by Maoist cadres since he had been involved in distributing compensation to the villagers and had been accused of stealing the

---

[134] "Naxalite attack on tendu leaf godown, also shooting," *Deshbandhu*, December 11, 1991.
[135] P. Shankar, *Yeh Jangal Hamara Hain*, p. 38.
[136] "Naxalio ne van vibhag ki do lakh ki lakri jalai," *Deshbandhu*, April 8, 1992 (Deshbandhu Archives, Raipur).
[137] "Naxalio ne Kashtagarh me aag lagai, aath lakh ki lakro jalee," *Samvet Sikhar*, April 6, 1994 (Deshbandhu Archives, Raipur).
[138] "Naxaliyon ne Koye Bauxite khadan bandh karwai," *Deshbandhu*, March 14, 1994.
[139] "Naxaliyon ne bauxite se bhara truck wa rakhni camp jalaya," *Dandakaranya Samachar*, March 11, 1994.
[140] "Maoists oppose Tata, Essar plants," *Central Chronicle*, May 18, 2006 (Deshbandhu Archives, Raipur).

funds.[141] After several renewals of the MoU agreement, Tata Steel decided to withdraw from its proposed 5.5 million tonne steel plant project in Lohandiguda in 2016.[142] Opposition from various *Adivasi* organizations and the Maoists may have delayed the acquisition of land from the *Adivasis* and led to this outcome.

The Maoists also opposed the NMDC plants in Kirandul. In June 2007, Naxals had attacked NMDC facilities and blown up "three 132 KVA towers in Narayanpur that had affected electricity supplies to Dantewada for 12 consecutive days" and the NMDC lost Rs. 160 crore. The very next year in April 2008, there was "disruption of power supplies in four districts of Chattisgarh by Maoist rebels" that resulted in NMDC losing around Rs 100 crore over eight days.[143] In May 2012, six Central Industrial Security Force (CISF) jawans patrolling the NMDC facility at Kirandul were ambushed and killed by the Maoists at night.[144] In 2014, a Rs. 607 crore expansion project of Deposit 11B mine of state-run miner NMDC at Bailadila in Chhattisgarh was set to be delayed further after "Naxals burnt part of a conveyor belt meant for evacuating the raw material."[145]

5.4   Scope Conditions: Timing of Onset of Insurgency and Rebel Agency

Historical institutions like colonial indirect rule do not explain the timing of onset of insurgency but only explain the spatial variation in rebel control after insurgency emerges and consolidates. The timing of emergence of the Maoists in Chhattisgarh was related to the ideological and strategic rethinking within the broader radical leftist movement in India in 1977–80 (Sinha 1989), which led to the emergence of the PWG in Telangana region of the former princely state of Hyderabad in the neighboring state of Andhra Pradesh in 1980. This was followed by a strategic decision by the PWG leadership to expand to neighboring Bastar region of Chhattisgarh in 1980s.[146] As the PWG cadres and leaders infiltrated into the Dandakaranya forested regions of Bastar princely state region of Chhattisgarh in 1990s–early 2000s, their ability to succeed or not was largely constrained by the political opportunity structures in the form of low state capacity and development, and the ethnic mobilization structures in the form of Gond tribes with grievances created by colonial indirect rule institutions (McAdam et al. 1996).

---

[141] Devjyot Ghoshal, "In Bastar, Tata Steel discovers a 'land' mine after troubled acquisition," *Business Standard*, January 24, 2013.

[142] "Tata Steel shelves Bastar project," *The Hindu*, August 28, 2016.

[143] "NMDC loses Rs 200 cr due to Naxal problems in Chhattisgarh," *Hindustan Times*, October 15, 2008.

[144] Deeptiman Tiwary, "Chhattisgarh: Exchange of fire between CISF and suspected Maoists in Dantewada, no casualties yet," *The Indian Express*, February 8, 2018.

[145] "Naxalite problem hits NMDC's Bailadila mine expansion," September 4, 2014, PTI.

[146] See Section 2.1 for details of the history of the movement in Chhattisgarh.

6 QUANTITATIVE ANALYSIS OF SPATIAL VARIATION IN MAOIST CONTROL IN CHHATTISGARH

To test for the causal effect of indirect rule on Maoist insurgency, I use a mixed-method research design (Goertz 2017; Lieberman 2005). In this section, I complement the qualitative process tracing of mechanisms of exploitation and weak state capacity with a novel sub-district dataset of Chhattisgarh to show that those areas that were part of a former princely state have a causal effect on Maoist insurgency. I present this briefly here, for details see my article in *World Development* and online appendices for this chapter.[147]

6.1 Addressing the Selection Issue – Using Instrument for Colonial Indirect Rule

In 1884, the chief commissioner of Central Provinces agreed that "Bastar is too poor to justify direct management by Government officers."[148] It was cheaper for the British to depend on a raja, to do the ruling on their behalf. Also, if there was tribal rebellion, it could be "blamed on the king's lack of concern for his subjects" (Sundar 2007: 103). Other pre-colonial qualities like hilly terrain, high forest cover, low potential revenue, and other unobserved qualities may also have led the British to select Bastar for indirect rule. Since these same pre-colonial qualities of these districts made them more prone to tribal rebellion in the future, there is potential selection bias in any quantitative analysis of the effects of princely state on Maoist insurgency.

I address the issue of selection bias in two ways. First, I do OLS analysis below to understand the effect of princely state on Maoist insurgency, in which I control for some observable determinants of indirect rule choice, like forest cover and elevation. Second, I exploit the random switch of the central districts of Bilaspur and Raipur to direct rule because of death of the king of Nagpur state as an instrument for choice of indirect rule in an IV-2SLS analysis.

Instrument for Indirect Rule through Princely States (instru_NagpurLapse): Following the defeat of Appa Sahib of the Marathas in 1817 by the British, the Nagpur state was managed by the British on behalf of the minor Bhonsla Raja Raghuji III, who "succeeded to the estates in 1830, but died without heirs in 1853, and the province lapsed to the British Government."[149] The reason for lapse of Nagpur state, ruled by the Bhonsla clan of the Marathas, to the British government due to death of the ruler was the existence of the Doctrine of Lapse

---

[147] For details of this quantitative analysis, see Mukherjee, "Historical Legacies of Colonial Indirect Rule: Princely States and Maoist Insurgency in Central India," *World Development* 111, pp. 113–29.

[148] Secy. Chief Commissioner, Central Provinces to Secy. Govt. of India, Foreign Department, 19 March 1884, Prog. No. 99 in *Foreign A-Political-I*, April 1884, Nos 99–103, *NAI*.

[149] Baden-Powell, *Land Tenure Systems of British India, Volume 1*, p. 47.

implemented by Governor General Lord Dalhousie (1847–56) under which any Indian ruler who died without a male heir would have to forfeit his kingdom to the British, and adoption of heirs would not be recognized. The switch to British direct rule was due to the random circumstance of the death of the ruler of Nagpur state without a male heir and was for reasons exogenous to the quality of the districts within Nagpur state. The central districts of current-day Chhattisgarh – Raipur, Bilaspur, Durg, Dhamtari, and Mahasamund – were part of Nagpur state in 1854, when they formed only two large districts of Raipur and Bilaspur. Since the reason for the switch of these districts to colonial direct rule was the natural death of the ruler of Nagpur state and was exogenous to the quality of these districts that could make them more prone to rebellion then or in the future, it can be used as an instrument for the British choice of direct/indirect rule in the Chhattisgarh area.

Exclusion Restriction: The only way by which the death of the Nagpur ruler is related to the outbreak of Maoist insurgency in the future is through the conversion of these districts to direct rule. This satisfies the requirement of the instrument being exogenous to the outcome being studied and fulfills the exclusion restriction condition of a good instrument. While it could be argued that the British wanted Nagpur state for its resources and there was selection involved, the British administrators could not have predicted the death of Raghuji III in 1854. So the actual timing of the switch to direct rule was randomly caused by his death and thus satisfies the exclusion restriction condition (Iyer 2010).[150] The only reason this was not exogenous would be if the British planned the death of the ruler, but there is no evidence of this.

Coding of the Instrument: See Online Appendix B for details of the coding of the instrument. The instrument is coded as those constituencies in Chhattisgarh state that were part of the colonial-era districts of Bilaspur and Raipur, since these two districts in the colonial era were part of erstwhile Nagpur state and today are part of Chhattisgarh. Some districts like Korba (three constituencies) and Janjgir-Champa (six constituencies) were British direct rule and not part of Nagpur princely state and did not become direct rule because of this random switch due to death of Nagpur ruler, and so they were not coded as part of the instrument.

6.2   OLS and IV-2SLS Regression Analysis

The following hypothesis is proposed based on the theory outlined previously:
   Hypothesis: Areas that had indirect colonial rule through princely states tend to have higher probability of Maoist insurgency in the future, even after

---

[150] Iyer, "Direct versus Indirect Colonial Rule in India," uses a similar instrument based on deaths of Indian rulers during the Doctrine of Lapse policy period of Lord Dalhousie for an all-India district-level IV-2SLS analysis. Here, I use this instrument only for the constituencies/districts in the state of Chhattisgarh.

controlling for various proximate measures of rebel opportunity and ethnic grievances.

6.2.1   Data and variables

MAPPING CENSUS DATA INTO ASSEMBLY CONSTITUENCIES In this chapter I use the *Vidhan Sabha* (State Assembly) constituency as the unit of analysis for the state of Chhattisgarh. This allows more fine-grained measurement of rebel control and colonial indirect rule, since district-level measurement masks sub-district variation in Maoist rebel control.[151] This is the first study on the Maoist insurgency in India to use the sub-district Assembly Constituency as the unit of analysis.

The state of Chhattisgarh has seventeen districts subdivided into ninety-seven *tehsils*, and ninety State Assembly Constituencies (ACs). Each district has one or more ACs. I develop a micro-level dataset for these ninety ACs. The dependent variable of *Maoist control* and the independent variable of *princely state* are measured at the AC level directly. Unfortunately, the Census 2001 socioeconomic, public good, and demographic data is in administrative units like district/*tehsils*, and there is not a perfect match geographically of *tehsil*/district boundaries with AC electoral boundaries.[152] To match the ninety constituencies to the ninety-seven *tehsils*, a map of district/*tehsil* boundaries of Chhattisgarh in 2001 was compared with constituency boundaries from an electoral map from 2003 State Assembly elections.[153] The *tehsil* boundaries and constituency boundaries were matched following the procedures of Banerjee and Somanathan (2007) and Thachil (2011). The coding procedure and data sources are described in more detail in Online Appendix C.

MEASURING MAOIST CONTROL AS THE DEPENDENT VARIABLE I explain spatial variation in *Maoist rebel control*, instead of killings or fatalities. It is important to distinguish between these concepts, since in those areas where the state is completely absent and the rebels have full control and set up alternate institutions of governance, there is probably less violence, and yet insurgency is most successful (Kalyvas 2006). In the case of Chhattisgarh, before the start of the *Salwa Judum* movement in 2005 that led to escalation of violence, the levels of rebel control were quite high in the southern districts like

---

[151] For example, the Indian state considers a district like Kanker in Chhattisgarh as under high Maoist influence, but it is the western areas of Kanker that are under higher Maoist control, while the eastern areas are not.

[152] Chandra, "Why Ethnic Parties Succeed" (pp. 159–60) notes: "government data, including data from the census, are reported by administrative subdivisions (district, tehsil, and block), which do not coincide with constituencies."

[153] Map 7: "Chhattisgarh Administrative Divisions 2001" in *Census of India 2001 Chhattisgarh Administrative Atlas*, p. 15, with Table 7: "List of Assembly Constituencies District-wise," pp. 15–17, and "Map of Assembly Segments," p. 18 of *Chhattisgarh State Assembly Election – 2003*.

Narayanpur and Dantewada, and yet levels of violence were relatively low, as shown in Figure 7.4. So using insurgency violence will not correctly measure the areas of rebel control in early 2000s before violence escalated in Chhattisgarh in 2005.

I follow the precedence of Mitchell (1968) and Kalyvas and Kocher (2009) and measure *Maoist control* based on government perception of rebel influence. Electoral data gives the percentage of polling stations within each Assembly Constituency that were Highly Sensitive, Sensitive, or Normal for the 2003 State Assembly elections and was collected during fieldwork.[154] I use the percentage of Highly Sensitive polling stations within each constituency as a proxy of Maoist control in that constituency. This is a measure of how politically sensitive a constituency was perceived to be, based on reports that the individual district administrations send to the chief election commissioner of the state prior to elections. This is a continuous measure and provides more information than a categorical measure of *rebel control* as used by Kalyvas (2006). There are possible biases in police perception with this measure, but the error in the measure of political sensitivity is not correlated with the independent variable of *colonial indirect rule*, since the police have the number of Maoist squads, the number of Maoist front organizations, and perhaps even the level of violence in mind when perceiving the level of Maoist control, but they are not thinking of historical institutions.[155] So, the OLS estimators are unbiased and consistent, though there will be larger variance in the error terms. For details on potential bias and how that is not an issue, see Online Appendix D for this chapter.

INDEPENDENT VARIABLES AND CONTROL VARIABLES
Independent variable: The main independent variable is *colonial indirect rule* through *princely states* in Chhattisgarh state.

Princely State: Princely state dummy was created by matching the 2003 Chhattisgarh Assembly Constituency Election Map[156] with the map of direct and indirect rule in Chhattisgarh from *The Imperial Gazetteer of India: Volume 26 – Atlas, Plate 39* (see Figure 7.2). This is coded as 1 if the constituency was earlier part of any of the princely states within Chhattisgarh area, and 0 if it was part of the British-governed areas of Raipur, Bilaspur, and Durg, which is possible since there are no constituencies today that were partly within British India and partly within princely states.

Control Variables: Electoral data at the constituency level was directly obtained from the Chhattisgarh State Election Commission. The socioeconomic and

[154] Table 22: "Assembly Segment Wise Highly Sensitive, Sensitive & Normal Polling Stations," *Chhattisgarh State Assembly Election – 2003*, p. 52.
[155] Interview with Inspector General of Police (Naxal operations), Giridhari Naik, Raipur, Chhattisgarh, 2009.
[156] "Map of Assembly Segments," p. 18 of *Chhattisgarh State Assembly Election – 2003*.

demographic data like literacy, unemployment, percentage of scheduled castes and tribes, provision of public goods, and so on was converted from Census of India 2001 data, using the procedure described earlier. Forest cover data is from the Forest Survey of India 2001 report. These variables and their sources are described in Online Appendix E for this chapter.

6.2.2 OLS Estimates of the Impact of Indirect Colonial Rule on Maoist Insurgency

(A)DIFFERENCE IN MEANS SHOWS EFFECTS OF COLONIAL INSTITUTIONS ON INTERMEDIARY MECHANISMS OF STATE CAPACITY AND DEVELOPMENT Table 7.5 gives the difference in means between direct rule and indirect rule constituencies of each variable for all constituencies in Chhattisgarh and shows significantly higher mean values of Maoist control for the constituencies that were under indirect rule through princely states. Table 7.5 also shows that former princely state constituencies have lower access currently to many public goods like schools, water tanks and tubewells, electricity, and literacy, while British direct rule areas have higher levels of access to paved roads and buses and show less average distance of villages from main town, that is, higher state penetration in these rural areas (Census 2001 data).

(B)MODEL SPECIFICATION The OLS regressions are of the form

$$Y_i = \alpha + \beta \; princely \; state_i + \delta \; X_i + \varepsilon_i,$$

where Y_i is the dependent variable of *Maoist control* for constituency i, *princely state$_i$* is the dummy for whether the constituency was earlier part of a princely state or British India, and X_i stands for other constituency characteristics controlled for, including forest cover, elevation, literacy, rurality, percentage of tribes and lower castes, and other variables usually included in civil war onset models; ε_i represents the error term.

The OLS model results are presented in Tables 7.6A and 7.6B. In all models, standard errors are clustered at the district level to account for unobserved district-level characteristics because constituencies in the same district are similar in terms of counterinsurgency, development policy, and other unobserved qualities.[157] In Table 7.6A, the baseline specification is Model 1, which has only the main independent variable – *princely state*, which is statistically significant at the 1 percent error level in predicting *Maoist control*. In Models 1B to 1D, *princely state* remains significant even after controlling for *forest cover* and *elevation*, which are two measures of terrain that could provide opportunity for rebellion and could also be considered pre-colonial qualities of these areas affecting selection by British.

---

[157] It is not possible to do district fixed effects estimation of *princely state* to control for any possible district-level unobservables, because there is little within-district variation in the *princely state* variable. See Gujarati, *Basic Econometrics*, pp. 640–51.

TABLE 7.5 *Summary statistics and difference in means by princely state*

Variable	No. of constituencies			Mean			Difference in means (standard errors in brackets)
	Total	British Empire	Princely States	Total	British Empire	Princely States	(British Empire) – (Princely State)
Maoist Rebel Control							
Percentage High Sensitive	90	52	38	10.66	2.17	22.26	– 20.09 *** (3.30)
Polling Stations							
Geography							
Forest Cover Percentage	90	52	38	30.83	19.18	45.68	– 25.70 *** (5.52)
Elevation (meters)	90	52	38	389.52	318.49	486.71	–168.22 *** (24.83)
Demography							
Scheduled Caste Percentage	90	52	38	11.88	15.51	6.93	8.58 *** (1.34)
Scheduled Tribe Percentage	90	52	38	33.24	20.03	51.31	–31.28 *** (4.03)
Population Density	90	52	38	293.93	366.47	194.69	171.78 *** (50.73)
Rural Percentage	90	52	38	84.70	81.48	89.12	–7.64 (4.83)
Socioeconomic							
Total Literacy	90	52	38	63.622	67.33	58.55	8.77 *** (2.39)
Male Literacy	90	52	38	76.65	81.21	70.41	10.79 *** (2.19)
Female Literacy	90	52	38	50.61	53.46	46.69	6.77 ** (2.65)
Male Unemployment	90	52	38	56.88	59.44	53.38	6.07*** (0.79)
Per Capita Income	90	52	38	603.29	747.55	405.89	341.66 (493.32)
State Capacity							
Post Office	90	52	38	0.18	0.19	0.15	0.04 ** (0.02)
Distance from Town (km)	90	52	38	31.36	22.58	43.39	–20.81 *** (4.69)

TABLE 7.5 *(continued)*

Variable	No. of constituencies			Mean			Difference in means (standard errors in brackets)
	Total	British Empire	Princely States	Total	British Empire	Princely States	(British Empire) – (Princely State)
Paved Road	90	52	38	0.36	0.41	0.30	0.11*** (0.04)
Railway Facility	90	52	38	0.007	0.008	0.005	0.003 (0.002)
Bus Facility	90	52	38	0.17	0.19	0.15	0.04** (0.02)
Education							
Middle School	90	52	38	0.29	0.31	0.26	0.05** (0.02)
Secondary School	90	52	38	0.09	0.11	0.07	0.04*** (0.01)
Water							
Tanks	90	52	38	0.384	0.518	0.202	0.316*** (0.094)
Tubewells	90	52	38	0.306	0.465	0.087	0.377*** (0.102)
Power							
Electricity	90	52	38	0.344	0.408	0.256	0.152*** (0.043)

Standard Errors in parentheses. * $p < 0.10$, ** $p < 0.05$, *** $p < 0.01$.
Source: All public goods data from Village Directory, Census of India 2001.

I include various postcolonial controls in Table 7.6A like *population density, rural percentage, per capita income,* as well as *male unemployment, male literacy, percentage of scheduled caste* and *scheduled tribes, access to electricity,* and the interaction term of *scheduled tribes* with *access to electricity.* Table 7.6B leaves out *per capita income* as a measure of state capacity and includes other proxies for state counterinsurgency capacity like *access to paved road, access to post office, railway station,* and *average distance of villages from nearest town* in a constituency. Model 8 includes effective number of political parties (ENPV) in constituencies (Wilkinson 2004) as a measure of political competitiveness.

The OLS models in Tables 7.6A and 7.6B show that *princely state* remains a statistically significant predictor of *Maoist control* even after controlling for more proximate measures of ethnic grievances, poverty, literacy, and different measures of state capacity, which are themselves the result of colonial rule institutions. This suggests that the colonial indirect rule institutions have their own separate effects, over and above the effects of contemporary factors like state capacity, ethnicity, and development of rebellion. However, the OLS results may possibly be biased due to selection into indirect rule of districts with more tribal rebellion and difficult terrain by the British colonial officers. The next section presents the IV-2SLS analysis to address selection bias.

6.2.3 2SLS Instrumental Variable Regression Model Estimation

In this section, I replicate the models from the OLS regressions in Tables 7.6A and 7.6B, using IV-2SLS analysis. I instrument for the potentially endogenous independent variable *princely state*, using *instru_Nagpur Lapse*, based on random annexation of Nagpur state due to the death of the ruler.

First Stage of IV-2SLS: The first stage regression for the IV strategy is

$$princely\ state_i = \alpha + \beta\ instru\_NagpurLapse_i + \delta\ X_i + \varepsilon_i$$

where *princely state$_i$* is the measure of *colonial indirect rule* for the *i*th constituency, as in the previous OLS regressions, and X_i stands for the same constituency characteristics controlled for in the OLS model. In the first stage of the IV-2SLS, I use *instru_NagpurLapse* as the instrument for the choice of direct vs. indirect rule in the British districts of Chhattisgarh based on the lapse of Nagpur state to British rule.

The results of the first stage of the IV-2SLS are presented in Table 7.7. Replicating Models 1A, 1B, 1C, 1D, 2A, and 2B from Table 7.6A of the OLS regressions, the first stage regressions generally show that *Instru_Nagpur Lapse* has a strong negative correlation with colonial indirect rule through princely states.[158] This is the result of these districts switching to direct British rule due to death of ruler. Bound, Jaeger, and Baker (1995) show how the IV-2SLS estimates may be somewhat biased in the same direction as OLS estimates in finite samples if there is weak correlation in the first stage between the instrument and the endogenous independent variables. The Angrist-Pischke F statistic of the instrument for *princely state* is larger than 10 in most models, which is the usual F statistic value required to suggest that instruments are sufficiently strong. So, it is possible to reject the null hypothesis of no correlation between instrument and endogenous regressors at the 95 percent confidence level, and this implies that the instruments are not weak.[159]

---

[158] Estimating first-stage regressions for Models 3–8 from Table 7.6B gives similar results that are not shown but are available on request.

[159] See Stock, Wright, and Yogo, "A Survey of Weak Instruments and Weak Identification in Generalized Method of Movement," for detailed discussion about weak instruments.

TABLE 7.6A *OLS estimates of impact of colonial institutions on Maoist rebellion*
Dependent variable: *Maoist control* (Percentage Highly Sensitive Polling Stations in each Constituency)

	Pre-colonial controls				Postcolonial controls	
	Model 1A	Model 1B	Model 1C	Model 1D	Model 2A	Model 2B
Princely State	20.09***	13.42***	17.83**	14.67**	15.55***	11.93***
	(0.001)	(0.004)	(0.044)	(0.042)	(0.005)	(0.002)
Forest Cover		0.260**		0.277**	0.281**	0.118
		(0.015)		(0.039)	(0.014)	(0.220)
Elevation			0.0134	−0.0101		−0.0304
			(0.569)	(0.724)		(0.173)
Popln Density					0.000250	0.00238
					(0.960)	(0.588)
Rural Percentage					0.0285	0.0688
					(0.636)	(0.178)
Per Capita Income					−0.000320	0.000172
					(0.476)	(0.483)
Male Unemployment					0.490	0.852*
					(0.260)	(0.064)
Scheduled Caste Percentage						−0.505**
						(0.038)
Scheduled Tribe Percentage						0.450***
						(0.009)
Electricity						26.93**
						(0.040)
ST% * Electricity						−1.029***
						(0.001)
Male Literacy						−0.481*
						(0.090)
Constant	2.173*	−3.013	−2.110	−0.151	−34.74	−13.86
	(0.061)	(0.136)	(0.774)	(0.984)	(0.203)	(0.749)
Observations	90	90	90	90	90	90
R^2	0.296	0.429	0.304	0.433	0.439	0.651

P-values in parentheses
Robust std. errors adjusted for 17 clusters by district.
* $p < 0.10$, ** $p < 0.05$, *** $p < 0.01$

Second Stage of IV-2SLS: The second-stage regression for the IV strategy estimates the impact of colonial indirect rule through *princely state* on *Maoist control* and has the same specification as the OLS model:

$$Y_i = a + b \text{ } princely \text{ } state_i + d \text{ } X_i + u_i,$$

TABLE 7.6 B *OLS estimates of impact of colonial institutions on Maoist rebellion*
Dependent variable: *Maoist control* (Percentage Highly Sensitive Polling Stations in each Constituency)

	Model 3	Model 4	Model 5	Model 6	Model 7	Model 8
Princely State	12.10***	11.34***	11.46***	11.62***	12.14***	12.87***
	(0.001)	(0.002)	(0.003)	(0.002)	(0.002)	(0.001)
Forest Cover	0.129	0.0916	0.105	0.116	0.115	0.109
	(0.194)	(0.384)	(0.226)	(0.227)	(0.230)	(0.241)
Elevation	−0.0310	−0.0289	−0.0287	−0.0287	−0.0314	−0.0265
	(0.167)	(0.164)	(0.190)	(0.180)	(0.157)	(0.226)
Population Density	−0.000349	0.00784	0.00217	0.00781	0.00266	0.00454
	(0.952)	(0.325)	(0.624)	(0.114)	(0.560)	(0.259)
Rural Percentage	0.0672	0.0811	0.0562	0.0799	0.0683	0.0853
	(0.181)	(0.181)	(0.312)	(0.130)	(0.203)	(0.136)
Per Capita Income					0.000177	0.000418
					(0.484)	(0.137)
Male Unemployment	0.839*	0.833*	0.763*	0.819*	0.869*	0.565
	(0.061)	(0.052)	(0.063)	(0.061)	(0.068)	(0.111)
Scheduled Caste Percentage	−0.431*	−0.454**	−0.449*	−0.556**	−0.492*	−0.741**
	(0.059)	(0.040)	(0.065)	(0.037)	(0.057)	(0.022)
Scheduled Tribe Percentage	0.462***	0.493***	0.393**	0.408**	0.461**	0.313**
	(0.008)	(0.006)	(0.031)	(0.017)	(0.011)	(0.046)
Electricity	26.34**	29.53**	24.15**	25.19**	26.04**	25.03**
	(0.033)	(0.023)	(0.032)	(0.047)	(0.026)	(0.024)
ST% * Electricity	−1.032***	−1.047***	−0.960***	−0.968***	−1.017***	−1.001***
	(0.001)	(0.001)	(0.001)	(0.001)	(0.001)	(0.000)
Male Literacy	−0.479*	−0.498*	−0.491*	−0.526*	−0.502	−0.476*
	(0.086)	(0.078)	(0.091)	(0.075)	(0.126)	(0.096)
Paved Road	7.410					
	(0.270)					
Post Office		−24.27				
		(0.334)				
Distance from Town			0.0691			
			(0.515)			
Railway Station				−170.3		
				(0.110)		
Voter Turnout 1985					0.0568	
					(0.760)	
ENPV 1998						6.374**
						(0.030)
Constant	−16.25	−12.00	−7.445	−8.116	−15.70	−11.82
	(0.708)	(0.775)	(0.859)	(0.846)	(0.720)	(0.770)
Observations	90	90	90	90	90	90
R^2	0.653	0.657	0.655	0.655	0.652	0.687

P-values in parentheses. Robust std. errors adjusted for 17 clusters by district.
* p < 0.10, ** p < 0.05, *** p < 0.01

TABLE 7.7 *First stage of IV-2SLS estimates of impact of colonial institutions on Maoist rebellion*
Dependent variable: *princely state*

	Pre-colonial controls				Postcolonial controls	
	Model 1A Princely State	Model 1B Princely State	Model 1C Princely State	Model 1D Princely State	Model 2A Princely State	Model 2B Princely State
Instrument (Nagpur Lapse, 1854)	-0.776*** (0.000)	-0.719*** (0.001)	-0.645*** (0.002)	-0.641*** (0.004)	-0.576*** (0.008)	-0.604*** (0.004)
Forest Cover		0.00229 (0.454)		0.000280 (0.902)	-0.00110 (0.621)	-0.00250 (0.262)
Elevation			0.000995 (0.114)	0.000970* (0.089)	0.000694 (0.134)	0.000446 (0.214)
Popln Density					-0.000124 (0.430)	0.0000304 (0.981)
Rural Percentage					-0.000635 (0.778)	-0.000100 (0.962)
Per Capita Income					0.00000732 (0.148)	0.00000500 (0.517)
Male Unemployment					-0.0249 (0.103)	-0.0224 (0.285)
Scheduled Caste Percentage						-0.00880 (0.463)
Scheduled Tribe Percentage						-0.00389 (0.562)
Electricity						-0.382 (0.138)

TABLE 7.7 (continued)

	Pre-colonial controls				Postcolonial controls	
	Model 1A Princely State	Model 1B Princely State	Model 1C Princely State	Model 1D Princely State	Model 2A Princely State	Model 2B Princely State
ST% * Electricity						0.00612 (0.340)
Male Literacy						-0.00658* (0.099)
Constant	0.776*** (0.000)	0.679*** (0.006)	0.329 (0.381)	0.328 (0.386)	1.950** (0.029)	2.696* (0.060)
Observations	90	90	90	90	90	90
R^2	0.611	0.626	0.676	0.676	0.707	0.728
Adjusted R^2	0.607	0.617	0.668	0.665	0.682	0.685
Weak Instrument Diagnosis:						
Angrist Pischke F statistic	37.27	17.44	12.95	11.36	9.08	11.63
Angrist Pischke p value	(0.000)	(0.000)	(0.0024)	(0.0039)	(0.0082)	(0.0036)
Kleibergen-Paap Wald statistic	37.27	17.44	12.95	11.36	9.08	11.63
Cragg-Donald Wald F statistic	138.49	99.56	89.38	82.18	61.25	60.97

P-values in parentheses
Robust std. errors adjusted for 17 clusters by district.
* $p < 0.10$, ** $p < 0.05$, *** $p < 0.01$

Tables 7.8A and 7.8B show the results of the second stage of the IV-2SLS regressions and are the same specifications as OLS models in Tables 7.6A and 7.6B.

6.2.4 Analysis and Discussion of Results

Colonial Institutions: In Table 7.8A, Model 1A, the instrumental variable regression yields a point estimate of 22.06 on *princely state* which is significant at the 99 percent confidence level. Moving a constituency from direct rule under the British to indirect rule through a princely state increases the percentage of Maoist-affected polling stations in the constituency by almost 22 percentage points. In Models 1B to 1D, including *forest cover* and *elevation, princely state* is still statistically significant and positively correlated with *Maoist control. These results suggest that controlling for pre-colonial determinants of choice of indirect rule, as well as using an instrument for indirect rule to address selection effects, princely state institutions have a separate causal effect on the probability of Maoist insurgency.* Forest cover or elevation possibly influenced the institutional selection of colonial indirect rule in some districts and areas of Chhattisgarh by the British, though not all. However, once these institutions were in place, they had an additional effect on state penetration and development that persisted through "sticky" path dependent mechanisms and created political opportunity structures for leftist insurgency, as demonstrated qualitatively earlier in the chapter.

Proximate Postcolonial Factors and Robustness Tests: In Table 7.8A, Model 2B, *scheduled tribe (ST) percentage* has a positive and significant coefficient, since the Maoists recruit mainly from the poor tribal populations in Chhattisgarh. Other papers like Gawande et al. (2017), Chandra and Garcia-Ponce (2019), and Gomes (2015) also find that scheduled tribes have a positive correlation with Maoist insurgency, and this is evidence for the Cederman et al. (2010) mechanism of ethnic grievances. *Scheduled caste (SC) percentage* has a negative and significant coefficient, because the lower castes in Chhattisgarh live in the central districts where there is no insurgency. Another interesting result is that *Male unemployment* has a positive and significant effect in the longer models, which could be support for both opportunity and grievance mechanisms, since unemployment may create lower opportunity costs to joining rebellion and also may generate grievance among tribal unemployed males. This supports the finding that the NREGS program reduces Maoist insurgency by providing employment in rural areas (Gawande et al. 2017; Hoelscher et al. 2012).

In Table 7.8B, I include various other postcolonial measures of state counterinsurgency capacity like access to paved roads and post offices and railway stations from Census of India data. The IV-2SLS results show *princely state* to be statistically significant.

TABLE 7.8A *IV-2SLS Estimates of impact of colonial Institutions on Maoist rebellion*
Dependent variable: *Maoist control* (Percentage Highly Sensitive Polling Stations in each constituency)

	Pre-colonial controls				Postcolonial controls	
	Model 1A	Model 1B	Model 1C	Model 1D	Model 2A	Model 2B
Princely State	22.06***	13.92***	20.81***	15.13**	16.47***	11.79**
	(0.000)	(0.000)	(0.007)	(0.011)	(0.005)	(0.037)
Forest Cover		0.256***		0.275**	0.290**	0.118
		(0.005)		(0.019)	(0.011)	(0.158)
Elevation			0.00737	-0.0109	-0.00716	-0.0303
			(0.744)	(0.680)	(0.792)	(0.144)
Popln Density					0.000179	0.00233
					(0.974)	(0.535)
Rural Percentage					0.0267	0.0686
					(0.652)	(0.120)
Per Capita Income					-0.000324	0.000172
					(0.446)	(0.424)
Male Unemployment					0.453	0.846*
					(0.293)	(0.052)
Scheduled Caste Percentage						-0.505**
						(0.013)
Scheduled Tribe Percentage						0.450***
						(0.001)

	(1)	(2)	(3)	(4)	(5)	(6)
Electricity						26.95**
						(0.016)
ST% * Electricity						-1.030***
						(0.000)
Male Literacy						-0.482*
						(0.061)
Constant	1.341**	-3.105*	-1.002	0.00386	-30.34	-13.42
	(0.023)	(0.085)	(0.889)	(1.000)	(0.343)	(0.752)
Observations	90	90	90	90	90	90
R^2	0.293	0.429	0.299	0.433	0.441	0.651
Adjusted R^2	0.285	0.416	0.283	0.413	0.393	0.597
Endogeneity and Over-Identification Test Diagnosis:						
Hansen's J statistic	†	†	†	†	†	†
Hansen's J (p-value)	†	†	†	†	†	†
Anderson-Rubin Wald test	na	9.54	5.29	5.33	4.25	2.10
Anderson-Rubin (p-value)	na	(0.0070)	(0.0352)	(0.0347)	(0.0559)	(0.1668)

P-values in parentheses
Robust std. errors adjusted for 17 clusters by district.
$*$ $p < 0.10$, $**$ $p < 0.05$, $***$ $p < 0.01$
†Hansen J Statistic (over-identification test of all instruments) is 0.000, since equation is exactly identified because the number of endogenous regressors equals the number of instruments.

TABLE 7.8B *IV-2SLS Estimates of impact of colonial Institutions on Maoist rebellion*
Dependent variable: *Maoistcontrol* (Percentage Highly Sensitive Polling Stations in each constituency)

	Model 3	Model 4	Model 5	Model 6	Model 7	Model 8
Princely State	12.15**	11.14**	11.75**	11.28*	12.44***	12.70**
	(0.024)	(0.040)	(0.041)	(0.051)	(0.009)	(0.018)
Forest Cover	0.130	0.0912	0.105	0.116	0.116	0.108
	(0.133)	(0.318)	(0.165)	(0.167)	(0.162)	(0.181)
Elevation	-0.0310	-0.0287	-0.0290	-0.0284	-0.0317	-0.0264
	(0.134)	(0.138)	(0.161)	(0.157)	(0.115)	(0.191)
Popln Density	-0.000337	0.00780	0.00226	0.00774*	0.00276	0.00448
	(0.947)	(0.272)	(0.555)	(0.063)	(0.439)	(0.148)
Rural Percentage	0.0673	0.0809	0.0568	0.0795*	0.0687	0.0850*
	(0.121)	(0.125)	(0.255)	(0.077)	(0.132)	(0.067)
Per Capita Income					0.000178	0.000417*
					(0.423)	(0.075)
Male Unemployment	0.841**	0.825**	0.776*	0.805*	0.881**	0.558
	(0.049)	(0.042)	(0.075)	(0.054)	(0.041)	(0.129)
Scheduled Caste Percentage	-0.431**	-0.454**	-0.449**	-0.557**	-0.491***	-0.741***
	(0.023)	(0.014)	(0.030)	(0.011)	(0.020)	(0.005)
Scheduled Tribe Percentage	0.462***	0.494***	0.393***	0.409***	0.461***	0.314**
	(0.001)	(0.000)	(0.009)	(0.003)	(0.001)	(0.014)
Electricity	26.33**	29.59***	24.12**	25.24*	25.96***	25.06***
	(0.012)	(0.007)	(0.010)	(0.020)	(0.008)	(0.008)
ST% * Electricity	-1.032***	-1.048***	-0.960***	-0.968***	-1.016***	-1.002***
	(0.000)	(0.000)	(0.000)	(0.000)	(0.000)	(0.000)
Male Literacy	-0.479*	-0.499**	-0.489*	-0.529**	-0.501***	-0.478*
	(0.059)	(0.049)	(0.064)	(0.049)	(0.083)	(0.066)

Paved Road	7.420				
	(0.214)				
Post Office		−24.42			
		(0.239)			
Distance from Town			0.0684		
			(0.488)		
Railway Station				−171.6*	
				(0.056)	
Voter Turnout 1985					0.0587
					(0.684)
ENPV 1998					6.364***
					(0.009)
Constant	−16.41	−11.37	−8.404	−7.016	−16.69 / −11.28
	(0.702)	(0.780)	(0.846)	(0.866)	(0.685) / (0.779)
Observations	90	90	90	90	90 / 90
R^2	0.653	0.657	0.655	0.655	0.652 / 0.687
Adjusted R^2	0.599	0.604	0.601	0.602	0.592 / 0.633
Endogeneity and Over-Identification Test Diagnosis:					
Hansen's J statistic	†	†	†	†	† / †
Hansen's J (p-value)	†	†	†	†	† / †
Anderson-Rubin Wald test	2.31	2.05	2.03	1.85	2.79 / 2.35
Anderson-Rubin (p-val)	(0.1484)	(0.1713)	(0.1734)	(0.1923)	(0.1141) / (0.1450)

P-values in parentheses

Robust std. errors adjusted for 17 clusters by district.

* p < 0.10, ** p < 0.05, *** p < 0.01

†Hansen J Statistic

(over-identification test of all instruments) is 0.000, since equation is exactly identified because the number of endogenous regressors equals the number of instruments.

I do various robustness checks, like robust clustering by colonial era princely state boundaries, using other measures of the dependent variable of *Maoist control*, and checking for spatial autocorrelation to control for diffusion of insurgency from neighboring districts, which are detailed in Online Appendix G of this chapter and my *World Development* article.

7   CONCLUSION: ENGAGING WITH THE NEXT CHAPTER ON MAOISTS IN TELANGANA

This chapter explored subnational variation within the Indian state of Chhattisgarh to show the historical origins of subnational variation in state capacity and tribal grievances, which were used by Maoist rebels to mobilize successfully. I use process tracing (George & Bennett 2005; Goertz 2017) to show how colonial indirect rule creates unequal land tenure systems and natural resource exploitation in the feudatory princely state of Bastar/ Kanker, and how this persists into the postcolonial period through path dependence (Mahoney 2000) and internal colonialism (Baruah 1999), and how these tribal grievances in the form of ethnic mobilization networks are then mobilized by Maoist rebel agents to create rebellion.

The next chapter analyzes the case of the PWG Maoists in the Telangana region of the former princely state of Hyderabad, in the neighboring state of Andhra Pradesh. Focusing on another state in the southern epicenter allows us to show the generalizability of the effects of *formal* colonial indirect rule through princely states on Maoist insurgency. At the same time, it helps push forward the research agenda of developing an understanding of variation in types of princely states that Wilkinson (2017) and Gerring et al. (2011) propose. While the same PWG Maoists operated in the Telangana region of Andhra Pradesh, the princely state of Hyderabad was not a feudatory princely state like in Chhattisgarh, but a successor state of the Mughal Empire ruled by the Nizam-ul-Mulk (Ramusack 2004). Yet this other type of princely state also had land inequality and Maoist insurgency. This helps us understand how different types of indirect rule within India can lead to the same outcome of Maoist insurgency and demonstrates equifinality.

Comparing the smaller feudatory princely states of Bastar/Kanker/Surguja in Chhattisgarh with the large Mughal successor state of Hyderabad in Andhra Pradesh also allows us to demonstrate that while there are lots of similarities, there is also some difference in the mechanisms created by these princely states in south-central India in their effects on rebellion. The Telangana region of the large princely state of Hyderabad in Andhra Pradesh experienced exploitation of peasants through the *deshmukhs* used by the Nizam of Hyderabad to collect land taxes (Sinha 1989; Thirumali 2003). This is similar to the despotic *malguzari* type land tenure systems practiced in Bastar state under the *Diwans* in the 1860 to the 1890s. There are also some differences, for example, the smaller feudatory princely states in Chhattisgarh have much lower levels of state and police capacity, while the larger princely state of Hyderabad was stronger in terms of state penetration. Also the terrain in Bastar was more forested than that in Telangana in Hyderabad. However, this difference did not prevent the PWG Maoists from being successful in Telangana. In fact, it was Telangana that was the crucible of peasant rebellion in India in the 1940s, much before the Maoists entered Bastar, as the next chapter shows.

8

Maoist Insurgency in Andhra Pradesh: The Nizam's Shadow on Telangana

I INTRODUCTION

In this chapter, I continue with the second part of the "nested analysis" research design (Lieberman 2005) by focusing on the Maoist rebellion in the South Indian state of Andhra Pradesh, which is the neighboring state just south of Chhattisgarh. I use the case of Andhra Pradesh as another *crucial pathway case* (Gerring 2007) to test my theory of colonial institutions of indirect rule shaping the structural conditions for Maoist insurgency. It is also a *process tracing case* (Goertz 2017) in which I trace the causal pathway linking indirect rule to insurgency. Similar to the chapter on Chhattisgarh, I use a mixed method research design and combine qualitative process tracing that demonstrates how land inequality and low development created by indirect rule persisted after independence in 1947, with a quantitative analysis of a novel constituency-level dataset within Andhra Pradesh.

While the new state of Telangana was created out of the state of Andhra Pradesh in 2014, the analysis is done on the older state of Andhra Pradesh, in which the northern part was indirectly ruled through the princely state of Hyderabad, and the southern part was under directly ruled Madras province. The princely state of Hyderabad created lower level of development (Lange 2009), as well as land inequality and despotic extraction (Boone 1994; Mamdani 1996), which then persisted into postcolonial times through path dependence (Mahoney 2000). The long history of leftist peasant rebellions in the state of Andhra Pradesh provided rebel agency that exploited these historically created structural inequalities. The Telangana peasant rebellion of 1946–49 in Hyderabad princely state was followed by the CPI-Marxist-Leninist movement in 1967–72 and finally culminated in the People's War Group (PWG) Maoist insurgency beginning in the 1980s. All these leftist rebellions succeeded in the Telangana districts of the former princely state of Hyderabad, and not in the British direct ruled areas of Madras province that had higher levels of development and less land inequality.

The chapter outline is as follows. In Section 2, I explain why I selected the case of Andhra Pradesh and then provide a history of the princely state of Hyderabad. In Section 3, I describe the mechanisms of land inequality and low public good provision created due to the policies of the Nizam of the princely state of Hyderabad, but higher development and more equal land tenure system in direct ruled Madras Presidency areas. In Section 4, I use qualitative data to demonstrate persistence of these effects into the postcolonial period through path dependence. Then in Section 5, I describe the history of the evolution of the PWG Maoists in Telangana region of Andhra Pradesh and show how rebel agency exploited the structural conditions to create successful Maoist insurgency. In Section 6, I describe the Assembly Constituency dataset for Andhra Pradesh and present regression analysis that shows that *princely state* has a significant and positive correlation with *Maoist control*. The concluding section compares the results with the case of the princely state of Chhattisgarh presented in the previous chapter.

2 THE CASE OF ANDHRA PRADESH

2.1 Why Select Andhra Pradesh?

The reason for selecting Andhra Pradesh is similar to that for choosing Chhattisgarh. It is one of the two main states in the southern epicenter of the Maoist insurgency, which represents the second causal pathway to Maoist insurgency outlined in Chapter 3, namely formal or de jure indirect rule through princely states creating conditions for Maoist insurgency.[1] Much like Chhattisgarh, the case of Andhra Pradesh also represents a crucial pathway case (Gerring 2007) that allows us to process trace this causal pathway linking indirect rule to Maoist insurgency. Like Chhattisgarh, there is variation of direct/indirect rule areas within Andhra Pradesh, which allows testing of the effect of indirect rule on inequality and conflict.

Focusing on a second case allows analytical comparison between different types of princely states, which create slightly different types of mechanisms that still lead to Maoist insurgency by the same PWG Maoist group, thus showing equifinality (Mahoney & Goertz 2006). The Chhattisgarh case shows how the small feudatory princely states with tribal populations ruled by Rajput "outsider" princes created conditions of weak state capacity and despotic extraction of land and natural resources. In comparison, the large princely state of Hyderabad in northern Andhra Pradesh represents a different type of

---

[1] There are also some small feudatory princely states that were in the southwestern part of the current state of Orissa that are not studied in my project and are also part of this southern epicenter of Maoist insurgency. Future studies could analyze these cases.

princely state that is a successor state of the Mughal Empire (Ramusack 2004), where the land tenure institutions allowed despotic extraction from peasants and low provision of public goods.

Wilkinson (2017) has criticized existing theories like those of Iyer (2010) and Verghese (2016a, 2016b) for failing to account for the heterogeneity in princely states in India. Analyzing another type of princely state that created conditions for Maoist insurgency provides a glimpse into the variation in types of princely states that were outlined in the typology of indirect rule in Chapter 6. It was the Telangana region of the successor state of Hyderabad, which had high levels of land inequality and caste oppression by *jagirdars* and *deshmukhs*, which was the crucible of various peasant rebellions in the colonial period, followed by the leftist-led Telangana rebellion of 1947–51, and finally the PWG Maoist–led rebellion starting in 1980. While Verghese (2016a) incorrectly claims that the "curious case" of Bastar in Chhattisgarh is not indirect rule, the same can hardly be said of Hyderabad, which was one of the largest princely states in British India, like Kashmir. For a colonial institutional theory to explain Maoist conflict in India, it is essential to explain why the Maoists succeeded in indirect rule areas of Telangana in former Hyderabad state, which studies like Verghese (2016a, 2016b) fail to do.

2.2   Hyderabad as a Successor State to the Mughals

Hyderabad was a large Muslim nobility-ruled princely state in southern India; along with Awadh and Bengal, it was one of the successor states of the Mughal Empire, where a Mughal provincial governor or military officer slowly became independent of Delhi and started his own revenue collection and appointed his own successors (Ramusack 2004: 24–27).

Before the Mughal era, this region in South India was ruled by various Hindu dynasties like the Chalukyas, Kakatiyas, and the Yadavas. The Muslim invasion started with Alauddin Khilji in 1294, and from 1340s, the Muslim Bahmani dynasty was founded and ruled the Telangana and neighboring areas till about 1518, ending with the death of Mahmud Shah Bahmani.[2] Amid the confusion following the death of Mahmud Shah, Kutb-ul-Mulk, who had been governor of the Golconda province under the Bahmanis, declared his independence and established the Kutb Shahi dynasty, which ruled from 1512 to 1687 with its capital at Hyderabad. In 1635, when Shah Jahan became the Mughal emperor, he sent a *firman* (royal edict) to Abdullah Kutb Shah at Golconda in return for his earlier help, and this was well received by the Kutb Shah king. The next Mughal emperor Aurangzeb invaded and plundered Hyderabad in 1655, but Abdullah Kutb Shah sued for peace. On Abdullah's death in 1674, his nephew Tana Shah succeeded him, but the Mughal Emperor Aurangzeb defeated and imprisoned Tana Shah in 1687, and he died in 1704 thus ending the Kutb Shahi dynasty.[3]

---

[2] *Imperial Gazetteer of India*, Hyderabad State, 1909, pp. 10–13.
[3] *Imperial Gazetteer of India*, Hyderabad State, 1909, p. 14.

This led to the founding of the Asaf Jahi dynasty by Asaf Jah, a distinguished general of Emperor Aurangzeb, who had been appointed *subedar* or viceroy of the Deccan in 1713 with the title of Nizam-ul-Mulk. With the death of Aurangzeb in 1707 and the gradual decline of the Mughal Empire, Asaf Jah asserted his independence from the Mughal throne in Delhi and fought against the Marathas who were attacking from the west. Asaf Jah defeated a Mughal army in 1724 and annexed Berar and set up his capital at Hyderabad; at the time of his death in 1748, he had established a sovereign kingdom of Hyderabad that became one of the successor states of the Mughal Empire.[4]

Following Asaf Jah's death in 1748, his son Nasir Jang got help from the English, and his grandson Muzaffar Jang got French support, thus involving the competing European colonizers in this region in the war of succession. Muzaffar Jang became the ruler and the French initially had control, but with his assassination, Dupleix, the French governor, selected Salabat Jang as Nizam in 1751. Salabat Jang was dethroned in 1761, and Nizam Ali Khan, the fourth son of Asaf Jah, became the Nizam with the help of the English and dismissed the French from his service.[5] Nizam Ali Khan ruled from 1762 to 1803, controlled the largest territorial base, and used direct revenues from the land to support his personal household and his administration and military, but he also gave out various lands and rights to revenue collection to feudal intermediaries like *jagirdars* and other landlords, which led to exploitation of peasants (Ramusack 2004: 26).

In 1766, under threat from the Marathas from the west, Nizam Ali Khan signed an initial treaty with the British, under which the East India Company promised to furnish a subsidiary force in time of war; in return the Nizam ceded the Northern Circars and promised tribute from Hyderabad. However, when the Nizam attacked the Marathas in 1795, the British governor general refused support because of a preexisting alliance with the Maratha peshwa. The Nizam again resorted to taking French assistance. In 1798, the annexationist governor general Lord Wellesley concluded a Treaty of Subsidiary Alliance with the Nizam that required Hyderabad to dismiss all French officials, disband its foreign troops, and pay Rs. 24 lakhs for the maintenance of a subsidiary force that would be integrated with the British army. Unlike the 1768 treaty, that was between equals, the 1798 treaty was between unequals and started the process of Hyderabad slowly coming under the indirect control of British colonialism (Ramusack 2004: 60–62).

In 1803, the British defeated the combined threat of Scindia and Holkar on the Nizam's territories in the Battle of Assaye and Argaon. Following Nizam Ali Khan's death in 1803, his son Sikander Jah succeeded him.[6] There slowly emerged a system of indirect rule in the 1800s, in which the British protected

---

[4] *Imperial Gazetteer of India*, Hyderabad State, 1909, p. 15.
[5] *Imperial Gazetteer of India*, Hyderabad State, 1909, pp. 15–16.
[6] *Imperial Gazetteer of India*, Hyderabad State, 1909, pp. 16–17.

Hyderabad from external enemies but continued to increase its influence in the internal administration of the state through the appointment of sympathetic *diwans*. The British rewarded Hyderabad with the fertile Berar province that they had taken from the Maratha-ruled Nagpur state but also forced Nizam Sikander Jah to accept Mir Alam as *diwan* (Ramusack, 2004: 63). In 1829, following Sikander Jah's death, his son Nasir-ud-Daula succeeded to the throne. In 1843, Siraj-ul-Mulk, the grandson of Mir Alam, was made the *diwan*; while he was removed following a serious Shia-Sunni riot in 1847, he was reinstated as *diwan* in 1851. In 1853, a new treaty was signed between the British and Hyderabad, in which the Nizam had to cede the revenues from Berar for the maintenance of troops. Soon after this new treaty, Siraj-ul-Mulk died and Salar Jang was appointed *diwan*.[7]

With the death of Nizam Nasir-ud-Daula in 1857, the new Nizam was Afzal-ud-Daula. In this period, Salar Jang I emerged as a powerful *diwan* who carried out several reforms in administration and land revenue and practically ruled the state and eclipsed the power of the Nizam. He coordinated with the British Resident and won such confidence of the British that they even permitted his minor son to succeed him as *diwan* on his death in 1883. According to Ramusack (2004), the criteria of indirect rule were clearly met for the case of Hyderabad in this period, since both sides acknowledged British control, the British were the dominant power, and all foreign and domestic rivals were excluded, and yet the Hyderabad administration continued to have control over internal affairs like collection of land revenues and judicial and legal jurisdiction of its subjects.[8]

3 BRITISH INDIRECT RULE SETTING UP CAUSAL PATHWAYS TO MAOIST INSURGENCY

The state of Andhra Pradesh was formed on November 1, 1956, during the linguistic reorganization of Indian states under Prime Minister Jawaharlal Nehru. In response to demands by Telugu-speaking peoples to have a unified state based on common language, the Telugu-speaking Telangana region of former Hyderabad state was unified with the Telugu-speaking regions of British Madras Presidency to form the new state of Andhra Pradesh.[9] The new state now had areas in the north from the princely state of Hyderabad and areas in the east and south from British direct rule Madras province. The eastern districts in Figure 8.1 of Hyderabad state and Figure 8.2 of Madras Presidency were combined to form Andhra Pradesh state in Figure 8.3. This internal variation

---

[7] *Imperial Gazetteer of India*, Hyderabad State, 1909, p. 17.

[8] Ramusack, *The Indian Princes and Their States*, p. 63.

[9] The Marathi-speaking regions of Hyderabad state joined Maharashtra state, and the non-Telugu regions of Madras Presidency where Tamil speakers dominated joined the new state of Tamil Nadu.

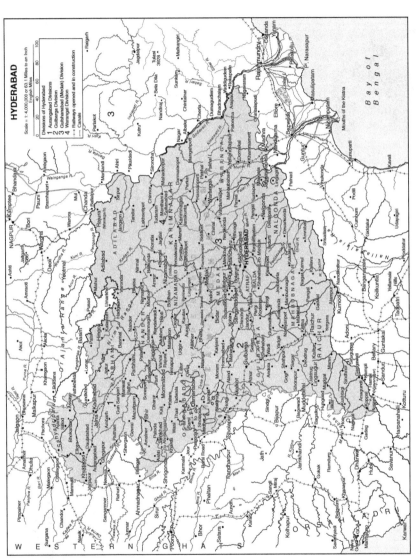

FIGURE 8.1 Map of princely state of Hyderabad: eastern districts of Adilabad, Karimnagar, Warangal, Nalgonda, Mahbubnagar, Medak and Nizamabad later became part of Andhra Pradesh state in 1956

Source: *The Imperial Gazetteer of India: Volume 26 – Atlas, Plate 40.* 1909. Available at https://dsal.uchicago.edu/reference/gaz_atlas_1909/pager.html?object=46

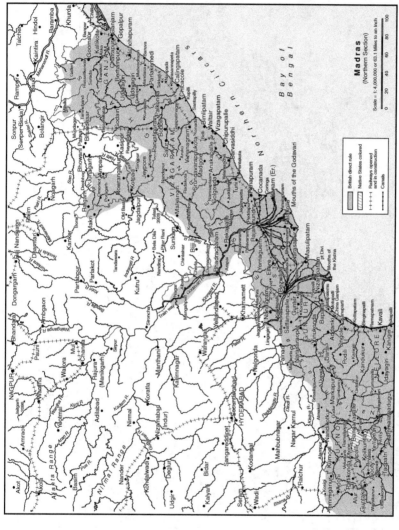

FIGURE 8.2 Map of Madras Presidency (northern section): coastal districts like Vizagapatam, Nellore, Kurnool, Guntur later became part of Andhra Pradesh state in 1956

Source: *The Imperial Gazetteer of India: Volume 26 – Atlas, Plate 42*. 1909. Available at http://dsal.uchicago.edu/maps/gazetteer/images/gazetteer_V18_pg250b.jpg

FIGURE 8.3 Map of Andhra Pradesh formed out of Telangana districts of Hyderabad princely state in north and Telugu-speaking districts of Madras presidency in south

makes Andhra Pradesh an ideal case to compare the historical legacies of indirect vs. direct rule on development and insurgency.

3.1 Effects of Colonial Indirect Rule in Andhra Pradesh

Formal indirect rule through the princely state of Hyderabad created two main mechanisms that did not occur in the neighboring areas in Madras province that were under direct British rule. First, the revenue collection institutions within Hyderabad state resulted in despotic extraction by various landlords, *jagirdars*, and other feudal intermediaries called *deshmukhs*. This resulted in higher levels of land and caste inequality than the districts that were formerly part of British direct rule as part of Madras province, which had more of the direct type of revenue collection systems, namely the *ryotwari* system, and did not create such high levels of extraction from peasants. Second, indirect rule in Hyderabad created lower levels of provision of public goods and lower levels of irrigation and agricultural productivity than direct rule in the coastal districts of Madras Presidency. Both these conditions persisted into the postcolonial period and created grievances among lower-caste/*Dalits* and indigenous tribals staying in the Telangana region of Hyderabad, thus creating ethnic mobilization networks that were mobilized by PWG Maoists beginning in the 1980s.

Mechanism 1: Exploitative Revenue Collection Systems in the Princely State of Hyderabad

The areas that were under British direct rule as Madras Presidency had different types of land tenure institutions than the areas that were under indirect British rule through the Nizam of Hyderabad.

Land Tenure in British Direct Rule Areas of Madras Presidency As described in Chapter 3, the four main types of land tenure systems within British India are *zamindari, ryotwari, mahalwari,* and *malguzari* land tenure systems.[10] The *zamindari* and *malguzari* systems had intermediaries collecting land revenues on behalf of the state and were indirect rule/revenue collection, while the *ryotwari* and *mahalwari* systems required that land revenue be collected directly from the peasants or villages and was direct rule/revenue collection.

In the state of Andhra Pradesh, the coastal Andhra and Rayalseema region districts had been under British direct rule as part of Madras Presidency. These were the districts of Srikakulam, Vizianagram, Vishakhapatnam, East Godavari, West Godavari, Krishna, Guntur, Prakasam, Cuddapah, Kurnool, Nellore, and Chittoor. In these former British direct rule districts, there was a mix of *zamindari* and *ryotwari* tenure systems. But there was a higher proportion of *ryotwari* or landlord type revenue collection and so there were lower levels of land inequality in this region than in the neighboring indirect rule areas of Hyderabad princely state. This resulted in more equal agrarian relations, less exploitation of the agricultural surplus of the land and labor, and greater agricultural productivity in these direct rule districts of Madras Presidency. The only exception was the *zamindari* areas in Srikakulam district in the northeastern tip of Madras Presidency, where the rebellion among the Girijan tribals took place in the 1960s. Other than this, there were no Maoist rebellions in these former directly ruled Andhra districts.

Land Tenure in Indirect Rule Areas of Hyderabad Princely State In Hyderabad princely state, the nomenclature for different types of land tenure was different from that in British-ruled Madras province, but the patterns were similarly based on whether or not the state collected land revenue directly from the *ryots* or indirectly through landlord-type intermediaries. The two main types of land tenure are outlined in Table 8.1, and both resulted in land inequality and exploitation of peasants.

---

[10] For descriptions of these land tenure systems, see Baden-Powell, *Land Systems of British India,* Volume 1.

TABLE 8.1 *Types of land tenure in areas in North Telangana districts of Hyderabad princely state*

Diwani lands (ryotwari)	Diwani lands (non-ryotwari)	Non-diwani lands (non-ryotwari)
1. *pattadari*	1. *pan-maqta* *	1. *sarf-e-khas*
2. *pot-pattadari*	2. *tahud/ sarbasta*	2. *samasthan / pesh*
3. *shikmidari*	*(deshmukhs)* *	*kash* *
4. *asami-shikmidari*	3. *ijara*	3. *jagir* *
	4. *ahrarar*	a) *paigah or jamiat jagirs*
		b) *al-Tamgha jagirs*
		c) *zat-jagirs*
		d) *tankha-jagirs*
		e) *mashrooti jagirs*
		f) *madad-maash jagirs*
		4. *inam*

*Indicates the most exploitative land tenure systems
Source: V. Ramakrishna Reddy, *Economic History of Hyderabad State (Warangal Suba: 1911–1950), Table VII, p. 88, 1987.*

1) Diwani/Khalsa Land Tenures and Their Effects on Peasant Welfare The first type of land tenure were the government lands also called the *diwani* or *khalsa* lands that were directly under the administration of the Nizam (prince) of Hyderabad, in which land revenue was collected by his revenue officials called *deshmukhs* and went directly into the Nizam's exchequer. According to Reddy (1987: 87): "In *Diwani* villages, *ryotwari* tenure based on the Bombay system was widely prevalent" and formed 60 percent to 70 percent of villages. The *Decennial Report* of the Nizam's administration confirms that "Diwani lands are invariably held on the purely ryotwari tenure. ... This tenure is practically a copy of the Bombay tenure."[11] Based on the theoretical framework outlined in earlier chapters, and Banerjee and Iyer's (2005) prediction, there should have been low levels of despotic extraction in these *diwani* lands under the Nizam. Yet, these officially *ryotwari* areas saw a lot of despotic exploitation that led to peasant rebellion.

This empirical puzzle is noted by the human rights activist K. Balagopal, who in an interview mentioned that "in Bihar ... it was in the Zamindari areas that we had the Communist movement, it was not in the Ryotwari areas. Here it is the opposite. Here the Telangana is in fact technically a ryotwari area, not Zamindari area. ... Communist movement was here in the ryotwari areas."[12]

[11] *Decennial Report on the Administration of H.E.H the Nizam's Dominions,* 1930, p. 75.
[12] Interview with K. Balagopal, Hyderabad, February 12, 2008.

The theoretical insight gained from studying the land tenure systems under the Nizam is that actual de facto land tenure on the ground is often different from de jure or official land tenure that is recorded by the state. While officially the *diwani/khalsa* lands under the Nizam were coded as *ryotwari*, in reality there was a lot of variation in types of land tenures. Some like the *pattedari* (owner or *pattedar* was himself the cultivator of land), *shikmidari* (protected tenants given the right to cultivate land), and *asami-shikmidari* (non-protected tenants) were like *ryotwari* tenure, others called *maqtas, tahuds/sarbastas, ijaras,* and *agrahars* were de facto non-*ryotwari* and had landlord-type actors who were exploitative. As Balagopal suggested insightfully, "The assumption is that ryotwari areas [are] full of small farmers, it is not necessarily so. In the name of ryotwari you can have a superior right-holder who can be terribly oppressive, whereas a zamindari area for whatever reason may not have a rebellion."[13]

The holders of these de facto non-*ryotwari* tenures were usually landlords or officials of power, and these tenures led to concentration of land in the hands of the landlord and excessive taxation causing misery among the peasants.[14] Of the different types of *diwani/khalsa* lands, the *tahud* or *sarbasta* type of tenure was the most unequal and most exploitative and coincides with the districts that later had the Telangana rebellion in the 1940s. Under this system, which was prevalent before 1866, wealthy and influential persons from the districts, called *deshmukhs*, served as tax farmers or contractors. These *deshmukhs* had to give a fixed amount to the treasury of the Nizam, but they extracted a lot more from the *ryots*/peasants and retained the excess taxes for themselves. They exploited the *ryots* and made them poor and miserable. Even though officially this was *diwani/ryotwari* tenure, in reality the emergence of landed intermediaries like *deshmukhs* made the system highly unequal and exploitative of the poor peasants and landless tenants, similar to that of the *zamindars* or landlords in the British direct rule areas.

In Telangana, the office of the *deshmukh* came into existence in the pre-colonial period. Since they were locally powerful, the Qutb Shah king first used them as revenue collectors. When Nizam-ul-Mulk, the Mughal governor of the Deccan formed the Asaf Jahi dynasty in Hyderabad, the *deshmukhs* were deeply entrenched into local social and political life and were difficult to dislodge, hence he decided to use them to carry out administration. With the onset of colonial indirect rule over Hyderabad, the *deshmukhs* were "integrated into the new system of control and exploitation, as revenue contractors" and were called *tahudars* or *sarbastadars*.[15] The *deshmukhs* under the new system became tax farmers with revenue contracts with the state and were only responsible for the

---

[13] Interview with K. Balagopal, Hyderabad, February 12, 2008.
[14] V. Ramakrishna Reddy, *Economic History of Hyderabad State*, pp. 86–109.
[15] Thirumali, *Against Dora and Nizam*, p. 22.

payment of revenue of the leased areas for specific periods to the state and could keep the excess revenue for themselves.

This led to "unscrupulous collection of land revenue by the *tahudars/ sarbastadars*" and increased usury, which culminated in an agrarian crisis in Telangana in the mid-nineteenth century and forced the British Resident at Hyderabad to appoint Salar Jung I as the new prime minister to carry out land reforms in 1853.[16] In 1854, under Salar Jung I, the revenue collecting powers were transferred to *taluqdars,* who were government-appointed tax collectors. By 1881, Hyderabad state was divided into fifteen districts headed by these *taluqdars,* who replaced the *deshmukhs.* The *deshmukhs* became *pattadars* (registered occupants of land) and were converted into legal landowners but lost the right to farm or collect land taxes from the peasants based on revenue contracts with the state.[17]

Unfortunately, these changes "did not affect much the strength and position of *deshmukhs* ... On the other hand it was further strengthened."[18] In lieu of the loss of tax-farming rights, the former *deshmukhs* were given land as compensation and were also allowed an annual pension on a hereditary basis called *rusumi-zamindari.* Thus, even after the introduction of Salar Jung I's reforms, the *deshmukhs* became big landlords, and their position became more permanent as compared with their previous uncertain and speculative *tahud* or *sarbasta* tenure.[19] They continued to consolidate their rural position by resorting to money lending and liquor and toddy contracts.

Also, due to pressure from the British Resident toward a cash crop economy, these *deshmukh* landlords started converting the service castes of the village into *vetti* or bonded labor to farm groundnuts, cotton, and other cash crops.[20] The exploitative practice of using *vetti* increased the suffering and deprivation of the poor landless lower-caste peasants and pushed them later toward participation in the Telangana rebellion of 1946. In his detailed study of land tenure in North Telangana, Reddy (1987: 104) writes, "all those Taluqs in the *Suba* where there was significant concentration of *Deshmukhs* ... witnessed in greater or lesser degree ... the peasant uprising."[21]

Sundarayya (1972) gives examples of several peasant movements under the leadership of the communists in Telangana in 1946–48, which highlights the exploitative role of landlords in these so-called *ryotwari* areas. For example, Mellacheruvu was a *ryotwari* village, and in reality

half of the land in this village was in the ownership of big landlords called *banjardars,* even though these lands were, from the beginning, cultivated by the peasants. The

[16] Thirumali, *Against Dora and Nizam*, pp. 23–25.
[17] Thirumali, *Against Dora and Nizam*, pp. 23–25.
[18] Reddy, *Economic History of Hyderabad State*, p. 99.
[19] Thirumali, *Against Dora and Nizam*, p. 24.
[20] Thirumali, *Against Dora and Nizam*, pp. 26–27.
[21] Reddy, *Economic History of Hyderabad State*, p. 104.

banjardars had all the rights, lease rights and possession rights. Many a time, the people had risen against these cruel *banjardars*, but every time, they were crushed down. The Andhra Mahasabha took the lead in uniting the people against landlord Chennur Veerabhadra Rao. … The people who were the target of his cruelty took revenge and murdered him in broad daylight.[22]

This supports Balagopal's claim that in Hyderabad state, landlords of different types often had de facto control over land and were exploitative of peasants, even though it was officially *ryotwari* land tenure.

2) Non-Diwani Land Tenures in Hyderabad Princely State and Their Effects on Peasant Welfare The second type of land tenure in Hyderabad was the non-government or non-*diwani* lands, which were divided into several categories – *sarf-e-khas*, *jagir*, *samasthanams*, and *inams* – and were different types of land grants to vassals of the Nizam (See Table 8.1). According to Thirumali (2003), the tenure holders of non-*diwani* areas had their own administrative machinery and were small feudatory states "independent" of the Nizam's government and carried out the administration "with the help of their own tehsildars and police officials."[23]

The *samasthanams* were several indigenous Hindu rajahs/chiefs scattered over the territory of the Nizam of Hyderabad. They had been given *sanads* or grants by the Mughal emperor, and the Nizam allowed them to continue to have some form of autonomous control over their territory, as long as they paid tribute called *peshkash*.[24] The second type were *sarf-e-khas* that were crown lands belonging to the Nizam. While *diwani* officials administered them, the revenues from these lands went into the *sarf-e-khas* treasury for the personal finances of the Nizam of Hyderabad and his family.[25] The third type were *jagirs*, which were land grants to noblemen made by the Nizam, in return for maintenance of household troops for the Nizam. The fourth type were called *inams* and were land grants by the Nizam's government to an individual in return for the performance of certain duties or as a reward to favorites.

Of these, the *sarf-e-khas* were less exploitative of peasants, because they "enjoyed the benefit of Survey and Settlement and the presence of the overlord of their villages on the spot."[26] *Inam* lands were also not very exploitative, because these landholders were not allowed to collect land revenue from the actual cultivators, unlike the *jagirdars*, *maqtadars*, and others.

The *samasthanams* were more exploitative because the raja's administration often made illegal demands on *ryots*. Another problem was the absenteeism of the raja and the frequent takeover of the *samasthan* administration by the Court of Wards for the settlement of disputes regarding succession as ruler of the area,

---

[22] P. Sundarayya, *Telangana People's Struggle and Its Lessons*, p. 22.
[23] Thirumali, *Against Dora and Nizam*, p. 19.   [24] Thirumali, *Against Dora and Nizam*, p. 18.
[25] Reddy, *Economic History of Hyderabad State*, p. 109.
[26] Reddy, *Economic History of Hyderabad State*, p. 113.

and the "administrative apathy and indifference exhibited by the *samasthandars* had contributed in a large measure for creating administrative vacuum ... which were fully exploited by *watandars,* big and immigrant merchants and forest officials in inflicting ... excesses on the ... tribal farmers and labourers."[27] A sense of frustration developed among the *Adivasis* in Palavancha *samasthanam* in Warangal district, and they started migrating to neighboring British direct ruled districts in the late 1930s–early 1940s.

Of the different non-*diwani* lands, the *jagirs* were the most exploitative and oppressive.[28] There were two types of *jagirs* – exempted and non-exempted. Exempted *jagirs* were often *jagirdars* who "functioned as independent princes having the administration of their territories completely at their disposal and this feature was so horrible that one shuddered at the very sight of it."[29] Non-exempted *jagirs* were smaller and more numerous and concentrated in the taluqs of Palvancha, Mahboobabad, Warangal, Karimnagar, and Kinwat within North Telangana.

In these smaller *jagirs,* the *jagirdars* started collecting huge revenue rents from their tenants, and as absentee landlords collected 25 percent to 50 percent more revenue than the *khalsa/diwani* villages. The majority of *jagirdars* also did not grant their *ryots* reduction of land revenue on the scale as was allowed by the Nizam government in *diwani* areas.[30] Also, the *jagirdars* forced various castes and groups to give them free labor or *vetti* and punished them through torture and deprivation of basic necessities of life on refusal. This use of *vetti* was one of the main causes for attacks against the *jagirdars* during the Telangana revolt of 1946. Since the *jagirdars* were mostly absentee landlords and lived outside their *jagir* areas, they could be easily overthrown, and so the Telangana rebellion then concentrated on fighting the *deshmukhs* who acted like exploitative landlords.[31]

Effects of Land Tenure Systems in Andhra Pradesh on Probability of Peasant Rebellion and Maoist Insurgency

What is the effect of these types of land tenure systems on the possibility of peasant rebellion in the 1940s, and Maoist insurgency in the 1980s? As shown earlier, the feudal exploitation of peasantry was most intense in the northeastern Telangana districts. Here some of the biggest landlords, whether *jagirdars* or *deshmukhs,* owned huge tracts of land in Nalgonda, Khammam, Karimnagar, and Warangal; so "it was this region which was the locus of the peasant insurrection in 1946–51."[32] Thirumali (2003) cites a police report that the Andhra Maha Sabha, which

---

[27] Reddy, *Economic History of Hyderabad State,* p. 114.

[28] D. N. Dhanagare, "Social Origins of the Peasant Insurrection in Telangana (1946–51)," p. 488.

[29] Reddy, *Economic History of Hyderabad State,* p. 117.

[30] Reddy, *Economic History of Hyderabad State,* p. 120.

[31] Thirumali, *Against Dora and Nizam,* p. 20.

[32] D. N. Dhanagare, "Social Origins of the Peasant Insurrection in Telangana (1946–51)," p. 489.

led the Telangana rebellion of 1946, came under the influence of communists "with the avowed object of eradicating jagirdars and Deshmukhs ... in Nalgonda district ... with its considerable number of Deshmukhs, Jagirdars and Maktadars, provided a good field for propaganda among the discontented villagers alleged to be groaning under the high heels of the feudal landlords."[33]

Looking at a map of land tenures in Hyderabad princely state in Figure 8.4, the Telangana peasant rebellion of 1946 was concentrated in the northeastern part of Hyderabad state, in the districts of Warangal, Nalgonda, Karimnagar, and Adilabad, which had more *diwani* lands with exploitative *deshmukhs*, as well as a number of smaller *jagirs* scattered in them, and a large *samasthanam* in Warangal. This was confirmed in an interview with Professor Kondadaram Reddy, who pointed out that in these northeastern districts of Telangana like Warangal, Karimnagar, and Adilabad "land was concentrated in the hands of a few people ... there were ... big landowners," while in the southwestern districts of Telangana like Medak, Rangareddy, and Mahbubnagar, there were more *samasthanams* or large Hindu states under the Nizam's rule where land revenue collection was more directly from the peasants and the oppression was "not as virulent as you can see in the eastern part." In response to this "oppressive landlordism," the Communist Party was strongest in the northeastern districts like Warangal, Karimnagar, and parts of Nizamabad, and they later "contributed the nucleus for the emergence of the Naxalbari movement," but in the southwestern Telangana districts, it was the Congress Party that became stronger.[34]

These land tenure institutions where landlords of different types, especially *deshmukhs* and *jagirdars*, collected land revenue and extorted the peasants not only led to the Telangana peasant rebellion of 1946–48, but also created path dependent effects that persisted and set up the political opportunity structures for future leftist movements like the People's War Group (PWG)–led insurgency starting in the 1980s. This can explain why the northeastern districts inside the Telangana region of the former Hyderabad state, like Warangal, Karimnagar, Adilabad, and Nizamabad, were the places that formed the nucleus of the initial PWG-led Maoist movement in the 1980s.

Table 8.2 provides data on the proportion of villages that were under official *diwani* vs. non-*diwani* areas in the Telangana districts of former Hyderabad princely state and combines this with the level of intensity of PWG-led Maoist rebellion (1980–2005). It shows some correlation between the districts that had higher proportion of *diwani* tenures, which have *deshmukhs,* and leftist rebellion.

---

[33] Thirumali, *Against Dora and Nizam*, p. 127, cites CID report, Sept. 1946, FN. 67/ AND/55 F. H. D. 1355 F. [1946] Andhra Pradesh State Archives.

[34] Interview with Kodandaram Reddy, Professor of Political Science, Nizam College, Osmania University. February 27, 2008. He later became Chairman of Telangana Joint Action Committee (T-JAC), which unified various organizations and helped create a separate Telangana state.

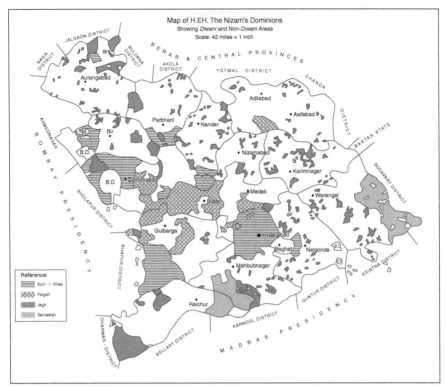

FIGURE 8.4 Map of Diwani and Non-Diwani Areas of Hyderabad State
Source: "Map of H.E.H. the Nizam's Dominions showing Diwani and Non-Diwani Areas," in *Report of the Royal Commission on Jagir Administration and Reforms*. 1947. Hyderabad: H.E.H. The Nizam's Government. Appendix 1, p. 136.

Mechanism 2: Lower Levels of Economic Development, Social Reforms, and State Capacity in the Princely State of Hyderabad

Besides land inequality and despotic extraction, the districts of Warangal, Khammam, Karimnagar, and Adilabad that were in the Telangana region of the princely state of Hyderabad had relatively lower levels of irrigation and agricultural and industrial development compared with the coastal Andhra districts of Krishna, Guntur, East Godavari, West Godavari, and Vishakhapatnam, which were part of the British Madras Presidency. (See Figure 8.1 for the Telangana districts of Hyderabad state and see Figure 8.2 for the British districts of Madras.) There were "distinct differences in the evolution of the socio-economic situation of both regions. While a well-defined middle class and a strong rich peasantry emerged in the Andhra region because of the growth of irrigation, development of modern education

TABLE 8.2 *Proportion of villages under diwani and non-diwani areas in Hyderabad princely state*

| | Number of villages under diwani and non-diwani areas | | | | | | |
| | Diwani | | Non-diwani | | | | |
Name of district	Deshmukh (de facto landlords)	Sarf-e-khas	Exempted jagirs	Non-exempted jagirs	Total villages	*diwani*/total	Maoist rebellion (1980s)
Atraf e Balda	0	573	78	225	876	0	Absent
Nizamabad	521	1	45	184	751	0.6937	High
Medak	551	13	157	207	928	0.5938	Low
Baght	83	1	117	77	278	0.2986	Low
Mahbubnagar	698	15	430	288	1431	0.4878	Low
Nalgonda	1002	15	27	212	1256	0.7978	High
Warangal	1177	4	83	208	1472	0.7996	High
Karimnagar	978	25	72	152	1227	0.7971	High
Adilabad	1881	0	71	191	2143	0.8777	High

Source: Report of the Royal Commission on Jagir Administration and Reforms, 1947, p. 37.

system and social reform movements, in the Telangana region oppressive political institutions prevented any social transformation."[35]

The districts of coastal Andhra were more developed than the districts of Telangana. The coastal Andhra districts were ruled directly by the British as part of Madras Presidency. The economic compulsions of the colonial regime and the chronic problems of flooding, waterlogging, and famines in these coastal delta districts led to the British constructing an anicut across the Krishna and Godavari Rivers in 1852.[36] With the goal of increasing the amount of revenue from agriculture, a large part of these coastal districts like Krishna and East Godavari were provided large-scale irrigation, which led to rapid commercialization of agriculture and generation and accumulation of agrarian surplus. This also led to increasing urbanization and growth of commerce, education, and even social reforms.

In contrast, no such irrigation schemes were put into place by the Nizam's government in the districts in the princely state of Hyderabad. Instead the feudal gentry like *jagirdars* and *deshmukhs* thoroughly exploited the landless peasants and *ryots* and extracted agrarian surplus, leaving not much for agricultural development and urban expansion.[37] The many *jagirdars* scattered across the Hyderabad state were not known for their efficiency in providing basic services and public goods to their citizens. These *jagirdars* made very poor contributions to the development of public goods like agriculture, irrigation, education, and health. There did not seem to be a single *jagir* "which spent at least one rupee out of hundred rupees on education. 75 percent of the villages did not seem to be having even primary schools."[38]

This difference meant that there were several reformist movements in the coastal Andhra districts of Guntur, Krishna, and East and West Godavari, but only violent radical movements in the Telangana districts. Linked to this agrarian development in the coastal Andhra districts was the emergence of enterprising Kamma and Reddy peasant middle castes. While the Reddy community joined the Congress Party, the Kammas took leadership positions in the Communist Party of India (CPI). The educated elites of these peasant middle castes led reformist movements in the coastal Andhra districts against the domination of the upper-caste Brahmins and also participated in anti-*zamindari* struggles that led to the abolition of the *zamindari* system and tenancy reforms in the postcolonial state and allowed the *ryots* of these peasant castes access to most of the fertile lands.[39] In contrast, in the

---

[35] Kodandaram, "Movement for Telangana State: A Struggle for Autonomy," *EPW*, January 13, 2007, p. 92.

[36] Haragopal, "The Telangana People's Movement: The Unfolding Political Culture," *EPW*, October 16, 2010, p. 52.

[37] Srinivasulu, "Caste, Class and Social Articulation in Andhra Pradesh," Working paper 179, ODI, September 2002, pp. 5–6.

[38] Reddy, *Economic History of Hyderabad State*, p. 120.

[39] Srinivasulu, "Caste, Class and Social Articulation in Andhra Pradesh."

Telangana region, there was no reformist anti-*zamindari* movement like that in the coastal Andhra region, and the "cumulative anger and anguish got expressed through the tribal revolts and later in the rise of Telangana armed struggle."[40] The *jagirdars* and *deshmukhs* had to be challenged by violence under the leadership of the CPI.

The gradual removal of the intermediary class of *zamindars* under the pressure of these social movements and the introduction of the *ryotwari* system in the coastal Andhra districts meant that a greater part of the agricultural surplus or profit now could be kept by the *ryot* or peasant cultivator. This increased agricultural productivity and growth, and the continued rise in price of grain in this period contributed to the growth of the economy and general increase in prosperity till 1930. With increase in irrigation, the coastal districts developed commercial agriculture of rice, and they changed from experiencing frequent famine to intensive commercial rice cultivation that supplied the other parts of Madras Presidency. The *ryotwari* system allowed even the smaller peasants to benefit to some extent from this.[41]

In contrast, the lack of irrigation facilities as well as the continuation of the *deshmukh* and *jagirdari* land tenure systems in Hyderabad state prevented the development of a similar commercialized agrarian economy in Telangana. In fact, the pressure of the colonial market to produce cash crops like groundnut and cotton led the *deshmukh* landlords in Hyderabad state to use the *vetti* system to exploit the peasant class and squeeze all agricultural surplus for themselves, leaving little for the poorest peasants and landless laborers.[42] There was no development of a vibrant agrarian economy with a free labor market and urban centers to support them.

4 PERSISTENCE OF THE EFFECTS OF THESE INSTITUTIONS INTO POSTCOLONIAL TIMES

Following Indian independence in 1947, Hyderabad princely state was incorporated as a part of the new state of Andhra Pradesh, which also included districts from the former direct ruled Madras Presidency. The Nizam of Hyderabad was abolished, and the Congress Party won elections and formed the government in Andhra Pradesh from the 1950s to 1970s and implemented land and irrigation reforms and tried to reduce the power of *zamindars/ jagirdars* in society. However, due to path dependence, both the mechanisms outlined earlier – land and class inequalities and lower levels of development – persisted into the postcolonial period in the Telangana region but were reduced further in the coastal Andhra region.

---

[40] Haragopal, "The Telangana People's Movement," p. 52.
[41] Carol Upadhya, "The Farmer-Capitalists of Coastal Andhra Pradesh," *EPW*, July 2, 1988, p. 1376.
[42] Thirumali, *Against Dora and Nizam*, pp. 26–27.

Path Dependent Mechanism 1: Persistence of Land Inequality in Telangana Region as Compared with Coastal Andhra through Continuing Power of Landlord and Elites

Prakash Singh, who was a senior police officer and had a lot of experience with counterinsurgency asked: "What led to the resurgence of Naxalism in the Telangana area? The region is of course dotted with rivers, hills and forests and thus provides an ideal setting for guerrilla activities. The basic reason, however, was the continued economic exploitation of the tribals by the landlords, traders and government officials, especially those of the Forest Department."[43] These landlords were created during the time of the Nizam of Hyderabad, and there were more such landlords in the areas within Telangana than in coastal Andhra. This implies that rebel opportunity like terrain and forest cover mattered (Fearon & Laitin 2003), but land inequalities created during the colonial era that persisted and created ethnic inequalities and exclusion from power of lower-caste *Dalits* and *Adivasis* were the main reason for Maoist recruitment (Cederman et al. 2010).

The leader of CPI-ML (Janashakti), during the peace talk negotiations with the Andhra Pradesh government in 2004, said,

The Telangana armed struggle is well known. However, the land relations have not undergone any basic change. For instance, the nature of control over the endowments land is evidence of continued landlordism. It is a contradiction that on the one hand, there are surplus as well as fallow lands and on the other hand, there are starvation deaths and farmers suicides.[44]

According to Dhanagare (1974: 513), "If ... a lasting dent in the agrarian structure and change in the conditions of its principal participants are viewed as the criterion then perhaps the Telangana insurrection was not more successful than other peasant resistance movements in India." This suggests that the earlier Telangana rebellion was not really successful in bringing about land reforms, but it possibly prepared the ground for future rebellions in the same areas.

Following the peasant rebellion in the Telangana region of Hyderabad state in 1946–51, the new Congress Party government promised to undertake significant land reforms. However, these land reforms were not successful in reducing land inequality. The Congress government in Andhra Pradesh introduced laws abolishing landlords like the Hyderabad Jagirdar Act, 1955, which abolished all the 975 *jagirs* in Telangana and the Inam (Abolition and Conversion into Ryotwari) Act, 1956. The government also introduced tenancy reforms, for example, the (Telangana Area) Tenancy and Agricultural Lands

[43] Singh, *The Naxalite Movement in India*, p. 130.
[44] Committee of Concerned Citizens, *Negotiating Peace: Peace Talks between Government of Andhra Pradesh and Naxalite Parties*, December 2006, p. 191.

Act, 1950 (amended 1954), by which tenants received protected tenancy status, minimum lease terms, and the right to purchase non-resumable lands.[45]

These official land reforms seemed to lack political will and were not really successful in improving the condition of the rural landless laborers. The regions with continuing peasant insurgencies led by various groups of Maoists are those where land reforms have not been very successful, whether in Andhra Pradesh and Bihar in India or Nepal or the Philippines.[46] While the Andhra Pradesh government reports that it assigned sixty lakh acres to the poor between 1955 and the 1980s, a figure that includes government, ceiling surplus, *inam*, and *bhoodan* lands, in contrast to West Bengal that has had more successful land reforms, Andhra Pradesh's land assignment suffered from lack of implementation. The few cases of successful land distribution occurred because of the efforts of individual officers, and not an effective program.[47]

According to the Andhra Pradesh government's own claims, by the 1970s, only 1,31,000 acres of dry land and 6,000 acres of wetland had been distributed among the landless, including the Girijan tribes of Srikakulam. In contrast, the land occupied by the peasants in Srikakulam and Telangana districts of Khammam, Warangal, Karimnagar, and East Godavari during the peasant rebellions of 1968–73 was 3,20,650 acres in 982 villages. So peasants "through their own struggles acquired 2.5 times as much land as was supposedly distributed by the Congress government."[48]

A committee set up by the Planning Commission to enquire into the failure of land reforms concluded that there was a lack of "political will" on part of the government that can explain this policy failure. This was probably because the rich peasant landlord class wielded a lot of influence on the government through its ethnic linkages with the politicians in power from their own Reddy or Kamma caste.[49] Even though *zamindari* and *jagirdari* land tenures had been abolished, and the *deshmukhs* of feudal times were no longer in existence after 1947, these erstwhile landlords and even the new ones continued to have their influence in industry and political life of Andhra Pradesh through their ethnic and patronage networks. This prevented the government from carrying out land reforms successfully, due to the vested interests of their own ethnic groups.[50] As

---

[45] For a list of different types of land reforms and tenancy reforms undertaken in different states of India, including Andhra Pradesh see Besley and Burgess, "Land Reform, Poverty Reduction, and Growth."

[46] DN, "Breaking the Deadlock: Land Reform Revisited," *Economic and Political Weekly*, June 29, 2002.

[47] Akella and Nielsen, "Building on Political Will," *Economic and Political Weekly*, 2005, p. 3719.

[48] "Andhra Pradesh: Peasants Struggle for Land," *Economic and Political Weekly*, October 1, 1977, p. 1694.

[49] "Andhra Pradesh: Peasants" Struggle for Land," *EPW*, October 1, 1977, p. 1693.

[50] Besley and Burgess, "Land Reform, Poverty Reduction, and Growth," suggest that of the different types of land reforms, abolition of *zamindaris* was easiest to implement and had the most political will backing it, while tenancy reforms were more difficult to implement because many state legislatures were controlled by the landlord class.

Herring (1983) concludes, it has been difficult to execute land reforms in India because land reform requires structural changes by using the very same institutions that reflect the existing distribution of power and resources. The problem is that land reforms are proposed by the ruling elites who are largely composed of, or structurally dependent upon, agrarian elites.

This was a clear case of persistence of the effects of certain colonial-era institutions even after their formal abolition. By the 1970s, the inability of the government to carry out successful land redistribution meant that the effects of land inequality in Telangana could no longer be removed and became path dependent and created the political opportunity structures for the new group of Maoist rebels to emerge and mobilize successfully. Path dependence of land inequality occurred through the power-based mechanism that Mahoney (2000) outlines, in which the continuing informal power of ex-landlords in the rural areas prevented effective land reforms from taking place. In contrast, since the initial level of land inequality and agrarian underdevelopment was lower in the coastal Andhra regions, it was easier for the new postcolonial government to implement land reforms in the coastal Andhra districts.

The reemergence of the Naxal movement in the 1970s and 1980s was partly to "complete the unfinished agenda of the Telangana armed struggle in the 1940s. . . . This was also a result of failures of the Congress in the 1950s to carry out its promise of land reforms peacefully through state measures."[51] The areas of Telangana that were less affected by the peasant rebellion of the 1940s continued to experience feudal oppression until the 1970s, and this created the political opportunity structures for the new peasant struggles under the Communist Party of India-Marxist Leninist (CPI-ML) and People's War Group (PWG) in the 1970s and 1980s in the Telangana region. While the initial Telangana rebellion (1946–51) was concentrated in Nalgonda and Khammam districts, with some spillover into Warangal and Adilabad districts toward the later phases, the later CPI-ML– and PWG-led movements in 1970s and 1980s occurred in Warangal, Adilabad, and Karimnagar districts, which were more peripheral in the initial struggle, and where the process of land distribution was not yet complete.

Path Dependence Mechanism 2: Persistence of Inequality in Development and Agriculture between Telangana and Coastal Andhra

Between 1930 and 1950, several events occurred that affected the agrarian and industrial development of the coastal Andhra region in the Madras Presidency. The Great Depression of the 1930s reduced agricultural prices, and the rural credit market collapsed. So the earlier pattern of investment of agricultural surplus into rural money lending and trade and the local agro industry had to stop. The rural elite of coastal Andhra district now started investing in urban

---

[51] Haragopal, "The Telangana People's Movement," p. 54.

industries and large sugar and cotton factories. World War II caused agricultural prices to rise again and increased the prosperity of the rural elite farmers of the Kamma castes of coastal Andhra, and the move to urban areas for better education and investment in big industries continued. Upadhya notes: "Following independence, the government began to play an increasingly active role in the rural economy, as promoter of agricultural modernisation, procurer of produce, provider of inputs and credit, and so on. Still, the path of agricultural and economic development and the social changes that accompanied them can be seen as continuations of what had begun earlier."[52]

The 1950s saw modest industrial growth in the coastal Andhra region, which was partly due to land reforms. The abolition of *zamindari* estates in 1949 "induced the more enterprising *zamindars* to convert their assets into industrial capital."[53] Thus the process of land reforms succeeded more in this region than in the Telangana districts, where the local *deshmukhs* and *jagirdars* even after abolition continued to influence government policy and prevent land redistribution. It is probably because of the previous trajectory of anti-*zamindari* reform movements and development of irrigation and agricultural sectors in the coastal Andhra regions that the former *zamindars* could transfer their agricultural surplus more easily into other sectors, which was not possible for the former landlords in the Telangana region.

The Green Revolution and the introduction of the high-yielding variety (HYV) seeds and modern fertilizers and pesticides since the 1960s also had a significant impact on agriculture and farming in the coastal Andhra districts. With improved irrigation, mechanization of agriculture, and modern technology of paddy farming, the big and medium landowning farmers in the region started obtaining larger agricultural surpluses, with higher yields from paddy production.[54] This of course increased the inequalities between smaller and larger farmers in the coastal Andhra region. More importantly, because these HYV seeds and fertilizers need a regular supply of water, this new agricultural process is water dependent. Since the coastal Andhra region has historically better irrigation facilities as compared with the Telangana region, which is more rain dependent, the outcome of the Green Revolution was an increasing gap in agricultural output between the coastal Andhra and Telangana regions. So the regional imbalances, which had started in the colonial period due to different colonial period policies, kept increasing in the postcolonial period.[55]

The new Congress government in Andhra Pradesh did not correct the irrigation imbalances between the different regions and in fact facilitated the Green Revolution in the coastal Andhra region because it was already well

---

[52] Upadhya, "The Farmer-Capitalists of Coastal Andhra Pradesh," *EPW*, p. 1378.
[53] Upadhya, "The Farmer-Capitalists of Coastal Andhra Pradesh," p. 1378.
[54] Upadhya, "The Farmer-Capitalists of Coastal Andhra Pradesh," p. 1378.
[55] Haragopal, "The Telangana People's Movement," p. 53.

endowed with water resources. The Congress government pumped in a lot of resources for development of canal irrigation and reduced support for tank irrigation between 1955 and 2000. This harmed the Telangana region, which had traditionally relied on tank irrigation. However, the loss of area under tank irrigation was not compensated with allocation of river waters through canal irrigation in Telangana region. Instead, the benefits of canal irrigation have gone to the coastal Andhra region, thus further increasing regional disparities.[56] Thus, erstwhile colonial institutions and their legacies continued to influence postcolonial government policies and resulted in a persistent and increasing agrarian and economic inequalities between the Telangana and coastal Andhra districts of Andhra Pradesh state.

5 POSTCOLONIAL RADICAL LEFTIST INSURGENCY IN ANDHRA PRADESH

5.1 Leftist Rebels Exploit These Structural Conditions of Land Inequality and Low Development in Indirect Rule Areas but Fail in Direct Rule Areas

The various peasant/tribal uprisings in Andhra Pradesh have found the most fertile ground in the northern Telangana districts that were part of the former princely state of Hyderabad. Few rebellions succeeded in the coastal Andhra and Rayalseema districts that were formerly part of British direct ruled Madras Presidency and had *ryotwari* land tenure systems.[57] This shows that while leftist rebels tried to mobilize *Dalits* and *Adivasis* in different parts of Andhra Pradesh, they mainly succeeded where the historically created opportunity structures in the form of severe land inequality were present in the former indirect rule areas of Telangana, where the grievances of the *Dalits* and *Adivasis* provided ethnic mobilization networks for Maoists with their ideological frames of rebellion to mobilize in the 1980s (McAdam et al. 1996). The leftist rebels could not succeed in the direct ruled areas where such historically created structural inequalities were not present. This demonstrates how colonial legacies of inequality were a necessary condition for rebel agency to succeed.

In her classic book on the Maoist movement in Andhra Pradesh, Shantha Sinha (1989) explains the failure of the Andhra Pradesh Revolutionary Communist Committee (APRCC) Maoist leaders like Chandra Pulla Reddy and T. Nagi Reddy to try and expand into the other regions of Andhra Pradesh. The APRCC Maoists had started their initial operations in the North Telangana region in the 1970s, which had been under colonial indirect rule as

---

[56] Kodandaram, "Movement for Telangana State," *EPW*, p. 92–93.

[57] The only exception was the 1968–71 movement in Srikakulam district in British direct ruled Madras province. Srikakulam however had *zamindari* estates and represents the first type of informal colonial indirect rule through landlords in my theoretical framework.

Hyderabad princely state. When they tried to similarly expand into the Rayalseema or coastal Andhra regions that had been under direct rule, they did not meet with as much success.

According to Sinha (1989, 166–69):

When the Maoists broke away from the CPI (M) they carried along with them large sections of the party members even in Coastal and Rayalseema districts. In these areas new committees were formed and T.N. and other leaders toured extensively propagating among the party members the APRCC line. However, in spite of having a strong organization of experienced communist cadre they were unable to start any militant mass movement here ... the reason for this lies in the fact that much of these areas had been settled according to the ryotwari tenancy system which did not allow glaring disparities in land holdings to arise. ...

[T]he very fact that the Maoists were more successful in Telangana than in these regions suggests another explanation for their failure. Unlike in Telangana which during the pre-independence period had been under the feudal political and administrative set up of the Nizam, the Coastal and Rayalseema areas had experienced some sort of liberal democratic politics. ... Further, having been part of the British Madras province the people of this region, had greater awareness of the governmental administrative machinery. The awareness coupled with the greater exposure to party politics had caused among the people of this region a tendency to adopt constitutional rather than ... violent methods, to solve their problems.

The PWG, which emerged as the most powerful rebel group since 1980, has also acknowledged the impact of historical choices of British indirect rule (Telangana) vs. direct rule (Coastal Andhra) on differences in land inequality and different patterns of development in the postcolonial period. In contrast to this higher level of agricultural and industrial development in the Andhra region that was under direct British rule, the PWG notes that the Telangana region that was under princely state rule of the Nizam of Hyderabad had much lower levels of agricultural development, due to more exploitative land revenue systems:

When compared with the growth of the coastal Andhra regions, Telangana is relatively backward. ... Because of Nizam's rule, Telangana region did not undergo much development. As the surplus from agriculture has to be paid in the form of taxes due to the exploitation by Deshmukhs and the nizam Nawab, the bourgeoisie of Telangana could not develop. As the land was concentrated in the hands of the Nizam feudal class, economic development did not take place.[58]

5.2 Evolution of Maoist Networks and Ideology and Patterns of Insurgency Violence in Andhra Pradesh

The history of leftist rebellion in Andhra Pradesh is long, and I divide it into three phases. The first phase was the historic Telangana peasant struggle from

[58] "Separate Telangana Movement – Development of Telangana – Our Programme," Central Committee, CPI (ML) People's War, pp. 1–3.

1946–51. The second phase was the peasant/tribal uprisings in the coastal Srikakulam region from 1968 to 1971, and the reemergence of Maoist movements in Telangana regions in 1968–78 under the APRCC. The third phase was the emergence of the Maoist movement under the PWG from the 1980s to the present period in the Telangana region.

Phase 1: Telangana Peasant Rebellion

The first outbreaks of agrarian discontent in Andhra Pradesh happened in 1944–46, in the districts of Warangal, Khammam, and Nalgonda in the Telangana region of the princely state of Hyderabad. The peasants felt oppressed and unhappy since the landlords were not protecting them from hunger and the moral economy of traditional village life was getting violated (Scott 1977). In the 1930–40s, the peasants tried various forms of protest like converting to Islam to avoid the *vetti* (bonded labor) that the landlords imposed on them, as well as forcibly opening the granaries of the landlords and publicly distributing grain, since it was the landlords' responsibility to keep them from starving.[59] However, most of these forms of protest were not effective and the landlords would refuse them work. In 1942–43, the communists in the Andhra Mahasabha started their movement in Nalgonda district in Telangana and opposed the local *deshmukh* Kunduri Lakshmi Kantha Rao, as well as the rice mill workers' strike for higher wages, which increased the "prestige of the communists in the eyes of the people."[60] The Communists also opposed *vetti* and encouraged the lower caste *Dalits* not to perform it.

Slowly communist activities began to spread in different villages in Nalgonda district from 1944 to 1946, and to some villages in Warangal and Karimnagar districts.[61] Following Indian independence in 1947, there was widespread opposition to the attempt by the Nizam, whose followers organized a paramilitary force of *razakars* to attack the communists and villages in Telangana. The communists organized armed squads to oppose the *razakars*, and this armed rebellion spread to Adilabad, Karimnagar, and Medak districts in 1948. Then on September 13, 1948, the Indian army marched into Hyderabad and the Nizam's army and the *razakars* surrendered and Hyderabad joined the Indian state. This reduced the relevance and support for the communists, and one group of communist leaders declared armed struggle to be over, under pressure from police action by the new Congress government.

Phase 2: 1968–72 The Srikakulam Movement and Andhra Pradesh Revolutionary Communist Committee (APRCC)

With the end of the Telangana movement, the Communist Party of India (CPI) focused on parliamentary politics and did not start any more armed rebellions

---

[59] Thirumali, *Against Dora and Nizam*, pp. 58–61.
[60] Thirumali, *Against Dora and Nizam*, p. 111.
[61] Dhanagare, "Social Origins of the Peasant Insurrection in Telangana (1946–51)," pp. 496–97.

in Andhra Pradesh. However, some radical factions within the CPI decided to restart the armed struggle, and there were three such groups. One group was the Srikakulam communists, the second group was led by T. Nagi Reddy, a third was the Central Organizing Committee (COC) from which the PWG later evolved.[62]

The Srikakulam rebellion occurred in the Srikakulam district in the northeastern corner of Andhra Pradesh, where the Girijan tribals were being exploited by non-tribal moneylenders who illegally took away their lands, and non-tribal landlords who exploited them and paid low wages.[63] The discontent among the Girijan tribals was mobilized by two schoolteachers, Vempatapu Satyanarayana and Adibatla Kailasam, who later joined the new CPI-Marxist (CPI-M) in 1964 following the split in the communist movement. The Naxalite movement, which started in 1967 under the leadership of the charismatic Charu Mazumdar in West Bengal, re-energized the Srikakulam movement, and it became more militant. The increase in violence led to the Andhra Pradesh government using police action; in August 1969, parts of Srikakulam district were declared disturbed areas, and by the mid-1970s, many of the leaders were killed and the movement slowly collapsed.[64]

The second group of communist leaders in Andhra Pradesh in this period was led by T. Nagi Reddy (T. N.), Chandra Pulla Reddy (C. P.), and D. Venkateshwara Rao (D. V.), who broke away from the CPI-Marxist to form the Andhra Pradesh Revolutionary Communist Committee (APRCC) on June 30, 1968. Unlike the CPI-ML, the APRCC leaders believed that while objectively there was a revolutionary situation in India, the people in all parts of the country were not subjectively ready for revolution.[65] The focus of the APRCC was to create mass movements like land occupation and create a united front of workers, students, and peasants, and not just a focus on armed struggle and annihilation of police/landlords as was the Charu Mazumdar/CPI-ML strategy in Bengal. The APRCC operated in Warangal, Khammam, and Karimnagar districts of Telangana, and East Godavari district, which was the only non-Telangana district where it was successful. The Koya and Gond tribes joined this rebellion, and their experience and social networks from the previous Telangana rebellion in the 1940s show organizational continuity from previous rebel movements.[66] These tribes provided the ethnic mobilization networks with their grievances created by colonial-era land tenure institutions. However, the movement faced reversals after initial success in land occupation programs in East Godavari district, in the face of police repression, since they were not ready with armed squads.[67] Following the arrest of Nagi Reddy and other leaders in December 1969, the APRCC movement continued with low levels of activity under the leadership of C. P. Reddy till the late 1970s.

---

[62] Mishra, *Barrel of the Gun*, p. 65.   [63] Mishra, *Barrel of the Gun*, pp. 66–67.
[64] Mishra, *Barrel of the Gun*, pp. 74–75.   [65] Sinha, *Maoists in Andhra Pradesh*, pp. 165–66.
[66] Mishra, *Barrel of the Gun*, p. 72.   [67] Singh, *The Naxalite Movement in India*, pp. 190–95.

The group that was more successful in Andhra Pradesh was the COC, which was formed by Suniti Ghosh and Soumya in November 1973. The COC disagreed with the earlier ideological and strategic errors of the Maoist movement under Charu Mazumdar, which was perceived as too focused on individual annihilations, and proposed instead a combination of armed squads with mass action. The COC was also against participation in elections, which was a strategy taken by certain other emerging Naxal groups, like the United CPI-ML of S. N. Singh.[68] The COC under the leadership of K. G. Satyamurthy and K. Sitaramaiah carried out several squad actions between 1971 and 1975. Different armed squads were organized under local leaders in Warangal, Khammam, Medak, and Nalgonda districts, all part of Telangana region of former Hyderabad state. The police were able to arrest some top leaders like Satyamurthy in November 1973, and the Khammam squad in 1974, which affected the movement somewhat, but the actions continued.[69]

With the imposition of the Emergency in 1975–77 by Indira Gandhi, many Naxalite/Maoist leaders were jailed. With end of the Emergency in 1977 and release of some of the leaders from jail, the Chandra Pulla Reddy group of CPI-ML decided to move toward electoral participation in 1978, to take advantage of the anti-Congress atmosphere post-emergency and won the Yellandu seat in Khammam.[70] This left the COC and the emerging PWG as the main active Maoist rebel groups.

Phase 3: 1980 Onward – Emergence of the People's War Group

The third phase of the movement in Andhra Pradesh started with K. Sitaramaiah breaking away from the COC and forming the PWG on April 22, 1980, Lenin's birth anniversary.[71] While Sitaramaiah had aligned himself with the COC in the post–Charu Mazumdar period in 1973, he continued to develop his own ideological formulation, which combined the annihilation theory of Mazumdar with dependence on mass movements. The PWG decided to adopt the tactic of "mass line *and* squad action."[72] Armed squad action was to be confined to the forest areas, and land occupation struggles and other mass movements would be used in the plains areas where the squads were susceptible to police attacks.

Under the leadership of Sitaramaiah and others like K. G. Satyamurthy, the PWG started organizing armed squads or *dalams* to create military strength. To complement the *dalams*, a number of overground front organizations were formed, like the Ryotu Coolie Sangham (RCS), which was the organization for workers and peasants; the Radical Students Union (RSU), which was the very active student union in Warangal and provided many recruits; the Radical

[68] Singh, *The Naxalite Movement in India*, p. 130, and *Echoes of Spring Thunder*, Report prepared by Left Wing Extremism Cell, Special Branch, West Bengal Police, p. 10.
[69] Mishra, *Barrel of the Gun*, p. 94. [70] Sinha, *Maoists in Andhra Pradesh*, pp. 274–75.
[71] Mishra, *Barrel of the Gun*, p. 103. [72] Sinha, *Maoists in Andhra Pradesh*, p. 291.

Youth Leagues (RYL); and the Singareni Karmika Samakhya (SIKASA), which was the coal miner's union in Singareni coal mines.[73] The RSU was important because the PWG used it to send batches of young urban students from Warangal to stay in the villages to acquaint themselves with the tribal peasants and the terrain in these areas.[74]

The increased strength of the PWG led to growing levels of violence from 1985 to 1990. The group targeted politicians, government property, and police officers. During the 1980s, the ruling Telugu Desam Party (TDP) workers were often targeted, especially because their leader and chief minister N. T. Rama Rao had initially called the Naxalites "freedom fighters" but later reneged on his promises. The most significant strike was the killing of Daggupati Chenchuramaiah, the son-in-law of N. T. Rama Rao in Prakasam district, which was supposed to be in retaliation for the killing of *Dalits* in the infamous Karamchedu massacre in July 1985, for which Chenchuramaiah was believed to have been responsible.[75]

In August 1991, K. Sitaramaiah was expelled by the PWG and Muppala Laxman Rao, popularly called Ganapathy, was made the general secretary of the PWG, over some internal leadership differences.[76] This started a new phase, and there was an increasing scale of attacks by the PWG against the police, and also against certain politicians. This forced Congress Chief Minister of Andhra Pradesh Chenna Reddy to adopt a more coercive counterinsurgency strategy by 1992. The PWG and its six front organizations were banned on May 20, 1992, and counterinsurgency operations resulted in the killing of 248 Naxalites and the arrest of 3,434 party activists 1992.[77]

Following the ban on PWG in 1992, the level of violence and activities of the PWG slowly fell. With the formation of a new TDP government under N. T. Rama Rao in Andhra Pradesh in 1995, a soft counterinsurgency policy was again adopted toward the PWG, and the ban was removed. The PWG again reorganized and formed guerrilla zones in North Telangana and Dandakaranya region, and levels of violence and extortion again increased. The Andhra Pradesh government, which by now had Chandrababu Naidu as the chief minister, was forced to reimpose the ban on July 23, 1996.[78]

In response to a government decision to launch coordinated action against the Naxalites by police forces of the various Indian states affected by Naxal violence, the PWG decided to form the People's Guerrilla Army (PGA) on January 2, 2001, in Andhra Pradesh, by reorganizing its guerrilla force.[79] Violence continued and

---

[73] Mishra, *Barrel of the Gun*, p. 103.   [74] Sinha, *Maoists in Andhra Pradesh*.
[75] Gossman, "Police Killings and Rural Violence in Andhra Pradesh," *Asia Watch*, September 20, 1992, pp. 12–13.
[76] Mishra, *Barrel of the Gun*, p. 110.   [77] Singh, *The Naxalite Movement in India*, p. 142.
[78] Mitra, *Genesis and Spread of Maoist Violence and Appropriate State Strategy to Handle It*, pp. 56–57.
[79] "People's Guerrilla Army, Left Wing Extremists," www.satp.org/satporgtp/countries/india/maoist/terrorist_outfits/peoples_guerrilla_arms_left_wing_extremists.htm

finally culminated in a landmine attack on Chandrababu Naidu's convoy, as he was returning from the temple town of Tirupati on October 1, 2003. Naidu and several other ministers were injured.[80] This was a major attack, which indicated the increased military skills and resolve of the PWG.

The Andhra Pradesh government responded by using special counterinsurgency units called Greyhounds to fight the PWG, besides paramilitary forces. The PWG kept hitting back by assassinating political leaders, destroying government property and private industries, thus intensifying the violence. In May 2004, the Congress Party was voted to power, and the new government lifted the ban on the PWG on July 22, 2004, based on electoral promises the Congress had made. Maoist leaders were given safe passage, and peace talks were held in the capital city, Hyderabad, from October 15–18, 2004. The Naxals presented an eleven-point charter of demands, including an independent commission to identify land to be distributed to the landless.[81]

There were several rounds of talks, but no agreement followed on various contentious issues like land distribution and whether the PWG cadre could carry arms. The Maoists claimed that the Congress government was not sincere about talks and was killing some of their cadres and trying to infiltrate their organization. According to senior Maoist leader Narayan Sanyal, the issue of carrying arms was nonnegotiable, because that is what gave the bargaining power to the Maoists; he claimed: "If we give up arms why we should talk to you?"[82] There were killings and counter killings by the PWG and police, culminating with the Naxals killing Narsi Reddy, a Congress Member of Legislative Assembly (MLA) on August 15, 2005, which led to the Congress government to reimpose the ban on the new Communist Party of India–Maoist (CPI-Maoist) on August 17, 2005.[83]

With the failure of the peace negotiations, the police intensified counterinsurgency operations, and the Maoist movement in Andhra Pradesh suffered setbacks with several top- and middle-ranked leaders killed. On October 14, 2004, the PWG had unified with the other main Maoist group, the MCC, to form the unified CPI-Maoist, and a tactical decision was made to reduce operations in the Telangana districts of Andhra Pradesh and to focus efforts in the Dandakaranya forested regions of Bastar in Chhattisgarh and Orissa. This caused the level of violence in Andhra Pradesh to fall after 2006; while a certain level of grievance continues among the tribal populations in the Telangana districts, the Maoists have not yet been able to increase their levels of operation in Andhra Pradesh. However, the unified CPI-Maoist now focuses its

---

[80] Singh, *The Naxalite Movement in India*, p. 168.

[81] For a record of the discussions, see *Negotiating Peace*, Committee of Concerned Citizens, December 2006, pp. 173–201.

[82] Interview with Narayan Sanyal (founder of Party Unity and former Politburo member of CPI-Maoist), Raipur Central Jail, Raipur, Chhattisgarh, 2008.

[83] Singh, *The Naxalite Movement in India*, pp. 170–72.

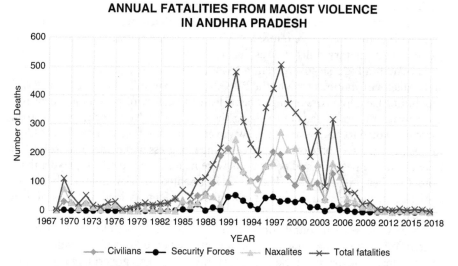

FIGURE 8.5 Annual fatalities from Maoist violence in Andhra Pradesh, 1968–2018
Source: www.satp.org/satporgtp/countries/india/states/andhra/data_sheets/annual_casu-
alties.htm for data till 2013, and www.satp.org/datasheet-terrorist-attack/fatalities/
india-maoistinsurgency-andhrapradesh for data from 2014 to 2018.

activities in the neighboring state of Chhattisgarh, and levels of violence
escalated there as violence decreased in Andhra Pradesh. Figure 8.5 shows the
patterns of violence for the Maoist insurgency in Andhra Pradesh.

5.3 How Maoist Rebel Agency Addressed *Dalit* and *Adivasi* Grievances of Land Inequality

In the initial phase of 1980–85, the PWG took up five major issues: (1)
distribution of land to the tiller; (2) occupying forest land and distributing
it to the tribals and the landless; (3) reduction in *arrack* (country liquor)
prices; (4) enhancement of wages of farm laborers, *beedi* makers, and
bamboo cutters; and (5) opposing harassment by landlords,
moneylenders, and corrupt government officials. The PWG would use its
dalams to enforce its decisions on these issues.[84] Justice was often delivered
in *jan adalats* (people's courts). In a famous incident at Indravelli in
Adilabad district on May 20, 1981, the PWG called a meeting of the
Gond tribals to protest against the influx of non-tribal Lambadas into the
area from neighboring Maharashtra state. The police fired on the gathering
crowds and killed thirteen Gond tribals, and the PWG cadres exploited

[84] Trinath Mishra, *Barrel of the Gun*, p. 105.

resultant tribal anger to consolidate their control over villages in Adilabad district.[85]

Following arrest in 1982 and subsequent escape in 1984 from the prisoner's ward of the hospital, K. Sitaramaiah was able to set up about fifty dalams of ten–twelve men in the Telangana district forests.[86] Using the pressure of their *dalams*, the PWG is believed to have redistributed nearly half a million acres of land across Andhra Pradesh in this period, by forcibly occupying the excess land of big landowners and giving it away to the landless or laborers working for the landlord. It also succeeded in raising the daily wages of landless laborers. Both these actions made the PWG very popular with the poorer populations in Telangana districts.[87]

In their banned publication *Vanguard*, the PWG notes that from February to May 1990, a number of large public rallies were organized by the Ryotu Coolie Sangham (RCS), the peasants' and workers' associations, in various towns in the North Telangana districts like Nizamabad, Warangal, Karimnagar, and Nalgonda. On May 5–6, 1990, there was a meeting in Warangal town that was attended by twelve lakh peasants, and a memorandum was presented to Chief Minister Chenna Reddy demanding *pattas* to "forest and banjar lands occupied by the peasantry since 1978. As per the detailed statistics provided in the memorandum ... a total of 190,122 acres of forest, banjar, ceiling, temple and other categories of lands in 929 villages spreading throughout the state have been occupied by the peasantry during the last one-decade under the leadership of the RCS."[88] After this conference, the local RCS helped the peasants occupy more lands from landlords, presented in Table 8.3, which shows that the Maoists were more successful in leading such agitations in the Telangana districts of Hyderabad state (indirect rule) than the Andhra districts that had been under Madras Presidency (British direct rule).

6 QUANTITATIVE ANALYSIS OF SPATIAL VARIATION IN MAOIST CONTROL IN ANDHRA PRADESH

6.1 Addressing the Selection Issue: Comparative Case Study of Hyderabad and Awadh Princely States

As explained in earlier chapters, it is possible that the British decided it was more economical and efficient to choose indirect rule for those areas or districts that were poor in agricultural productivity, intrinsically low revenue, and more difficult to govern due to difficult terrain or rebellious tribal populations. This creates a problem of selection bias when studying the long-term effects of colonizer choices on economic or political

---

[85] Prakash Singh, p. 132.   [86] Trinath Mishra, p. 106.   [87] Prakash Singh, p. 134.
[88] *Vanguard*, May–June 1991, p. 20.

TABLE 8.3 *Land redistributed by peasants and RCS in 1990 movement*

Name of district (direct or indirect rule)	No. of villages covered	No. of landlords	Occupied land in acres	No. of people participated and other details
Warangal (Telangana)	77	107	3,015	700 families for agriculture and 500 house sites
Karimnagar (Telangana)	48	24	4,238	3,516 persons participated; 600 acres of forest land included
Adilabad (Telangana)	47	136	1,919 +501	lands surrendered by landlords voluntarily
Nizamabad (Telangana)	10	15	348	40 acres forest lands included
East Godavari (Madras presidency)	48	97	4,341	2,200 acres forest land and 175 acres fruit gardens included
Visakhapatnam (Madras presidency)	7	6	423	50 families
Guntur (Madras presidency)	5	1	480	430 acres Temple lands
Anantapur (Madras presidency)	13	–	722	Temple and Banjarlands
Cuddapah (Madras presidency)	1	1	40	Recaptured from landlord
Srikakulam (Madras presidency)	20	1	173	Cashew tope
Medak (Madras presidency)	2	1	16	Temple lands held by landlords
Chittoor (Madras presidency)	1	–	40	held by 60 families
Gadchiroli (Maharashtra)	8	15	434 +65	Voluntarily surrendered by landlords

Source: Vanguard, *May–June 1991, p. 20, www.bannedthought.net/India/Vanguard/index.htm*

outcomes, because these particular pre-colonial attributes of the colony may be the reason for the postcolonial outcome of low levels of development and Maoist rebellion.

Fortunately, this is not as much of a problem for the case of Hyderabad state, which remained under indirect rule, not because the area was unproductive and low revenue, but because historical contingency prevented the British from annexing it and setting up direct rule. In a detailed comparative analysis of Hyderabad with the princely state of Awadh in Chapter 6, I show that Lord Dalhousie, the governor general from 1848 to 1856, desired to annex the rich state of Hyderabad as much as Awadh. Yet, the British were able to annex Awadh into direct rule in 1856 but unable to do the same for Hyderabad. The reason for the difference in British choice of rule between Hyderabad and Awadh can be traced to the difference in geopolitical constraints facing these two otherwise similar states.[89] This difference in external geopolitical circumstances led to variation in financial relations, which explains why Awadh was annexed into direct rule but Hyderabad was not. This Most Similar Systems case comparison design demonstrated that it was historical contingency and not selection by the British administrators that determined indirect rule in Hyderabad.

6.2 OLS and Logistic Regression Analysis

I test my theory of indirect rule creating structural conditions for Maoist insurgency by exploiting spatial variation at the sub-district level in Maoist control in the state of Andhra Pradesh. The following hypothesis is proposed based on the theory outlined in earlier chapters:

Hypothesis: Areas that had indirect colonial rule through princely states tend to have higher probability of Maoist insurgency in the future, even after controlling for various proximate measures of rebel opportunity and ethnic grievances.

6.2.1 Data and Variables

Mapping Census Data into Assembly Constituencies Like the sub-district econometric analysis for Chhattisgarh, I use the Vidhan Sabha (State Assembly) constituency (AC) as the unit of analysis. The Assembly Constituency is located below the district level and allows a more disaggregated analysis and measurement of *rebel control* than can be done at the district level.

The administrative map of erstwhile Andhra Pradesh consists of 22 districts subdivided into 1,110 *mandals* (sub-districts), and the electoral map consists of 294 Assembly Constituencies.[90] Each district had several Assembly Constituencies, and I develop a new dataset for these 294 constituencies. I measure the dependent variable *Maoist control* and the independent variable

[89] Fisher, *Indirect Rule in India*, pp. 399–400.
[90] The sub-district units in Chhattisgarh are called *tehsils*; in Andhra Pradesh, they are called *mandals*.

of *princely state* directly at the constituency level. However, control variables like *unemployment, literacy, provision of electricity, schools and irrigation facilities, access to roads and railways* are available in administrative units like village/*mandal*/district from the Census of India 2001 Village Directory (VD) dataset, and not in electoral constituency units. As explained in Chapter 7 on Chhattisgarh, this creates the problem of converting census data into constituency units, since sub-district and Assembly Constituency boundaries do not always match spatially. Fortunately, for Andhra Pradesh this problem is easier to solve, because following the reorganization of the electoral map during a delimitation process in 2007, the *mandals* fit perfectly within each Vidhan Sabha constituency, and there are no *mandals* that cross constituency boundaries.[91] Using information from the 2007 Delimitation Commission and by comparing the map of *mandal* boundaries of Andhra Pradesh in 2001 from the *Census of India 2001 Andhra Pradesh Administrative Atlas*,[92] with the constituency boundaries in 2009 *Andhra Pradesh Assembly Constituency Election Map*,[93] the census data for all the *mandals* within each constituency were aggregated up to that constituency level. Details are in Online Appendix A for this chapter.

Measuring *Maoist Control* as the Dependent Variable As already discussed in Chapter 7, I prefer to use *rebel control* as my dependent variable, and not killings/fatalities. As Kalyvas (2008: 401) notes, in a civil war, "the absence of fatalities from a particular location may be indicative of two distinct ... states of the world: either a total state monopoly of violence (which is what most studies assume is the case) or a total absence of the state." Similarly, Zukerman-Daly (2012: 6) suggests that "violence is not a perfect indicator of successful insurgency as insurgents in the forest do not need to carry out violence if they have no competition."

For Andhra Pradesh I measure *Maoist control* using data from the State Election Commission in Andhra Pradesh, which ranks Vidhan Sabha Assembly constituencies on their level of political sensitivity, based on reports that the district superintendent of police (SP) and district magistrate (DM) send to the chief election commissioner prior to elections. Unfortunately, the State Election Commission booklets for the 2004 and 2009 Assembly Constituency elections in Andhra Pradesh have the categorization of percentage of "Sensitive," "Hyper Sensitive," and "Extremist Affected" polling stations at the district level and not at the constituency level. Luckily during fieldwork in the capital city

---

[91] *Delimitation of Parliamentary and Assembly Constituencies in the State of Andhra Pradesh*, 2007.

[92] Plate 11: "Andhra Pradesh: Changes in Administrative Boundaries: 1991–2001," *Census of India 2001: Andhra Pradesh Administrative Atlas*, p. 14

[93] "Assembly and Parliamentary Constituencies of Andhra Pradesh, 2009 Elections," from *General Elections to the House of People and Andhra Pradesh Legislative Assembly, 2009.*

Hyderabad, I was able to collect data on the political sensitivity of each constituency for the 2009 Assembly elections, from the State Election Commission.[94] The data explicitly states whether a constituency is "Naxal Affected" or "Communally Sensitive" or "Faction Ridden" or has "Important Leaders," and some are left blank indicating there are no political tensions. I coded those constituencies that are marked as "Naxal affected" as 1 and coded the other constituencies as 0, and I use this binary measure of *Maoist control* for the 294 assembly constituencies as the dependent variable.

Possible Bias in Government Perception of Maoist Control: Like other measures of rebel control based on government perception (Kalyvas and Kocher 2009; Mitchell 1968), there may be bias in government perception of Maoist control. For example, Mitchell (1968) used military maps reported in newspapers to measure rebel control during the Vietnam War, but this measure could possibly be biased because it is based on government information. Similarly, district police chiefs and magistrates could overestimate or underestimate Maoist control in constituencies in their districts in Andhra Pradesh. For example, the district police could possibly overestimate the degree of Maoist control in a constituency in their district to get more troops and counterinsurgency funds. However, the measurement error in the dependent variable is uncorrelated with the independent variable, since the police use various criteria to determine their threat perception of Maoist influence but do not consider historical indirect rule.[95] So the regression estimators are unbiased and consistent, though there will be larger variance in the error terms.[96]

Independent Variable: I measure colonial indirect rule as a 0–1 dichotomous variable named *princely state,* which is created by matching the 2009 *Andhra Pradesh Assembly Constituency Election Map*[97] with the maps of direct and indirect rule in Andhra Pradesh from *The Imperial Gazetteer of India*: Volume 26 – Atlas, Plates 40 and 41 (see Figures 8.1 and 8.2). This is coded as 1 if the constituency was earlier part of the princely state of Hyderabad, and 0 if it was part of the British directly ruled Madras Presidency.

Control Variables: Socioeconomic and demographic data like literacy; per capita income; unemployment; percentage of scheduled castes and tribes; and provision of public goods like electricity, irrigation, schools, primary health centers comes from the Census of India 2001. Geographic data like forest cover

---

[94] This data was gathered from an administrative officer in the State Election Commission, Hyderabad, for research purposes and is available on request. I cannot identify the officer to protect identity.

[95] While interviewing police officers, I realized that they depend on various factors to categorize constituencies or districts as under high or medium or low Maoist control, but they are not thinking of colonial indirect rule.

[96] See Gujarati, *Basic Econometrics*, pp. 524–28.

[97] "Assembly and Parliamentary Constituencies of Andhra Pradesh, 2009 Elections."

and elevation is developed from Forest Survey of India and other GIS data sources. Voting and electoral data like voting turnout, electoral competitiveness, is directly obtained from the Andhra Pradesh State Election Commission reports.

6.2.2 Regression Analysis of the Impact of Colonial Indirect Rule on Maoist Control

(a) Difference in Means Shows Effects of Colonial Institutions on Intermediary Mechanisms of State Capacity, Public Goods, and Literacy Table 8.4 shows difference in means between direct rule and indirect rule constituencies for various measures of public goods, socioeconomic factors, and state capacity. *Maoist control* has a higher mean value of 0.521 for the constituencies that were under princely state, and a much lower mean value of 0.097 for those constituencies that were under direct British rule.

Using Census 2001 data, both male and female literacy is significantly higher in British direct rule constituencies, and male unemployment is higher on average in those constituencies that were in the erstwhile princely state of Hyderabad. This is important since higher male unemployment implies lower opportunity costs for joining rebellion, and hence the possibility of higher Maoist rebellion (Dasgupta et al. 2017). Also, former princely state constituencies have lower connectivity of rural areas to urban centers, significantly lower access to bus and railway stations and post offices, implying lower counterinsurgency capacity for the state (Fearon & Laitin 2003).

(b) Logistic Regression Model Specification Since the dependent variable *Maoist control* is binary, I use a logistic regression

$$logit\ (\pi) = \alpha + \beta\ princely\ state_i + \delta\ X_i + \varepsilon_i,$$

where *logit* (π) is the logistic function of probability that a constituency i is under Maoist control, and *princely state*$_i$ is the dummy for whether the constituency was earlier part of indirect rule or British direct rule; X_i stands for other constituency characteristics like forest cover, elevation, literacy, access to public goods, state capacity, and other variables usually included in civil war onset models; ε_i represents the error term.

I present regression models in Table 8.5. The basic model specification is Model 1, which includes only *princely state*. Model 2 includes *forest cover* and *elevation* (proxying for mountainous terrain) as controls. Models 3 to 8 control for literacy, percentage of scheduled castes and scheduled tribes, as well as proxies for state/counterinsurgency capacity like access to paved roads, post office, and railway stations and average distance of villages from closest town.

Standard errors are clustered at the district level, since constituencies that are part of the same district may have a common set of unobservable properties

TABLE 8.4 *Summary statistics and difference in means by princely state*

| | Observations | | | Mean | | | Difference in Means |
Variable	Total	British Empire	Princely States	Total	British Empire	Princely States	(British Empire) – (Princely State)
Maoist Control							
Naxal-Affected Polling Stations	294	175	119	0.268	0.097	0.521	−0.424 *** (0.047)
Geography							
Forest Cover Percentage	293	174	119	11.12	9.22	13.89	−4.67 ** (2.23)
Elevation (meters)	264	163	101	247.15	174.82	363.88	−189.06 *** (22.96)
Demography							
Scheduled Caste Percentage	264	163	101	16.87	16.62	17.29	−0.68 (0.76)
Scheduled Tribe Percentage	264	163	101	7.25	5.64	9.87	−4.23 *** (1.46)
Population Density	256	158	98	955.63	1307.91	387.65	920.26 (724.27)
Population	264	163	101	264,774.3	265,895.8	262,964.4	2931.36 (3279.09)

(continued)

Variable	Total	British Empire	Princely States	Total	British Empire	Princely States	(British Empire) − (Princely State)
Socioeconomic							
Total Literacy	264	163	101	56.46	58.96	52.43	6.53 *** (1.31)
Male Literacy	264	163	101	66.88	68.43	64.36	4.07 *** (1.19)
Female Literacy	264	163	101	45.89	49.34	40.33	9.01 *** (1.52)
Male Unemployment	264	163	101	48.96	46.99	52.15	−5.16 *** (0.79)
Per Capita Income	256	158	98	38.66	37.68	40.22	−2.54 (8.32)
State Capacity							
Post Office	259	161	98	0.63	0.67	0.57	0.10 *** (0.02)
Distance from Town (km)	259	161	98	28.69	28.06	29.73	−1.67 (2.26)
Paved Road	259	161	98	1.12	1.10	1.16	−0.06 ** (0.04)
Railway Facility	259	161	98	1.77	1.81	1.71	0.097 ** (0.041)
Bus Facility	259	161	98	1.01	1.05	0.94	0.11 *** (0.03)

Education							
Primary School	259	161	98	2.79	3.09	2.31	0.78 **** (0.17)
Middle School	259	161	98	0.69	0.64	0.76	−0.12 *** (0.04)
Secondary School	259	161	98	0.34	0.33	0.37	−0.04 * (0.02)
Health							
Hospitals	259	161	98	0.019	0.021	0.015	0.005 * (0.003)
Primary Health Centers	259	161	98	0.075	0.087	0.055	0.032 *** (0.007)
Maternity and Child Welfare Center	259	161	98	0.018	0.022	0.014	0.008 (0.009)
Water							
Tanks	259	161	98	1.52	1.44	1.67	−0.23 *** (0.094)
Tubewells	259	161	98	1.47	1.42	1.54	−0.12 * (0.102)
Power							
Electricity	259	161	98	0.947	0.942	0.954	−0.012 (0.014)

P-values in parentheses. * p < 0.10, ** p < 0.05, *** p < 0.01
Source: All socio-economic and public goods data from Census of India 2001. Forest cover data from Forest Survey of India.

unique to the district, which make them more or less prone to Maoist rebellion. It is not possible to include district-specific fixed effects, because lack of within-district variation in the *princely state* variable, results in princely state being dropped from the fixed effect analysis.[98]

6.2.3   Analysis and discussion of results:

Colonial Indirect Rule Institutions: In Table 8.5, Model 1, *princely state* is statistically significant at the 99 percent confidence level, and positively correlated with *Maoist control*. In Model 2, I control for *forest cover* and *elevation*, which are possible pre-colonial factors influencing British selection of indirect rule in this area, and *princely state* is still strongly statistically significant and positively correlated. This means that once the institutions of indirect rule were chosen, they had their own independent effect through land inequality and low development. In Models 3 to 8, where I control for more postcolonial socioeconomic outcomes and demographic factors, *princely state* remains a significant predictor of *Maoist control*, which indicates the independent effect of colonial indirect rule beyond the effects of proximate measures of ethnic grievances and weak state capacity on Maoist control.

Terrain and Pre-Colonial Determinants of Choice of Princely State: The *forest cover* variable is also statistically significant and positively correlated in all models in Table 8.5. This is expected, since the Maoist insurgency occurred in the Dandakaranya forested areas and also in the Nallamala forested areas in the northern Telangana districts of Andhra Pradesh. This means that opportunity for rebellion existed in Andhra Pradesh, because constituencies that have high forest cover tend to have more Maoist control. Well-known Maoist sympathizer and balladeer Gaddar pointed out the importance of not only feudal exploitation but also terrain to hide from the police. According to Gaddar, the Nallamala forests bordering Telangana were probably not as dense and useful in providing cover for the Maoists as the denser Dandakaranya forests in the Abujhmarh area of Chhattisgarh where he had once been part of an underground cadre. He emphasized that for successful attacks by Maoists on police stations or armories, "there must be a retreating place in the guerrilla war, waise terrain hona chahiye waha pe chhipne ke liye (there has to be terrain for hiding)."[99]

However, *elevation* has a negative and statistically significant correlation with *Maoist control* in all models, which goes against the expectation that bad

---

[98] See Gujarati, *Basic Econometrics*, pp. 640–51 for why lack of within-group variation for a variable causes the variable to be omitted from the fixed effects analysis by STATA. As in Chhattisgarh, in Andhra Pradesh there has not been much change in the district boundaries since British times, and the new districts have been created by splitting larger districts into smaller ones; they do not have areas that were inside both princely state territory and British rule territory.

[99] Interview with Gaddar, Hyderabad, February 18, 2008.

TABLE 8.5 *Logit estimates of impact of colonial institutions on Maoist rebellion in Andhra Pradesh*
Dependent variable: Maoist control

	Model 1	Model 2	Model 3	Model 4	Model 5	Model 6	Model 7	Model 8
Princely State	2.313*** (0.001)	3.560*** (0.002)	3.083*** (0.005)	2.906*** (0.007)	2.852*** (0.008)	2.799*** (0.007)	3.209*** (0.003)	3.005*** (0.001)
Forest Cover		0.0638*** (0.000)	0.0423** (0.035)	0.0459** (0.024)	0.0447** (0.025)	0.0451** (0.025)	0.0421** (0.045)	0.0470** (0.015)
Elevation		−0.00351 (0.196)	−0.00624*** (0.008)	−0.00641*** (0.005)	−0.00635*** (0.008)	−0.00601*** (0.006)	−0.00684*** (0.003)	−0.00663*** (0.004)
Population Density			−0.00215 (0.143)	−0.00228 (0.167)	−0.00231 (0.150)	−0.00230 (0.182)	−0.00146 (0.306)	−0.00242 (0.183)
Per Capita Income			0.00237** (0.048)	0.00232* (0.063)				
Male Unemployment			0.204 (0.219)	0.241 (0.163)	0.256 (0.137)	0.257 (0.154)	0.251 (0.123)	0.256 (0.139)
Scheduled Caste Percentage			0.0492 (0.460)	0.0577 (0.362)	0.0661 (0.300)	0.0575 (0.383)	0.0535 (0.338)	0.0611 (0.334)
Scheduled Tribe Percentage			0.0631** (0.017)	0.960 (0.371)	1.127 (0.325)	1.065 (0.346)	1.460 (0.152)	1.060 (0.330)
Male Literacy			0.00391 (0.924)	−0.00363 (0.925)	0.00349 (0.932)	−0.00737 (0.848)	−0.00658 (0.866)	0.000136 (0.997)
Electricity				13.40 (0.229)	11.84 (0.320)	12.91 (0.282)	16.91 (0.126)	11.28 (0.385)

(continued)

TABLE 8.5 (continued)

	Model 1	Model 2	Model 3	Model 4	Model 5	Model 6	Model 7	Model 8
ST% * Electricity				-0.940 (0.395)	-1.125 (0.339)	-1.048 (0.368)	-1.482 (0.159)	-1.043 (0.352)
Paved Road					2.163 (0.296)			
Post Office						0.698 (0.652)		
Distance from Town							0.0354** (0.017)	
Railway Station								1.039 (0.586)
Constant	-2.229*** (0.000)	-2.596*** (0.000)	-12.38 (0.146)	-26.61** (0.031)	-28.69** (0.027)	-27.04** (0.039)	-31.33** (0.020)	-27.39** (0.031)
Observations	294	263	255	255	255	255	255	255
Pseudo R^2	0.1925	0.3857	0.4521	0.4600	0.4622	0.4581	0.4723	0.4588
Log Likelihood	-138.16	-97.68	-85.57	-84.34	-84.002	-84.65	-82.43	-84.53
Percentage Correctly Predicted	74.83%	84.03%	83.92%	85.10%	85.49%	85.49%	85.10%	83.92%
Area under ROC Curve	0.7598	0.8854	0.9108	0.9124	0.9135	0.9124	0.9176	0.9130

p-values in parentheses. * $p < 0.10$, ** $p < 0.05$, *** $p < 0.01$
All models include district fixed effects. Not possible to calculate district fixed effects due to lack of intra-district variation in indirect rule measure.

terrain reduces state counterinsurgency capacity and makes it easier to sustain rebellion. It is possible that this is because of multicollinearity, and the coefficient for *elevation* is biased and it is not possible to interpret the regression coefficient on *elevation*. Also, the Telangana region is not very hilly unlike in Kashmir or some regions in India's northeast that also have insurgency, and so this may not be a good measure of rebel opportunity in this area.

Proximate Postcolonial controls: I include *Scheduled Caste Percentage* and *Scheduled Tribe Percentage* in Models 3 and 4, since the Maoists tend to recruit mainly from these socially and economically disadvantaged groups. *Scheduled Tribe Percentage* is statistically significant in Model 3, but not in any other models, and *Scheduled Caste Percentage* is not statistically significant in any model. The *Scheduled Caste Percentage* result may point to regional variation in Maoist insurgency in India: in the northern epicenter of the insurgency, especially in the state of Bihar, lower castes are more numerous than tribes, but in Andhra Pradesh the insurgency is supported by tribes, like in Chhattisgarh, which provide the *ethnic mobilization networks* for the rebels.

Male *literacy* and *male unemployment* are statistically nonsignificant once *princely state* is included in the models 3 to 8 in Table 8.5. However, the difference of means in Table 8.4 shows *male literacy* is lower and *male unemployment* is higher in constituencies that were earlier part of the princely state of Hyderabad than in areas that were under direct British rule in Madras Presidency. So this is an indication of the long-term structural effects of indirect rule, leading to lower levels of employment, literacy, and public good provision, thus setting up the political opportunity structures for leftist insurgency in the future. Instead of interpreting this as lack of support for *grievance* theories, it may imply that the conditions of grievances were created by long-term historical legacies of colonial indirect rule.

An interesting result that seems difficult to explain is that in Models 3 and 4, *per capita income* (aggregated from village-level data on income up to the constituency level) has a positive and sometimes statistically significant correlation with Maoist control. At this low level of aggregation, *per capita income* is not a proxy for state capacity, unlike in Fearon and Laitin (2003), which uses country level *per capita income* as a proxy for state counterinsurgency capacity. The *per capita income* measure probably reflects the level of development, or income at the village level in Andhra Pradesh, aggregated up to the constituency level. The positive correlation seems to imply that those constituencies that have a higher mean value of village income tend to have more Maoist insurgency on average, keeping other variables at their mean values.

While this seems counterintuitive at first glance, it possibly makes sense if we take into account Maoist strategic doctrine, which suggests that the poorest villages are not always considered the ones most amenable to rebellion. Rather, those villages, or areas, that have a lot of exploitation of lower castes and tribes and high levels of inequality and at the same time are above a certain threshold level of economic development or natural resources are more ready for revolution. These areas have high relative deprivation but also provide greater opportunity for the Maoist rebels to tax forest officials or business owners running steel, coal, or iron ore factories.[100]

According to former director general of police (DGP) in Andhra Pradesh, Swaranjit Sen, the Maoists were strategic in choosing their areas of operation, and there was no strong correlation between the poverty level of an area and whether it would become a Maoist stronghold.[101] Noted human rights activist, K. Balagopal mentioned that there is no direct link between lack of development and Naxalism, else the poorer districts like Mahbubnagar in Telangana would have been under Maoist influence first. Rather it was feudal oppression and the presence of former Communist Party of India-Marxist members that explains spatial variation in success of Maoist insurgency in Andhra Pradesh.[102] According to Professor G. Haragopal, the districts in Telangana that were most affected by Maoist movement like Karimnagar and Warangal have seen more development than the districts that were less affected by Naxalism like Mahbubnagar and Medak. This implies that the Naxals have been successful in acting as pressure groups, and the "political system there responded ... they also took some development projects there."[103] So, levels of development are possibly endogenous to conflict and could be one reason why per capita income has a positive correlation with insurgency.

In Models 5 to 8 in Table 8.5, I replace *per capita income* with other proxies of local counterinsurgency capacity, like *access by paved road*, *post office*, *railway station*, and *average distance of villages in constituency from nearest town* drawn from Census of India 2001 data. State capacity is not easy to measure at this low level of spatial disaggregation, but these are more accurate measures of state counterinsurgency capacity at the local level than per capita income. For example, whether or not a village has access to a paved road is a good indication of how quickly police forces can reach the village in response to a security threat. The only state capacity measure that is statistically significant is *distance from nearest town*, which shows that those constituencies that tend to have more villages that are remote from urban centers have a higher

---

[100] See *Strategy and Tactics of the Indian Revolution*, 2004 (final version), pp. 57–58, in which the PWG Maoists write: "In accordance with our general line of establishing Base Areas first in the backward countryside and then gradually expanding to the advanced areas and finally encircling the cities, we have to first select the strategic areas to continue our rural work. ... The question of economic self-reliance should also be a factor while selecting the area keeping in view the perspective of building and sustaining the Base area."

[101] Interview with Swaranjit Sen, ex-DGP of Andhra Pradesh, Hyderabad, February 26, 2008.

[102] Interview with K. Balagopal, Hyderabad, February 8, 2008.

[103] Interview with G. Haragopal, professor of political science, Hyderabad Central University, Hyderabad, February 6, 2008.

probability of Maoist control. This provides support for opportunity-based theories of civil war, like those of Fearon and Laitin (2003) or Collier and Hoeffler (2004), but with much more fine-grained measures of state capacity than possible in these cross-national studies.

Substantive Interpretation of Results and Discussion of Causal Mechanisms Interpreting coefficients of logistic regression is challenging because of the nonlinearity of the underlying relationship.[104] The substantive impact of each variable can be understood by analyzing the impact on the predicted probability of *Maoist control*, when that variable is changed from its minimum to maximum observed value, holding the other variables at their mean values. Table 8.6 shows the changes in predicted probabilities of *Maoist control* for the variables in Table 8.5, using the S-POST statistical package in STATA created by Long and Freese (2006).[105] In Model 1, changing the value of *princely state* from its minimum value of 0 to its maximum value of 1 increases the predicted likelihood of a constituency having *Maoist control* by 42.39 percentage points. This is a relatively large substantive effect and seems robust to different model specifications. In Model 4, where many of the control variables are included, the effect of being part of a princely state increases the probability of Maoist control by 28.02 percentage points.

6.2.4 Robustness Checks

I do some robustness checks and present the results briefly here, and in more detail in Online Appendix B for this chapter. I filed a Right to Information Act (RTI) application to obtain the data on "Sensitive," "Hyper-sensitive," and "Extremist Affected" polling stations in each constituency; after several attempts, the Andhra Pradesh Police Department sent me the data at the constituency level.[106] I use this data to develop a continuous measure of *Maoist control* as "percentage of polling stations in constituency that were Extremist Affected." This is similar to the continuous measure of Maoist control in Chapter 7. I use this measure of Maoist control for both 2004 and 2009 elections, and Table 8.7 shows that *princely state* is statistically significant for the *Maoist control_continuous_2004* measure but is not statistically significant for the *Maoist control_continuous_2009* measure. A possible reason is that following the 2004 elections, a Congress Party government was formed in Andhra Pradesh that fulfilled its electoral promise of negotiating with the Maoists in 2004. However, following the failure of the high-profile peace talks, the government escalated counterinsurgency operations, and the Andhra Pradesh police under the leadership of DGP Swaranjit Sen and the Greyhounds specialized counterinsurgency unit was able to destroy the Maoist networks by

---

[104] See Long, *Regression Models for Categorical and Limited Dependent Variables*.
[105] Long and Freese, *Regression Models for Categorical Outcomes Using Stata*.
[106] This demonstrates the challenges of collecting data on a sensitive topic like the Maoist insurgency in India since government officials are not always willing to share data.

TABLE 8.6 *Changes in predicted probabilities of key independent variables* (change in percentage points of Maoist control as each independent variable is changed from its minimum value to maximum value, keeping the other independent variables at their mean value)

Dependent variable: *Maoist control*

	Model 1 (S-POST)	Model 2 (S-POST)	Model 3 (S-POST)	Model 4 (S-POST)
Princely State	42.39% ***	64.26%	31.59%	28.02%
Forest Cover		86.82%	64.47%	69.54%
Elevation		−36.64%	−26.46%	−26.24%
Population Density			−32.81%	−34.13%
Per Capita Income			30.24%	28.35%
Male Unemployment			36.98%	45.35%
Scheduled Caste Percentage			11.38%	13.05%
Scheduled Tribe Percentage			89.26%	99.99%
Male Literacy			1.23%	−1.10%
Electricity				11.04%
ST% * Electricity				−97.84%

P-values in parentheses. * p < 0.10, ** p < 0.05, *** p < 0.01
The predicted values were estimated using the commands *prvalue, prchange* in the S-POST package available in STATA.

2005–7, and the Maoist leadership made the strategic decision to relocate its activities to the neighboring south Chhattisgarh forested areas in Bastar. So, by 2009 the level of Maoist control in the original core areas in Telangana districts of Hyderabad princely state areas was reduced.

I also control for other measures of political disorder like Hindu-Muslim communal tensions, which I discuss in more detail in Online Appendix B for this chapter. To check whether the measure of Maoist control is influenced by government perceptions of other types of political disorder like language movements or Hindu-Muslim riots, I control for these other measures of political disturbance in Table 8.8. The data I gathered during fieldwork explicitly states whether a constituency is "Naxal Affected," "Communally Sensitive," "Faction Ridden," or has "Important Leaders."[107] I code as 1

---

[107] The constituencies that were called "Important Leaders" had important political leaders. The district administration wants to provide more forces to ensure peaceful elections. The "Communally Sensitive" constituencies were those that had a history of Hindu-Muslim riots. Many constituencies in the Rayalseema region districts were called "Faction Ridden," because these areas are famous for factional feuds between political families based partly on caste.

TABLE 8.7 *OLS estimates of impact of colonial institutions on Maoist rebellion in Andhra Pradesh*
Dependent variable: Continuous measure of Maoist control for both 2004 and 2009

	2004 Model 1 District cluster	2004 Model 2 Constituency cluster	2004 Model 3 District cluster	2004 Model 4 Constituency cluster	2009 Model 5 District cluster	2009 Model 6 Constituency cluster	2009 Model 7 District cluster	2009 Model 8 Constituency cluster
Princely State	9.508** (0.014)	9.508*** (0.000)	7.482* (0.069)	7.482*** (0.002)	2.405 (0.249)	2.405* (0.075)	-2.186 (0.488)	-2.186 (0.326)
Forest Cover			0.199** (0.015)	0.199*** (0.005)			0.167* (0.080)	0.167** (0.018)
Elevation			0.00479 (0.409)	0.00479 (0.290)			0.00626 (0.145)	0.00626* (0.054)
Population Density			-0.00005 (0.498)	-0.00005 (0.493)			-0.00002 (0.698)	-0.00002 (0.740)
Per Capita Income			-0.0228*** (0.009)	-0.0228*** (0.004)			0.00382 (0.592)	0.00382 (0.615)
Male Unemployment			0.0857 (0.864)	0.0857 (0.770)			0.241 (0.238)	0.241 (0.170)
Male Literacy			-0.0443 (0.700)	-0.0443 (0.686)			-0.0791 (0.257)	-0.0791 (0.149)

(continued)

	District cluster	Constituency cluster	District cluster	Constituency cluster	District cluster	Constituency cluster	District cluster	Constituency cluster
Scheduled Caste Percentage			0.0935 (0.637)	0.0935 (0.450)			0.139 (0.186)	0.139* (0.059)
Scheduled Tribe Percentage			1.149 (0.259)	1.149 (0.293)			4.361*** (0.003)	4.361*** (0.001)
Electricity			2.080 (0.924)	2.080 (0.913)			18.59 (0.150)	18.59 (0.145)
ST% * Electricity			-1.068 (0.340)	-1.068 (0.364)			-4.128*** (0.006)	-4.128*** (0.005)
Constant	3.666*** (0.001)	3.666*** (0.000)	-3.072 (0.915)	-3.072 (0.880)	3.058** (0.011)	3.058*** (0.001)	-28.49 (0.107)	-28.49* (0.060)
Observations	265	265	231	231	294	294	255	255
R^2	0.123	0.123	0.330	0.330	0.011	0.011	0.547	0.547
Adjusted R^2	0.120	0.120	0.296	0.296	0.007	0.007	0.527	0.527

P-values in parentheses

Models include district robust cluster standard errors, or constituency robust cluster standard errors. Not possible to calculate district fixed effects due to lack of intra-district variation in indirect rule measure.

* $p < 0.10$, ** $p < 0.05$, *** $p < 0.01$

those constituencies that were marked *communally sensitive* as a measure of Hindu-Muslim political disturbances in the past. The data also has a column grading each constituency as A+, A, B, or C, which is a general measure of political disturbance. I convert this into a categorical measure of 0 to 4 and use it as a proxy for *general political sensitivity*.

The results in Table 8.8 show that *communal sensitivity* has a strong negative correlation with *Maoist control*, while *princely state* remains a significant predictor of *Maoist control*. This is expected because as Varshney (2002) and Wilkinson (2004) point out, Hindu-Muslim riots are an urban phenomenon in India, while the Maoist insurgency occurs in rural areas. Also, *general political sensitivity* has a positive correlation with *Maoist control*, but *princely state* is still strongly positively correlated with Maoist influence. This shows that the measure of *Maoist sensitivity* actually measures Maoist rebel control, and not political disturbances like communal riots or other kinds of political unrest.

7 CONCLUSION – COMPARING CHHATTISGARH AND ANDHRA PRADESH CASES

This chapter advances our understanding of how British colonial institutions affected Maoist insurgency in India by making both conceptual and empirical contributions. Conceptually, it analyzes another state in the southern epicenter of the insurgency, where the same PWG Maoist group operated as in Chhattisgarh, and where indirect rule through a different type of princely state also created structural conditions for leftist rebellion. While the case of Chhattisgarh in Chapter 7 showed how small feudatory princely states with Rajput rulers from other regions led to low state capacity, land inequality, and natural resource extraction, the case of Hyderabad shows how a successor state of the mighty Mughal Empire could also lead to land inequality. The mechanisms of despotic extraction from peasants by native intermediaries are similar – it is through *zamindars* and *diwans* in Chhattisgarh and *deshmukhs* and *jagirdars* in Andhra Pradesh. Also, both cases have indirect rule leading to lower levels of development and public goods. This shows similarity in outcomes in two very different types of princely states. The main difference is that there was natural resource extraction in Bastar princely state in Chhattisgarh, while in Hyderabad, there was less natural resource extraction. Also, in terms of police/state capacity, Hyderabad was stronger. But both places still had Maoist rebellion, which shows equifinality and multiple causal paths leading to the same outcome (Mahoney & Goertz 2006).

Empirically, I develop a sub-district dataset for Andhra Pradesh, similar to the dataset for Chhattisgarh – these are the first Vidhan Sabha Constituency datasets for studying insurgency in India. I also use the measure of Maoist control for both Andhra Pradesh and Chhattisgarh, based on threat perception of police from State Election Commission data collected during

TABLE 8.8 *OLS Estimates of impact of colonial institutions on Maoist rebellion in Andhra Pradesh*
Dependent variable: *Maoist control* (continuous measure) 2004

	Model 1	Model 2	Model 3	Model 4	Model 5	Model 6	Model 7	Model 8
Princely State	8.697** (0.019)	7.935** (0.040)	7.283* (0.073)	8.013** (0.016)	7.387** (0.039)	7.125* (0.082)	6.653** (0.034)	6.783* (0.093)
Communally Sensitive	-5.478** (0.011)	-1.063 (0.309)	-2.025 (0.286)				-7.010*** (0.006)	-2.915 (0.177)
General Sensitivity				1.975** (0.014)	1.085 (0.213)	0.991 (0.260)	2.401*** (0.008)	1.147 (0.216)
Forest Cover		0.271*** (0.000)	0.193** (0.015)		0.263*** (0.000)	0.193** (0.019)		0.185** (0.022)
Elevation		0.00547 (0.330)	0.00401 (0.501)		0.00499 (0.364)	0.00390 (0.469)		0.00263 (0.645)
Population Density			-0.0000462 (0.486)			-0.0000433 (0.480)		-0.0000441 (0.461)
Per Capita Income			-0.0225*** (0.009)			-0.0224*** (0.007)		-0.0219*** (0.006)
Male Unemployment			0.0700 (0.888)			0.0344 (0.947)		0.00373 (0.994)

(continued)

	(1)	(2)	(3)	(4)	(5)	(6)	(7)	(8)
Male Literacy			-0.0360			-0.0497		-0.0385
			(0.763)			(0.673)		(0.754)
Scheduled Caste Percentage			0.126			0.0563		0.0977
			(0.546)			(0.778)		(0.635)
Scheduled Tribe Percentage			1.178			1.034		1.058
			(0.243)			(0.305)		(0.292)
Electricity			2.801			-0.113		0.578
			(0.898)			(0.996)		(0.979)
ST% * Electricity			-1.084			-0.961		-0.966
			(0.330)			(0.389)		(0.385)
Constant	4.850***	0.800	-3.654	-1.322	-2.011	0.233	-0.880	-0.0835
	(0.000)	(0.350)	(0.900)	(0.531)	(0.269)	(0.994)	(0.660)	(0.998)
Observations	265	235	231	265	235	231	265	231
R^2	0.145	0.312	0.332	0.153	0.319	0.336	0.188	0.339
Adjusted R^2	0.139	0.300	0.295	0.147	0.307	0.299	0.179	0.300

P-values in parentheses
Models include district robust cluster standard errors. Not possible to calculate district fixed effects due to lack of intra-district variation in indirect rule measure.
* $p < 0.10$, ** $p < 0.05$, *** $p < 0.01$

fieldwork. Perhaps future studies of insurgency in India can use similar data to measure rebel control for other insurgencies, like in Kashmir or Nagaland. My data on rebel control is a useful empirical contribution that complements the Gawande et al. (2017) dataset on Maoist violence.

Having completed providing empirical evidence to demonstrate that different types of indirect rule in India created conditions for Maoist insurgency in two states in India, by using process tracing and micro-level datasets, I now turn to checking for the external validity of my theory in the next two chapters. Certain cases in India were historically part of *zamindari* estates or part of princely states, yet there was no Maoist insurgency. I study the cases of Kerala and Karnataka as apparent exceptions in the next chapter and try to show that these are not really exceptions, but influential cases (Gerring 2007) where there were the warrior or conquest princely states of Mysore and Travancore, which were different from the feudatory princely state of Bastar and the successor princely state of Hyderabad. These warrior princely states of Mysore and Travancore had fought the European colonizers using European strategy and arms and had developed a more centralized bureaucracy with more intrusive and direct land revenue collection systems. Also, in these states the mechanisms of land inequality could be reversed, and there was no path dependence, because of the role of progressive postcolonial political parties. Then in Chapter 10, I show how colonial indirect rule created conditions for insurgency in other cases within India like Kashmir and North East, and cases outside India, like the Taliban insurgency in Pakistan and the various ethnic secessionist insurgencies in Burma's frontier districts.

PART III

GENERALIZABILITY

9

Explaining Partial Success of Maoists in Kerala and Karnataka

I INTRODUCTION

The book starts with the question of what explains the peculiar spatial variation of Maoist insurgency in India. In the previous chapters, I have demonstrated using both qualitative and quantitative analysis that districts in India that had been previously exposed to colonial indirect rule through princely states in Andhra Pradesh/Chhattisgarh/Orissa region or colonial indirect revenue collection through *zamindari* land tenure in Bengal/Bihar region had a higher chance of successful Maoist insurgency in the future. Using rich archival and interview data, I have done process tracing of the causal mechanisms to show that colonial legacies of land inequality and low development persisted in Chhattisgarh and Andhra Pradesh, thus creating structural conditions for Maoist insurgency.

However, in certain states within India, princely states and *zamindari* tenure did not lead to the same level of Maoist success. For example, the south Indian state of Kerala was formed out of the former princely states Cochin and Travancore as well as British direct ruled Malabar district that had *zamindari* land tenure. While there was Naxalite mobilization in the first phase of the movement in the 1960s in Kerala, the Maoists were not very successful in that state since their resurgence in the 1980s in other parts of India. Similarly, another south Indian state of Karnataka, which neighbors Andhra Pradesh, includes the area where the princely state of Mysore was located. While CPI-Maoist attempted to gain control in certain parts of Karnataka near the hilly Western Ghats in 2005–7, they were not as successful as in neighboring Andhra Pradesh.

What explains these exceptional cases? Closer analysis of these cases shows that these are not really exceptions but rather *influential cases* (Gerring 2007a: 108) where "apparent deviations from the norm are not *really* deviant, or do not challenge the core of the theory, once the circumstances of the special case or cases are fully understood." Examining these cases in fact further strengthens the theory by showing that based on the theoretical framework outlined earlier in Chapter 3, some conditions varied in these cases that led to the lower chance of Maoist success. In that sense, these are exceptions that prove the rule.

To explain these influential cases, in this chapter I use the *typology* of different types of princely states that I presented earlier in Chapter 6, drawing on the historiography by Ramusack (2004). Such a typology provides more fine-grained variation of types of princely states, thus building on the idea of scholars like Mahoney (2010) and Wilkinson (2017) that there are different types of indirect rule. Using this typology of princely states, I show that these so-called exceptional cases of Kerala and Karnataka were actually a different type of indirect rule through *warrior* or *conquest* states like Mysore or Travancore that resulted in higher levels of centralization and state capacity than the *feudatory/ tributary* princely states in Chhattisgarh or the *successor state* of Hyderabad in Andhra Pradesh discussed in earlier chapters that had despotic extraction and low state capacity.

Another reason why the Maoists have not been as successful in Kerala and Karnataka was that land inequality was reversed by progressive postcolonial political parties enacting land reforms, particularly in the case of Kerala. This demonstrates that the effects of colonial land tenure and path dependent persistence of power of princes and landlords can be reversed, as Lange (2009) shows in cases like Botswana in Africa, and Acemoglu et al. (2013) show for the cases of Sierra Leone and Uganda in Africa.

2   INFLUENTIAL CASES WHERE COLONIAL INDIRECT RULE/REVENUE COLLECTION DOES NOT LEAD TO POSTCOLONIAL MAOIST INSURGENCY

Analyzing the spatial variation of the core areas of Maoist insurgency in the late 1990s to the early 2000s shows that most of these areas were formerly either princely states in Andhra Pradesh/Chhattisgarh/Orissa region or *zamindari* land tenure in Bihar/Bengal/Jharkhand areas, which makes indirect rule a necessary condition for Maoist insurgency. However, certain states within India had former princely states and *zamindari* tenure but have not seen successful Maoist insurgency in the second phase, like Kerala and Karnataka, though there has been some resurgence since 2005 in these states. This makes colonial indirect rule a necessary but not a sufficient condition for Maoist rebellion.

Before explaining these influential or exceptional cases, it is important to start with the caveat that the theory has broad generalizability within India, since it is tested on a district-level dataset in earlier chapters and includes state fixed effects that take into account state level heterogeneity. So these apparent exceptions do not disprove the theory, since some level of Maoist influence has been developing in recent times in Kerala and Karnataka, though not as successfully as the core base areas and guerrilla zones that the Maoists created in Telangana and Bastar.

It also needs to be considered that almost all other insurgencies in India occur in areas that were historically under some form of indirect rule. The ongoing ethnic insurgency in Kashmir, as well as several secessionist insurgencies in the northeastern states like Tripura, Manipur, Nagaland, and even some districts in Punjab all were previously colonial indirect rule. Also, areas that were indirectly ruled on the frontiers in the North West Frontier Province (NWFP) in Pakistan developed the Taliban insurgency, and the long-lasting Baluchi insurgency occurred in the former princely state areas like Kalat in Pakistan. Similarly, most of the Frontier-ruled areas of Burma like the Shan, Kachin, and Chin states were indirectly ruled by the British, and later they all had long-lasting ethnic secessionist insurgencies. Telescoping away from the Maoist conflict and taking a broader look at insurgencies in general in South Asia, we find broad support for my theory of different types of indirect rule creating conditions for ideological as well as secessionist insurgency.

Focusing on these apparently exceptional cases of Maoist failure in Kerala and Karnataka, we find that they had certain forms of indirect rule that led to better development and less land inequality that prevented Maoist groups from being as successful as in Chhattisgarh, Andhra Pradesh, Bihar, and Jharkhand. Also, postcolonial governments in Kerala and Karnataka did some land reforms to reverse path dependence of effects of unequal colonial land tenure systems, which most other state governments in India like in Bihar, Andhra Pradesh, or Madhya Pradesh were unable to do. This chapter shows that because of these two reasons indirect rule did not create the same extent of land inequality and low development, and also some of the pernicious effects of indirect rule were reversed in Kerala and Karnataka. As a result, the Maoists in Kerala and Karnataka were not as successful as in the other states like Chhattisgarh, Andhra Pradesh, and Bihar where the legacies of indirect rule and *zamindari* land tenure was typically high land inequality and low development.

2.1   A Typology of Different Types of Princely State and de Facto Direct Influence of British Administrators

Mysore and Travancore princely states that became part of Kerala and Karnataka states were different from the feudatory princely states of Chhattisgarh and Orissa in central-eastern India and had progressive rulers and good administrators like the *diwan* Madhav Rao of Travancore. Also, many of the well-governed princely states, such as Mysore, Travancore, Baroda, and Kolhapur, had institutions and laws similar to those in directly ruled British India provinces like Bombay and Madras, and part of the reason for this was that "these states enjoyed for many years the control and guidance of British officials, and the restoration of Home Rule has to only a limited extent involved some reversion to the methods of administration that were for a time altered."[1]

The princely state of Mysore was under British de facto rule for almost sixty years after the defeat of Tipu Sultan in 1799, and the British continued to have control through regents in the court even after they formally handed Mysore back to the Hindu Wodeyar dynasty. The ruler of Travancore carried out reforms when faced with a threat from the British to annex the state, but these extensive reforms were in a way under the direct supervision and influence of the British resident. Fisher (1991: 214) notes that despite the official policy of nonintervention, the Resident continued to interfere in the state administration, and that the "high officials of the state each used to report to the Resident twice every week 'to report extraordinaries, and to confer on public Business.'" So Travancore and Mysore princely states while officially indirect rule, were de facto direct rule for long periods of time and are not really exceptions to my theoretical prediction.

However, a deeper reason traces back to pre-colonial times for why these kingdoms of Travancore and Mysore were more centralized and had higher state capacity and development outcomes. There were different types of princely states in India, and some were more prone to despotic extraction and underdevelopment than others, as outlined in detail in Chapter 6. I briefly recount here the types of princely states and their effects on state capacity, development, and land revenue institutions, which helps understand why the Maoists were not as successful in Kerala and Karnataka.

Tributary/Feudatory States: The princely states in the central-eastern regions of Orissa, Chhattisgarh, and Chhota Nagpur (Jharkhand) could be categorized as tributary/feudatory states and were ruled by Rajput and Maratha princes who were ethnically quite different from the native populations of these regions (Lee 2017). They defeated the Gond and Bhil tribes in central-eastern India and were quite exploitative and extractive. These states often allied with the British and did not oppose them; hence, they were given protection by the colonizers that added to their ability to be extractive. A good example was the Bastar feudatory state, which had Rajput rulers from outside the region, who allowed exploitation of land resources of the Gond tribals under their rule, leading to several tribal rebellions and later Maoist insurgency by the People's War Group (PWG) since 1980s.[2]

Successor States: The princely state of Hyderabad, though much larger in size, was what Ramusack (2004) called one of the successor states of the

---

[1] Lee-Warner, *The Native States of India*, p. 132.
[2] The case of Bastar princely state and how it created conditions for Maoist insurgency in southern Chhattisgarh is analyzed in detail in Chapter 7.

Mughal Empire. It did not have the capacity to resist and was forced to ally with the British and never developed a highly centralized state bureaucracy and tax capacity. Also, the Nizam of Hyderabad was Muslim while the majority of his subjects were Hindus, and he used *deshmukhs* to collect land revenue and extract taxes from his poor peasants. Such despotic extraction and land inequality increased grievances among *Dalits* and *Adivasis* that the Maoists were able to mobilize successfully. Other successor states were Bengal and Awadh in the east. Bengal had a *zamindari* land tenure system and land inequality, which led to the initial Naxalite movement in the 1960s.

Warrior/Conquest States: In contrast, the princely state of Mysore under Tipu Sultan, which formed the rump of the current state of Karnataka, as well as Travancore under Martanda Varma, which became part of the current state of Kerala, were warrior or conquest states and quite different from the successor state of the Mughal Empire that was Hyderabad, or the small feudatory/tributary states in Chhattisgarh and Orissa region (Ramusack 2004). Travancore and Mysore did not ally with the Europeans or get protection from them; thus, they did not develop the pattern of despotic extraction as happened in Hyderabad and Bastar. Mysore under Hyder Ali and then his son Tipu Sultan fought and defeated the British in several wars in the 1760–1780s before Tipu was finally defeated in 1799 in the siege of Seringapatnam. Travancore under Martanda Varma defeated the Dutch East India Company in the 1740s and modernized the army along European lines. Such warfare increased the state capacity of these so-called warrior states that were forced to increase taxation and develop a more efficient police and bureaucracy. Also, the Hindu rulers of Travancore and Cochin were from the region and were focused on providing development to the people who were from their own ethnic group (Lee 2017). While Haider Ali and Tipu Sultan were Muslim rulers of Hindu subjects, they had many Hindu Brahmin officials and ministers. The official rulers of Mysore were the Hindu Wadiyar dynasty to whom the British returned the kingdom after defeating Tipu in 1799.

These differences explain why these warrior states of Travancore/Cochin and Mysore were different and more developed and progressive than the interior protected tributary Chhattisgarh states of Bastar and Surguja, or the successor state of Hyderabad. This variation in type of princely state also explains why there was more development and a more centralized state historically in Travancore and Mysore states that translated into higher levels in the postcolonial period in Kerala and Karnataka respectively (Ramusack 2004). This led to very different patterns of state formation and land inequality in these states, which decreased the chances of success of radical Maoist insurgency later.

See Figure 9.1 for a map of these warrior states of Travancore, Cochin and Mysore.

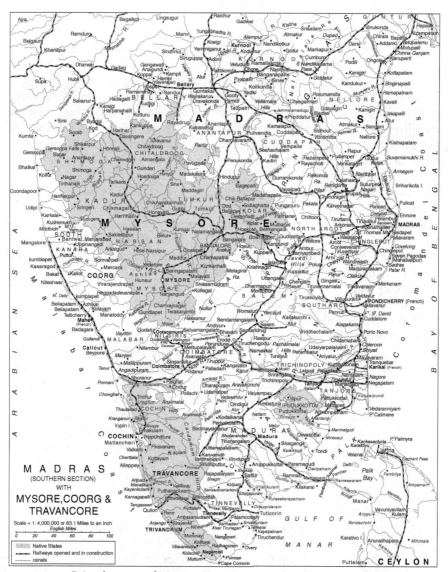

FIGURE 9.1 Princely states of Mysore, Travancore, and Cochin, surrounded by British direct ruled Madras Presidency areas
Source: *Imperial gazetteer of India. Oxford: Clarendon Press, 1907–1909.* Volume 18, opposite page 250. Available from http://dsal.uchicago.edu/maps/gazetteer/images/gazetteer_V18_pg250.jpg

2.2 Path Dependence Reversed by Liberal Postcolonial Governments:

Another reason why these states like Kerala, and Karnataka did not have successful Maoist insurgency since the 1990–2000s is that the postcolonial governments in these provinces reversed some of the historically created land inequality. Theories of colonial legacies are not deterministic, and as Lange (2009) shows, the effect of colonial indirect rule may or may not become path dependent depending on the contingent conditions of particular cases, and in particular the role of postcolonial political elites or parties. In Lange's (2009) analysis of the path dependent effect of British indirect rule, he shows that while many countries that had British direct rule had better developmental outcomes, there are some cases that had British indirect rule like Botswana but reversed path dependence to develop good institutions, and some cases that had British direct rule but still had inefficient institutions. What determines whether or not path dependence is established or broken is whether the postcolonial political elite was able to reverse path dependent mechanisms. In a paper comparing the effects of chieftaincies between Uganda and Sierra Leone, Acemoglu et al. (2013) suggest that colonial indirect rule institutions may or may not lead to ethnic insurgency depending on the relationship of dominant postcolonial politicians with colonial-era chiefs. In Uganda, the postcolonial politicians forced the chiefs of the powerful Buganda kingdom into exile, and this prevented the chiefs from continuing in power, while in Sierra Leone the postcolonial politicians were closely related to the chiefs and allowed chiefly power to continue, which led to despotism continuing and civil war in Sierra Leone.

The contingent postcolonial conditions that Kerala experienced was rule under the Communist Party of India-Marxist–led governments at the state level since the 1960–1970s, alternating with Congress governments. The leftist party-led governments carried out more serious land reform than seen in most other states in India that did not have such progressive leftist parties in power at the state level (Herring 1983; Kohli 1987). In these rare cases like Kerala where the Communist Party of India-Marxist won elections and carried out significant land reforms to reverse path dependence, the pernicious effects of indirect rule and landlordism were reversed (Herring 1983).[3] While the Congress government in Karnataka did not do such comprehensive land reforms in the 1970s, a modicum of progressive policies like tenancy reforms still occurred, particularly in the districts that were part of Mysore princely state that the Maoists later targeted (Kohli, 1987). As a consequence, land inequalities and low levels of development that had been created by the former colonial institutions of princely states and *zamindari* estates were partly reversed by postcolonial governments, and these mechanisms could not become path dependent, which made it difficult for Maoists to mobilize ethnic grievances of tribals and *Dalits*.

---

[3] The state of West Bengal also had CPI-Marxist led left front governments in power since 1970s and did significant land tenancy reforms, which could be part of the explanation for why the Maoists were not as successful in the second phase of Maoist rebellion since 1980s, even though the original CPI-ML led Naxalite movement had started in West Bengal in the 1960s.

Applying these influential cases of Karnataka, and Kerala to the schematic diagram of my theory of indirect rule setting up conditions for insurgency (see Figure 3.3), the causal pathway after India's independence does not move in the direction of path dependence of mechanisms of land inequality. As Bhaskar notes in the Maoist journal *People's March*: "More than six hundred states and all zamindari estates, the colonial legacy of the hated Permanent Settlement, were formally abolished. ... Some land reform programmes were initiated by various ruling class governments in the next decades, most notably in Kashmir, Keralam, Karnataka and, to a lesser degree, in Paschim Banga."[4] This shows even Maoist writers are aware that land reforms were more effective in Kerala, Karnataka, and West Bengal than in other states in India. In these cases where leftist parties or a Congress Party leader with an antipoverty agenda emerged to carry out land reforms or reduce the local power of previous landlords and princes, the chances of Maoist insurgency later in the 1980s were reduced.

This is in contrast to the Congress and Janata Dal Party governments in the states of Madhya Pradesh/Chhattisgarh and Bihar, and the Congress and Telugu Desam Parties in Andhra Pradesh that did not do serious land reforms since the middle- and upper-caste landlords who were part of the ruling classes had vested interests and prevented such reforms, thus paving the way for Maoist insurgency later. Unlike the cases of Chhattisgarh, Andhra Pradesh, Bihar, Orissa, and Jharkhand, where inequalities persisted and became path dependent, these exceptional cases of Kerala and Karnataka saw path dependence being reversed by progressive postcolonial political parties, which led to lower inequality and thus less chance of success of Maoist rebels. Studying these cases thus validates my theory of colonial legacies and shows that the theory is not deterministic and allows for the possibility of reversal of path dependence by a political party that is committed to reforms. These are what Gerring (2007) calls influential cases where the apparent deviations or exceptionalism does not really challenge the theory, once the exact circumstances have been analyzed. Instead, it reveals certain other conditions that once explained enrich the theory and allow it to explain these cases of Karnataka and Kerala.

3   WHY MAOISTS WERE NOT AS SUCCESSFUL IN KARNATAKA

In this section, I focus on the case of Karnataka state in India to demonstrate how being a different type of princely state and having progressive political parties that did land reforms reduce the chances of successful Maoist mobilization.

---

[4] Bhaskar, "A Decade of 'Developing' Displacement," in *People's March Supplement: A Decade of Struggle and Sacrifice*, September 2014.

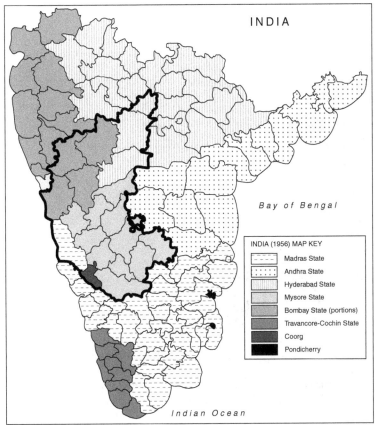

FIGURE 9.2 Map of Karnataka, formed out of various princely states and British direct rule areas following the linguistic reorganization of Indian states in 1956
Source: https://en.wikipedia.org/wiki/Mysore_State#/media/File:Karnataka_1965_Reorg
.svg

Karnataka was formed on November 1, 1956, following linguistic reorganization in the 1950–1960s by combining districts that had Kannada-speaking people from former Mysore princely state, Hyderabad princely state, and a few districts that were part of Bombay and Madras Presidency that were colonial direct rule. This is clear by comparing the maps in Figures 9.2 and 9.3 of current Karnataka state and how this was formed out of the former British direct and indirect ruled areas. The state of Karnataka provides an ideal case in which different types of princely states and British direct rule left legacies and is useful to study its long-term effects on the ability of the Maoists to mobilize successfully. I use qualitative data for this brief analysis, but future research could build sub-district datasets for Karnataka and do quantitative testing, as I have done for Andhra Pradesh and Chhattisgarh in previous chapters.

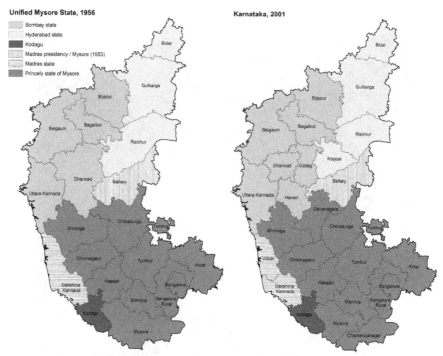

FIGURE 9.3A,B Comparing current districts of Karnataka with colonial era princely states and British direct rule
Source: www.censusindia.gov.in/maps/State_Maps/StateMaps_links/karnataka01.html and https://en.wikipedia.org/wiki/Mysore_State#/media/File:Mysore_1956.jpg

3.1   Maoists Attempts in Malnad Region of Karnataka State Not Fully Successful

The Maoists often strategically targeted certain regions that they believed were ripe for rebellion based on the terrain as well as socioeconomic conditions of the people. In 2001, the PWG Maoists planned to expand into the Malnad area in Karnataka state along the Western Ghats. The Karnataka unit of the PWG had been formed in 1980; after its failure to establish a base in Raichur district, the PWG recognized the Malnad area along the hilly Western Ghats range that spanned from north to south across several districts of Karnataka as a viable area, and twenty-five trained cadres were sent there in 2001.[5] They had previously surveyed this area in a report called *Perspective for Agrarian Work in Karnataka, 1987,* since they considered the terrain as well as social conditions to be conducive for revolution.

[5] Suba Chandran and Chari (eds.), *Armed Conflicts in South Asia 2011,* p. 271

In a report based on socioeconomic investigation in Karnataka, the CPI-ML (People's War) wrote as follows:

The Western Ghats ... runs from North to South for about 2,200 kms. ... It passes through Kerala, TN, Karnataka, Goa, Maharashtra and Gujarat. ... The Western Ghats that runs through Karnataka is called as the Malnad. ... The Western Ghats has its strategic significance for peoples' war in India owing to the forest and mountainous terrain. The population of Malnad is about one-tenth of that of the entire state. ... It passes through 10 of Karnataka's 27 districts. ... While its terrain is of strategic value for ppw in India, the above mentioned additional factors enhance its strategic significance. ...

The Perspective Area falls in the central part of Malnad. ... It includes parts ... of the forested areas of Udupi, Shimoga, Chikmagalur and Dakshina Kannada districts. It covers an area of about 10,000 sq kms in eight taluks. By deploying adequate squads, organizing the masses in class struggle and conducting guerrilla warfare here, the Perspective Area will gradually emerge as a Guerrilla Zone. *Hence the Perspective Area is that area which we plan to develop as a Guerrilla Zone.* ... Today we have initiated our work in one part of the Perspective Area. We are currently working in parts of five taluks.[6]

In spite of their careful plans in 2001, the PWG Maoists were not as successful in expanding to and setting up base areas in the Malnad zone in Karnataka. Another document released during the 9th Unity Congress held in 2007 by the CPI-Maoist notes that the Maoists were working in five squad areas composed of four districts and five urban centers in five districts in this area. However, the "movement in the strategic area is still weak. Our mass base is not very strong. There is a serious shortcoming from the SC in concentrating on the area and consolidation."[7] The Central Committee member of PWG and Karnataka State Committee Secretary Sende Rajamouli was arrested in Kollam in Kerala on June 22, 2007, and his successor Nandakumar was arrested on June 1, 2010, in Hyderabad, which reduced the ability of the CPI-Maoist to expand much in the Malnad area. Some level of violence continued with fifteen Naxalites, nine security forces, and six civilians having lost their lives in 2005–2011 (Suba Chandran & Chari 2012: 272). On June 5, 2017, three Maoists surrendered to the police in Chikmagalur district in Karnataka, taking the total number who surrendered to thirteen since 2010. This seems to be an indication of the failing Maoist movement and its reduced organizational capacity in the Malnad area.[8]

In fact, early on, there was a split in the Maoist movement, with one group suggesting that it was not possible to mobilize successfully in the Malnad area

---

[6] CPI-ML (PW), *Karnataka: Social Conditions and Tactics.*

[7] CPI-Maoist, *Political Organization Review of CPI (Maoist)*, January 2007, p. 29.

[8] "Naxal movement fading away in Karnataka," *The Hindu*, June 7, 2017; see also, "Naxalite movement at a low ebb in Malnad region as 3 more surrender," June 5, 2017, www.news-karnataka.com

and they should focus on urban areas. This was rejected as "right opportunism" by the CPI-Maoist leadership, who continued to insist that there were still feudal relationships in the Malnad, and they should keep trying to mobilize in this area.[9] This resulted in this group leaving and forming the Karnataka Maoist Independence Center, which was later renamed Revolutionary Communist Party of Karnataka (RCP) in 2007. The RCP noted that "choosing Malnad as perspective area was a strategic goof up, as though Malnad's topography favoured guerrilla warfare but the region was relatively developed with people growing commercial crops" (Suba Chandran & Chari 2012: 271).

3.2 Direct Intervention by British in Warrior State of Mysore for Long Periods of Time Increased State Capacity and Development

Why did the CPI-Maoist fail to convert the Malnad region along the Western Ghats into a Maoist guerilla zone, as it planned to do as early as 2001? Why has the movement petered out? It seems that the analysis of the Revolutionary Communist Party of Karnataka (RCP), which split from the CPI-Maoist because of a difference of opinion on the viability of Maoist success in the Malnad region was possibly correct. Maybe the Chikmagalur, South Kannada, Udupi, and Shimoga districts in the Malnad region of current Karnataka that were targeted by the CPI-Maoist did not have the conditions of landlord-based domination and high levels of land inequality as prevalent under the *zamindari* land tenure systems in Bihar or the *deshmukh*-based land tenure systems in Hyderabad.

Looking at Figure 9.2, which is the historical map of which princely states and direct rule areas formed Karnataka, and Figure 9.3, which compares the district map of current Karnataka state with colonial era boundaries of direct and indirect rule, it is clear that two of the coastal region districts of South Kannada and Udupi that were part of the Malnad region targeted by the Maoists had been part of British direct rule as Madras province. They had thus been exposed to higher levels of governance and public good distribution. Since Madras province had *ryotwari* land tenure, which was relatively more equal in terms of land revenue structures, so these districts did not have as much feudal relations and land inequality as in the Telangana region of former Hyderabad princely state. The CPI-Maoist thus was not as successful in South Kannada and Udupi. This is well explained by my theoretical framework that directly ruled areas in colonial times had relatively better development and less land inequality, and thus less chance of insurgency.

Looking at Figures 9.3A and 9.3B, we can also see that two of the other districts targeted by the Maoists – Shimoga and Chikmagalur – had been part of the former Mysore princely state. However, Mysore under rulers like Haidar Ali and then later his son Tipu Sultan was a warrior/conquest state (Ramusack 2004), which fought four wars against the British between 1766 and 1799 and

---

[9] See CPI-ML (PW), *Karnataka: Social Conditions and Tactics.*

built up a strong army and bureaucracy and infrastructure, as compared with weaker feudatory states like Bastar or Orissa, or successor states like Hyderabad, which never confronted the British. Under Haider Ali and Tipu Sultan, Mysore state became highly centralized and developed higher levels of public goods.

The region of Mysore was traditionally ruled by the Hindu Wadiyar dynasty dating back to 1399. The Wadiyars were petty chieftains in the ancient Vijayanagara Empire and by 1610 the last agent of the Vijayanagara king sold Seringapatnam fort to Raja Wadiyar, after which the Wadiyars evolved from petty chieftains to royal rulers and expanded Mysore state (Ramusack 2004: 29–30; Stein 1985). The increase in state capacity of Mysore can be traced to the reign of Chikkadevaraja Wadiyar, who ruled from 1672 to 1704 and increased general revenue collected by state officials and also exempted lands held by his soldiers from revenue demand, thus substantially increasing his centralized military capacity (Stein 1985: 400–401).

Disputes over succession to the throne in the mid-eighteenth century led Krishnaraja Wadiyar II (1734–65) to seek the help of a Muslim general Haidar Ali (1722–82). Haidar Ali carried out a successful coup in 1761 and became the de facto ruler of Mysore from 1761 to 1782, though officially he continued to accept the suzerainty of the Wadiyar king and also sought legitimacy from the Mughal Empire (Ramusack 2004: 30). Haidar Ali modernized his army along European lines and 8,000 of his infantry were armed with musket and 4,000 with matchlocks, and mercenary Eurasian officers led them (Roy 2005: 668).[10] During Haidar Ali's reign, a new system of fiscalism was built upon the foundations laid by Chikkadevaraja Wadiyar. Large territories were auctioned to powerful Hindu warriors who became tax farmers or *amildars* and extracted taxes from lesser chieftains and passed them on to the Mysore treasury (Stein 1985: 401).

Tipu Sultan (1753–99) succeeded his father Haidar Ali in 1782; he further tried to create a "centralized military machine" for which he increased state control of local political units and increased state revenues. To finance his expanding military, cash crops such as sugar cane were encouraged, and state-supported trading centers were opened that allowed the state to penetrate more deeply into the local rural economy and undermine the power of intermediary chiefs and revenue farmers. Overall, Tipu tried to develop a centralized state and revenue system to fund his wars and this led to bureaucratic development and modernization (Ramusack 2004: 31).

Stein (1985: 391–92) describes this development in Mysore under Haidar Ali and Tipu Sultan as military fiscalism. Under Tipu Sultan, the "Mysore system of military fiscalism was brought to its highest point" (Stein 1985: 401). To strengthen the land revenue collection system, Tipu directly appointed provincial governors or *asaf*, who appointed *amildars* or tax collectors. Each

---

[10] Roy, "Military Synthesis in South Asia."

amildar was assisted by two *sheristadars*. In this centralized system, village settlements were made with hereditary headmen who had to be active cultivators, and accountants kept revenue records of each village (Stein 1985: 402). Bayley (1988: 28) notes that "Haidar Ali and Tipu Sultan tried to eliminate all intermediaries between themselves and the peasant farmers, subjecting them to new demands for the punctual payment of revenue." Thus it was a more intrusive and equitable system of land revenue, similar to the *ryotwari* land tenure systems developed later by Thomas Munro in Madras, and resulted in more land revenue and also less land inequality.

Foa (2016: 21) suggests that such warrior state regimes established a stock of "infrastructural power" at the local level to mobilize revenue and personnel. It required the expansion of bureaucratic capacity in the form of an army of civil servants and a documentary system to keep track of land surveys and rights. Bayley (1983) estimates that between 1600 and 1800, Mysore "upped its nominal tax revenue from under 10 percent of the gross produce to about 40 percent under Tipu Sultan in 1790s." See Table 9.1 for revenue and tax rates of warrior and successor states in pre-colonial India.

Following the defeat of Tipu Sultan in the Battle of Seringapatnam in 1799, Governor General Lord Wellesley decided to restore to the throne the "ancient" Hindu Wadiyar dynasty: he believed it was not feasible for the East India Company to provide the personnel to administer such a large region (Fisher 1991: 404–6). Wellesley appointed Purnia, who was one of Tipu Sultan's former ministers to the post of *diwan* and appointed a British officer as Resident to the court of the Wadiyar prince who was a minor. The first twelve years with Purnia resulted in excellent governance and generated huge revenue surpluses. However, with the coming of age of the Wadiyar prince, he

TABLE 9.1 *Revenue and taxation per capita in pre-colonial India*
Taxation figures refer to dates from the period 1770–1820

Polity	Revenue (£m)	Population (m)	Tax per capita (£)
Warrior/Conquest States			
Maratha Peshwa	4.0	5.0	0.80
Mysore Empire	4.0	8.0	0.50
Travancore	0.25	0.9	0.27
Successor States			
Bengal	5.8	40	0.15
Hyderabad	1.5	10.7	0.14
Awadh	0.79	6.5	0.12

Source: Adapted from Foa, *Ancient Polities, Modern States*, p. 174.

demanded his rights in 1811, and disagreements between the king and Purnia resulted in dismissal of the minister. Within a few years, the British Resident reported that the new Wadiyar ruler was being accused of misrule and the revenue surpluses had disappeared (Fisher 1991: 408–10).

As a result of this perceived misadministration, Governor General Bentinck decided to intervene and from 1831 to 1881, Mysore was ruled by the British through a commission that administered the state through British officers appointed by the Company (Fisher 1991: 410–11). This period of direct British administration led to the adoption of some of the British structures of administration and governance into princely Mysore, and probably left bureaucratic organizational residues that persisted into the postcolonial period when Mysore became part of the state of Karnataka.[11]

During this period under direct British tutelage, the state centralization and more direct land revenue collection systems continued to build on the earlier institutional development under Tipu Sultan. The policy of military fiscalism was continued by the British in Madras Presidency, and the East India Company continued to have high military expenditure as a percentage of total expenditure in Madras Presidency from 1804 to 1816, which forced it to increase its total revenue collections (Stein 1985: 404–5). Another element of continuity was that Sir Thomas Munro who was a well-known advocate for the *ryotwari* land tenure system in Madras Presidency in the 1820s was the joint secretary of commissioners for the Settlement of Mysore. Munro tried to remove the power of the local chiefs or *poligars*, as Tipu Sultan had done, and used nonnative administrators like Maratha Brahmins to collect land revenues directly from the villages. The elimination of the "stratum of chiefly authorities – raja and poligar – was as assiduously pressed by Munro as it had been by Tipu Sultan" and he opposed the use of chiefly intermediaries like *poligars* and *zamindars* (Stein 1985: 406). This may have resulted in a more direct and relatively equitable land revenue collection system in Mysore, as compared with the *zamindari* land tenure system in Bengal.

The long-term effects of having warrior/conquest states and then continuation of similar policies of land tenure and state centralization resulted in the districts of old Mysore state having low levels of inequality in distribution of land, and the state had "one of the highest proportions of owner-cultivators and lowest incidences of landlessness in the subcontinent" (Manor 1980: 202). Further evidence comes from a study by a team of people from the Center for Socialist Studies, Bangalore, which did social investigations in the Maoist-affected Malnad area on March 11–12, 2005, and found that the feudal system and economic inequalities that are usually found in other areas with Maoist influence were not found in this area.[12] The study found that the main

---

[11] Manor, *Political Change in an Indian State*; Gustafson, "Mysore 1881–1902," and other studies discuss the dynamics of development in Mysore princely state.

[12] Raviprasad Kamila, "Study reveals causes for Naxalism in Malnad," *The Hindu*, September 1, 2005.

Districts in the North and East of Karnataka Have Very High Poverty

District-level poverty, 2012

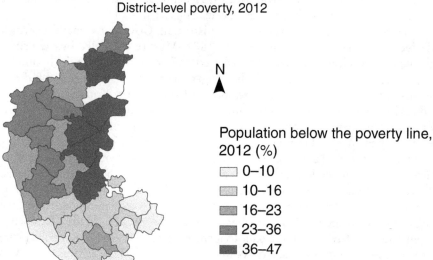

N
▲

Population below the poverty line, 2012 (%)

▢ 0–10
▨ 10–16
▩ 16–23
◪ 23–36
◼ 36–47
▢ No data

FIGURE: 9.4 Karnataka district-level poverty, 2012
Source: World Bank Document, *Karnataka – Poverty, Growth, Inequality,* http://documents.worldbank.org/curated/en/479831504091412309/pdf/119189-BRI-P157572-Karnataka-Poverty.pdf

grievance among the tribals was not to do with feudal relations but rather the establishment of the Kudramukh National Park, which proposed to displace tribals and forest dwellers, and led to some support for Naxalites.[13]

Figure 9.4 shows a map from a World Bank report on Karnataka that if compared with Figure 9.3 shows that the northern districts that were part of Hyderabad princely state were worse off in terms of poverty, while southern and eastern districts that were part of Mysore princely states were better off. Since the Maoists targeted the eastern and coastal districts, they did not find very high levels of inequality and poverty there.

Foa (2016: 24, footnote 15), in his dissertation on the long-term effects of pre-colonial kingdoms, finds that Karnataka state raises 9.8 percent of its gross state product in taxation, which is the highest level in India, a country where most states have weak fiscal compliance. Foa (2016: 24) proposes that it is plausible that Karnataka, which was known as "new Mysore" till 1973 and was built around the region that had the Mysore kingdom, has "drawn on the

---

[13] Raviprasad Kamila, "Kudremukh issue gave rise to Naxalism," *The Hindu,* November 8, 2011.

loyalties, organization, and bureaucratic infrastructure generated by the Mysore Empire, the key challenger to British hegemony in eighteenth-century southern India." Foa (2016: 117) also cites survey evidence that shows that there is intrastate variation within Karnataka in "level of confidence in local government to implement public projects." While the northern parts of Karnataka that were not part of Mysore state had much lower levels of confidence, the southern parts that had been part of Mysore had much higher levels of confidence.

Because Mysore state was a warrior/conquest state under Tipu Sultan and then later from 1831 to 1881 was practically under direct rule/control of the British Residents, it had higher levels of bureaucratic/state capacity and development and lower land inequality than most other princely states. As a consequence, while the CPI-Maoist correctly analyzed the Malnad area as favorable in terms of terrain, it did not have the same historically created inequalities and low development, which the Maoists found in Telangana, Bastar, or Bihar/ Jharkhand. This case is a good example of how rebel agency is constrained by the lack of historically created ethnic mobilization networks. This explains why the Maoists did not succeed in creating guerrilla zones in Shimoga and Chikmagalur districts of Karnataka that had been part of Mysore state.

3.3 Successful Land Tenancy Reforms in Karnataka Partly Reversed Path Dependence

Another reason why it was challenging for the Maoists to succeed in the hilly terrain of the Malnad districts was the relatively successful land reforms in Karnataka in the 1970s. This reduced grievances and did not provide the Maoists with the ethnic mobilization networks discussed in my theoretical framework. Not only did some of these districts have higher development and state capacity to start with because they had been part of Mysore warrior princely state, but also this effect was multiplied by relatively successful land tenancy reforms in some of these districts targeted by the Maoists.

Studies by James Manor (1980) find that there was successful land reforms in Karnataka, under Devraj Urs who became the chief minister of Karnataka in 1972 and ruled till 1980. He was primarily appointed by Prime Minister Indira Gandhi to overthrow the old Congress leaders following the split in the Congress due to Indira Gandhi leaving the old Congress and forming her own Congress (I). Till then, the dominant Vokkaliga and Lingayat castes had controlled Karnataka politics, and Devraj Urs was the first chief minister of Karnataka who was not from these dominant caste groups, but from a small *jati*/caste. For his own survival, he had to "mobilize support among the less powerful sections of society" who formed more than 60 percent of the state's population and included various backward castes.[14] He did this by several progressive policies, in particular land tenancy reforms introduced in 1973

---

[14] James Manor, "Pragmatic Progressives in Regional Politics", p. 202.

that were particularly successful in the districts of South and North Kannada along the coastal region.

According to Manor (1980: 203), while there was corruption and pressure in the tribunals that were supposed to administer the applications for tenancy, overall there was success for these new tenancy reforms. Manor reports that by the end of November 1979, a total of 798,582 applications had been received from people claiming to be tenants "who qualified for ownership of the lands they worked. Of these applications, 530,441 had been dealt with by land tribunals. 319,909 or 60.3 % of these cases had been decided in favour of tenants, with 1,249,174 acres being thus distributed."

Kohli (1987) provides a contrasting evaluation of the success of land reforms in Karnataka: while Devraj Urs started a land reform program in Karnataka, it was not entirely successful. While there was some success in tenancy law reforms, there was not much of an attempt to redistribute surplus lands, and the powerful landlords of the Vokkaliga and Lingayat castes often did not lose their lands and continued to have political power in the state, which shows the reproduction of landed elite power through path dependence, as suggested by Mahoney (2000). Kohli (1987: 155) suggests this occurred even though Chief Minister Devraj Urs was a populist because the land reform program was merely a ploy to get the votes of the poor and lower castes. Unlike the Communist Party of India-Marxist (CPI-M) government in West Bengal that believed in class conflict, for the Congress government in Karnataka in the 1970s, while "the needs of the lower classes were emphasized, this was not at the cost of expropriating the propertied or even disrupting the class structure."[15] While Devraj Urs moved away from dependence on the existing landowning elite from the Vokkaliga and Lingayat dominant castes, and brought several Backward Castes into the ruling coalition, his "ideological principles did not hold out any real threat to the propertied as a whole" (Kohli 1987: 156).

This analysis by Kohli (1987) matches with the claim by the CPI-Maoist, who similarly suggest in their document *Social Conditions and Tactics in Karnataka* that the land reforms did not really change much on the ground, and that "former landlords continue to enjoy their big landlord status even after the land reform in most of the cases" and that "land reform has not fetched land to the Dalits who were the bonded laborers in the households of landlords."[16] Maybe this is what prompted the Maoists to try to mobilize in the Malnad region of Karnataka where terrain was also favorable.

However, a more detailed analysis shows that while surplus land redistribution did not succeed in Karnataka's 1974 land reform, there was higher success in tenancy reforms, as was the case in West Bengal. According to new tenancy laws introduced in Karnataka, those who were tenants on

---

[15] Kohli, *The State and Poverty in India*, p. 155.
[16] CPI-ML (PW), *Karnataka: Social Conditions and Tactics*, pp. 22–23.

March 1, 1974, when the tenancy law was passed would have occupancy rights to the land and could not be evicted from the land they were cultivating. The state would compensate the landlords for their lands (Kohli 1987: 167). Tribunals were set up to hear cases and there were 800,335 applications filed by tenants involving 42.7 millions of acres between 1975 and 1980, of which 342,843 applications were decided in favor of tenants (Kohli 1987: 168–69, table 4.6). By the end of the program in 1981, "185 million acres of land was legally transferred to tenants" (Kohli 1987:172). This shows some level of success in tenancy reforms as compared with other states in India, where land reforms were a failure.

Kohli (1987: 175) also finds subregional variation within Karnataka in the success of such tenancy reforms. The coastal districts of North and South Kannada were targeted by the Maoists, but as is clear by comparing Figures 9.3A and 9.3B, these areas had been part of Bombay and Madras Presidency, which were directly ruled and supposed to have *ryotwari tenure*. This may explain why Table 9.2 shows that they had almost 99.25 percent of their land under tenancy, and landlords were not from dominant Vokkaliga and Lingayat castes. Also, Devraj Urs found it easier to do land reforms in these former direct ruled districts, and as Table 9.2 shows, they had almost 60 percent success in tenancy reforms, which again made it difficult for Maoists to succeed later in these districts, because of lower land inequality to start with and then relatively more successful land tenancy reforms.

TABLE 9.2 *Regional variations in Karnataka's land reforms*

Region (districts)	Land under tenancy in early 1970s (A)	Land acquired by former tenants (B)	Rate of success (percentage of B to A)
Coastal (North and South Kannada* districts)	5240 (99.25%)	3138	60 %
Eastern (Chikmagalur,* Coorg, Hassan, and Shimoga* districts)	1675 (8.19%)	1157	70 %
Southern (Bangalore, Kolar, Mandya, Mysore, Tumkur)	5417 (9.69%)	755	14 %
Northern (Belgaum, Bellary, Bidar, Bijapur, Chitradurga, Dharwar, Gulbarga, and Raichur districts)	25,772 (18.29%)	7955	31 %
Karnataka total	38,086 (17.14%)	13,005	34 %

* = *districts targeted by Maoists in Malnad region*
Source: Kohli, *The State and Poverty in India*, table 4.10, p. 175.

The Maoists also targeted the districts of Chikmagalur and Shimoga in the hilly Western Ghats in the Malnad, which were part of the eastern region. As Table 9.2 shows, Chikmagalur and Shimoga had an almost 70 percent success rate in tenancy reforms. Comparing Figures 9.3A and 9.3B, it is clear that these districts were formerly part of Mysore princely state. Tenancy reforms in Chikmagalur and Shimoga districts were relatively successful, may have reduced inequality to some extent, and reversed some of the potential path dependence, thus making it even more difficult for the CPI-Maoist to successfully recruit in this region in 2005–7, by not providing them with the historically created ethnic mobilization networks from tribals with grievances due to land inequality. Interestingly, it was the northern and southern region districts in Table 9.2 that were not part of Malnad hilly region and so were not targeted by the Maoists that had much lower (31 percent and 14 percent) levels of success in tenancy reforms. Unfortunately for the Maoists, it seems they got their strategic calculations wrong about which districts to target in Karnataka.

4   MAOIST FAILURE IN KERALA

Due to space constraints, I briefly explain why the Maoists did not succeed in Kerala, which future research can analyze in more detail. In the initial phase of 1967–76, Naxalite groups emerged in Kerala, accompanying the "Spring Thunder" that was happening in Bengal and Andhra Pradesh. The first ever incident was a raid on the Thalassery police station in North Malabar's Kannur district on November 21, 1968. The attack was not successful, since of the 1,000 Naxals who were supposed to take part in the raid, only 315 turned up; when the lone grenade launched failed to explode, the group fled. Two days later, there was a successful attack carried out on the Pulpalli police wireless station that resulted in the deaths of some policemen. The Congress government responded to these increasing attacks on police stations and landlords by launching a counterinsurgency operation that led to several Naxal leaders being arrested and prominent leader Arikkad Verghese being killed, and the incipient movement was crushed by 1976. Since then Maoist insurgency in Kerala declined and did not escalate in the 1980–90s as compared with other states like Bihar, Chhattisgarh, and Andhra Pradesh where the MCC and PWG slowly developed and expanded their operations.[17]

In recent times, there has been some resurgence by the CPI-Maoist, targeting certain districts in the Wayanad region of Kerala. For example on December 7, 2014, personnel of Thunderbolt, the elite paramilitary commando unit of the Kerala Police had an encounter with a six-member team of the Communist Party of India-Maoist (CPI-Maoist) at the Chappa forest area located on

---

[17] Bibhu Routray, "Return of the Native: CPI-Maoist in Kerala," March 16, 2015, www.ipcs.org/comm_select.php?articleNo=4850

Kozhikode-Wayanad border.[18] There have been media reports of some resurgence of Maoists in the Karnataka-Kerala-Tamil Nadu tri-junction area since 2018, with the hilly tracts of the Western Ghats in the southern Karnataka-Kerala border region being used as a safe haven for cadres and Maoist camps.[19] However, the level of violence has never increased very much and it seems that CPI-Maoist does not consider Kerala as a central part of its strategic plan, but more as a safe haven for camps.

This seems to make Kerala an exception to my theoretical prediction, since Kerala is composed of the two princely states of Travancore and Cochin in the south and the Malabar districts of Madras Presidency in the north that, though directly ruled, had extractive *zamindari estates* that resulted in rack renting (Herring 1983). However, much like the case of Karnataka, the princely states of Travancore and Cochin in Kerala were warrior states, which led to increased state capacity and progressive policies, and there were communist parties in Kerala that built on these progressive policies from the past.

Warrior/Conquest State: In 1729, Martanda Varma became the raja of the medieval kingdom of Venad, which he converted into the state of Travancore (Panikkar, 1960). He tried to create a centralized state after executing his Nayar chiefs and selling their wives and children into slavery. He started conquering and absorbing the territories of neighboring chiefs; by 1758 when he died, Travancore included around 7,000 square miles of territory. He brought in Tamil and Maratha brahmins to administer the new territories and removed the local chiefs, much like Tipu Sultan removed the local *poligar* chiefs (Ramusack 2004: 33–34). Having displaced the Nayar chiefs, Varma worked with the priests to create an efficient bureaucracy and in 1750 formalized the alliance by dedicating the entire territory of Travancore state to the deity *Sri Padmanabha* of whom he was the first servant (Foa 2016: 93).

To fund his increasing military expenditures, Martanda Varma introduced a low land tax in 1739, but the majority of revenues was generated from an "elaborate system of personal taxes and fines, covering not only life rituals such as marriages, childbirth, and death, but also the consumption and export of commodities (salt and pepper), personal and capital goods such as country boats, ploughs" (Foa 2016: 93–94). The net effect was that in 1853 per capita taxation in Travancore was among the highest in India, even though land revenue was low. This high level of revenues allowed Travancore state to build a "highly centralized military force" and invest large amounts for construction of fortification and temples. Varma defeated the Dutch East India Company in 1741 in the Battle of Colachel and appointed its captured Flemish captain, De

---

[18] Routray, "Return of the Native."
[19] Shaswati Das, "Naxals regrouping in Tamil Nadu, Kerala, Karnataka: Police," July 4, 2018, www.livemint.com/Politics/sSFEYAkyS22Kei4ioHUNkI/KeralaKarnatakaTN-sees-strong-Maoist-resurgence-Intellige.html

Lannoy, as the general of his own army and tried to develop a European-style army focused on cannons, infantry, and firearms (Foa 2016: 94).

The centralized state started by Martanda Varma is considered to be the starting point for the future development of Travancore. During the reign of the next king Rama Varma, Travancore faced threats from Mysore; in 1795, the Travancore king concluded a treaty of subsidiary alliance with the East India Company (Ramusack 2004: 34). This increased indirect control by the British Resident over Travancore beginning in 1805, when the East India Company helped subdue a rebellion by the Nayar castes. In 1811, *Diwan* Colonel John Munro reduced the power of local court officials, abolished various taxes, and tried to create an administrative structure like districts and sub-districts in British India. Thus British indirect control and threat of annexation may have also played a role in the continuing reforms by the Travancore rulers (Desai 2005: 465).

Jeffrey (1976: 64–103) discusses the modernization in land revenue collection, the inclusion of Western-educated bureaucrats like the *Diwan* Madhava Rao at the helm of the administration, and the expansion of the Public Works Department (PWD) leading to expansion of the road network in princely Travancore since 1863. Jeffrey (1978) points out that the social reforms like temple-entry movement for lower castes in the 1950s were unintentional consequences of previous political-administrative reforms in the 1860s by Travancore's rulers. Desai (2005: 459) notes that Travancore was set apart even from other princely states that undertook reforms because of the vast public health measures it undertook, which required an "expansion in the capacity of the state – the collection of vital statistics and the administration of public health measures." These reforms led to the growth of the infrastructural power of the state, which was "arguably more far-reaching than in most directly ruled British provinces" (Desai, 2005: 483).

Desai (2005) describes how in 1865, the Travancore monarchy gave full ownership rights of land to state tenants and allowed them to transfer or sell their lands. This resulted in untouchable castes like Ezhavas and Syrian Christians to use cash savings to acquire small parcels of land. Land concentration among the upper castes was thus reduced. This presaged future land reforms by the Communist Party in the 1960s. According to Desai, these state formation and welfare policies and land reforms undertaken by the princely states during the nineteenth century had a path dependent influence on the ability of the Communist Party governments to carry out even more extensive reforms after the 1960s, by mobilizing the lower castes, and further deepening these institutions of good governance.

Communist Party Rule Reversed Path Dependence

Kerala has seen the parliamentary leftist parties like the Communist Party of India-Marxist (CPI-M) being successful electorally, forming governments since the 1960s, and carrying out an extensive land reform program, besides other progressive politics (Herring 1983).

Heller (1995: 648–49) discussed how the undivided Communist Party of India (CPI) won elections in Kerala in 1957 on the basis of radical redistributive demands. While Nehru dismissed the communist government in 1959 and imposed President's Rule, the CPI-M returned to power in 1967 and started redistributive political program and land reforms. Since the CPI-M was a highly disciplined cadre-based party, it was able to successfully consolidate a "broad-based alliance of poor peasants, agricultural labourers and workers into a political class" and through various agitational methods like strikes and land-grab movements in 1970s was able to take on the alliance of landlords, plantation owners, upper castes who sided with the Congress Party and opposed such land reforms (Heller 1995: 648). Thus the vested interest of upper-caste elites and landlords who prevented land reforms in other states in India like Andhra Pradesh and Bihar was overcome, and the path dependent effects of indirect revenue collection institutions like *zamindari* or *deshmukh* tenure was reversed in Kerala. This reduction in inequality meant that Maoist rebels did not have historically created ethnic inequalities and weak state capacity to mobilize *Dalits* and tribals for successful rebellion in the 1980–90s.

5 CONCLUSION

Addressing these seemingly exceptional cases of Karnataka and Kerala in this chapter shows that they are not really exceptions once the nuances of these cases are understood in detail. In fact, both these cases were a different type of princely state from that of Hyderabad in Andhra Pradesh and Bastar in Chhattisgarh that we analyzed in earlier chapters. Also there was direct British intervention and administration for long periods of time in Mysore and Travancore that did not happen as much in Hyderabad and Bastar. Finally, progressive political parties in Kerala and Karnataka reversed path dependence, which did not happen in Chhattisgarh and Andhra Pradesh.

In this chapter we looked at potential exceptions and showed that these are influential cases (Gerring 2007) that are actually well predicted by my theory of colonial legacies once the nuances of the cases are understood. In the next chapter, I look beyond India to see if the theory of colonial legacies of indirect rule has broader applicability. In particular, I focus on the cases of British indirect rule in Burma and Pakistan, which were also part of the British Empire in South Asia. I also briefly discuss other cases of British and Spanish colonialism beyond South Asia where the theory travels, which could be analyzed in more detail in future research. While the concept of direct-indirect rule does not directly apply to Spanish colonialism in Latin America and elsewhere, it is still useful to see how dependence on pre-colonial intermediaries in other empires lead to similar outcomes of ethnic and land inequalities and sometimes rebellion.

Frontiers of Empire: Indirect Rule and Insurgency in Burma and Pakistan

I INTRODUCTION

This book focuses on the case of the Maoist insurgency in India to show that historical institutions like colonial indirect rule created structural conditions of ethnic inequality among *Dalits* and *Adivasis* that were later used by Maoist rebels to mobilize these ethnic groups. Does colonial indirect rule have similar effects in other cases of British colonialism in South Asia and beyond? How generalizable is this theory to other colonizers besides the British, for example, Spanish and French colonial rule? This chapter analyzes other cases of British and Spanish colonial rule, to show that the mechanisms of land and natural resource extraction and lower development that are evident in India are also to be found in other countries. The goal of this chapter is not to provide detailed micro-level evidence and causal analysis of path dependence but to provide broad descriptive evidence through some case studies of how colonial indirect rule has long-term causal effects leading to insurgency. While this book uses fine-grained analysis of the Maoist insurgency in India to show that colonial indirect rule caused weak state capacity, ethnic grievances, and insurgency, future scholarship needs to analyze if similar colonial legacies created conditions for insurgency in other countries within South Asia and beyond.

In India, the erstwhile princely state of Kashmir has had secessionist insurgency since 1989 (Bose 2003; Ganguly 1996), which declined in violence in recent times but flared up again in 2019 following the BJP government in India removing Kashmir's special autonomy status. Several northeastern states of India like Manipur, Nagaland, Tripura, and Mizoram have had colonial indirect rule in tribal areas and have seen multiple ethnic secessionist insurgencies after independence (Baruah 2005). Marwah (2009: 176) notes about India's northeast that "The British had realized the difficulties of directly ruling this region. Unfortunately, the policy of colonial neglect has continued even in the post-independence era. The British had segregated the area into three broad categories: regulated areas, scheduled districts, backward tracts and partially or excluded areas."

A deeper look into the past reveals that within India almost all the states that have had insurgency were previously exposed to some form of colonial indirect rule. According to Jafa (1999),

A number of areas which the British ruled indirectly through native princes or tribal chiefs up to 1947 have shown a tendency to resist integration or ... have been in the forefront of dissent or open armed defiance of the central authority. The Nagas and the Mizos were ruled through the tribal chieftains and headmen, Manipur and Tripura through their respective Maharajas. Jammu and Kashmir was ruled indirectly through the Maharaja. The Jat-Sikh heartland of Punjab, which has spawned ethno-nationalism and separatism among the Sikhs, is co-terminus with the cis-Sutlej area whose Sikhs helped the British defeat the trans-Sutlej Sikhs and which later constituted the princely states of Patiala, Nabha, Faridkot, Jind, Malerkotla, Kalsia and Kapurthala.

These cases need to be analyzed with similar subnational datasets that measure colonial institutions and insurgency, though that is beyond the scope of this book.

Before partition and Indian independence in 1947, the British used indirect rule in the "frontier" areas to India's west and east, in what is today Pakistan and Myanmar/Burma respectively, and this created structural conditions for insurgency. Within Pakistan, both the Tehrik-e-Taliban insurgency beginning in the mid-2000s in the Federally Administered Tribal Areas (FATA) in the North Western Frontier Province (NWFP) and the recurrent Baluchi secessionist movements since the 1960s have occurred in areas of erstwhile British indirect rule (Ali 2005; Naseemullah 2014). Looking east to Myanmar/Burma, there have been multiple ethnic secessionist insurgencies in Burma's periphery that were "frontier areas" under British indirect rule (Smith 1999). In this chapter, I analyze these two cases of how indirect rule created structural conditions for insurgency.

In addition, Lord Lugard is said to have used indirect rule extensively in West Africa, which raises the question of whether some of the insurgency movements we have seen in Sub-Saharan Africa since the 1980s were partly facilitated by colonial indirect rule. Acemoglu et al. (2013) find that some African countries like Sierra Leone did not abolish colonial indirect rule systems, creating grievances that led to ethnic insurgencies, whereas others like Uganda and Ghana were able to reduce the powers of pre-colonial–era chiefs and avoid such problems. Studies like those of Sampson (2014: 312–15) and Babalola (2013: 13–16) have noted the role of British indirect rule in allowing the Islamic caliphate and sharia law to continue in the north of Nigeria, and more direct rule creating a Western secular Christian/animist culture in the south, thus creating conditions for Islamic movements since 1980s and more recently the emergence of the Boko Haram insurgency in Nigeria's north.

Various scholars have noted that different colonizers have varying effects on development and conflict even in similar areas (Blanton et al. 2001; Lee & Schultz 2012). Can my theory be generalized to Spanish colonialism, especially since Latin America has had so many cases of leftist insurgencies since the 1960–1970s? The leftist Revolutionary Armed Forces of Colombia (FARC) insurgency in Colombia happened in areas of historically low state penetration (Robinson 2013), and Zukerman-Daly (2012) shows how the La Violencia conflict from the past left organizational legacies that led to the FARC insurgency. Later in this chapter, I briefly describe two cases of Spanish colonial land tenure institutions creating inequalities and leftist insurgency. One case is of Spanish rule in Mexico, which created conditions for the Zapatista insurgency, and another case is of Spanish and then American rule in the Philippines, which resulted in the New People's Army (NPA) insurgency.

2   BRITISH INDIRECT RULE ALONG THE FRONTIER IN SOUTH ASIA – BURMA AND PAKISTAN

Territorial expansion of the British East India Company in India finally led to its annexing Punjab in the west from the Sikh descendants of Ranjit Singh in the 1840s, and Assam beyond Bengal in the east. Beyond Punjab lay the Afghan Empire across the Hindu Kush Mountains and Russian influence in Central Asia, and beyond Assam in the northeast lay Indo-China under French influence. The British Empire was now facing the frontiers of its rule. In the NWFP of Pakistan, the British used a form of indirect rule that depended on tribal chiefs. In the northeast frontier of India, the British depended on indirect rule through the various chiefs of ethnic clans along the Burmese border. Unlike the successor state of Hyderabad and feudatory state of Bastar, these were a different type of indirect rule through frontier states that helped the British protect the interiors of their empire in India from foreign threats at a low cost. However, it resulted in low ethnic integration and weak state capacity, which later led to multiple insurgencies in Pakistan and Burma after the British left.

2.1   Case 1: British Colonial Indirect Rule and Ethnic Secessionist Insurgency in Myanmar/ Burma

In Myanmar, the British used direct rule in the central territories called "Ministerial Burma" subject to British administrative, legal, and revenue institutions, and indirect rule in the peripheral Frontier regions that had lower state capacity. Many of the protracted ethnic insurgencies by the Karen, Kachin, and Shan ethnic groups have occurred in these peripheral regions traditionally ignored by the central state (Callahan 2003). These Frontier or Excluded Areas were rugged hilly tracts and home to various minority ethnic groups who were historically not affected by the government in the plains. These areas continued as Frontier Areas of indirect rule under the British. Smith (1999: 27) notes that it was "in these remote ethnic minority areas that insurgent movements have remained most firmly entrenched since independence, as attempts by successive governments to extend authority into the hills have met with resistance." The only exception to this was the Communist Party of Burma (CPB)–led insurgency, which occurred in the Ministerial Burma areas that were directly ruled under the British. However, with the fall of the CPB's last strongholds in the Pegu Yomas in the mid-1970s, the CPB's remaining "liberated zones" have been located in Kachin and Shan state areas in the Frontier ethnic minority areas (Smith 1999: 27–29).

History: Conflict with the Burmese king over the regions that bordered the Burmese kingdom and British territory in Bengal led to deteriorating Burmese-British relations and the first Anglo-Burman War of 1824–26, which led to British annexation of Arakan and Tenasserim and also Assam and Manipur that remained in India. The Second Anglo-Burmese War of 1852–53 led to the annexation of Lower Burma. Facing threat from the French motivated the British to complete the final and complete annexation of the territory of Upper Burma with the British victory in the Third Anglo-Burman War of 1886 (Smith 1999: 40). Following this, the British deposed Burmese King Thibaw, and Burma was assimilated into the British Empire as a province of India. It was divided into the central lowlands of "Burma proper," where the majority of Burman and Mon speakers lived, and the surrounding ethnic minority-populated Frontier Areas on the periphery of the state (South 2008: 10).

Since there was general unrest in the newly obtained colony, the British began a process of "pacification" to bring the "disturbed areas" under control by subduing military resistance and instituting revenue-collection measures (Aung-Thwin 1985). As pacification proceeded, the central plains were brought under control first, following which expeditionary efforts were made into the hilly areas to secure the frontiers. Pre-colonial power relations between the residents of the plains, mainly ethnic Burmans who formed the Burmese kingdom, and the hill peoples (Chins, Kachins, Karens, and some Shan) operated on the basis of a tributary system whereby the chiefs of the peripheral hill tribes recognized the authority of the Burmese kingdom and paid allegiance to the royalty while maintaining equal dominance in the areas they commanded (Aung-Thwin 1985). The Burmese kings usually abstained from interference in the internal affairs of the petty states and tribal chieftains in the periphery, who were allowed to rule their own people, and it was a type of indirect rule (Furnivall 1958: 6–8). When the British arrived, they co-opted these existing structures of indirect rule through local chiefs, while also introducing new rules and patterns of governance that changed the previously fluid interactions.

Indirect Rule: In October 1886, as British forces still struggled to quell resistance on the central plains, Lord Dufferin wrote to the secretary of state for India in London, Viscount Cross, outlining the policy of indirect rule he intended to follow in the hills: "The Shans, Kachins and other mountain tribes live under the rule of hereditary Chiefs, whose authority is generally sufficient to preserve order amongst them. ... If we secure the allegiance of these rulers, we obtain ... most of what we require" (Smith 1999: 41). The main motivation for the British using indirect rule in the frontier areas was to rule at the least possible cost and with minimal interference, so as to maintain a strategic buffer zone against China and France. As Smith (1999: 42) notes, on the eve of World War II, there were just forty members of the Burma Frontier Service administering the entire Scheduled Areas, which shows the relatively low state and administrative capacity used to rule these frontier regions through indirect rule.

Based on this assessment, the tribal governance of hill peoples under their hereditary chiefs or princes was to continue in the peripheral regions as it had been under the monarchy. To achieve such compliance, the British undertook the local custom of "visiting" each tribal authority figure, albeit with a strong military force. Resistance was met with force, if necessary, and a compliant chief replaced a defiant one if the need arose (Aung-Thwin 1985: 253). The British confirmed those local chiefs who would recognize the new colonial government and replaced those who were recalcitrant by more willing rivals (Furnivall 1958: 8).

Such arrangements began with the Shans and were extended to other hill tribes. At first, the Federated Shan states were recognized as quasi-autonomous areas ruled by hereditary Shan chiefs known as *Sawbwas* (Report of the Frontier Areas Committee of Enquiry 1947). The Chin Hills consisted of some unadministered areas and others under petty Chin chiefs who did not have the same powers as the Shan *Sawbwas* (Furnivall, 1948). As such, a superintendent and four assistant superintendents governed parts of Chin Hills. Karenni remained nominally independent as it was never formally annexed and was classified as a feudatory state but was required to pay an annual tribute and comply with the British political officer stationed in the state (Report of the Frontier Areas Committee of Enquiry 1947). The British administration implemented a similar frontier policy in other hill tribes, whereby partial sovereignty was granted in return for an annual tribute similar to what was required under the Burman kings (Aung-Thwin 1985: 253). This ensured that the revenue received was enough to run the costs of maintaining a garrison of soldiers with a political officer in strategic locations to ensure a thin but nonetheless visible British presence in these areas (Smith 1999).

Direct Rule: In contrast to the system of indirect rule through preexisting chiefs in the hills, the British used much more direct forms of rule in the Burman-dominated plains, where "the monarchy was abolished and in 1888 a new system of administration was introduced, following the existing practice in India, and the old township and circle units and the powers of the local

Myothugyis (hereditary rulers) was broken up. Instead, authority was devolved to individual headmen (*thugyi*) for each of Burma's 17–18,000 village tracts" (Smith 1999: 41).

In central Burma, the administrative system of the *Hutladaw*, the royal court or the Great Council of State, was dissolved and replaced by British deputy commissioners and police officers who divided Burma into fourteen districts (Aung-Thwin 1985). Each district was to be secured by a civil and a military British officer replicating the earlier roles of the *myowin* and the *sitke*, respectively (Aung-Thwin 1985). After the third Anglo-Burman War of 1886, Sir Charles Crosthwaite, who was appointed the new chief commissioner, devised a plan to restructure the Burmese system of local administration based on "a circle under a hereditary circle headman, exercising a personal authority over his own people but not necessarily the overlord of all the inhabitants of the circle" into "village communities with recognized heads" as was the system in India on which his plan was based (Furnivall 1948: 74). As per this plan, the circle was broken up with the civil officer appointing local headmen (*thugyi*) for each village unit who were willing to serve the new colonial powers in all of Burma's village tracts (Aung-Thwin 1985; Smith 1999). The British civil officers were responsible for "the restoration of order, the protection of life and property and the assessment and collection of the ordinary revenue" while "most of the unimportant criminal work and nearly all the civil suits [were to] be disposed of by the native officials, subject to the check and control of the district officer" (Aung-Thwin 1985: 253). As such, the indigenous circle headmen were partially transformed into officials and the circle of self-government was transformed into village administrative units for colonial convenience (Furnivall 1948).

Persistence over Time: With the Government of Burma Act in 1935, and Burma's independence from India in 1937, the "distinction in rule between the hills and plains that had evolved during the process of annexation came to be encoded in law" (Smith 1999: 42). Burma remained divided into two distinct areas, one was Ministerial Burma or old Burma Proper, which had a parliament with elections and a limited form of local democracy. The other was the vast hill tracts of the Frontier Areas, which were renamed as Scheduled/Excluded Areas. This was composed of the Karenni and Shan states and chunks of the Arakan, Chin, Kachin and Naga Hills and remained "under the loose supervision of the local residents of the Burma Frontier Service," though all civil, criminal, and financial affairs continued to be administered by the hereditary rulers and chiefs (Smith 1999: 43).

Effects of Indirect Rule: Indirect rule had different effect in the Frontier Areas that became causal conditions for the ethnic secessionist insurgencies after Burmese independence. First, when relying on the traditional chiefs in the Frontier Areas, the British protected the hereditary chiefs without allowing the traditional mechanism of ousting inefficient headmen or rulers. This restricted the political development of these ethnic groups, as the chiefs were no longer accountable to their constituency as had been the case and were now "immovable tyrants sanctioned by British law" (Smith 1999: 47). This was similar to the mechanism of lack of accountability and despotic chiefs in Africa (Boone 2014; Mamdani 1996) and was one of the reasons for ethnic grievances and rebellion. For example, in the southern Shan states, the rulers of several *Sawbwa* families were corrupt, which led to rebellion in 1936–38 by Kayan villagers of the small sub-state of Mongpai against one particularly inept ruler. Similarly, the Pao and Kayan rebellions that have occurred since Burmese independence have been a "residue of resentment against their treatment by the Shan *Sawbwas* under the British" (Smith 1999: 47).

Another mechanism created by the division of these territories into direct rule in the Burman-dominated plains versus indirect rule in the Frontiers with these ethnic minority groups was the crystallization of ethnic identities and divisions between the ethnic majority Burmans and the ethnic minorities like Shans/Karens/Kachins. While these ethnic differences had existed before colonialism, indirect rule made them more politically salient. For example, in response to the colonial policy of separatism, in the 1930s a nationalist party emerged in Ministerial Burma that demanded the Burmanization of schools and unification of all people under Burman rule. This scared the ethnic minorities and led to "sharper distinctions between its ethnic groups" than had existed previously under the Burmese monarchial system (Silverstein 1959: 98). This is similar to the case of British colonialism making caste divisions and Hindu-Muslim religious identities more salient in India (Dirks 2001; Pandey 1990).

A third mechanism similar to the case of Hyderabad in India was the low development of the indirect-ruled Frontier areas due to chronic economic neglect. The British had little incentive to invest funds for the development of the hilly peripheries, since there was enough rice production and profitable timber and oil extraction in the central plains area of Ministerial Burma, which was sufficient to cover the imperial costs of maintaining these buffer zones. The few industries that developed in the Frontier Areas were small and inefficient and depended on imported labor from India, like a tea factory at Namhsam, lead/silver mines at Bawdin and Namtu in the Shan states, and wolfram mines at Mawchi in Karenni states. This unequal level of development continued till the 1990s, with whatever development there was occurring in the Burman heartland areas and little in the Frontier ethnic minority areas (Smith 1999: 47).

Colonial Policy of Divide and Rule

These ethnic and economic differences between direct and indirect rule areas were further aggravated by colonial policy of *divide and rule* in which the British intentionally favored recruitment into the army of ethnic minorities from the Frontier regions, while excluding the Burman or Bamar majority from the central plains. The purpose was to balance against the majority Bamars by giving more power to the minority Karens/Kachins/Shans in the army.

Historically, the Karen had served as guides for the British army in the First and Second Anglo-Burmese Wars of 1824–25 and 1852–53, and Karens had been recruited to help overthrow the Burmese king Thibaw in 1885 and suppress the rebellions in Lower Burma in 1886 (Smith 1999: 44). The British thought of the Karens as well as the Chins and Kachins, as "martial races" better suited to warfare, similar to their view of the Sikhs and Gurkhas in India (Wilkinson 2015). By the early twentieth century, these minority ethnic groups from the hills had established themselves as the military manpower of the British army (Selth 1986: 488). In 1925, a decision was taken to recruit only Chins, Kachins, and Karens. All Burmans in the army were discharged because it was considered unwise to retain them due to their perceived lack of loyalty as nationalist mobilization increased. After 1935, the British recognized the need to open the ranks to Burmans, but little effort was made to do so (Selth 1986: 488). Using 1931 census data, Furnivall (1948: 183–84) shows that in 1939 only 472 Burmans were members of the regular armed forces though they were 75.11 percent of the country's population, but there were 1,448 Karens, 868 Chins, and 881 Kachins, though these minority ethnic groups were only a small part of the population (see Table 10.1).

Such a recruitment pattern led to a clear divide along ethnic lines as World War II broke out. The Burma Independence Army (BIA) organized by Burman nationalists was formed on the basis of recruitment from the mainly Burman groups. As the war progressed and the BIA received support from Japan, it committed violent atrocities against the minority ethnic groups (Fredholm, 1993). On the other side, the Karen, Chin, and Kachin remained loyal to the British and received weapons to fight as guerrillas against the Japanese and the

TABLE 10.1 *Racial constitution of the Burma army, 1939*

Race	Percentage of Population	Number in the Army
Burmese	75.11 %	472
Karen	9.34 %	1448
Chin	2.38 %	868
Kachin	1.05 %	881
Other		
– Native	2.38 %	168
– Foreign	9.74 %	

Source: J. S. Furnivall, 1948, *Colonial Policy and Practice*, p. 184.

BIA (Fredholm 1993; Smith 1999: 62–65). Such ethnic fighting led to destruction/deaths for both sides and helped create unity among the minority ethnic groups and also intensified their grievances and hatred for the majority Burmans. It led to demands for greater autonomy and finally for secession by the ethnic minorities in post-independence Burma, which led to the various ethnic secessionist insurgencies (Behera 2017).

Effects of These Colonial Policies on Insurgency

As decolonization progressed and independence drew closer in the 1940s, there were growing demands from the chiefs of the semi-autonomous tribes for independent statehood. The British solution was to combine Scheduled and Ministerial Burma into a union thereby offering ethnic minorities some level of continued autonomy (Fredholm 1993). The minorities objected to this and demanded complete independence. After decades of colonial meddling that overthrew the previous structures of ethnic relations, these contestations were now left to the newly formed Burmese government to solve.

Despite attempts to devise a mutually agreeable solution at the Panglong Conference in 1947 in which General Aung San of the Burmans promised that if Burmans received one *kyat,* then the minorities would also receive one *kyat,* the Burman majority and the various ethnic minorities could not reconcile their differences (Fredholm 1993; Smith 1999: 78). Different ethnic minority groups like the Karens and Kachins started armed rebellions demanding independence in the Frontier areas in the 1950s. The Karen National Union (KNU) in southeast Burma and the Kachin Independence Organisation (KIO) in the northeast developed liberated zones with their own governments, education departments and armies among these ethnic minority groups that had always been on the periphery of pre-colonial and colonial states.

The Shans and Kachins decided to adopt a wait-and-watch policy in the 1950s. Frustration was growing among the Shans, which was shared by all the minority ethnic groups in Burma that the government in Rangoon was becoming more and more centralized and Burmanized and the ethnic minorities were losing out in terms of power sharing (Smith 1999: 192). The immediate spark for the start of the Shan rebellion in 1958 was the invasion of the Kuomintang (KMT) from China and the intrusion of the Burmese army into the Shan states to deal with this threat, thus leading to violence. However, the deeper structural conditions had been created by the 1947 constitution written after the Panglong Conference, in which the Shan state had the right to secession after a ten-year trial period, and the administrative powers of the state had been given to the traditional chiefs/*Sawbwas*, in the hope that they could persuade the Shan people to join the Burmese federation. Following independence, the *Sawbwas* came under a lot of pressure from the Burmese nationalist movement and their own subjects to renounce their political powers. In 1957–58, with the time limit for the right to secession approaching, this pressure increased. In a

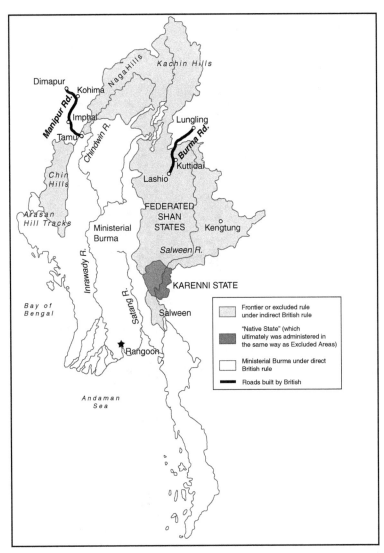

FIGURE 10.1A British colonial direct and indirect rule in Burma
Source: Callahan, Mary. 2003. *Making Enemies: War and State Building in Burma*.
Ithaca: Cornell University Press, p. 28, Map 3.

ceremony in April 1959, attended by General Ne Win of the Burmese Army
(*tatmadaw*), the thirty-four remaining *Sawbwas* of Shan state gave up their
rights. Following this, the military government in Rangoon headed by Ne Win
pressured the new Shan government to give up its right to secede (Smith 1999:
192–94).

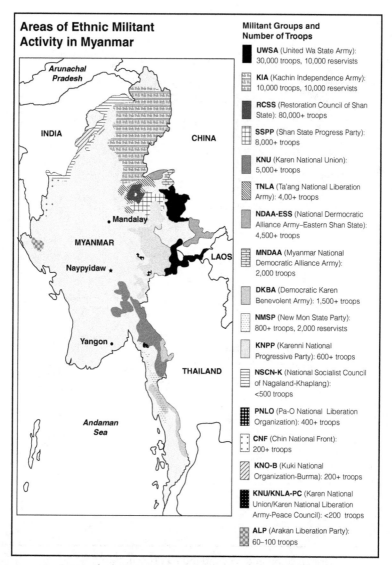

FIGURE 10.1B Areas of ethnic insurgency in Burma
Source: https://worldview.stratfor.com/article/path-peace-myanmar-bends-toward-china

This threatened to disrupt the power balance between the Burman government and the Shan states, guaranteed by the 1947 constitution. In June–July 1961, a minority people's conference was organized by Shan leaders and included Kachin, Karens, and Chin leaders. The solution proposed was a "loose federalized form of constitution with powers shared equally between the minority states and the Burman-majority areas."

However such a solution was not acceptable to Ne Win and the *Tatmadaw* leaders of Burman origin, and the Burmese army enacted a coup on March 2, 1962, to avoid federalism and destruction of unified Burma (Smith 1999: 195–96). Following the coup and the arrest of the Shan/Kachin/Chin leaders who had been proposing more federalism, the elected Shan administration collapsed and the state came under military occupation. On April 22, 1964, the three largest rebel Shan organizations, the Shan State Independence Army (SSIA), the Shan National United Front (SNUF), and the Kokang Resistance Force agreed to join forces to create the Shan State Army (SSA), thus starting a long-lasting insurgency in these former Frontier State Areas (Smith 1999: 220).

Various other ethnic minorities also started their own rebellions in the other Frontier Areas. In 2006, there were at least forty-one armed ethnic rebel groups, of which the Karen National Union (KNU), the Karen National Progressive Party (KNPP), Shan State Army–South (SSA-South), and the Chin National Front (CNF) maintained forces of several hundred troops. Of these almost two-thirds had reached some form of ceasefire with the military government, while ten groups had not. The three major non-ceasefire groups were the SSA-South, the Karen National Liberation Army (KNLA), and the Karenni Army (Cline 2009: 579). Figure 10.1A shows areas of British colonial direct and indirect rule in Burma, and Figure 10.1B shows areas of ethnic insurgency. Comparing these two maps shows a high overlap between the frontier/excluded indirect rule areas and ethnic insurgencies in Burma.

Another interesting aspect of colonial indirect rule that may have facilitated rebel mobilization after Burmese independence is that many of the royal families of former chiefs, who could draw on traditional systems of patronage, led or joined the insurgency movement (Smith 2007:13). In the Shan and Karenni states, relatives of the hereditary *Sawbwa* families joined the insurrections. Prominent members of royal households who organized insurgent movements after independence include "Sao Shwe who led the first rebellion in the Karenni state; Chao Tzang Yawnghwe, who was son of Sao Shwe Thaike (Burma's first president) and co-founder of the SSA; ... and the present-day Wa National Organization president Maha San" (Smith 2007: 14).

To summarize, the effects of colonial indirect rule combined with the effects of colonial divide and rule created demands by these ethnic minorities for independence and translated into secessionist insurgencies. Colonial indirect rule had intensified the ethnic differences between the majority Burman and minority ethnic groups and increased the grievances of the minorities due to low development of these frontier areas. At the same time, colonial divide and rule created ethnic inclusion of minorities and ethnic exclusion of majority Burmans from army and government. Following independence, the minority ethnic groups continued to demand more power in the new state. However, the ethnic majority Burmans were not willing to satisfy the demand of the ethnic minorities, which led the ethnic minority groups to escalate their demands and ask for independence and finally led to secessionist movements. These colonial policies had resulted in greater power for ethnic minorities in the Army and intensifying grievances: their sudden ethnic exclusion from power following independence led to insurgency (Cederman et al. 2010).

Bringing historical institutions back into the analysis of recent insurgencies in Burma allows us to understand that the reason for so many ethnic secessionist insurgencies rests in "Burma's complex ethnic past" (Smith 1999: 89). It provides a historically rooted explanation for the ethnic insurgencies.

2.2 Case 2: Taliban Insurgency in Pakistan

The Tehrik-e-Taliban Pakistan (TTP) insurgency (2001–10) occurred in the Federally Administered Tribal Areas (FATA) region of the North West Frontier Province (NWFP) of Pakistan, where historically the British had used a hybrid type of indirect rule in these frontier territories bordering Afghanistan. As Naseemullah (2014: 502) notes, "The proximate causes of this insurgency are not obscure: the US invasion of Afghanistan in 2001, the ouster of the Taliban shortly thereafter, Pakistan's security alliance with US in the 'War on Terror.'"

However, the reason for the success of the Taliban in the FATA region of NWFP could also be explained by the Pakistani state's abysmal lack of state capacity in this region (Fearon & Laitin 2003), which was driven by the indirect rule institutions used since colonial times. The British had relied on "state-financed tribal militias, constabularies, and the *political agents* of the state rather than civilian bureaucrats and provincial police forces" that had created this weak state capacity in the first place (Naseemullah 2014: 502), which allowed the Taliban to easily consolidate in these former indirectly ruled areas on Pakistan's frontier. Most scholars ignore the long-term effects of indirect rule in creating and sustaining such weak state capacity and a strong Pashtun ethnic identity averse to assimilation into a nation-state, as factors that created opportunity structures for rebellion and also the ethnic mobilization networks for recruitment by the Taliban in the future.

History: The Pashtuns living in the northwest frontier of Pakistan bordering Afghanistan were independent and warlike tribes, including the Wazirs, Mehsuds, and Afridis, who prided themselves on never having their land conquered by outsiders and refused to pay taxes to any state (Johnson & Mason 2008: 50–52). Previous attempts to conquer them by Mughal emperors had failed, and Emperor Akbar saw his army destroyed and 8,000 lives lost in 1586 to the Yusufzai of Peshawar Valley, while Aurangzeb lost 10,000 soldiers and had 20,000 captured in an operation to subdue the Afridi tribe that controlled the Khyber Pass (Akins 2017: 5). With the arrival of the British, the East India Company fought several wars to control the Pashtun tribes of Afghanistan. The First Anglo-Afghan War ended in disaster, with an army of 18,000 killed by the frontier tribes in 1842 as they retreated from Kabul and only Dr. William Brydon surviving to reach the British fort at Jalalabad. When asked where the rest of the army was, the exhausted doctor replied, "I am the army."[1]

Once Punjab and the territories around the Indus River were acquired after the second Anglo-Sikh war of 1848–49, the British had to decide where to set the western borders. Brothers Henry and John Lawrence, two administrators stationed in Punjab in the 1840s and 1850s perfected the "Punjab school of governance." In their dealings with the northwest frontier, they championed local knowledge and had officers who were prone to "going native" (White 2008: 222). There were debates between a *forward policy* of conquering the tribes and ruling them directly and a *closed-border policy* of giving independence to the frontier tribes, but the actual policy oscillated between these options and was usually a type of hybrid indirect rule (Naseemullah 2013: 509). Initially Lord Lytton, the British viceroy in the 1870s was in favor of the forward policy. The British got control of the State of Kalat (in Baluchistan) in 1876 under the Treaty of Jacobabad and occupied Quetta in 1877. In 1878–79, the Second Anglo-Afghan War occurred and the British invaded and occupied Afghanistan. On May 26, 1879, under the Treaty of Gandmark, Amir Dost Mohammad of Afghanistan agreed to conduct his foreign affairs according to the advice of the British government, but the Afghans attacked the British Mission and massacred Chief Cavagniari and his men on September 3, 1879. The British sent an army that deposed Amir Dost Mohammad, and they handed the crown over to Abd-ur-Rahman Khan, who maintained stability and cordial relations with the British (Yousafzai & Yaqubi 2017: 80–81). A team of British surveyors negotiated the Durand Line in 1893 under Sir Mortimer Durand to formalize the border between British India and Afghanistan (Johnson & Mason 2008).

Motivations for Indirect Rule: Based on their experiences in the Anglo-Afghan wars, the British realized that it was difficult to conquer these frontier tribes. According to Sir Olaf Caroe, the last governor of NWFP, "if you want to get anything done in dealing with tribes, work through the tribal organization; let the tribal leaders produce the goods in their own way. In other words, it was the principle of indirect rule."[2] In 1901, Viceroy Lord Curzon created the new North West Frontier Province (NWFP) by taking the districts of Hazara, Peshawar, Kohat, Bannu, Dera Ismail, and Dera Ghazi Khan of Punjab province and making them part of the new NWFP.[3] The NWFP consisted of the tribal Pashtun-dominated buffer region along the Durand Line, the international border between British India and Afghanistan.

Lord Curzon decided to use indirect rule in the NWFP, using the legal framework of the Frontier Crimes Regulation (FCR). Along the whole

---

[1] Ahmed, *The Thistle and the Drone*, p. 155.   [2] Caroe, *The Pathans*, p. 398.
[3] Michael Callen, Saad Gulzar, Arman Rezaee, and Jacob Shapiro, "Choosing Ungoverned Space: Pakistan's Frontier Crimes Regulation," Manuscript, 2018.

frontier, from Chitral to Seistan, regular troops were withdrawn and replaced by tribal militia or levies, with the goal of cultivating friendly relations with the tribes and not giving them any excuse for aggression.[4] In his speech to the tribal chiefs of the NWFP at Peshawar on April 26, 1902, Curzon outlined his policy and assured them that "The policy of the Government of India towards the trans-border men is very simple. . . . We have no wish to seize your territory or interfere with your independence."[5] However, he also warned that if there continued to be attacks and disorder by the tribals in the name of *jihad*, then he would crush it. He also assured them that they would continue to receive tribal allowances for helping to maintain peace and keeping the various roads and passes open, and that the British were fine with "whatever form of Government or authority the particular tribe prefers," thus providing them with internal political autonomy.[6]

The British sought to control the FATA districts of the NWFP "through indirect rule, and to use the tribal areas as a buffer zone against Russian expansionism in the region" (Ali 2018: 4). Johnson and Mason (2008: 52) describe the British approach to the frontier areas as "masterly inactivity" that "essentially used the tribesmen as a buffer between India's northern frontier and the approaching Russian Empire in Central Asia." Lord Curzon feared that Russia would take advantage of any disruptions along the northwestern borders with Afghanistan to try and interfere in the British domain of India, as part of the Great Game between Russia and Britain in trying to control Central Asia. In a speech in 1904, he said that the northwest frontier of India was "a land frontier 5700 miles in length, peopled by hundreds of different tribes. . . . A single outbreak at a single point may set entire sections of that frontier ablaze. Then, beyond it . . . are the muffled figures of great European Powers, advancing nearer and nearer."[7]

Indirect Rule and its Historical Legacies

Naseemullah (2014: 507, 511–13) describes British administration in the frontier regions as a form of hybrid governance or indirect rule composed of overlapping spheres of coercive organizations and institutions. First, the British allied with tribal *maliks* or leaders, who were part of the tribal *Jirga* or consultative assembly, to maintain order and provide justice to the tribes under their jurisdiction. Second, stipends or allowances were given to the *maliks* to recruit *khassadars* and tribal levies, who were armed militiamen used to maintain law and order and were under the command of both tribal *maliks* and British political agents. The recruitment of *khassadars* was

---

[4] *Lord Curzon in India: Being a Selection From His Speeches as Viceroy & Governor-General of India, 1898–1905*, pp. xi–xii (Introduction), and p. 418 (Extract from Budget Speech, March 26, 1902).

[5] *Lord Curzon in India*, p. 423 (Durbar at Peshawar).

[6] *Lord Curzon in India*, p. 423 (Durbar at Peshawar).   [7] *Lord Curzon in India*, p. 37.

considered a cost-effective way of addressing the security challenge facing the British. Third, a paramilitary militia known as the Frontier Constabulary was established in 1913 and was recruited from the tribes to maintain political order over roads and mountain passes. Its function was to uphold the law in *external* relations between settled districts and frontier tribes, but it never really developed the coercive capacity vis-à-vis the tribes.

These institutions of hybrid indirect rule were underpinned by the Frontier Crimes Regulation (FCR) legal system, under which the local governor appointed political agents, who would send criminal cases to the local council of elders/*maliks*, known as the *Jirga*, for trial. The political agent could approve of the *Jirga's* ruling or could overturn it (Callen et al. 2018).[8] If there were crimes or violations of the peace, then the FCR legal system would be used to impose punishment on individuals or even entire tribes under the collective responsibility clause of the FCR (Ali 2018: 4).

Several mechanisms were created as a result of the use of hybrid indirect rule that facilitated Taliban insurgency in the future. First, it resulted in a weak state and police capacity in this region because of the British decision to depend on the *khassadars* instead of developing a regular civilian police force in FATA. The Frontier Constabulary was developed by the British to police the FATA; although it had potential to increase the state's monopoly over coercive violence in these frontier regions, it remained underdeveloped. Naseemullah (2014: 511) cites an intelligence report to the provincial governor that mentions that "in 1942, there were 425,197 fighters among the various tribal groups in the agencies, with 236,218 breech-loading and 25,677 muzzle-loading firearms. This yields a ratio of one Constabulary member for every 55 armed tribesmen," which is a low ratio of formal police capacity to military capacity of the tribesmen. Also there was dependence on tribal levies to control the area; for example, Lord Curzon in his speech to the tribal chiefs mentioned the opportunity of tribal employment in the *levies* of "Swat, Dir and Chitral" and also the "Khyber Rifles, the Samana Rifles, the Kurram Militia, and the Waziristan Milita."[9] The use of informal tribal *levies* and vigilantes was a type of organizational legacy that could later be used by armed insurgent groups like the Taliban. This legacy of weak police capacity in this frontier region continued under the Pakistani government, making it difficult to do effective counterinsurgency operations against the Taliban.

Second, in these far-flung areas, the level of development and public goods was very low, compared with the more directly ruled areas like Punjab and Sindh provinces in Pakistan. According to Akins (2017: 7–8), because of the geographic and administrative isolation of the tribal areas, there was "lack of development within the region, with a striking dearth of schools, hospitals, and

---

[8] Michael Callen, Saad Gulzar, Arman Rezaee, and Jacob Shapiro, "Choosing Ungoverned Space: Pakistan's Frontier Crimes Regulation." Manuscript.

[9] *Lord Curzon in India*, p. 424.

infrastructure by the end of British rule." Because of the unique political position of FATA within Pakistan, this region faced "chronic underdevelopment as access and economic opportunities are severely restricted." (Akins 2017: 10) Also, this region had low literacy rates, varying "between 26.77% (North Waziristan) and 57.2% (Khyber) for men and 1.47% (North Waziristan) and 14.4% (Kurram) for women" (Akins 2017: 10).[10] This possibly increased the ability of the Taliban to recruit from young men with low literacy in this frontier region.

Third, the use of tribal *maliks,* who were partly protected by the colonizers in return for maintaining order, meant that there was potential for despotic rule and the development of political and economic inequality, much like the Nizam of the princely state of Hyderabad depending on *deshmukhs.*[11] These tribal elders had a lot of power, since they were the main actors who helped resolve disputes through the *Jirga* system of tribal council (Ali 2018: 5). There have been allegations that the FCR and the use of tribal *maliks* have allowed the spread of corruption because of the power and privileges granted to the *maliks.* This has caused resentment between the "political have-nots" of a younger generation called *kashar* and the privileged elder *maliks* or *mashars* (Akins 2017: 10–11). From his fieldwork experience in the tribal areas of FATA, the anthropologist Akbar Ahmad cites one Shamshur Rahman, a schoolteacher in the Agency and a *kashar,* who said: "These Maliks are of the British rule which is a great injustice. Our Maliks destroyed the qualities of their forefathers, they are toady now and drinking wine so how they will do the services of their tribe, khel or nation?"[12] When the Taliban arrived in the FATA post-2001, they killed around 800 tribal *maliks* by 2012, and the existing grievances by the younger generation against the *maliks* may have helped them recruit from the Pushtun youth of this region (Akins 2017: 12).

A fourth effect of using indirect rule and a policy of noninterference with these Pashtun tribes was "an upward spiral of violence and ceding of influence to the mullahs" (Tripodi 2008: 141–42). There were several tribal rebellions against the British inspired by Muslim religious figures, and "in 1908, 1915, 1927, 1933 and 1935 the Mohmand tribe alone engaged in large-scale military activity against the British presence. Each time, their actions were inspired by the urgings of senior religious figures such as the Haji of Turangzi and the Fakir of Alinga" (Tripodi 2008: 141–42). Johnson and Mason (2008: 53–54) note that "A figure remarkably similar to Taliban leader Mullah Mohammed Omar, Mirza Ali Khan – a Tori Khel Waziri Pashtun known to the West as the Fakir of Ipi – led British and later Pakistani security forces on a frustrating chase around

---

[10] *Multiple Indicator Cluster Survey (MICS): Federally Administered Tribal Area (FATA) Pakistan,* Planning & Development Department, FATA Secretariat, 2009, pp. 26–27.

[11] See Chapter 8 for analysis of the princely state of Hyderabad and its effects on Maoist insurgency in India.

[12] Ahmed, *Pukhtun Economy and Society,* p. 144.

the frontier for thirty years. Protected by his Pashtun tribal supporters in the mountains, he was never caught." These previous colonial-era rebellions provided legacies of organizational networks and ideological repertoires of militant Islam that the Taliban were able to draw upon (Tarrow 1998).

Persistence over Time

After Pakistan's independence following 1947, the FATA region continued to be ruled using political agents and tribal *maliks* and the FCR continued to be used along with *Jirgas* for legal purposes.[13] The FCR persisted after independence and was integrated as articles 246–47 of Pakistan's 1973 Constitution (Naseemullah 2014: 507). Soon after independence, the founding leader of Pakistan, Muhammad Ali Jinnah removed the army from the frontier areas and promised to allow the FCR to continue in the tribal Pashtun areas of FATA. He also agreed to continue the allowances that the tribal elders had received under the British (Ali 2018: 4).

Why was indirect rule through local elites continued by the postcolonial Pakistani state? The motivation was partly that it would have been costly to bring these frontier areas under direct state control, and it would have been more cost-effective to allow the colonial-era institutions to continue. On April 17, 1948, Jinnah gave a speech to the leaders of the tribal *Jirgas*, in which he said:

Pakistan has no desire to unduly interfere with your internal freedom. On the contrary, Pakistan wants to help you and make you … self-reliant and self-sufficient and help in your educational, social and economic uplift, and not be left as you are dependent on annual doles, as has been the practice hitherto. … You know that the Frontier Province is a deficit province, but that does not trouble us so much.[14]

Another reason for continuing the FCR system in the FATA border areas was that the new state of Pakistan felt threatened by Afghanistan, which had irredentist claims to the Pashtun populated tribal areas and North Western Frontier Province and declared the Durand Line separating the Pashtuns on both sides of the border invalid. The Pakistani leaders believed that it would be best to let the status quo in FATA continue because disrupting the already "precarious balance within the region" may have caused the Pushtun tribes to try to secede from Pakistan and join their ethnic kin across the border in Afghanistan. So, Jinnah's successors continued the FCR in FATA to maintain peace in the region. Much like under British rule, the purpose of the continuing

---

[13] Michael Callen, Saad Gulzar, Arman Rezaee, and Jacob Shapiro, "Choosing Ungoverned Space: Pakistan's Frontier Crimes Regulation," Manuscript, pp. 7–8.

[14] See https://united4justice.wordpress.com/tag/muhammad-ali-jinnah-address-to-the-tribal-jirga-at-government-house/

FCR was simply to protect the interests of the Pakistani state rather than ensuring any notion of justice or civil rights for FATA residents (Akins 2017: 9).

In more recent times, the FCR is slowly being withdrawn from the region following increasing criticism that *Jirga* decisions are not always fair, are influenced by the stronger party, and are also biased against women (Ali 2018: 6). In 2011, President Asif Ali Zardari amended the FCR through a presidential order, which placed limits on the collective action clause and the powers of the political agent. However, the underlying framework of the law still remained, leading to a string of protests under the "Go, FCR, Go" movement calling for the repeal of the British-era law (Akins 2017: 13).

2.5 Effects of These Colonial Policies on Insurgency

In 2001, the United States and NATO started the War on Terrorism and attacked the Taliban regime in Afghanistan. Following the collapse of the Taliban in Afghanistan, many of these militants including the entire Taliban leadership retreated across the Durand Line into the historically indirectly ruled region of FATA in NWFP in Pakistan, where the relatively weak state presence allowed the Taliban to flourish (Johnson & Mason 2008: 42). See Figure 10.2A for a map of British direct and indirect rule areas in the North Western Frontier Province and Figure 10.2B for a map of location of the Taliban insurgency in early 2000s.

The Taliban regime in Afghanistan in 1996–2001 had been able to slowly replace the system of tribal *maliks* with "conservative politico-religious cells comprising local mullahs known as ulemas" (Johnson & Mason 2008: 54–55). This process had started with the Soviet invasion of Afghanistan in 1979 and the *mujahideen* campaign against the Russians, with the traditional *maliks* being replaced by religious leaders. Thus, one historical legacy of indirect rule in the form of *maliks* and tribal agents was slowly being superseded by another historical legacy in the form of religious *mullahs* who provided the ideological repertoires for recruiting Pashtun youth to the Taliban. The Taliban had an advantage in that they had been in Afghanistan for a longer period and thus it was not as short lived as the previous religious movements against the British colonizers (Johnson & Mason 2008: 54). Between 2005 and 2006, the Taliban targeted and killed more than 200 tribal elders who resisted Taliban domination in FATA districts of NWFP in Pakistan (Johnson & Mason 2008: 57). Also, the relatively weak police and military presence in FATA provided the opportunity structures for the Taliban to mobilize the youth.

The Pakistan army under US pressure launched counterinsurgency operations that failed and then in 2006 tried unsuccessfully to negotiate with these militants through various ceasefires, which soon failed as well. In 2007, these militants formed the umbrella organization Tehrik-e-Taliban Pakistan (TTP or Pakistani Taliban), which started a war against the Pakistani state and carried out many suicide attacks with high casualty rates across the country

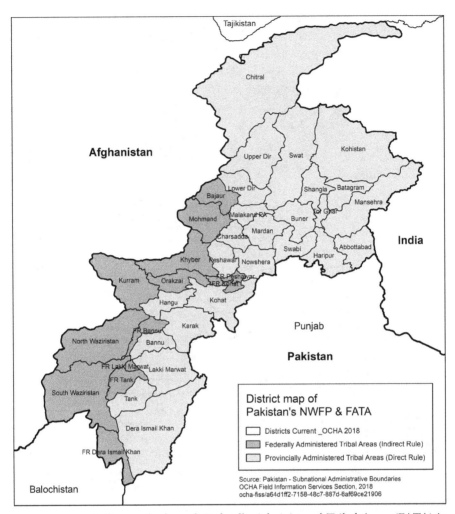

FIGURE 10.2A Indirect rule through Federally Administered Tribal Areas (FATA) in North Western Frontier Province (NWFP) in Pakistan
Source: https://commons.wikimedia.org/wiki/File:NWFP_and_FATA.jpg and https://upload.wikimedia.org/wikipedia/commons/1/17/NWFP_and_FATA.jpg

(Ali 2018: 6–7). The Pakistan army and air force conducted dozens of local military operations in FATA; however, as the army was already dealing with multiple conflicts on other fronts, it was reluctant to go after the main sanctuaries of militants and start an all-out counterinsurgency against the militants in North Waziristan Tribal Agency, despite domestic and international pressure to do so. This allowed the insurgents to further increase their capacity and recruitment and continue to inflict violence (Ali 2018: 7).

FIGURE 10.2B Taliban insurgency in NWFP and FATA in Pakistan
Source: Bill Rogio, "Taliban Insurgency Expands into Punjab," *The Long War Journal*,
February 7, 2009, at hwww.longwarjournal.org/archives/2009/02/taliban_insurgency_
e.php

In June 2014, the Pakistan Armed Forces launched the joint military
offensive Zarb-e-Azb ("Sharp and Cutting Strike") against various militant
groups hiding in North Waziristan sanctuaries. There was a brutal attack by
the TTP in December 2014 on the Army Public School Peshawar, which caused
the deaths of 132 students and resulted in increasing public support for the
counterinsurgency against the Taliban. Since. then, the Pakistan army has
launched an ambitious counterterrorism strategy known as the National

Action Plan, and attempts were launched to integrate FATA into the rest of NWFP. Levels of insurgent violence have since reduced, and the Pakistan army now claims that it has cleared major areas of the FATA region of militants (Ali 2018: 7).

3 BRIEF DESCRIPTIONS OF OTHER CASES FOR FUTURE RESEARCH

The cases of Pakistan and Burma show how British indirect rule along the frontiers of India resulted in insurgencies. They showcase that along with successor states of the Mughals like Hyderabad and Bengal, and feudatory/tributary states in Chhattisgarh and Orissa, frontier princely states that had been useful for the British for geostrategic purposes also tended to have weak state capacity and ethnic grievances that were conducive to insurgency in the future.

However, all these are cases within the British Empire in South Asia. Does my theory apply to cases beyond the British colonial empire? In this section, I briefly sketch a few cases that experienced Spanish colonial rule and had leftist insurgencies, which could be analyzed in future research. These are the leftist insurgencies in the Philippines and Mexico, which had been under Spanish colonial rule that created landlords and land inequality and have similar mechanisms as the Maoist insurgency case in India.

3.1   Spanish Colonial Rule in Latin America and the Philippines and Leftist Insurgencies

The Spanish did not use the concept of direct vs. indirect rule, unlike the British. Instead, they used central vs. peripheral rule in Latin America (Mahoney 2010). However, it is possible to broaden the concept beyond the narrow institutional definition of indirect rule to the choice by colonizers to depend on local elites to collect land revenue and rule on their behalf (Sartori 1970). Such a broader conceptualization of colonial indirect rule can be used to check whether insurgencies occur in the areas of colonial dependence on native intermediaries in other regions beyond South Asia.

Several leftist insurgencies occurred in Latin America – in Peru, Colombia, Mexico, and El Salvador – where the Spanish colonizers used various types of institutions to extract resources. There was also Spanish and later American colonialism in the Philippines. I focus on the cases of leftist insurgency in the Philippines and in Mexico and show that the land inequality and state weakness that were the proximate causes for rebellion were themselves created by institutional choices in the past by the Spanish colonizers.

3.2   New People's Army Insurgency in the Philippines

The Philippines had a communist-led insurgency, popularly known as the Huk rebellion in the 1940s. Following this was the emergence of the New People's Army (NPA) insurgency that started in the 1960s and is the longest-lasting Maoist rebellion in Asia. There are deep Spanish colonial roots for the Huk rebellion, as well as the NPA rebellion since the 1960s in the Philippines. The Spanish colonial period (1521–1898) saw the Spaniards build on the traditional village organization system in the Philippines, which co-opted the traditional village feudal leaders and confirmed their status over the serfs and enslaved people. This "system of *indirect rule* helped create the Filipino upper class, the *principals.*"[15] The Spanish colonizers created the *encomienda* system in 1570, which was a system of collecting tribute from a group of natives under the *encomendero* who was responsible for the welfare of the people in his *encomienda*. However, the *encomienda* developed into an exploitative system when the *encomenderos* forced the villagers to pay more than was required of them, which led to despotic extraction (Ligot 1994: 4). In their study of causes of indirect rule, Gerring et al. (2011) suggest that the *encomienda* system was a type of indirect rule.

While the *encomienda* system was abolished in the seventeenth century, the land inequalities persisted, and the "life of the peasant during the Spanish period was characterized by absolute poverty and humiliation" (Ligot 1994: 5–6). Following the Filipino rebellion against Spain in 1896, the American colonizers took over the Philippines from 1898 to 1946. Reforms followed, and an economic system of free enterprise and equal opportunities was introduced, but the economic inequalities in rural areas created during the Spanish period persisted; there were several peasant rebellions even during American rule, for example, the "colorum" religious uprisings of 1923 in Mindanao, the Tanggulan uprising of 1931, and the "sakdalista" peasant revolt of 1934 (Ligot 1994: 8).

Following the Japanese invasion during World War II, the Hukbalap rebellion occurred in the Philippines, between 1946 and 1960. The Huks were organized based on "peasant associations with loose linkages to the Philippine Communist Party" or PKP (P Staniland 2014: 193). With the end of the Huk rebellion in the 1950s, radical elements within the PKP, led by Jose Sison, broke off to form the Communist Party of Philippines – Marxist-Leninist-Maoist (CPP-MLM) – in 1968. They launched the armed group called the New People's Army (NPA; CPP-NPA) the next year and started a protracted people's war based on Maoist principles. There was a ceasefire attempt by the newly elected Corazon Aquino government in 1986, but this was short lived and followed by renewed military operations against the NPA. In the late 1980s and

---

[15] Jacinto Ligot. 1994. "Communist Insurgency in the Philippines." Thesis submitted to Naval Postgraduate School, Monterey, California.

early 1990s, the CPP-NPA suffered various organizational losses. The Philippine government captured key leaders, and internal purges again resulted in deaths of dozens of CPP-NPA members.[16] In more recent times, there has been a resurgence of support for the NPA and increasing violence after Duterte became president of the Philippines in 2016 and the number of NPA attacks spiked from 60 in 2016 to 260 in 2017. [17]

3.3 Zapatistas in Mexico:

The Ejercito Zapatista de Liberacion Nacional (EZLN) rebellion in Mexico led by Subcomandante Marcos fought for indigenous rights against neoliberal policies and had historical roots in indigenous/peasant mobilization and land inequality (Harvey 1998; Womack 1999). The Zapatista rebels in Chiapas province in Mexico wanted to preserve their "own traditional forms of organization, as well as local governance of the economy" when challenged by forces of globalization and Mexico's signing of NAFTA in 1994, which led to the outbreak of the revolt in Chiapas and the EZLN taking over several towns (Karklins 2009: 104). Trejo (2012) shows how the EZLN in Chiapas and the EPR in Oaxaca, Guerrero, and other southern states of Mexico represented a rebellion that mobilized indigenous people for grievances of land exploitation by landlords.

However, there were deeper historical roots to the outburst of the Zapatista/ EZLN rebellion in 1994. Karklins (2009: 104) writes:

zapatismo has its roots in the long history of colonialism in Latin America. ... The Mexican state, like many in Latin America, is a colonial construction, with rigid borders that oftentimes cut across ethnic and tribal lines. Furthermore, the prevalence of mestizos in the central government since Mexico's independence has privileged policies of assimilation over those privileging indigenous identity ... This has resulted in significant conflict in areas where the concentration of indigenous populations is high, such as Oaxaca and Chiapas, where the local residents have sought to maintain their indigenous identities.

Harvey (1998: 36) analyzes how there was a previous history of peasant/ indigenous opposition to rural bossism or *caciquismo*. This phenomenon emerged with Spanish colonial conquest of the Chiapas province in 1524–27, which saw the colonizers use rural elites or *caciques* to try and control Indian land and labor, resulting in rebellions in 1712 and 1867–70. This control by rural elites or *caciques,* which was a form of colonial indirect rule in Latin America, continued into the postcolonial period and "is a visible legacy of

---

[16] "Communist Party of the Philippines–New People's Army," http://web.stanford.edu/group/mappingmilitants/cgi-bin/groups/view/149

[17] Amy Chew, "A resurgent communist New People's Army in southern Philippines raises security threat in Mindanao," October 18, 2018, www.channelnewsasia.com/news/asia/communist-new-peoples-army-philippines-security-threat-mindanao-10841242

colonialism and nineteenth-century liberalism in Chiapas" (Harvey 1998: 36). Continuities of legacies of *caciquismo* can be found because the "caciques who would be challenged by peasant movements in the municipalities of Venustiano Carranza and Simojovel in the 1970s were descendants of the dominant families in the same regions in 1911" (Harvey 1998: 52). The Zapatista rebellion can thus be seen as the latest in a history of rebellions by indigenous people for land and dignity in the Chiapas region, similar to the Maoist rebellion in Chhattisgarh or Jharkhand in India.

4   CONCLUSION

In this chapter, I have tried to show how colonial indirect rule created long-term legacies for both ethnic and ideological insurgencies of different types in countries other than India. Future research should try to find other such cases and analyze them in more detail, using both archival data and micro-level datasets. It is clear even from a cursory study of these cases that colonial indirect rule had different kinds of effects through various channels, which were later exploited by rebel leaders. The mechanisms created by indirect rule that led to these insurgencies in Burma and Pakistan were similar to the mechanisms of weak state capacity, low development and ethnic exclusion that are to be found in the case of Maoist insurgency in Chhattisgarh and Andhra Pradesh in India. Spanish colonial rule resulted in dependence of colonizers on local elites like *caciques* in Mexico and *encomenderos* in Philippines to collect land revenue, which caused land inequality and rebellion. This was similar to the *zamindari* land tenure system in Bihar and Bengal in India. While the exact form of indirect rule and mechanisms varied in regions beyond South Asia, there are broad similarities that demonstrate generalizability of the theory.

The role of rebel agency is also crucial, but this study hopes to show that many of the conditions of ethnic inequality and grievances, as well as state weakness, which are taken as the causes by the civil war literature are themselves created by deeper historical processes and institutions. Taking a step back in time, and bringing history back into the study of insurgency, allows us as scholars to develop a more holistic and deeper understanding of insurgency. It also explains why there is persistence of conflict in some regions, whether in Mexico, India, or Nigeria, with peasant or tribal rebellions in the colonial period being crushed to later reemerge in different forms in the same region in the future.

Conclusion: Policy Implications and Future of the Maoist Conflict

The book starts by asking if current insurgencies and civil wars have deep roots in history. It analyzes subnational variation of the Maoist insurgency in India to show that different types of British colonial indirect rule – through landlords and princes – created structural inequalities and despotic extraction, which persisted as enabling conditions for leftist rebellion. The previous chapter shows that there is broad generalizability of this theory to other cases in South Asia, like the ethnic secessionist insurgencies in Burma and the Taliban insurgency in Pakistan, where different forms of British indirect rule created conditions for insurgency. Future research needs to analyze how historical institutions created similar conditions of state weakness and inequalities that were conducive to insurgency in other cases in Africa and South America.

I end the book by bringing the focus back to the case of the Maoist insurgency in India and engaging with a pertinent question – are there any policy implications of my theory based on colonial institutions? A likely criticism of a theory based on colonial legacies is that the structural conditions created by colonialism are persistent and sticky and cannot be changed. So, once such conditions are created, there is not much a government can do to prevent insurgency and inequality in that region, and there are no relevant policy suggestions that can be derived from such a theory.

Another possible critique of a theory based on colonial legacies is whether it can explain changing patterns of violence and how long a persistent insurgency like the Maoist conflict will last. This question becomes relevant since the level of violence in the Maoist conflict has declined since 2013–14; the number of surrenders by Maoist cadres has increased in recent years, but low-level violence and attacks against security forces continue. Is there a chance that the Maoist leaders will negotiate a peace agreement as the FARC rebels did in Colombia? Does my theory based on colonial legacies have any predictions for patterns of violence and duration of insurgency? I address these issues in this concluding chapter.

I   POLICY IMPLICATIONS OF COLONIAL LEGACIES

Are there possible policy implications of my theory that long-term patterns of
state formation dating from the colonial period create legacies for postcolonial
conflict in India, for the current Indian government? More generally, for
theories that emphasize the role of colonial factors in predicting postcolonial
outcomes like those of Acemoglu et al. (2001) and Mahoney (2010), what are
the possible policy implications for the current period? If the long-term causal
mechanisms that lead to Maoist insurgency in India are irreversible in the
postcolonial period, then one possible implication could be that nothing much
can be done by postcolonial governments to change the undesirable outcomes of
past historical institutions. There is a path dependence and stickiness of the
mechanisms unleashed by these historical institutions that are very difficult to
reverse.

Kohli (2004: 421) in his analysis of the effects of colonialism on postcolonial
industrial development in developing countries like South Korea, Brazil, India,
and Nigeria addresses the issue of policy implications by suggesting that "To
stand the old master Karl Marx on his head, far too many scholars and
practitioners have been trying to change the developing world; the point is
also to understand it. And yet if a problem has been understood well, it ought
to have some implications for how to deal with it in the future." In this spirit,
there are two possible ways to think of policy implications of my theory. First, if
it is true that choices of indirect rule by empires lead to lower development,
ethnic grievances, and other undesirable outcomes, then countries should avoid
using convenient deals with local actors to carry out governance. For example,
the United States should not try to use alliances with warlords and ethnic chiefs
in Iraq or Afghanistan, since this will again backfire in the future. The Indian
central government has often continued the policies of indirect rule developed
by the British toward the ethnic groups in India's northeast, but a more direct
form of administration might have prevented the many ethnic insurgencies in
this region from breaking out. Thus, lessons from the past can guide policy
choices in the present.

The second way to draw policy implications is to realize that while the effects
of these colonial institutions from the past are persistent and sticky, they are not
irreversible if the right combination of political will and social/ethnic demands
forces the government to try and reverse some of the pernicious effects of
indirect colonial rule institutions. The causal logic that leads from past
historical institutions of indirect rule to postcolonial outcomes is not
deterministic. It is possible for certain postcolonial provincial governments to
reverse the pernicious effects of indirect rule at certain critical junctures, and if
these opportunities are not taken, then *lock-in* occurs and the effects of earlier
institutions persist. This is apparent in both the Indian Maoist insurgency case
and other cases of colonial indirect rule in the British Empire. For example, in
Chapter 9, I explain the exceptional states of Kerala and Karnataka within

India, which had indirect rule through princely states under the British and yet no Maoist insurgency since the 1980s: progressive political parties were able to carry out land reforms in the postcolonial period and break the power of landed elites to some extent in these states. This matches with Kohli's (2004: 424–25) suggestion that while institutional shocks and changes usually come from large-scale events like colonialism or anti-colonial freedom movements, small-scale incremental changes through political parties to reverse long-term institutional effects are possible in certain cases, where the overall state capacity and institutions are not very low.

Finally, a direct policy implication of my theory for Indian policy makers and government is regarding the anti-Maoist *Salwa Judum* vigilante movement in Chhattisgarh between 2005 and 2007. The *Salwa Judum* was indirectly supported by the ruling Bharatiya Janata Party (BJP) in the state and led to escalation of interethnic violence and displacement of large numbers of *Adivasis* from Dantewada district, many of whom have yet to return to their villages, thus creating a long-term negative impact on the education and health of these displaced tribal families. Looking back at history, the government had to rely on vigilante groups like *Salwa Judum* because of historically low levels of state/police capacity in these areas of former colonial indirect rule, which meant that the local police force was not strong enough to tackle the insurgency (Miklian 2009). It was lack of formal state capacity through police that forced the government to rely on vigilante groups to tackle the Maoist menace. Also, many of the leaders of the *Salwa Judum*, like Mahendra Karma, were tribal landlords, whose land, property, and status in their rural community were threatened by the Maoists. These landlords were local elites whose predecessors had emerged during colonial indirect rule and whose power persisted through path dependent mechanisms into the 1980s. Similar use of upper caste-based armies like the *Ranvir Sena* in Bihar in the 1990s to fight the Maoists, also intensified caste violence in India. Upper-caste landlords descended from the *zamindars* of colonial times continued to remain powerful in these areas and created vigilante groups to fight the Maoists and stop them from distributing land to the lower-caste peasants and *Adivasis* in Bihar and Chhattisgarh. Historical legacies of landlordism and a weak state could be useful to understand the pattern of counterinsurgency in these areas and have deep lessons for the current Indian government.

A direct policy implication of my theory is that the state should try to overcome the path dependent persistence of low police capacity and develop a stronger police force in states like Bihar and Chhattisgarh and provide better development in tribal areas, and not rely on tribal elites to do counterinsurgency operations on its behalf. The state should also try to enact land reforms, as done by Communist Party–led governments in states like Kerala and West Bengal, which will reduce the power of landlords and prevent them from using vigilantism. Avoiding such policies of indirect rule and exploitation would have possibly prevented successful Maoist mobilization in former princely state areas of Chhattisgarh. Future studies could analyze the effect of historical institutions on other such counterinsurgency choices.

2   ENDGAME OF THE MAOIST CONFLICT, OR RECURRENCE IN THE FUTURE?

2.1   What Explains the Recent Reduction of Violence in 2011–2014?

In this book, I have tried to explain how initial areas of Maoist control in the second phase of Maoist insurgency in the 1980s–90s emerged in areas where there were historically indirect forms of rule and revenue collection. In fact, the first phase of insurgency in 1967–73 inspired by Charu Mazumdar and Kanu Sanyal also occurred in areas of *zamindari* tenure in Naxalbari in Bengal and Srikakulam in Andhra. Does such a theory based on historical legacies allow us to understand the more recent dynamics of the Maoist conflict? Can my theory explain why there was a sudden rise of violence between 2005 and 2011 and then a rapid decline since 2012–13? See Figures 11.1 and 11.2 in Section 2.2 for patterns of violence.

As described in detail in the section on the history of the insurgency in Chapter 4, the unification of the PWG and MCC to form the CPI-Maoist in 2004 led to escalation in levels of attacks by the Maoists and rapid geographic spread. The Indian state also responded in the form of higher counterinsurgency, in particular the *Salwa Judum* vigilante movement in the state of Chhattisgarh, which also contributed to the sudden escalation in violence from 2005 to 2009. Following the decline of the *Salwa Judum* in Chhattisgarh and its official ban by the Supreme Court in response to a petition filed by Nandini Sundar and other human rights activists, the central state used other counterinsurgency strategies like Operation Greenhunt in 2009–11 that tried to coordinate state police and paramilitary forces across all Maoist-affected states, with the goal of destroying the Maoist base areas in Jharkhand and Chhattisgarh. The Maoists responded with several attacks, the most high profile being an ambush that killed seventy-five Central Reserve Police Force (CRPF) troops in Dantewada district in Chhattisgarh in April 2010, which destroyed political consensus and weakened Operation Greenhunt.

With the end of Operation Greenhunt, the levels of violence sharply declined in 2012–15. Why did insurgency violence levels fall? One of the reasons could be that the development programs by the central and state governments like the Integrated Action Plan (IAP), road-building projects, and building police stations in vulnerable areas have finally succeeded. These were started by the previous Congress government (2005–9 and 2009–14) and are being continued by the current BJP government since 2014 (Mukherjee 2018b). The study by Dasgupta et al. (2017) finds that those districts where the National Rural Employment Guarantee Scheme (NREGS) was implemented by the government tended to see a reduction in the level of Maoist violence, by providing employment opportunities to poor people in Maoist-affected areas. The effect of the NREGS scheme is more visible in Andhra Pradesh and Chhattisgarh, which are "star states" with more efficient bureaucracies than states like Jharkhand, Bihar, and Orissa, which are low-capacity states with less efficient bureaucracies (Dasgupta et al. 2017).

Since coming to power, the BJP government in New Delhi has also continued several of these development policies, along with increased counterinsurgency efforts. It has replaced the IAP of the Congress government with a new scheme started in 2017–18, known as the "Special Central Assistance for the most LWE Affected Districts" to fill up critical gaps in public infrastructure and services with an outlay of INR 30 billion, with INR 10 billion per annum. In March 2018, the government had informed Parliament that under the Road Requirement Plan-I (RRP-I), of the sanctioned 5,422 kilometers roads in thirty-four Maoist-affected districts, 4,537 kilometers of road had been completed, while the remaining 885 kilometers were "under construction."[1]

Besides development, the central and various state governments have been increasing counterinsurgency efforts, which may be bearing fruit. The *Annual Report of the MHA, 2018–19* claims that the recent fall in Maoist violence can be "attributed to greater presence and increased capacity of the Security Forces across the LWE affected States, better operational strategy and better monitoring of development schemes."[2] One important counterinsurgency scheme started by the Congress government was the Security Related Expenditure (SRE) scheme, which allowed state governments to reimburse 50 percent of their expenses on provisions like insurance plans for police personnel, community policing, rehabilitation of surrendered Maoists, and other security-related items. Recently, the BJP government raised the SRE reimbursement to up to 100 percent and also allowed the advance release of funds to the Maoist-affected states.[3] The central government has helped states raise fourteen specialized commando battalions (CoBRA) that are "equipped and trained in guerrilla and jungle warfare techniques and deployed to the worst-affected districts." It has also helped in creating several Counter Insurgency and Anti-Terrorism Schools (CIAT), similar to the Counter Terrorism and Jungle Warfare College (CTJW) in Kanker, Chhattisgarh, to train police for counterinsurgency operations.[4]

Another reason for the reduction in violence could have to do with counterinsurgency success in arresting or killing Maoist leaders at various levels. As Table 11.1 shows, between 2010 and 2017, around 949 Maoist leaders at the national, state, and local levels were arrested, killed, or

---

[1] Deepak Kumar Nayak, "Maoists: Wounded, not Vanquished," *South Asia Intelligence Review*, Vol. 17, no. 40, April 1, 2019. www.satp.org/south-asia-intelligence-review-Volume-17-No-40#assessment1

[2] Annual Report, Ministry of Home Affairs, 2018–19, p. 10.

[3] Niranjan Sahoo, "Half a Century of India's Maoist Insurgency: An Appraisal of State Response," ORF Occasional Paper 198, June 2019.

[4] Sahoo, "Half a Century of India's Maoist Insurgency."

TABLE 11.1 *Maoist leadership neutralized during
2010–17*

Category	Killed	Arrested	Surrendered	Total
National	3	15	1	19
State	20	163	31	214
Local	102	335	279	716
Total	125	513	311	949

Source: www.satp.org/south-asia-intelligence-review-Volume-16-No-
22#assessment1
For more detailed breakdown by locality of arrests, surrenders,
deaths, see www.satp.org/satporgtp/countries/india/maoist/
data_sheets/LWE_2016.htm

surrendered, which lends some credence to theories of *leadership decapitation*. These included at least 19 national-level leaders, 214 state-level leaders, and 716 local-level leaders. Security forces arrested 513 leaders, including 15 national-level leaders, 163 state-level leaders, and 335 local-level leaders. There was also the surrender of 311 Maoist leaders, including one national-level leader, 31 state-level leaders, and 279 local-level leaders.[5]

Also, the Maoist leadership is undergoing a crisis because of deaths of leaders and an aging leadership. At the time of its formation in 2004, the CPI-Maoist had a sixteen-member strong Politburo, the outfit's highest decision-making body, led by General Secretary Muppala Lakshmana Rao. Of this, only eight members remain, with two having been killed, two died due to illness, and four have been arrested. Similarly, the CPI-Maoist originally had a thirty-four-member strong Central Committee (CC), the second-highest decision-making body in the outfit, which included all the sixteen members of the Politburo and another eighteen members. Of the latter eighteen, at least two have been killed, nine arrested, one surrendered, and one died due to illness, leaving only five of the original eighteen.[6]

Many of the CPI-Maoist leaders in the Politburo and the CC are aging and suffering from health issues – seven are older than 60 years. Ganapathy was sixty-seven and the oldest leader Prashant Bose was sixty-nine in 2017. In the meeting of the CC in February 2017, this issue of aging leadership was meticulously discussed, and a resolution adopted. According to the newspaper *Telangana Today*, which was able to access these reports from the Central Committee meeting, the CPI-Maoist party has decided to relocate those aging leaders to safer locations in urban areas and has urged the veteran leaders to

---

[5] Ajit Kumar Singh, "Rudderless Reds," *South Asia Intelligence Review*, Volume 16, No. 22, November 27, 2017. www.satp.org/south-asia-intelligence-review-Volume-16-No-22#assessment1
[6] Deepak Kumar Nayak, "Maoists: No Takers," *South Asia Intelligence Review*, Vol. 18, No. 12, September 16, 2019. www.satp.org/south-asia-intelligence-review-volume-18-no-12#assessment2

come forward on their own "in the revolutionary spirit" and "step down" from their positions to set an example for others. This may be the reason General Secretary Ganapathy stepped down in 2018, making way for his second in command, Basavaraj, to take over the leadership role. The news report suggests that this could result in "significant change in the strategies and tactics of the Indian revolutionary movement" given the "penchant of young leaders to opt for more intensified military actions."[7]

2.2 Temporary Dip Followed by Return to Usual Pattern of Low Intensity, Persistent Conflict?

Does the gradual reduction in level of violence signal the end of one of India's longest and most protracted insurgencies? It is better to be cautious before making a theoretical claim or prediction since it is still not clear if this is a temporary dip in violence levels or a permanent end to this long-lasting Maoist conflict.

While the levels of violence have been reduced to below the *average* of 500 deaths per year of the 1990s, there continue to be low levels of violence in the range of 400 deaths per year. In Figure 11.1, I present data on violence levels

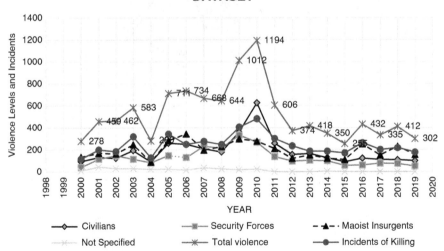

VIOLENCE LEVELS AND INCIDENTS IN MAOIST INSURGENCY (2000–19) FROM SATP DATASET

FIGURE 11.1 Violence levels and incidents in Maoist insurgency from SATP data
Source: See www.satp.org/datasheet-terrorist-attack/fatalities/india-maoistinsurgency (downloaded and updated with 2019 data on July 14, 2020)

---

[7] K. Srinivas Reddy, "Maoists to relieve 'veteran comrades' of key roles," *Telangana Today*, September 27, 2017.

from the SATP database on the Maoist insurgency, which shows that the total
fatalities of security forces, Maoists and civilians was 432 deaths in 2016, 335
in 2017, and 412 in 2018.[8] It seems after the really low dip in violence in 2015,
the levels of violence are again close to the 400 deaths per year average it was
at before the merger of the PWG and MCC. Also, the number of violent
incidents is 262 in 2016, 200 in 2017, and 217 in 2018 respectively,
which shows that number of attacks by Maoists may also be falling in recent
years, which suggests that the number of Maoist squads on the ground are
diminishing.

I also present data in Figure 11.2 on Maoist insurgency violence from
Ministry of Home Affairs (MHA) government data, which I obtained from
the www.satp.org data archives. This MHA data is more comprehensive than
that presented in Figure 4.2 in Chapter 4 from MHA Annual Reports, because it
also includes *Naxal/Maoist deaths*. This MHA data also shows that *total*

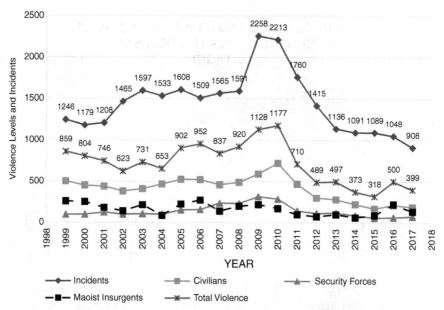

**VIOLENCE LEVELS AND INCIDENTS OF
MAOIST VIOLENCE (MHA DATA)**

FIGURE 11.2 Violence levels and incidents in Maoist insurgency from government data
Source: Fatalities in Left-wing Extremism (Ministry of Home Affairs) at www.satp.org
/satporgtp/countries/india/maoist/data_sheets/fatalitiesnaxalmha.htm

[8] See www.satp.org/datasheet-terrorist-attack/fatalities/india-maoistinsurgency for updated data
till 2019–20.

violence peaks at 1,177 deaths in 2010 and then starts to decline. It was 500 deaths in 2016 and 399 deaths in 2017, which shows that there is still some low-intensity violence continuing in recent years. The *incidents of violence* in the MHA data in Figure 11.2 are much higher than in the SATP events data in Figure 11.1 and are in the range of 1,000 incidents average per year in 2014–17, which shows that the number of incidents may not have declined that much, though levels of violence have fallen.

While there have been increasing rates of surrenders by Maoist cadres, and the ability of the Maoists to recruit seems to have gone down in recent years, they still seem to retain their ability to carry out occasional large attacks. For example, on April 24, 2017, the Maoists attacked a CRPF convoy and killed twenty-five *jawans* and injured six in an ambush in the Burkapal area of Sukma in Chhattisgarh. This was the single largest attack since the 2010 attack on CRPF in the same Sukma area that resulted in the deaths of seventy-five CRPF soldiers. The attack took place more than a month after thirteen CRPF *jawans* were killed in a similar ambush at a road-opening party on the Injeram-Bhejji stretch, around 60 kilometers from this ambush spot.[9] This may have been a desperate attempt by the local Maoist leadership to demonstrate their ability, but it still shows that it may be premature to assume that the insurgency has ended, even though recruitment levels are falling.[10]

As mentioned earlier, the Maoist leadership was aware of the problem of the aging leadership in the Politburo and on November 5, 2018, replaced the long-serving General Secretary Ganapathy (Muppala Laxmana Rao) with his "second-in-command" Nambala Keshava Rao *aka* Basavaraj. Basavaraj had been the head of the CPI-Maoist's military wing, the People's Liberation Guerrilla Army (PLGA) and had a reputation for a greater tendency to use violence and was suspected to be behind the planning of recent attacks in Chhattisgarh.[11] This was announced by the CPI-Maoist Central Committee in a press statement, which confirmed that "In view of his growing ill-health and advancing age in the past few years and with the aim of strengthening the Central Committee and with a vision of the future, Comrade Ganapathy voluntarily withdrew from the responsibilities of General Secretary."[12]

---

[9] Deeptiman Tiwary, Dipankar Ghose, and Rahul Tripathi, "Worst in Chhattisgarh in seven years: 25 CRPF men killed by Maoists in Sukma," *Indian Express*, April 25, 2017. https://indianexpress.com/article/india/worst-in-chhattisgarh-in-seven-years-26-crpf-men-killed-by-maoists-in-sukma-4626755/

[10] "Murder at noon: On Maoist attack in Chhattisgarh's Sukma," *The Hindu*, April 27, 2017. www.thehindu.com/opinion/editorial/murder-at-noon/article18209974.ece

[11] Nayak, "Maoists: Wounded, not Vanquished."

[12] *Communist Party of India-Maoist, Central Committee*, Press Release, November 10, 2018. www.bannedthought.net/India/CPI-Maoist-Docs/Statements-2018/181110-CC-GeneralSecretaryChange-Eng.pdf

In 2017, Madvi Hidma, a tribal battalion commander from Bastar, was inducted into the Central Committee (CC), which made him the second tribal and the youngest CC member. The reason could be to promote him as the "'tribal face" of the CPI-Maoist, besides recognition of his skills as the military commander of the Sukma battalion that had carried out some of the daring attacks on the CRPF. Hidma's battalion "has been exceptionally successful in combat against the security forces. It has less than 10% casualty ratio in every combat compared to the security forces and its morale is extremely high."[13] Promoting him into the CC, in combination with attempts to get the aging veteran leadership to retire and allow new leadership to emerge may be a signal that the Maoists are aware of their weakening capacities on the ground, which they are trying to rectify.

The CPI-Maoist is reportedly trying to strengthen its Central Military Commission (CMC), the group's principal fighting force. According to a September 10, 2019 report, intelligence inputs suggest that around 250 Maoist cadres have recently joined the CMC.[14] To add a cautionary note, the Maoist insurgency has gone through phases of low violence in the past, only to escalate again. Prakash Singh, a former police chief with considerable counterinsurgency experience, commented that the patterns of violence in the Maoist insurgency seem to escalate in a cyclical manner every ten years, as they did in 1971, 1991, and 2001–1981 with only ninety-two deaths being the only exception.[15] Violence did escalate again around 2010–11, and so it is still possible that we may see a resurgence of the insurgency in the 2020s!

It seems that the Maoist insurgency falls into the pattern of low intensity but persistent conflict that can be seen in many other insurgencies in India, like the Naga insurgency and Manipur insurgency in the northeast, and even the ethnic secessionist insurgency in Kashmir, which has seen lower levels of violence since 2010 but recent escalation since 2016 following the killing of popular rebel leader Burhan Wani (Mukherjee 2018b). Attempts to sign a peace agreement with the PWG Maoists failed in Andhra Pradesh in 2004, and similar attempts at peace with the CPI-Maoist in Jharkhand in 2010 have also failed. While initial levels of violence in the 1990s were in the 400–500 deaths per year range, counterinsurgency escalation by state governments in Andhra Pradesh and Chhattisgarh in 2005–10 led to a sudden rise in levels of violence. While levels of Maoist violence have decreased since 2013, it is not clear whether this implies a complete end to violence or just a return to the pattern of low-intensity persistent insurgency.

Narayan Sanyal, one of the founders of Party Unity (PU) in the Bihar-Jharkhand zone who helped forge unity between the different Maoist outfits that led to the formation of the CPI-Maoist in 2004 was arrested in 2005 and

[13] Pavan Dahat, "CPI (Maoist) commander Hidma promoted to Central Committee," *The Hindu*, September 10, 2017.
[14] Nayak, "Maoists: No Takers."   [15] Singh, *The Naxalite Movement in India*, pp. 164–65.

kept in Raipur Central Jail. When asked about the possibility of success of the revolution in his lifetime, he said: "this movement is not going to win immediately or in the near future" and it "may be a generation or more before the movement succeeds." While accepting that the Maoist movement in India would not succeed in his lifetime, he believed that the current "socioeconomic conditions will allow it to continue" since inequalities still existed.[16] This attitude of one of the high level leaders of the CPI-Maoist shows that Maoist leaders believe in protracted insurgency and have long-time horizons and are willing to tolerate ups and downs in the success of the insurgency movement.[17]

Ganapathy, erstwhile general secretary of CPI-Maoist, accepted that the Maoists had made tactical errors in expanding their areas of influence and escalating violence, which resulted in escalation in counterinsurgency tactics of the security forces and serious loss of cadres and leaders. He writes in 2014: "leadership losses began since May 2005 itself, they increased gradually after Unity Congress and the situation took a serious turn by 2011 end. The leadership failed to a large extent in defending itself and the ranks. ... This failure is a very severe one" (Ganapathy 2014). In order to avoid such errors which had led to the demise of the Sendero Luminoso Maoist leadership in Peru, Ganapathy suggested that the CPI-Maoist must follow tactics that allows it to protect and preserve their forces. It is possible that the CPI-Maoist leadership decided to start a phase of "tactical retreat" where the Maoist leadership is trying to consolidate its capacity and make changes in leadership and plan for a different strategy in the future.[18]

Another explanation for the persistence of the Maoist conflict is based on state side motivations. Staniland (2012b) has shown that the state is often willing to agree to shadowy bargains that allow it to "keep a lid" on peripheral insurgencies, whether in Nagaland in north east India, the FATA region in Pakistan, or other places, as long as they do not escalate. Similarly, Mukherjee (2014) suggests that "middle capacity" states like India, Pakistan, Burma, and Indonesia in South and Southeast Asia have been willing to live with and contain peripheral insurgencies that are not very threatening, especially when faced with *multiple* insurgencies that force the state to prioritize which ones to tackle effectively (Mukherjee 2014). This could explain the violence patterns of the Maoist insurgency, where the escalation of violence in 2005–10 was due to increased threat perception of state from the rebels due to sudden escalation of attacks by Maoists. This led the central state to respond, but once the levels of violence return to earlier lower levels, the state may be willing to

---

[16] Interview with Narayan Sanyal (founder of Party Unity and former Politburo member of CPI-Maoist), Raipur Central Jail, Raipur, Chhattisgarh, 2008.

[17] For analysis of how long-time horizons of rebel leaders influences conflict duration, see Monica Toft, "Issue Indivisibility and Time Horizons as Rationalist Explanations for War."

[18] Pradhan, "Maoists: Tactical Retreat," *South Asia Intelligence Review*, Vol. 11, No. 36, 2013.

allow the Maoist conflict to persist as long as it remains localized. It is possible the Maoist insurgency has returned to this pattern of low-intensity violence following an escalation due to changing insurgency strategy in 2005–10.

3 DOES MY THEORY PREDICT THIS CHANGING PATTERN OF VIOLENCE?

Scope Condition – Colonial Institutions Only Explain Origins and Not Intensity and Duration of Insurgency

Regardless of whether the decline in Maoist attacks signals an end to the insurgency or only a different low-intensity phase, the pertinent question is whether my theory on colonial legacies predicts this changing pattern of violence.

One of the scope conditions of my theory is that colonial institutions can only explain the initial spatial variation of insurgency and not future dynamics. In Chapter 3, Section 4.4, I explain that my theory of colonial indirect rule only explains variation in rebel control till the initial consolidation of the Maoist conflict in 2004. Following the unification of the Maoist Communist Center (MCC) and People's War Group (PWG) to form the CPI-Maoist in 2004, the Maoists developed a much higher level of organizational capacity and also changed its tactics, which allowed it to expand beyond the initial core areas that were historically part of indirect rule and revenue collection. Historically created inequality and low state capacity no longer retained the same capacity to constrain rebel mobilization and patterns of violence.

Once an insurgency movement consolidates, new dynamics emerge within the rebel movement and within the state counterinsurgency operations that start playing a more important role in predicting the pattern of insurgency. Similarly, intensification in state counterinsurgency could also lead to losses of Maoist cadre and leadership capture that could lead to a reduction in violence. My theory based on historical institutions does not claim to explain the changing patterns of violence and the duration of insurgency, which are better explained by Maoist strategy and state counterinsurgency policies in states like Chhattisgarh, Bihar, West Bengal and Andhra Pradesh.

However, the initial core areas of Maoist control in the second phase of Maoist mobilization in the 1980s–90s in Bihar, Andhra Pradesh, and Chhattisgarh are well predicted by my theoretical framework, since they occur in areas of *zamindari* land tenure, or the feudatory or successor type of princely states. Even the initial phase in 1967–73 of Naxal or Maoist rebellion in the Naxalbari region of north Bengal and the Srikakulam region of Andhra Pradesh were in zones of *zamindari* land tenure, which is a form of indirect revenue collection in my theoretical framework. This initial outbreak of tribal rebellion in 1967–73 thus occurred in areas of land revenue exploitation based on unequal land tenure systems and is also well predicted by my theoretical framework.

4 RECURRENCE OF REBELLION HISTORICALLY

This brings us back to the question of whether we are seeing the endgame of one of India's longest-running insurgencies or whether Maoist violence can recur in some other form in the future. This book focuses on explaining spatial variation of Maoist control since the 1990s for the second phase of the insurgency. However, the first phase of the insurgency occurred in Naxalbari in Bengal in 1967–73 and in Srikakulam in Andhra Pradesh in the 1970s and was crushed by the state. Before that, a Communist Party–led peasant rebellion took place in the Telangana region in Andhra Pradesh in 1947–51 as well as the Tebhaga peasant rebellion in Bengal in the 1940s. Earlier, there were various tribal and peasant rebellions in colonial times like the Birsa Munda–led tribal rebellion in Jharkhand in 1899–1900 and the Gunda Dhar–led tribal rebellion in Bastar in Chhattisgarh in 1910.

There seems to be a recurrence of peasant and tribal rebellion in these areas from colonial and even pre-colonial times. Gough (1974: 1406) mentions seventy-seven such colonial-era rebellions, and while these revolts have been widespread and of different types, "certain areas have an especially strong tradition of rebellion," in particular both rural and urban Bengal, the Santhal areas of Bihar and Bengal, the tribal areas of Andhra Pradesh and eastern Orissa, the southern Chhattisgarh area (Gough 1974). These endemic rebellions occurred mostly in areas with indirect revenue collection systems like the *zamindari* land tenure system in the Bengal/Bihar zone or indirect rule through small and large feudatory-type princely states in central India and the large successor princely state of Hyderabad in Andhra Pradesh.

These grievances persisted into the postcolonial era. The peasant and tribal rebellions in these same regions led by Maoist intellectuals since 1980s are just a new version of earlier rebellions against the state, except that the earlier versions were led by indigenous leaders. It is state policies of exploitation of natural and land resources and extremely high land revenue taxation that often led to these rebellions during colonial times; since these inequalities persisted, future rebellions have continued, only their form and leadership have changed. According to Sundar (2006), the Maoists are the true heirs to the Bhumkal rebellion in Chhattisgarh in the colonial period. They have tried to mobilize the tribals by providing them protection from the outsider *thekedars* and forest guards, who represent an alien ethnic group, and from a central state that is led by non-tribals (Sundar 2006). The Maoist ideologue Nitin depicts the *Adivasi* support of the PWG since 1980s to oppose government policies that deprive them of their rights over forests and land, as a "continuation of their 150 year long tradition of militant protests and armed rebellions" (Nitin 2006: 11).

This long-lasting arc of rebellion in these regions in India demonstrates why it is important to bring back the role of historical institutions and conflict to the analysis of civil wars, because it allows us to explain persistence and historical recurrence of conflict, which existing theories of civil war are not good at explaining. Other regions like Africa and Latin America also have such long-lasting effects of historical institutions that create inequality and weak state capacity, for example, the *mita* system of labor exploitation in Peru that may have had indirect effects on inequality and the Shining Path insurgency that need to be analyzed in future research. Colonial indirect rule in Nigeria may have laid the grounds for the Boko Haram insurgency, due to divergent types of pre-colonial and colonial-era empires in northern and southern Nigeria. Besides indirect rule, other types of colonial institutions that constructed ethnic identities may also play a role in creating ethnic grievances. Understanding such different types of historical legacies of conflict is crucial for studies of civil war.

Bibliography

BOOKS AND ARTICLES

Acemoglu, Daron, Simon Johnson, and James Robinson. 2001. "The Colonial Origins of Comparative Development: An Empirical Investigation." *American Economic Review* 91 (5): 1369–401.

Acemoglu, Daron, Isaias Chaves, Philip Osafo-Kwaako, and James Robinson. October 2013. "Indirect Rule and State Weakness in Africa: Sierra Leone in Comparative Perspective." NBER paper.

Ahmed, Akbar S. 1980. *Pukhtun Economy and Society: Traditional Structure and Economic Development in a Tribal Society.* London; Boston: Routledge & Kegan Paul.

2013. *The Thistle and the Drone: How America's War on Terror Became a Global War on Tribal Islam.* Washington, DC: Brookings Institution Press.

Akella, Karuna and Robin Nielsen. 2005. "Building on Political Will: Next Step for Land Reform." *Economic and Political Weekly*, August 20.

Akins, Harrison. 2017. "FATA and the Frontier Crimes Regulation in Pakistan: The Enduring Legacy of British Colonialism," *Policy Brief 5:17*, Baker Center for Public Policy.

Alam, Muzaffar, and Sanjay Subrahmanyam, eds. 1998. *The Mughal State, 1526–1750.* Delhi; New York: Oxford University Press.

Alam, Sanjeer. 2010. "On Matching Census Tracts and Electoral Boundaries: The Bottom-up Aggregation Approach." *Economic and Political Weekly*, August 21.

Ali, Imtiaz. 2005. "The Balochistan Problem." *Pakistan Horizon* 58 (2): 41–62.

2018. "Mainstreaming Pakistan's Federally Administered Tribal Areas Reform Initiatives and Roadblocks." *United States Institute of Peace Special Report.*

"Andhra Pradesh: Peasants' Struggle for Land." 1977. *Economic and Political Weekly*, October 1.

Angrist, Joshua D. and Jorn-Steffen Pischke. 2009. *Mostly Harmless Econometrics: An Empiricist's Companion.* Princeton, NJ: Princeton University Press.

Anselin, Luc. 1988. *Spatial Econometrics: Methods and Models.* Dordrecht; Boston: Kluwer Academic Publishers.

2000. "GIS, Spatial Econometrics and Social Science Research." *Journal of Geographical Systems* 2 (1): 11–15.

Arjona, Ana. 2017. *Rebelocracy: Social Order in the Colombian Civil War.* Cambridge: Cambridge University Press.

Arnson, Cynthia, ed. 1999. *Comparative Peace Processes in Latin America*. Stanford, CA: Stanford University Press.

Aung-Thwin, Michael. 1985. "The British 'Pacification' of Burma: Order without Meaning." *Journal of Southeast Asian Studies* 16 (2): 245–61.

Babalola, Dele. 2013. "The Origins of Nigerian Federalism: The Rikerian Theory and Beyond." *Federal Governance* 10 (1): 43–54. https://nbn-resolving.org/urn:nbn:de:0168-ssoar-346764

Balagopal, K. 1988. *Probings in the Political Economy of Agrarian Classes and Conflict*. Hyderabad: Perspectives.

   2006a. "Chhattisgarh: Physiognomy of Violence." *Economic and Political Weekly* 41 (22), June 3: 2183–86.

   2006b. "Maoist Movement in Andhra Pradesh." *Economic and Political Weekly* 41 (29), July 22: 3183–87.

Balcells, Laia and Stathis Kalyvas. 2010. "Did Marxism Make a Difference? Marxist Rebellions and National Liberation Movements." Paper prepared for the Annual Meeting of the American Political Science Association, Washington, DC, September 2–5.

Banerjee, Abhijit and Lakshmi Iyer. 2005. "History, Institutions and Economic Performance: The Legacy of Colonial Land Tenure Systems in India." *American Economic Review* 95 (4): 1190–213.

Banerjee, Abhijit and Rohini Somanathan. 2007. "The Political Economy of Public Goods: Some Evidence from India." *Journal of Development Economics* 82: 287–314.

Banerjee, Sumanta. 1980. *In the Wake of Naxalbari: The Naxalite Movement in India*. Calcutta: Subarnarekha Press.

   1984. *India's Simmering Revolution*. New Delhi: Select Book Syndicate.

Baruah, Amit. 1990. "Bastar of the Tribals." *Frontline*, May 12–25.

Baruah, Sanjib. 1999. *India against Itself: Assam and the Politics of Nationality*. Philadelphia: University of Pennsylvania Press.

   2005. *Durable Disorder: Understanding the Politics of Northeast India*. New Delhi: Oxford University Press.

Baum, C. F., M. E. Schaffer, and S. Stillman. 2007a. "Enhanced Routines for Instrumental Variables: Generalized Method of Moments Estimations and Testing." *The Stata Journal* 7 (4): 465–506.

   2007b. "*ivreg2*: Stata Module for Extended Instrumental Variables/2SLS, GMM and AC/HAC, LIML, and K-class Regression." Boston College Department of Economics, Statistical Software Components S425401. Downloadable from http://ideas.repec.org/c/boc/bocode/s425401.html.

Bayly, C. 1983. *Rulers, Townsmen and Bazaars: North Indian Society in the Age of British Expansion, 1780–1870*. Oxford: Oxford University Press.

   1988. *Indian Society and the Making of the British Empire*. Cambridge; New York: Cambridge University Press.

Behera, Anshuman. 2017. "Development as a Source of Conflict: The Sahukars, Displaced People and the Maoists in Koraput." *The Round Table* 106 (5): 543–56.

Besley, Timothy and Robin Burgess. 2000. "Land Reform, Poverty Reduction, and Growth: Evidence from India." *Quarterly Journal of Economics* 115 (2): 389–430.

Besley, Timothy, and Marta Reynal-Querol. 2014. "The Legacy of Historical Conflict: Evidence from Africa." *American Political Science Review* 108 (2): 319–36.

Bhatia, Bela. 2005. "The Naxalite Movement in Central Bihar." *Economic and Political Weekly* 40 (14): 1536–49.

Bhavnani, Rikhil R., and Bethany Lacina. 2015. "The Effects of Weather-Induced Migration on Sons of the Soil Riots in India." *World Politics* 67 (4): 760–94.

Blanton, Robert T., David Mason, and Brian Athow. 2001. "Colonial Style and Post-Colonial Ethnic Conflict in Africa." *Journal of Peace Research* 38 (4): 473–91.

Blattman, Chris and Edward Miguel. 2010. "Civil War." *Journal of Economic Literature* 48 (1): 3–57.

Boone, Catherine. 1994. "States and Ruling Classes in Postcolonial Africa: The Enduring Contradictions of Power." In J. Migdal, A. Kohli, and V. Shue, eds., *State Power and Social Forces: Domination and Transformation in the Third World*. New York: Cambridge University Press.

2003. *Political Topographies of the African State: Territorial Authority and Institutional Choice*. New York: Cambridge University Press.

2014. *Property and Political Order in Africa*. New York: Cambridge University Press.

2017. "Sons of the Soil Conflict in Africa: Institutional Determinants of Ethnic Conflict Over Land." *World Development* 96: 276–93.

Bose, Sumantra. 2003. *Kashmir: Roots of Conflict, Paths to Peace*. Cambridge, MA: Harvard University Press.

Bound, John, David Jaeger, and Regina Baker. 1995. "Problem with Instrumental Variables Estimation When the Correlation Between the Instruments and the Endogenous Explanatory Variable Is Weak." *Journal of the American Statistical Association* 90 (430): 443–50.

Brass, Paul. 1997. *Theft of an Idol*. Princeton, NJ: Princeton University Press.

Callahan, Mary. 2003. *Making Enemies: War and State Building in Burma*. Ithaca, NY: Cornell University Press.

Caroe, Olaf. 1976. *The Pathans: 550 B.C.–A.D. 1957. With a New Epilogue*. Oxford; New York: Oxford University Press.

Cederman, Lars-Erik, Andreas Wimmer, and Brian Min. 2010. "Why Do Ethnic Groups Rebel? New Data and Analysis." *World Politics* 62 (1): 87–119.

Cederman, Lars-Erik, Nils Weidmann, and Kristian Gleditsch. 2011. "Horizontal Inequalities and Ethnonationalist Civil War: A Global Comparison." *American Political Science Review* 105 (3): 478–95.

Cederman, L., K. Gleditsch, and H. Buhaug. 2013. *Inequality, Grievances, and Civil War*. Cambridge Studies in Contentious Politics. Cambridge: Cambridge University Press.

Chakraborty, Debashish. 2009. "Maoists in West Bengal." *Economic & Political Weekly* 44 (46): 17–19.

Chandra, Kanchan. 2004. *Why Ethnic Parties Succeed: Patronage and Ethnic Headcounts in India*. Cambridge, UK; New York: Cambridge University Press.

Chandra, Kanchan and Steven Wilkinson. 2008. "Measuring the Effect of 'Ethnicity'." *Comparative Political Studies* 41 (4/5): 515–63.

Chandra, Kanchan, and Omar García-Ponce. 2019. "Why Ethnic Subaltern-Led Parties Crowd Out Armed Organizations: Explaining Maoist Violence in India." *World Politics* 71 (2): 367–416.

Cline, Lawrence E. 2009. "Insurgency in Amber: Ethnic Opposition Groups in Myanmar." *Small Wars & Insurgencies* 20 (3–4): 574–91.

Collier, Paul and Anke Hoeffler. 2004. "Greed and Grievance in Civil War." *Oxford Economic Papers* 56: 563–95.

Copland, Ian. 1982. *The British Raj and the Indian Princes: Paramountcy in Western India, 1857–1930*. New Delhi: Orient Longmans Ltd.

Cunningham, H. S. 1891. *Earl Canning*. Oxford: Clarendon Press.

Curzon of Kedleston, George Nathaniel Curzon, and Thomas Raleigh. 1906. *Lord Curzon in India: Being a Selection from His Speeches as Viceroy & Governor-General of India, 1898–1905. Introduction by Sir Thomas Raleigh*. London: Macmillan.

Dasgupta, Aditya, Kishore Gawande, and Devesh Kapur. 2017. "(When) Do Anti-Poverty Programs Reduce Violence? India's Rural Employment Guarantee and Maoist Conflict." *International Organization* 71 (3): 605–632

Dell, Melissa. 2010. "The Persistent Effects of Peru's Mining Mita." *Econometrica* 78 (6): 1863–1903.

Desai, Manali. 2005. "Indirect British Rule, State Formation, and Welfarism in Kerala, India, 1860–1957." *Social Science History* 29 (3): 457–88.

Dhanagare, D. N. 1974. "Social Origins of the Peasant Insurrection in Telangana (1946–51)." *Contributions to Indian Sociology* 8 (1): 109–34.

Dincecco, Mark, and Mauricio Prado. 2012. "Warfare, Fiscal Capacity, and Performance." *Journal of Economic Growth* 17 (3): 171–203.

Dirks, Nicholas. 2001. *Castes of the Mind: Colonialism and the Making of Modern India*. Princeton, NJ: Princeton University Press.

Djankov, Simeon, and Marta Reynal-Querol. 2010. "Poverty and Civil War: Revisiting the Evidence." *The Review of Economics and Statistics* 92 (4): 1035–41.

DN, 2002. "Breaking the Deadlock: Land Reform Revisited." *Economic and Political Weekly* June 29.

Do, Quy-Toan, and Lakshmi Iyer. 2010. "Geography, Poverty and Conflict in Nepal." *Journal of Peace Research* 47 (6): 735–48.

Dunning, Thad. 2008. "Model Specification in Instrumental-Variables Regression." *Political Analysis* 16 (3): 290–302.

Duyker, Edward. 1987. *Tribal Guerillas: The Santals of West Bengal and the Naxalite Movement*. New Delhi: Oxford University Press.

Economist, Feb 25, 2010, "Ending the Red Terror."

Fearon, James, and David Laitin. 2001. "Ethnicity, Insurgency, and Civil War." Presented at the 2001 Annual Meetings of the American Political Science Association, San Francisco, CA, August 30–September 2.

2003. "Ethnicity, Insurgency, and Civil War." *American Political Science Review* 97 (1): 75–90.

2011. "Sons of the Soil, Migrants, and Civil War." *World Development* 39 (2): 199–211.

Fisher, Michael H. 1987. *A Clash of Cultures: Awadh, the British and the Mughals*. New Delhi: Manohar Publications.

1991. *Indirect Rule in India. Residents and the Residency System, 1764–1858*. New Delhi: Oxford University Press.

Foa, Roberto. 2016. *Ancient Polities, Modern States*. Doctoral dissertation, Harvard University, Graduate School of Arts & Sciences.

Fredholm, Michael. 1993. *Burma: Ethnicity and Insurgency*. Westport, CT: Praeger.

Furnivall, J. S. 1948. *Colonial Policy and Practice: A Comparative Study of Burma and Netherlands India*. Cambridge: Cambridge University Press.

1958. *The Governance of Modern Burma*. New York: International Secretariat, Institute of Pacific Relations.

Ganguly, Sumit. 1996. "Explaining the Kashmir Insurgency – Political Mobilization and Institutional Decay." *International Security* 21 (2): 76–107.

Ganguly, Sumit, Manjeet Pardesi, and Nicolas Blarel eds. 2018. *The Oxford Handbook of India's National Security*. New Delhi: Oxford University Press.

Garg, Ruchir. 2008. "Roots and Causes: The Case of Dandakaranya." In Ramana, P. V., and Observer Research Foundation, eds., *The Naxal Challenge: Causes, Linkages, and Policy Options*. New Delhi: Pearson Education, 25–28.

Gawande, Kishore, Devesh Kapur, and Shanker Satyanath. 2017. "Renewable Natural Resource Shocks and Conflict Intensity: Findings from India's Ongoing Maoist Insurgency." *Journal of Conflict Resolution* 61 (1): 140–72.

Gennaioli, Nicola, and Ilia Rainer. 2007. "The Modern Impact of Precolonial Centralization in Africa." *Journal of Economic Growth* 12 (3): 185–234.

George, Alexander L., and Andrew Bennett. 2005. *Case Studies and Theory Development in the Social Sciences*. Cambridge, MA: MIT Press.

Gerring, John. 2007a. *Case Study Research: Principles and Practices*. Cambridge University Press.

Gerring, John. 2007b. "Is There a (Viable) Crucial-Case Method?" *Comparative Political Studies* 40 (3): 231–53.

Gerring, John, Daniel Ziblatt, Johan Van Gorp, and Julian Arevalo. 2011. "An Institutional Theory of Direct and Indirect Rule." *World Politics* 63 (3): 377–433.

Goertz, Gary. 2017. *Multimethod Research, Causal Mechanisms, and Case Studies: An Integrated Approach*. Princeton, NJ: Princeton University Press.

Goertz, Gary, and James Mahoney. 2005. "Two-Level Theories and Fuzzy-Set Analysis." *Sociological Methods & Research* 33(4): 497–538.

Gomes, Joseph Flavian. 2015. "The Political Economy of the Maoist Conflict in India: An Empirical Analysis." *World Development* 68: 96–123.

Goodwin, Jeff, and Theda Skocpol. 1989. "Explaining Revolutions in the Contemporary Third World." *Politics and Society* 17 (4): 489–509.

Gordon, Stewart. 1993. *The Marathas 1600–1818*. Cambridge; New York: Cambridge University Press.

Gossman, Patricia. 1992. "Police Killings and Rural Violence in Andhra Pradesh." *Asia Watch* September 20: 12–13.

Gough, Kathleen. 1974. "Indian Peasant Uprisings." *Economic and Political Weekly* 9 (32): 1391–412.

Gould, Roger. 1991. "Multiple Networks and Mobilization for the Paris Commune." *American Sociological Review* 56 (6): 716–29.

Griffin, Lepel Henry. 1898. *Ranjit Singh and the Sikh Barrier between Our Growing Empire and Central Asia*. Oxford: Clarendon Press.

Guardado, Jenny. 2016. "Forced Labor, Ethnicity and Conflict: Evidence from the Peruvian *Mita*." Manuscript, presented at OSU conference on colonialism, April 29.

Guha, Ramachandra. 1983. "Forestry in British and Post-British India: A Historical Analysis." *Economic and Political Weekly* 18 (45/46), October 29: 1940–47.

Gujarati, Damodar N. 2003. *Basic Econometrics*. 4th ed. Boston: McGraw-Hill.

Gurr, Ted Robert. 1970. *Why Men Rebel*. Princeton, NJ: Princeton University Press.

Gustafson, Donald R. 1968. *Mysore 1881–1902: The Making of a Model State*. PhD Thesis, University of Wisconsin, Madison.

Gutiérrez-Sanın, Francisco and Elisabeth Wood. 2014. "Ideology in civil war: Instrumental Adoption and Beyond." *Journal of Peace Research* 51 (2): 213–26.

Habib, Irfan. 1999. *The Agrarian System of Mughal India 1556–1707*. New Delhi; New York: Oxford University Press.

    1984. *Peasant and Artisan Resistance in Mughal India*. McGill Studies in International Development, No. 34. McGill University.

Haragopal, G. 2010. "The Telangana People's Movement: The Unfolding Political Culture." *Economic and Political Weekly*, October 16.

Harvey, Neil. 1998. *The Chiapas Rebellion: The Struggle for Land and Democracy*. Durham, NC: Duke University Press.

Hassner, Ron. 2003. "To Halve and to Hold: Conflicts over Sacred Space and the Problem of Indivisibility." *Security Studies* 12 (4): 1–33.

Hechter, Michael. 2000. *Containing Nationalism*. New York: Oxford University Press.

Hegre, Havard, and Nicholas Sambanis. 2006. "Sensitivity Analysis of Empirical Results on Civil War Onset." *Journal of Conflict Resolution* 50 (4): 508–35.

Hegre, Havard, Tanya Ellingsen, Scott Gates, and Nils Peter Gledisch. 2001. "Towards a Democratic Civil Peace? Democracy, Political Change, and Civil War, 1816–1992." *American Political Science Review* 95: 33–48.

Heller, Patrick. 1995. "From Class Struggle to Class Compromise." *The Journal of Development Studies* 31 (5): 645–72.

Herbst, Jeffrey Ira. 2000. *States and Power in Africa: Comparative Lessons in Authority and Control*. Princeton, NJ: Princeton University Press.

Herring, Ronald J. 1983. *Land to the Tiller: The Political Economy of Agrarian Reform in South Asia*. New Haven, CT: Yale University Press.

Hoelscher, K., Jason Miklian, and Krishna Chaitanya Vadlamannati. 2012. "Hearts and Mines: A District-Level Analysis of the Maoist Conflict in India." *International Area Studies Review* 15 (2): 141–160.

Horowitz, Donald. 1985. *Ethnic Groups in Conflict*. Berkeley; Los Angeles: University of California Press.

Hurd, John. 1975. "The Economic Consequences of Indirect Rule in India." *Indian Economic Social History Review* 12: 169–81.

Iyer, Lakshmi. 2010. "Direct versus Indirect Colonial Rule in India: Long Term Consequences." *The Review of Economics and Statistics* 92 (4): 693–713.

Jafa, Vijendra Singh. 1999. "Administrative Policies & Ethnic Disintegration: Engineering Conflict in India's North East." *Faultlines: Writings on Conflict & Resolution*, Vol. 2. www.satp.org/faultline/Volume-2

Jaffrelot, Christophe. 2003. *India's Silent Revolution – The Rise of the Lower Castes in North India*. New York: Columbia University Press; New Delhi: Permanent Black.

Jeffrey, Robin. 1976. *Decline of Nayar Dominance: Society and Politics in Travancore, 1847–1908*. New York: Holmes & Meier Publishers.

    ed. 1978. *People, Princes and Paramount Power: Society and Politics in the Indian Princely States*. Delhi: Oxford University Press.

Jha, Sanjay. 2008. "Political Bases and Dimensions of the Naxalite Movement." In *The Naxal Challenge*, ed. P. V. Ramana.

Jha, Saumitra. 2013. "Trade, Institutions, and Ethnic Tolerance: Evidence from South Asia." *American Political Science Review* 107 (4): 806–32.

Jha, Saumitra, and Steven Wilkinson. 2012. "Does Combat Experience Foster Organizational Skill? Evidence from Ethnic Cleansing during the Partition of India." *American Political Science Review* 106 (4): 883–907.

Johnson, Thomas H., and M. Chris Mason. 2008. "No Sign until the Burst of Fire: Understanding the Pakistan-Afghanistan Frontier." *International Security* 32 (4): 41–77.

Joshi, G. M. 1990. *Tribal Bastar and British Administration*. New Delhi: Indus Publishing Company.

Joshi, Madhav, and T. David Mason. 2010. "Land Tenure, Democracy, and Patterns of Violence during the Maoist Insurgency in Nepal, 1996–2005." *Social Science Quarterly* 91 (4): 984–1006.

Karklins, Alexander. 2009. "The Colonial Legacy and Human Rights in Mexico: Indigenous Rights and the Zapatista Movement." *Human Rights and Human Welfare Research Digest*. www.du.edu/korbel/hrhw/researchdigest/latinamerica2/digest-human%20rights%20in%20latin%20america%20vol%202-mexico.pdf

Kalyvas, Stathis. 2006. *The Logic of Violence in Civil War*. Cambridge; New York: Cambridge University Press.

2008. "Promises and Pitfalls of an Emerging Research Program: The Microdynamics of Civil War." In Stathis Kalyvas, Ian Shapiro, and Tarek Masoud, eds. *Order, Conflict, and Violence*. Cambridge; New York: Cambridge University Press, 397–421.

Kalyvas, Stathis and Matthew Kocher. 2009. "The Dynamics of Violence in Vietnam: An Analysis of the Hamlet Evaluation System (HES)." *Journal of Peace Research* 46 (3): 335–55.

Kennedy, Jonathan and Lawrence King. 2013. "Adivasis, Maoists and Insurgency in the Central Indian Tribal Belt." *European Journal of Sociology*, LIV.

Kennedy, Jonathan, and Sunil Purushotham. 2012. "Beyond Naxalbari: A Comparative Analysis of Maoist Insurgency and Counterinsurgency in Independent India." *Comparative Studies in Society and History* 54 (4): 832–62.

Khan, Muhammad Khaili, and Lu Wei. 2016. "When Friends Turned into Enemies: The role of the National State vs. Tehrik-i-Taliban Pakistan (TTP) in the War against Terrorism in Pakistan." *The Korean Journal of Defense Analysis* 28 (4): 597–626.

King, Gary, Michael Tomz, and Jason Wittenberg. 2000. "Making the Most of Statistical Analyses: Improving Interpretation and Presentation." *American Journal of Political Science* 44: 341–55.

Kocher, Matthew, Thomas Pepinsky, and Stathis Kalyvas. 2011. "Aerial Bombing and Counterinsurgency in the Vietnam War." *American Journal of Political Science* 55 (2): 201–18.

Kohli, Atul. 1987. *The State and Poverty in India: The Politics of Reform*. Cambridge: Cambridge University Press.

ed. 2001. *The Success of India's Democracy*. Cambridge: Cambridge University Press.

2004. *State Directed Development: Political Power and Industrialization in the Global Periphery*. New York: Cambridge University Press.

2012. *Poverty Amid Plenty in the New India*. New York: Cambridge University Press.

Krishna, Anirudh. 2017. *The Broken Ladder: The Paradox and Potential India's One-Billion*. Cambridge: Cambridge University Press.

Kujur, Rajat. 2008. "Naxal Movement in India: A Profile." *IPCS Research Papers*. New Delhi: Institute for Peace and Conflict Studies.

Kulke, Hermann, and Dietmar Rothermund. 2004. *A History of India*. 4th ed. Milton Park, Abingdon, Oxfordshire; New York: Routledge.

Laitin, David. 1985. "Hegemony and Religious Conflict." In P. Evans, D. Rueschemeyer, and T. Skocpol, eds., *Bringing the State Back In*. Cambridge; New York: Cambridge University Press, 285–316.

1986. *Hegemony and Culture: Politics and Religious Change among the Yoruba*. Chicago: University of Chicago Press.

Lange, Matthew. 2009. *Lineages of Despotism and Development: British Colonialism and State Power*. Chicago: University of Chicago Press.

Lange, Matthew and Andrew Dawson. 2009. "Dividing and Ruling the World? A Statistical Test of the Effects of Colonialism on Postcolonial Civil Violence." *Social Forces* 88 (2): 785–818.

Lange, Matthew and Dietrich Rueschemeyer, eds. 2005. *States and Development: Historical Antecedents of Stagnation and Advance*. New York: Palgrave Macmillan Press.

Lange, Matthew, James Mahoney, and Mathias vom Hau. 2006. "Colonialism and Development: A Comparative Analysis of Spanish and British Colonies." *American Journal of Sociology* 111 (5): 1412–62.

Lawrence, Adria. 2010. "Triggering Nationalist Violence: Competition and Conflict in Uprisings against Colonial Rule." *International Security* 35 (2): 88–122.

Lee, Alexander. 2017. "Ethnic Diversity and Ethnic Discrimination: Explaining Local Public Goods Provision." *Comparative Political Studies* 51 (10): 1351–83.

2019. "Land, State Capacity, and Colonialism: Evidence from India." *Comparative Political Studies* 52 (3): 412–44.

Lee, Alexander, and Kenneth A. Schultz. 2012. "Comparing British and French Colonial Legacies: A Discontinuity Analysis of Cameroon." *Quarterly Journal of Political Science* 7 (4): 365–410.

Lee-Warner, Sir William. 1910. *The Native States of India*. London: Macmillan and Co., Ltd.

Levi, Margaret. 1988. *Of Rule and Revenue*. Berkeley: University of California Press.

Lichbach, Mark I. 1994. "What Makes Rational Peasants Revolutionary? Dilemma, Paradox, and Irony in Peasant Collective Action." *World Politics* 46 (3): 383–418.

Lieberman, Evan. 2005. "Nested Analysis as a Mixed-Method Strategy for Comparative Research." *American Political Science Review* 99 (3): 435–452.

2015. Nested Analysis: Toward the Integration of Comparative-Historical Analysis with Other Social Science Methods. In J. Mahoney and K. Thelen, eds., *Advances in Comparative-Historical Analysis*. Strategies for Social Inquiry. Cambridge: Cambridge University Press, 240–63.

Ligot, Jacinto. 1994. "Communist Insurgency in the Philippines." Thesis submitted to Naval Postgraduate School, Monterey, California.

Long, J. Scott. 1997. *Regression Models for Categorical and Limited Dependent Variables*. Thousand Oaks; London: Sage Publications.

Long, J. Scott, and Jeremy Freese. 2006. *Regression Models for Categorical Outcomes Using Stata*. 2nd ed. College Station, TX: Stata Press.

Louis, Prakash. 2002. *The Naxalite Movement in Central Bihar*. New Delhi: Wordsmiths.

Lugard, Sir F. D. 1926. *The Dual Mandate in British Tropical Africa*. Edinburgh: William Blackwood & Sons.

Lyall, Alfred C. 1910. *The Rise and Expansion of the British Dominion in India*. 5th ed. London: J. Murray.

Maclagan, Michael. 1962. *"Clemency" Canning*. London: MacMillan and Company Ltd.

Maddison, Angus. 2003. *The World Economy: Historical Statistics*. Paris: Organisation for Economic Co-operation and Development.

Mahoney, James. 2000. "Path Dependence in Historical Sociology." *Theory and Society* 29 (4): 507–48.

2010. *Colonialism and Postcolonial Development: Spanish America in Comparative Perspective*. New York: Cambridge University Press.

Mahoney, James and Gary Goertz. 2006. "A Tale of Two Cultures: Contrasting Quantitative and Qualitative Research." *Political Analysis* 14: 227–49.

Mamdani, Mahmood. 1996. *Citizen and Subject*. Princeton, NJ: Princeton University Press.

2001. *When Victims Become Killers*. Princeton, NJ: Princeton University Press.

Mampilly, Zachariah. 2011. *Rebel Rulers: Insurgent Governance and Civilian Life during War*. Ithaca, NY: Cornell University Press.

Manor, James. 1978. *Political Change in an Indian State: Mysore 1917–1955*. Columbia, MO: South Asia Books.

1980. "Pragmatic Progressives in Regional Politics." *Economic and Political Weekly* 15 (5/7): 201–13.

Marshall, P. J. 1987. *Bengal – The British Bridgehead: Eastern India, 1740–1828*. Cambridge: Cambridge University Press.

Marwah, Ved. 2009. *India in Turmoil: Jammu and Kashmir, the North East and Left Extremism*. New Delhi: Rupa & Co.

Mayaram, Shail. 2003. *Against History, Against State: Counterperspectives from the Margins*. New York: Columbia University Press.

McAdam, Doug. 1986. "Recruitment to High-Risk Activism: The Case of Freedom Summer." *American Journal of Sociology* 92: 64–90.

McAdam, Doug, John D. McCarthy, and Mayer N. Zald, eds. 1996. *Comparative Perspectives on Social Movements: Political Opportunities, Mobilizing Structures, and Cultural Framings*. Cambridge; New York: Cambridge University Press.

McCarthy, John D, and Mayer N. Zald. 1973. *The Trend of Social Movements in America: Professionalization and Resource Mobilization*. Morristown, NJ: General Learning Press.

1977. "Resource Mobilization and Social Movements: A Partial Theory." *American Journal of Sociology* 82: 1212–41.

McEvedy, Colin, and Richard Jones. 1978. *Atlas of World Population History*. New York: Penguin Books.

Metcalf, Thomas R. 1979. *Land, Landlords and the British Raj: Northern Indian in the Nineteenth Century*. Berkeley: University of California Press.

Michalopoulos, Stelios, and Elias Papaioannou. 2013. "Pre-Colonial Ethnic Institutions and Contemporary African Development." *Econometrica* 81 (1): 113–52.

Migdal, Joel. 1988. *Strong Societies and Weak States: State-Society Relations and State Capability in the Third World*. Princeton, NJ: Princeton University Press.

Miguel, Edward, Shanker Satyanath, and Ernest Sergenti. 2004. "Economic Shocks and Civil Conflict: An Instrumental Variables Approach." *Journal of Political Economy* 112 (4): 725–53.

Miklian, Jason. 2009. "The Purification Hunt: The Salwa Judum Counterinsurgency in Chhattisgarh, India." *Dialectical Anthropology* 33: 441–59.

Misra, Babu Ram. 1942. *Land Revenue Policy in the United Provinces under British Rule*. Benares: Nand Kishore & Brothers.

Mishra, Trinath. 2007. *Barrel of the Gun: The Maoist Challenge and Indian Democracy*. New Delhi: Sheriden Book Co.

Mitchell, Edward. 1967. "The Significance of Land Tenure in the Vietnamese Insurgency." *Asian Survey* 7 (8): 577–80.

   1968. "Inequality and Insurgency: A Statistical Study of South Vietnam." *World Politics* 20 (3): 421–438.

Mohsin, Amena. 2003. *The Chittagong Hill Tracts, Bangladesh*. Boulder, CO: Lynne Rienner Publishers.

Mukherjee, Nilmani. 1962. *The Ryotwari System in Madras 1792–1827*. Calcutta: Firma K. L. Mukhopadhyay.

Mukherjee, Shivaji. 2014. "Why Are the Longest Insurgencies Low Violence? Politician Motivations, Sons of the Soil, and Civil War Duration." *Civil Wars* 16 (2): 172–207.

   2018a. "Colonial Origins of Maoist Insurgency in India: Historical Institutions and Civil War." *Journal of Conflict Resolution* 62 (10): 2232–2274.

   2018b. "Historical Legacies of Colonial Indirect Rule: Princely States and Maoist Insurgency in Central India." *World Development* 111: 113–29.

   2018c. "Insurgencies in India – Origins and Causes," in S. Ganguly, M. Pardesi, N. Blarel (eds.), *The Oxford Handbook of India's National Security*. New Delhi: Oxford University Press, 209–28.

Murillo, Mario. 2007. "Indigenous Communities Caught in the Crossfire." September 25. https://nacla.org/article/indigenous-communities-caught-crossfire

Murshed, S. Mansoob, and Scott Gates. 2005. "Spatial-Horizontal Inequality and the Maoist Insurgency in Nepal." *Review of Development Economics* 9 (1): 121–34.

Naseemullah, Adnan. 2014. "Shades of Sovereignty: Explaining Political Order and Disorder in Pakistan's Northwest." *Studies in Comparative International Development* 49: 501–22.

Naseemullah, Adnan, and Paul Staniland. 2016. "Indirect Rule and Varieties of Governance." *Governance* 29 (1): 13–30.

Nayak, Deepak Kumar. 2019a. "Maoists: Wounded, not Vanquished." *South Asia Intelligence Review* 17 (40). www.satp.org/south-asia-intelligence-review-Volume-17-No-40#assessment1

   2019b. "Maoists: No Takers." *South Asia Intelligence Review* 18 (12). www.satp.org/south-asia-intelligence-review-volume-18-no-12#assessment2

Nunn, Nathan, and Diego Puga. 2012. "Ruggedness: The Blessing of Bad Geography in Africa." *The Review of Economics and Statistics* 94(1): 20–36.

Oppenheim, Ben, and Michael Weintraub. 2017. "Doctrine and Violence: The Impact of Combatant Training on Civilian Killings." *Terrorism and Political Violence* 29 (6): 1126–48.

Paige, Jeffery M. 1975. *Agrarian Revolution: Social Movements and Export Agriculture in the Underdeveloped World*. New York: Free Press.

Pandey, Gyanendra. 1990. *The Construction of Communalism in Colonial North India*. Delhi; New York: Oxford University Press.

Panikkar, K. M. 1960. *A History of Kerala 1498–1801*. Annamalainagar, India: Annamalai University, Historical Series, no. 15.

Petersen, Roger. 2002. *Understanding Ethnic Violence: Fear, Hatred, and Resentment in Twentieth Century Eastern Europe.* Cambridge Studies in Comparative Politics. Cambridge: Cambridge University Press.

Pierson, Paul. 2000. "Increasing Returns, Path Dependence, and the Study of Politics." *American Political Science Review* 94 (2): 251–67.

Pradhan, Fakir Mohan. 2013. "Maoists: Tactical Retreat." *South Asia Intelligence Review* 11 (36). www.satp.org/satporgtp/sair/Archives/sair11/11_36.htm#assessment2

Qunungo, Suniti. 1998. *Chakma Resistance to British Domination, 1772–1798.* Chittagong: Shanti Press.

Rabitoy, Neil. 1975. "System v. Expediency: The Reality of Land Revenue Administration in the Bombay Presidency, 1812–1820." *Modern Asian Studies* 9 (4): 529–46.

Ragin, Charles C. 1987. *The Comparative Method: Moving beyond Qualitative and Quantitative Strategies.* Berkeley: University of California Press.

Rana, R. P. 1981. "Agrarian Revolts in Northern India during the Late 17th and Early 18th Century." *The Indian Economic and Social History Review* 18 (3–4): 287–322.

Reddy, V. Ramakrishna. 1987. *Economic History of Hyderabad State (Warangal Suba: 1911–1950).* Delhi: Gian Publishing House.

Reddy, Kodandaram. 2007. "Movement for Telangana State: A Struggle for Autonomy." *Economic and Political Weekly* 42 (2): 90–94.

Ramusack, Barbara N. 2004. *The Indian Princes and Their States.* The New Cambridge History of India, Volume III.6. Cambridge; New York: Cambridge University Press.

Regmi, Mahesh Chandra. 1976. *Landownership in Nepal.* Berkeley: University of California Press.

Reynal-Querol, Marta. 2002. "Ethnicity, Political Systems and Civil War." *Journal of Conflict Resolution* 46 (1): 29–54.

Robinson, James. 2013. "Colombia: Another 100 Years of Solitude?" *Current History* February.

Ross, Michael L. 2004. "How Do Natural Resources Influence Civil War? Evidence from Thirteen Cases." *International Organization* 58 (1): 35–67.

Roy, Kaushik. 2005. "Military Synthesis in South Asia: Armies, Warfare and Indian Society, c. 1740–1849." *The Journal of Military History* 69 (3): 651–90.

Roy, B. K., and Vijay Verma. "Regional Divisions of India – A Cartographic Analysis: Occasional Papers." *IAS*, Series 1, Volume XI, Madhya Pradesh.

Russett, Bruce. 1964. "Inequality and Instability: The Relation of Land Tenure to Politics." *World Politics* 16 (3): 442–54.

Sahni, Ajai. 2007. "Asleep in Chhattisgarh." *South Asia Intelligence Review* 6 (1). www.satp.org/satporgtp/sair/Archives/6_1.htm#assessment1

Sahoo, Niranjan. 2019. "Half a Century of India's Maoist Insurgency: An Appraisal of State Response," ORF Occasional Paper *198*, June.

Sambanis, Nicholas. 2001. "Do Ethnic and Non-Ethnic Civil Wars Have the Same Causes?" *Journal of Conflict Resolution* 45 (3): 259–82.

Sambanis, Nicholas. 2004. "What Is Civil War?" *Journal of Conflict Resolution* 48 (6): 814–58.

Sampson, Isaac Terwase. 2014. "Religion and the Nigerian State: Situating the de Facto and de Jure Frontiers of State – Religion Relations and Its Implications for National Security." *Oxford Journal of Law and Religion* 3 (2): 311–39.

Sartori, Giovanni. 1970. "Concept Misformation in Comparative Politics." *The American Political Science Review* 64 (4): 1033–53.

Schwartzberg, Joseph E., ed. 1992. *A Historical Atlas of South Asia. Second Impression, with Additional Material*. New York; Oxford: Oxford University Press.

Scott, James. 1977. *The Moral Economy of the Peasant*. New Haven, CT: Yale University Press.

2009. *The Art of Not Being Governed: An Anarchist History of Upland Southeast Asia*. New Haven, CT: Yale University Press.

Selth, Andrew. 1986. "Race and Resistance in Burma, 1942–1945." *Modern Asian Studies* 20 (3): 483–507.

Sen, Ilina. 2006. "Ground Clearing with the Salwa Judum." *Himal, South Asia* 19 (8): 42–44.

Seshan, Radhika. 2014. "The Maratha State: Some Preliminary Considerations." *Indian Historical Review* 41 (1): 35–46.

Shah, Alpa. 2010. *In the Shadows of the State: Indigenous Politics, Environmentalism, and Insurgency in Jharkhand, India*. Durham, NC: Duke University Press.

2013. "The Agrarian Question in a Maoist Guerrilla Zone: Land, Labour and Capital in the Forests and Hills of Jharkhand, India." *Journal of Agrarian Change* 13 (3): 424–50.

Silverstein, Josef. 1959. "The Federal Dilemma in Burma." *Far Eastern Survey* 28 (7): 97–105.

Singh, Ajit Kumar. 2017. "Rudderless Reds." *South Asia Intelligence Review* 16 (22). www.satp.org/south-asia-intelligence-review-Volume-16-No-22#assessment1

Singh, Prakash. 1995. *The Naxalite Movement in India*. New Delhi: Rupa Publications.

Singh, Prerna. 2016. *How Solidarity Works for Welfare: Subnationalism and Social Development in India*. New York: Cambridge University Press.

Sinha, Shantha. 1989. *Maoists in Andhra Pradesh*. New Delhi: Gian Publishing House.

Sivaramakrishnan, K. 1999. *Modern Forests: Statemaking and Environmental Change in Colonial Eastern India*. Stanford, CA: Stanford University Press.

Skocpol, Theda. 1979. *States and Social Revolutions: A Comparative Analysis of France, Russia, and China*. Cambridge; New York: Cambridge University Press.

1982. "What Makes Peasants Revolutionary?" *Comparative Politics* 14 (3): 351–75.

Slater, Dan, and Daniel Ziblatt. 2013. "The Enduring Indispensability of the Controlled Comparison." *Comparative Political Studies* 46 (10): 1301–27.

Smith, Martin J. 1999. *Burma: Insurgency and the Politics of Ethnicity*. 2nd (updated) ed. Dhaka: The University Press; Bangkok: White Lotus; London: Zed Books.

2007. *State of Strife: The Dynamics of Ethnic Conflict in Burma*. Institute of Southeast Asian Studies. Singapore; Washington, DC East-West Center.

Snow, David A., Louis A. Zurcher, and Sheldon Ekland-Olson. 1980. "Social Networks and Social Movements: A Microstructural Approach to Differential Recruitment." *American Sociological Review* 45: 787–801.

South, Ashley. 2008. *Ethnic Politics in Burma: States of Conflict*. Abingdon; New York: Routledge.

Srinivasulu, K. 2002. "Caste, Class and Social Articulation in Andhra Pradesh: Mapping Differential Regional Trajectories." Working paper 179, ODI, September, pp. 5–6.

Staiger, D., and J. H. Stock. 1997. "Instrumental Variables Regression with Weak Instruments." *Econometrica* 65: 557–86.

Staniland, Paul. 2012a. "Organizing Insurgency: Networks, Resources, and Rebellion in South Asia." *International Security* 37 (1): 142–77.

2012b. "States, Insurgents, and Wartime Political Orders." *Perspectives on Politics* 10 (2): 243–64.

2014. *Networks of Rebellion: Explaining Insurgent Cohesion and Collapse*. Ithaca: Cornell University Press.

Stein, Burton. 1985. "State Formation and Economy Reconsidered: Part One." *Modern Asian Studies* 19 (3): 387–413.

Stock, J. H., J. H. Wright, and M. Yogo. 2002. "A Survey of Weak Instruments and Weak Identification in Generalized Method of Moments." *Journal of Business and Economic Statistics* 20: 518–29.

Stokes, Eric. 1978. "The Land Revenue Systems of the North-Western Provinces and Bombay Deccan 1830–1948: Ideology and the Official Mind." In *The Peasant and the Raj: Studies in Agrarian Society and Peasant Rebellion in Colonial India*, ed. Eric Stokes. Cambridge: Cambridge University Press.

Suba Chandran, D., and P. R. Chari, eds. 2012. *Armed Conflicts in South Asia 2011: The Promise and Threat of Transformation*. London; New York: Routledge.

Sundar, Nandini. 2006. "Bastar, Maoism and Salwa Judum." *Economic and Political Weekly* 41 (29): 3187–92.

2007. *Subalterns and Sovereigns: An Anthropological History of Bastar (1854–2006)*. Delhi: Oxford University Press.

Sundarayya, P. 1972. *Telengana People's Struggle and Its Lessons*. Calcutta: Communist Party of India (Marxist).

Tarrow, Sidney G. 1998. *Power in Movement: Social Movements and Contentious Politics*. 2nd ed. Cambridge; New York: Cambridge University Press.

Thachil, Tariq. 2011. "Embedded Mobilization: Nonstate Service Provision as Electoral Strategy in India." *World Politics* 63 (3): 434–69.

2014. *Elite Parties, Poor Voters: How Social Services Win Votes in India*. New York: Cambridge University Press.

Thirumali, Inukonda. 2003. *Against Dora and Nizam: People's Movement in Telangana 1939–1948*. New Delhi: Kanishka Publishers.

Tilly, Charles. 1978. *From Mobilization to Revolution*. Reading, MA: Addison-Wesley.

Toft, Monica. 2006. "Issue Indivisibility and Time Horizons as Rationalist Explanations for War." *Security Studies* 15 (1): 34–69.

Tomz, Michael, Jason Wittenberg, and Gary King. 2001. "Clarify: Software for Interpreting and Presenting Statistical Results." Manuscript, Stanford University. http://gking.harvard.edu/clarify/clarify.pdf

Topalova, Petia. 2005. "Trade Liberalization, Poverty and Inequality: Evidence from Indian Districts." NBER working paper no. 11614.

Trejo, Guillermo. 2012. *Popular Movements in Autocracies: Religion, Repression and Indigenous Collective Action in Mexico*. New York: Cambridge University Press.

Tripodi, Christian. 2008. "Peacemaking through Bribes or Cultural Empathy? The Political Officer and Britain's Strategy towards the North-West Frontier, 1901–1945." *Journal of Strategic Studies* 31 (1): 123–51.

Troyan, Brett. 2008. "Ethnic Citizenship in Colombia," *Latin American Research Review* 43 (3): 166–91.

Upadhya, Carol. 1988. "The Farmer-Capitalists of Coastal Andhra Pradesh." *Economic and Political Weekly* 23 (27), July 2: 1376-82.

Vanden Eynde, Oliver. 2018. "Targets of Violence: Evidence from India's Naxalite Conflict." *Economic Journal* 128 (609): 887–916.

Vanneman, Reeve, and Douglas Barnes. 2000. "*Indian District Database, 1961–1991*," machine-readable data file and codebook. College Park, MD: Center on Population, Gender, and Social Inequality. www.bsos.umd.edu/socy/vanneman/districts/index.html

Varshney, Ashutosh. 1998. "Why Democracy Survives." *Journal of Democracy* 9 (3): 36–50.

   2002. *Ethnic Conflict and Civic Life: Hindus and Muslims in India.* New Haven, CT: Yale University Press.

Verghese, Ajay. 2016a. "British Rule and Tribal Revolts in India: The Curious Case of Bastar." *Modern Asian Studies* 50 (5).

   2016b. *The Colonial Origins of Ethnic Violence in India.* Stanford, CA: Stanford University Press.

Verghese, Ajay, and Emmanuel Teitelbaum. 2019. "Conquest and Conflict: The Colonial Roots of Maoist Violence in India." *Politics and Society* 47 (1): 55–86.

Weiner, Myron. 1978. *Sons of the Soil: Migration and Ethnic Conflict in India.* Princeton, NJ: Princeton University Press.

Weinstein, Jeremy M. 2007. *Inside Rebellion: The Politics of Insurgent Violence.* Cambridge; New York: Cambridge University Press.

White, Joshua T. 2008. "The Shape of Frontier Rule: Governance and Transition, from the Raj to the Modern Pakistani Frontier." *Asian Security* 4 (3): 219–43.

Wilkinson, Steven. 2004. *Votes and Violence: Electoral Competition and Ethnic Riots in India.* Cambridge; New York: Cambridge University Press.

   2015. *Army and Nation: The Military and Indian Democracy since Independence.* Cambridge, MA: Harvard University Press.

   2017. "Looking Back at the Colonial Origins of Communal and Caste Conflict in India," February 21, *The Wire.* https://thewire.in/110535/communal-violence-caste-colonialism/

Womack, John. 1999. *Rebellion in Chiapas: An Historical Reader.* New York: New Press.

Wood, Elisabeth. 2003. *Insurgent Collective Action and Civil War in El Salvador.* New York: Cambridge University Press.

Wucherpfennig, Julian, Philipp Hunziker, and Lars-Erik Cederman. 2016. "Who Inherits the State? Colonial Rule and Post-Colonial Conflict." *American Journal of Political Science* 60 (4): 882–98.

Yousafzai, Iftikhar, and Himayatullah Yaqubi. 2017. "The Durand Line." *Journal of Research Society of Pakistan* 54 (1): 78–97.

Zukerman-Daly, Sarah. 2012. "Organizational Legacies of Violence: Conditions Favoring Insurgency Onset in Colombia, 1964–1984." *Journal of Peace Research* 49 (3): 473–91.

CONTEMPORARY GOVERNMENT DOCUMENTS/ REPORTS (POST-1947)

Annual Reports, Ministry of Home Affairs, India, 2010–19.

"Assembly and Parliamentary Constituencies of Andhra Pradesh, 2009 Elections," from *General Elections to the House of People and Andhra Pradesh Legislative Assembly, 2009, Volume II, Statistical Report,* Andhra Pradesh.

Census of India, 1951, Volume VII, Madhya Pradesh, Part 1-A Report, Nagpur, Govt. Printing, 1953.

Census of India, 2001, Andhra Pradesh Administrative Atlas, published by Directorate of Census Operations, Andhra Pradesh.

Census of India, 2001, Chhattisgarh Administrative Atlas, published by Directorate of Census Operations, Madhya Pradesh and Chhattisgarh.

Chhattisgarh State Assembly Election – 2003, published by the Chief Electoral Officer, Chhattisgarh.

Committee of Concerned Citizens. 2006. *Negotiating Peace: Peace Talks between Government of Andhra Pradesh and Naxalite Parties.*

Delimitation of Parliamentary and Assembly Constituencies in the State of Andhra Pradesh, Andhra Pradesh Gazette Part V Extraordinary (Lr. No.790IElecs.-A/ 2004, Genl.Admn. (Elecs.-A) Department, dated 31–05-2007).

"Echoes of Spring Thunder," Report prepared and compiled by Left Wing Extremist Cell, Special Branch, Kolkata, 2001.

Mitra, D. M. 2012. *Genesis and Spread of Maoist Violence and Appropriate State Strategy to Handle It.* New Delhi: Bureau of Police Research and Development, Ministry of Home Affairs, Government of India

Ministry of Home Affairs, India. February 11, 2005. "Revision of guidelines for Re-Imbursement of Security Related Expenditure (S.R.E) to Naxal affected states under S.R.E. Scheme." MHA Memo Number 11–18015/4/03-IS.III.

Madhya Pradesh Congress Committee. 1966. *Report of the Bastar Study Team of the State Congress.* Bhopal: Madhya Pradesh Congress Committee.

"Muhammad Ali Jinnah Address to the Tribal Jirga at Government House." United4justice's Weblog. https://united4justice.wordpress.com/tag/muhammad-ali -jinnah-address-to-the-tribal-jirga-at-government-house/

Report of an Expert Group to Planning Commission. 2008. *Development Challenges in Extremist Affected Areas.* New Delhi: Government of India Publications.

Speech of Home Minister P. Chidambaram on 14th September 2009 on the Occasion of the DGPs/IGPs Conference – 2009. http://mha.nic.in/pdfs/HM-DGP-CONF140909.pdf.

"Hindustan Steel Limited: Preliminary Report on Site Location for Bailadila-Vizag Area Steel Plant," January 1963 in "Proposal for the Setting up of a Steel plant in Bailadilla Vishakhapatnam area during the 4th Plan," Dept: Railways, Branch: Planning, Year: 1963. File No: 63/PL/4/4 (5)/ 1–22, National Archives of India.

"Broad Gauge Line to Iron Ore Belt." *The Statesman.* November 18, 1963, *Dept: Railways, Branch: Planning, Year: 1963. File No: 63/PL/4/4 (5)/ 1–22.*), National Archives of India.

ARCHIVAL GOVERNMENT DOCUMENTS/ REPORTS (PRE-1947)

Aitchison, C. U. 1892. *A Collection of Treaties, Engagements and Sanads relating to India and Neighbouring Countries.* Volumes I–XIII. Calcutta: Government of India Central Publication Branch.

Baden-Powell, Baden Henry. 1892. *The Land-systems of British India: Being a Manual of the Land-Tenures and of the Systems of Land-Revenue Administration Prevalent in the Several Provinces*, Volumes 1–3. Oxford: Clarendon Press.

de Brett, E. A. 1909. *Central Provinces Gazetteers: Chhattisgarh Feudatory States.* Bombay: The Times Press.

Foreign Political-A, August 1876, Program No. 163–172. "Disturbances at Bastar," National Archives of India.

Foreign Political-A, August 1876, Program No. 170, National Archives of India. "Report from H. MacGeorge, Deputy Commissioner Godavari district to Secretary to the Chief Commissioner," Central Provinces, 22 April 1876, in "Disturbances at Bastar."

Foreign A-Political-I, January 1884, Prog. Nos. 117–125, National Archives of India. "Report on the Administration of Bastar State," by H. C. E. Ward, Addl. Commissioner, Chhattisgarh Division. Prog. No 122.

Foreign A-Political-I, January 1884, Prog. Nos. 117–125, National Archives of India. "Letter from W. B. Jones, Chief Commissioner, Central Provinces to Raja Bhyro Deo, Bastar," Prog. No. 120.

Foreign A-Political-I, January 1884, Prog. Nos. 117–125, National Archives of India. "Memo by Chief Commissioner, Central Provinces," Prog. 118, para 6, 40.

Foreign A-Political-I, April 1884, Prog. Nos. 99–103, National Archives of India. "Letter from Raja Bhairo Deo to Chief Commissioner Bastar," No. 100.

Foreign A-Political-I, April 1884, Nos. 99–103, National Archives of India. Secy. Chief Commissioner, "Central Provinces to Secy. Govt. of India, Foreign Department," Prog. No. 99.

Foreign Political-I, September 1884, Prog. No. 32, paras 9, 18 (memo), National Archives of India.

Foreign Political-I, November 1891, Pros. Nos. 103–106, National Archives of India.

Foreign Secret-I, September 1910, Progs. No. 16, Enclosure 1, paras. 3–4, National Archives of India.

Foreign Secret-I, September 1910, Prog. No. 16 Enclosure 1, Para 16, National Archives of India. "Report on connection . . ."

Foreign Secret-I, September 1910, Prog. No. 16, Enclosure 3, Para 5, National Archives of India. R. H. Craddock, Chief Commissioner, Central Provinces, "Note on connection of Lal Kalendra Singh with the rebellion in Bastar State . . ."

Foreign, Secret-I, August 1911, Prog. No. 37. Enclosure no. 1, para 7, National Archives of India. "Report by E. A. DeBrett."

Foreign and Political Department, Internal Branch, File No. 328-I, 1926, National Archives of India. "Renewal of the prospecting license for iron ore in the Bastar State in favour of the Tata Iron and Steel Company, Ltd., for one year at a time, for a further period of three years."

Fraser, A. H. L. 1892. "Tour Notes on the Bastar State," Compilation No. XXXVIII, Paragraph 6, Jagdalpur Collectorate Records Room.

Government of Hyderabad. 1930. *Decennial Report on the Administration of H.E.H the Nizam's Dominions* (6th October 1912 to 5th October 1922 A.D.), *Companion Volume to the Administration Report for 1331 F*. Hyderabad-Deccan Government Central Press.

"Holt Mackenzie, Memorandum," July 1, 1819, para. 550, *Selections from the Revenue Records of the N.W. Provinces 1818–1820* (Calcutta, 1866).

Minute by Sir Bartle Frere on the subject of adoption as affecting successions in Native States. Foreign Department Proceedings. June 1860. No. 261 Part A. National Archives of India.

Report of the Royal Commission on Jagir Administration and Reforms. Hyderabad: H. E.H. The Nizam's Government, 1947.

Report on the Administration of the Central Provinces and Berar, for the year 1909–10. Nagpur: Printed at the Secretariat Press, 1911.

Report on the Police Administration of the Central Provinces and Berar for the year 1910. Nagpur: Government Press, 1911.

Report on the Administration of the Central Provinces and Berar, for the year 1915–16. Nagpur: Printed at the Secretariat Press, 1917.

Report on the Administration of the Central Provinces and Berar, for the year 1920–21. Nagpur: Printed at Government Press, 1922.

Report on the Administration of Bastar state, for the year 1944.

Annual Report on the Police Administration of the Central Provinces, 1920.

Report of the Frontier Areas Committee of Enquiry, 1947. www.burmalibrary.org /docs14/Frontier_Areas_Committee_of_Enquiry-1947-full.pdf

The Imperial Gazetteer of India, Volumes 1–26. 1908. Oxford: Clarendon Press.

The Imperial Gazetteer of India, Hyderabad State, 1909.

Nelson, A. *Central Provinces District Gazetteer: Bilaspur District*, 1909.

Nelson, A. *Central Provinces District Gazetteer: Raipur District*, 1909.

Temple, Sir Richard. 1863. *Reprint of Report on the Zamindaris and Other Petty Chieftancies in the Central Provinces in 1863.* Nagpur: Government of India.

NAXAL/ MAOIST DOCUMENTS

30 years of Naxalbari – An Epic of Heroic Struggle and Sacrifice. Kolkata: Revolutionary publications. http://naxalresistance.wordpress.com/2007/09/17/30-years-of-naxalbari/

Banerjee, Aloke. June 2003. *Inside MCC Country (MCC er Deshe).*

Bhaskar, "A Decade of 'Developing' Displacement," in *People's March Supplement: A Decade of Struggle and Sacrifice – 10 Years of the CPI-Maoist*, September 2014. www .bannedthought.net/India/PeoplesMarch/ePM/PM-V13-Supplement-Sep2014.pdf

Central Committee (P) CPI-Maoist. 2001. *We Humbly Bow Our Heads – Self-Criticism of the MCCI and the CPI-(ML) [PW] On Strained Relations.*

Central Committee, CPI (ML) People's War. Undated document. "Separate Telangana Movement—Development of Telangana—Our Programme." Obtained from Archives on Contemporary History, Jawaharlal Nehru University, New Delhi.

CPI-Maoist Central Committee. 2007. *Political Organization Review of CPI (Maoist) (Passed in the Unity Congress – 9th Congress in January 2007).*

CPI-ML (People's War) Central Committee. May 1999. *Guerilla Zones – Our Perspective.* (Draft).

CPI-ML (People's War). March 2001. *Strategy and Tactics, Adopted in Second Congress,* (preliminary draft).

CPI-Maoist Central Committee. March 2001. *Strategy and Tactics of the Indian Revolution* (final version).

CPI-Maoist Central Committee. 2004. *Strategy and Tactics of the Indian Revolution.* (final version)

CPI-ML (People's War). 2004. "Social Investigation – South Bastar, March 2004." www .satp.org/satporgtp/countries/india/maoist/documents/papers/SouthBastar.htm

CPI-ML (People's War). 2002. "Karnataka: Social Conditions and Tactics – A report based on preliminary social investigation conducted by survey teams October 2001 in the

Perspective Area." www.satp.org/satporgtp/countries/india/maoist/documents/papers/socialcondition.htm

CPI-ML (People's War). "Social Investigation of North Telangana." www.satp.org/satporgtp/countries/india/maoist/documents/papers/Socialinvestigation_Northtelangana.pdf

CPI-Maoist Central Committee. 2007. *Political Organization Review of CPI (Maoist) (Passed in the Unity Congress – 9th Congress in January 2007)*.

CPI-Maoist, Central Committee, Press Release, November 10, 2018. www.bannedthought.net/India/CPI-Maoist-Docs/Statements-2018/181110-CC-GeneralSecretaryChange-Eng.pdf

Dandakaranya Special Zonal Committee, CPI-Maoist. 12 Aug 2005. *Jan Jagran Nahi, Jan Daman Abhiyan*.

Ganapathy, "Lessons and Challenges of the Indian Revolution," in *People's March Supplement: A Decade of Struggle and Sacrifice - 10 Years of the CPI-Maoist*, September 2014. www.bannedthought.net/India/PeoplesMarch/ePM/PM-V13-Supplement-Sep2014.pdf

Maoist Communist Center of India. 2004. *Rajneetik Sangathanik—Samiksha Report*. Obtained from West Midnapore Police.

Nitin. 2006. "The Forest Is Ours – Assert the Indigenous Adivasi Inhabitants of Dandakaranya and the Vast Hinterland of India." *People's March*, Vol. 7, No. 1, January 2006.

Vanguard, May–June 1991. www.bannedthought.net/India/Vanguard/index.htm

HUMAN RIGHTS GROUP DOCUMENTS

Asian Center for Human Rights (ACHR). March 2006. *The Adivasis of Chhattisgarh–Victims of the Naxalite movement and Salwa Judum campaign*.

Committee Against Violence on Women (CAVOW). December 2006. *Salwa Judum and Violence on Women in Dantewara, Chhattisgarh*.

Human Rights Forum. December 2006. *Death, Displacement and Deprivation: The War in Dantewada*.

Human Rights Watch. July 2008. *Being Neutral Is Our Biggest Crime*.

Independent Citizen's Initiative. 2006. *War in the Heart of India*.

People's Union of Civil Liberties (PUCL) et al. June 1985. *Bastar: Ek Muthbher ki Jaanch (Investigation into an Encounter)*.

People's Union of Civil Liberties (PUCL). July 1989. *Bastar: Development and Democracy*. Madhya Pradesh.

People's Union of Democratic Rights (PUDR) et al. 2006. *When the State Makes War on Its Own People*. New Delhi.

Shankar, P. 2006. *Yeh Jangal Hamara Hain*. New Vistas Publications.

Vanaja, C. April 10, 2005. "Janatana Sarkar: A Parallel Government in the Dandakaranya." *Andhra Jyothi*.

Index

Books in the Series

9 781108 844994